Communication
Yearbook
25

Communication Yearbook 25

WILLIAM B. GUDYKUNST
EDITOR

Published Annually for the
International Communication Association

LAWRENCE ERLBAUM ASSOCIATES, PUBLISHERS

2001   Mahwah, New Jersey   London

Lawrence Erlbaum Associates, Inc., Publishers
10 Industrial Avenue
Mahwah, NJ 07430

P 87
. C 5974
Vol. 25
ρ D3176048

Library of Congress:
ISSN: 0147-4642
ISBN: 0-8058-4034-6 (hardcover)

Cover design by Kathryn Houghtaling-Lacey

Managing Editor: Barbara Stooksberry, ICA Headquarters
Production Editor: Shannon Smithson, ICA Headquarters

CONTENTS

*The review of these manuscripts was begun under the editorship of Michael Roloff.

THE INTERNATIONAL COMMUNICATION ASSOCIATION

The International Communication Association (ICA) was formed in 1950, bringing together academics and other professionals whose interests focus on human communication. The Association maintains an active membership of more than 3,000 individuals, of whom some two thirds are teaching and conducting research in colleges, universities, and schools around the world. Other members are in government, law, medicine, and other professions. The wide professional and geographic distribution of the membership provides the basic strength of the ICA. The Association is a meeting ground for sharing research and useful dialogue about communication interests.

Through its divisions and interest groups, publications, annual conferences, and relations with other associations around the world, the ICA promotes the systemic study of communication theories, processes, and skills. In addition to *Communication Yearbook,* the Association publishes the *Journal of Communication, Human Communication Research, Communication Theory, A Guide to Publishing in Scholarly Communication Journals,* and the *ICA Newsletter.*

For additional information about the ICA and its activities, visit online at www.icahdq.org or contact Michael L. Haley, Executive Director, International Communication Association, P.O. Box 9589, Austin, TX 78766 USA; phone (512) 454-8299; fax (512) 451-6270; email: ica@icahdq.org

Editors of the *Communication Yearbook* series:

Volumes 1 and 2, Brent D. Ruben
Volumes 3 and 4, Dan Nimmo
Volumes 5 and 6, Michael Burgoon
Volumes 7 and 8, Robert N. Bostrom
Volumes 9 and 10, Margaret L. McLaughlin
Volumes 11, 12, 13, and 14, James A. Anderson
Volumes 15, 16, and 17, Stanley A. Deetz
Volumes 18, 19, and 20, Brant R. Burlson
Volumes 21, 22, and 23, Michael E. Roloff
Volumes 24, 25, and 26, William B. Gudykunst

INTERNATIONAL COMMUNICATION ASSOCIATION
EXECUTIVE COMMITTEE

President and Chair
Joseph N. Cappella, *University of Pennsylvania*

President-Elect
Cindy Gallois, *University of Queensland*

President-Elect Select
Jennings Bryant, *University of Alabama*

Immediate Past President
Linda L. Putnam, *Texas A&M University*

Finance Chair
Peter Monge (ex-officio), *University of Southern California*

Executive Director
Michael L. Haley (ex-officio), *ICA Headquarters*

Associate Executive Director
Robert L. Cox (ex-officio), *ICA Headquarters*

BOARD OF DIRECTORS

Members-at-Large
Barbara O'Keefe, *University of Illinois*
Sandra Ball-Rokeach, *University of Southern California*
Daniel Hallin, *University of California, La Jolla*

Student Members
Sarah J. Tracy, *Arizona State University*
Kristine Nowak, *University of Connecticut*

Division Chairs and Vice Presidents

Information Systems
Michael Shapiro, *Cornell University*

Interpersonal Communication
Laura Stafford, *Ohio State University*

Mass Communication
Sharon Strover, *University of Texas, Austin*

Organizational Communication
Patrice Buzzanell, *Purdue University*

Intercultural & Development Communication
Bella Mody, *Michigan State University*

Political Communication
Steve Reese, *University of Texas, Austin*

Instructional & Developmental Communication
Jake Harwood, *University of Kansas*

Health Communication
Kim Witte, *Michigan State University*

Philosophy of Communication
John M. Wise, *Arizona State University*

Communication & Technology
Joseph Schmitz, *University of Tulsa*

Feminist Scholarship
Dafna Lemish, *Tel Aviv University*

Communication Law & Policy
Louise Benjamin, *University of Georgia*

Language & Social Interaction
Robert E. Sanders, *University of Albany/SUNY*

Popular Communication
Sharon R. Mazzarella, *Ithaca College*

Public Relations
Dean Kruckeberg, *University of Northern Iowa*

Special Interest Group Chairs

Visual Communication
Ann Marie Barry, *Boston College*

Gay, Lesbian, Bisexual, & Transgender Studies
John Nguyet Erni, *University of New Hampshire*
Sue Lafky, *University of Iowa*

CONSULTING EDITORS

The following scholars made this volume of *Communication Yearbook* possible. The editor thanks them for their assistance in reviewing one or more manuscripts.

*C*OMMUNICATION *Yearbook* is devoted to publishing state-of-the-art literature reviews in which authors critique and synthesize a body of communication research. The first volume under my editorship was devoted to publishing state-of-the-art essays in which authors summarized the state of theory and research in each of the divisions and interest groups in the International Communication Association (ICA). This volume returns to the tradition of publishing critical, integrative reviews of specific lines of research. In addition, this volume includes two senior scholars' reviews of their lines of theory and research. I had hoped to include reviews of research published in languages other than English, but no complete manuscripts were submitted.

The chapters in this volume should be of interest to a large number of communication scholars. The chapters cover research from several different areas of study in the field, and they will be useful to researchers in a variety of the ICA's divisions and interest groups.

Teresa Harrison and Lisa Falvey examine the role of new media technologies in democracy. They isolate theses that are used in the research on new communication technologies: decentralization-centralization, information access, interactional access, liberal democracy, and deliberative democracy. Harrison and Falvey then examine the role of these theses in new communication technologies in democracy within the contexts of interpersonal, organizational, government-political, and community networking.

Philip Napoli reviews the theoretical perspectives used to explain the Federal Communications Commission (FCC) policymaking process and research on that process. He concludes that most research has focused on explaining past FCC behavior and that there has been little effort devoted to developing and testing theories that predict FCC behavior. Napoli argues that there is a need for research that tests competing theoretical perspectives of FCC behavior.

William Eveland and Sharon Dunwoody examine the implications of theory and research on the uses and effects of hypermedia for the World Wide Web. They argue that research on hypermedia is fragmented across disciplines, with little cross citation. This has led to inconsistent use of concepts and inconsistent methods of measuring similar concepts. Given these problems, Eveland and Dunwoody provide an initial attempt to specify a causal model of the ordering of the variables using an information-processing perspective. Based on the causal model and their review, they generate numerous plausible hypotheses for future research.

Amy Nathanson reviews research on the parents' and other adults' mediation of children's television viewing. She finds that the concept of mediation has not been defined consistently in previous research and suggests that mediation be conceptualized to include active mediation, restrictive mediation, and coviewing. Nathanson concludes that some forms of active and restrictive mediation can have positive outcomes for children (e.g., help them understand the difference between television and reality), but it appears that coviewing does not. She suggests that future research on mediation needs to be content specific, and researchers must control for the total amount of television viewing.

Shelton Gunaratne examines research on the "Third Communication Revolution—the convergence of the telecommunication, computers, and digitalization" (p. 153). He isolates variables from the study of modernization (i.e., urbanization, literacy, education, media participation) that explain "informatization" (i.e., economic status, telephone density, Internet host penetration).

Richard Johannesen argues that ethics are central theoretically and professionally in the field of communication. He isolates major trends in research on ethics (e.g., recognition of the interrelationships between freedom and responsibility; a feminist "ethic of care"). Given the major trends, Johannesen discusses challenges for the study of ethics in the field (e.g., development of a "postmodern" ethic; the role of diversity in developing communication ethics).

John Oetzel, Trudy Burtis, Martha Chew Sanchez, and Frank Pérez review the research on communication in culturally diverse work groups. They argue that previous research can be classified on the basis of the role communication performs in the group: (a) The group's communication is influenced by cultural or contextual factors, (b) communication influences the group outcomes, and (c) communication is a defining element of the group's culture. They conclude by isolating questions for future research (e.g., "How does communication function to create inclusive and divisive groups?").

Ernest Bormann, John Cragan, and Donald Shields review the development and use of symbolic convergence theory (SCT). SCT explains the role of fantasy sharing in human action. Bormann et al. summarize the concepts used in SCT and their interrelationships. They also present research using SCT to solve "real-world" problems (e.g., creating a new corporate identity and culture). They conclude by addressing criticisms of SCT and providing suggestions for future research using the theory.

James Honeycutt and Sherry Ford review research on imagined interactions, mental imagery in which individuals imagine conversations with others. Research on imagined interactions is based in symbolic interactionism and is used as an approach to the study of interpersonal communication. In addition to summarizing previous research and addressing criticisms of the line of research, Honeycutt and Ford outline current and future work on imagined interactions.

Aaron Cargile and James Bradac examine attitudes toward language by reviewing research on evaluations of speakers' language. They argue that language attitudes play only a small role in hearers' reactions to speakers. Cargile and Bradac, therefore, present a "general process" model of hearers' evaluations of speakers. Their model incorporates variables such as the hearers' perceptions of speakers' language and nonlanguage behavior, speakers' attributes, and the hearers' attitudes and individuating information, and hearers' information processing.

Each of the chapters in this volume makes a unique contribution to the field, yet several of the chapters contain concepts that can be linked with each other. Oetzel and his associates, for example, review research on the role of communication in culturally diverse work groups, though one of the factors that should play a role— hearers' evaluations of speakers, the focus of Cargile and Bradac's chapter—is not discussed. Oetzel et al.'s chapter also summarizes research that addresses at least one of the challenges Johannesen raises regarding studying ethics in the future. Similarly, Harrison and Falvey's chapter is related to Gunaratne's chapter. These are only a few of the linkages among the chapters in this volume.

Before concluding, I want to thank the people who made this volume possible. Michael Roloff, the preceding editor of *Communication Yearbook*, oversaw most of the review process for two of the chapters in this volume. I thank the authors of these chapters for being patient and waiting for their chapters to be published so that volume 24 (the first under my editorship) could focus on theory and research in the ICA's divisions and interest groups. The volume would not exist in its present form without the authors' contributions and the reviewers' suggestions for improving the chapters. The School of Communications and the Department of Speech Communication at California State University, Fullerton, provided release time for me to work on *Communication Yearbook*.

Bill Gudykunst,
Laguna Beach, CA

CHAPTER CONTENTS

1 Democracy and New Communication Technologies

TERESA M. HARRISON
LISA FALVEY
Rensselaer Polytechnic Institute

The communication discipline has harbored a long interest in the relationship between communication technology and democracy. In this review, we assess the literature addressing this relationship in the context of new communication technologies. We begin by exploring the way that causal claims have been conceptualized and go on to consider 5 "root theses" that represent the major currents of thought that flow through this literature. Each of the five root theses is itself an umbrella for a cluster of similar hypotheses: *decentralization-centralization, information access, interactional access, liberal democracy*, and *deliberative democracy*. We then consider how these theses are implicated in four major sites of theorizing about the democratizing effects of new technologies—the interpersonal, organizational, government-political, and community networking contexts.

THE newest of the most recent round of new communication technologies, which center on computer networks and the various modalities of computer-mediated communication that networks enable, have set off an avalanche of speculation regarding their prospects for improving, supplementing, or extending democratic practices in our society. The idea that communication technology can be used in the service of democratic political aspirations has been inspirational for many. However, those born prior to the diffusion of television are likely to find such prognostications familiar and naive; at one time, television was seen to hold considerably greater promise for enhancing democracy than it has lived up to (Abrahamson, Arterton, Orren, 1988; McQuail, 1995).

In fact, the history of documented attempts to understand the relationship between communication media and democracy is much older than the example of television. Rhetorical theorists remind us that one approach to the study of com-

Correspondence: Teresa M. Harrison, Language, Literature & Communication, Rensselaer Polytechnic Institute, Troy, NY 12180; email: harrison@rpi.edu.

munication originated in the political conditions of ancient Greece, which relied upon oral expression as the medium through which citizens participated in self-government (Corbett, 1990; Kennedy, 1994). Some of the very first communication theories were based on the study of rhetorical communication practiced by citizens in the ancient democratic polis, which represented some of the earliest manifestations of civic life (Deethardt, 1983).

Although theorists have pursued different research trajectories in the twentieth century, interest in the relationship between democracy and communication has endured and ranged widely. Social theorists have tended to focus on the social and interactional foundations of democracy, with attention to concepts such as plurality (see, e.g., Arendt, 1958), community (see, e.g., Dewey, 1916), and the distinction between public and private (see, e.g., Habermas, 1989; Fraser, 1992), or, conversely, with attention to the problems of achieving a genuine democratic dialogue in the postmodern world (see, e.g., Baudrillard, 1983). Contemporary rhetorical theorists, for example, have focused on the impact and symbolic value of oral and printed expression as it relates to democracy (see, e.g., Parry-Giles,1993). Communication theorists are frequently concerned with issues related to equality in the distribution of information (see, e.g., Markus, 1987; Ritchie, 1991; Thorn & Connolly, 1987). Mass communication theorists have focused on how particular media and their contents involve audiences in political processes, (e.g., Bennett 1992) as well as on the ways that economic factors and public policy bear upon the media's representation of divergence and plurality in democratic cultural systems (e.g., Murdock, 1995). However, in an important sense, all these are studies of the relationship between communication media and democracy, since all seek to understand how some qualities that we associate with democracy can be preserved, promoted, extended, or in some way improved through some of the many forms of communication behavior that take place through diverse forms of communication media.

Thus, the last decade of speculation about the effects of new communication technologies on democratic forms and practices may be seen as an extension of the discipline's traditional concern with communication and democracy. In the current context, the technologies generally referred to as the new communication and information media technologies—"those communication technologies, typically involving computer capabilities (microprocessor or mainframe), that allow or facilitate interactivity among users or between users and information" (Rice, 1984, p. 35)—are radically new and present us with potentials not yet well understood. Included within this category are forms of communication made possible through computing and computer networking technologies, including electronic mail, electronic conferences, work group support systems, and information sharing capabilities made available through local area networks, the Internet, and the World Wide Web. Indeed, we now appear to be entering a period of rapid, almost dizzying, cross breeding between microprocessor-based and traditional analog business and entertainment-based media. The near future holds the prospect of hybrid media forms, part television and part computer, part telephone and part radio. Delivery technologies also appear to be poised for rapid cross-breeding with cable television networks already carrying wide area Ethernet, and Ethernet carrying video and telephony. It is anticipated that existing electric utility wiring may prove capable of delivering high speed digital communication at the same time it performs as usual to bring electricity to buildings.

From the time that futurists such as Naisbitt (1982) and Toffler (1981) first popularized their predictions about their effects on democracy, the latest new communication technologies have developed rapidly. The World Wide Web, which many believe is as revolutionary as the television, was first introduced to the public in 1991. It is time to recognize and begin to approach more systematically the discipline's long preoccupation with democracy and communication media. The latest new communication technologies are not just radically new; the pervasiveness and speed of their diffusion promise to impact most of the discipline's traditional categories of study. Indeed, the variety of democratic visions to which communication technologies have given rise suggest that the yearning for democracy is expressed in many different ways across numerous traditional communication contexts.

A casual glance at the literature will confirm there are many more claims about the nature of the relationship between technology and democracy then there is actual research. But it is as important to understand the nature of these claims as it is to understand what the research reports, first, because these claims express the kinds of democratic goals to which we aspire for communication technology. Many democratic visions are no doubt utopian, as Carey (1988) warns us, but they articulate what we yearn for in our society and what we think we are or should be trying to achieve. As Carey further reminds us, it is not always the case that more involvement, more decentralization, and more communication are necessarily desirable.

It is also important to recognize that much of the research exploring the relationship between democracy and communication has both a critical and a practical dimension (Fay, 1987). That is, those who conduct such research tend to recognize that democracy as we currently experience it, in whatever venue and form, is not as good as it could be. Further, it implies that communication practices can and should be designed in ways that improve democracy. Those who wish to employ technology for democratic aims will need to specify the kinds of designs and design processes that should be supported. To make good on such intentions requires that we understand what we mean by democracy, how it is enacted through communication practices, how technology may be designed to facilitate democratic goals, and the social milieu in which technologies for democratization are deployed.

In the space allocated to this chapter, it will not be possible to construct a general framework for understanding the relationship between communication technology and democracy or to elaborate any particular technological designs for improving democracy. But we do intend to undertake some conceptual work with the aim of creating a foundation for working toward such goals. Our analysis will begin by exploring the way that causal relationships between communication technology and democracy have been conceptualized in the literature. We then consider the various ways that democracy is expected to be related to technology in this literature. It will become apparent that democracy is a "contested" term (Cheney, 1995), and when invoked in the context of new communication technologies, it may refer to a wide range of individual behaviors, social and political structures, and particular philosophical and social conditions. We organize our analysis of the technology-democracy relationship in terms of five root theses and countertheses, which we believe broadly represent the predominant currents of thought that flow through this literature.

From there, we explore four major sites of theorizing about the democratizing effects of new communication technologies. These sites—interpersonal, organizational, government-political, and community networking—may be loosely conceived as social contexts in which theorists or practitioners have argued that the introduction of new communication technologies has the potential to reorganize or stimulate new behavior on the part of an individual or collectivity in ways that are viewed as somehow more democratic than was previously the case.

CAUSAL CLAIMS ABOUT COMMUNICATION
TECHNOLOGY AND DEMOCRACY

In a strong sense we might say that the first systematic study of communication arose under conditions of political exigency: the need to understand how to communicate within the context of a new form of citizen decision making. According to Corbett (1990), following the overthrow of Thrasybulus, the tyrant of Syracuse, a form of democratic decision making was established in which ordinary citizens seeking to recover lost property were required to make claims in court. Corax of Syracuse formulated and codified a set of guidelines to help citizens in developing effective speeches. This depiction of events may be the first to suggest a causal relationship between a particular set of social and political conditions (democratized decision making) and the development of a communication technology (the speech). In this view, communication technology is seen as a product or accomplishment of a set of historical-cultural conditions. Since the "discovery" of rhetoric by the early Greeks, freedom of speech, and subsequently freedom of press, have been regarded as important prerequisites to the maintenance of democratic political conditions.

More recently, attempts to understand the relationship between democracy and technology have focused primary attention on the role of technology in maintaining or altering social and cultural conditions. Marshall McLuhan focused attention squarely on the formative role that communication technologies in general play in creating culture and society by altering cognition. As Slack (1984) points out,

McLuhan's theory rests on a simple causal determinism that views communication technology such as the phonetic alphabet as "the technology that created civilized man" (McLuhan, 1964/1995, p. 84), considers the advent of print literacy as creating conditions enabling the development of logic and reason (p. 85), credits typography with the development of industrialism, centralization, and nationalism, and finds the "eager assertion of individual rights" (McLuhan, 1962, p. 220) as much a feature of literacy and print as is nationalism.

Whereas McLuhan's analysis has certainly created a new appreciation for the role of communication technology in the formation of social life, the causality implied in such claims is best understood as retrospective. Looking back, we can see how developments in social and political life were made possible by technologies such as print, but that does not mean that such developments were always inevitable consequences of the development of print. A more systematic approach to understanding the nature of the relationship between democracy and communication technology demands a clear conceptualization of complex and interdependent material and social processes. Unfortunately, contemporary discussions of the relationship between technology and its outcomes are still frequently cast in simple, deterministic terms in which outcomes are envisioned to be the direct result of a particular technological solution (Marvin, 1988; Winner, 1986). Consider, for example, the democratic utopianism of Meeks (1997) who proclaims that in the twenty-first century, technology will reclaim democracy by binding communities together. "Street by street, housing tract by housing tract, in a kind of societal guerilla warfare, people will begin to use the technology of telecommunications, of the net and all it has become by then, to reach out to one another" (p. 76). This process will begin in the schools, which will use technology for mini-town hall meetings, and then extend to electronic voting in local, then state, and then "it's a small leap" (p. 77) to the national level.

Such conceptualizations obscure the important social and cultural processes that are implicated in the diffusion of innovative technology. A more complex ontology suggests that social processes and culture interact with material technologies and, in so doing, alter the conditions under which technologies are used, diffused, and acquire meaning (Flichy, 1995; Harrison & Stephen, 1996). Although, ultimately, the consequences of technology will be dependent on social processes, technologies themselves are never neutral. Technologies present the social world with new "liberties of action" (Cherry, 1985) making it physically possible to engage in new actions, to build new things. The material possibilities presented by technologies of communication are characterized by a "bias" (Innis, 1951) that creates the grounds for, but not the inevitability of, particular forms of social organization.

Theorists sensitive to the need for more complex conceptualizations of causality have nonetheless shown a keen appreciation for the novel behaviors and modes of organization that new communication technologies offer. The promise of these new "liberties" is in part greatly responsible for the bubbling democratic optimism that continues to permeate academic and popular commentary about the new technologies. Lievrouw (1994) points out that, in contrast to the "informing" orientation of traditional mass media, the new communication media are more "involving," allowing for more interaction and the expression of multiple perspectives than before. Berman and Weitzer (1997) add that the channels required for engaging in such interaction appear to be abundant and affordable for the average citizen, and that the ease of participating in online interaction or setting up one's own website makes it, in principal, a useful tool for organizing effective and speedy political action.

On the other hand, not all theorists are as sanguine about the democratic potential of new communication technologies. Innis's (1951) extensive historical analysis suggests that communication technology has evolved in ways that run directly contrary to democratic visions. By enabling individuals to overcome constraints on action due to space, Innis believed that communication technologies advanced the possibilities for centralization and imperialism. Drawing on this analysis, Gillespie and Robins (1989) argue that new communication technologies enable centrally located organizations to penetrate and control peripheral regions, presenting an "inherent centralizing bias" (p. 11). Similarly, other theorists have argued new technologies present greater possibilities for programs of surveillance, control, and disinformation. Some of the very capabilities that allow users to share information with each other may also be used to enable others to acquire and store information about individuals without their permission, or used to track consumer and employee behavior and target individuals in particular categories for particular kinds of information or advertising (e.g., Gurak, 1997; Raab, 1997; Rheingold, 1993b; Roszak, 1994; Winner, 1986; Zuboff, 1988).

Theorists who recognize particular potentials of new technologies (as opposed to their inevitable effects) emphasize that whether or not their predictions are realized will depend on how individuals choose to use the technology as well as on the particular governmental policies that are created to shape or define particular outcomes (see, e.g., Braman, 1994; Doctor, 1991). Pool (1983), subscribing to a "soft technological determinism," argues that electronic technology is "conducive" to freedom and that only political errors will make computerized information networks less free than the printing press. For these theorists, the future is open-ended and scholarship about the future will help to create it.

But even those who agree that the future is open-ended may disagree over how open-ended it can be. Webster and Robins (1986) suggest that the choices posed by information technology are not as unlimited as they are presented to be, that the rhetoric that encompasses this discussion obscures certain economic, corporate, and global forces whose realities limit our abilities to make genuine choices more than we might realize. They believe that "purposeful control over destinies can only come about when real social processes are revealed" (p. 80). Clearly, it behooves us to consider the social, economic, and material conditions in all their complexity under which new communication technologies offer grounds for increasing democratization or the erosion of civil liberties. On the other hand, a simpler ontology, one based squarely on human will and opposition, is offered in a recent article in *The Nation* that proclaims "The net could become a vibrant alternative to the media oligopoly. The message to progressives is clear: Don't whine, go online" (Shapiro, 1998).

WHAT DEMOCRACY MEANS

When talking about democracy, people appear to mean many different things (Cheney, 1995), and this is no less true in the context of new communication technology. It would thus be useful to begin with some foundational definitions and distinctions to serve as a basis for the discussion that will ensue. For example, following David Beetham (1993), we might view democracy as "a mode of decision-making about collectively binding rules and policies over which the people exercise control" (p. 55). The most democratic arrangement would therefore be one "where all members of the collectivity enjoy effective equal rights to take part in such decision-making directly" and one that "realizes to the greatest conceivable degree the principles of popular control and equality in its exercise" (p. 55). However, this definition is open to many important subsidiary questions, such as, which technological and communicative conditions must prevail in order for members to "enjoy effective equal rights," what means are provided for individuals to take part in "decision-making about collectively binding rules and policies," and how is "the greatest conceivable degree" of "popular control and equality" best insured. In research on democracy and technology, the devil is in the details, and researchers differ markedly on which details their work addresses.

The literature does not lend itself to a single orientation to democracy. Researchers are rarely explicit about their orientations, and they do not always base their analysis on the literature of democratic theory. Instead, they frequently assume one or more particular orientations to democracy and proceed from there. Furthermore, claims in the literature about the interrelationships between technology and democracy seem to be distributed between positive and negative prognostications, regardless of the particular orientation(s) of democracy at issue. Thus, it seemed more useful to represent the literature by organizing our analysis around a set of root theses that are frequently invoked about the relationship between democracy and new communication technologies. It is important to note that the theses we identify are not completely independent of each other; indeed, it will become apparent that they overlap in some respects and build upon each other. We will see how these theses are implicated in each of the four substantive research domains that we consider later.

Decentralization-Centralization Theses

Everyone agrees that new communication and information technologies have the potential to improve the quantity and quality of available information. Such is the nature of these technologies: Their basic purposes are to generate and disseminate information. Discussions about the relationship between technology and democracy frequently focus on the effects of information produced in and through these technologies, taking two general routes. In the first case, theorists argue that the ability to generate and disseminate new information will have the effect of decentralizing decision making in a wide variety of contexts or, as the counterthesis suggests, will contribute to already existing trends toward centralization. In the second case, discussed in the next section, what is at issue is the extent of information distribution and access: Theorists argue that new information generated by information and communication technologies should, but may not, be distributed widely and equitably, with corresponding positive or negative effects on the nature of democratic practices.

The decentralization-centralization theses are not strictly about democracy in a political sense. Based on the assumption that hierarchical and bureaucratic social structures were created originally to cope with limitations on the quality and quantity of information, the decentralization thesis suggests that increased information generation and distribution will make it possible to allocate participation in decision making more widely, creating autonomy, freedom, and pluralism. As O'Toole (1990) puts it "Since information is a requisite of power in organizations as well as in nations, when information is shared the power of the central authority is diminished, and all those who now have access to the information are, to some extent, *empowered*" (p. 238).

Business and industrial organizations are the most frequent contexts for these discussions; however, Cleveland (1985), announcing the "twilight of hierarchy," suggests that more knowledgeable people and the informatization of society will destabilize hierarchies that have existed historically on the basis of control, secrecy, ownership, structural unfairness, and location. Discussing political, social, and cultural democracy, Tehranian (1990) suggests that, if democracy is conceived as a "cybernetic social system of networks in which there are many autonomous and decentralized nodes of power and information with their own multiple channels of communication" (p. 6), then new communication media present the preconditions for such a system: interactivity, the potential for universality, channel capacity, content variety, low noise, and high speed.

Doubting that new technologies will have a direct effect on political participation, Schickler (1994) suggests that they can instead decentralize two traditional political hierarchies: the news media's monopoly over dissemination and interpretation of information and the dominance of political and economic elites over decision making. New technologies give citizens the ability to gather their own information, disperse it widely, scrutinize the performance of elites, and question officials and candidates. These capabilities will not be used by everyone; however, they can be used by oppositional groups to create uncertainties for current elites and to generate hierarchies of counterelites. O'Toole (1990) points out that, counter to dire predictions of Orwellian surveillance, information technologies used in Communist countries enabled the development of pluralism, which he describes as "the particular enemy of totalitarianism" (p. 220).

With respect to organizational hierarchies, Sproull and Kiesler (1991) have argued that new technologies have the potential to alter processes of organizational information distribution by speeding them up, widening networks of delivery and exchange, and bypassing traditional gatekeepers. In so doing, these new technologies alter the nature of influence, participation, and control within organizations. For Zuboff (1988), the "informating" power of networked computerized information can universalize access to organizational data, enabling blue collar workers to engage their intellectual skills in work, creating an increased sense of empowerment and commitment. Further, widespread access to data can flatten the traditional stratification of workers and managers, since managers' claim to authority has rested on their monopoly over information, although Evans (1991) argues that such democratization will take place only with further and more radical changes to the workplace.

Sproull and Kiesler (1991) and Zuboff (1988) also call attention to the potential for information exchanged in electronic conferencing in organizations to increase the knowledgability and expertise of employees. But a possible disincentive to the advantages of widespread information distribution is losing the unfettered ability of elite decision makers to manipulate and choose between options. Mantovani's (1994) position is that no particular application of information technology in organizations is inherently democratic; organizations must choose whether to use new communication technologies to empower and "informate" their employees, thus creating the potential for a different form of organizational structure, or use them to collect information about employees' behavior and diminish employees' discretion, thus preserving management's prerogatives (Clement, 1988).

Other theorists doubt that such choice has ever been genuinely available and assert the counterthesis: that information technology ultimately leads to increased centralization on the part of global corporations and the state. For Hamelink (1986), the promise of decentralization is an illusion fostered by those who have the most to gain in an information society. Webster and Robins (1986) acknowledge that decentralization is taking place, but only under the auspices of more centralized and integrated structures that enable an increasing level of "coordination and observation from the center" (p. 321) making it possible to overcome spatial constraints and "orchestrate widely disseminated sites of production as if they were centralized." Ultimately, the danger of these capabilities is centralized surveillance and control by corporate and state bureaucracies (Gandy, 1989). The outcomes envisioned are illustrated in Webster and Robins's (1986) reference to two popular metaphors: H.G. Wells's World Brain, which "anticipates what we see as an emerging regime of information production, circulation, consumption and control" (p. 343) and the Panopticon, Jeremy Bentham's model for an architecture of control designed originally for prisons, factories, and schools, that due to new technological capabilities, can now be applied to the social totality.

Information Access Theses

The other information-centered root thesis frequently at the heart of democracy-technology claims consists of two conjoined ideas: that access to and use of relevant and credible information is a precondition for certain kinds of practices required for democratic participation and that technology is increasingly the means by which such information is or should be made available. The set of premises that suggest that "good information" is required for "good democracy" and that such information needs to be made available to all in a democracy, regardless of individual economic and social resources, is described by Dervin (1994) as a "narrative with near-mythic cultural status" that has justified social policies aimed at increasing access to new communication technologies.

Information is viewed as critical to democratic practices in a number of respects. At the most general level, it is suggested that the ability of political groups to organize and mobilize for political action is based on the extent to which they can receive and distribute information rapidly; this ability is likely to be enhanced by new communication technologies (Braman, 1994; Hiltz & Turoff, 1993). However, others argue that information is essential to the development of more basic democratic competencies. Formulating opinions, creating preferences, testing choices, and acting in decision-making arenas are fundamental to possessing equal rights and opportunities to participate in democratic decision making (Doctor, 1992; van Dijk, 1996). Another way of looking at these capabilities is in terms of power, and it is such capabilities that seem to be at the heart of the aphorism that "information is power" (Johnson, 1997). At an even more basic level, Bowie (1990) has argued that access to information and to information technology is required for the effective exercise of one's First Amendment rights to free speech. Without access to information and the technology used to disseminate information, it is impossible to formulate or communicate opinions that can compete effectively in the marketplace of ideas; thus, those who lack access to information and information technology are deprived of the ability to have effective voice.

It has been suggested that the information dissemination capabilities of new technologies may have the effect of destabilizing existing political systems because of new opportunities to more rapidly and effectively organize oppositional political interest groups (Braman, 1994); but theorists are more frequently concerned about the dangers posed by lack of access. Doctor (1992) formulated the concept of "information democracy" to refer to the need to provide access to information resources and the means for individuals to use information in their daily lives. Access to information requires that individuals also have access to hardware and software, as well as the training, literacies, and competencies required to receive and understand such information (Bowie, 1990; Doctor, 1991; Gandy, 1988).

In the treatments above, information is conceptualized as a social good (Ansah, 1986; Schiller, 1996) that needs to be available to all in order to live responsibly in a democratic society just as other basic needs are provided. However, Gandy (1988) has argued that new technologies will increase the disparity between those who have access to information and technology and those who lack it. Doctor (1992) has reviewed the historical evidence, which confirms the presence of a persistent gap between the rich and the poor in areas of computers and education, telephone service, and public library services.

Although information in democratic systems should be treated as a social good, it is more frequently treated as a commodity, controlled and manipulated as a source of growth for the market system (Schiller, 1988; 1996). From this perspective, information takes on a sinister quality and is associated with a counterthesis: that "bad information" can limit the degree of freedom and privacy enjoyed by individuals, threatening the quality and character of a democratic system. The same technologies that enable individuals to access and distribute information are also able to collect information about their users. Here though, rather than a single or centralized bureaucratic "inspective force" such as the state or corporation, theorists warn of multiple, business-oriented data gatherers engaging "in ordinary and routine surveillance activities, undertaken from more diffuse and numerous power centers" (Robins & Webster, 1988, p. 60).

Traditionally, the threat posed by using technology to gather information has centered on invasions of privacy (Westin, 1971); however, more recently, this threat has centered on how information about individuals is used for market research (Curtis, 1988). Elmer (1997) describes the ways in which "transaction-generated information" about the user is accumulated when using the Web. Such information can be used to sort consumers into stratified categories based on economic, racial, and ethnic variables (Curtis, 1988). Consumers are then targeted for particular kinds of information about products, topics, and so forth, based on their presumed levels of interest and ability to pay.

Interactional Access Theses

Whereas much commentary on the democratic potential of the new technologies has focused on information, even more has been directed at the quality and level of interactional access and expressive freedom these technologies afford to individual communicators. Relatively early in the diffusion of computer networking, when the Internet and its predecessors were still used predominantly by academic and government researchers, scholars observed that the medium democratizes elitist and exclusionary research networks by allowing interaction to become accessible and visible through computer conferencing (Baird & Borer, 1987; Pfaffenberger, 1986). In the ensuing decade of experimentation, it has become evident that this effect takes both interpersonal and intellectual dimensions.

In particular, researchers and participants have commented on the ability to participate on a more equal basis in interpersonal conversation, which involves being heard by others, expressing opinions that are respected, and being treated fairly by other interactants. This equalizing effect has been attributed to the impersonality of computer interaction compared to face-to-face interaction, which minimizes interpersonal and professional status cues, making it easier to disagree and to argue in favor of unpopular opinions (Hiltz, 1977; Lerch, 1983).

Harasim (1993, 1996) has observed that interacting through computer networks creates a new kind of social space, an interactional environment characterized by diminished social presence cues and more opportunities for individuals to think about their responses to others. It is the absence or reduction of such social cues that has led many to describe online interaction as functioning more democratically than face-to-face interaction (Kiesler, Siegel, & McGuire, 1984). Researchers have found these effects extending to educational discourse where teachers and students may become more equal participants in class-oriented computer conferences, (Faigley, 1992; Tuman, 1992) and organizational settings where computer conferencing and group decision support systems may enhance egalitarian interaction between managers and their subordinates (Nunamaker, Dennis, Valacich, Vogel, & George, 1991; Sproull & Kiesler, 1991; Zuboff, 1988). For some theorists (e.g., Ess, 1996; Herring, 1993), Habermas's (1970) ideal speech situation sets the standard for democratic discourse, ruling out as violations of democratic norms those behaviors that impede the realization of Habermas's ideal.

Other academic researchers have imputed a democratizing quality to the multimedia and hypertextual nature of information distributed through the Internet and World Wide Web, not because such information becomes economically or distributionally accessible as we argued above, but because the interactive and playful character of such media make texts of all kinds intellectually accessible to and under the control of learners and readers. As Tuman (1992) puts it, "computer technology has the potential to open up the entire process of reading and writing, undermining a stolid entrenched literary tradition of 'classic' authors and in turn allowing everyone to read and write, to exchange texts, on an equal basis" (p. 19). The interactivity of navigational control of hypertext allows electronic readers to "genuflect before the text or spit on its altar, add to a text or subtract from it, rearrange it, revise it, suffuse it with creativity," according to Lanham (1993, p. 6). He further envisions the possibility for a multimedia discourse consisting of words, images, sounds, and color that produces a literature in which the expressive arts are interchangeable, thus re-enfranchising those who lack a natural proclivity for print.

As experience with the new technologies has accumulated, however, important questions have been raised about the actual extent and usefulness of the expressive freedom afforded through computer-mediated communication. Empirical examinations of online interaction have found that the uninhibited character of online interaction gives rise to the disinhibited phenomenon of "flaming," which, as we discuss in detail below, discourages participation particularly among women. Furthermore, the pristine and initially cueless online interactional environment can be modified by the purposeful introduction of identity cues afforded by the institutional contexts in which online discussions occur. And the seemingly normless and anarchic character of online interaction gives way over time to self-censorship (MacKinnon, 1995), and attempts, if not yet succeeds, at institutional censorship (Shade, 1996). Johnson (1997) warns that online discussions may produce insularity—"free" discussions between those who already agree—rather than the engagement with difference required in democratic deliberation. Finally and perhaps most to the point, we must consider seriously the argument posed by Schudson (1997), who takes issue with the assumption that conversation is inherently democratic and suggests instead that democratic norms and institutions are required for the existence of democratic conversation. His position raises the question of whether the potentially democratizing effects of egalitarian access to interaction through technology must ultimately rest on a more sturdy foundation of democratic philosophy.

Liberal Democracy Theses

So far, we have considered centralization, information, and interaction as sites of discourse about the potentially democratic character of new communication technologies. But these qualities are best viewed as some of the necessary communicative conditions for equal participation in governance; so far we have not addressed the means by which participation in governance takes place or how the greatest conceivable degree of popular control in governance might be exercised.

In the literature of democracy, scholars have debated the merits of direct versus representative democracy as two forms of democratic governance structures. Participatory democracy is the earliest form of democracy, based on the model of the Athenian polis, in which there is no distinction between those who govern and those who are designated as citizens (Held, 1996). Through oral discussion and debate, citizens participated directly in decision making about their civic affairs.

In liberal or representative democracy, on the other hand, decisions are made by representatives whom citizens vote into or out of office. The system of democracy in the U.S. and most contemporary democratic governments is predicated on this model. Since this form of democracy is based on elected decision makers comprising a state that could deprive citizens of their rights to democracy, liberal philosophy also extends to citizens' certain basic rights—for example, to freedom of speech, freedom of press, freedom of assembly, and rights to privacy—that protect them from potential abuses of power (Held, 1996).

Many political theorists who advocate the need for significant reinvigoration of democracy are motivated by concern for declining participation in western representative democracies, as indicated by decreases in the number of eligibles who vote in elections and by waning interest in state and local decision making (Barber, 1984; Pateman, 1970). Although few believe genuine participatory democracy is plausible, it has now become commonplace in the popular and academic literature to suggest that new communication technologies can increase political participation and involvement in some of the primary decision making or deliberative processes involved in democratic life.

Theorists typically split in two broad directions over the particular form of political participation and involvement they believe needs to be addressed. Those following in the path of the electronic democracy or "teledemocracy movement" of the 1980s are oriented toward using technology to improve the individual's direct participation in registering opinions about political decision making as well as making it easier for citizens to vote. According to Brants, Huizenga, and van Meerten (1996), this "decision making sphere," where preferences are expressed and incorporated into policy, is analytically distinct from the political process of the "discursive public sphere," in which deliberation takes place. The public sphere and other approaches to deliberative democracy are discussed in the next section.

The teledemocracy movement began nearly two decades ago, motivated by the development of new communication technologies that antedated the popularization of the Internet and the invention of the World Wide Web and centered on enhancements to television and telecommunication. According to Becker and Scarce (1987, p. 264),

> teledemocracy is the use of telecommunications technology to promote, improve, and expand (a) direct, pure democratic forms such as town meetings, initiative, referendum and recall; and (b) the citizen informational and feedback functions of indirect democratic forms such as republics, where the population elects various legislative and executive officials to plan, promulgate, and carry out public policy.

What was especially exciting at that time was the development of two-way communication capabilities in media that had traditionally been one-way; for example, cable television could be equipped with a means for registering feedback instantly from viewers. Thus, "by its very nature," this two-way capacity for communication "helps systematize the distribution of information and debate, stimulates interest and participation, involves many who don't want to or can't leave home, and has great promise to maximize the voting turnout" (Becker & Scarce, 1987, p. 283).

As one might imagine, considerable energy has been directed at describing how the two-way communication capabilities of the Internet and World Wide Web can be used to supplement and enhance communication channels between representative governments and their constituencies. Proponents argue that webpages, electronic mail, and computer conferencing can provide the material infrastructure to bring citizens in closer contact with their elected representatives, with local governments, and with candidates for office; further, theorists speculate that this infrastructure offers the possibility of decentralizing and de-bureaucratizing government functions, making them more responsive to citizens (Brants, 1996; Connell, 1996; Frissen, 1997; Hacker & Todino, 1996; Loader, 1997). As Street (1997) points out, the assumption behind using technology for these purposes is that technology solves problems in time, size, knowledge, and access that have inhibited participation or interaction with government representatives in the past.

Grossman (1995) argued that two "inexorable" forces in our society are moving the United States toward more direct forms of government: a historical trajectory of ever increasing social and political equality among citizens and the coming synergy of television, telephone, satellites, cables, and computer networking. He foresees a future that can swing easily in the direction of electronic plebiscites in which individuals pursue their own self-interest or toward participatory decision making aimed at maximizing the common good.

Theorists do not look upon democracy by plebiscite with relish; this "debased form of democracy" (Street, 1997, p. 32) is seen as a significant drawback to the greater direct participation afforded by the new technologies. The problem is that plebiscites do not necessarily involve a deliberative process as part of citizen decision making. New technologies exacerbate this, as their instantaneous interactivity makes it possible to register instant responses, discourages second thoughts, and invites the participation of demagogues and egomaniacs (Schlesinger, 1997). Abrahamson, Arteron, and Orren (1988) fear that government will act on the basis of citizen feedback formulated without the benefit of discussion that focuses on concerns relevant to the common good, as well as the equally unpalatable outcome that government by plebiscite will become government by majority rule, endangering the principle that individual and minority rights will be respected in a democracy.

Deliberative Democracy Theses

It is clear from the literature that many theorists also harbor the hope that new communication technologies will enable citizens to engage in more productive political dialogue and in so doing contribute to a reconstitution of what they regard as the deliberative substance of democracy. This literature is old in the life span of computer networking and conferencing technologies, reaching back to Hiltz and Turoff's (1978/1993) earliest set of predictions regarding their impact on politics. At that time, Hiltz and Turoff waxed optimistic regarding the positive outcomes of using computer conferences to involve citizens in online political discussions. They also predicted that online information and conferencing services could be used for people-to-people exchanges of information, ideas, and action plans.

As Bertelsen (1992) and Hacker (1996) point out, the model of participatory democracy animates much of the discussion about the democratic potential of new communication technologies, which seem to make feasible new ways to include individual voices in political discourse and, in so doing, reinvigorate civic life. A major difference between representative and participatory democracies, as Rucinski (1991) suggests, lies in the greater level of knowledge that individuals must have about the perspectives of others and the interests that underlie those perspectives for participatory democracy; she notes that interactive communication technologies bear the promise, if not yet the reality, of facilitating the development of such knowledge.

Despite the common discussion of more deliberative approaches to democracy, there is considerable divergence in the political and communication theories that form the foundation for these aspirations. One strand of thought is situated in the role that media play in animating political discourse within a democracy, expressed originally in the observations of Alexis de Tocqueville about media use in America. Davis (1997) uses Tocqueville's observations to call attention to a parallel with contemporary political uses of the Internet. According to Davis, Tocqueville was impressed by the unrestrained and competitive political quality of the media in the United States, particularly newspapers, which "individuals and groups used to reach out to the like-minded, forming invisible threads of community" (p. 122) and which became the foundation for political discussion and debate. She suggests that the same eagerness to "push ideas, argue cases, and advocate courses of action that animated the American polity of the 1830s" (p. 123–124) can be found in the way that individuals interact in Internet conferences and use the Web in cyberspace today.

Keane (1991) differs somewhat from Davis in his view of the press, but comes to the same conclusions regarding the potential for animating discourse through new technologies. He argues that the traditional relationship between communication media and democracy is predicated on the model of face-to-face communication in the Greek polis, in which it was assumed that all citizens could speak to each other directly. In such a context, traditional assurances of freedom of speech and freedom of the press could be assumed sufficient to guarantee democratic expression. However, this model fails to acknowledge that individuals in modern civil society enjoy differential access to the means of communication because market competition prevents some individuals from access to the media of public communication. He argues in favor of a model of public service media to check the concentration of market-based media, a model made economically feasible in part through the availability of digital technologies, which would allow independents and smaller-scale, decentralized operations to "narrowcast" to audiences.

The role of media in providing the information and opportunities for democratic discourse becomes more explicit in the theorizing that has centered on Habermas's (1989) concept of the public sphere. Habermas believed that the link between the people and a democratic government was forged through the social intercourse that took place between citizens who discussed issues of common concern in a variety of public places—coffee houses, salons, and journals of opinion. Habermas's ideal of free-flowing conversation was characterized by rational-critical debate as the standard for argument, the bracketing of status differentials, the ability to problematize any area of discussion, and a conception of the public that was inclusive in principle (Calhoun, 1992). Critical to the efficacy of the public sphere was the rise of capitalism and the commodification of information made possible through the development of a competitive press, and subsequently the development of the mass media, which provided the basis for informed opinion and the opportunity for public expression.

The public sphere for Habermas is an ideal, predicated on his analysis of discourse in the political arena of eighteenth century democracies. It has been heavily criticized for its inaccurate depictions of public media and political discourse (Schudson, 1992), for its neglect of a plebian public sphere operating in parallel to the bourgeois public sphere (Garnham, 1992), and for its failure to consider that its conceptualization rests on historical conditions that excluded the participation of women and discussion of issues in the "private" realm relevant to them (see e.g., Fraser, 1992; McLaughlin, 1993). Nevertheless, the concept of the public sphere has been inspirational for democratic communication theorists because it focuses analysis on the media as the central link between the mass public communication and democratic politics and calls attention to the material communicative conditions for democratic public discourse (Garnham, 1992). Thus, the promise of using the discourse and information dissemination capabilities of new communications technology to reconstitute the public sphere laces the prognostications of a significant number of political and communication theorists (Hacker & Todino, 1996; Kellner, 1997; Sassi, 1996; Bryan, 1996).

A second and somewhat complementary route toward the enhancement of the deliberative quality of democracy is through communitarian philosophies and their offshoots. Communitarian democracy stresses decision making in the service of the common good, instead of that which serves the interests of individuals or specific groups (Abrahamson, Arterton, & Orren, 1988; Ess, 1996). This model and its contemporary analogues or extensions (e.g., "strong democracy," Barber, 1984) is viewed as offering a superior vision of civic life, marked by community involvement, civic commitment, and rational deliberation. Community deliberation and persuasion in decision making are foregrounded in this model of democracy; participation in these activities is regarded as a transformative process in understanding and creating the common good (Abrahamson, Arterton, & Orren, 1988).

Communitarian democracy seeks to reinvigorate the idea of a public space in which members of a community meet to engage in the communication activities that both create and sustain community life (Doheny-Farina, 1996). Proponents of new communication technologies have been quick to point out the paucity of neutral public gathering places, or "great good places" (Oldenberg, 1989) in contemporary life. They suggest that cyberspace may present an important alternative where individuals can meet virtually to engage in the kind of discourse that is critical to the reconstitution of a vibrant community life (Doheny-Farina, 1996; Rheingold, 1993b; Schuler, 1995).

From the communitarian perspective, communication between members of the community takes place largely within public contexts. An alternative to this view is presented by Friedland (1996) who draws on Putnam's theory of social capital to argue that communities should be seen as "social capital networks," rather than simply or only as discourse communities. Putnam (1993, 1995) argued that the social connections in a community that are the basis for effective democratic governance are those implicated in his concept of social capital, a resource created in the patterns of interpersonal, conversational association between actors in the community that form the basis for cooperative relationships and mutual trust. Social capital enables "participants to act together more effectively to pursue shared objectives" (Putnam, 1996, p. 31). Putnam found these associations between citizens in geographic space, that is, in church membership, participation in social clubs and sports teams, and other forms of civic association.

For Putnam (1996), whether or not social capital can be created in the interaction that takes place in online forums remains to be seen; he was not particularly optimistic, suspecting that only face-to-face relationships inspired the kind of mutual engagement required. However, Friedland (1996) has argued that electronic networks provide the opportunity for citizens to build new networks of association, create new norms for sharing and reciprocity, and erect new foundations for trust. In the concrete uses of computer networking through which individuals and groups are creating new networks of civic engagement, Friedland suggests that new technologies are extending democratic practices, "even though they are embedded in an oligopolistically networked capitalist marketplace" (p. 187).

A third approach to technology and deliberative democracy lies in Deetz's (1992) perspective on democracy as participation. Deetz (1992) extends Barber's conception of strong democracy as "a participatory process of ongoing, proximate self-legislation and the creation of political community" (Barber, 1984, p. 151) by arguing that democratic participation must begin not with differing issue positions, but with communicative processes of identity formation and experience that are inherently political. Through communication, particularly language, individual subjects and their experiences are socially constructed, taking on the character of socially inscribed differences, values, and ideologies. However, this process is not a monolithic one because "the subject is subject to a range of discourses, some of which conflict"; thus, the point of participation in democracy is to "reclaim the conflicts that keep one ideological formation from ruling or becoming treated as self-evident or natural" (Deetz, 1992, p. 138). In this perspective, technologies can enhance participation or control based on "how different groups utilize the technologies and what they do to people's capacity to express different kinds of meaning. Each technology, because of its nature and structural place, privileges certain groups of people and certain types of meaning" (p. 109). For Deetz, the question of how new communication technologies will affect the constitution of meaning in democratic participation requires further research.

The counter to each of these strands of the deliberative democracy theses is the possibility that spaces for discussion now opened by the new technologies will eventually become colonized and controlled by media oligopolies or other global corporations. One possible result is that the deliberative, expressive character of discourse afforded by the new technologies will be available only to elite, upper and middle class participants in political processes, whereas the interaction of others is confined to consumer-oriented activities structured for consumer-oriented purposes (Calabrese & Borchert, 1996; Hardt, 1996). Barber (1997) is more pessimistic about the eventual outcome of corporate control of online media. He acknowledges the potentially pluralizing effects of new technologies and his own past support for their democratizing potential, but now argues that technology may come ultimately to mirror the society in which it is introduced. He points to current tendencies on the part of corporations to vertically integrate, by purchasing material infrastructure and content, warning that talk of diversity will come quickly to mask "a new form of totalism all the more dangerous because it boasts of choice and is sold in the language of freedom" (p. 216).

SITES FOR RESEARCH ABOUT DEMOCRACY AND TECHNOLOGY

The root theses we have explored above provide a descriptive vocabulary for assessing the kinds of claims made about the relationship between new communication technologies and democracy. Our next task is to explore the ways in which these claims take form in the specific theories and empirical research that address the nature and extent of democracy in each of four particular contexts: interpersonal, organizational, governmental-political, and community networking. In the analysis that follows, space constraints will not permit a thorough review of the literature in each of the areas addressed; instead we examine themes expressed in the literature related to the promise, empirical effects, and significance of new communication technologies for the nature of democracy, as we have defined it above.

The Interpersonal Context

Rheingold (1993a) proclaims that the democratic promise of new communication technologies lies in the ability to turn the average person "into a publisher, an eyewitness reporter, an advocate, an organizer, a student or teacher, and potential participant in a worldwide citizen-to-citizen conversation" (p. 131). His and others' claims about the democratic possibilities of new communication technologies for people interacting with other people rest on three of the theses examined above: (a) that individuals will have access to the information provided by new technology, (b) that interaction using new technologies will prove more democratic than in face-to-face contexts, and (c) that citizens can use new technologies to exercise their free speech rights in the context of liberal democracy.

We begin by exploring themes related to the economics of access to information. In only a few instances is communication technology made available to all members of a community without some sort of cost: for equipment, service, and particular skill and knowledge requirements required to use computers and computer networks. The widening gap between rich and poor in America affects the number of individuals who can own and maintain computers, modems, and Internet connections at home, producing what theorists fear is a technological gap between the "haves" and "have-nots" (Firestone & Schneider, 1996; Jacobson, 1996; Schiller,

1995). Rates of access to the Internet, although difficult to assess, offer support for the contention that relatively few in America and around the world can participate in the kinds of endeavors Rheingold writes about (Loader, 1997).

Computer manufacturers, telephone companies, and other businesses that support network infrastructure, poised to profit greatly from the current communication revolution, commodify goods and services offered through the network in ways that keep the poor from buying and using technology (Schiller, 1995; Sclove, 1995). Perelman (1998) notes that anytime a thing is commodified, there must be scarcity in order to make a profit. Information, however, is a difficult thing to make scarce; thus artificial barriers must be created to keep in those who have paid for it and keep out those who cannot or will not pay for it. As an example, Jacobson (1996) points to the unwillingness of telephone companies to upgrade necessary technology infrastructures (such as wiring) in poor communities.

In addition to difficulties in gaining access due to socioeconomic status, gender has also been a factor in physical access problems. Balka (1993) found that women have greater access difficulties than men, which are compounded by problems getting necessary technical support to set up and maintain access to the network. However, when community public access is extended to all citizens (which we will discuss in more detail below), evidence exists that women's participation rates do increase (Collins-Jarvis, 1993).

Even if universal access were a possibility for all citizens, once online some groups still experience difficulties in achieving interactional equality, mainly due to pressure from dominant online groups. Studies of Usenet groups often reveal that their ranks are made up primarily of men (Anderson, 1996; Brail, 1996; Clerc, 1996; Smith, McLaughlin, & Osborne, 1997; Sutton, 1994). One way that Usenet populations ensure more male members is through surveying and policing membership ranks, exerting pressure by making sexual advances, limiting the discussion to women's bodies, or dismissing women's topics of conversation (Anderson, 1996; Balka, 1993; Brail, 1996; Clerc, 1996; Kramarae & Taylor, 1993; Smith et al., 1997; Sutton, 1994). Clerc (1996) writes that "a direct ploy for dissuading women from posting is to send them offensive email" (p. 82).

In some environments, men control access to their online hangouts. Gilboa (1996) relates her own experience with hacker culture as one in which women are often forbidden from participating in hacker forums. However, the potentially unlimited number of channels on the network means that women and other special interests can and do find ways to create their own virtual spaces; in the process they may also find greater memberships and establish stronger ties because of common interests (Wellman, 1997). Baym (1997) describes a soap opera Usenet group that attracts and supports female membership; mailing lists such as Systers and SAPPHO are dedicated to providing women-only access to women's issues (Borg, 1994; Camp, 1996; Hall, 1996). These forums, however, are often under male scrutiny because they too pose equally difficult access and participation questions (Hall, 1996).

The fact that social presence cues are diminished in online interaction is one of the most frequently cited reasons for the expectation of democratic online interaction. Reduced cues, however, have also been implicated in the antidemocratic phenomenon of flaming (Kiesler et al., 1984). Although flaming has been defined in very different ways, it is considered to be insulting, inflammatory, or harassing speech. Research on flaming has often centered on the hypothesis that reduced social cues, anonymity, and reduced self-awareness produces users who are more likely to behave in unregulated ways (Kiesler et al., 1984; Lea & Spears, 1991; Spears, Lea, & Lee, 1990; Sproull & Kiesler, 1991). In the deindividuation model, users are more likely to be absorbed by the group, and therefore think little about themselves or the effects of their online behaviors.

Further research into the deindividuation model led to the social identity/deindividuation or SIDE model (Spears & Lea, 1992; Spears & Lea, 1994), which discriminates more closely between the roles of social and individual identity by suggesting that if social identity is most salient, the online environment will lead to deindividuation, and if individual identity is at the fore, group influence will lessen and individual responsibility will increase. In the SIDE model, deindividuation occurs because, as users try to assess others' individual identity, they rely on sparse cues, and therefore make stereotypical judgments about others (Matheson, 1991; Matheson & Zanna, 1988; Spears & Lea, 1992, 1994).

Some research is critical of the concept of flaming (Lea, O'Shea, Fung, & Spears, 1992; Thompsen, 1996) since definitions in the literature range from "hostile expressions of strong emotions" (Lea et al., 1992) to "speaking incessantly" (Kiesler et al., 1984). Questions have also focused on how often it really happens (Lea et al. 1992), and whether it is simply context dependent, depending on the degree to which such behavior is tolerated or expected (Siegel, Dubrovsky, Kiesler, & McGuire, 1986).

Flaming has been blamed for unequal participation, particularly between men and women. Herring (1993) found greater participation by men in an online academic discussion; when women's participation increased, men tried to discourage women from participating through flaming. She also found that men's style of talking was more aggressive and challenging. These findings have been substantiated in other studies (Herring, Johnson, & DiBenedetto, 1992, 1995). Similarly, Collins-Jarvis (1997) found that male participants engaged in aggressive behavior at the expense of female participation until restrictions on verbal behavior were placed on participants. A recent study, however, found that, in certain populations, male flaming did not exceed female flaming, although women tended to use slightly more graphic accents (ASCII pictures of smiling faces, for example) than men—perhaps as a way to soften their communication style (Witmer & Katzman, 1997).

Beyond flaming, women in online environments are often subject to sexual harassment and physical threats. The "Bungle" rape case, where a man (presumably) in an online environment proceeded to "rape" a female, is often used as an example of sexual harassment online (Dibbell, 1993). Although this case is often cited, it is an isolated incident. More likely, however, are the feelings of frustration many women may experience in response to continued sexual advances made by men (Balsamo, 1993; Brail, 1996; Clerc, 1996; Deuel, 1996; Lipton, 1996).

The online environment presents the opportunity to play with identity in ways that some find related to democratic interaction. Virtual reality and online role-playing environments, such as MUDs (multi-user dungeons), are hailed as forums that provide users with an opportunity to free themselves from traditional constructions of gender and race by taking on new identities. These assertions are predicated on the belief that freedom from restrictions associated with identity will lead to increased participation and online equality. Much of the interaction takes place in MUDs between gender-neutral personas or characters (Deuel, 1996; Hall, 1996; Kendall, 1996; Lipton, 1996; Turkle, 1995). This genderless notion of sex appeals to many theorists, including post-feminists such as Haraway (1985), who believe that gender categories should be dismantled. The counterthesis to the disembodied, genderless, multiplicity of identities that are possible in MUDs is the assertion that new roles are often merely a reconstruction of power rather than a freedom from real-life constructed roles (Balsamo, 1993; Kendall, 1996).

The desire to protect women from sexually harassing electronic forums has led to other problems related to freedom of speech. At one university, for example, students were blocked from access to Usenet groups where the topic was related to sex, in order to protect women from harassment and avoid law suits from female students who could claim no safe space was made available to them on campus (Riley, 1996). However, other researchers believe that sexual harassment online is unsubstantiated, and that protection against perceived online harassment is only likely to perpetuate women's status as victims (Miller, 1995).

Do citizens use new technologies to support their rights to free speech in liberal democracy? Increased citizen participation is seen by democratic theorists as a function of better opportunities for free speech as well as increased access of citizens to voting registration and voter information and cheaper, faster access to parties and politicians (Corrado, 1996; Firestone & Schneider, 1996), removal of physical barriers to voting (Corrado, 1996), and removal of intermediaries to political information (such as journalists; Firestone & Schneider, 1996). We discuss more systematic participation in political activities in a section below. Here we focus on free speech within online environments.

The passing of the Communications Decency Act, subsequently struck down by the Supreme Court, presented a major blow to the anarchic, ungoverned nature of the Internet. Marshall (1998) notes, however, that greater threats to free speech have come from outside the government through private interests who put pressure on those who engage in less popular speech acts. Whine (1997) reports incidents of online vigilantism designed to police the environment. In cases of hate speech, individuals have been "run out of town" through expansive email campaigns by individuals and groups on the Internet.

Online service providers, system administrators of Usenets, and listserv own ers also act as gatekeepers for what can be said online. In many cases, behavior restrictions are based on a community code of moral and ethic behavior (Collins-Jarvis, 1997; Rheingold, 1993b). In most Usenets, listservs, and MUDs, system administrators have the right to delete offensive material, remove the offender from the forum, or let offensive material remain.

The U.S. Congress is currently trying to revive legislation that would limit online speech. But even in the shadow of potential threats to freedom of speech, the Internet still represents a potentially rich ground for reimagining democratic processes. Researchers have found examples of ways in which the technology has facilitated public electronic meeting spaces, providing a "place" to speak, as well as a faster rate of dissemination of information and a widened geographic population from which to draw—often, as of yet, without much government or corporate interference (Rheingold, 1993b). Grossman (1995), for instance, recounts the events that unfolded after a proposed amendment to a recent education bill that would have made it extremely difficult to homeschool children legally. The message of the upcoming vote on the bill spread quickly over a bulletin board service. The electronic homeschooling community quickly called their ranks to arms, and their congressional representatives were soon inundated with calls, faxes, and letters. The amendment was defeated.

On the Systers Usenet group (comprised of women in math and science), news of Mattel's newest talking Barbie ("Math is hard!") spread quickly and widely enough to generate a massive online protest, which resulted in talking Barbie's removal from the toy shelves (Camp, 1996). Grassroots efforts to stop the distribution of Lotus MarketPlace (which stored demographic information about millions of Americans) and the Clipper chip (an industry standard proposed to insure that all new electronic devices could be monitored by the government) were also successful due to speedy and broad dissemination efforts (Gurak, 1996, 1997). While these examples of organizing in the electronic public sphere show how new communication technologies can be used to resist power, they are not without problems. Gurak (1997) notes that the speed with which information can be disseminated can often pose a risk for misinformation. Rumors easily run rampant on electronic channels.

The Organizational Context

For researchers in the organizational context, new technologies have the potential to democratize by removing or reducing information gatekeepers, and in so doing diminishing the effects of hierarchy. Email, bulletin boards, and conferencing systems expand vertically and horizontally the amount and kinds of information disseminated in the organization, thus providing the potential for decision making to be decentralized among diverse organizational actors, as well as for improved access to decision-oriented interaction in the organization. On the other hand, it is also apparent that new technologies will not be a mechanism for "public sphere" discussion on the part of employees; the evidence suggests that new technologies are far more frequently used to gather information about employees than they are appropriated by employees for their own purposes.

Barley (1986, 1990) has argued that new technologies may alter existing organizational structures by changing the patterns of action associated with particular tasks, which may in turn alter the interaction networks required to support particular organizational processes. More specifically with respect to communication technologies, Zuboff's (1988) ethnographic studies found that computer conferencing and email increased the level of information exchanged among subordinates and between superiors and subordinates and created more collaborative working relationships for employees across organizational divisions. Sproull and Kiesler (1991) also found evidence to support decentralization, noting in particular that peripheral employees often felt more connected through the use of these media and that email presents the ability to speak directly with superiors, bypassing secretarial gatekeepers.

More recent research has been conducted in "virtual organizations" or VOs, which Adams (1997) defines as "any group of persons who organize through computer-mediated means of communication for some end or work" (p. 138). In VOs members are "less physically tangible," and they have more "democratic arenas" available to them in the form of chat lines, listservs, and WWW pages (Adams, 1997). Ahuja and Carly's (1998) study of hierarchies in VOs revealed that "virtual organizations may well be non-hierarchical and decentralized from an authority standpoint" but that individuals had to travel across or up several "layers" in their information seeking behavior and other communication acts. This led them to conclude that, "from a communication standpoint [VOs] may still be hierarchical and somewhat centralized. The reason for this rests in the communicative efficiency and robustness of the hierarchical form and in the benefits of role specialization."

Much of the research on reduced social cues, deindividuation, and flaming was conducted originally within small group and organizational contexts. Similar to the interpersonal context, new technologies are thought to facilitate more equal participation in organizational decision making due to reduction of social cues, even though email users are not always likely to be anonymous. This research has also sought to test the efficacy of group decision support systems (GDSS), which are designed to facilitate group decision processes through the use of computer-mediated communication channels such as email, electronic voting systems, and synchronous, sometimes anonymous, chat.

Studies have found that computer-mediated interaction in small groups is associated with more equal amounts of participation due to reduced social cues and deindividuation (Adrianson & Hjelmquist, 1991; DeSanctis, Poole, Lewis, & Desharnais, 1992; Dubrovsky, Kiesler, & Sethna, 1991; Kraemer & Pinsonneault, 1990; McLeod, Baron, Weighner Marti, & Yoon, 1997; Siegel et al., 1986; Straus, 1997). Equalization occurs because computer-mediated communication focuses attention on the text and deflects social cues such as high status or a dominating interactional style (Siegel et al., 1986). Not surprisingly, research on GDSS systems reflects incidents of increased flaming as well (Gallupe, DeSanctis, & Dickson, 1988; Siegel et al., 1986; Valacich & Schwenk, 1995).

However, more recent research has failed to consistently find differences in participation between face-to-face and CMC conditions (Savicki, Kelley, & Lingenfelter, 1996; Weisband, Schneider, & Connolly, 1995). Other studies have found decreases in participation equalization for CMC groups (Galegher & Kraut, 1994), or that participation is dependent on task type (Hiltz, Johnson, & Turoff, 1986). Weisband et al. (1995) failed to find status-equalizing effects in computer-mediated anonymous or nonanonymous conditions. Further, questions have been raised about the validity of equalization studies by researchers (Spears & Lea, 1994; Straus, 1997) who argue that computer-mediated communication reduces the amount of communication from all interactants and that equality of participation has no impact on productivity, satisfaction, or cohesiveness.

Additional concerns have been raised about the validity of GDSS studies. Researchers have argued that the ability of zero-history groups (usually in university labs) to simulate or generalize to actual organizational contexts is limited (Kraemer & Pinsonneault, 1990; Walther, 1992). Analysis of lab versus field studies finds that field studies reap similar results more consistently than lab studies (Dennis, Nunamaker, & Vogel, 1991). The use of timed studies has also been questioned, because groups using CMC take more time to communicate and therefore take longer to go through typical group stages such as task-orientation, conflict, and solidarity (Walther, 1992).

Because corporate success relies on the participation of all relevant employees in technological work processes, access to new technology is rarely an issue (see Allen, 1995, however, for evidence of gender-based distinctions in off-site connectivity to computer systems favoring males). More common are issues related to organizational access to electronic information about employees' activities. According to Gandy (1995), networked computers facilitate the gathering of information about keystrokes, transactions, email, and "even the tone of voice" of telemarketers, agents, and claims processors. Management's right to scrutinize employees' interaction, including email, computer conferencing transcripts, telephone logs, and other records has been upheld in court; further, management's proclivity to read, print, and sometimes disseminate employees' email has also been documented (Branscomb, 1994; Sproull & Kiesler, 1991; Weisband & Reinig, 1995; Zuboff, 1988). Alder and Tompkins (1997) reviewed evidence suggesting that electronic performance monitoring is extensive and argued that, without employees' involvement in setting its scope and conditions, such monitoring may give rise to resistance. On the other hand, Sewell (1998) contends that electronic surveillance combined with the peer group scrutiny characteristic of work teams enables organizations to "cede a degree of discretion to teams while increasing the probability that it is then exercised in line with the organization's goals and objectives" (p. 422).

Although Habermas (1989) did not include organizations in what he meant by the public sphere, there are several documented examples of employees' efforts to seize control of network resources and use them to generate alternative discourse within the organization. Sproull and Kiesler (1991) discuss the history of an IBM computer network that managers and staff used to publish an underground electronic newsletter in which they argued with management policies. Management responded by restricting access and monitoring network use. Further, Zuboff (1988) described a number of failed attempts to use computer conferencing systems to address employees' nonbusiness objectives, including a conferencing system originally intended for business productivity that became a social network. Through surveillance of conference transcripts, management discovered this unwelcome transition and coerced employees into ceasing their participation. A further example was a grassroots effort to establish an invitation-only list, whose members would defend the list's secrecy. Participation trailed off as managers inaugurated stricter surveillance tactics. Finally, women in the office seeking to create an "old girls network" formed a computer conference of their own. Management eventually cracked down on that conference too, applying even more direct surveillance techniques.

Because of improved surveillance techniques and stricter usage regulations, it is likely that these kinds of grassroots efforts will be minimized. Even so, it remains possible for employees to use new technologies to advance their own interests. In a case study of GDSS use, one researcher relates an incident in which a vice president informed subordinates that the board had just made a very unpopular decision; they subsequently turned on the GDSS system and started to try to generate ways to overcome the unpopular decision (Kettelhut, 1994). The vice president eventually calmed the insurrection, but the incident gives rise to the possibility that democratic interaction cannot always be predicted.

Government and Political Contexts

For at least 2 decades, social scientists and political leaders have been alive to the potential for new technologies to connect citizens with the political process and with politicians in general. Early experiments with teledemocracy demonstrated that plebiscitary democracy was technologically, if not socially, feasible and that technology could be used to bring citizens into greater contact with public officials (Arterton, 1987). With the rise of the Internet and World Wide Web, theorists and practitioners have begun to explore how these technologies can be used in the service of liberal democracy. However, the literature indicates that in this context, as in others, research and theory has also relied on assumptions related to access to information, decentralization, and deliberative democracy.

Certainly political parties are using the Net to keep connected with their constituencies and to provide them with information about the candidates. During the 1996 campaign, for example, Bob Dole's website received three million hits during its first 6 months, recruiting 10,000 people to join an email list and 1,700 individuals to volunteer (Corrado, 1996). Internet use was not limited to the presidential race. By January 1996, 70 senators and nearly 200 members of Congress had gotten email systems or websites (Corrado, 1996). Of potentially greater impact, though, is the ability for multiparty systems to emerge as a result of greater connections with voters. Because it is inexpensive to reach a large number of voters, and because it is not (yet) controlled by mass media or journalists, smaller, third party politicians have a greater opportunity to appeal to the electorate (Firestone & Schneider, 1996). The rise of additional political parties poses the possibility of engaging an otherwise apathetic voter population (Corrado, 1996; Firestone & Schneider, 1996).

The White House also maintains a sophisticated website, designed to create citizen empowerment by making information from the executive branch available to citizens (Hacker, 1996; Hacker & Todino, 1996). The White House site distributes documents related to the presidency and directs citizens to electronic forums for political discourse. Grassroots efforts to use the network to educate voters have arisen in the U.S., Canada, and England (Clift, 1998). In the U.S., Minnesota e-Democracy, established in 1994 to promote political participation, provides information about elections in Minnesota and hosts electronic debates for gubernatorial candidates, most recently in February 1998 (Raney, 1998).

Bimber (1998) is among the few who have collected empirical data assessing who is using the Internet to contact voters, finding that large, traditionally influential political organizations are the most active in using the Internet. He also found that nontraditional alternative organizations are actively engaged in contacting their constituencies; they reach fewer voters but rely more extensively on email for communication. In other research (Bimber, 1998), he has found that women are less likely to use technology in their political activities; in particular women are less likely to see candidates' websites, use the Web to read news, or send email to their representatives.

Kedzie (1995) has published perhaps the only empirical analysis of the general relationship between new technologies and liberal democracy, which assessed the relationship between the quality of interconnectivity as provided by four global computer networks (Internet, Bitnet, UUCP, and FidoNet), and the ranking of 141 countries on measures of their citizens' political rights to participate in policymaking and civil rights, such as freedom of speech. He found consistent univariate and multiple correlations between democracy and interconnectivity in analyses that suggest the causal force of technology.

States, such as California and Oregon, are using the Internet and Web to make certain liberal democratic practices, such as voter registration, easier. When online security becomes more robust and reliable, it will be possible for voting to occur online as well, perhaps benefiting voters who are physically challenged (Corrado, 1996). Of course, access issues play an important role in the Internet's ability to reinvigorate liberal democracy; no voting body is complete unless everyone who wants to can participate and, until that condition occurs, liberal claims about the democratizing power of the Internet will be restricted (Corrado, 1996; Firestone & Schneider, 1996; Jarvis, 1996; Loader, 1997).

Beyond using new technologies for election-oriented activity, local governments around the world are making considerable strides in designing online systems for accessing traditional local services and officials (Loader, 1997). Among the most famous of these is the Manchester Information City project in Manchester, England. According to Bryan (1996), the local political system in Manchester was a critical force in shaping the structure and objectives of the online system, which was oriented originally toward economic development. But she argues further that the development of Internet-related skills empowers citizens to participate in electronic democracy and encourages them to articulate their democratic ideals. Carter (1997) provides more detail about the specific projects that have comprised the project, which have focused on providing access to the Internet, training, technical support, and employment opportunities related to new technologies. He also describes the Telecities Network, a coalition of 50 cities across Europe actively pursuing online methods for providing access to government services. The online collection, *Democracy and Government On-Line Services*, (Ostberg & Clift, 1998) provides a more in-depth look at government-sponsored Internet services aimed at raising awareness of government processes, making government information available, facilitating feedback, enabling participation in government, and providing direct support for democratic (i.e., liberal democratic) processes.

Amsterdam and the Netherlands have been quite active in incorporating new technologies into the delivery of government services and information, with the anticipated effect, as Frissen (1997) predicts, of decentralizing the bureaucratic structures of public administration. Brants, Huizenga, and van Meerten (1996) discuss two specific Internet applications sponsored by the Amsterdam local government. "City Talks" consisted of discussions between representatives of political parties and nongovernmental organizations on local issues selected by representatives of social movement organizations and made possible through the use of cable television, telephone, teletext, and computers in public places. "City Consultations," a less successful application, was an interactive electronic questionnaire that the user accessed through so many different technologies that the complexity of the process probably operated as a disincentive. A third Internet application is the "Digital City" of Amsterdam, a citizen-initiated community network, which we discuss below.

Finally, we turn to the Santa Monica Public Electronic Network (PEN) project, introduced in 1989 as the first government-sponsored computer networking application oriented toward objectives that embraced both liberal and deliberative democracy. PEN designers provided city residents with free access to the system as well as publicly available access sites, so that even homeless individuals were able to become consistent users. PEN designers were also committed to creating the conditions for discussion of issues and access to local officials, which they addressed by creating online conferences devoted to community topics. O'Sullivan

(1995) found that the project succeeded in meeting certain criteria for evaluating teledemocracy projects; Collins-Jarvis (1993) examined the relatively low participation of females in PEN's electronic conferences; two articles have focused on electronic deliberations over the issue of homelessness (Rogers, Collins-Jarvis, & Schmitz 1994; Schmitz, Rogers, Phillips, & Paschal, 1995). Dutton (1996) identified five different viewpoints on the rights and responsibilities of participants in electronic discourse; his analysis suggests that interaction needs to be governed by contextual norms and conventions in order to accomplish the goals of liberal democratic discourse.

Community Networking

Most academics and practitioners celebrate the Internet and the World Wide Web as technologies that are overcoming limitations on communication traditionally imposed by geography. However, a rapidly growing community networking movement has chosen instead to use these technologies to enhance the development of their local communities. According to Schuler (1996a), an estimated 390 community networking services currently exist or are under development in the United States and around the world. This phenomena has become known by many different names—free-nets, community computing, community telecomputing, community bulletin boards, civic networking, telecommunity systems, and community information services—but what they share is a grass-roots orientation toward bringing community members from diverse walks of life together, meeting community needs and problems, and representing local culture, pride, and community ownership (Morino, 1994).

Community networks attempt to accomplish these goals by making community-related information or services (e.g., webpages for organizations, electronic conferences devoted to local issues) available online, through the World Wide Web, electronic mail, or a dial-in bulletin board. These services often focus on bringing the resources of information technology to bear upon traditional issues in community development: unemployment, economic stimulation, health and social welfare, environmental concerns, educational needs, and so forth.

An important objective for some developers has been to use community networks to provide equal access to information and computer networking technology, which has generally been accomplished by making equipment for accessing network services available to the public by placing computing equipment with modem connections in public spaces, as well as by offering free access to the Internet. Thus, many community networks have so far been created by activists whose primary interest centers on free or inexpensive access to the Internet (Tillman, 1997), to "democratize the Information SuperHighway" in the words of LaMendola and Rueda (1997). Doctor (1992) describes the free-net concept as holding "the greatest promise for realizing information democracy objectives" (p. 70).

Other theorists view community networks as the site for a significant reinvigoration of community life, a fulfillment of the communitarian vision of democracy

(Doheny-Farina, 1996; Schuler, 1995). According to London (1997), community networks have the potential to enhance civic discourse, by nurturing the development of dialogue and deliberation and by cultivating trust, connectedness, and cooperation.

Consistent with this perspective is the philosophy articulated by proponents of "civic networking," who, following the establishment of the U.S. Advisory Council on the National Information Infrastructure in 1993, argued the case for using information technology to revitalize both civic and economic institutions at the local level, believing that this would lead to a revitalization of civic culture in general (Civille, 1993; Civille, Fidelman, & Altobello, 1993; Fidelman, 1994; Sharp & Beaudry, 1994). Civille, Fidelman, and Altobello (1993) of the Center for Civic Networking outlined a general policy of widespread public access to networked information for the purpose of stimulating economic development, improving education, reducing the costs of government services, health care, pollution, and layoffs, and reviving civic institutions and discourse.

So far there has been little empirical research addressing community networks at all, much less that aimed at examining the effectiveness with which community networks have been able to achieve any of their goals. Some research has focused on describing the history of the development of particular community networking projects and their social, cultural, and economic contexts (see, for example, Harrison, Zappen, Stephen, Garfield, & Prell, 2001; Uncapher, 1991). Other research, such as that of Brants, Huizenga, and van Meerten (1996), describes characteristics of specific networking services. The Digital City of Amsterdam in The Netherlands, for example, provides access to the administrative information system of local government and also provides electronic conferences on computer technology, art and culture, and the relationship between information technology and democracy. Taking perhaps the first step at attempting to systematize the description of community networks, Doctor and Ankem (1996) have assessed over 600 services provided by four community networking systems in order to develop a taxonomy of information needs and services (education, social services, etc.) and the kinds of help provided by the system (factual, counseling, advocacy, etc.). Contractor, Zink, and Chan (1998) describe the development of software that community networks can use to assess the overlap in links between participating organizations in an effort to use their resources effectively in mobilizing for collective action.

Research has also studied demographic characteristics of the user populations of particular community networks with the purpose of determining how successful these projects have been in attracting a broad cross section of the community population; that research suggests that, so far at least, well-educated males are the heaviest consumers of community networking resources (see, e.g., Patrick & Black, 1996, on the National Capital FreeNet of Ottawa; Patterson & Kavanaugh, 1996, on the Blacksburg Electronic Village; and Schalken & Tops, 1994, on the Digital City in Amsterdam, The Netherlands).

A small number of studies have looked at the democratizing aspects of community networks. Harrison and Stephen (1998) found that the vast majority of the 40 community networks in their sample not only subscribed to the goal of providing equal access to information, but also made good on it by supplying free access to the network and, in many cases, equipment in public venues to use in obtaining access.

Law and Keltner (1995) conducted interviews with key individuals at five "civic networks" with the aim of describing the individual, group, and social benefits and disadvantages of providing access to networked technologies for individuals that are traditionally underserved. They found, first, civic networks provide access to information resources for those who would not otherwise enjoy access. Second, they found that all five networks engaged in activities designed to increase their users' involvement in politics and government. Finally, they found evidence that civic networks were able to create social capital by strengthening interpersonal relationships, bringing community members together, and helping nonprofit organizations to organize and function more effectively.

By interviewing individuals involved in the community networking movement, Friedland (1996) has also arrived at the conclusion that these projects create social capital. He suggests that the impact of a community network should not be measured in terms of numbers of users, but rather by the "ripple effects of secondary social network influences" (pp. 196–197). In particular, he advocates using social network theory to evaluate the formation and circulation of social capital in electronic networks.

Principally a practitioner, Schuler (1997) has invited academic researchers to participate in the creation of community networks and to investigate the factors that enable networks to succeed. But project developers are advised to build democratic decision making into the structure of the project. For Schuler (1996b), the best way to "kill" a community network is to fail to involve the community in the development of the service. Gygi (1996) has advised project developers that "Community-based organizations and other key stakeholders need to be involved in project planning and implementation. The degree of outside control and representativeness of the organizational structure will likely influence the community economic development and political participation outcomes associated with the project."

Two studies have attempted to evaluate the extent to which community networks themselves engage in democratic practices, although each cautions that they are only preliminary studies. Doctor and Hardy (1996) found that 80% of the 25 computerized community information systems in their sample were governed nondemocratically; that is, members or users had no formal voice in governance. Harrison and Stephen (1998) essentially replicated these results, finding that only approximately one-quarter of the services in their sample provided for democratic participation in the form of becoming a formal "member," attending meetings, or having the right to vote on issues.

CONCLUSION

Our review of four sites of research exploring the relationship between democracy and new technologies underscores that the five root theses defined earlier provide a useful basis for examining this broad area of study. It is apparent that each of these theses is well represented in our discussion of the research, although clearly some sites of research seem more focused on particular democratic perspectives than others. For example, research in government and political contexts tends to center on liberal democracy more than other theses, but not exclusively so. We see issues associated with access, decentralization, and deliberative democracy as well represented in this section of the review.

We began with the observation that researchers have not always agreed on the meaning of democracy and have subsequently seen how variable those meanings are and how significantly this variability permeates the literatures in each of the four contexts. Clearly, it will no longer do to speak simply of "democracy"; for the sake of clarity as well as progress, we need to acknowledge that the literature is comprised of at least five theoretical visions of democracy. In the future, research must begin by spelling out as explicitly as possible its particular perspective on democracy and locating itself within that particular tradition of thought. Only then can any significant advances in theory building and testing take place.

This review has also suggested that relatively little is actually known about the validity of the five root theses that we have introduced and assessed, or their countertheses. In nearly every context, research is embryonic, still addressing primarily descriptive questions in an effort to learn more about the form and shape of particular phenomena. But we do not regard this state of affairs with any particular alarm. The conceptual confusion over democracy that we have been complaining about is due to the exceptional richness of the concept, and the ability of new technologies to excite our imaginations about democracy has generated novel technological designs that are stimulating enormous public experimentation with new behaviors. While this period of intense social experimentation continues it is unlikely that definitive answers will be obtained.

It is important nonetheless to continue this research. As van Dijk (1996) suggests, the types of communication technologies designed will be strongly related to one's vision of democracy as different models call for different capabilities on the part of citizens and decision makers. And, as we have seen, each model of democracy we have considered entails different kinds of communicative action. For example, efficient and effective information distribution—a transmission model of communication—is only a prerequisite for some but entirely sufficient for other approaches to democracy. Hacker (1996) suggests that we need to understand the communicative dimensions of our theories of democracy in order to create applications that will enhance democracy, whatever we may mean by that term. That can only happen with greater effort to discern the connections between democracy and communication and to test those connections with technological applications used by people.

We are in a time of tremendous social, political, and economic ferment as myriad institutions jockey for position in the new information age. Castells's (1996, 1997) analysis helps us to understand the contours of the forces that are forging a new economic, societal, and cultural world: the loss of legitimacy and power of the nation-state, a global economy characterized by flows and networks of labor, materials, and information; the dissolution of the shared identities that are required for citizenship in a democracy; and the fragmentation of democratic political systems. He identifies three trends relevant to the "informational politics" that he foresees with the capacity for reconstructing democracy in the network society (Castells, 1997). First, in spite of the global economy currently under construction, politics will become reoriented around the local, with the "most powerful trends legitimizing democracy in the mid-1990s . . . taking place, worldwide, at the local level" (p. 350). Second, politics will become "symbolic" with political mobilization oriented increasingly around nonpolitical causes with wide consensus (e.g., humanitarian causes such as Amnesty International or Oxfam). Finally, the potential offered by computer-mediated communication to engage in online information diffusion and retrieval, to conduct issue referendums, to organize new political formations that circumvent traditional political structures, and to foster grass-roots deliberation and debate provide one final "path of democratic reconstruction" with outcomes as potentially forbidding as they are promising.

It seems fairly safe to say that computer-mediated communication will play an important role in the evolution of democracy as the world transitions to network society. Thus, it behooves us to work actively to express and test our democratic preferences—through theory development, research, and critique. Street (1996) reminds us that "the idea of democracy to which we aspire must be understood as partly a product of the technology that surrounds it" (p. 39). Thus, although we argued above that the design of technology depends in part upon our models of communication and democracy, it is important to recognize that our democratic aspirations will be influenced by the technology that we create. In the final analysis, the applications that survive will play a significant role in influencing the way that we think about democracy in the future.

REFERENCES

Abrahamson, J., Arterton, C., & Orren, G. (1988). *The electronic commonwealth: The impact of new media technologies on democratic politics*. New York: Basic Books.

Adams, T. L. (1997). Follow the yellow brick road: Using diffusion of innovations theory to enrich virtual organizations in cyberspace. *Southern Communication Journal, 62*(2), 133–148.

Adrianson, L., & Hjelmquist, E. (1991). Group processes in face-to-face and computer-mediated communication. *Behavior and Information Technology, 10*, 281–296.

Ahuja, M. K., & Carly, K. M. (1998). Network structure in virtual organizations. *Journal of Computer-Mediated Communication, 3*(4), [Online]. Available: http://www.ascusc.org/jcmc/vol3/issue4 ahuja.html

Alder, G. S., & Tompkins, P. K. (1997). Electronic performance monitoring: An organizational justice and concertive control perspective. *Management Communication Quarterly, 10*, 259–288.

Allen, B. J. (1995). Gender and computer-mediated communication. *Sex Roles, 32*(7– 8), 557.

Anderson, J. (1996). Not for the faint of heart: Contemplations on Usenet. In L. Cherny & E. R. Weise (Eds.), *Wired women: Gender and new realities in cyberspace* (pp. 126–138). Seattle, WA: Seal.

Ansah, P. A. V. (1986). The struggle for rights and values in revolution. In M. Traber (Ed.), *The myth of the information revolution* (pp. 64–83). London: Sage.

Arendt, H. (1958). *The human condition*. Chicago: University of Chicago Press.

Arterton, F. C. (1987). *Teledemocracy: Can technology protect democracy*? Newbury Park, CA: Sage.

Baird, P. M., & Borer, B. (1987). An experiment in computer conferencing using a local area network. *The Electronic Library, 5*(3), 162–169.

Balka, E. (1993). Women's access to on-line discussions about feminism. *Electronic Journal of Communication/La revue electronique de communication, 3*, [Online]. Available: http://www.cios.org/getfile/Balka_v3n193

Balsamo, A. (1993). Feminism for the incurably informed. *South Atlantic Quarterly, 92*, 681–712.

Barber, B. (1984). *Strong democracy*. Berkeley: University of California Press.

Barber, B. (1997). The new telecommunications technology: Endless frontier or the end of democracy? *Constellations, 4*(2), 208–228.

Barley, S. (1986). Technology as an occasion for structuring: Evidence from observations of CT scanners and the social order of radiology departments. *Administrative Science Quarterly, 31*, 78–108.

Barley, S. (1990). The alignment of technology and structure through roles and networks. *Administrative Science Quarterly, 35*, 61–103.

Baudrillard, J. (1983). *In the shadow of the silent majorities or, The end of the social and other essays*. P. Foss, J. Johnston, & P. Patton (Trans.). New York: Semiotext(e).

Baym, N. K. (1997). Interpreting soap operas and creating community: Inside an electronic fan culture. In S. Kiesler (Ed.), *Culture of the Internet* (pp. 103–120). Mahwah, NJ: Erlbaum.

Becker, T., & Scarce, R. (1987). Teledemocracy emergent: State of the American art and science. In B. Dervin & M. Voigt (Eds.), *Progress in Communication Sciences, Vol. 8*, (pp. 263–287). Norwood, NJ: Ablex.

Beetham, D. (1993). Liberal democracy and the limits of democratization. In David Held (Ed.), *Prospects for democracy* (pp. 55–73). Palo Alto, CA: Stanford University Press.

Bertelsen, D. (1992). Media form and government: Democracy as an archetypal image in the electronic age. *Communication Quarterly, 40*, 325–337.

Bennett, W. L. (1993). White noise: The perils of mass mediated democracy. *Communication Monographs, 59*, 401–406.

Berman, J., & Weitzer, D. J. (1997). Technology and democracy. *Social Research, 64*(3), 1313–1319.

Bimber, B. (1998). The Internet and political mobilization: Research note on the 1996 election season. *Social Science Computer Review, 16*(4), 391–401.

Bimber, B. (2000). Measuring the gender gap on the Internet. *Social Science Quarterly, 81*(3). 868–876.

Borg, A. (1994). Women defining technology for the 21st century: A report from America. In J. E. A. Adam, E. Green, & J. Owen (Eds.), *Women, work and computerization: Breaking old boundaries— Building new forms* (pp. 231–238). New York: Elsevier.

Bowie, N. (1990). Equity and access to information technology. *The Annual Reviews—1990* (pp. 131–177). Queenstown, MD: Institute for Information Studies.

Brail, S. (1996). The price of admission: Harassment and free speech in the wild, wild west. In L. Cherny & E. R. Weise (Eds.), *Wired women: Gender and new realities in cyberspace* (pp. 141–157). Seattle, WA: Seal.

Braman, S. (1994). The autopoietic state: Communication and democratic potential in the net. *Journal of the American Society for Information Science, 45*(6), 358–368.

Branscomb, A. W. (1994). *Who owns information? From privacy to public access*. New York: Basic Books.

Brants, K. (1996). Policing democracy: Communication freedom in the age of Internet. *Javnost, 3*, 57–70. Reprinted in the *Electronic Journal of Communication/La revue electronique de communication, 6*, [Online]. Available: http://www.cios.org/www/ejc/v6n296.htm

Brants, K., Huizenga, M., & van Meerten, R. (1996). The new canals of Amsterdam: An exercise in local electronic democracy. *Media, Culture, and Society, 18*, 233–247.

Bryan, C. (1996). Manchester: Democratic implications of an economic initiative. *Javnost, 3*, 103–116. Reprinted in the *Electronic Journal of Communication/La revue electronique de communication, 6*(2), [Online]. Available: http://www.cios.org/www/ejc/v6n296.htm

Calabrese, A., & Borchert, M. (1996). Prospects for electronic democracy in the United States: Rethinking communication and social policy. *Media, Culture, and Society, 18*(2), 249–268.

Calhoun, C. (1992). Introduction: Habermas and the public sphere. In C. Calhoun (Ed.), *Habermas and the public sphere* (pp. 1–48). Cambridge, MA: MIT Press.

Camp, L. J. (1996). We are geeks, and we are not guys: The Systers mailing list. In L. Cherny & E. R. Weise (Eds.), *Wired women: Gender and new realities in cyberspace* (pp. 114–126). Seattle, WA: Seal.

Carey, J., with James J. Quirk. (1988). The mythos of the electronic revolution. In J. Carey (Ed.), *Communication as culture: Essays on media and society* (pp. 113–141). Boston: Unwin Hyman.

Carter, D. (1997). Digital democracy or information aristocracy: Economic regeneration and the information economy. In B. D. Loader (Ed.), *The governance of cyberspace* (pp. 136–152). London: Routledge.

Castells, M. (1996). *The information age: Economy, society and culture. Vol. I: The rise of the network society*. Oxford, UK: Blackwell.

Castells, M. (1997). *The information age: Economy, society and culture. Vol. II: The power of identity*. Oxford, UK: Blackwell.

Cheney, G. (1995). Democracy in the workplace: Theory and practice from the perspective of communication. *Journal of Applied Communication Research, 23*, 167–200.

Cherry, C. (1985). *The age of access: Information technology and social revolution*. W. Edmondson (Ed.). London: Croom Helm.

Civille, R. (1993). *The Internet and the poor*, [Online]. Available: gopher://nic.merit.edu:7043/00/confererence.proceedings/network.communities/internet-poor.txt

Civille, R., Fidelman, M., & Altobello, J. (1993). *A national strategy for civic networking: A vision of change*, [Online]. Available: gopher://gopher.civic.net:2400/00/ssnational strat/national strategy.txt.

Clement, A. (1988). Office automation and the technical control of information workers. In V. Mosco & J. Wasko (Eds.), *The political economy of information* (pp. 217–246). Madison: University of Wisconsin Press.

Clerc, S. (1996). Estrogen brigades and "big tits" threads: Media fandom online and off. In L. Cherny & E. R. Weise (Eds.), *Wired women: Gender and new realities in cyberspace* (pp. 73–97). Seattle, WA: Seal.

Cleveland, H. (1985). The twilight of hierarchy: Speculations on the global information society. In B. Guile (Ed.), *Information technologies and social transformation* (pp. 55–79). Washington, DC: National Academy Press.

Clift, S. (1998). Democracy is online. *OnTheInternet*, March/April, [Online]. Available: http://www.e-democracy.org/do/article.html

Collins-Jarvis, L. (1993). Gender representation in an electronic city hall: Female adoption of Santa Monica's PEN system. *Journal of Broadcasting and Electronic Media, 37*, 49–65.

Collins-Jarvis, L. (1997, November). *Discriminatory messages and gendered power relations in online discussion groups*. Paper presented at the annual meeting of the National Communication Association, Chicago.

Connell, I. (1996). Cyberspace: The continuation of political education by other means. *Javnost, 3*, 87–102. Reprinted in the *Electronic Journal of Communication/La revue electronique de communication, 6*, [Online]. Available: http://www.cios.org/www/ejc/v6n296.htm

Contractor, N., Zink, D., & Chan, M. (1998). IKNOW: A tool to assist and study the creation, maintenance, and dissolution of knowledge networks. In T. Ishida (Ed.), *Lecture Notes in Computer Science, 1519. Community computing and support systems* (pp. 201–217). New York: Springer-Verlag.

Corbett, E. P. J. (1990). *Classical rhetoric for the modern student* (3rd ed.). New York: Oxford University Press.

Corrado, A. (1996). Elections in cyberspace: Prospects and problems. In A. Corrado & C. M. Firestone (Eds.), *Elections in cyberspace: Toward a new era in American politics* (pp. 1–31). Washington, DC: Aspen Institute.

Curtis, T. (1988). The information society: A computer-generated caste system. In V. Mosco & J. Wasko (Eds.), *The political economy of information* (pp. 95–107). Madison: University of Wisconsin Press.

Davis, G. (1997). Alexis de Tocqueville and the Internet. *Press/Politics, 2*(2), 120–126.

Deethardt, J. (1983). Inventing democracy: Future alternatives for social action. *Communication Education, 32,* 153–166.

Deetz, S. (1992). *Democracy in an age of corporate colonization.* Albany: SUNY Press.

Dennis, A. R., Nunamaker, J. F., Jr., & Vogel, D. R. (1991). A comparison of laboratory and field research in the study of electronic meeting systems. *Journal of Management Information Systems, 7*(3), 107–135.

DeSanctis, G., Poole, M. S., Lewis, H., & Desharnais, G. (1992). Using computing in quality team meetings: Initial observations from the IRS-Minnesota project. *Journal of Management Information Systems, 8*(3), 7–26.

Dervin, B. (1994). Information-democracy: An examination of underlying assumptions. *Journal of the American Society for Information Science, 45*(6), 369–385.

Deuel, N. R. (1996). Our passionate response to virtual reality. In S. Herring (Ed.), *Computer-mediated communication: Linguistic, social and cross-cultural perspectives* (pp. 129–146). Philadelphia: John Benjamins.

Dewey, J. (1916). *Democracy and education.* New York: Macmillan.

Dibbell, J. (1993, December 21). A rape in cyberspace, or, How an evil clown, a Haitian trickster spirit, two wizards and a cast of dozens turned a database into a society. *Village Voice,* pp. 36–43.

Doctor, R. D. (1991). Information technologies and social equity: Confronting the revolution. *Journal of the American Society for Information Science, 42*(3), 216–228.

Doctor, R. D. (1992). Society equity and information technologies: Moving toward information democracy. In M. E. Williams (Ed.), *Annual review of information science and technology, 27,* 43–96.

Doctor, R. D., & Ankem, K. (1996). An information needs and services taxonomy for evaluating computerized community information systems. *Proceedings of the American Society for Information Science Mid-Year Meeting* (pp. 275–283). Medford, NJ: Information Today.

Doctor, R., & Hardy, C. (1996). *Democracy and governance in computerized community information services,* [Online]. Available: http://www.laplaza.org/cn/local/doctor2.html

Doheny-Farina, S. (1996). *The wired neighborhood.* New Haven, CT: Yale University Press.

Dubrovsky, V. J., Kiesler, S., & Sethna, B. N. (1991). The equalization phenomenon: Status effects in computer-mediated and face-to-face decision making groups. *Human Computer Interaction, 6,* 119–146.

Dutton, W. (1996). Network rules of order: Regulating speech in public electronic fora. *Media, Culture, & Society, 18,* 269–290.

Elmer, G. (1997). Spaces of surveillance: Indexicality and solicitation on the Internet. *Critical Studies in Mass Communication, 14,* 182–191.

Ess, C. (1996). The political computer. In C. Ess (Ed.), *Philosophical perspectives on computer-mediated communication* (pp. 197–230). Albany, NY: SUNY Press.

Evans, F. (1991). To "informate" or "automate": The new information technologies and democratization of the workplace. *Social Theory and Practice, 17*(3), 409–439.

Faigley, L. (1992). The achieved utopia of the networked classroom. In L. Faigley (Ed.), *Fragments of rationality: Postmodernity and the subject of composition* (pp. 163–199). Pittsburgh, PA: University of Pittsburgh Press.

Fay, B. (1987). *Critical social science.* Ithaca, NY: Cornell University Press.

Fidelman, M. (1994). *Life in the fast lane: A municipal roadmap for the information superhighway*, [Online]. Available: http://civic.net/fastlane.html

Firestone, C. M., & Schneider, P. A. (1996). Forward. In A. Corrado & C. M. Firestone (Eds.), *Elections in cyberspace: Toward a new era in American politics* (pp. v–x). Washington, DC: Aspen Institute.

Flichy, P. (1995). *Dynamics of modern communication: The shaping and impact of new communication technologies*. London: Sage.

Fraser, N. (1992). Rethinking the public sphere: A contribution to the critique of actually existing democracy. In C. Calhoun, *Habermas and the public sphere* (pp. 109–142). Cambridge, MA: MIT Press.

Friedland, L. (1996). Electronic democracy and the new citizenship. *Media, Culture, and Society, 18*, 185–212.

Frissen, P. (1997). The virtual state: Postmodernisation, informatisation, and public administration. In B. Loader (Ed.), *The governance of cyberspace* (pp. 111–125). London: Routledge.

Galegher, J., & Kraut, R. E. (1994). Computer-mediated communication for intellectual teamwork: An experiment in group writing. *Information Systems Research, 5*(2), 110–138.

Gallupe, R. B., DeSanctis, G., & Dickson, G. W. (1988). Computer-based support for group problem-finding: An experimental investigation. *MIS Quarterly, June*, 277–296.

Gandy, O. (1988). The political economy of communications competence. In V. Mosco & J. Wasko (Eds.), *The political economy of information* (pp. 108–124). Madison: University of Wisconsin Press.

Gandy, O. (1989). The surveillance society: Information technology and bureaucratic social control. *Journal of Communication, 39*(3), 61–76.

Gandy, O. H., Jr. (1995). It's discrimination, stupid! In J. Brook & I. A. Boal (Eds.), *Resisting the virtual life: The culture and politics of information* (pp. 35–47). San Francisco: City Lights.

Garnham, N. (1992). The media and the public sphere. In C. Calhoun (Ed.), *Habermas and the public sphere* (pp. 359–376). Cambridge, MA: MIT Press.

Gilboa, N. (1996). Elites, lamers, narcs and whores: Exploring the computer underground. In L. Cherny & E. R. Weise (Eds.), *Wired women: Gender and new realities in cyberspace* (pp. 98–113). Seattle, WA: Seal.

Gillespie, A., & Robins, K. (1989). Geographical inequalities: The spatial bias of the new communications technologies. *Journal of Communication, 39*(3), 7–18.

Grossman, L. (1995). *The electronic republic: Reshaping democracy in the information age*. New York. Viking.

Gurak, L. J. (1996). The rhetorical dynamics of a community protest in cyberspace: What happened with Lotus MarketPlace. In S. Herring (Ed.), *Computer-mediated communication: Linguistic, social, and cross-cultural perspectives* (pp. 264–277). Philadelphia: John Benjamins.

Gurak, L. J. (1997). *Persuasion and privacy in cyberspace*. New Haven, CT: Yale University Press.

Gygi, K. (1996). *Uncovering best practices: A framework for assessing outcomes in community computer networking*, [Online]. Available: http://www.laplaza.org/about lap/archives/cn96/gygi.html

Habermas, J. (1970). Towards a theory of communicative competence. *Inquiry, 13*, 360–375.

Habermas, J. (1989). *The structural transformation of the public sphere* (T. Burger, Trans.). Cambridge, MA: MIT Press.

Hacker, K. (1996). Missing links in the evolution of electronic democratization. *Media, Culture, & Society, 18*, 213–232.

Hacker, K., & Todino, M. (1996). Virtual democracy at the Clinton White House: An experiment in electronic democratisation. *Javnost, 3*, 71–86. Reprinted in the *Electronic Journal of Communication/La revue electronique de communication, 6*(2), [Online]. Available: http://www.cios.org/www/ejc/v6n296.htm

Hall, K. (1996). Cyberfeminism. In S. Herring (Ed.), *Computer-mediated communication: Linguistic, social and cross-cultural perspectives* (pp. 147–170). Philadelphia: John Benjamins.

Haraway, D. (1985). A manifesto for cyborgs: Science, technology, and socialist feminism in the 1980s. *Socialist Review, 15*, 65–107.

Hamelink, C. (1986). Is there life after the information revolution? In M. Traber (Ed.), *The myth of the information revolution* (pp. 7–20). London: Sage.

Harasim, L. (1993). Networks: Networking as social space. In L. Harasim (Ed.), *Global networks* (pp. 15–34). Cambridge, MA: MIT Press.

Harasim, L. (1996). Online education: The future. In T. Harrison & T. Stephen (Eds.), *Computer networking and scholarly communication in the twenty-first century university* (pp. 203–214). Albany, NY: SUNY Press.

Hardt, H. (1996). The making of the public sphere: Class relations and communication in the United States. *Javnost, 3*, 7–23. Reprinted in the *Electronic Journal of Communication/La revue electronique de communication, 6*, [Online]. Available: http://www.cios.org/www/ejc/v6n296.htm

Harrison, T., & Stephen, T. (1996). Computer networking, communication, and scholarship. In T. Harrison & T. Stephen (Eds.), *Computer networking and scholarly communication in the twenty-first century university* (pp. 3–36). Albany, NY: SUNY Press.

Harrison, T., & Stephen, T. (1998). Researching and creating community networks. In S. Jones (Ed.), *Doing Internet research*. Newbury Park, CA: Sage.

Harrison, T., Zappen, J., Stephen, T., Garfield, P., & Prell, C. (2001). Building electronic community: A town-grown collaboration. In E. Rothenbuhler & G. Shepherd (Eds.), *Communication and community*. Mahwah, NJ: Erlbaum.

Held, D. (1996). *Models of democracy* (2nd ed.). Stanford, CA: Stanford University Press.

Herring, S. (1993). Gender and democracy in computer-mediated communication. *Electronic Journal of Communication/La revue electronique de communication, 3*, [Online]. Available: http://www.cios.org/www/ejc/v3n393.htm

Herring, S., Johnson, D., & DiBenedetto, T. (1992). Participation in electronic discourse in a "feminist" field. In K. Hall, M. Bucholtz, & B. Moonwomon (Eds.), *Proceedings of the second Berkeley Women and Language Conference, Vol. 1: Locating power*. Berkeley, CA: Berkeley Women and Language Group.

Herring, S., Johnson, D., & DiBenedetto, T. (1995). This discussion is going too far! In K. Hall & M. Bucholtz (Eds.), *Gender articulated* (pp. 67–96). New York: Routledge.

Hiltz, S. R., Johnson, K., & Turoff, M. (1986). Experiments in group decision making: Communication process and outcome in face-to-face versus computerized conferences. *Human Communication Research, 13*(2), 225–252.

Hiltz, S. (1977). Computer conferencing: Assessing the social impact of a new communications medium. *Technological Forecasting and Social Change, 10*, 223–238.

Hiltz, S., & Turoff, M. (1993). *The network nation: Human communication via computer* (rev. ed.). Cambridge, MA: MIT Press. (Original work published 1978)

Innis, H. (1951). *The bias of communication*. Toronto, Canada: University of Toronto Press.

Jacobson, R. (1996). "Are they building an off-ramp in my neighborhood?" and other questions concerning public interest in the access to the information superhighway. In L. Strate, R. Jacobson, & S. B. Gibson (Eds.), *Communication and cyberspace: Social interaction in an electronic environment* (pp. 143–153). Cresskill, NJ: Hampton Press.

Jarvis, S. R. (1996). Assessing the impact of new technologies on the political process. In A. Corrado & C. M. Firestone (Eds.), *Elections in cyberspace: Toward a new era in American politics* (pp. 35–45). Washington, DC: Aspen Institute.

Johnson, D. (1997). Is the global information infrastructure a democratic technology? *Computers and Society, 27*(3), 20–26.

Kedzie, C. (1995). International implications for global democratization. In R. H. Anderson (Ed.), *Universal access to e-mail: Feasibility and societal implications* (pp. 151–168). Santa Monica, CA: Rand.

Keane, J. (1991). *The media and democracy*. Cambridge, UK: Polity Press.

Kellner, D. (1997). Intellectuals, the public sphere, and new technologies. *Research in Philosophy and Technology, 16*, 15–31.

Kendall, L. (1996). MUDder? I hardly know 'er! Adventures of a feminist MUDder. In L. Cherny & E. R. Weise (Eds.), *Wired women: Gender and new realities in cyberspace* (pp. 207–223). Seattle, WA: Seal.

Kennedy, G. (1994). *A new history of classical rhetoric*. Princeton, NJ: Princeton University Press.

Kettelhut, M. C. (1994). How to avoid misusing electronic meeting support. *Planning Review, 22*(4), 34–38.

Kiesler, S., Siegel, J., & McGuire, T. W. (1984). Social psychological aspects of computer-mediated communication. *American Psychologist, 39*, 1123–1134.

Kraemer, K. L., & Pinsonneault, A. (1990). Technology and groups: Assessment of the empirical research. In J. Galegher, R. E. Kraut, & C. Egido (Eds.), *Intellectual teamwork: Social & technological foundations of cooperative work* (pp. 375–405). Mahwah, NJ: Erlbaum.

Kramarae, C., & Taylor, H. J. (1993). Women and men on electronic networks: A conversation or a monologue? In H. J. Taylor, C. Kramarae, & M. Ebben (Eds.), *Women, information technology and scholarship* (pp. 52–61). Urbana, IL: Center for Advanced Study.

LaMendola, W. F., & Rueda, P. (1997). *An evaluation of the Colorado Access-Value-Content Project*, [Online]. Available: http://bcn.boulder.co.us/~rueda/aclin.html

Lanham, R. (1993). *The electronic word: Democracy, technology, and the arts*. Chicago: University of Chicago Press.

Law, S. A., & Keltner, B. (1995). Civic networks: Social benefits of on-line communities. In R. H. Anderson (Ed.), *Universal access to e-mail: Feasibility and societal implications* (pp. 119–150). Santa Monica, CA: Rand.

Lea, M., O'Shea, T., Fung, P., & Spears, R. (1992). "Flaming" in computer-mediated communication: Observations, explanations, implications. In M. Lea (Ed.), *Contexts of computer-mediated communication* (pp. 89–112). New York: Harvester-Wheatsheaf.

Lea, M., & Spears, R. (1991). Computer-mediated communication, deindividuation and group decision-making. *International Journal of Man-Machine Studies, 34*, 283–301.

Lerch, I. A. (1983). Computer conferencing—A new tool for scientific communication. *Physics Today, 36*(8), 9, 90.

Lievrouw, L. (1994). Information resources and democracy: Understanding the paradox. *Journal of the American Society for Information Science, 45*(6), 350–357.

Lipton, M. (1996). Forgetting the body: Cybersex and identity. In L. Strate, R. Jacobson, & S. B. Gibson (Eds.), *Communication and cyberspace: Social interaction in an electronic environment* (pp. 335–349). Cresskill, NJ: Hampton Press.

Loader, B. (1997). The governance of cyberspace: Politics, technology and global restructuring. In B. D. Loader (Ed.), *The governance of cyberspace* (pp. 1–19). London: Routledge.

London, S. (1997). Civic networks: building community on the net, [Online].Available: http://www.west.net/~insight/london/networks.htm.

MacKinnon, R. (1995). Searching for the Leviathan in Usenet. In S. Jones (Ed.), *CyberSociety* (pp. 112–137). Thousand Oaks, CA: Sage.

Mantovani, G. (1994). Is computer-mediated communication intrinsically apt to enhance democracy in organizations? *Human Relations, 47*, 45–62.

Markus, L. (1987). Toward a "critical mass" theory of interactive media. *Communication Research, 14*, 491–511.

Marshall, J. M. (1998). Will free speech get tangled in the Net? *American Prospect, Jan/Feb*(36), 46–50.

Marvin, C. (1988). *When old technologies were new*. Oxford, UK: Oxford University Press.

Matheson, K. (1991). Social cues in computer-mediated negotiations: Gender makes a difference. *Computers in Human Behavior, 7*, 137–145.

Matheson, K., & Zanna, M. P. (1988). The impact of computer-mediated communication on self-awareness. *Computers in Human Behavior, 4*, 221–233.

McLuhan, M. (1962). *The Gutenberg galaxy.* Toronto, Canada: University of Toronto Press.

McLuhan, M. (1964/1995). *Understanding media.* Cambridge, MA: MIT Press.

McLaughlin, L. (1993). Feminism, the public sphere, media and democracy. *Media, Culture, and Society, 15,* 599–620.

McLeod, P. (1992). An assessment of the experimental literature on electronic support of group work: Results of a meta-analysis. *Human-Computer Interaction, 7,* 257–280.

McLeod, P. L., Baron, R. S., Weighner Marti, M., & Yoon, K. (1997). The eyes have it: Minority influence in face-to-face and computer-mediated group discussion. Journal of Applied Psychology, 82, 706–718.

McQuail, D. (1995). New roles for new times. *Media Studies Journal, 9*(3), 11–19.

Meeks, B. (1997). Better democracy through technology. *Communications of the ACM, 40*(2), 75–78.

Miller, L. (1995). Women and children first: Gender and the settling of the electronic frontier. In J. Brook & I. A. Boal (Eds.), *Resisting the virtual life: The culture and politics of information* (pp. 49–57). San Francisco: City Lights.

Morino, M. (1994). Assessment and evolution of community networking, [Online]. Available: http://www.morino.org/under_sp_asse.asp

Murdock, G. (1995). Across the Great Divide: Cultural analysis and the condition of democracy. *Critical Studies in Mass Communication, 12,* 89–95.

Naisbitt, J. (1982). *Megatrends: Ten new directions transforming our lives.* New York: Warner Books.

Nunamaker, J. F., Dennis, A. R., Valacich, J. S., Vogel, D. R., & George, J. F. (1991). Electronic meeting systems to support group work. *Communications of the ACM, 34*(7), 40–61.

Oldenberg, R. (1989). *The great good place.* New York: Paragon House.

O'Sullivan, P. (1995). Computer networks and political participation: Santa Monica's teledemocracy project. *Journal of Applied Communication Research, 23,* 93–107.

Ostberg, O., & Clift, S. (1998). *Democracy and government on-line services,* [Online]. Available: http://www.state.mn.us/gol/democracy.

O'Toole, J. (1990). Information and power: Social and political consequences of advanced tele/computing technology. *The Annual Review—1990* (pp. 211–249). Queenstown, MD: Institute for Information Studies.

Parry-Giles, S. J. (1993). The rhetorical tension between propaganda and democracy: Blending competing conceptions of ideology and theory. *Communication Studies, 44,* 117–131.

Pateman, C. (1970). *Participation and democratic theory.* Cambridge, UK: Cambridge University Press.

Patrick, A. S., & Black, A. (1996). *Rich, young, male, dissatisfied computer geeks? Demographics and satisfaction from the National Capital FreeNet,* [Online]. Available: http://debra.dgbt.doc.ca/services-research/survey/demographics/paper/.

Patterson, S., & Kavanaugh, A. (1996). *Summary of user profiles and expectations,* [Online]. Available: http://www.bev.net/research/Users.2_96.html

Perelman, M. (1998). *Class warfare in the information age.* New York: St. Martin's Press.

Pfaffenberger, B. (1986). Research networks, scientific communication and the personal computer. *IEEE Transactions on Professional Communication, PC 29*(1), 30–33.

Pool, I. de Sola. (1983). *Technologies of freedom.* Cambridge, MA: Harvard University Press.

Putnam, R. (1993). *Making democracy work: Civic traditions in modern Italy.* Princeton, NJ: Princeton University Press.

Putnam, R. (1995). Bowling alone: America's declining social capital. *Journal of Democracy, 6*(1), 65–78.

Putnam, R. (1996). The strange disappearance of civic America. *Policy: A Journal of Public Policy, 12*(1), 31–43.

Raab, C. (1997). Privacy, democracy, information. In B. D. Loader (Ed.), *The governance of cyberspace* (pp. 155–174). London: Routledge.

Raney, R. F. (1998, March 2). In online debate, candidates focus on issues without spin. *New York Times Cybertimes,* [Online]. Available: http://www.nytimes.com/library.cyber/articles/02minnesota.html

Rheingold, H. (1993a). A slice of life in my virtual community. In L. Harasim (Ed.), *Global networks: Computers and international communication* (pp. 57–80). Cambridge, MA: MIT Press.

Rheingold, H. (1993b). *The virtual community.* Reading, MA: Addison-Wesley.

Rice, R. (1984) *The new media: Communication, research, and technology.* Beverly Hills, CA: Sage.

Riley, D. M. (1996). Sex, fear and condescension on campus: Cybercensorship at Carnegie Mellon. In L. Cherny & E. R. Weise (Eds.), *Wired women: Gender and new realities in cyberspace* (pp. 158–168). Seattle, WA: Seal.

Ritchie, L. D. (1991). Another turn of the information revolution: Relevance, technology, and the information society. *Communication Research, 18,* 412–427.

Robins, K., & Webster, F. (1988). Cybernetic capitalism: Information, technology, everyday life. In V. Mosco & J. Wasko (Eds.), *The political economy of information.* Madison: University of Wisconsin Press.

Rogers, E., Collins-Jarvis, L., & Schmitz, J. (1994). The PEN project in Santa Monica: Interactive communication equality, and political action. *Journal of the American Society for Information Science, 45,* 401–410.

Roszak, T. (1994). *The cult of information* (rev. ed.). Berkeley: University of California Press.

Rucinski, D. (1991). The centrality of reciprocity to communication and democracy. *Critical Studies in Mass Communication, 8,* 184–194.

Sassi, S. (1996). The network and the fragmentation of the public sphere. *Javnost, 3.* Reprinted in the *Electronic Journal of Communication/La revue electronique de communication, 6,* [Online]. Available: http://www.cios.org/www/ejc/v6n296.htm

Savicki, V., Kelley, M., & Lingenfelter, D. (1996). Gender and group composition in small task groups using computer-mediated communication. *Computers in Human Behavior, 12*(2), 209–224.

Schalken, K., & Tops, P. (1994). *The digital city: A study into the backgrounds and opinions of its residents,* [Online]. Available: http://cwis.kub.nl/~frw/people/schalken/schalken.htm

Schickler, E. (1994). Democratizing technology: Hierarchy and innovation in public life. *Polity, 27*(2), 175–199.

Schiller, D. (1988). How to think about information. In V. Mosco & J. Wasko (Eds.), The political economy of information (pp. 27–43). Madison: University of Wisconsin Press.

Schiller, H. I. (1995). The global information highway: Project for an ungovernable world. In J. Brooks & I. A. Boal (Eds.), *Resisting the virtual life: The culture and politics of information* (pp. 17–33). San Francisco: City Lights.

Schiller, H. I. (1996). *Information Inequality: The deepening social crisis in America.* New York: Routledge.

Schlesinger, A. (1997) Has democracy a future? *Foreign Affairs, 76*(5) 2–12.

Schmitz, J., Rogers, E., Phillips, K., & Paschal, D. (1995). The Public Electronic Network (PEN) and the homeless in Santa Monica. *Journal of Applied Communication, 23,* 26–43.

Schudson, M. (1992). Was there ever a public sphere? If so, when? Reflections on the American case. In C. Calhoun (Ed.), *Habermas and the public sphere* (pp. 142–163). Cambridge, MA: MIT Press.

Schudson, M. (1997). Why conversation is not the soul of democracy. *Critical Studies in Mass Communication, 14,* 297–309.

Schuler, D. (1995). *Creating public space in cyberspace: The rise of the new community networks,* [Online]. Available: http://scn.org/ip/commnet/iwdec.html

Schuler, D. (1996a). *New community networks: Wired for change.* Reading, MA: Addison-Wesley.

Schuler, D. (1996b). *How to kill community networks. Hint: We may have already started,* [Online]. Available: http://www.scn.org/ip/commnet/kill-commnets.html

Schuler, D. (1997). *Community computer networks: An opportunity for collaboration among democratic technology practitioners and researchers,* [Online]. Available: http://www.scn.org/ip/commnet/oslo-1997.text

Sclove, R. E. (1995b). Making technology democratic. In J. Brooks & I. A. Boal (Eds.), *Resisting the virtual life: The culture and politics of information* (pp. 85–101). San Francisco: City Lights.

Sewell, G. (1998). The discipline of teams: The control of team-based industrial work through electronic and peer surveillance. *Administrative Science Quarterly, 43,* 397–428.

Shade, L. R. (1996). Is there free speech on the net? In R. Shields (Ed.), *Cultures of Internet: Virtual spaces, real histories, living bodies* (pp. 11–32). London: Sage.

Shapiro, A. (1998, June 6). New voices in cyberspace. *The Nation,* [Online]. Available: http://past.thenation.com/issue/980608/0608shapiro.shtml

Sharp, M. Beaudry, A. (1994). *Communications as engagement: The Millennium report to the Rockefeller Foundation,* [Online]. Available: http://www.cdinet.com/Millennium

Siegel, J., Dubrovsky, V., Kiesler, S., & McGuire, T. (1986). Group processes in computer-mediated communication. *Organizational Behavior and Human Decision Processes, 37,* 157–187.

Slack, J. D. (1984). *Communication technologies and society: Conceptions of causality and the politics of technological intervention.* Norwood, NJ: Ablex.

Smith, C. B., McLaughlin, M. L., & Osborne, K. K. (1997). Conduct control on Usenet. *Journal of Computer-Mediated Communication, 2*(4), [Online]. Available: http://www.ascusc.org/jcmc/vol2/issue4/smith.html

Spears, R., & Lea, M. (1992). Social influence and the influence of the "social" in computer-mediated communication. In M. Lea (Ed.), *Contexts of computer-mediated communication* (pp. 30–65). New York: Harvester-Wheatsheaf.

Spears, R., & Lea, M. (1994). Panacea or panopticon? The hidden power in computer-mediated communication. *Communication Research, 21,* 427–459.

Spears, R., Lea, M., & Lee, S. (1990). De-individuation and group polarization in computer-mediated communication. *British Journal of Social Psychology, 29,* 121–134.

Sproull, L., & Kiesler, S. (1991). *Connections: New ways of working in the networked organization.* Cambridge, MA: MIT Press.

Straus, S. G. (1997). Technology, group process, and group outcomes: Testing the connections in computer-mediated and face-to-face groups. *Human-Computer Interaction, 12,* 227–266.

Street, J. (1997). Remote control? Politics, technology and electronic democracy. *European Journal of Communication, 12*(1), 27–42.

Sutton, L. A. (1994, February). *Using USENET: Gender, power and silence in electronic discourse.* Paper presented at the annual meeting of the Berkeley Linguistics Society, Berkeley, CA.

Tehranian, M. (1990). *Technologies of power: Information machines and democratic prospects.* Norwood, NJ: Ablex.

Thorn, B., & Connolly, T. (1987). Discretionary data bases: Theory and some experimental findings. *Communication Research, 14,* 512–528.

Thompsen, P. A. (1996). What's fueling the flames in cyberspace? A social influence model. In L. Strate, R. Jacobson, & S. B. Gibson (Eds.), *Communication and cyberspace: Social interaction in an electronic environment,* (pp. 297–315). Cresskill, NJ: Hampton Press.

Tillman, C. (1997). *Thinking about the future: The National Capital FreeNet/Libertel de la Capitale Nationale,* [Online]. Available: http://www.si.umich.edu/Community/pro ncf.html

Toffler, A. (1981). *The third wave.* New York: Morrow.

Tuman, M. (1992). *Word perfect: Literacy in the computer age.* Pittsburgh, PA: University of Pittsburgh Press.

Turkle, S. (1995). *Life on the screen: Identity in the age of the Internet.* New York: Simon & Schuster.

Uncapher, W. (1991). Rural grassroots telecommunication: Big Sky Telegraph and its community. [Online]. Available: http://www.well.com:70/0/Community/communets/bigsky.txt

Valacich, J. S., & Schwenk, C. (1995). Devil's advocacy and dialectical inquiry effects on face-to-face and computer-mediated group decision making. *Organizational Behavior and Human Decision Processes, 63*(2), 158–173.

van Dijk, J. (1996). Models of democracy—Behind the design and use of new media in politics. *Javnost, 3,* 43–56. Reprinted in the *Electronic Journal of Communication/La revue electronique de communication, 6,* [Online]. Available: http://www.cios.org/www/ejc/v6n296.htm

Walther, J. B. (1992). Interpersonal effects in computer-mediated interaction: A relational perspective. *Communication Research, 19*, 52–90.

Webster, F., & Robins, K. (1986). *Information technology: A Luddite analysis*. Norwood, NJ: Ablex.

Weisband, S. P., & Reinig, B. A. (1995). Managing user perception of email privacy. *Communications of the ACM, 38*(12), 40–47.

Weisband, S. P., Schneider, S. K., & Connolly, T. (1995). Computer-mediated communication and social information: Status salience and status differences. *Academy of Management Journal, 38*(4), 1124–1151.

Wellman, B. (1997). An electronic group is a social network. In S. Kiesler (Ed.), *Culture of the Internet* (pp. 179–205). Mahwah, NJ: Erlbaum.

Westin, A. (1971). Civil liberties issues in public databanks. In A. Westin (Ed.), *Information technology in a democracy* (pp. 301–310). Cambridge, MA: Harvard University Press.

Witmer, D. F., & Katzman, S. L. (1997). On-line smiles: Does gender make a difference in the use of graphic accents. *Journal of Computer-Mediated Communication, 2*(4), [Online]. Available: http://www.ascusc.org/jcmc/vol2/issue4/witmer1.html

Whine, M. (1997). The far right on the Internet. In B. D. Loader (Ed.), *The governance of cyberspace* (pp. 209–227). London: Routledge.

Winner, L. (1986). *The whale and the reactor*. Chicago: University of Chicago Press.

Zuboff, S. (1988). *In the age of the smart machine*. New York: Basic Books.

CHAPTER CONTENTS

2　The Federal Communications Commission and the Communications Policymaking Process: Theoretical Perspectives and Recommendations for Future Research

PHILIP M. NAPOLI
Fordham University

Recent developments in communications policy have increased the need for a thorough understanding of the behavior of the Federal Communications Commission and the dynamics of the communications policymaking process. This theoretical and methodological review and critique of the literature devoted to FCC behavior and communications policymaking outlines the diversity of theoretical approaches to the FCC that have evolved over time and the specific processes by which the FCC can be influenced by outside stakeholders. This review concludes that there have been far too few efforts to subject these diverse theoretical perspectives to inclusive analyses, in which competing theories of regulatory behavior are tested simultaneously. In addition, researchers have focused primarily on explaining past Commission actions, making relatively few efforts to develop and test predictive theories of FCC behavior. In addressing these gaps in the literature, future research should (a) explore more context-specific models of FCC behavior; (b) focus on issue-type distinctions; and (c) address the possibility that different types of FCC behavior may demonstrate different characteristics. Attention to these areas may help to reconcile the diversity of theories of FCC behavior that have received empirical support.

S TUDIES of the FCC's role in communications policymaking have originated from a variety of disciplines, including political science, law, and sociology. However, as media policy issues have become increasingly common subject matter for communications research, the need to understand the behavior of the Federal Communications Commission has become more central to the field and attention to FCC behavior among communications researchers has increased.

Correspondence: Philip M. Napoli, Graduate School of Business, Fordham University, 113 West 60th St., New York, NY 10023; email: pnapoli@fordham.edu

Communication Yearbook 25, pp. 45–77

The FCC's authority to regulate the structure, content, and technologies of an industry that has the capacity to affect the cultural and political attitudes and values of the nation places it in a powerful position of indirect social influence. Thus, "it is as important to understand how the regulations within the [FCC] are constructed as understanding the specific regulations" (Krugman & Reid, 1980, p. 311).

Recent developments have magnified the need to devote research attention to the FCC. First, somewhat paradoxically, the latest efforts at deregulating the communications industry have, in many ways, actually increased the prominence and potential influence of the FCC. In the Telecommunications Act of 1996, which was widely hailed as a landmark in communications deregulation, the term "deregulation" appears only twice, whereas variants of the term "regulation" appear 202 times. In addition, there are 353 specific references to the FCC and 80 formal proceedings that the Commission had to initiate (Neuman, McKnight, & Solomon, 1997, p. 31). Congress's tendency to pass broad and ambiguous legislation has placed most of the policymaking burden squarely on the FCC's shoulders (see Braun, 1997; Olufs, 1999). Consequently, even in this era of supposed deregulation, the FCC's budget and staff size have continued to grow (Egan, 1996; Huber, 1997), and its centrality to communications policy may actually be increasing rather than diminishing.

In addition, the communications industry is growing increasingly complex, with new technologies giving rise to new markets and institutions. New and different organizations are making inroads into the communications marketplace, while the traditional separations between industries are blurring (Neuman et al., 1997). These evolutionary trends within the communications industry increase the complexity of the policymaking process. Today, a greater diversity of interests vie for favorable government policies, the intersections and overlaps of interests have grown more complex, and the influence potential of the various industry segments has shifted in response to changes in the competitive environment. Given these new developments within the industry, models and assumptions developed as recently as ten years ago may no longer adequately capture the intricacies of communications policymaking.

This review is intended as a foundation upon which future research and theory development can address these important changes It outlines the current state of theory and research within the field of FCC behavior, identifying its methodological gaps and critiquing its theoretical weaknesses. It also identifies avenues for future research.

REGULATORY BEHAVIOR AND THE FCC

Studies of the FCC's role in the communications policymaking process draw heavily upon the extensive literature (developed largely within the fields of political science and economics) on regulatory behavior. Researchers have developed—

and found empirical support for—a diverse array of theories of regulatory behavior (see Horwitz, 1989). Similar diversity characterizes the research devoted specifically to the FCC. This section outlines the primary theoretical approaches to FCC behavior, frequently referring to the broader literature on regulatory behavior in order to better chart the interdisciplinary influences on this area of research.[1]

Public Interest Theories

The Communications Act of 1934, the document which gave birth to the Federal Communications Commission, mandates that the FCC serve the "public interest, convenience, or necessity" (see Communications Act, 1934; Robinson, 1989). The concept of the public interest is not unique to communications regulation. The terminology was in fact borrowed from utilities and transportation regulation (Caldwell, 1930) and has become a guidepost for many regulatory agencies. As the foundation principle for industry regulation, the public interest functions as both a normative theory of how a regulatory agency should behave, as well as an explanatory theory for how it does behave. The earliest theoretical approach to regulatory behavior naturally assumed that regulatory agencies functioned according to the principles under which they were created. This approach assumes that regulators' decisions are primarily guided by their expert perceptions of what best serves the interests of the public. However, when assessing the public interest as an explanatory theory of FCC behavior, the key question that arises is where exactly does the theory draw its predictive or explanatory power? There are in fact two different interpretations of how this question should be answered.

The public interest as the public's influence. The first interpretation places the preferences and input of the public in a position to significantly impact policy decisions (labeled a "preponderance" theory of the public interest by Held, 1970; see also Frazer, 1997). Consequently, the key assumption is that the regulators operate under a fairly accurate impression of the public's preferences regarding policy issues. As Cass (1981) argues, "The articulated meaning of the term public interest is that it reflects some composite of the views of the citizenry" (p. 57). During the first year of the Federal Radio Commission, Commissioner Henry Bellows proclaimed, "We can only do what you tell us you want done" (Baughman, 1985, p. 4), reflecting the degree to which public input was expected to guide regulatory behavior. In sum, this "preponderance" approach to the public interest concept places the regulatory agency in the mediating position of responding to the policy preferences of the public.

Some studies of the FCC have suggested that this variant of the public interest theory provides a viable predictive model of Commission behavior. Many studies have found evidence of "public interest" groups exerting a strong influence on FCC adjudicatory or policy decisions (Fife, 1984; Grundfest, 1976; Nord, 1978; Slavin & Pendleton, 1983), with some interpreting these findings as supporting the public interest theory. However, such conclusions place the predictive power of the public interest theory within the preferences and influences of special interest groups, which is a somewhat controversial interpretation (Schubert, 1960, pp. 13–32). It is questionable whether evidence of responsiveness to individual interest groups can be interpreted as support for the public interest theory of regulatory behavior. As McQuail (1992) points out, a public interest approach that relies on the will of the people would depend upon majority preferences for its predictive power, something that is not inherent in the influence of individual public interest groups.

Other studies have found evidence that the FCC largely ignores the input of the public in the formulation of its decisions, or that representatives of the public lack the resources necessary to affect the policy process. According to McGregor (1986), although the FCC does an admirable job of soliciting public comments on policy issues, it does a poor job of processing these comments and routing them to the relevant personnel. In addition, McGregor (1986) found no evidence that any of the informal comments submitted directly affected the Commission's decision making (p. 423). Kim's (1995) analysis of the formulation of Direct Broadcast Satellite policy concluded that citizen participation was "weak and ineffective," due in large part to the declining financial resources of citizens' groups (p. 59).

Public influence over communications regulation was expected to increase with the DC circuit court's decision in the *Office of Communication of the United Church of Christ v. Federal Communications Commission* (1966). This decision established the right of representatives of the general public to intervene in broadcast license proceedings before the FCC. Prior to this decision, citizens had no legal rights to participate in this process. However, research by McLauchlan (1977) concluded that intervenors seldom appeared and had little effect on decision outcomes (p. 305). McLauchlan gathered statistics on a sample of decisions for different types of adjudicatory matters, including petitions, licenses, forfeiture liability, and cease and desist orders, for the 1972 and 1974 fiscal years (p. 278); however, his analysis did not go beyond calculating percentages according to case types, involved parties, and outcomes. Research by Linker (1983) built upon McLauchlan's approach, employing more sophisticated statistical analyses. Linker focused on the effects of intervenors on broadcast adjudicatory decisions, finding that adjudicatory decisions were more likely to favor broadcasters when an intervenor was present. From these results, Linker concluded that the presence of an intervenor representing the public may in fact lead the Commission to become more convinced of the validity of broadcasters' arguments, due to the intervenors' inferior abilities and resources in terms of presenting arguments before the Commission. Of course it is also possible that intervenors only appeared when there was a greater likelihood of a probroadcast decision. Ultimately, these results cast doubt on the predictive value of any variant of the public interest theory that depends upon the influence of citizens or citizens' groups.

Though the failure of the public to influence policy may be a result of resource inequities or negligence on the part of the FCC, we must also address the fact that the public has long been characterized as apathetic regarding matters of broadcast regulation (Baughman, 1985, p. 19; Ulloth, 1979, p. 231). Survey data indicate that over 44% of respondents do not know the main purpose of the FCC (Kim, 1992a).[2] As McGregor (1986) has pointed out, most FCC proceedings involve technical, legal, or economic issues that attract little attention from the public, though nontechnical issues, such as children's television, do in fact generate substantial amounts of public comment (p. 421). However, research by Napoli (1997) shows that high-profile, nontechnical issues in areas such as content and ownership regulation comprise only a very small fraction of the FCC's broadcast policy output (p. 199). As McQuail (1992) states, this majoritarian variant of the public interest theory is "generally insensitive, or just irrelevant, to some key issues, especially matters of a longer term, minority or technical character" (p. 25). Thus, a variant of the public interest theory that relies on the opinions and influence of the public for its explanatory power is not likely to have generalizability across issue types.

A "unitary" public interest theory. Some analysts have argued that the "preponderance" theory outlined above has historically been inadequate for understanding communications regulation, given the fact that many policymakers have rejected the notion that satisfying the preferences of the majority of the public alone serves the public interest (Held, 1970, pp. 84–93). Perhaps, then, the second variant of the public interest theory is more appropriate. This variant places the established principles guiding regulator decision making in the central predictive position. Under this "unitary theory" approach, "a single ordered and consistent scheme of values" represents the "public interest" and provides the predictive power for anticipating decision outcomes (McQuail, 1992, p. 23; see also Held, 1970).

One of the earliest studies of FCC behavior (which focused on radio licensing) concluded that the Commission did indeed make decisions in accordance with public interest principles (Edelman, 1950). Barton (1979, 1984) also found support for this "unitary" public interest theory in her study of FCC broadcast licensing decisions. Her analysis indicated that the public interest criteria outlined in the 1965 Policy Statement on Comparative Broadcast Hearings were effective predictors of an applicant's likelihood of being granted a broadcast license (Barton, 1979, p. 409). Specifically, the greater the degree to which the applicant met the criteria outlined in the Policy Statement, the greater was the likelihood of that applicant being granted a broadcast license.

Beyond these studies, however, there has been little evidence supporting the "unitary" approach as a predictive model. The reason lies primarily in the fact that the guiding principles of the "public interest" have remained ambiguous and malleable in nature (broadcast licensing is one of the few areas in which public interest criteria have been explicitly defined). Within the context of communications regulation, the ambiguity of the phrase "public interest, convenience, or necessity" has been particularly pronounced (see Friendly, 1962, pp. 54–56; Napoli, 2001). The term has been associated with a broad array of objectives, ranging from diversity to localism, to character and integrity (Crane, 1982; Federal Radio Commission, 1928; Ford, 1961; Krugman & Reid, 1980). In addition, different Commissions have offered conflicting interpretation of how best to achieve these objectives (Napoli, 2001). This combination of ambiguity, multiplicity of dimensions, and conflicting interpretations has made it difficult for the public interest to acquire a definite meaning within communications policymaking (Coase, 1959, pp. 8–9; Napoli, 2001). Consequently, turning to a single ordered and consistent scheme of values for guidance in predicting FCC behavior is virtually impossible, thus the explanatory power of the "unitary" public interest theory quickly breaks down.

Clearly, there are major problems inherent in both variants of the public interest theory of regulatory behavior. Given these weaknesses, it is perhaps not surprising that the theory has been extensively criticized (see Posner, 1974) and largely abandoned as an analytical tool for understanding and anticipating the behavior of the Federal Communications Commission.

Moving Beyond the Public Interest

Analysts of FCC behavior have, over time, become much more sophisticated in their theoretical approach, acknowledging that Commission decisions are likely the product of a much more complex set of factors. One of the earliest examples can be seen in Lichty's (1961/1962, 1962) analysis of the relationship between the backgrounds of the FCC commissioners and policy shifts throughout the history of the Commission. Lichty (1962) concluded that professional backgrounds, education, and political affiliations all appeared to be factors related to the FCC's policy direction.

Whereas this approach offers a more sophisticated perspective on FCC behavior, it still neglects significant elements in its research approach. Lichty (1962) acknowledged this fact, stating that "there have been other influences and pressures on the FRC and FCC (e.g., the President, Congress, public opinion, and the broadcasting industry) in the absence of a specific definition of the 'public interest, convenience or necessity'" (p. 108). Lichty (1962) did not attempt to incorporate these potential influences into his research design, though he did offer one of the earliest outlines of the interplay of influences at work upon the FCC. Lichty's approach was later duplicated and updated by Williams (1976, 1993), who largely affirmed Lichty's findings in historical studies covering the years 1962 to 1975 and 1975 to 1990. Like Lichty (1962), Williams (1993) acknowledged that "many other forces affect the regulation of the communications industry" (p. 59).

Capture theory. Lichty's work is important not only for the series of follow-up studies it inspired, but also because it provides some of the earliest (though tentative) support for the possibility that the regulated industries are capable of influencing FCC decisions. This process, commonly referred to as the "capture" theory of regulatory behavior, has remained a prominent framework for understanding FCC decision making.

Capture theory has been conceptualized in a number of different ways, though all begin with the assumption of a public interest origin of regulatory agencies (Horwitz, 1989, p. 29). Some definitions strictly limit the concept to situations in which regulators consciously and voluntarily make decisions favoring the regulated industries (Kalt & Zupan, 1990, p. 107; Levine & Forrence, 1990, p. 169), whereas others emphasize that regulators can be unconsciously captured (Mitnick, 1980). An important point raised by Horwitz (1989) is that for capture to exist, regulators must systematically favor the regulated industries and ignore the public interest (p. 20).

Lichty's (1962) analysis emphasized a component of the "revolving door hypothesis";\ specifically, that FCC commissioners drawn from the regulated industries are more likely to make decisions favoring the regulated industries (see Berner, 1976). According to this hypothesis, regulators drawn from the regulated industry are inherently more sympathetic to industry interests than regulators without industry experience. This has been called the "entry" portion of the "revolving door" hypothesis. The "exit" portion of the revolving door hypothesis asserts that the promise of lucrative postregulatory employment within the regulated industries compels regulators to make pro-industry decisions in order to curry favor with potential employers (Gormley, 1979, p. 667; Mitnick, 1980; Noll, Peck, & McGowan, 1973, p. 123; Quirk, 1981). Along these lines, Schwartz (1959) relates an instance in which FCC Chairman George McConnaughey negotiated an agreement to go into law practice with a Pittsburgh attorney, who represented an applicant for a contested Pittsburgh TV channel, while the case was pending before the Commission. All of this took place while McConnaughey was still a member of the Commission (Schwartz, 1959, pp. 142–143). The FCC awarded the TV station to the attorney's client less than a month after McConnaughey left the Commission (p. 143). In response to the fear such instances provoked of the "revolving door" affecting policy decisions, Congress passed an ethics bill in 1978 placing limits on the services former regulatory agency commissioners and high-level staff members could provide to the regulated industries upon leaving the Commission (Ethics in Government Act, 1978).

The decades following Lichty's (1962) work have seen a number of studies supporting variants of the capture theory. Cohen (1986) found weak statistical evidence supporting the "exit" portion of the revolving door hypothesis. His analyses indicated that commissioners who accepted post-FCC employment in the regulated industries were more likely to cast pro-industry votes. He also found that a commissioner in his or her last year of FCC service was more likely to cast pro-industry votes—evidence suggesting that commissioners begin to behave in a manner more favorable to the regulated industries as concerns regarding post-FCC employment become more immediate. Gormley (1979) found qualified support for the "entry" portion of the revolving door hypothesis. Analyzing commissioner voting data for the years 1974 through 1976, Gormley found that commissioners with prior broadcast industry experience tended to vote as a separate, identifiable bloc, and that this bloc was more likely to cast probroadcast industry votes; however, the party affiliation of the commissioner had even greater explanatory power, a conclusion also reached in a similar, unpublished, analysis conducted by Wollert (1977) for the years 1966 thorough 1975.[3]

Of course, the means by which a regulatory agency becomes captured by the industry it regulates are not confined to questions of pre- and postregulatory agency employment. Other factors can come into play as well. For example, some analysts have emphasized the high levels of interaction among regulators and representatives of the regulated industry and the possible effects that the personal relationships that develop can have on regulatory decisions (Cole & Oettinger, 1978). Others have highlighted the fact that the regulated industries are frequently the source of information that regulators utilize when making decisions, and the opportunities that this situation poses for introducing biased information into the decision-making process (Johnson & Dystel, 1973). Finally, the regulated industry monitors and participates in the Commission's decision making with much more regularity and intensity than the general public, public interest groups, or any other interested stakeholders (Napoli, 2001). This situation further allows for the possibility of decision making that systematically favors industry interests over other interests (Crotts & Mead, 1979).

Beyond the quantitative investigations of the revolving door hypothesis described above, a number of case studies of FCC decision making have also supported the capture model (Berner, 1976; Cole & Oettinger, 1978). Kim (1995) found that industry interest groups dominated the FCC's rulemaking process for Direct Broadcast Satellite, despite efforts by individual citizens, citizens groups, and noncommercial broadcast groups. In an extensive historical analysis of the FCC's regulation of cable television, LeDuc (1973) concluded that, "the FCC, from its initial microwave rules in 1962 through its third report a decade later, has used only one basic technique—restriction of cable signal carriage—to achieve one goal—protection of the broadcasters' economic markets" (p. 202).

LeDuc's (1973) conclusion helps illustrate some of the problems inherent in applying traditional versions of the capture theory to contemporary FCC behavior. Specifically, how do we adapt capture theory to a situation (such as the FCC's) in which the regulatory agency oversees multiple, increasingly interrelated industries, each with potentially divergent preferences regarding individual policy decisions? Clearly, in the FCC's early years it was relatively easy to place the broadcast industry alone in the position of dominance, as LeDuc (1973) does. In the past, broadcasting has frequently been singled out as the area which receives the greatest amount of attention and resources from the FCC as a whole, and from the commissioners in particular (Cole & Oettinger, 1978; McLauchlan, 1977). Also, until recently, the bulk of the commissioners who could be characterized as having any kind of prior communications industry experience came almost exclusively from the broadcast industry (see Flannery, 1995). In fact, the overwhelming majority of the FCC behavior literature has focused exclusively on the Commission's decision making activity within the context of broadcasting (e.g., Cohen, 1986; Cole & Oettinger, 1978; Krasnow, Longley, & Terry, 1982; Mahan & Schement, 1984; Ray, 1990). However, the rise of cable television, the growth of direct broadcast satellite, changes within the telephone industry, and the increasing prominence of the computer industry in communications policy debates (see Seel, 1997) all undermine the simplicity with which capture theory typically has been formulated and applied.

Also, within more narrowly defined industry segments, conflicts of interest are still likely to take place (see R. J. Williams, 1976, p. 336). For instance, it is not uncommon for the broadcast networks and the local stations to be on opposite sides of a policy issue, or for the networks to occasionally diverge from each other in their policy preferences (Napoli, 1997, p. 162). In these situations, it becomes even more difficult to apply a meaningful interpretation of capture theory, as determining which decision option accurately reflects industry interests becomes increasingly difficult.

At the most basic level, capture theory does not account for any of the multitude of instances in which the FCC has made decisions opposed by the regulated industries (see R. J. Williams, 1976, p. 338). For example, Teske (1990) discusses how capture fails to explain the Commission's relationship with AT&T during the 1970s (p. 19). Thus, although the regulated industry may be a powerful influence on the behavior of regulatory agencies such as the FCC, the capture model may be an oversimplification of a much more complex process (see Reagan, 1987, pp. 62–64). The theory's continued prominence within the regulatory behavior literature has led Baughman (1985) to argue that capture has "had a deadening effect on the study of the administrative process" (p. xv). At the very least, much work needs to be done in developing and testing more sophisticated formulations of capture theory that account for multiple industry interests and variation in their ability to influence policy outcomes.

Rethinking capture theory. Capture theory has also come under criticism by members of the FCC. According to former FCC Commissioner Glen O. Robinson (1978), capture theory is

> a somewhat superficial explanation for a more complex phenomenon. . . . The chief weakness of the industry capture thesis . . . is that it personalizes what is all too often an institutional bias of regulation itself. It is true that the regulator tends to develop a familiarity and an empathy with regulated interests. What is not true is the inference that this familiarity and empathy are necessarily contrary to the political intent and purpose of regulation. In communications, as in many other regulated sectors of the economy, regulation has generally been instituted or extended on the initiative (or at least the consent) of the regulated interests. . . . Thus, it is not simply that regulators have become tools of private interests, but that regulation has become a tool of private interests. (pp. 395–396)

Robinson's perspective is particularly important, as it reflects an increasingly prevalent assertion in recent FCC research—that the assumption that the regulatory process was ever actually free to become captured needs to be questioned, as does the notion that the FCC was actually created with the primary intention of serving the public interest. It may be that a regulatory agency is in fact created primarily to serve the interests of the industry it regulates. Such an agency is the product of what Wilson (1989) describes as "client politics"—a situation in which all or most of the benefits of regulation go to a single, reasonably small, interest group (p. 76). Wilson (1989) classifies the FCC as a prime example of an agency created out of client politics (p. 76). Along similar lines, Owen and Braeutigam (1978) used case studies to demonstrate how industries can exploit the regulatory process to their advantage in a variety of fields, including telecommunications.

The argument that the FCC was never actually free for the capturing has received support from historical research on the origins of broadcast regulation by Hazlett (1990), McChesney (1994), and Rosen (1980). These authors provide compelling evidence of the extent to which government regulation originated at the behest of large commercial broadcasters, was shaped with their input, and was implemented in ways that advantaged them over smaller, noncommercial broadcasters. Such conclusions reflect an increasingly prominent critical theory perspective on communications policymaking. The underlying assumption of this perspective is that the entirety of the regulatory process is structured around the accommodation of industry interests. Along these lines, Rowland (1997b) and Streeter (1996) argue that a careful analysis of the history of the public interest standard and its application in broadcast regulation indicates that the term can be very closely tied with accommodating the interests of commercial broadcasters (see also Hazlett, 1990; Williams, R.J., 1976), so much so that the common characterization of the "ambiguous" public interest standard may need to be reevaluated (Rowland, 1997a). Historical research by Shipan (1997) has, however, reached a less extreme conclusion. Shipan (1997) emphasizes that Congress did more than just reflect interest group pressures when designing the communications regulatory system, instead designing a system that reflected its own best interests as well.

As with the more traditional capture theory, this "capture from inception" approach may have diminished predictive utility for the present and future communications policy landscape, in which broadcasters represent just one of many distinct industrial interests. Specifically, though this research has provided evidence that the communications regulatory process generally conforms with industrial interests, like the traditional capture theory approach it does not adequately account for those instances in which policy outcomes contradict industry preferences (see above). Nor does this perspective provide adequate tools for anticipating the outcome of individual decisions in which different powerful industry segments are on opposing sides of an issue. Certainly in some such situations policy compromises manage to accommodate multiple interests (e.g., the Telecommunications Act of 1996), but in other instances there are distinct winners and losers (see Seel, 1997). On the other hand, a situation such as the cable industry's eventual success at convincing the FCC to lift stifling regulations represented a defeat on the part of the broadcast industry (see Streeter, 1987). Though the ultimate winner may once again be one of the regulated industries (perhaps over the best interests of the public), the capture from inception approach provides little guidance in anticipating the victors of such increasingly prevalent interindustry policy conflicts.

Consequently, this perspective, though valuable as a piece of historical revisionism, is of questionable utility for explaining current policy outcomes. Indeed, it may be that the critical theory perspective functions primarily as a macrolevel theory of the policymaking process (given its focus on the factors affecting the institutional design and structure of the policymaking process) that requires supplemental theoretical approaches for those instances in which the researcher is interested in understanding the factors affecting the outcomes of specific policy decisions (i.e., taking a more microlevel approach).

Organizational analyses. When analysts within the fields of economics and organizational behavior began to turn their attention to the FCC, the role of structural and organizational factors in affecting Commission decision making received increased attention. The development of this approach owes much to Downs's (1967) classic analysis of bureaucratic behavior. The first of Downs's major arguments is that an "ossification syndrome" afflicts many bureaucratic organizations (p. 158). This syndrome is characterized by an overwhelming tendency to preserve the status quo. Causes include increased control from monitoring agencies, increased specialization, and the escalation of operating authority. The end result is an inability to take fast or novel action (Downs, 1967, pp. 158–159). Downs (1967) also argues that regulatory bureaucrats, primarily concerned with main taining and improving their position, either consciously or unconsciously make decisions that preserve or expand the existing bureaucracy, regardless of whether such decisions are in the public interest (p. 8). Related to this point is what is perhaps Downs's most important argument: "bureaucratic officials, like all other agents in society, are significantly—though not solely—motivated by their own self-interests" (p. 2). This perspective is central to classic theories of regulatory behavior developed later by Stigler (1971) and Peltzman (1976).

Downs's (1967) arguments permeate a number of analyses of the FCC. The assumption of self-interested regulators is central to Noll et al.'s (1973) theory of FCC behavior (pp. 120–121). Also echoing Downs, LeDuc (1973) argues that the FCC makes decisions primarily intended to expand its own bureaucracy (pp. 27–28). Downs's (1967) perspective has also been used to explain why, even during eras of "deregulation," the FCC's budget and staff size continue to grow (Egan, 1996; Mosco, 1990, pp. 38–40). FCC analysts have also frequently argued that the Commission is predisposed to maintaining the status quo, particularly when faced with complex decisions posed by new communications technologies (Braun, 1994; Goldin, 1970; Goodwin, 1973; Stern, 1979).

Although bureaucratic self-interest may factor into this tendency to preserve the status quo, another commonly cited reason is the Commission's inadequate information gathering and processing resources (Mosco, 1975, 1979; Johnson & Dystel, 1973; Napoli, 1999; Schulman, 1979, pp. 87–88). LeDuc (1973) argues that this situation accounted for the FCC's mishandling of cable television. However, he also argues that the same situation has been in effect since the Commission's inception:

> There is no effective information gathering process within the FCC capable of providing the material necessary to evaluate the potential for public service of new communications techniques. During the 1930s this defect led to a policy discouraging the development of television in the United States. (LeDuc, 1973, p. 28)

Mosco's (1975) analysis of a number of policymaking cases concluded that, in the face of complex situations (such as the advent of a new technology), the FCC imposes a simplifying analytical framework that interprets the new technology in terms of existing technologies (see also Stern, 1979, p. 355), whereas Weare (1996) argues that the lack of analytical resources contributes to a process of "disjointed incrementalism," in which regulators avoid larger issues and focus on incremental changes that may lack any coherent direction over time. All of these arguments naturally conclude that these characteristics of the FCC result in suboptimal decision making.

It has often been pointed out that insufficient information gathering and analytical resources can cause a regulatory agency to rely on the regulated industries for information necessary to make decisions (Mitnick, 1980). This problem appears to be particularly acute within the FCC (Cole & Oettinger, 1977; Crotts & Mead, 1979, p. 49). LeDuc's (1973) study of the FCC's handling of cable television regulation revealed that "Lacking the resources to obtain . . . information, the Commission had to place its reliance upon research supplied by an industry [the broadcast industry] whose presentation might not be altogether free from self-serving coloration" (p. 28). Obviously, in this situation an organization-level factor such as inadequate information gathering and processing resources provides greater opportunities for the regulated industries to influence FCC decision making.

Organization-level analyses have also frequently focused on the qualifications and expertise of FCC personnel. One common argument is that the comparably low pay of government work and the lack of upward mobility act as deterrents to talented and motivated personnel, and create high levels of turnover (Emery, 1971; Stern, 1979, p. 360). The end result is that the Commission functions at a low level of efficiency and effectiveness (Emery, 1971, p. 393; Stern, 1979, pp. 359–361). This argument has been a recurring theme in an extensive series of government-commissioned studies of FCC performance (Napoli, 1998).

A number of questions arise regarding the applicability of many of the common assumptions of organization-based analyses to FCC behavior. First, given the degree to which FCC employment can enhance the market value of a communications professional, and the opportunities that usually exist to "cash in" on a few years of government work, it may be that the assumption of undertalented FCC personnel ignores the realities of the nature of government service. Also, the common criticism that the FCC lacks analytical resources may be less accurate in light of the creation in 1973 and subsequent growth of the Office of Plans and Policy within the Commission. This office, which focuses on research and long-range planning, was created in response to the superior analytical resources present in the White House's Office of Telecommunications Policy (Will, 1978, pp. 136–137). Though the Commission's analytical resources may still be considered insufficient, it is important to recognize that capacity in this area has changed over time and, thus, that the strength of this argument may be in decline. Finally, the key issue that arises in terms of organization-centered analyses is whether the FCC indeed has the degree of autonomy that would allow its structures, personnel, and institutional needs to be the primary determinants of regulatory decisions. Although the FCC theoretically functions as an "independent" regulatory agency, purely organization-centered perspectives suggest that the Commission functions in a vacuum. Though an understanding of organizational factors provides a logical foundation upon which to build more sophisticated models of the regulatory process, the following section demonstrates that it may be necessary to place FCC behavior within a larger political context.

Political theories. Proponents of the organizational perspective tend to argue that regulatory agencies are capable of resisting external influences and functioning with a certain degree of autonomy from their overseers. According to this perspective, the regulatory agencies remain genuinely independent from political influence. However, during the 1980s, the dominant paradigm of regulatory behavior theory underwent a shift from one emphasizing the difficulty that elected officials have in controlling bureaucratic organizations to one emphasizing the potency of these institutions in affecting bureaucratic behavior, and the numerous control mechanisms available to them (Wood & Waterman, 1991, p. 801). The past two decades have therefore produced an extensive literature demonstrating the extent to which political actors, such as Congress or the president, are the primary factors influencing regulatory behavior. These conclusions have been prominent in the FCC behavior research in recent years as well.

Congressional dominance. The congressional dominance model of course asserts the centrality of Congress in determining the behavior of regulatory agencies. The relevant subcommittees, in particular, are considered the locus of influence (Arnold, 1979; Heffron, 1983, p. 45; Ogul, 1976, p. 184; Tunstall, 1986, pp. 245–246). Congressmembers' committee assignments can be thought of as the result of a loss-gain calculus, in which individual members actively seek the committee assignments that will maximize their utility in terms of both political benefits and personal satisfaction (Hamm, 1983, pp. 383–385; Weingast, 1989, p. 150). Thus, members of congressional committees who are in oversight positions over regulatory agencies are likely to have substantial motivation to maintain an active interest in the oversight of the relevant bureaucratic agency (Ogul, 1976, pp. 182–183).

In terms of the FCC, Krasnow et al. (1982) argue that the chairpeople of the relevant congressional oversight subcommittees historically have been able to dominate the behavior of the Commission (p. 88). Jung (1996) argues that an influx of Democratic congressmembers into the subcommittees overseeing the FCC brought a halt to Chairman Mark Fowler's deregulatory activities (p. 145–149). Similarly, membership changes in Congress during the 1970s have been associated with more aggressive policymaking activity (Rowland, 1982a).

Congressional influence can be achieved through a variety of methods. It is important, however, to recognize the distinction between Congress's ability to control procedure and its ability to control substance (Gruber, 1987, pp. 13–14). Thus, regulatory agency behavior can be influenced in terms of the process by which policy is made, or more directly, in terms of specific policies (i.e., passing legislation that creates policy changes that the agency must then institute). The methods discussed below typically fall into the former category. These methods represent efforts by Congress to affect communications policy via influencing the FCC without resorting to direct legislation.

The most commonly identified method of congressional influence over regulatory agencies is the appropriations process, whereby the "power of the purse" is used to constrain the behavior of wayward regulators and to motivate them to successfully and obediently pursue the congressional mandate. According to Owen and Braeutigam (1978), "The most powerful tool of congressional control is the budget process" (p. 26) This power resides primarily within the subcommittees of the Appropriations Committee of each house of Congress (Krasnow et al., 1982, p. 96). According to Gellhorn (1978), congressional appropriation power has four effects on the FCC: (a) It provides some assurance that the FCC will order its priorities and performance to obtain congressional approval; (b) it fosters informal contact between the agency's leadership and Congress; (c) individual congressmembers can carry disproportionate authority; and (d) FCC leadership realizes the agency will encounter the least congressional criticism by avoiding controversial policies and acting cautiously (p. 452). The FCC's deregulatory initiatives of the 1980s have been characterized as due in large part to its reduced appropriations during the Reagan administration (Krasnow et al., 1982, p. 99).

The power of the purse can become particularly direct and potent in the form of appropriations riders (see Devins, 1993, p. 167), through which funding is made contingent upon particular policies being maintained, initiated, or altered (Krasnow et al., 1982, p. 99; Reagan, 1987, p. 157; Rowland, 1982a, pp. 129–130). For example, the 98th Congress used an appropriations bill rider to block the FCC's plan to liberalize television group ownership rules. Another rider directed the FCC to consider alternatives to repealing the Fairness Doctrine (Shooshan & Krasnow, 1987, pp. 628–630).

One particularly important development in the Congress-FCC relationship is the 1971 legislation that changed the FCC from a permanently authorized agency to one requiring reauthorization every 2 years. According to Shooshan and Krasnow (1987), this congressionally instituted change was an effort by Congress to create "another pressure point to enhance its control over FCC decision-making" (p. 626). The authors also argue that the switch was designed to affect the distribution of influence within Congress:

> Since the use of annual authorizations reduces the time available for consideration by . . . the appropriations committees, it virtually insures that the legislative committees will retain primary oversight and policy responsibility. While the constraints on the appropriations process are less severe with multi-year authorizations, the need for Congress to authorize an agency on a periodic basis nonetheless strengthens the oversight power of legislative committees. With regard to the FCC authorization, the Senate and House Commerce Committees are the legislative committees which have gained additional power. (Shooshan & Krasnow, 1987, p. 624)

Another important influence tool is the Senate's power to approve the president's FCC commissioner nominations (see Graham & Kramer, 1976). This authority provides the Senate with the opportunity to filter out those appointees not likely to serve congressional interests. Some researchers have argued that the Senate is quite active in influencing the appointment process, though this influence is seldom visible in the form of rejecting a nominee. This action is seldom necessary, "because conflicts between the Senate and the President, or between committees and nominees, are nearly always worked out at some earlier stage in the appointment process" (Mackenzie, 1981, p. 168). Thus, rejection "is a step [the Senate is] likely to take only when all of the compromise mechanisms available to them have been explored and exhausted" (Mackenzie, 1981, p. 168). On the other hand, Graham and Kramer (1976) argue that the Senate has traditionally not imposed strict standards on the President's FCC nominations, instead assuming that the appointees were fit by the fact that they had been nominated (p. 402).[4]

Other methods of congressional influence include the threat of direct legislation (Ferejohn & Shipan, 1989b), the design and alteration of administrative procedures (Borchardt, 1962), and Congress's oversight and investigation authority (Devins, 1993; Emery, 1971; Laffont & Tirole, 1990; Scher, 1960; Wilson, 1989). Oversight hearings have the potential to have an enormous influence on FCC behavior (Kim, 1991). Krasnow et al. (1982) documented a number of examples of congressional preferences expressed in oversight hearings quickly being translated into Commission policy activity (pp. 112–114). For instance, in 1971 the chairman of the House Communications Subcommittee suggested that the FCC establish an office to deal specifically with children's television. This suggestion was quickly acted upon by then-Chairman, Dean Burch (Krasnow et al., 1982, p. 113). In his review of congressionally commissioned analyses of the FCC, Napoli (1998) concluded that they were used not only to signal displeasure with FCC performance, but also as analytical ammunition in an ongoing struggle with the executive branch for greater influence over the FCC.

It should be emphasized that, with each of these modes of influence, there may not be evidence of direct influence activity; rather, "Control may occur through a process of anticipated reactions" (Gruber, 1987, p. 13). Reagan (1987) characterizes these indirect methods as "soft" oversight, as opposed to "hard" oversight (direct control over agency activity; p. 158). Weingast and Moran's (1983) frequently cited model of congressional dominance presumes that congressional influence is always present but seldom easily visible. Instances of highly visible congressional activity, such as investigations, hearings, or legislation, can be interpreted as instances in which the informal methods of influence have broken down (Ogul, 1976, p. 161). From this perspective, the passage of Telecommunications Act of 1996 can be interpreted as evidence of the FCC failing to satisfactorily respond to congressional policy preferences. Similarly, in 1996, Representative Jack Fields, then Chairman of the House Telecommunications and Finance Subcommittee, introduced a bill designed to reduce the responsibilities of the FCC and to keep a tighter reign on Commission chairpersons by limiting their travel privileges (Braun, 1997, p. 12). The bill did not pass, however, which may be due largely to the fact that much proposed legislation is intended primarily to threaten the Commission into changing its behavior. Such an approach relies upon anticipated reactions to legislative threats.

However, it may very well be an oversimplification to treat congressional influence as a constant. There are factors that can potentially cause variation in the intensity and effectiveness of congressional oversight. For instance, the subject matter in question can have an impact. Specifically, the more technical and complex the subject matter, the less Congress may be able to influence the bureaucracy in question. Overseeing complex subject matter is more time consuming and may require more specialized knowledge than congressmembers are likely to have (Ogul, 1976, pp. 14–15). Consequently, Congress may be incapable of accurately determining the policy direction that best serves its interests, as well as less able to influence the FCC in the desired direction.

Compounding this situation is the likelihood that a congressmember will generally allocate personal resources in accordance with the allocation's likely political benefits (Moe, 1984, p. 767). Given that voters' levels of interest and their abilities to determine the policy decision that maximizes their utility generally decrease in situations involving highly technical matters, congressmembers are less motivated to involve themselves in these matters than they are for less technical issues (Stigler, 1971, pp. 10–11). This is particularly relevant in terms of the FCC, given that the vast majority of its decisions fit into the highly technical category.

Some analysts have argued that regulatory decision making is effectively beyond congressional control, or, at the very least, that Congress is one of a number of influences affecting regulatory behavior, and that the notion of congressional "dominance" is too extreme (Moe, 1987; Woolley, 1993). In terms of the FCC, according to Symons (1989), Congress has:

Acted too slowly, and too much in response to the initiates of the agencies, to influence the overall development of policy. While this behavior could be interpreted as assent to these policies, it may be more accurate to say that events have moved too quickly, and underlying politics have been too conflictual, for politically sensitive officials to take charge. (p. 278)

The result is a "fragmented" policy process that does not reflect the influence of any single institution (Symons, 1989, p. 280). Similarly, from case studies of FCC decisions regarding access charges and price caps, Ferejohn and Shipan (1989a) concluded that the policy outcomes ultimately "reflected a mix of bureaucratic autonomy and congressional influence" (p. 302).

Quantitative tests of congressional dominance on the FCC have been few in number. Though these analyses have found evidence of relationships between congressional variables and FCC behavior, these relationships are generally not strong enough to support a "dominance" theory (see Napoli, 1997, 2000). For example, Cohen (1986) found that the strength of the conservative coalition in Congress significantly increased the likelihood of a commissioner casting probroadcasting votes, though this variable was only one of a number of variables found to be significantly related to commissioner voting behavior. Hill (1991) coded 199 FCC decisions regarding satellite broadcasting in terms of whether they hurt, benefited, or had no effect on the various interested parties. Her analyses indicated that there was a greater than chance proportion of decisions that fell into the category identified as representative of congressional interests; however, the absence of any evidence of intercoder reliability for the very complex coding scheme undermines the strength of this conclusion.

Similar coding problems plague many of the quantitative analyses discussed here (e.g., Canon, 1969; Cohen, 1986; Gormley, 1979), highlighting one of the major difficulties in analyzing FCC behavior, both from a quantitative and a qualitative perspective. Specifically, how does one say with confidence that a decision is best classified as serving Congress's interests over the "public interest" or the interests of the regulated industry? It may not often be obvious whose interests are really being served by a particular decision. It is also possible that multiple interests are being served. It is certainly possible that the public interest could coincide with the industry's interests (Krugman & Reid, 1980, p. 316; R. J. Williams, 1976, p. 339) or Congress's interests in a particular situation. For example, the decision to repeal the Fairness Doctrine may have served the public interest by eliminating the "chilling effect" on the presentation of controversial issues. At the same time, the decision to repeal was certainly supported by broadcasters, who were happy to be free of the financial and editorial burdens associated with the Fairness Doctrine. The fact that these various interests need not, and in fact may not, be mutually exclusive complicates making objective determinations of whose interests are actually being served by individual policy decisions.

In contrast to the moderate findings of the quantitative research, a number of case studies have concluded that Congress is central to FCC behavior (Ferejohn & Shipan, 1989a, 1989b; Krasnow et al., 1982; Krasnow & Shooshan, 1973). Some, however, have concluded that Congress is not always successful (Devins, 1993; Shields, 1991) and that the balance of power is shifting away from Congress and toward the FCC (Markin, 1991).

Presidential influence. Whereas there has been no expressed theory of "presidential dominance" of the FCC, theoretical approaches that incorporate significant presidential influence certainly run counter to the long-held assumption that there is generally no presidential influence on regulatory behavior (Moe, 1987). The notion of the "independent" regulatory commission has long been assumed to apply primarily to intervention by the president (Scher, 1960, p. 912). However, research by Moe (1982, 1987) in particular has provided evidence that the president plays a central, if not dominant, role in regulatory behavior. FCC-specific researchers have paid considerable attention to the potential role of the president in affecting communications policymaking as well.

Many scholars have claimed that all presidents attempt to influence regulatory behavior (Bernstein, 1955, p. 109; Mackenzie, 1981; Schwartz, 1959, p. 204), though some have characterized presidential influence as "more often focused on the macro level of regulation" than the "highly particularistic" influence efforts of congressmembers (Reagan, 1987, p. 156). Of course, the degree of influence may well vary across administrations, due in part to varying degrees of interest (see Rourke & Brown, 1996). In terms of the FCC, Franklin D. Roosevelt was very interested in policy decisions (Kang, 1987), whereas Harry Truman showed little or no interest in Commission policies (Krasnow et al., 1982, p. 67). Other active presidents included Kennedy, Johnson (due of course to his extensive family broadcast holdings), Nixon (see Porter, 1976; Powe, 1987; Spievak, 1970), Carter, and Reagan (Markin, 1991), whereas Ford has been characterized as playing a relatively passive role in the operation of the FCC (Krasnow et al., 1982, p. 67). Rowland (1982b) argues that the influence of the president in telecommunications policymaking began in the late 1960s, at which point the executive branch intruded upon a process previously dominated by Congress and the regulated industries (pp. 22–23).

There are a number of influence tools available to the president. The president has the power to appoint FCC commissioners and designate the chairperson. The president can also recommend individuals for lower level, "career service" positions within the Commission (Wiley, 1988). Appointment power has been characterized as the president's most potent tool of influence over regulatory agency behavior (Bernstein, 1955, p. 109). The power of appointment can clearly be utilized by the president to staff the FCC with like-minded personnel (Williams, 1993, p. 47). The appointment process has also been recognized as a form of political patronage, wherein loyal campaign contributors or operatives are awarded regulatory agency positions (Cohen, 1986, p. 705; Eckert, 1981, p. 118; Williams, 1993, p. 44). The end result is a commissioner who is very likely to adhere closely to the appointing president's perspective on regulatory matters (Moe, 1982). Of course, given the Senate's role in approving appointments, this process has been characterized as "a persistent struggle" between the Senate and the executive branch "to shape the contours of public policy" (Mackenzie, 1981, p. 95).

Also, given that the president's power to designate the FCC's chairperson is not subject to approval by Congress (though the nominee must still receive congressional approval), some have suggested that, through the chairperson, the president is able to significantly affect the policy direction and the decision making of the FCC (Devins, 1993; Williams, 1993, p. 48). Though each commissioner is technically co-equal, the chairperson has a major impact on the preparation of the agenda at Commission meetings, and on personnel decisions ranging from lower level staff to bureau chiefs, and even new commissioners (Krasnow et al., 1982, p. 44). Of course chairperson influence cannot be treated as a constant. Chairman Richard Wiley, for instance, has been described as remarkably effective in determining the course of FCC activity, taking an active role in hiring decisions and minimizing dissenting opinions. Wiley's successor, Charles Ferris, on the other hand, has been characterized as less successful in influencing the behavior of the Commission, due primarily to resistance from Commission staff (Krasnow et al., 1982, pp. 44–45).

Other potential methods of presidential influence include utilizing the Office of Management and Budget, the Justice Department, and other executive offices to pressure the FCC. For example, Nixon's creation of the Office of Telecommunications Policy was intended in part to allow greater executive branch participation in FCC decisions (Lucoff, 1977; Miller, 1982; Porter, 1976). Finally, the president may achieve influence via the power and prestige associated with the presidency. According to Moe (1982), the stature of the presidency has a significant impact on regulators' responsiveness to presidential preferences on regulatory matters (pp. 201–202).

Evidence of presidential influence on the FCC has appeared in both quantitative and qualitative studies of Commission behavior. Quantitative studies of FCC decision making have found the party of the appointing president to be a significant predictor of commissioner voting behavior (Canon, 1969; Cohen, 1986), with Republican-appointed commissioners casting more pro-industry votes than Democratic appointees. Historical studies by Lichty (1961/1962, 1962) and Williams (1976, 1993) have reached similar conclusions, with Williams (1993) concluding that the regulatory philosophy of the appointing president is the single best predictor of commissioner voting behavior (p. 45). Case studies by Devins (1993) and Kang (1987) also have attributed substantial influence to the president.

However, the exponential growth of the federal government has created a situation in which the president cannot possibly know a broad enough range of qualified people to only choose appointees with whom he or she is personally familiar (Mackenzie, 1981, p. 3). This makes control via appointment potentially much more difficult now than in the past. In addition, according to Weingast (1981), matters related to the regulatory agencies generally fall below the president's threshold of interest; thus, "For most agencies, the influence of the president is sporadic or unimportant" (p. 150). It may be that we can only expect presidential influence on FCC behavior for those issues with high levels of national visibility or significance.

DISCUSSION AND CRITIQUE

This review has attempted to compartmentalize the various theoretical approaches to FCC behavior. However, this is always dangerous exercise, as it suggests that the different theoretical perspectives are mutually exclusive approaches to explaining behavior. It is important to emphasize that there are areas of theoretical intersection and overlap. For example, the assumption of self-interested regulators that characterizes many organization-level analyses obviously has an important linkage with capture theory. Should the regulated industries offer the greatest benefits in reward for particular decisions, then the likelihood of capture increases. Similarly, the information processing issue common to organization-level analyses can also overlap into capture theory. Regulators dependent upon the regulated industries for information may become unwillingly captured by making decisions based upon biased information (Mitnick, 1980). Despite these areas of overlap, it is still safe to say that the research on FCC behavior reflects a diversity of distinct—and occasionally contradictory—perspectives, and has yet to adhere around a core of theoretical consistency.

This state of theoretical diversity highlights the need for research approaches that incorporate a broad range of possible influence sources. One of the few (and certainly the most well-known) of these more inclusive theoretical approaches is the Krasnow et al. (1982) "broadcast policymaking model." Developed initially by Longley (1969), this model has undergone a series of evolutions (Krasnow & Longley, 1973, 1978; Krasnow et al., 1982) and has inspired a number of case studies based on the model (Cooper, 1996; Kim, 1992b; Nord, 1978; Seel, 1997; Tucker & Safelle, 1982). Consistent through the various formulations of the model is the presumption that broadcast regulation is fundamentally a political process that is not dominated by any one participant. Where major evolution has taken place is in the outline of the major participants in the process. The original model described three participants: the FCC, Congress, and the regulated industry. The next formulation added citizen groups, the courts, and the White House (Krasnow & Longley, 1973).[5] Subsequent applications of the model have recommended additional revisions, such as incorporating the computer industry as a major participant in the policymaking process (Seel, 1997).

Clearly, Krasnow et al.'s (1982) approach involves conducting what have been described as "stakeholder analyses" (Dutton, 1992a, p. 66), in which the focus is on the interplay of interest groups. Thus, it is less a model of FCC behavior than a broader model of the policymaking process; however, the FCC does maintain the central position in the model. For the Krasnow et al. (1982) model to remain a viable representation of the policymaking process, it may need to expand further. The authors last revised their model in 1982, and future revisions may need to incorporate stakeholders such as the cable industry, the telephone industry, and even the utilities industry, all of whom may soon become—or already are—active participants in broadcast policy issues due to their financial interests in competing delivery technologies.

However, simply identifying additional stakeholders is only a small step toward reaching a deeper understanding of the factors affecting FCC behavior. This is due in part to the fact that the Krasnow et al. (1982) model does not articulate predictive propositions. Thus, while it has functioned as a useful explanatory tool for FCC behavior, its utility for anticipating decision outcomes is limited (Krasnow et al., 1982, p. 134). This shortcoming of the Krasnow et al. (1982) model is characteristic of the entirety of the FCC behavior literature. There have been far too few efforts at constructing and testing generalizable predictive models of Commission behavior. To date, analysts of the FCC have provided us with a deep understanding of the past, but few tools with which to anticipate the future.

Beyond the Krasnow et al. (1982) model and its offspring, there have been relatively few research efforts that have taken a more inclusive approach to FCC behavior (for exceptions, see Baughman, 1985; R. J. Williams, 1976). The tendency to create and test "artificially dyadic" theoretical models within the broader literature on regulatory behavior (Moe, 1985, p. 1114) has characterized the study of the FCC as well. The bulk of the analyses of the FCC have focused on the possible impact of one particular factor on the FCC while neglecting to incorporate and explore competing explanations. Some studies have focused exclusively on the influence of the courts (see Jameson, 1979; Ulloth, 1979), whereas others have focused exclusively on Congress (Shooshan & Krasnow, 1987), the president (Kang, 1987), or citizens' groups (Slavin & Pendleton, 1983) while neglecting simultaneously to investigate other possible influence sources.

However, the greater problem is that most studies have focused on very narrow time frames or issues. This may be due in part to the fact that the majority of the research on FCC behavior has taken a case study approach (see Braun, 1994; Cole & Oettinger, 1978; Ferejohn & Shipan, 1989a, 1989b; Fife, 1984; Hart, 1994; Johnson, 1973; Kim, 1992b, 1995; Markin, 1991; Slavin & Pendleton, 1983), though many of the quantitative analyses have focused on very narrow time frames or issue areas as well (Canon, 1969; Gormley, 1979; Hill, 1991). Studies that focus on the FCC's handling of a particular policy issue (Braun, 1994, Hill, 1991; Kim, 1995; Park, 1973), or a particular administrative regime (Canon, 1969; Grubb, 1996; Krasnow & Shooshan, 1973) can provide only tentative claims of generalizability. The conclusions may be largely a product of the contextual factors at that particular point in time. In addition, those issues chosen for case study analysis are typically those of high visibility and widely acknowledged social or political significance. For example, previous case study research has focused on such high profile areas as cable regulation (LeDuc, 1973; Park, 1973), children's television (Markin, 1991; Tucker & Safelle, 1982), minority ownership (Fife, 1984), and television violence (Cooper, 1996). Decisions in these areas represent a very small fraction of the FCC's total policy output (see Napoli, 1997, p. 199). Thus they do not necessarily provide an accurate reflection of typical FCC behavior. These factors may help explain why such a diversity of theoretical perspectives have received support in the FCC literature.

Cohen's (1986) research provides an indication of how future research can address these issues. Cohen's analysis of FCC decisions covered a broad time period (1955 through 1974) and incorporated variables pertaining to a range of regulatory behavior theories into the analysis. His results suggested that multiple influences are working simultaneously on the Commission. However, the overall predictive power of his model was rather weak (Cohen, 1986, p. 701), suggesting that such quantitative investigations of FCC behavior need to go beyond simply simultaneously accounting for multiple influence sources. However, at this point, there is little theoretical guidance for how to proceed.

One strategy that could aid in disentangling the multiple competing theories is taking a more "situational" approach to investigating the behavior of the FCC. Policy decisions need to be analyzed within the unique political, social, and economic context in which they arise (see Sabatier, 1977). A focus on contextual variables, such as variations in citizen interest, industry pressure, industry resources, and congressional and presidential monitoring, could provide a starting point for explaining why some analyses of the FCC have, for example, strongly supported the capture model, whereas others have supported competing perspectives, such as congressional dominance. Most theoretical formulations of FCC behavior and communications policymaking to date have not built situational variables into their models. Dutton's (1992a) application of the "ecology of games" to communications policymaking is an exception, given its emphasis on "interactions across different domains of corporate and public affairs" (p. 66; see also Dutton, 1992b, 1995). This approach highlights the need to consider the effects of political and economic developments outside the immediate communications policy realm on decision outcomes. Another exception is the "systems" model (structured very similarly to the Krasnow et al., 1982, model) outlined by Labunski (1981), in which a wide variety of situational variables are identified and operationalized in an effort to determine "the circumstances under which certain actors affect policy decisions" (p. 164). Unfortunately, Labunski (1981) does not test the proposed model with actual data, and there have been no subsequent efforts to gather and analyze the data necessary to test the model. Nonetheless, these approaches emphasize the importance of placing communications policymaking within a broader political and economic context and provide useful tools for further analyses of the policymaking process.

The agency theory literature, developed primarily within economics, also could be useful in developing and testing more context-specific models of FCC behavior. Agency theory focuses on the relationship between the agent (in this case, the FCC) and those monitoring the agent's behavior, the principals (e.g., citizens, Congress, the president, the regulated industries). Agency theory emphasizes the idea that the intensity of influence is not a constant, but is in fact a function of "monitoring costs"—the costs associated with effectively monitoring an agent to minimize self-interested behavior (these costs can vary from issue to issue as well; see Alchian & Demsetz, 1972; Jensen & Meckling, 1976). This theoretical approach has provided useful insights into the behavior of other regulatory agencies (see Spiller, 1990; Weingast, 1989; Weingast & Moran, 1983), but has yet to be applied to the analysis of the FCC.

A starting point for such an approach could involve following Levine and Forrence's (1990) recommendation to focus on the degree to which particular policy issues have become a part of the "public agenda" (pp. 192–193), in order to gain a sense of the monitoring costs involved for that particular issue. Quantifying the volume and position of formal and informal comments for each policy decision could also be a useful analytical approach, as it would provide an indication of who was monitoring issues and the intensity which with they were participating in the policy debate (Napoli, 2001). Other possibilities include incorporating measures of congressional subcommittee activity, perhaps in terms of numbers of hearings, amount of time, or amount of legislation directed toward the FCC and communications issues. If, as Crotts and Mead (1979) contend, the FCC responds to whomever is paying attention, then more thorough investigations into levels of monitoring may provide important insights into the dynamics of FCC behavior.

Along related lines, there should be greater attention to the characteristics of individual issue types and how issue type distinctions might be related to FCC behavior patterns. Should we expect the same behavioral patterns for a highly publicized, nontechnical policy decision, such as one involving children's television programming, as we would for a decision involving a more obscure technical issue, such as one involving permissible transmission power? Probably not. Cary (1967) advocates making a distinction between "matters in the limelight . . . where there is a public controversy, and those of a more technical nature" (p. 57). Addressing the question above would tie in closely with the monitoring costs issue, as some issue types are certainly more costly to monitor effectively than others. We see relatively few instances of issue-type distinctions being made within the FCC literature. One exception is Canon's (1969) analysis of two years of commissioner votes, which found that partisan differences in voting patterns vanished for certain issue areas, such as statutory interpretation and cable television (p. 609). More recent research by Napoli (2000) also found evidence of different influence patterns across issue types, with presidential influence appearing only across the full range of issue types and congressional influence appearing within more specific issue areas. These results suggest that issue types offer a potentially fruitful intervening variable for providing a more complete understanding of FCC behavior.

More attention also needs to be devoted to the different representations of FCC behavior. Some studies have focused on the FCC's policymaking activity, while others have focused on adjudicatory activity, with little acknowledgment that behavioral patterns may vary across activity types. It may be that these two representations of regulatory behavior are not interchangeable. As Moe (1987) states:

> Rule-making is politically much more dangerous than adjudication. Case-by-case adjudication allows agencies to pick off firms and individuals one by one; only the unlucky or the particularly egregious violators are dragged through the enforcement machinery. Industries as a whole are not roused to political action. . . . Adjudication is a method tailor-made for bureaucratic survival and security. (p. 504)

This perspective receives support from research by Napoli (1997), which found that stakeholder influence on FCC behavior appeared much stronger for Commission enforcement activity than for its policymaking activity. Within the FCC research, the qualitative literature has focused exclusively on policymaking (see Braun, 1994; Krasnow et al., 1982; Lichty, 1962; Williams, 1976, 1993). In contrast, the quantitative FCC studies have focused either on adjudicatory behavior (Barton, 1979; Linker, 1983) or on voting behavior in the aggregate, with no distinction made between adjudicatory and policymaking functions (Canon, 1969; Cohen, 1986; Gormley, 1979). There has also developed a small body of studies that has focused exclusively on the FCC's enforcement activity. These studies have provided chronological listings of Commission broadcast enforcement activities such as license revocations, license renewal denials, and fines and forfeitures (Abel, Clift, & Weiss, 1970; Clift, Abel, & Garay, 1980; Stanley, 1964; Weiss, Ostroff, & Clift, 1980). Unfortunately, none of these studies has made any effort to provide causal explanations for shifts in the levels of enforcement activity over time, instead remaining purely descriptive. Clearly, the broad construct of FCC behavior can be operationalized in a variety of ways. The fact that these different operationalizations may not be perfectly interchangeable from a theoretical perspective may help explain the diversity of empirical findings regarding FCC behavior.

Finally, it is important that future research attempts to look beyond the behavior of the five commissioners. A number of analysts of regulatory agencies in general, and of the Federal Communications Commission in particular, have emphasized the role that lower level staffers and the individual bureaus play in affecting decision making. At the general level, Welborn (1977) points out:

> Commission decisions almost without exception are preceded by staff work and are . . . based upon analyses and recommendations of staff associated with the various bureaus . . . and offices. The stakes in staff work include much more than the choices made in particular substantive determinations. Regulatory agendas and priorities are shaped at the staff level and have their largest reflections there. (p. 87)

In terms of the FCC, Williams (1976) has highlighted the potential influence of Commission staffers, as has Goodwin (1973), who says, "In the typical rulemaking proceeding, the Commission is somewhat at the mercy of the line bureau involved" (p. 45). However, the process by which the Commission's staff affects decision outcomes has received virtually no empirical investigation.[6] This is most likely due to the fact that data regarding their activity and positions on policy issues are difficult to obtain. Representations of commissioner positions and behavior, on the other hand, are relatively easy to obtain, in the form of votes and written opinions. However, it is essential for future research to focus on the workings of the staff level of the FCC and the interaction process between staff members of the individual bureaus and the commissioners. This focus could provide insights into the earlier stages of the FCC's decision-making processes, before matters reach the commissioners or are presented in Notices of Proposed Rulemaking. Looking beyond the commissioners should provide a more complete portrait of FCC behavior.

CONCLUSION

As this review has indicated, research on FCC behavior has reached a point where several compelling theories have received at least some empirical support. The task at hand now is to try to reconcile these disparate perspectives and integrate them into a broader, more generalizable theory of FCC behavior, with an emphasis on predicting future FCC behavior as opposed to explaining past behavior. Some of these gaps in the literature have been recognized in the past (Krasnow et al., 1982), yet they persist today. In order to address these areas, greater attention needs to be paid to the contextual factors surrounding individual decisions. These factors need to become integrated into theoretical models of FCC behavior. Along similar lines, FCC behavior needs to be studied across an extended time span and across a diversity of issues, with less emphasis placed on individual issues or administrative regimes. Such research approaches are sorely lacking in the literature to date.

A possible strategy for addressing these gaps in the literature would be to approach FCC behavior from broader, more inclusive quantitative perspectives. This has been a common and informative approach among political scientists studying the behavior of other regulatory bureaucracies, including the FDA, the EPA, the FTC, the NLRB, and the SEC (e.g., Moe, 1982, 1985; Weingast, 1989; Weingast & Moran, 1983; Wood & Waterman, 1991). In contrast to these regulatory agencies, the published quantitative research on FCC behavior is quite sparse and dated. Thus, the methodological, theoretical, and statistical advances that have taken place over the past decade have not been represented in this research approach. Along related lines, the many insights developed within the numerous case studies of FCC behavior conducted over the past decade need to be applied and tested over time and across issue areas.

Of course, not all of the theoretical perspectives outlined in this chapter may be equally amenable to the methodological suggestions offered here. For instance, the central tenets of the critical theory perspective lend themselves more to broad historical analysis. Indeed, the research suggestions above reflect an orientation more toward the "microdynamics" of the policymaking process (e.g., the factors affecting individual decision outcomes) than the "macrodynamics" of the policymaking process (e.g., the factors affecting the institutional design and structure of the policymaking process). These research suggestions are, however, a function of the gaps identified in the literature to date. The limited quantity of studies that have taken a broader quantitative approach suggests that a number of potentially viable methodological strategies have not been explored. This review has offered both theoretical and methodological suggestions for how future research of this sort might proceed.

NOTES

1. For more general reviews of the regulatory behavior literature, see Horwitz (1989) and Mitnick (1980).
2. However, these results should be qualified by the fact that residents from a single state (Kentucky) participated in the study.
3. See Canon (1969) for the first study of this type, in which the techniques of bloc analysis and Guttman scaling (methods typically used to study judicial voting behavior) are applied to the voting behavior of FCC commissioners.
4. We should be skeptical of this conclusion, however, given that it comes from a Senate-sponsored analysis.
5. For an extended discussion of the evolution of the model, see Kim (1992b).
6. For exceptions see Quirk (1981) and Welborn (1977), though these studies do not focus exclusively on the FCC.

REFERENCES

Abel, J. D., Clift, C., & Weiss, F. A. (1970). Station license revocations and denials of renewal, 1934–1969. *Journal of Broadcasting, 14*(4), 411–421.
Alchian, A. A., & Demsetz, H. (1972). Production costs, information costs, and economic organization. *American Economic Review, 62*, 777–795.
Arnold, R. D. (1979). *Congress and the bureaucracy: A theory of influence.* New Haven, CT: Yale University Press.
Barton, M. F. (1979). Conditional logit analysis of FCC decisionmaking. *Bell Journal of Economics, 10*, 399–411.
Barton, M. F. (1984). Modeling FCC decision-making. *Political Methodology, 10*(4), 495–511.
Baughman, J. L. (1985). *Television's guardians: The FCC and the politics of programming, 1958–1967.* Knoxville: University of Tennessee Press.
Berner, R. O. (1976). *Constraints on the regulatory process: A case study of regulation of cable television.* Cambridge, MA: Ballinger.

Bernstein, M. H. (1955). *Regulating business by independent commission.* Princeton, NJ: Princeton University Press.

Borchardt, K. (1962). Congressional use of administrative organization and procedures for policy-making: Six case studies and some conclusions. *George Washington Law Review, 39*(2), 429–466.

Braun, M. J. (1994). *AM stereo and the FCC: Case study of a marketplace shibboleth.* Norwood, NJ: Ablex.

Braun, M. J. (1997, April). *The Telecommunications Act of 1996—An evaluation of the Act's impact after the first year: FCC issues.* Paper presented at the meeting of the Broadcast Education Association, Las Vegas, NV.

Caldwell, L. G. (1930). The standard of public interest, convenience or necessity as used in the Radio Act of 1927. *Air Law Review, 1*(3), 295–330.

Canon, B. C. (1969). Voting behavior on the FCC. *Midwest Journal of Political Science, 13,* 587–612.

Cary, W. L. (1967). *Politics and the regulatory agencies.* New York: McGraw-Hill.

Cass, R. A. (1981). *Revolution in the wasteland: Value and diversity in television.* Charlottesville: University of Virginia Press.

Clift, C., Abel, J., & Garay, R. (1980). Forfeitures and the Federal Communications Commission: An update. *Journal of Broadcasting, 24*(3), 301–310.

Coase, R. H. (1959). The Federal Communications Commission. *Journal of Law & Economics, 2,* 1–40.

Cohen, J. E. (1986). The dynamics of the "revolving door" on the FCC. *American Journal of Political Science, 30*(4), 680–708.

Cole, B., & Oettinger, M. (1977). Covering the politics of broadcasting. *Columbia Journalism Review, 16*(4), 58–63.

Cole, B., & Oettinger, M. (1978). *Reluctant regulators: The FCC and the broadcast audience.* Reading, MA: Addison-Wesley.

Communications Act of 1934. 48 Stat. 1064 (1934).

Cooper, C. A. (1996). *Violence on television: Congressional inquiry, public criticism and industry response: A policy analysis.* Lanham, MD: University Press of America.

Crane, J. S. (1982). Issues of public interest regulation in Supreme Court decisions: 1927–1979. In J. J. Havick (Ed.), *Communications policymaking and the political process* (pp. 109–124). Westport, CT: Greenwood Press.

Crotts, G., & Mead, L. M. (1979). The FCC as an institution. In L. Lewin (Ed.), *Telecommunications: An interdisciplinary study* (pp. 39–119). Dedham, MA: Artech House.

Devins, N. (1993). Congress, the FCC, and the search for the public trustee. *Law and Contemporary Problems, 56*(4), 145–188.

Downs, A. (1967). *Inside bureaucracy.* Boston: Little, Brown.

Dutton, W. H. (1992a). The ecology of games in telecommunications policy. In H. M. Sapolsky, R. J. Crane, W. R. Neuman, & E. M. Noam (Eds.), *The telecommunications revolution* (pp. 65–88). New York: Routledge.

Dutton, W. H. (1992b). Ecology of games shaping telecommunication policy. *Communication Theory, 2*(4), 303–328.

Dutton, W. H. (1995). The ecology of games and its enemies. *Communication Theory, 5*(4), 379–392.

Eckert, R. D. (1981). The life cycle of regulatory commissioners. *Journal of Law & Economics, 24,* 113–120.

Edelman, M. (1950). *The licensing of radio services in the United States, 1927–1947: A study in administrative formulation of policy.* Urbana: University of Illinois Press.

Egan, B. L. (1996). Abolish the FCC. *Telecommunications Policy, 20*(7), 469–474.

Emery, W. B. (1971). *Broadcasting and government: Responsibilities and regulations.* East Lansing: Michigan State University Press.

Ethics in Government Act of 1978, Pub. LA. No, 95–521, 92 Stat. 1824 (1978).

Federal Radio Commission (1928). Statement made by the Commission on August 23, 1928, relative to the public interest, convenience, or necessity. Reprinted in F. J. Kahn (Ed.). (1984). *Documents of American Broadcasting* (4th ed., pp. 57–62). Englewood Cliffs, NJ: Prentice-Hall.

Ferejohn, J. A., & Shipan, C. R. (1989a). Congress and telecommunications policy. In P. R. Newberg (Ed.), *New directions in telecommunications policy: Vol. 1. Regulatory policy: Telephony and mass media* (pp. 301–314). Durham, NC: Duke University Press.

Ferejohn, J. A., & Shipan, C. R. (1989b). Congressional influence on administrative agencies: A case study of telecommunications policy. In L. C. Dodd & B. I. Oppenheimer (Eds.), *Congress reconsidered* (4th ed., pp. 393–410). Washington, DC: Congressional Quarterly.

Fife, M. D. (1984). *FCC policy on minority ownership in broadcasting: A political systems analysis of regulatory policymaking.* Unpublished doctoral dissertation, Stanford University, Stanford, CA.

Flannery, G. (Ed.). (1995). *Commissioners of the FCC, 1927–1994.* Lanham, MD: University Press of America.

Ford, F. (1961). The meaning of the "public interest, convenience or necessity." *Journal of Broadcasting, 5,* 205–218.

Frazer, K. D. (1997, May). *Organizations, resources, and political participation: Public interest groups and new technologies in the policy making process.* Paper presented at the annual conference of the International Communication Association, Montreal, Canada.

Friendly, H. J. (1962). *Administrative agencies: The need for better definition of standards.* Cambridge, MA: Harvard University Press.

Gellhorn, E. (1978). The role of Congress. In G. O. Robinson (Ed.), *Communications for tomorrow: Policy perspectives for the 1980s* (pp. 445–462). New York: Praeger.

Goldin, H. H. (1970). *Innovation and the regulatory agency: FCC's reaction to CATV.* Report prepared for the Sloan Commission on Cable Communications.

Goodwin, K. R. (1973). Another view from the Federal Communications Commission. In R. E. Park (Ed.), *The role of analysis in regulatory decisionmaking* (pp. 43–61). Lexington, MA: Lexington Books.

Gormley, W. T. (1979). A test of the revolving door hypothesis at the FCC. *American Journal of Political Science, 23*(4), 665–683.

Graham, J. M. & Kramer, V. H. (1976). *Appointments to the regulatory agencies: The Federal Communications Commission and the Federal Trade Commission (1949–1974).* Committee on Commerce. Washington, DC: U.S. Government Printing Office.

Grubb, M. V. (1996, August). *Nicholas Johnson: The public's defender on the Federal Communications Commission, 1966–1973.* Paper presented at the meeting of the Association for Education in Journalism and Mass Communication, Anaheim, CA.

Gruber, J. E. (1987). *Controlling bureaucracies: Dilemmas in democratic governance.* Berkeley: University of California Press.

Grundfest, J. A. (1976). *Citizen participation in broadcast licensing before the FCC.* Santa Monica, CA: Rand.

Hamm, K. E. (1983). Patterns of influence among committees, agencies, and interest groups. *Legislative Studies Quarterly, 8*(3), 379–426.

Hart, J. A. (1994). The politics of HDTV in the United States. *Policy Studies Journal, 22*(2), 213–228.

Hazlett, T. W. (1990). The rationality of U.S. regulation of the broadcast spectrum. *Journal of Law & Economics, 31,* 133–175.

Heffron, F. (1983). The Federal Communications Commission and broadcast deregulation. In J. J. Havick (Ed.), *Communications policy and the political process* (pp. 39–70). Westport, CT: Greenwood Press.

Held, V. (1970). *The public interest and individual interests.* New York: Basic Books.

Hill, A. E. (1991). *Tests of theories of regulatory agency behavior: The Federal Communications Commission and the establishment of the international satellite communications system.* Unpublished doctoral dissertation, Harvard University, Cambridge, MA.

Horwitz, R. B. (1989). *The irony of regulatory reform: The deregulation of American telecommunications.* New York: Oxford University Press.

Huber, P. (1997). *Law and disorder in cyberspace: Abolish the FCC and let common law rule the telecosm.* New York: Oxford University Press.

Jameson, K. C. (1979). *The influence of the United States Court of Appeals for the District of Columbia on federal policy in broadcast regulation.* New York: Arno Press.

Jensen, M. C., & Meckling, W. H. (1976). Theory of the firm: Managerial behavior, agency costs, and ownership structure. *Journal of Financial Economics, 3,* 305–360.

Johnson, N. (1973). Institutional pressures and response at the FCC: Cable and the Fairness Doctrine as a case study. In G. Gerbner, L. P. Gross, & W. H. Melody (Eds.), *Communications technology and social policy* (pp. 113–145). New York: Wiley.

Johnson, N., & Dystel, J. J. (1973). A day in the life: The Federal Communications Commission. *Yale Law Journal, 82,* 1575–1634.

Jung, D. J. (1996). *The Federal Communications Commission, the broadcast industry, and the Fairness Doctrine, 1981–1987.* Lanham, MD: University Press of America.

Kalt, J. P., & Zupan, M. A. (1990). The apparent ideological behavior of legislators: Testing for principal-agent slack in political institutions. *Journal of Law & Economics, 34,* 103–131.

Kang, J. (1987). Franklin D. Roosevelt and James L. Fly: The politics of broadcast regulation, 1941–1944. *Journal of American Culture, 10,* 23–33.

Kim, H. (1991, August). *Congress and the FCC: An analysis of congressional hearings on nominations of FCC commissioners.* Paper presented at the meeting of the Association for Education in Journalism and Mass Communication, Boston, MA.

Kim, H. (1992a). *How to talk back to your television set: A survey of Kentuckians.* Unpublished master's thesis, University of Kentucky, Lexington.

Kim, H. (1992b). Theorizing deregulation: An exploration of the utility of the "broadcast policy-making system" model. *Journal of Broadcasting & Electronic Media, 36*(2), 153–172.

Kim, H. (1995). The politics of deregulation: Public participation in the FCC rulemaking process for DBS. *Telecommunications Policy, 19*(1), 51–60.

Krasnow, E. G., & Shooshan, H. M. (1973). Congressional oversight: The ninety-second Congress and the Federal Communications Commission. *Federal Communications Bar Journal, 26,* 81–117.

Krasnow, E. G., & Longley, L. (1973). *The politics of broadcast regulation.* New York: St. Martin's Press.

Krasnow, E. G., & Longley, L. (1978). *The politics of broadcast regulation* (2nd ed.). New York: St. Martin's Press.

Krasnow, E. G., Longley, L. D., & Terry, H. A. (1982). *The politics of broadcast regulation* (3rd ed.). New York: St. Martin's Press.

Krugman, D. M., & Reid, L. R. (1980). The "public interest" as defined by FCC policy makers. *Journal of Broadcasting, 24*(3), 311–325.

Labunski, R. E. (1981). *The First Amendment under siege: The politics of broadcast regulation.* Westport, CT: Greenwood Press.

Laffont, J., & Tirole, J. (1990). The politics of government decision making: Regulatory institutions. *Journal of Law, Economics, & Organization, 6*(1), 1–31.

LeDuc, D. R. (1973). *Cable television and the FCC: A crisis in media control.* Philadelphia: Temple University Press.

Levine, M. E., & Forrence, J. L. (1990). Regulatory capture, public interest, and the public agenda: Toward a synthesis. *Journal of Law, Economics, & Organization, 6,* 167–198.

Lichty, L. W. (1961/1962). Members of the Federal Radio Commission and the Federal Communications Commission 1927–1961. *Journal of Broadcasting, 6,* 23–34.

Lichty, L. W. (1962). The impact of the FRC and FCC commissioners' background on the regulation of broadcasting. *Journal of Broadcasting, 6,* 97–110.

Linker, J. (1983). Public intervenors and the public airwaves: The effect of interest groups on FCC decisions. In J. J. Havick (Ed.), *Communications policy and the political process* (pp. 149–170). Westport, CT: Greenwood Press.

Longley, L. D. (1969). *The politics of broadcasting: Industry, Congress, and the FCC.* Unpublished doctoral dissertation, Vanderbilt University, Nashville, TN.

Lucoff, M. (1977). Telecommunications management and policy: Who governs? *Journalism Monographs, 51.*

Mackenzie, G. C. (1981). *The politics of presidential appointments.* New York: Free Press.

Mahan, E., & Schement, J. R. (1984). The broadcast regulatory process: Toward a new analytical framework. In B. Derva & M. J. Voigt (Eds.), *Progress in communication sciences: Vol. 4* (pp. 1–22). Norwood, NJ: Ablex.

Markin, K. (1991, August). *Congress, the FCC, and children's television regulation: A shift in the balance of power.* Paper presented at the meeting of the Association for Education in Journalism and Mass Communication, Boston, MA.

McChesney, R. W. (1994). *Telecommunications, mass media, & democracy: The battle for the control of U.S. broadcasting, 1928–1935.* New York: Oxford University Press.

McGregor, M. A. (1986). The FCC's use of informal comments in rule-making proceedings. *Journal of Broadcasting & Electronic Media, 30*(4), 413–425.

McLauchlan, W. P. (1977). Agency-clientele relations: A study of the Federal Communications Commission. *Washington University Law Quarterly, 77*(2), 257–306.

McQuail, D. (1992). *Media performance: Mass communication and the public interest.* Newbury Park, CA: Sage.

Miller, J. (1982). Policy planning and technocratic power: The significance of the OTP. *Journal of Communication, 32*(1), 53–60.

Mitnick, B. M. (1980). *The political economy of regulation: Creating, designing and removing regulatory reforms.* New York: Columbia University Press.

Moe, T. (1982). Regulatory performance and presidential administration. *American Journal of Political Science, 26*(2), 197–224.

Moe, T. (1984). The new economics of organization. *American Journal of Political Science, 28,* 737–777.

Moe, T. (1985). Control and feedback in economic regulation: The case of the NLRB. *American Political Science Review, 79*(4), 1094–1116.

Moe, T. (1987). An assessment of the positive theory of "congressional dominance." *Legislative Studies Quarterly, 12*(4), 475–520.

Mosco, V. (1975). *Broadcasting in the United States: A comparative analysis.* Cambridge, MA: Harvard University Program on Information Technologies and Public Policy.

Mosco, V. (1979). *Broadcasting in the United States: Innovative challenge and organizational control.* Norwood, NJ: Ablex.

Mosco, V. (1990). The mythology of telecommunications deregulation. *Journal of Communication, 40*(1), 36–49.

Napoli, P. M. (1997). *Regulatory behavior and the Federal Communications Commission: An analysis of broadcast policy making and enforcement activity.* Unpublished doctoral dissertation, North western University, Evanston, IL.

Napoli, P. M. (1998). Government assessment of FCC performance: Recurring patterns and implications for recent reform efforts. *Telecommunications Policy, 22*(4/5), 409–418.

Napoli, P. M. (1999). The unique nature of communications regulation: Evidence and implications for communications policy analysis. *Journal of Broadcasting & Electronic Media, 43*(4), 565–581.

Napoli, P. M. (2000). The Federal Communications Commission and broadcast policymaking—1996–1995: A logistic regresion analysis of interest group influence. *Communication Law and Policy, 5*(2), 203–233.

Napoli, P. M. (2001). *Foundations of communications policy: Principles and process in the regulation of electronic media.* Cresskill, NJ: Hampton Press.

Neuman, W. R., McKnight, L., & Solomon, R. J. (1997). *The Gordian knot: Political gridlock on the information highway.* Cambridge, MA: MIT Press.

Noll, R. G., Peck, M. J., & McGowan, J. J. (1973). *Economic aspects of television regulation.* Washington, DC: Brookings Institution.

Nord, D. P. (1978). The FCC, educational broadcasting, and political interest group activity. *Journal of Broadcasting, 22*(3), 321–338.

Office of Communication of the United Church of Christ v. Federal Communications Commission, 359 F.2d 994 (D.C. Circuit 1966).

Ogul, M. S. (1976). *Congress oversees the bureaucracy: Studies in legislative supervision.* Pittsburgh, PA: University of Pittsburgh Press.

Olufs, D. W. (1999). *The making of telecommunications policy.* Boulder, CO: Lynne Rienner.

Owen, B. M., & Braeutigam, R. (1978). *The regulation game: Strategic use of the administrative process.* Cambridge, MA: Ballinger.

Park, R. E. (1973). *The role of analysis in regulatory decisionmaking: The case of cable television.* Lexington, MA: Lexington Books.

Peltzman, S. (1976)). Toward a more general theory of regulation. *Journal of Law & Economics, 18,* 211–240.

Porter, W. E. (1976). *Assault on the media: The Nixon years.* Ann Arbor: University of Michigan Press.

Posner, R. A. (1974). Theories of economic regulation. *Bell Journal of Economics, 5*(2), 335–358.

Powe, L., Jr. (1987). *American broadcasting and the first amendment.* Berkeley: University of California Press.

Quirk, P. J. (1981). *Industry influence in federal regulatory agencies.* Princeton, NJ: Princeton University Press.

Ray, W. B. (1990). *FCC: The ups and downs of radio-TV regulation.* Ames: Iowa State University Press.

Reagan, M. D. (1987). *Regulation: The politics of policy.* Boston: Little, Brown.

Robinson, G. O. (1978). The Federal Communications Commission. In G. O. Robinson (Ed.), *Communications for tomorrow: Policy perspectives for the 1980s* (pp. 353–400). New York: Praeger.

Robinson, G. O. (1989). The Federal Communications Act: An essay on origins and regulatory purpose. In M. D. Paglin (Ed.), *A legislative history of the Communications Act of 1934* (pp. 3–24). New York: Oxford University Press.

Rosen, P. T. (1980). *The modern stentors: Radio broadcasters and the federal government, 1920–1934.* Westport, CT: Greenwood Press.

Rourke, F. E., & Brown, R. E. (1996). Presidents, professionals, and telecommunications policy making in the White House. *Presidential Studies Quarterly, 26*(2), 539–549.

Rowland, W. D. (1982a). The process of reification: Recent trends in communications legislation and policy-making. *Journal of Communication, 32*(4), 114–136.

Rowland, W. D. (1982b). The illusion of fulfillment: The broadcast reform movement. *Journalism Monographs, 79.*

Rowland, W. D. (1997a). The meaning of "the public interest" in communications policy, Part I: Its origins in state and federal regulation. *Communication Law and Policy, 2*(3), 309–328.

Rowland, W. D. (1997b). The meaning of "the public interest" in communications policy, Part II: Its implementation in early broadcast law and regulation. *Communication Law and Policy, 2*(4), 363–396.

Sabatier, P. A. (1977). Regulatory policymaking: Toward a framework of analysis. *Natural Resources Journal, 17,* 415–460.

Scher, S. (1960). Congressional committee members as independent agency overseers: A case study. *American Political Science Review, 54,* 911–920.

Schulman, H. J. (1979). Is structural and procedural change a better answer for consumers than the "reform" or abolishing the FCC? In T. R. Haight (Ed.), *Telecommunications policy and the citizen* (pp. 65–94). New York: Praeger.

Schwartz, B. (1959). *The professor and the commissions.* New York: Knopf.

Schubert, G. (1960). *The public interest: A critique of the theory of a political concept.* Glencoe, IL: Free Press.

Seel, P. B. (1997, August). *Conflict and resolution at the FCC: Computer industry opposition to the proposed national HDTV standard.* Paper presented at the meeting of the Association for Education in Journalism & Mass Communication, Chicago, IL.

Shields, P. (1991). The politics of the telecommunications policy process: The example of the FCC's price cap initiative. *Policy Studies Journal, 19*(3–4), 495–513.

Shipan, C. R. (1997). *Designing judicial review: Interest groups, Congress, and communications policy.* Ann Arbor: University of Michigan Press.

Shooshan, H. M., III, & Krasnow, E. G. (1987). Congress and the Federal Communications Commission: The continuing contest for power. *COMMENT, 9*(14), 619–633.

Slavin, S., & Pendleton, M. S. (1983). Feminism and the FCC. In J. J. Havick (Ed.), *Communications policymaking and the political process* (pp. 127–148). Westport, CT: Greenwood Press.

Spievak, E. B. (1970). Presidential assault on telecommunications: Reorganization plan no. 1 of 1970. *Federal Communications Bar Journal, 23*(3), 155–181.

Spiller, P. T. (1990). Politicians, interest groups, and regulators: A multiple principals agency theory of regulation, or "Let them be bribed." *Journal of Law & Economics, 33,* 65–99.

Stanley, E. R. (1964). Revocation, renewal of license, and fines and forfeiture cases before the Federal Communications Commission. *Journal of Broadcasting, 8*(4), 371–382.

Stern, R. H. (1979). *The Federal Communications Commission and television: The regulatory process in an environment of rapid technical innovation.* New York: Arno Press.

Stigler, G. J. (1971). The theory of economic regulation. *Bell Journal of Economics and Management, 2*(2), 3–21.

Streeter, T. (1987). The cable fable revisited: Discourse, policy, and the making of cable television. *Critical Studies in Mass Communication, 4,* 174–200.

Streeter, T. (1996). *Selling the air: A critique of the policy of commercial broadcasting in the United States.* Chicago: University of Chicago Press.

Symons, H. J. (1989). The communications policy process. In P. R. Newberg (Ed.), *New directions in telecommunications policy: Vol. 1. Regulatory policy: Telephony and mass media* (pp. 276–300). Durham, NC: Duke University Press.

Teske, P. E. (1990). *After divestiture: The political economy of state telecommunications regulation.* Albany: State University of New York Press.

Tucker, D. E., & Safelle, J. (1982). The Federal Communications Commission and the regulation of children's television. *Journal of Broadcasting, 26*(3), 657–669.

Tunstall, J. (1986). *Communications deregulation: The unleashing of America's communications industry.* New York: Basil Blackwell.

Ulloth, D. R. (1979). *The Supreme Court: A judicial review of the Federal Communications Commission.* New York: Arno Press.

Weare, C. (1996). The illusion of reform: The dilemma of structural telecommunications policy. *Telecommunications Policy, 20*(6), 415–427.

Weingast, B. R. (1981). Regulation, reregulation and deregulation: The foundation of agency-clientele relationships. *Law and Contemporary Problems, 44*(1), 147–177.

Weingast, B. R. (1989). The congress-bureaucratic system: A principal agent perspective (with applications to the SEC). *Public Choice, 44*(1), 147–191.

Weingast, B. R., & Moran, M. J. (1983). Bureaucratic discretion or congressional control? Regulatory policymaking by the Federal Trade Commission. *Journal of Political Economy, 91*(5), 765–800.

Weiss, F. A., Ostroff, D., & Clift, C. E. (1980). Station license revocations and denials of renewal, 1970–1978. *Journal of Broadcasting, 24*(1), 69–77.

Welborn, D. M. (1977). *Governance of federal regulatory agencies.* Knoxville: University of Tennessee Press.

Will, T. E. (1978). *Telecommunications structure and management in the executive branch of government, 1900–1970.* Boulder, CO: Westview Press.

Wiley, R. E. (1988). "Political" influence at the FCC. *Duke Law Journal, 1988,* 280–285.

Williams, R. J. (1976). The politics of American broadcasting: Public purposes and private interests. *Journal of American Studies, 10*(3), 329–340.

Williams, W. (1976). Impact of commissioner background on FCC decisions: 1962–1975. *Journal of Broadcasting, 20*(2), 239–260.

Williams, W. (1993). Impact of commissioner background on FCC decisions, 1975–1990. In R. J. Spitzer (Ed.), *Media and public policy* (pp. 43–60). Westport, CT: Praeger.

Wilson, J. Q. (1989). *Bureaucracy: What government agencies do and why they do it.* New York: Basic Books.

Wollert, J. A. (1976). *Regulatory decision-making: The Federal Communications Commission (1966–1975).* Unpublished doctoral dissertation, Michigan State University, Easr Lansing.

Wood, B. D., & Waterman, R. W. (1991). The dynamics of political control of the bureaucracy. *American Political Science Review, 85*(3), 801–828.

Woolley, J. T. (1993). Conflict among regulators and the hypothesis of congressional dominance. *Journal of Politics, 55*(1), 92–114.

CHAPTER CONTENTS

3 Applying Research on the Uses and Cognitive Effects of Hypermedia to the Study of the World Wide Web

WILLIAM P. EVELAND, JR.
Ohio State University

SHARON DUNWOODY
University of Wisconsin-Madison

This article situates the technological and historical origins of the World Wide Web in hypermedia systems that were conceptualized during the World War II era and first developed decades before the Web. The article then reviews the cross-disciplinary literature on hypermedia, which has developed over the past decade or so in education and educational technology, computer science, library and information science, psychology, and even geography. This review begins with a summary of underlying theory relevant to hypermedia, then focuses on the existing research on both the uses and the effects of hypermedia. The article discusses how the theory and research on hypermedia may or may not be extended to apply to the uses and effects of the Web. Finally, the implications of hypermedia theory and research, and its connections to traditional communication uses and effects research, are identified to provide suggestions for future research on the Web in the field of communication.

T HOSE who are interested in conducting research on the uses and effects of the World Wide Web may believe that, because searches of electronic data bases and recent communication journal articles produce few studies with "World Wide Web" or "Internet" in their titles or abstracts, research in this area must start from scratch. To the contrary, the literature on hypermedia uses and

AUTHORS' NOTE: Initial manuscript submitted April 26, 1999. Revised manuscript submitted September 1, 1999. The research reported in this article was supported by a cooperative agreement between the National Science Foundation and the University of Wisconsin-Madison (No. RED-9452971). At UW-Madison, the National Institute for Science Education is a collaborative effort of the College of Agricultural and Life Sciences, the School of Education, the College of Engineering, and the College of Letters and Science, joined by the National Center for Improving Science Education, Washington, DC. Opinions, findings, and conclusions in this manuscript are those of the authors and do not necessarily reflect the views of the supporting agencies.

Correspondence: William P. Eveland, Jr., School of Journalism & Communication, Ohio State University, 3139 Derby Hall, 154 N. Oval Mall, Columbus, OH 43210; email: eveland.6@osu.edu effects, in conjunction with research on the uses and effects of other media, can offer useful starting points for research on the World Wide Web. This article focuses on the theories and empirical studies that make up the hypermedia literature because they are less familiar and less readily available to communication researchers. However, it also addresses some points of intersection between the hypermedia and communication literature that can guide future World Wide Web research in the field of communication. We hope that this article will encourage the application of hypermedia theory and research to the study of the uses and effects of the Web among communication scholars.

BACKGROUND

In 1945 Vannevar Bush, then director of the U.S. Office of Scientific Research and Development, predicted in *Atlantic Monthly* that technology would shape the ways in which knowledge would be stored and accessed in the future (Bush, 1945). In that article he proposed a device called a "memex," which would serve as "a sort of mechanized private file and library" (p. 106). Among the unique features of the memex was the manner in which users could access and annotate its contents. Bush (1945) claimed:

> It affords an immediate step . . . to associative indexing, the basic idea of which is a provision whereby any item may be caused at will to select immediately and automatically another. This is the essential feature of the memex. The process of tying two items together is the important thing. (p. 107)

The key reason for the development of the memex, in Bush's opinion, was that the traditional mode of accessing and processing information in libraries did not mesh well with the workings of the human mind. He asserted that the human mind "operates by association. With one item in its grasp, it snaps instantly to the next that is suggested by the association of thoughts, in accordance with some intricate web of trails carried by the cells of the brain" (p. 106).

Thus, more than 50 years ago, Vannevar Bush had the foresight to propose the creation of a database that afforded instantaneous access to information through associational links. The technology behind this idea would later be updated (Bush envisioned the use of microfilm) and expanded upon. For instance, Ted Nelson built upon the thinking of Bush, combining word processing with document annotation, storage, and retrieval, and began actual development of a computer program to implement his ideas beginning in the 1960s (Nelson, 1993). This "Xanadu" program, which Nelson believed would ultimately change the way humans read and write, has been developed and modified over the course of the past four decades. Nelson also coined the term "hypertext" in the 1960s (Bevilacqua, 1989; Heller, 1990; Nelson, 1993; Tsai, 1988–1989). The term hypertext is now being replaced by the term "hypermedia" (also coined by Nelson) because of the use of multimedia in many hypertext systems. Therefore, for simplicity's sake, we will use the term "hypermedia" as an inclusive label.

The defining feature of hypermedia is the use of nodes (packets of information, typically in the form of a "page") connected by links that may be traversed easily at the whim of the user (Horney, 1991; Nelson, 1993; Shirk, 1992). As such, hypermedia is distinguished from traditional media by a high level of user control over the pace, order, and content of the medium, thus allowing use to be nonlinear or nonsequential (Duchastel, 1990; Horney, 1993; Nelson, 1979; Shin, Schallert, & Savenye, 1994), although hypermedia is not precluded from being linear and sequential (Nelson, 1993).

Nearly 5 decades after Bush's classic article, the idea of the memex—in the form of hypermedia—would take the United States by storm in the guise of the World Wide Web (The Internet, 1997). The World Wide Web is a graphics-based interface that is the most popular application available on the larger, more inclusive Internet (Rada, 1995). The Web was initially created in the early 1990s, but its entry into popular consciousness did not occur until almost mid-decade. The Web is, in effect, a massive hypermedia system (Astleitner & Leutner, 1995) that links together content as diverse as pornography and religion, science and myth, politics and pop culture. Unfortunately, the fact that the Web is a hypermedia system and that hypermedia systems have been studied for quite some time seems to have been lost on many of those with an interest in the Web (Buckingham, Shum, & McKnight, 1997).

Recent statistics on the popularity of the Internet and the World Wide Web reveal the massive growth in this medium over the past few years. A Harris Poll conducted in December 1997 and January 1998 (Taylor, 1998) revealed that over one third of all U.S. adults use the Internet. This compared to only 7% using the Internet in a similar Harris Poll in September 1995 (Taylor, 1998). Mediamark (1998) places the proportion of U.S. adults using the Internet at a more conservative 23%, an increase of 260% since they began tracking Internet use. A poll conducted in the fall of 1998 (Pew Research Center, n.d.) found that over 40% of American adults used the Internet, with nearly half of those beginning using the Net during the past year. Finally, a series of studies conducted by Bimber (1999) found that Internet access among American adults has increased from 26% in October 1996 to 46% in February 1998 and 55% in March 1999. Whereas some of the discrepancy in these estimates is likely caused by a lack of clarity in questions about use of the Internet (does it mean World Wide Web, use of electronic mail, or something else?), it is clear that a substantial proportion of the U.S. population is making use of this technology today, and that use has been increasing rapidly over the past several years.

Considering that the World Wide Web is in its infancy relative to other popular electronic media such as television and radio, this level of usage is quite dramatic. However, like most innovations that enter a social system, adoption of the World Wide Web has not occurred equally across social strata. For example, early research by Wirthlin Worldwide (1996) reported that the online audience was "well-educated, wealthy, and younger than the national average." Hoffman and Novak (1998) also described racial biases in Web use that were evident from their study. CommerceNet (1997) noted a bias toward males and people from higher social strata among Internet users. However, by this time they began to notice that these disparities were declining compared to past surveys. Most recently, the Pew Research Center (n.d.) concluded from their study that "increasingly people without college training, those with modest incomes, and women are joining the ranks of Internet users, who not long ago were largely well-educated, affluent men." All of these biases—and their reduction over time—is just what we would expect based on the study of the diffusion of other new information technologies (Compaine, 1988).

The World Wide Web is the world's largest hypermedia system. Although it is not yet truly a "mass" medium, its level of use and substantial growth in recent years leads us to believe that it will soon follow the pattern of many other new communication technologies, such as radio and television, and become a mass medium with widespread access and appeal. The success of the Web compares favorably to early diffusion rates of AM radio, black-and-white television, color television, and the telephone, which took 10, 10, 17, and 70 years, respectively, to spread to half of the population (Rice, 1984). It is important to note, however, that only about 40% of households owned a personal computer by 1996 (Nielsen Media Research, 1996) compared to 31% in 1994 and 36% in 1995 (Times Mirror, 1995), though many people (54%) have access to computers at work or school if not at home (Times Mirror, 1995). Since Web use is increasing much more quickly than computer ownership, ownership or access may, in time, limit the growth of Web use. However, the elimination of the need for a large financial investment and high levels of technical know-how is now being reduced by the introduction of devices (e.g., Web TV©) that allow individuals to access the Web through a typical television set for an initial investment of only a few hundred dollars. This technological development may serve to reduce some of the social status and gender biases in Web use as well.

With the increasing popularity of the World Wide Web, the time has come for communication researchers to explore its uses and effects from a theoretical and empirical perspective as they have already done with the other dominant media of our time. In order to begin this research effort it would be useful to have a strong foundation in research and theory to turn to for insight. We will discuss the value of research on the uses and effects of other media for this endeavor, but this article focuses on an additional literature—the literature on the uses and effects of hypermedia—as part of the basis for a communication research program on the uses and effects of the World Wide Web.

Areas of Study Relevant to Research on the World Wide Web

The preceding section makes the argument that when we discuss the World Wide Web, we are not dealing with something completely new but instead with an extension of hypermedia systems, which themselves have been available and studied closely for more than a decade. It thus makes sense for any research that attempts to examine the uses and effects of the World Wide Web to first consult the literature on the uses and effects of hypermedia. Although we make no claim that the uses and effects of hypermedia will be the same as those of the World Wide Web (indeed, later we will discuss likely differences), we do believe that important theoretical and methodological insights may be gained from the hypermedia literature.

Any suggestion that researchers embark on a reading of "the hypermedia literature" begs the questions "What is the hypermedia literature, and where do I find it?" The hypermedia literature is clearly cross-disciplinary, scattered across at least four different fields: cognitive psychology, computer or library information science, educational technology, and geography. In general, the focus of these four relatively distinct literatures can be described as follows: Research in cognitive psychology—the smallest component of hypermedia research—examines the structure of human memory and information processing and attempts to link it to the structure of computer information systems (e.g., Quillian, 1968; Wild, 1996). The computer and library information science literature looks at the usability and effectiveness of different human-computer interfaces—of which hypermedia is but one—for different tasks (e.g., Campagnoni & Ehrlich, 1989; Carmel, Crawford, & Chen, 1992; Thüring, Hannemann, & Haake, 1995). The research in educational technology is concerned with the design and application of hypermedia systems for classroom or individual instruction. The primary focus tends to be on either comparing the instructional effectiveness of entirely different media (e.g., hypermedia vs. print) or different hypermedia designs (e.g., hierarchically structured vs. unstructured), often focusing on the role of individual differences, such as user age and expertise, as predictors of effectiveness (e.g., Lanza & Roselli, 1991; Yang & Moore, 1995–1996). Finally, research originating in geography (and based on cognitive psychology) examines people's ability to represent physical and virtual spaces, including hypermedia, in memory and thus navigate effectively through these spaces (Crampton, 1992; Darken & Sibert, 1996; Kim & Hirtle, 1995; Kitchin, 1994; Shum, 1990). It also considers the potential influence of individual differences and external factors (such as characteristics of the space) on the effectiveness of navigation or "wayfinding expertise."

THEORY APPLICABLE TO USES AND EFFECTS
OF THE WORLD WIDE WEB

Several domains of theory pertaining to hypermedia may help communication researchers theorize about the uses and effects of the World Wide Web, including research on the structure of human memory and the link between that structure and the structure of hypermedia systems. Other theories consider the impact of user control of instruction and motivation on the uses and effects of media. Early in the 1990s, hypermedia theorist David Jonassen argued that "hypertext design is theory-rich and research-poor" (Jonassen, 1992, p. 125). Seven years after this statement was made, we would still agree with its first component but less so with the second. Therefore, we will begin by briefly addressing the first part of the statement, grouping the theories into three general domains applicable to World Wide Web uses and effects.

Structural Similarities Between Human Memory and Hypermedia

Psychologists studying the structure of human memory have proposed many theories about the way our minds work. Although a complete discussion of these models—and their similarities and differences—is well beyond the scope of this or any single article, a brief description of one of the more popular conceptualizations will be illustrative. As the earlier quote by Bush (1945) revealed, many psychologists believe that bits of information in human memory are organized through their connections to each other on some (typically semantic) level. Theories taking this perspective on human memory exist in many fields and include research on schemas (e.g., Schallert, 1982; Wicks, 1992), levels of processing (e.g., Craik & Lockhart, 1972; Greenwald & Leavitt, 1984), domains of memory (e.g., Kintsch, 1972; Tulving, 1985), priming (e.g., Collins & Loftus, 1975; Iyengar & Kinder, 1986), and connectionism (e.g., McClelland, 1988; Smith, 1996). The act of learning, from this perspective, is thus in large part a process of creating and maintaining meaningful links among concepts in memory (Jonassen, 1988; Nelson & Palumbo, 1992).

Theorists interested in the uses and effects of hypermedia frequently argue that the structure of hypermedia and the process of its use mimics this common conception of the structure of human memory and the function of information processing (e.g., Bieber, Vitali, Ashman, Balasubramanian, & Oinas-Kukkonen, 1997; Churcher, 1989; Jonassen & Wang, 1993; Kozma, 1987; Lucarella & Zanzi, 1993; Marchionini, 1988; Shin et al., 1994; Shirk, 1992). Jonassen (1988) notes that "because hypertext is a node-link system based upon semantic structures, it can map fairly directly the structure of knowledge it is representing" (p. 14). Claims such as these are used as theoretical evidence for the hypothesized superiority of hypermedia as a learning tool compared to other, more constrained and linear media that do not represent a knowledge domain so precisely. Churcher (1989) argues that "where hypertext is highly structured and indeed is the structure of the domain of knowledge and that structure/system is to eventually become the users [sic] conceptual model it strongly suggests hypertext as a more effective learning environment" (p. 245). Thus, the argument made by many hypermedia advocates is that, because hypermedia can be designed to emulate the appropriate (based on domain experts) links among concepts in a particular knowledge domain, learners will more easily be able to build their own mental models from the model used in the hypermedia system (e.g., Churcher, 1989; Jonassen, 1988; Jonassen & Wang,

1993). In effect, in most theoretical approaches the user is assumed to employ the hypermedia system to shape his or her own mental representations of the domain of knowledge—both in terms of content and structure—thereby emulating the knowledge structure of the domain expert whose advice influenced the design of the hypermedia system itself. However, some theorists believe that there are important differences between the structure and use of hypermedia systems and those of human memory. For instance, Nelson and Palumbo (1992) argue that in reality:

> At present, most hypermedia systems support linkages indicating only that one unit of information is somehow related to another unit of information, without specifying the nature of this relationship and a rationale for its existence. . . . In contrast, human memory supports a much stronger linking mechanism that both establishes a relationship and conveys information about the associational nature of the link. (p. 290)

Despite this and other criticisms of the link between human memory and hypermedia, most hypermedia researchers who take a stance on the issue seem to agree that the similarities between the two are many and theoretically important.

The argument for the superiority of hypermedia over other media for learning is linked closely with theories about the most appropriate designs for hypermedia, which are again based on theories of human memory and information processing. Suggested designs include those that are unstructured (so that the user may be completely free to choose his or her own path), hierarchically structured, structured as a network, or structured based on the "true" form of the domain of knowledge (e.g., Churcher, 1989; Nelson & Palumbo, 1992; Shirk, 1992; Yang & Moore, 1995–1996). Evidence pertaining to these theories will be discussed in the section below on hypermedia research.

Learner Control

One of the more prevalent notions in educational technology theory is the role of learner or user control of instruction. Theoretically, the argument is that, when students are given the opportunity (or required) to control the (a) pace, (b) order, or (c) content of instruction, they will not only be able to "design" a more meaningful and individualized (and thus effective) lesson than a teacher but they will also be able to maintain their motivation to learn and interest in the content so that the likelihood of future learning is enhanced (Kinzie, 1990; Kinzie, Sullivan, & Berdel, 1988; Milheim & Martin, 1991; Steinberg, 1989). The use of computer-aided instruction, especially via hypermedia, has been proposed as one possible means of providing different levels of learner control.

Shin and her colleagues argue that "in a hypertext environment, use of learner control is inevitable, because hypertext creates nonsequential, dynamic, and multiple structures of information that allow learners with different interests to navigate multiple pathways through the information" (Shin et al., 1994, p. 33). Learner control should have several related effects on users. It should engage users in the content because they must take part in its creation (in the sense that making choices about links to follow is creating content) and thus they take a more active role in their own learning (Landow, 1997). Learner control also requires more effortful processing of the information and precludes passivity that may be permitted using other media, like television. Learner control also increases the likelihood that the content will be of interest to and relevant to the learning of the user because the user can avoid information that is irrelevant, too complex, or too simple. Advanced users can skim introductory information and thus devote more effort to learning new information, whereas novices can devote the time necessary to learn the basics before advancing to more difficult information. According to the theory of learner control, all of these factors suggest that the positive effects of hypermedia on learning should be greater than those of other modes of instruction that do not afford a similar level of control and interactivity. However, as will be discussed later, the requirement of learner control may also have negative effects, such as increasing cognitive load, that can detract from learning.

The theory of learner control has implications for the design of hypermedia systems in much the same way as do theories of human memory and information processing. Specifically, learner control can be conceptualized as a continuum ranging from complete control for the learner ("learner control") to complete control for the system or teacher ("program control"; Milheim & Martin, 1991). The level of control afforded the learner is a direct function of the design of the system, with less structured systems providing more user control than systems with a clear structure, such as hierarchical or expert-based systems. In addition, some systems offer what has been termed "instructional advisement," which can be considered a limited type of program control in that the system makes suggestions about the most appropriate movements but the user can override the suggestions at any time (Shin et al., 1994). A "guided tour" with no real alternatives except for when to move to the next page would represent the minimum level of learner control in a hypermedia system—only control over pace is provided. The appropriate level of learner control to be built into a system—to encourage the positive outcomes described above without overburdening users with cognitive load—has become an empirical question, however, and will be addressed in a later section of this article.

Motivation

One of the important mediators of the hypothesized effects of learner control on learning is the motivation produced (or maintained) by being in control of one's own instruction (Kinzie, 1990; Steinberg, 1989). Independent of the effects of learner control on motivation, however, variations in motivation have been hypothesized as important factors in learning from hypermedia. The motivational impact of self-efficacy—the feeling that one is capable of performing at a certain level—is an oft-cited predictor of learning (e.g., Bandura, 1982; Schunk, 1991).

Using somewhat more complex models of learning, other researchers have theorized that many different motivational variables, such as perceptions of the medium, self-efficacy, or gratifications sought, influence the cognitive effort invested in learning from any medium, which in turn influences learning directly (Elliott & Dweck, 1988; Eveland, 1997a, 1997b, 1998; Kelleher, 1996; Multon, Brown, & Lent, 1991; Salomon, 1983, 1984). Similarly, it has been argued that beneficial cognitive effects of the use of hypermedia will occur only for those who are highly motivated to learn from the content available via this technology (e.g., Kinzie & Berdel, 1990). Jonassen and Grabinger (1993) offer an eloquent theoretical statement about the impact of motivations on learning from hypermedia:

> Learning depends on the purpose for using the hypertext, which in turn drives the level of processing. . . . Learners can learn from hypertext, we argue, only if they actively construct knowledge, which they will do if they are accessing the information to fulfill a personally meaningful purpose and have a reasonable level of prior knowledge and interest in the topic. (p. 21)

EMPIRICAL RESEARCH ON THE USES OF HYPERMEDIA

As noted earlier, it was once argued that the topic of hypermedia was "theory-rich and research-poor" (Jonassen, 1992, p. 125). Although in some cases this is still true (for instance, little research has been conducted on the influence of hypermedia use on the structure of human memory), and in other cases the research evidence on a particular point is inconsistent, there has been a flowering of empirical research concerning hypermedia topics during the 1990s. It is to this literature that we now turn.

Like most other areas of media research, studies of the uses and effects of hypermedia vary greatly in terms of methodology and the quality of the application of those methods. Three research traditions dominate empirical research on hypermedia: traditional experimentation, qualitative and think-aloud interviews, and collection of computer logs of hypermedia use. In addition, many studies employ a mixed methods approach, using two or more of these methods in order to answer their research questions.

In this section, we will focus on research into how people use hypermedia. We will begin with a discussion of how hypermedia use has been measured and analyzed. From there, we will move to an important question about hypermedia usage: Do people take advantage of the opportunities afforded them to move nonlinearly through the information in the hypermedia system and, if so, how? We then will examine some of the important independent variables that influence the uses of hypermedia, such as system design, motivations, and individual differences. After our discussion of the uses of hypermedia, the next section of this article will deal with research on the cognitive effects of hypermedia use.

Measurement and Analysis of Hypermedia Use

Traditional experimentation, as well as qualitative and think-aloud interviewing, are such common procedures in social science research that little needs to be said about the use of these methods here. Most introductory methods books do a much more complete job than we could do. We will discuss briefly, instead, the use of the least common method, which has traditionally been called "keystroke data" (e.g., Card, Moran, & Newell, 1983) but now should be more appropriately called "mouse-click data" or "hypermedia audit trails" (Eveland & Dunwoody, 1998; Misanchuk & Schwier, 1992). Whatever the term one chooses to use (we will use "hypermedia audit trails"), the meaning is the same: temporally coded data indicating the behaviors (selecting objects with a mouse or keystrokes) of those using computers.

Researchers have often cited the benefits of this type of data compared to other forms of data. First, because hypermedia audit trails are unobtrusively collected observational data, the problem of social desirability—which can often influence the validity of self-report measures of media use (Rice & Borgman, 1983; Rice & Rogers, 1984)—is removed. Even when social desirability is not a problem, random and systematic error in the recall of media use can introduce error in self-report measures; this, too, is avoided by audit trail data (Ettema, 1985; Huff & Rosenberg, 1989). Second, because this type of data collection requires little human effort, the amount of data that may be collected is limited only by the needs of the investigator, the amount of time available for data collection, and data storage capacity. No time or effort need be expended in the entry of data, either, because this is done automatically by the computer. Statistical power is rarely a concern of researchers using computer-collected data because of the ease of collecting large quantities of data or the census (as opposed to sample) nature of the data collected. Finally, computer-collected data users are often able to obtain longitudinal data because of the simplicity with which data can be collected over time.

At first glance, it would appear that the measurement of hypermedia use is quite simple because of the automation involved and the large (especially for social science research) quantity of data produced. Why, then, do so many researchers who use audit trail or other computer-collected data warn novices about the difficulties of this form of data collection and analysis (e.g., Marchionini, 1989; Rice & Borgman, 1983; Rice & Rogers, 1984; Smith, Smith, & Kupstas, 1993)? Despite the ease of collection, longitudinal nature of the data, and the potentially large sample sizes when studying hypermedia audit trails, this method of data collection and analysis has just as many pitfalls as other methods. Two of these pitfalls are problems of measurement error and sense-making or data analysis.

First, while computer-collected data can minimize some types of measurement error, other types still play an important role, especially for research concerning the World Wide Web (see Berthon, Pitt, & Watson, 1996, for a detailed discussion of these problems). The most important aspect of measurement error using this type of data is that it is likely to be primarily systematic rather than random, and thus is likely to introduce bias into results.

The second, and often most difficult, problem in using hypermedia audit trails is making sense of the data beyond a simple qualitative analysis. Marchionini (1989, p. 62) points out that "a general characteristic of search patterns that makes them difficult to compare is that they are unique entities," noting that in his data the length of individual search patterns ranged from 2 to 51 moves. This presents a problem when attempting to compare the nth move of one user to others, because the number of missing cases for any one move (say, the 27th) may be substantial, especially when the data are highly skewed with low median values as research has shown website use to be (Huberman, Pirolli, Pitkow, & Lukose, 1998). Further, raw hypermedia audit trails are very microscopic measures, often only becoming interpretable when aggregated in some way, much like other longitudinal observational data (see Olson, Herbsleb, & Reuter, 1994; van Hooff, 1982). However, the appropriate means of aggregation is not always clear because many options for aggregation are available.

One can take several possible approaches to the analysis of computer-collected data. The first, as implied earlier, is to analyze small bits of the data qualitatively (either avoiding numeric summaries altogether or avoiding the use of either parametric or nonparametric statistics to test hypotheses), an approach taken by many hypermedia researchers (e.g., Hill & Hannafin, 1997; Horney & Anderson-Inman, 1994; Leventhal, Teasley, Instone, Rohlman, & Farhat, 1993; Schroeder & Grabowski, 1995). Second, the data may be aggregated into many different structures and described statistically, effectively attacking the problem at many different units of analysis in order to answer all of one's research questions (e.g., Eveland & Dunwoody, 1998). A third analytical strategy—suggested by many authors but rarely used—is employing models of temporal dependency (i.e., Markov models) between requests (e.g., Chapman, 1981; Marchionini, 1989; Qiu, 1993; Rice & Borgman, 1983). Markov models are used to represent the relationship between temporally contiguous categorical behaviors; that is, they can be used to determine how users' current movements are dependent upon their previous movements.

Whereas we have focused here on the use of computer-collected data, other methods, such as qualitative interviews, experimental methods, and even sample surveys, in conjunction with computer-collected data, are likely to produce the most accurate picture of the uses of the World Wide Web. We now move on to discuss the results of research on the uses of hypermedia conducted to date. We will first identify two research domains: descriptive research on the process of moving through a hypermedia system and explanatory research that examines the contingent conditions that may influence such movement.

Patterns of Movement Through Hypermedia

As previously noted, one of the defining attributes of hypermedia (and thus of the World Wide Web) is its associational organizational structure, which allows users to navigate in a nonlinear or nonsequential manner (Duchastel, 1990; Nelson, 1993; Shin et al., 1994). However, because of the control users have over the content of hypermedia systems, nonlinear navigation is a possibility but not a requirement for those who choose to maintain a linear reading strategy. As Horney (1993) has noted, "Determined readers can . . . remain bound within a narrow pattern of behavior despite the presence of rich webs of opportunities" (p. 74). So, while a hypermedia system can be categorized as more or less nonlinear in its structure, so can the use of any hypermedia system be categorized as more or less nonlinear. These two measures are likely to be correlated, but rarely perfectly correlated. The question then becomes: How do people use hypermedia systems?

Few researchers have addressed the linearity of hypermedia usage directly, and the heterogeneity of terms and definitions in the few studies that have examined this issue make conclusions tenuous (see Campagnoni & Ehrlich, 1989; Carmel et al., 1992; Eveland & Dunwoody, 1998; Leventhal et al., 1993; Marchionini & Shneiderman, 1988). In most cases, linearity of use is operationalized as observation of a direct path to goal-relevant information via a table of contents, "next" buttons, an index, or keyword search (e.g., linear use, hierarchical use, or "searching"). By contrast, the "Web surfing" equivalent in hypermedia research (e.g., nonlinear use, nonhierarchical use, or "browsing") refers to following associational links among concepts, often serendipitously or possibly with interest as the only motivation.

As with traditional media use studies, the hypermedia literature indicates that movement through a site is often governed by contingent conditions. Unfortunately, differences found within studies are difficult to compare across studies because of the plethora of different operationalizations and terminology in the literature. The reader should take this into account when reading the remainder of this article.

Influences on Hypermedia Use

At least two categories of variables seem to have some influence on the uses of hypermedia: motivations and individual differences. Motivations typically refer to the task assigned to the user (external motivations), although motivations may come from within the person (internal motivations) as well. The individual difference variable of primary concern to researchers is expertise (either "domain" or "system"), but differences in cognitive ability or style, age, and gender have also been addressed. It is important to note that most studies examine only one or a few variables and thus do not typically control for confounding factors statistically. However, the homogeneous subjects used in many studies may provide some means of control through design by holding some of these potential confounding factors constant.

Motivations. Marchionini and Shneiderman (1988) have argued that patterns of hypermedia use vary depending on the task to which users are assigned, with browsing a function of less well-defined problems compared to searching, which takes place when problems are more precisely defined. Similarly, Gray and Shasha (1989) claim that links are most useful when searches are undirected and much less useful when one needs to answer a direct question. Strong empirical evidence was brought to bear on this issue by Qiu (1993). He demonstrated significant differences in the Markov models of system use based on whether the users were completing general or specific tasks. The general path produced more wandering (browsing) whereas the specific path producing a more directed search. Most recently, Barab, Fajen, Kulikowich, and Young (1996) found significantly different navigation patterns for a group given a precise problem to solve with a hypermedia system versus a group simply told to use the system in preparation for a test. Specifically, the group given the precise problem to solve tended to more closely follow the "ideal path" (identified a priori by the researchers) through the content than did the test group.

Individual differences. Many hypermedia researchers have called for the examination of individual differences in the study of the uses and effects of the medium (e.g., Jonassen, 1988; Marchionini, 1989; Nielsen, 1995). Although many types of individual differences may be important, the literature has tended to focus on *system expertise* (experience with and skill using the hypermedia system) and *domain expertise* (experience with and knowledge of the content area under study) as key factors, with much less effort devoted to a few other individual differences, such as cognitive ability or style, age, and gender.

Scholars have argued that "expert users who are specialists in the task domain will welcome the great power and control [of hypermedia], but novices to the system and task domain will likely benefit from limited menus and less [user] control" (Marchionini & Shneiderman, 1988, p. 78). A similar argument has been made by Leventhal and her associates (1993), who claim (and provide some evidence) that novices tend to make use of a hierarchical structure, when provided, rather than use the nonlinear options available in hypermedia. As they gain experience, they begin to move away from the structure, much like a child will remove the training wheels from a first bicycle after gaining some experience (for additional evidence, see Leventhal, Teasley, Instone, & Farhat, 1994).

Qiu (1993) found significant differences in the Markov models of hypermedia use of system experts and novices. His interpretation of the data was that experienced users of a hypermedia system tended to make use of the nonlinear options provided, whereas inexperienced users tended to engage in more "linear browsing." Carmel et al. (1992) found that domain experts tended to browse fewer topics in more depth while novices tended to browse more topics in less depth. The overall differences in hypermedia use were moderate, however, because despite different methods of browsing, both novices and experts tended to browse as opposed to using a search strategy.

However, some potentially inconsistent findings on the relationship between hypermedia use and expertise do exist. Hirsch and Borgman (1995), examining a system which provided opportunities for both keyword searching and browsing, found that those with less domain expertise were more likely to restrict themselves to browsing. Their explanation of this finding is that keyword systems require some domain knowledge but that hypermedia systems can allow novices to browse and thus gain some understanding of the domain, a function that keyword search systems cannot provide.

In addition to expertise, at least four other factors have also been linked to patterns of hypermedia use: cognitive ability or style, gender, and age. As would be expected because of the relatively unstructured nature of hypermedia, people with greater visualization ability—the ability to perceive patterns of objects in space—are more capable of nonlinear browsing, whereas those with lesser abilities tend to make more frequent use of a hierarchical structure (Campagnoni & Ehrlich, 1989). In a study of the influence of cognitive style on hypermedia uses and effects, Leader and Klein (1996) found significant differences between field-independent (i.e., analytical style) and field-dependent (i.e., global or holistic style) learners. Specifically, field-independent learners needed to access fewer than half of the number of screens to find information in a hypermedia database than did field-dependent learners. Beasley and Vila (1992) found that general intellectual ability, as measured by ACT scores, was unrelated to either linear or nonlinear (measured separately) patterns of hypermedia use.

Demographic factors have also proven to be important in the uses of hypermedia. For instance, based on a test of differences between Markov models, Qiu (1993) found that males are significantly different from females in terms of their hypermedia usage patterns. He interpreted his data to indicate that males are significantly more likely to use search-type strategies, whereas females tend to browse linearly through the content; however, the meaning of this interpretation is clouded somewhat by a lack of definition of these terms. Beasley and Vila (1992) found that females used a more linear strategy (defined as the frequency of using a "Next" button) compared to males, although this relationship only bordered on statistical significance. Because of different operationalizations, it is unclear whether this result is consistent or inconsistent with that of Qiu (1993).

Finally, Leventhal et al. (1994) compared the patterns of hypermedia use of adults (college students) and children (fourth graders) and concluded that the younger users tended to employ more exploratory strategies while the older users tended to be more structured in their searches of the system.

Whereas these limited and sometimes conflicting findings do not do much to illuminate the reasons behind individual differences in hypermedia use, they do point to the necessity of considering them for future research. What is most important for future research is to begin to develop consistent conceptualizations and operationalizations of concepts such as search strategies or linearity of use so that studies are directly comparable. Unfortunately, space does not permit us to develop arguments for our own specific recommendations of conceptualizations and measurements, although we have addressed the issue in our empirical work (Eveland & Dunwoody, 1998).

In addition to developing consistent conceptualizations and operationalizations, there should be a greater effort to include controls for demographic variables such as age and gender when examining the effects of independent variables such as expertise, because these independent variables may be highly correlated with both demographics and hypermedia use and thus represent spurious effects. Social scientists have long known that understanding reality typically requires a multivariate, not bivariate, approach, and this knowledge should be applied to the study of hypermedia and the Web.

EMPIRICAL RESEARCH ON THE COGNITIVE EFFECTS OF HYPERMEDIA

By comparison to the research on the uses of hypermedia, the available evidence on the effects of hypermedia is much more developed from both a theoretical and empirical perspective. A number of studies have examined the influence of hypermedia use on criterion variables such as interest or motivation and knowledge. Researchers have compared the relative effectiveness and efficiency of using hypermedia versus traditional paper text for learning, and they have examined how hypermedia structure, motivations, and individual differences can moderate the influence of hypermedia use. We will examine each of these topics in turn, beginning with a discussion of the criterion variables that have traditionally concerned hypermedia researchers.

Criterion Variables

Theories of the uses and effects of hypermedia discussed previously suggest that many possible variables may be influenced by the use of hypermedia. Theories of learner control predict that hypermedia use will increase or maintain the motivation of users because of its greater user control and ability to permit individualized content in comparison to other media. Similarly, many different theories suggest that the characteristics of hypermedia can lead to increased knowledge of relevant content domains. Less common but still present in the literature are claims that hypermedia use can influence the structure of knowledge through the format of the hypermedia system itself. Research has at least begun to examine all of these effects, with a primary focus on the acquisition of content knowledge, sometimes measured as the effectiveness of finding (but not necessarily being able to recall or recognize at a later time) relevant information.

Paper Text vs. Hypermedia

Research comparing the effectiveness of different media (e.g., print vs. television vs. radio) for learning has a long tradition that continues today (e.g., Furnham, Gunter, & Green, 1990; Gunter, Furnham, & Gietson, 1984; Neuman, Just, & Crigler, 1992). This research tradition has continued in the realm of computer versus paper text comparisons (e.g., DeFleur, Davenport, Cronin, & DeFleur, 1992; Obourne & Holton, 1988; Reinking, 1988; Rice, 1994) and has recently spawned research on the relative effectiveness of hypermedia versus paper text (Gray, Barber, & Shasha, 1991; Psotka, Kerst, & Westerman, 1993; Sundar, Narayan, Obregon, & Uppal, 1998). However, during the past decade or so, this research has become a rather controversial matter in some circles.

The criticisms of general media comparison research, of which the hypermedia versus paper comparisons are part, center on the confound between medium and content. The critics of these research efforts claim that any "effects" of one medium over another may be spurious because of differences in content or instructional strategy used in different media (e.g., Clark, 1983, 1985; Hagler & Knowlton, 1987). Others counter that when studies are properly conducted and interpreted, comparisons can produce useful and theoretically meaningful results (e.g., Kozma, 1994; Morrison, 1994; Shrock, 1994). With others, we feel the argument for continuing this line of research is most effectively justified by the fact that, in the real world, content and instructional strategy do vary across media because of the ease of their application in one medium compared to another; thus, to control this difference would produce studies with little ecological validity (Ross & Morrison, 1993).

If the above argument is accepted, the question becomes: From which medium—hypermedia or traditional print—do people learn more effectively? Although some of the results have been qualified by interactions with other variables, the general conclusion in the literature, based on a meta-analysis conducted by Chen and Rada (1996), is that hypermedia is more effective (though not necessarily more efficient) at producing information gain than paper text (see also Gray et al., 1991; Psotka et al., 1993). Of specific interest to researchers concerned with learning from the World Wide Web is that some limited evidence suggests that hypermedia is more effective for incidental learning (Leventhal et al., 1993). Some have found, however, that the superiority of hypermedia for learning generally may be moderated by the task at hand (e.g., Leventhal et al., 1993; Rada & Murphy, 1992). This point offers a fortuitous segue into research on the variables that have been found to influence the effectiveness of hypermedia for learning.

Moderators of Hypermedia Effects

Researchers studying the influence of hypermedia use have identified several variables that may increase or decrease the effectiveness of this medium for learning. Much like the research on the moderators of hypermedia use, the most important variables include hypermedia structure, motivations, and individual differences such as learning strategies or expertise. We will examine the research evidence concerning each of these variables in turn.

Hypermedia structure. As predicted by learner control theory, the structure and amount of control afforded users in hypermedia have exercised a significant impact on the cognitive effects of the system in many studies. Early research conducted by Gray (1987) found that, when given greater control of the sequence of instruction, users comprehended more of the content immediately after exposure, although a retention test a week later indicated no differences between groups given greater or lesser control. Providing high levels of control of the content to users, but combining that flexibility with instructional advisement, increased learning for those groups who had difficulty dealing with the greater levels of control. However, the user control-instructional advisement combination did not influence, positively or negatively, those who could learn well without the advisement (Lee & Lehman, 1993).

In the context of learning from media, cognitive overhead may be defined as the amount of mental effort required to locate specific information and to understand how this information is oriented within a larger information source (i.e., a chapter in a book or a page in a website). Generally speaking, hypermedia use demands more cognitive overhead than the use of printed text because hypermedia use requires "a certain overhead of metalevel decision making, an overhead that is absent when the author has already made many of these choices for you" (Conklin, 1987, p. 40). One impact of different hypermedia structures could be to exacerbate the cognitive overhead hypermedia place on users (Oliver, 1996). Much of the theory and research on hypermedia systems has described user feelings of being "lost" in hyperspace (Conklin, 1987) or, more generally, "disorientation" (e.g., Calvi, 1997). These feelings may be caused by both inexperience with the medium or content as well as poor site design (Landow, 1997). In any case, disorientation will increase the cognitive overhead required to make use of the site.

It is assumed by most psychologists that the capacity to process information is finite and is often exceeded by the information available in the environment. In order to deal with this limitation in cognitive capacity, users may not always devote an optimum amount of cognitive effort to all tasks. Therefore, if a website's design requires substantial cognitive effort simply to navigate through it (cognitive overhead), less effort will be available to invest in actual learning processes such as integration and elaboration (Eveland & Dunwoody, 2000). Since the amount of mental effort devoted to learning processes is a very important correlate of actual learning, site designs that are overly complex or not intuitive can cause disorientation, leading to increased effort devoted to cognitive overhead and thus a reduction in learning. Thus, it is not total effort expended, but specific types of effort, that encourage learning. But even setting immediate learning aside, if the site is too complex it might discourage individuals from ever returning or from seeking information elsewhere in the future, which may be an even more danger-ous effect of poor site design and high cognitive load.

Some hypermedia system designs attempt to provide features to reduce the cog-nitive load imposed by the technology. Some research has focused on variables related to identifying in-text links (e.g., Carlson & Kacmar, 1999; Kahn & Locatis, 1998). Other studies have examined the role of window size and the amount of text per node in producing disorientation and reducing search effectiveness (Kim & Eastman, 1999). A meta-analysis by Chen and Rada (1996) demonstrated that, consistent with the claims of some designers (e.g., Bieber et al., 1997), providing a graphical overview of the structure of the hypermedia system can increase the effectiveness as well as the efficiency of hypermedia use. Although there is no direct evidence, it is likely that features such as maps reduce the cognitive load of using hypermedia systems and thus allow users to devote more effort to the pro-cesses of elaboration, synthesis, and integration, which promote learning. A useful next step in this area of research would be to directly measure the cognitive load imposed by the site design, potentially making use of work in engineering that has attempted to address similar constructs (e.g., Wickens, 1992). This would allow researchers to determine empirically if the impact of site design on learning is truly mediated by the effect of site design on cognitive overhead. Similarly, re-searchers should make an effort to directly measure the amount of cognitive effort devoted to mental processes beneficial to learning, such as elaboration, as indi-viduals use websites (Eveland & Dunwoody, 2000).

Examining just a few types of hypermedia structure variations, then, the evi-dence indicates that the structure of a hypermedia system can have a significant impact on learning from the system. However, the direction of the effects are not always in favor of greater freedom of navigational control. Whereas greater con-trol may provide opportunities for individualized learning and continuing motiva-tion, some designs may turn over too much control to the user, thereby increasing cognitive load and decreasing learning.

Motivations. Scholars have argued that any sort of motivation may conceivably influence the effectiveness of hypermedia use (e.g., Jonassen & Grabinger, 1993; Kinzie & Berdel, 1990); however, the focus of research has been on external mo-tivations as moderators of learning. Internal motivations would include the inter-est and desire to learn or goals determined by the individual. External motivations, on the other hand, are typically operationalized as tasks assigned to users by a teacher or experimenter and are typically categorized as either "search" goals or "browse" goals (or sometimes labeled "closed" and "open" tasks, respectively). Search goals, or closed tasks, commonly entail finding a specific unit of informa-tion in a single location. Browse goals, or open tasks, typically require the integra-tion of small bits of information from several locations.

A meta-analysis of the literature on the influence of external motivations on the effectiveness of learning from hypermedia (Chen & Rada, 1996) indicates strong support for the assertion that hypermedia is much more effective for learning on open tasks (those having general goals) than closed tasks (those having specific goals). According to the authors, each of seven studies identified as testing this hypothesis found supportive evidence, with a large average effect size ($r = .63$). Using more complex distinctions by asking several different types of questions that varied in their level of openness, Leventhal et al. (1993) found differences in the relative effectiveness of hypermedia versus print based on question type. A close reading of their tables reveals that the variability in effectiveness across all question types was much higher for the control group using a paper version of the content (mean scores ranging from 0.29 to 1.76 for the paper group, compared to 1.16 to 1.51 for the hypermedia group). This greater variance in effectiveness due to question type for the paper version indicates that the moderating effects of task (i.e., question type) are in fact greater for paper than hypermedia. Clearly, however, the external task assigned to hypermedia users has some influence on the effectiveness of the medium, which is better suited to browsing and integrating tasks.

Individual differences. As with any medium, many individual-level variables may influence the amount of learning from hypermedia. Most research on individual differences in hypermedia effects has focused on two key variables: expertise and cognitive/learning styles.

Earlier, we noted that theories of learner control predict that greater levels of control for the user should produce higher levels of learning (Kinzie et al., 1988). However, reviews of the learner control literature have not found strong support for this hypothesis; instead, it appears that learner control is effective only for those subjects who are highly motivated or have greater expertise in the content domain, and thus are better prepared to structure their own learning processes (e.g., Gay, 1986; Milheim & Martin, 1991; Park, 1991; Steinberg, 1989).

Consistent evidence for the importance of expertise is available from the hypermedia literature. Rada and Murphy (1992), for instance, found that hypermedia was a more effective search tool than printed text in a sample of system (hypertext) experts but that print was clearly more effective for novices. In a more direct test of the learner control hypothesis, Shin et al. (1994) found no difference between free-access and limited-access conditions for a group with substantial prior knowledge. However, a low-prior-knowledge group of users scored significantly lower on an achievement test in the free-access system than in the limited-access system.

Several recent studies have examined how cognitive strategies and learning strategies may moderate the cognitive effects of hypermedia use and have concluded that more active, conceptually based, and analytical learning styles are more conducive to learning from this medium. Lee and Lehman (1993) found that those with passive learning styles (operationalized as those scoring more than one-half standard deviation below their sample mean on an index called the "Passive Active Learning Scale") achieved lower learning scores than active and neutral learners when using a hypermedia system without instructional cues. Another study

(Esichaikul, Smith, & Madey, 1994) demonstrated that, when using hypermedia, those with learning styles favoring abstract conceptualization produced higher quality solutions to problems than those with learning styles favoring more concrete experience. Similarly, a study by Leader and Klein (1996) discussed earlier indicated that field-dependent learners (those who have a global or holistic cognitive style) produced significantly fewer correct answers in their search of a hypermedia system than field-independent learners (those who have a more analytic cognitive style). However, significant interactions with the type of search tool available indicated that this pattern only held in two of the four experimental conditions.

DIRECTIONS FOR FUTURE RESEARCH

Criticisms of and Conclusions From the Hypermedia Literature

The study of the uses and effects of hypermedia is a classic example of cross-disciplinary research. Seldom, if ever, do researchers in one domain cite the research in other domains. Some existing literature reviews completely ignore theory and research conducted outside of their home field. This review has tried to demonstrate the cross-disciplinary nature of hypermedia research. At the same time, as communication researchers ourselves, we have attempted to make this theory and research more accessible to those in communication and related disciplines.

As a cross-disciplinary area of theory and research, the hypermedia literature tends to be fragmented and to suffer from broad and inconsistent use of terminology and operationalizations. Thus, despite the existence of a substantial literature (only a part of which has been reviewed here), few studies on any single topic are truly comparable. This has forced the few laudable attempts at meta-analysis to rely on an extremely small number of studies composed largely of unpublished dissertations and conference papers that are not widely available to communication researchers (see Chen & Rada, 1996).

Further, even in published studies, statistical analyses are often not correctly applied or, even worse, the appropriate designs for accurate tests of hypotheses (e.g., use of control groups or comparisons of effects between hypermedia and other media) are not implemented. Astleitner and Leutner (1995, p. 395) have noted, "A lot of the research in the field of learning with hypermedia still comes from computer scientists who, in general, do not dispose of that high-quality methodological repertoire concerning empirical investigation which is usually common to social scientists." For instance, one glaring omission in this research is the design of studies to test for interactions between medium and background characteristics like expertise in order to determine whether the effects of expertise on learning from hypermedia are particularly acute for hypermedia or simply another manifestation of effects that occur with any medium.

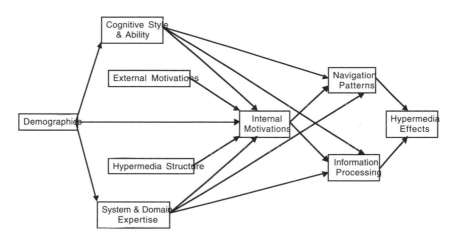

Figure 1. A hypothesized model of hypermedia uses and effects.

Aside from flaws in research design (i.e., lack of random assignment) or analytical errors, two other consistent drawbacks in the empirical research on the uses and effects of hypermedia are (a) the failure to control for extraneous variables in observational research and the use of extremely homogeneous samples—typically either elementary students or graduate students—in experimental studies; and (b) the failure to measure and analyze theoretically meaningful mediator variables such as perceived user control, motivation, and cognitive load.

All these factors make it difficult to derive any solid generalizations from the existing hypermedia literature. Instead, the literature on hypermedia uses and effects more realistically can provide communication researchers with a template for choosing potentially important independent and moderator variables for further study in the context of the World Wide Web, and to learn from the early attempts of others.

In order to facilitate future multivariate research, we have arranged those variables that have been commonly studied in the hypermedia literature into a preliminary causal model based on an information processing perspective (Figure 1). This model represents our view of how these variables should be arranged; although many of the links have been consistently supported by research, in general this is a hypothesized model. Table 1 presents specific hypotheses for each link based primarily on the literature reviewed in this article.

In this model, demographic variables are considered exogenous. Demographic variables are presumed to directly influence levels of expertise, cognitive style and ability variables, and internal motivations (e.g., gratifications sought, self-efficacy). External motivations (i.e., tasks), hypermedia structure, cognitive style/ability, and expertise are also believed to have an impact on internal motivations.

TABLE 1
Hypothesized Effects on Key Variables in Predicted Model

Variable	*Factors influencing variable*
Cognitive style & ability	1) Younger children will have lower levels of cognitive ability than older children and adults.
System & domain expertise	1) Older children and younger adults will be more likely to have system expertise than younger children and older adults.
	2) Females will be less likely to have system expertise than males.
	3) Those of low socio-economic status (SES) will be less likely to have system expertise than those of high SES.
	4) Depending on topic, domain expertise will vary by gender, age, SES, and other demographic factors.
Internal motivations	1) Depending on topic, gender, SES, or age may influence internal motivations.
	2) External motivations often influence internal motivations.
	3) Hypermedia structure, through learner control, motivates users.
	4) Expertise using the system or in the domain increases self-efficacy.
Navigation patterns	1) Those with greater visualization skills and cognitive ability will be better able to engage in nonlinear navigation.
	2) Those with greater domain and system expertise will engage in more nonlinear navigation patterns and be less likely to become disoriented and lost.
	3) Search tasks produce linear navigation, whereas browse tasks produce nonlinear navigation.
Information processing	1) Those with greater cognitive ability will be better able to engage in productive information processing behaviors such as elaboration.
	2) Those with greater domain expertise will be more effective at engaging in productive information processing behaviors such as elaboration.
	3) Those who are motivated to learn will engage in elaborative forms of information processing.
Hypermedia effects	1) Those who engage in nonlinear navigation patterns that follow their interests and abilities will learn more than those who follow a strict and predetermined linear pattern.
	2) Those who engage in productive information processing activities such as elaboration will learn more from hypermedia than those who engage in less of this form of information processing.

Internal motivations, cognitive style/ability, and expertise are expected to directly influence navigation patterns through hypermedia and information processing in the form of elaboration on content and amount of invested effort. These navigation patterns and information processing activities, in turn, serve as the key mediating variables for hypermedia effects. It should be noted that this model is a slightly modified version of the cognitive mediation model advocated by the first author (Eveland, 1997a, 1997b, 1998).

A concrete example combining experimental manipulations, self-report mea surement of exogenous and mediating variables, and electronic observation of navigation patterns will help to illustrate this model. Learning from a Web site could be examined by altering the hypermedia structure to produce a simple, relatively "linear" and a sophisticated, relatively "nonlinear" version of the site. Participants would be randomly assigned to one or the other of these versions, using instructions to provide *external motivations* for (randomly) either learning or entertainment. Both the site structure and the assigned motivation would contribute to perceptions of self-efficacy—which is one form of *internal motivation*—for completing the assigned task. Self-efficacy would also likely be influenced by preexisting levels of cognitive ability and expertise with both the system (in this case, the Web) and the content of the site (e.g., health information, current affairs), as well as by demographic variables such as socio-economic status or gender.

Self-efficacy, cognitive ability, and both forms of expertise would likely have substantial impact on the qualitative type and quantity of *information processing* (e.g., more effort spent elaborating, integrating and synthesizing vs. simple repetition or selective scanning) and the electronically observed *patterns of navigation* (e.g., seeking additional information available about certain subtopics) through the site. Finally, these navigation patterns (which determine the content, order, and length of exposure to specific information in the site) and information processing activities are the direct determinants of learning.

Why Might Web Uses and Effects Differ From Those of Hypermedia?

Despite our focus on the hypermedia literature, we do not take the position that the uses and effects of the World Wide Web itself will perfectly mirror those of other hypermedia systems. Indeed, the Web is unlike any other hypermedia system in existence because of its massive size, broad access, and multiple, independent authors. Thus, the direct and automatic application of all hypermedia research to the Web context without consideration of these differences is probably inappropriate (Smith, Newman, & Parks, 1997).

Two of the most important variables identified in hypermedia research are expertise and motivation. In most of the studies described above, the variance in each of these variables was rather limited. Motivation has typically been based on directions from teachers or experimenters to conduct a focused search versus a less focused browse of a small hypermedia system. On the Web, the variety of motivations is likely to be much greater and more likely to be internally generated, as would be expected considering the differences in context between classroom learning from a hypermedia system and "surfing the Web." How will this increased variance in motivation influence the uses and effects of the Web? Similarly, the level of expertise of users of the Web varies widely, from first-time users to computer programmers and from elementary school children to Ph.D.'s in a content domain. How will this wide variety in expertise influence the uses and effects of the Web?

The World Wide Web is also infinitely larger than the largest hypermedia system examined in the studies above. This can only exacerbate the problems of disorientation or being "lost in hyperspace" (Calvi, 1997; Dias & Sousa, 1997; Kahn & Landow, 1993; McKnight, Dillon, & Richardson, 1989; Psotka et al., 1993; Roselli, 1991) that users have felt in the smaller systems. In addition, the much wider variety of content on the Web means that someone who is a domain expert at one moment may become a complete domain novice with the click of a mouse button. How will this great variety of content and massive size influence World Wide Web uses and effects? This is an important question for those who plan to conduct research in this area.

Another variable on the Web that is not studied in the hypermedia literature is the perceived credibility of the source. Whereas a hypermedia system used in a classroom or experimental setting is likely to come from a single source and be given high ratings for credibility, the information on the World Wide Web varies tremendously in origin and credibility. How will user credibility judgments influence the uses and effects of the Web? What role will skepticism, cynicism, trust, and quality assessment skills play in learning from the Web? These are important questions that research in communication is only beginning to address (e.g., Johnson & Kaye, 1998a; Sundar, 1998).

Integrating Hypermedia and Communication Research for Web Applications

Although mass media scholarship to date emphasizes traditional information channels—newspapers, television, and radio—its conceptual efforts may be quite generalizable to the Web context. Just as it is important to avoid neglecting the hypermedia literature available in other disciplines, so it is useful to incorporate relevant theory from communication. The question then becomes: How might the research on hypermedia and traditional communication research be integrated into the study of the uses and effects of the World Wide Web? We envision connections between these two literatures both at the level of Web use and Web effects.

Use of the Web. One important issue that has been examined in the context of other communication technologies is how users combine their use of the Web with other media. The first issue should be the demographic correlates of Web use. As with most new technologies, use of the Web has been shown to correlate positively with income and education (CommerceNet, 1997; Wirthlin Worldwide, 1996). However, as the technology diffuses, will the correlates of Web use resemble those of traditional print channels such as news magazines and newspapers or will they appear more like those of television?

The second issue relates to the influence of Web use on other mediated and interpersonal means of communication. Chaffee and Mutz (1988) argued that mass mediated and interpersonal communication serve complementary, not competitive roles. Should we expect that the same applies to the use of the World Wide Web and traditional media? The research examining the impact of use of other new communication technologies appears to be mixed (e.g., Becker, Dunwoody, & Rafaeli, 1983; Bromley & Bowles, 1995; James, Wotring, & Forrest, 1995; Reagan, 1989). What about the relationship between Web use and face-to-face communication, especially considering the ability to communicate interpersonally via the Web in real time and even with video images? Will the use of the Web supplement or supplant the use of more traditional media and face-to-face communication? Future studies of Web use should examine this issue closely, and they may learn from research studying other new technologies like electronic mail, bulletin boards, and cable television.

Researchers interested in patterns of television exposure have studied the influence of inheritance effects on program viewing (Eastman, Newton, Riggs, & Neal-Lunsford, 1997; Tiedge & Ksobiech, 1986; Webster, 1985). Since the remote control became commonly available, its influence on inheritance effects, and the phenomenon of channel changing more generally, has been examined (Eastman & Newton, 1995; Ferguson, 1994; Kaye & Sapolsky, 1997; Walker, 1988). Despite the relative ease with which the television channel may be changed in this age of the remote control, television content is still designed to be watched in increments of about a half hour at minimum. However, the Web is a medium designed to be surfed, and "channel changing" takes place much more frequently. How might the research on flow through television content and the use of the remote control be applied to the study of Web use using audit trail data, especially as full-motion video and audio content become more widely available on websites and more accessible with faster modems? Those currently studying the remote control as a means for frequent content selection should devote some of their efforts to the use of the computer mouse for the same purpose.

A strong connection may be made between research on the gratifications sought from media and the role of motivations in hypermedia research. Although hypermedia research has typically only considered the influence of externally imposed goals on the uses of hypermedia, communication researchers have studied the importance of internally developed goals. Some research has examined differences between the (actual or normative) uses made of traditional media and new technologies (e.g., Perse & Courtright, 1993; Williams, Phillips, & Lum, 1985; Williams, Strover, & Grant, 1994), and this research is beginning to examine the gratifications sought from the Web (Eighmey & McCord, 1998; Kaye, 1998). Is Web use primarily instrumental or is it merely the act of surfing, a ritualized motive, that Web users are seeking? Other research in communication is now beginning to apply other types of motivations, including notions of self-efficacy, to research on the use of the Web (Fredin & David, 1998).

Effects of the Web. In many cases the theory and research findings from the hypermedia literature can be interpreted in light of traditional mass media effects research. This may be most true when considering the role of expertise in learning from hypermedia. The evidence from the hypermedia literature described above indicates that those higher in expertise are more likely to learn from hypermedia and are more capable of making use of the availability of learner control it affords. Almost 30 years ago, Tichenor, Donohue, and Olien (1970) suggested that education (as an indicator of socio-economic status) should facilitate learning from mass media channels, leading to increasing knowledge gaps between those of higher and lower education levels. This hypothesis remains one of the more popular topics in mass media effects research (see Gaziano, 1997; Viswanath & Finnegan, 1996). In their original discussion of the knowledge gap hypothesis, Tichenor et al. suggested that greater cognitive ability, communication skills, and access to media sources (plus a few other variables) were the immediate causes of differential knowledge acquisition. Thus, the application of the socio-structural knowledge gap framework for research on learning from the Web may provide new insights into the effects of the medium while providing a new context for knowledge gap research.

In addition to research in the knowledge gap tradition, research on the acquisition of public affairs knowledge in political science and mass communication has taken a more psychological approach in examining the role of education, expertise, and prior knowledge (e.g., Fiske, Lau, & Smith, 1990; Rhee & Cappella, 1997), focusing on the benefits of more developed schemas for information acquisition, structuring, retention, and recall. This approach, then, can also provide additional theory that may be applied to learning from the Web in the same way it has been applied to traditional news media. Researchers have recently begun to compare the relative learning from the Web and other sources of mediated information in real-world contexts, such as presidential election campaigns (e.g., Johnson, Braima, & Sothirajah, 1999).

Just as gratifications sought have been hypothesized to have effects on media uses, researchers have also hypothesized that these motivations may have some influence on media effects (e.g., Blumler, 1979). This is consistent with the hypermedia research finding that externally imposed motivations can have some influence on the effects of hypermedia. Presumably, then, internally developed motivations for Web use (i.e., gratifications sought from Web use or from use of particular types of Web content) may influence the effects of Web use. For instance, those who seek information from the Web—whether internally or externally driven—may process the content to which they are exposed in more depth. Research concerned with more traditional media has demonstrated that this deeper, more elaborative processing can lead to greater learning (e.g., Eveland, 1997a, 1997b). On the other hand, those who have either entertainment or ritualized (e.g., to pass time when bored) motivations for Web use may be less cognitively engaged with the content and thus learn little from the information to which they are exposed.

Few studies of hypermedia consider effects beyond the cognitive (for exceptions, see Hoffman & Novak, 1996; Johnson et al., 1999). However, communication researchers have traditionally been interested in affective and behavioral effects as well. Can World Wide Web use influence people's attitudes toward science, religion, politics, and other—sometimes controversial—topics? Can Web use lead to greater participation in public life, or does it just lead to cynicism and withdrawal (Johnson & Kaye, 1998b)? What are the effects of the Web relative to traditional mass mediated channels such as television, newspapers, and radio? Are advertising effects stronger or weaker on the Web compared to other media? These are questions to which researchers should devote more attention.

One characteristic of the Web that may influence its attitudinal effects relative to traditional media is the diversity of its content. A key assumption of several prominent mass communication theories, such as the spiral of silence (Noelle-Neumann, 1993) and cultivation theory (Gerbner, Gross, Morgan, & Signorielli, 1994), is that mass media content, particularly television, is consonant. The argument is that media content is homogeneous because the ability to express oneself via the media is limited to those in positions of power, and those in power share the same interests. Thus the content of the media is homogeneous in that it represents only the interests of those in power. Although we will leave this debate in the context of television for others (Signorielli, 1986; Webster, 1986), observers have noted that the Web makes access to a worldwide audience infinitely more democratic. Never before has it been so easy for a single individual to express his or her views to such a far-reaching audience; indeed, the freedom and ease of expression on the Web has led to calls for censorship from many sectors of society. Therefore, whereas traditional media content may or may not be consonant, the content of the Web is unlikely to be consonant and, thus, cultivation effects or a spiral of silence may be less likely to occur based on exposure to the Web.

Robert Putnam (1995a, 1995b) has argued that television has led to an erosion of "social capital," which includes interpersonal trust and involvement in associations and groups. This effect, he claims, takes place through two separate processes. First, the time displacement hypothesis suggests that the more time spent watching television, the less time is available for engaging in social activities with others (Moy, Scheufele, & Holbert, 1999). This logic could also be applied to the Web, and at least some evidence from psychology indicates that Internet use generally may have such an effect (Kraut et al., 1998). The second process is likened to cultivation, in which the consonant, violent images on television produce fear and, more generally, perceptions of a mean and dangerous world. These feelings lead individuals to avoid social contact and mistrust others, thus reducing social capital. However, if the argument about the diversity of content on the Web described above is true, use of the Web may or may not produce feelings of fear. The effect should depend on the specific content used, just as some have argued for the role of television in the destruction of social capital (Shah, 1998).

CONCLUSION

There is a substantial literature dispersed across several fields that addresses the uses and effects of hypermedia systems, of which the World Wide Web is by far the largest and most complex. In order to make this literature more readily available to communication researchers engaged in the nascent study of the World Wide Web, in this article we have reviewed this cross-disciplinary literature and indicated points of intersection between it and traditional communication theory.

Due to its cross-disciplinary nature, the hypermedia literature uses a variety of conflicting conceptualizations and operationalizations that make generalizable patterns of findings difficult to identify. However, communication researchers can learn from and build upon this literature by understanding the important issues that have been raised and clarifying ambiguities due to poor definitions of concepts and inconsistent operationalizations. It is only by addressing these problems that the study of hypermedia and the World Wide Web can move forward.

It is our hope that this review will encourage communication scholars to delve into the hypermedia literature and make use of it in developing their own theories and research projects concerning the uses and effects of the World Wide Web. Whereas the hypermedia literature does not provide any definitive or generalizable answers for us, it does have a decade head start on us in asking important and relevant questions, and thus we still have much to learn from it.

REFERENCES

Astleitner, H., & Leutner, D. (1995). Learning strategies for unstructured hypermedia—A framework for theory, research, and practice. *Journal of Educational Computing Research, 13*, 387–400.

Bandura, A. (1982). Self-efficacy mechanism in human agency. *American Psychologist, 37*, 122–147.

Barab, S. A., Fajen, B. R., Kulikowich, J. M., & Young, M. F. (1996). Assessing hypermedia navigation through Pathfinder: Prospects and limitations. *Journal of Educational Computing Research, 15*, 185–205.

Beasley, R. E., & Vila, J. A. (1992). The identification of navigation patterns in a multimedia environment: A case study. *Journal of Educational Multimedia and Hypermedia, 1*, 209–222.

Becker, L. B., Dunwoody, S., & Rafaeli, S. (1983). Cable's impact on use of other news media. *Journal of Broadcasting, 27*, 127–140.

Berthon, P., Pitt, L. F., & Watson, R. T. (1996). The World Wide Web as an advertising medium: Toward an understanding of conversion efficiency. *Journal of Advertising Research, 36*(1), 43–54.

Bevilacqua, A. F. (1989). Hypertext: Behind the hype. *American Libraries, 20*, 158–162.

Bieber, M., Vitali, F., Ashman, H., Balasubramanian, V., & Oinas-Kukkonen, H. (1997). Fourth generation hypermedia: Some missing links for the World Wide Web. *International Journal of Human-Computer Studies, 47*, 31–65.

Bimber, B. (1999). *Data on Internet users and on political use of the Internet* [Online]. Available: http://www.polsci.ucsb.edu/~bimber/research/demos.html

Blumler, J. G. (1979). The role of theory in uses and gratifications studies. *Communication Research, 6*, 9–36.

Bromley, R. V., & Bowles, D. (1995). Impact of Internet on use of traditional news media. *Newspaper Research Journal, 16*(2), 14–27.

Buckingham Shum, S., & McKnight, C. (1997). World Wide Web usability: Introduction to this special issue. *International Journal of Human-Computer Studies, 47*, 1–4.

Bush, V. (1945, July). As we may think. *Atlantic Monthly, 176*, 101–108.

Calvi, L. (1997). Navigation and disorientation: A case study. *Journal of Educational Multimedia and Hypermedia, 6*, 305–320.

Campagnoni, F. R., & Ehrlich, K. (1989). Information retrieval using a hypertext-based help system. *ACM Transactions on Information Systems, 7*, 271–291.

Card, S. K., Moran, T. P., & Newell, A. (1983). *The psychology of human-computer interaction.* Hillsdale, NJ: Erlbaum.

Carmel, E., Crawford, S., & Chen, H. (1992). Browsing in hypertext: A cognitive study. *IEEE Transactions on Systems, Man, and Cybernetics, 22*, 865–884.

Carlson, J. R., & Kacmar, C. J. (1999). Increasing link marker effectiveness for WWW and other hypermedia interfaces: An examination of end-user preferences. *Journal of the American Society for Information Science, 50*, 386–398.

Chaffee, S. H., & Mutz, D. C. (1988). Comparing mediated and interpersonal communication data. In R. P. Hawkins, J. M. Wiemann, & S. Pingree (Eds.), *Advancing communication science: Merging mass and interpersonal processes* (pp. 19–43). Newbury Park, CA: Sage.

Chapman, J. L. (1981). A state transition analysis of online information-seeking behavior. *Journal of the American Society for Information Science, 32*, 325–333.

Chen, C., & Rada, R. (1996). Interacting with hypertext: A meta-analysis of experimental studies. *Human-Computer Interaction, 11*, 125–156.

Churcher, P. R. (1989). A common notation for knowledge representation, cognitive models, learning and hypertext. *Hypermedia, 1*, 235–254.

Clark, R. E. (1983). Reconsidering research on learning from media. *Review of Educational Research, 53*, 445–459.

Clark, R. E. (1985). Confounding in educational computing research. *Journal of Educational Computing Research, 1*, 137–148.

Collins, A. M., & Loftus, E. F. (1975). A spreading activation theory of semantic processing. *Psychological Review, 82*, 407–428.

CommerceNet. (1997). *"Startling increase" in Internet shopping reported in new CommerceNet /Nielsen Media Research study* [Online]. Available: http://www.commerce.net/work/pilot/nielsen_96/press_97.html

Compaine, B. M. (1988). Information gaps: Myth or reality? In B. M. Compaine (Ed.), *Issues in new information technology* (pp. 179–191). Norwood, NJ: Ablex.

Conklin, J. (1987). Hypertext: An introduction and survey. *IEEE Computer, 20*(90), 17–41.

Craik, F. I. M., & Lockhart, R. S. (1972). Levels of processing: A framework for memory research. *Journal of Verbal Learning and Verbal Behavior, 11*, 671–684.

Crampton, J. (1992). A cognitive analysis of wayfinding expertise. *Cartographica, 29*(3–4), 46–65.

Darken, R. P., & Sibert, J. L. (1996). Navigating large virtual spaces. *International Journal of Human Computer Interaction, 8*, 49–71.

DeFleur, M. L., Davenport, L., Cronin, M., & DeFleur, M. (1992). Audience recall of news stories presented by newspaper, computer, television and radio. *Journalism Quarterly, 69*, 1010–1022.

Dias, P., & Sousa, A. P. (1997). Understanding navigation and disorientation in hypermedia learning environments. *Journal of Educational Multimedia and Hypermedia, 6*, 173–185.

Duchastel, P. C. (1990). Examining cognitive processing in hypermedia usage. *Hypermedia, 2*, 221–233.

Eastman, S. T., & Newton, G. D. (1995). Delineating grazing: Observations of remote control use. *Journal of Communication, 45*(1), 77–95.

Eastman, S. T., Newton, G. D., Riggs, K. E., & Neal-Lunsford, J. (1997). Accelerating the flow: A transition effect in programming theory? *Journal of Broadcasting & Electronic Media, 41*, 265–283.

Eighmey, J., & McCord, L. (1998). Adding value in the information age: Uses and gratifications of sites on the World Wide Web. *Journal of Business Research, 41*, 187–194.

Elliott, E. S., & Dweck, C. S. (1988). Goals: An approach to motivation and achievement. *Journal of Personality and Social Psychology, 54,* 5–12.

Esichaikul, V., Smith, R. D., & Madey, G. R. (1994). The impact of learning style on problem-solving performance in a hypertext environment. *Hypermedia, 6,* 101–110.

Ettema, J. S. (1985). Explaining information system use with system-monitored vs. self-reported use measures. *Public Opinion Quarterly, 49,* 381–387.

Eveland, W. P., Jr. (1997a, May). *Motivation, information processing, and learning from the news: Toward a synthesis of paradigms.* Paper presented at the annual meeting of the International Communication Association, Montreal, Quebec.

Eveland, W. P., Jr. (1997b). *The process of political learning from the news: The roles of motivation, attention, and elaboration.* Unpublished doctoral dissertation, University of Wisconsin-Madison.

Eveland, W. P., Jr. (1998, August). *The cognitive mediation model: A framework for studying learning from the news with survey methods.* Paper presented at the annual meeting of the Association for Education in Journalism and Mass Communication, Baltimore, MD.

Eveland, W. P., Jr., & Dunwoody, S. (1998). Users and navigation patterns of a science World Wide Web site for the public. *Public Understanding of Science, 7,* 285–311.

Eveland, W. P., Jr., & Dunwoody, S. (2000). Examining information processing on the World Wide Web using think aloud protocols. *Media Psychology, 2,* 219–244.

Ferguson, D. A. (1994). Measurement of mundane TV behaviors: Remote control device flipping frequency. *Journal of Broadcasting & Electronic Media, 38,* 35–47.

Fiske, S. T., Lau, R. R., & Smith, R. A. (1990). On the varieties and utilities of political expertise. *Social Cognition, 8,* 31–48.

Fredin, E. S., & David, P. (1998). Browsing and the hypermedia interaction cycle: A model of efficacy and goal dynamics. *Journalism & Mass Communication Quarterly, 75,* 35–54.

Furnham, A., Gunter, B., & Green, A. (1990). Remembering science: The recall of factual information as a function of the presentation mode. *Applied Cognitive Psychology, 4,* 203–212.

Gay, G. (1986). Interaction of learner control and prior understanding in computer-assisted video instruction. *Journal of Educational Psychology, 78,* 225–227.

Gaziano, C. (1997). Forecast 2000: Widening knowledge gaps. *Journalism & Mass Communication Quarterly, 74,* 237–264.

Gerbner, G., Gross, L., Morgan, M., & Signorielli, N. (1994). Growing up with television: The cultivation perspective. In J. Bryant & D. Zillmann (Eds.), *Media effects: Advances in theory and research* (pp. 17–41). Hillsdale, NJ: Erlbaum.

Gray, S. H. (1987). The effect of sequence control on computer assisted learning. *Journal of Computer-Based Instruction, 14,* 54–56.

Gray, S. H., Barber, C. B., & Shasha, D. (1991). Information search with dynamic text vs. paper text: An empirical comparison. *International Journal of Man-Machine Studies, 35,* 575–586.

Gray, S. H., & Shasha, D. (1989). To link or not to link? Empirical guidance for the design of nonlinear text systems. *Behavior Research Methods, Instruments, & Computers, 21,* 326–333.

Greenwald, A. G., & Leavitt, C. (1984). Audience involvement in advertising: Four levels. *Journal of Consumer Research, 11,* 581–592.

Gunter, B., Furnham, A., & Gietson, G. (1984). Memory for the news as a function of the channel of communication. *Human Learning, 3,* 265–271.

Hagler, P., & Knowlton, J. (1987). Invalid implicit assumption in CBI comparison research. *Journal of Computer-Based Instruction, 14,* 84–88.

Heller, R. S. (1990). The role of hypermedia in education: A look at the research issues. *Journal of Research on Computing in Education, 22,* 431–441.

Hill, J. R., & Hannafin, M. (1997). Cognitive strategies and learning from the World Wide Web. *Educational Technology Research & Development, 45*(4), 37–64.

Hirsch, S. G., & Borgman, C. L. (1995). Comparing children's use of browsing and keyword searching on the Science Library Catalog. *Proceedings of the American Society for Information Science, 32,* 19–26.

Hoffman, D. L., & Novak, T. P. (1996, July). Marketing in hypermedia computer-mediated environments: Conceptual foundations. *Journal of Marketing, 60,* 50–68.

Hoffman, D. L., & Novak, T. P. (1998, April 17). Bridging the racial divide on the Internet. *Science, 280,* 390–391.

Horney, M. A. (1991). Uses of hypertext. *Journal of Computing in Higher Education, 2*(2), 44–65.

Horney, M. (1993). A measure of hypertext linearity. *Journal of Educational Multimedia and Hypermedia, 2,* 67–82.

Horney, M. A., & Anderson-Inman, L. (1994). The Electro-Text project: Hypertext reading patterns of middle school students. *Journal of Educational Multimedia and Hypermedia, 3,* 71–91.

Huberman, B. A., Pirolli, P. L. T., Pitkow, J. E., & Lukose, R. M. (1998, April 3). Strong regularities in World Wide Web surfing. *Science, 280,* 95–97.

Huff, C. W., & Rosenberg, J. (1989). The online voyeur: Promises and pitfalls of observing electronic interaction. *Behavior Research Methods, Instruments, & Computers, 21,* 166–172.

The Internet: Bringing order from chaos. (1997). *Scientific American, 276*(3), 50–51.

Iyengar, S., & Kinder, D. R. (1986). *News that matters: Television and American opinion.* Chicago: University of Chicago Press.

James, M. L., Wotring, C. E., & Forrest, E. J. (1995). An exploratory study of the perceived benefits of electronic bulletin board use and their impact on other communication activities. *Journal of Broadcasting & Electronic Media, 39,* 30–50.

Johnson, T. J., Braima, M. A. M., & Sothirajah, J. (1999). Doing the traditional media sidestep: Comparing the effects of the Internet and other nontraditional media with traditional media in the 1996 presidential campaign. *Journalism & Mass Communication Quarterly, 76,* 99–123.

Johnson, T. J., & Kaye, B. K. (1998a). Cruising is believing? Comparing Internet and traditional sources on media credibility measures. *Journalism & Mass Communication Quarterly, 75,* 325–340.

Johnson, T. J., & Kaye, B. K. (1998b). A vehicle for engagement or a haven for the disaffected? Internet use, political alienation, and voter participation. In T. J. Johnson, C. E. Hays, & S. P. Hays (Eds.), *Engaging the public: How government and the media can reinvigorate American democracy* (pp. 123–135). Lanham, MD: Rowman & Littlefield.

Jonassen, D. H. (1988). Designing structured hypertext and structuring access to hypertext. *Educational Technology, 28*(11), 13–16.

Jonassen, D. H. (1992). Designing hypertext for learning. In E. Scanlon & T. O'Shea (Eds.), *New directions in educational technology* (pp. 123–130). Berlin, Germany: Springer-Verlag.

Jonassen, D. H., & Grabinger, R. S. (1993). Applications of hypertext: Technologies for higher education. *Journal of Computing in Higher Education, 4*(2), 12–42.

Jonassen, D. H., & Wang, S. (1993). Acquiring structural knowledge from semantically structured hypertext. *Journal of Computer-Based Interaction, 20,* 1–8.

Kahn, K., & Locatis, C. (1998). Searching through cyberspace: The effects of link cues and correspondence on information retrieval from hypertext on the World Wide Web. *Journal of the American Society for Information Science, 49,* 1248–1253.

Kahn, P., & Landow, G. P. (1993). The pleasures of possibility: What is disorientation in hypertext? *Journal of Computing in Higher Education, 4*(2), 57–78.

Kaye, B. K. (1998). Uses and gratifications of the World Wide Web: From couch potato to Web potato. *New Jersey Journal of Communication, 6,* 21–40.

Kaye, B. K., & Sapolsky, B. S. (1997). Electronic monitoring of in-home television RCD usage. *Journal of Broadcasting & Electronic Media, 41,* 214–228.

Kelleher, T. (1996, August). *Amount of invested mental effort and learning from media: A conceptual review.* Paper presented at the annual meeting of the Association for Education in Journalism and Mass Communication, Anaheim, CA.

Kim, H., & Hirtle, S. C. (1995). Spatial metaphors and disorientation in hypertext browsing. *Behaviour & Information Technology, 14,* 239–250.

Kim, S. H., & Eastman, C. M. (1999). An experiment on node size in a hypermedia system. *Journal of the American Society for Information Science, 50,* 530–536.

Kintsch, W. (1972). Notes on the structure of semantic memory. In E. Tulving & W. Donaldson (Eds.), *Organization of memory* (pp. 247–308). New York: Academic Press.

Kinzie, M. B. (1990). Requirements and benefits of effective interactive instruction: Learner control, self-regulation, and continuing motivation. *Educational Technology Research and Development, 38*, 5–21.

Kinzie, M. B., & Berdel, R. L. (1990). Design and use of hypermedia systems. *Educational Technology Research and Development, 38*, 61–68.

Kinzie, M. B., Sullivan, H. J., & Berdel, R. L. (1988). Learner control and achievement in science computer-assisted instruction. *Journal of Educational Psychology, 80*, 299–303.

Kitchin, R. M. (1994). Cognitive maps: What are they and why study them? *Journal of Environmental Psychology, 14*, 1–19.

Kozma, R. B. (1987). The implications of cognitive psychology for computer-based learning tools. *Educational Technology, 27*(11), 20–25.

Kozma, R. B. (1994). Will media influence learning? Reframing the debate. *Educational Technology Research and Development, 42*(2), 7–19.

Kraut, R., Patterson, M., Lundmark, V., Kiesler, S., Mukopadhyay, T., & Scherlis, W. (1998). Internet paradox: A social technology that reduced social involvement and psychological well-being? *American Psychologist, 53*, 1017–1031.

Landow, G. P. (1997). *Hypertext 2.0: The convergence of contemporary critical theory and technology*. Baltimore, MD: Johns Hopkins University Press.

Lanza, A., & Roselli, T. (1991). Effects of the hypertextual approach versus the structured approach on students' achievement. *Journal of Computer-Based Instruction, 18*, 48–50.

Leader, L. F., & Klein, J. D. (1996). The effects of search tool type and cognitive style on performance during hypermedia database searches. *Educational Technology Research & Development, 44*(2), 5–15.

Lee, Y. B., & Lehman, J. D. (1993). Instructional cuing in hypermedia: A study with active and passive learners. *Journal of Educational Multimedia and Hypermedia, 2*, 25–37.

Leventhal, L. M., Teasley, B. M., Instone, K., & Farhat, J. (1994). Age-related differences in the use of hypertext: Experiment and design guidelines. *Hypermedia, 6*, 19–34.

Leventhal, L. M., Teasley, B. M., Instone, K., Rohlman, D. S., & Farhat, J. (1993). Sleuthing in HyperHolmes: An evaluation of using hypertext vs. a book to answer questions. *Behavior & Information Technology, 12*, 149–164.

Lucarella, D., & Zanzi, A. (1993). Browsing and searching in hypertext systems. *Journal of Computing in Higher Education, 4*(2), 79–105.

Marchionini, G. (1988). Hypermedia and learning: Freedom and chaos. *Educational Technology, 28*(11), 8–12.

Marchionini, G. (1989). Information-seeking strategies of novices using a full-text electronic encyclopedia. *Journal of the American Society for Information Science, 40*, 54–66.

Marchionini, G., & Shneiderman, B. (1988). Finding facts vs. browsing knowledge in hypertext systems. *IEEE Computer, 21*(1), 70–80.

McClelland, J. L. (1988). Connectionist models and psychological evidence. *Journal of Memory and Language, 27*, 107–123.

McKnight, C., Dillon, A., & Richardson, J. (1989). Problems in hyperland? A human factors perspective. *Hypermedia, 1*, 167–178.

Mediamark. (1998). *44 million American adults regularly use Internet* [Online]. Available: http://www.mediamark.com/mri/docs/98may22.html

Milheim, W. D., & Martin, B. L. (1991). Theoretical bases for the use of learner control: Three different perspectives. *Journal of Computer-Based Instruction, 18*, 99–105.

Misanchuk, E. R., & Schwier, R. A. (1992). Representing interactive multimedia and hypermedia audit trails. *Journal of Educational Multimedia and Hypermedia, 1*, 355–372.

Morrison, G. R. (1994). The media effects question: "Unresolvable" or asking the right question. *Educational Technology Research and Development, 42*(2), 41–44.

Moy, P., Scheufele, D. A., & Holbert, R. L. (1999). Television use and social capital: Testing Putnam's time displacement hypothesis. *Mass Communication & Society, 2,* 27–45.

Multon, K. D., Brown, S. D., & Lent, R. W. (1991). Relation of self-efficacy beliefs to academic outcomes: A meta-analytic investigation. *Journal of Counseling Psychology, 38,* 30–38.

Nelson, T. H. (1979). Electronic publishing and electronic literature. In E. C. DeLand (Ed.), *Information technology in health science education* (pp. 211–216). New York: Plenum Press.

Nelson, T. H. (1993). *Literary machines 93.1.* Sausalito, CA: Mindful Press.

Nelson, W. A., & Palumbo, D. B. (1992). Learning, instruction, and hypermedia. *Journal of Educational Multimedia and Hypermedia, 1,* 287–299.

Neuman, W. R., Just, M. R., & Crigler, A. N. (1992). *Common knowledge: News and the construction of political meaning.* Chicago: University of Chicago Press.

Nielsen, J. (1995). *Multimedia and hypertext: The Internet and beyond.* Boston: AP Professional.

Nielsen Media Research. (1996). *Home technology report* [Online]. Available: http://www.nielsenmedia.com/news/hotech-summary.html

Noelle-Neumann, E. (1993). *The spiral of silence—Our social skin* (2nd ed.). Chicago: University of Chicago Press.

Oborne, D. J., & Holton, D. (1998. Reading from screen versus paper: There is no difference. *International Journal of Man-Machine Sudies, 28,* 1–9.

Oliver, R. (1996). Measuring users' performance with interactive information systems. *Journal of Computer Assisted Learning, 12,* 89–102.

Olson, G. M., Herbsleb, J. D., & Reuter, H. H. (1994). Characterizing the sequential structure of interactive behaviors through statistical and grammatical techniques. *Human-Computer Interaction, 9,* 427–472.

Park, O. (1991). Hypermedia: Functional features and research issues. *Educational Technology, 31*(8), 24–31.

Perse, E. M., & Courtright, J. A. (1993). Normative images of communication media: Mass and interpersonal channels in the new media environment. *Human Communication Research, 19,* 485–503.

Pew Research Center. (n.d.). *Online newcomers more middle-brow, less work-oriented: The Internet audience goes ordinary* [Online] Available: www.people-press.org/tech98sum.htm

Psotka, J., Kerst, S., & Westerman, T. (1993). The use of hypertext and sensory-level supports for visual learning of aircraft names and shapes. *Behavior Research Methods, Instruments, & Computers, 25,* 168–172.

Putnam, R. D. (1995). Bowling alone: America's declining social capital. *Journal of Democracy, 6,* 65–78.

Putnam, R. D. (1995). Tuning in, tuning out: The strange disappearance of social capital in America. *PS: Political Science & Politics, 28,* 664–683.

Qiu, L. (1993). Markov models of search state patterns in a hypertext information retrieval system. *Journal of the American Society for Information Science, 44,* 413–427.

Quillian, M. R. (1968). Semantic memory. In M. Minsky (Ed.), *Semantic information processing* (pp. 227–270). Cambridge, MA: MIT Press.

Rada, R. (1995). Hypertext, multimedia and hypermedia. *The New Review of Hypermedia and Multimedia 1995: Applications and Research, 1,* 1–21.

Rada, R., & Murphy, C. (1992). Searching versus browsing in hypertext. *Hypermedia, 4,* 1–30.

Reagan, J. (1989). New technologies and news use: Adopters vs. nonadopters. *Journalism Quarterly, 66,* 871–875, 887.

Reinking, D. (1988). Computer-mediated text and comprehension differences: The role of reading time, reader preference, and estimation of learning. *Reading Research Quarterly, 23,* 484–498.

Rhee, J. W., & Cappella, J. N. (1997). The role of political sophistication in learning from news. *Communication Research, 24,* 197–233.

Rice, G. E. (1994). Examining constructs in reading comprehension using two presentation modes: Paper vs. computer. *Journal of Educational Computing Research, 11,* 153–178.

Rice, R. E. (1984). *The new media: Communication, research, and technology.* Beverly Hills, CA: Sage.

Rice, R. E., & Borgman, C. L. (1983). The use of computer-monitored data in information science and communication research. *Journal of the American Society for Information Science, 34*, 247–256.

Rice, R. E., & Rogers, E. M. (1984). New methods and data for the study of new media. In R. E. Rice (Ed.), *The new media: Communication, research, and technology* (pp. 81–99). Beverly Hills, CA: Sage.

Roselli, T. (1991). Control of user disorientation in hypertext systems. *Educational Technology, 31*(12), 42–46.

Ross, S. M., & Morrison, G. R. (1993). In search of a happy medium in instructional technology research: Issues concerning external validity, media replications, and learner control. *Educational Technology Research & Development, 37*, 19–33.

Salomon, G. (1983). The differential investment of mental effort in learning from different sources. *Educational Psychologist, 18*, 42–50.

Salomon, G. (1984). Television is "easy" and print is "tough": The differential investment of mental effort in learning as a function of perceptions and attributions. *Journal of Educational Psychology, 76*, 647–658.

Schallert, D. L. (1982). The significance of knowledge: A synthesis of research related to schema theory. In W. Otto & S. White (Eds.), *Reading expository material* (pp. 13–48). New York: Academic Press.

Schroeder, E. E., & Grabowski, B. L. (1995). Patterns of exploration and learning with hypermedia. *Journal of Educational Computing Research, 13*, 313–335.

Schunk, D. H. (1991). Self-efficacy and academic motivation. *Educational Psychologist, 26*, 207–231.

Shah, D. V. (1998). Civic engagement, interpersonal trust, and television use: An individual-level assessment of social capital. *Political Psychology, 19*, 469–496.

Shin, E. C., Schallert, D. L., & Savenye, W. C. (1994). Effects of learner control, advisement, and prior knowledge on young students' learning in a hypertext environment. *Educational Technology Research and Development, 42*(1), 33–46.

Shirk, H. N. (1992). Cognitive architecture in hypermedia instruction. In E. Barrett (Ed.), *Sociomedia: Multimedia, hypermedia, and the social construction of knowledge* (pp. 79–93). Cambridge, MA: MIT Press.

Shrock, S. A. (1994). The media influence debate: Read the fine print, but don't lose sight of the big picture. *Educational Technology Research and Development, 42*(2), 49–53.

Shum, S. (1990). Real and virtual spaces: Mapping from spatial cognition to hypertext. *Hypermedia, 2*, 133–158.

Signorielli, N. (1986). Selective television viewing: A limited possibility. *Journal of Communication, 36*(3), 64–76.

Smith, E. R. (1996). What do connectionism and social psychology offer each other? *Journal of Personality and Social Psychology, 70*, 893–912.

Smith, J. B., Smith, D. K., & Kupstas, E. (1993). Automated protocol analysis. *Human-Computer Interaction, 8*, 101–145.

Smith, P. A., Newman, I. A., & Parks, L. M. (1997). Virtual hierarchies and virtual networks: Some lessons from hypermedia usability research applied to the World Wide Web. *International Journal of Human-Computer Studies, 47*, 67–95.

Steinberg, E. R. (1989). Cognition and learner control: A literature review, 1977–1988. *Journal of Computer-Based Instruction, 16*, 117–121.

Sundar, S. S. (1998). Effect of source attribution on perception of online news stories. *Journalism & Mass Communication Quarterly, 75*, 55–68.

Sundar, S. S., Narayan, S., Obregon, R., & Uppal, C. (1998). Does Web advertising work? Memory for print vs. online media. *Journalism & Mass Communication Quarterly, 75*, 822–835.

Taylor, H. (1998). *The remorseless rise of the Internet* [Online]. Available: http://www.louisharris.com/poll/1998polls/Feb1998.html

Thüring, M., Hannemann, J., & Haake, J. M. (1995). Hypermedia and cognition: Designing for comprehension. *Communications of the ACM, 38*(8), 57–66.

Tichenor, P. J., Donohue, G. A., & Olien, C. N. (1970). Mass media flow and differential growth in knowledge. *Public Opinion Quarterly, 34,* 159–170.

Tiedge, J. T., & Ksobiech, K. J. (1986). The "lead-in" strategy for prime-time TV: Does it increase the audience? *Journal of Communication, 36*(3), 51–63.

Times Mirror Center for the People & the Press. (1995, October 16). *Technology in the American household.* Press release.

Tsai, C. J. (1988–1989). Hypertext: Technology, applications, and research issues. *Journal of Educational Technology Systems, 17,* 3–14.

Tulving, E. (1985). How many memory systems are there? *American Psychologist, 40,* 385–398.

van Hooff, J. A. R. A. M. (1982). Categories and sequences of behavior: Methods of description and analysis. In K. R. Scherer & P. Ekman (Eds.), *Handbook of methods in nonverbal behavior research* (pp. 362–439). Cambridge, UK: Cambridge University Press.

Viswanath, K., & Finnegan, J. R., Jr. (1996). The knowledge gap hypothesis: Twenty-five years later. In B. R. Burleson (Ed.), *Communication yearbook 19* (pp. 187–227). Thousand Oaks, CA: Sage.

Walker, J. R. (1988). Inheritance effects in the new media environment. *Journal of Broadcasting & Electronic Media, 32,* 391–401.

Webster, J. G. (1985). Program audience duplication: A study of television inheritance effects. *Journal of Broadcasting & Electronic Media, 29,* 121–133.

Webster, J. G. (1986). Audience behavior in the new media environment. *Journal of Communication, 36*(3), 77–91.

Wickens, T. D. (1982). *Models for behavior: Stochastic processes in psychology.* San Francisco, CA: W. H. Freeman.

Wicks, R. H. (1992). Schema theory and measurement in mass communication research: Theoretical and methodological issues in news information processing. In S. A. Deetz (Ed.), *Communication yearbook 15* (pp. 115–145). Newbury Park, CA: Sage.

Wild, M. (1996). Mental models and computer modeling. *Journal of Computer Assisted Learning, 12,* 10–21.

Williams, F., Phillips, A. F., & Lum, P. (1985). Gratifications associated with new communication technologies. In K. E. Rosengren, L. A. Wenner, & P. Palmgreen (Eds.), *Media gratifications research: Current perspectives* (pp. 241–252). Beverly Hills, CA: Sage.

Williams, F., Strover, S., & Grant, A. E. (1994). Social aspects of new media technologies. In J. Bryant & D. Zillmann (Eds.), *Media effects: Advances in theory and research* (pp. 463–482). Hillsdale, NJ: Erlbaum.

Wirthlin Worldwide. (1996, September). *Internet market share size and demographics* [Online]. Available:http://www.ttalk.com/pn.html

Yang, C. S., & Moore, D. M. (1995–1996). Designing hypermedia systems for instruction. *Journal of Educational Technology Systems, 24,* 3–30.

CHAPTER CONTENTS

4 Mediation of Children's Television Viewing: Working Toward Conceptual Clarity and Common Understanding

AMY I. NATHANSON
Ohio State University

Despite decades of research on parents' or other adults' mediation of children's television viewing, we still have a rather limited understanding of its potential to promote positive effects and prevent negative outcomes. One reason for this is that a consensus regarding the proper conceptualization of mediation has not yet been reached. As a result, the term has been used inconsistently and produced a body of literature that is difficult to synthesize. The purpose of this paper is to review how mediation has been regarded in past work and to develop a clear conceptualization of this construct. In addition, previous research on the effects of mediation is synthesized to provide a summary of its potential to affect children's reactions to television. Common themes, especially those relevant to explaining how mediation influences children, are identified and discussed.

A FTER years of research on the effects of television, we have learned that watching television is related to a number of undesirable outcomes among children. Among other things, children who watch more television are at risk for becoming more aggressive (Paik & Comstock, 1994), learning stereotypes (McGhee & Frueh, 1980; Morgan, 1982), experiencing fright reactions (Cantor, 1994), and developing cultivation-like attitudes (Ridley-Johnson, Chance, & Cooper, 1984). On the other hand, television can also have a positive effect on children (e.g., learning of educational content, promoting prosocial behaviors), especially when adults are present to facilitate the development of these outcomes (Corder-Bolz, 1980; Eron & Huesmann, 1984; Friedrich & Stein, 1975; Rushton, 1982). Television, then, is not inherently bad or good for children—its potential is shaped, in part, by how the children view the material.

Correspondence: Amy Nathanson, School of Journalism & Communication, Ohio State University, 3062 Derby Hall, 154 N. Oval Mall, Columbus, OH 43210; email: nathanson.7@osu.edu

Communication Yearbook 25, pp. 115–151

Parents play a vital role in shaping how their children watch television (Bryce & Leichter, 1983). For decades, researchers from various fields (including communication, psychology, and education) have been interested in the potential for parents to intervene in or "mediate" children's television viewing. Some researchers have explored how parents or other adults can facilitate prosocial effects from watching television whereas others have focused on developing methods for reducing children's vulnerability to experiencing antisocial effects. As a result, research on "mediation" has been accumulating over the past 30 years. This body of work is important because it contains an answer to a question that plagues both researchers and the public: How can we cope with the unavoidable presence of television in children's lives?

Unfortunately, it is difficult to find an answer to this question in the mediation literature. This is not to say that mediation research has not yielded useful findings—quite the contrary, as much of the work in this area has produced interesting and thought-provoking results that have important implications. Rather, the problem lies in the fact that research in this area has not proceeded from a common understanding. This problem is most evident in the lack of consensus regarding what the term mediation means. The mediation construct itself has not been adequately defined, leaving us with only a vague idea of what specific behaviors it encompasses. The lack of attention to the conceptualization of mediation has helped create a body of research that investigates the impact of a wide variety of behaviors, all under the heading of "mediation research."

Given the variety of ways that researchers have defined and used mediation, it is very difficult to make sense of the empirical findings that are based on very different operationalizations. Austin, Bolls, Fujioka, and Engelbertson (1999) lamented that "many of the studies that have examined parent-child interaction and the media are difficult to compare due to inconsistent definitions and measurement techniques across studies, and apparently contradictory and potentially misleading findings" (p. 176). In addition, some important research that has clearly addressed mediation issues does not even use the term mediation, making it extremely difficult to even identify relevant work in this area. The lack of agreement regarding this construct severely limits this literature's potential to grow in a meaningful direction. It is essential, then, that scholars researching this area both identify mediation as the label given to the phenomenon they are investigating and come to a consensus regarding its conceptualization so that research can advance from a common understanding.

The purpose of this paper was to make a first step at working toward that common understanding. Specifically, this paper engaged in some conceptual work on the construct of mediation by (a) reviewing how it has been defined and operationalized in the past, (b) identifying and considering key issues in developing this construct, and (c) coming to a conclusion regarding an appropriate conceptualization of mediation. Additionally, in an effort to synthesize the disparate studies conducted in this area, this paper reviewed the research on the effects of mediation, including studies that are clearly relevant but did not use this terminology. Particular attention was paid to identifying and discussing common themes underlying the research findings, especially those that justify speculations regarding why mediation is associated with certain outcomes. It is hoped that this synthesis of research from a variety of fields will provide a common base of literature that future work can use to advance theoretical arguments and predictions regarding mediation.

THE CONCEPTUALIZATION OF MEDIATION

At the most general level, mediation refers to interactions with children about television. This interaction can take place before, during, or after viewing. Mediation can be performed by a number of different individuals, although most research assumes that it is done by parents (the term "parental mediation" is often used in this case). Studies of parental mediation typically use survey research (e.g., Austin, 1993a; Desmond, Singer, Singer, Calam, & Colimore, 1985; Nathanson, 1999), although a few studies have recruited parents to participate in experiments regarding the effects of parental mediation (e.g., Mattern & Lindholm, 1983; Matthews & Desmond, 1997; Prasad, Rao, & Sheikh, 1978; Salomon, 1977). Other studies (mostly experiments) have explored the effects of mediation offered by other adults, such as teachers (e.g., Corder-Bolz, 1980; Corder-Bolz & O'Bryant, 1978) and experimental confederates (e.g., Collins, Sobol, & Westby, 1981; Nathanson & Cantor, 2000; Valkenburg, Krcmar, & de Roos, 1998). A handful of studies has also considered the role of mediation provided by siblings (Alexander, Ryan, & Munoz, 1984; Haefner & Wartella, 1987; Lawrence & Wozniak, 1989; McDonald, 1986; Wilson & Weiss, 1993) and peers (Nathanson, in press-a).

Specifications regarding what kind of interactions mediation encompasses vary. Some say that mediation refers to communicative behaviors, such as discussion and explanation (Desmond, Hirsch, Singer, & Singer, 1987). Other researchers use the term to reflect the use of rules and restrictions regarding television (e.g., Abelman, 1990); still others equate mediation with simply watching television with children (e.g., Dorr, Kovaric, & Doubleday, 1989; Haefner & Wartella, 1987). Moreover, some researchers include multiple forms of behavior relating to television as part of the mediation construct, such as both discussion and rule-making (Lin & Atkin, 1989).

Mediation Versus General Communication

Given the wide variety of ways that mediation has been regarded in the past, it is important to draw some boundaries regarding what behaviors it encompasses so we can develop a more precise conceptualization of the term. One distinction that is useful to make is between interactions with children that focus on television and the more general forms of mediation-like behaviors that parents perform. That is, some researchers use the mediation term very generally and include both parental behaviors relating to television and parents' general communication style and disciplinary orientation.

The decision to consider parental communication and disciplinary styles as efforts at mediation has it roots in the literature on family communication patterns. Family communication patterns have been studied in the contexts of marital relationships and parent-child relationships (Meadowcroft & Fitzpatrick, 1988), with the latter context bearing relevance to the mediation of children's television viewing. Family communication patterns can be thought of varying along two primary dimensions, which interact to produce a four-fold typology (Chaffee & McLeod, 1972; Chaffee, McLeod, & Atkin, 1971; McLeod, Atkin, & Chaffee, 1972b). The first dimension, called "socio-oriented," reflects families that encourage children to avoid conflict and sacrifice the expression of personal feelings to preserve harmonious relationships. The second dimension, called "concept-oriented," describes families that encourage children to debate issues and express their opinions regardless of whether they conflict with others. Depending on whether families earn high or low scores on both dimensions, they are classified into one of the following four categories: laissez faire (families who score low on both dimensions), consensual (families who score high on both dimensions), protective (families who score high on socio-orientation but low on concept-orientation), and pluralistic (families who score high on concept orientation but low on socio-orientation).

According to Chaffee et al. (1971), family communication patterns "help guide the child in his 'cognitive mapping' of situations he encounters outside the immediate family context, e.g., at school, in relation to public affairs issues, and mass media use" (p. 331). Hence, family communication patterns have been considered mediation in that parents are believed to provide children with a frame of reference for selecting and interpreting television.

In fact, family communication patterns have been related to a number of media outcomes. In some of the earliest work in this area, it was found that adolescents' interest in television and news media was related to each of the four categories of family communication patterns (Chaffee et al., 1971; McLeod et al., 1972b). Other research has found that family communication patterns are related to children's or adolescents' cognitive activities while viewing (Thompson, Pingree, Hawkins, & Draves, 1991), social uses of television (Lull, 1980), political development (McLeod & Chaffee, 1972; Meadowcroft, 1986), and aggression (McLeod et al., 1972b).

Based on recent reconceptualizations of the two fundamental dimensions of family communication, researchers have found that parents who emphasize control and power assertion are more likely to direct children's media decision-making than parents who emphasize open and supportive communication (Krcmar, 1996). In a related vein of research not explicitly couched within the literature on family communication patterns, researchers have found that, compared to children of parents who use inductive disciplinary styles that emphasize reasoning and explanation, children of parents who use sensitizing disciplinary techniques that highlight physical punishment and force are more aggressive (Desmond et al., 1987; Singer, Singer, & Rapaczynski, 1984), more affected by antisocial television, and less affected by prosocial television (Abelman, 1985). Inductive parenting styles often are related to positive effects, such as a greater understanding of televised plots and commercials (Desmond et al., 1987; Singer, Singer, Desmond, Hirsch, & Nicol, 1988).

Certainly, these general communication styles and disciplinary orientations are relevant variables to mediation research. In fact, parental communication styles have been shown to be related to television-focused communication (Austin, 1993a; Austin, Roberts, & Nass, 1990; Desmond et al., 1985; Fujioka & Austin, 1999; Rose, Bush, & Kahle, 1998). However, for clarity's sake, a clear distinction needs to be made between these kinds of behaviors and those that are focused on children's television viewing. Without this kind of distinction, mediation can refer to such a broad class of behaviors that the term itself means very little.

One solution to this problem is to reserve the term mediation for interactions with children about television and to use labels such as "communication style" and "disciplinary style" to refer to the more general forms of interactions that parents have with their children. Some researchers have used to term "television mediation" to highlight the television-focused nature of the interactions (Nathanson, 1998; Valkenburg, Krcmar, Peeters, & Marseille, 1999). However, this specificity might not be necessary if the label "mediation" was only used to refer to interactions regarding television.

For the purpose of this review, mediation means interactions with children about television. It is hoped that future research will adopt this definition, and use other labels to refer to parent-child interactions that do not concern television. The focus of this paper is mediation.

A Three-Dimensional Conceptualization of Mediation

As noted above, mediation has been inconsistently used to refer to a wide variety of behaviors. Because researchers have identified so many forms of mediation, a useful strategy for making sense of this construct is to consider mediation as a higher order construct that encompasses a variety of distinct behaviors. Although a multidimensional conceptualization of mediation is not typically used in the literature, it is not a completely novel idea. Bybee, Robinson, and Turow (1982) argued for a three-dimensional conceptualization of mediation, which has been adopted in subsequent research (e.g., van der Voort, Nikken, & van Lil, 1992; Weaver & Barbour, 1992). However, recent work showed that the distinctions among their factors were unclear and that an alternative three-dimensional conceptualization is more useful (Valkenburg et al., 1999).

In the following portion of this paper, I identify the three primary forms of mediation that researchers have studied: active mediation, restrictive mediation, and coviewing. Although not all of the research has used these labels per se, the work reviewed in each section has focused on the same kinds of general behaviors.

To highlight the similarities and slight deviations among the various conceptualizations, a review of how each of these forms of behavior have been defined in the past is also provided. This review includes recommendations for future conceptualizations that hopefully will reduce some of the confusion regarding this multifaceted concept.

Active mediation. Nearly all of the research on mediation acknowledges that the concept refers to conversations that parents (or other adults) have with children about television. Some call this "active mediation" (e.g., Austin, 1993a; Nathanson, 1999) to reflect the active discussion of television, whereas others refer to this as "evaluative guidance" (e.g., Bybee et al., 1982; van der Voort et al., 1992). The evaluative guidance label may be misleading, however, as television-related talk can be neutral and nonevaluative. The active mediation label may be more useful for this reason and the fact that it explicitly refers to the higher order construct, mediation.

It is typically assumed that parents initiate active mediation in order to assist their children in critical viewing. However, children may induce active mediation by engaging their parents in television-related discussions. In their observational study of nine families, Reid and Frazer (1980) found that five- to nine-year-old children encouraged active mediation by asking their parents questions about special effects techniques. Further, in a naturalistic, in-home study of mother-child pairs, Stoneman and Brody (1982) found that, while viewing situation comedies, children were more likely to ask their mothers questions concerning character motivations and intentions than to comment on the material themselves. This suggests that children can desire parental assistance during viewing and will initiate active mediation sessions. Hence, the individual who initiates television-related talk can vary. Although the effects of active mediation could be shaped, in part, by who instigates it, the mere identification of active mediation should be based only on its presence and not its instigator.

Measures of active mediation often tap the frequency with which parents engage in the following forms of television-related talk: discussing the reality status of programs, making critical comments about behaviors witnessed on television, and providing supplemental information about topics introduced by television. There is good reason for this operationalization, as these are the television-related topics that parents most frequently discuss with their children (Messaris, 1982).

However, it is unclear whether all three types of communication should be combined into one index. That is, it is uncertain what the combination of these three activities reflect, theoretically speaking. Moreover, it is difficult to imagine which child-related outcomes an index reflecting all three forms of conversation should be related to, unless we suspect that increased frequency of television-related talk—regardless of its content—makes children more sophisticated television viewers.

Certainly, the content of parents' communication about television should be important in determining the kinds of messages that children receive about television and how they are ultimately affected by it. For example, television-related talk that is generally positive in tone (e.g., endorsements of television content) should be differentially related to children's outcomes than television-talk that is generally negative (e.g., criticisms of television content). In fact Austin et al. (1999) argued that "scholars must distinguish between positive and negative reinforcement of content, which can be characterized by different motivations and different behaviors" (p. 177). As a result, Austin et al. (1999) made the distinction between "positive mediation" and "negative mediation."

More specifically, positive active mediation can include pointing out the good things that characters do, agreeing with televised messages, encouraging children to adopt the behavior of characters, and conveying that portrayals are realistic. These kinds of comments serve as endorsements of television content and may increase the chances that children will accept or imitate what they view.

On the other hand, negative active mediation focuses on getting children to understand the negative aspects of televised portrayals through such activities as condemning the behavior of characters, disagreeing with televised messages, discouraging children from adopting characters' behaviors, or explaining that portrayals are not realistic. These kinds of comments challenge or contradict televised content and serve as an opportunity for parents to use a concrete television situation to communicate what is not acceptable behavior. As a result, this kind of active mediation should lead children to be skeptical of what they see on television and less likely to accept and imitate television content.

Given the conceptual difference between positive and negative active mediation, Austin (1992) suggested that we examine "the motivations behind and effects of positive and negative strategies separately" (p. 359) rather than combine items tapping each concept into one index. In addition, neutral forms of active mediation are possible (e.g., providing supplemental information, clarifying content) and should be considered. In the future, then, it is important for researchers not only to recognize the multifaceted nature of active mediation, but also to pinpoint which form of active mediation is most relevant to their predictions.

Restrictive mediation. Restrictive mediation involves setting rules about how much, when, and which types of television can be viewed (Weaver & Barbour, 1992). Some work has used the term "restrictive guidance" to tap the same concept (e.g., Bybee et al., 1982; van der Voort et al., 1992); however, the term restrictive mediation seems especially useful given its reference to the higher order construct.

Most of the studies that have explored this dimension of mediation have used single-item measures to tap whether parents enforce any rules regarding television viewing. However, Bybee et al. (1982) introduced a more extensive, five-item measure that reflects more aspects of restrictive mediation and appears to have face validity. For example, in addition to asking whether parents restrict viewing, their measure taps how often parents restrict certain programs and if they specify when children can watch. Although the authors did not report the reliability of their restrictive mediation index, van der Voort et al. (1992) found that the same index had a reliability of .75 in their Dutch sample. Tangney (1988) also used a multi-item restrictive mediation index by assessing if parents restrict viewing hours, the nature of the restrictions on both weekends and weekdays, whether they restricted access to certain programs, and if viewing was used as a reward or punishment.

Overall, there has not been much controversy regarding the conceptualization of restrictive mediation. However, even though its conceptualization appears rather straightforward, researchers may want to complicate it to arrive at a richer construct. Currently, the concept reflects the enforcement of parent-generated rules about television, regardless of the child's input. This implies that restrictive mediation reflects an authoritarian parenting style. However, research indicates that restrictive mediation is qualitatively different from authoritarianism. For example, McLeod, Atkin, and Chaffee (1972a) found that the relationships between restrictive mediation and other parenting measures, such as the use of physical, verbal, and restrictive punishment, were either nonsignificant or weak. Instead, they found that restrictive mediation was positively related to parental affection. McLeod et al. (1972b) also found that parental control over television was related to both a socio-orientation and a concept orientation.

This suggests that restrictive mediation is a more complex construct than current measurement allows us to detect. Parents who use it are not inherently authoritarian but may discuss and negotiate with children to determine viewing boundaries. Future research should include measures that address the process of determining and enforcing viewing rules so that a fuller understanding of restrictive mediation can be developed.

Another minor limitation in the conceptualization of restrictive mediation is that it is often thought of in terms of its frequency of occurrence. That is, restrictive mediation items are often phrased so that parents must report how often they enforce rules and restrictions about viewing. However, if rules are already in place and well understood, parents may not need to reiterate them. For example, whereas some parents may restrict children's viewing on a case-by-case basis, depending on the circumstances, others may establish firm rules about the viewing of certain programs. When asked how often they restrict their children's access to a certain kind of program, parents with these firm rules may be unsure how to respond. That is, perhaps these parents have only needed to remind their children of the rule once or twice. Despite the fact that they enforce a very strict viewing rule, the parents may earn rather low scores on such restrictive mediation measures.

Perhaps a useful method of assessing restrictive mediation is to assess the kinds of rules parents have and how strict they are in enforcing them. With this kind of approach, researchers can not only understand if parents have rules for television viewing, but also gain a sense of how restrictive the rules are and how strictly they are enforced. This method should produce a more accurate and informative restrictive mediation measure than methods that assess the sheer frequency of restrictive mediation behaviors.

Coviewing. Probably the least clarity in the mediation literature involves coviewing. Coviewing behaviors are often subsumed within the labels of "unfocused guidance" (Bybee et al., 1982; van der Voort et al., 1992) or "nonrestrictive guidance" (Atkin, Greenberg, & Baldwin, 1991). However it is most useful to focus on coviewing per se, which refers to parents watching television with their children. Coviewing should not imply that any conversation takes place between them; it only means that parents and children are in the same room and are watching the same television program (Valkenburg et al., 1999).

However, coviewing is often equated with active mediation. This is most evident in the rationales that researchers provide to justify their predictions regarding the effects of coviewing. For example, Dorr et al. (1989) predicted that coviewing would be related to children's social reality judgments regarding family series because "parents will comment at least occasionally on the plausibility and representation of the content they are coviewing with their children" (p. 39). Bybee et al.'s (1982) work also subsumed both coviewing and discussion of content under the general heading of unfocused guidance. For example, their unfocused guidance index reflects items assessing how often parents "watch TV with child," "talk about a show while viewing," and "discuss a show just viewed or about to be viewed" (p. 704).

Valkenburg et al. (1999) argued that the unfocused guidance style of mediation is really a "methodological artifact resulting from a forced interpretation of items that loaded on a 'left-over' factor" (p. 54). They pointed out that the items comprising this scale are conceptually unrelated and therefore lack face validity. Moreover, their factor analysis of items tapping active mediation, restrictive mediation, coviewing, and Bybee et al.'s (1982) unfocused guidance items failed to identify an unfocused guidance factor, leading them to conclude that "the unfocused mediation style identified in several earlier studies . . . is an invalid style of mediation" (p. 62). Valkenburg et al. argued that unfocused guidance should be abandoned and instead, attention should be directed toward one aspect of unfocused guidance—social coviewing.

The underlying assumption appears to be that while coviewing television, parents will talk to their children about the content. Certainly, coviewing and active mediation are related concepts. However, coviewing is not a necessary condition for active mediation to occur—parents can discuss television programs with children before or after watching. Similarly, not all coviewing experiences involve parent-child conversations (Austin et al., 1999). Oftentimes, parents simply watch television in the presence of their children but do not comment on the material. It is important, then, to distinguish between these two concepts rather than meld them together. Future work should acknowledge the distinction between these concepts, advance separate predictions about the effects of each, and develop measures or analyses that preserve their differences.[1]

The Importance of Content

One conceptual oversight that has affected the measurement of all three forms of mediation is the role of television content in parents' mediation behaviors. With some exceptions (e.g., Austin et al., 1990; Dorr et al., 1989; Messaris & Kerr, 1984; Nathanson, 1999), measures of mediation do not ask parents to think about certain kinds of content or genres when estimating how frequently they talk about, restrict, or coview television with their children. These nonspecific mediation measures, then, ask parents to generalize their mediation behaviors across all kinds of content types—a task that may be very difficult for parents to complete and may yield inaccurate responses.

For example, it is likely that parents will engage in different mediation behaviors depending on the kind of television their children are watching. For example, parents might restrict their children's access to violent programming, but encourage them to view educational television. Further, they may engage in negative active mediation of violent content, but use positive active mediation when their children view prosocial content. Thus, measures that tap parents' mediation of specific types of television content should provide the most accurate data.

Reports From Parents Versus Children

Another methodological issue that affects the conceptualization of mediation is whether researchers should gather mediation data from parents or children. Although data are typically gathered based on convenience or accessibility, this choice is theoretically important.

Most assessments of mediation come from parents. However, research has shown that parent and child reports of the family environment often differ (Tolan, Gorman-Smith, Huesmann, & Zelli, 1997). For example, Greenberg, Ericson, and Vlahos (1972) found that reports of the frequency of family interaction by fourth and fifth graders and their mothers were only moderately correlated. Although the researchers found a relatively strong correlation between mother and child reports of parental coviewing, they failed to find a significant correspondence in reports of television viewing rules. Further, Austin (1993b) found varying degrees of correspondence between parent and child reports of family communication dimensions.

The proper measurement of the family environment, including parent-child interactions, is an issue that is debated in other fields. The preferred method appears to be observational (Grotevant & Carlson, 1987), although self-report measures are also used and considered useful for tapping the subjective experiences of family members (Carlson, 1990). Unfortunately, there is not much research attesting to the validity of various sources of self-report measures of the parent-child relationship (Carlson, 1990). As Grotevant and Carlson (1989) note, most measures of family functioning rely on parent or adolescent reports, perhaps due to the fact that younger children may be unable to provide reliable and valid assessments.

Certainly, as the ones who provide mediation, parents appear to be the ideal respondents for providing accurate data. On the other hand, parents are likely to want to provide socially desirable responses. That is, parents may distort their answers to mediation questions in order to convince the researchers that they are "good" parents. As Hoffman and Lippitt (1960) acknowledge, the desire to appear socially desirable may be particularly strong in research on families. Some communication research corroborates this finding by demonstrating, for example, that parents report more family interaction and acknowledge less television viewing (especially violent television viewing) on their children's part than the children report (Greenberg et al., 1972).[2] Despite the concern over social desirability, however, few researchers have explicitly assessed the degree to which social desirability affects the quality of their measures (Grotevant & Carlson, 1989).

Children's reports of family processes are often desirable for theoretically different reasons. According to Grotevant and Carlson (1989), these kinds of reports are especially valuable to the phenomenological tradition, which suggests that perceptions of parents' behaviors play a more significant role in the development of personality than the actual behaviors themselves. That is, children's perceptions of their parents' behaviors may be important intervening variables in the relationship between the actual behaviors and children's outcomes (Hoffman & Lippitt, 1960). Austin (1993b) asserted that "since what 'occurs' in family communication may differ in fundamental ways, depending on the perspective and cognitive abilities of the family member one asks, the patterns the child perceives may prove at least as important for media uses and effects as the patterns the parent reports" (p. 566).

Regardless of which population is used, the decision to collect data from either parents, children, or both should be theoretically driven. However, because mediation research is vague about how parents' behaviors regarding television influence children, it is not clear which of these approaches is most appropriate. It is very important, then, that theories of mediation effects be developed—not only to aid our understanding of how mediation works but also to permit sound decisions regarding respondent selection to be made. In the meantime, researchers should consider the theoretical statements they inevitably make when selecting research participants and whether their targeted population is justified.

The Need for Statistical Control

One analytical issue is especially important to preserving an appropriate conceptualization of mediation. When researchers assess the relationship between mediation and outcomes, it is essential that they statistically control for the amount of television (or specific genres of television) that children view. This procedure is important for two reasons. First, controlling for the amount of television that children view eliminates the possibility that any relationships observed between mediation and children's outcomes are spurious due to the influence of children's television viewing.

For example, one alternative explanation for the finding that mediation is related to prosocial outcomes in children is that children whose parents mediate simply watch less television than other youngsters. As a result, it could be that relationships between mediation and outcomes are really spurious due to the influence of children's television viewing. This explanation is particularly likely in the case of restrictive mediation, as children whose parents restrict their television viewing usually watch less television than other children (Abelman, 1999; Brown, Childers, Bauman, & Koch, 1990; Brown & Linne, 1976; Roberts, 1981). As a result, television viewing should be controlled when assessing the effects of mediation on children.

Second, controlling for the influence of television viewing should maintain the conceptual clarity of the mediation construct. For example, conceptually, television mediation is not meant to reflect how much television children view. However, when television viewing is not controlled in statistical analyses, mediation measures may reduce to rough assessments of the amount of time spent viewing television. Although the results of previous work suggest that mediation makes children less vulnerable to experiencing negative effects from television, when researchers do not control for the influence of television viewing, we cannot rule out the possibility that these findings simply replicate the well-known finding that children who watch less television are less aggressive.

Because what we are really interested in is the effects of mediation above and beyond how much television children view, it is important to control for the potentially confounding influence of television viewing. This practice is necessary to both preserving the proper conceptualization of mediation and providing a more appropriate and stringent test of mediation's effects.

Summary

The mediation concept has been used and defined very inconsistently. As a result, the body of research addressing mediation issues is rather disorganized and difficult to digest. In this paper, it is proposed that mediation be defined as a three-dimensional construct that encompasses the following types of interactions with children about television: active mediation, restrictive mediation, and coviewing. It has been recommended that behaviors that do not involve television be labeled differently. In addition, because mediation practices are likely to vary depending on the type of television programming, researchers have been urged to develop content-specific mediation predictions and measures. It has also been recommended that researchers carefully consider the theoretical implications of selecting who their respondents will be. Finally, to distinguish the effects of mediation from those associated with levels of television viewing, it has been suggested that all analyses addressing mediation effects statistically control for the amount that children watch television.

THE EFFECTS OF MEDIATION ON CHILDREN

This section of the paper reviews research on the effects of the three primary forms of mediation on children. To remain consistent with the conceptual framework developed in the preceding section, research exploring the effects of active mediation, restrictive mediation, and coviewing will be reviewed, regardless of whether these specific labels were used by the authors (e.g., research exploring the effects of evaluative guidance can be found under the heading "active mediation"). Because few studies have explored explanations for mediation effects, the existing research is used to advance speculations regarding why mediation is linked with particular outcomes.

Active Mediation

Before reviewing the effects of active mediation, it is first useful to describe who tends to engage in and receive this form of mediation. Research has shown that mothers (Valkenburg et al., 1999; van der Voort et al., 1992) are especially likely to engage in active mediation. Further, the propensity to engage in positive active mediation is related to having a relatively low income, positive attitudes toward television, and believing that television is a good learning tool, whereas the tendency to use negative active mediation is related to parental skepticism toward television (Austin et al., 1999; Austin, Knaus, & Meneguelli, 1998). The relationship between active mediation and education is unclear; whereas some work demonstrates that highly educated parents are likely to use active mediation (van der Voort et al., 1992), other work has found no relationship between education and the tendency to engage in negative, positive, or nonvalenced active mediation (Austin et al., 1998). Most of the research indicates that the provision of active mediation does not depend on the child's age or gender (Bybee et al., 1982; van der Voort et al., 1992).

Relative to the other forms of mediation, active mediation has been subjected to empirical testing the most often, in both survey and experimental contexts. In general, researchers have found that children who receive active mediation are more sophisticated and less vulnerable television viewers. This conclusion is based on research assessing the impact of active mediation on one of four classes of outcomes: children's comprehension of or learning from televised material, their social attitudes or perceptions, their emotional responses, and their real-world behaviors.

Active mediation and children's understanding of or learning from television. The most formal efforts at active mediation are not performed by parents in the home but via in-school curricula designed to increase children's media literacy. In general, media literacy projects have shown that active mediation can help children think more critically about television (Abelman & Courtright, 1983; Hobbs

& Frost, 1997; Rapaczynski, Singer, & Singer, 1982; Roberts, Christenson, Gibson, Mooser, & Goldberg, 1980; Singer, Zuckerman, & Singer, 1980). As Singer and Singer (1998) describe, the two major goals of most media literacy programs is to increase children's understanding of (a) the technical aspects of television (e.g., how television works, how to distinguish between what's real and fantasy) and (b) the literary devices used to create program content (e.g., plot lines, character development). For example, Dorr, Graves, and Phelps (1980) found that lessons about television, taught in school, were successful in teaching children how television programs are made and how to form judgments about the reality status of televised material. Further, Matthews and Desmond (1997) showed that even less direct efforts, such as training parents to encourage their children's critical viewing of advertisements, can make children more sophisticated consumers of television.

As Singer and Singer (1998) explain, media literacy programs improve children's comprehension of television by, in part, increasing their attention to the content. They stated that "it is important for viewers to attend to and concentrate on content if, indeed, they are to process the information in a critical manner" (p. 166). When viewers are encouraged to use an active viewing style, then, they learn more from the content.

However, parents do not need to teach media literacy lessons to improve their children's understanding of television. Instead, active mediation strategies that clarify the content of programs or provide relevant supplemental information promotes greater comprehension as well. For example, Collins et al. (1981) explored the impact of adult comments about television on children's comprehension of inferences that were necessary to understand a television plot. In their study, second graders watched an edited version of an action adventure program. One group of children watched the program with an adult who made "facilitating comments," or remarks that clarified important inferences in the story. The other group of children heard an adult make neutral comments (i.e., comments that simply described the actions taking place) at the same points in the program.

Not surprisingly, the authors found that children in the treatment condition understood the inferences necessary to grasp the plot better than control-group children. Even more important, however, they found that the children in the treatment group were better able to make inferences about the story that did not directly relate to the facilitating comments themselves. The authors suggested that by providing facilitating comments, the children's cognitive burden for processing the plot may have been lessened, thereby allowing the children to devote more processing energy to other aspects of the program.

Corder-Bolz and O'Bryant (1978) also found that when preschoolers heard teachers provide supplemental information about a topic introduced by televised entertainment, the youngsters understood more of the content than children who heard only neutral comments. Similarly, Valkenburg et al. (1998) found that children who received additional comments about opera while viewing a children's cultural program recalled more information about opera than children who coviewed the same program with an adult who did not provide the additional comments. Finally, Watkins, Calvert, Huston-Stein, & Wright (1980) found that preschoolers and kindergartners who heard an adult experimenter summarize the important elements and inferences of a prosocial cartoon they were watching were better able to recall aspects of the cartoon than children who either received no mediation or the same information via the audio track of the cartoon.

Other work exploring the impact of active mediation on children's learning of educational television has found similar results (e.g., Ball & Bogatz, 1970). For example, Corder-Bolz (1980) found that when teachers provided additional information about the grammar lessons taught in an episode of the *Electric Company* (e.g., "That's called an apostrophe," "There's that silent 'e' again."), first and second graders learned more of the content than when an adult simply directed their attention to the program in general. This finding only held true, however, for learning tasks that were geared toward the learning ability of the children. That is, mediation had no impact for material that pretesting determined was either very difficult or very easy for the children.

Therefore, it seems that adults can improve children's processing and understanding of television by either involving them in formal media literacy programs or making comments that provide clarifying or supplemental information on topics introduced by television. Because many of these studies involved experiments where some children are given additional information and others are not, one could argue that what this work really explores is children's ability to recall supplemental information provided by adults during television viewing. However, an even more convincing test of the benefits of active mediation for children's comprehension of television would be to compare reports of ongoing parental mediation, as it occurs in the home, to children's ability to comprehend television when their parents are not present. This kind of study would allow us to assess whether children who receive active mediation in the home (and not minutes before taking a television comprehension test) actually apply more critical viewing skills to their television viewing than other youngsters.

In fact, Desmond et al. (1985) provided such a study. They examined the relationship between parental reports of the frequency of active mediation and children's ability to comprehend a 15-minute segment of *Swiss Family Robinson* shown in the laboratory. The authors found a positive relationship between active mediation and children's comprehension scores. Thus, Desmond et al.'s study suggests that talking to children about television may better prepare them to process and understand other television programs even when they view without mediation.

It seems clear, then, that active mediation can enhance children's comprehension of television. The next question becomes: Why? Although there has been little research examining why this relationship holds, a few studies have laid the groundwork that might help us answer this question. Reiser, Tessmer, and Phelps (1984) speculated that one particular form of active mediation—asking children questions about television while they are viewing—might be particularly beneficial to children's learning because of how it affects children's perceptions of and involvement in the content. They argued that asking questions might focus children's attention on important aspects of the presentation (which children might not be able to discern on their own) and encourage them to become active participants in viewing, which previous work has found to result in increased learning (Schramm, 1972, 1977). Interestingly, this explanation is very similar to Singer and Singer's (1998) explanation for how media literacy programs work.

To explore this hypothesis, Reiser et al. (1984) tested the impact of asking preschool children questions about television content on the children's learning of material from the program presented. In the experimental treatment, children viewed three edited versions of *Sesame Street* over a 5-day period with an adult who asked the children questions about the material (e.g., "What number is that?"). Regardless of the children's response to the question, the adults also provided feedback in the form of the correct answer (e.g., "That is a six."). The control-group children watched the same videotapes over the same period in the presence of an adult who did not ask questions or provide any feedback. In a comprehension test administered three days after the children viewed the last videotape, the authors found that preschoolers in the experimental group earned higher scores than control-group children.

Reiser et al.'s (1984) study demonstrated that mediation in the form of questions significantly increases children's learning from educational television. However, the authors confounded the question-asking manipulation with the provision of feedback. Because the feedback offered in their study is similar to the kinds of active mediation strategies tested in other experiments (e.g., providing supplemental information, clarifying important content information), Reiser et al.'s study may have simply replicated many of the findings discussed earlier. As a result, their study does not tell us whether question-asking per se is a useful active mediation strategy.

In a follow-up study, Reiser, Williamson, and Suzuki (1988) sought to correct some of the shortcomings of their previous work. In this study, preschoolers were assigned to one of four conditions. In the first condition, children viewed, over a 5-day period, three videotapes of *Sesame Street* with an adult who asked the children questions about the material and provided feedback (as in their first study). Children in the second condition viewed the tapes with an adult who simply asked children questions about the material and provided no feedback. In a third condition, children viewed the tapes with an adult who only directed their attention to important parts of the program (e.g., "Let's watch this," "That looks like a good part."). This condition was added to understand whether question-asking is equivalent to simply drawing children's attention to important parts of a program, or whether it encourages children to process the material more deeply. Finally, the control-group children watched the tapes with an adult who did not make any comments during viewing.

Reiser et al. (1988) found that in the posttest (which was administered 3 days after viewing the last tape), children who either heard the questions and the feedback or the questions alone earned significantly higher scores than children in the control condition. Children in the attention group had higher scores that control-group children, but this difference was not significant. Since there was no significant difference between the scores of children in the questions-feedback condition and the questions-only condition, it appeared that the provision of questions during viewing was particularly important in increasing children's learning. In fact, hearing questions about the content was equally beneficial to children's learning as hearing the questions and answers.

Reiser et al.'s (1988) study is particularly useful because it offers an explanation for why active mediation should be linked to increased learning of educational content. The authors argued that questioning children during viewing may have elevated the amount of effort they invested in the program while viewing. They also speculated that the mere activity of asking children questions may have led children to believe that the program was important, demanding, and should be taken seriously.

In this sense, the authors imply that active mediation is important, not so much for its specific content, but for its ability to send a message to children about the value and importance of televised content and how much attention it deserves. Hence, children's perceptions of and involvement in televised material may be important intervening variables that explain how active mediation affects children's television comprehension.

Active mediation and children's attitudinal or perceptual outcomes. Although much of the work on active mediation has explored its impact on children's comprehension of and learning from television, some research has focused on the influence of active mediation on attitudinal or perceptual outcomes. For example, Corder-Bolz (1980) found that active mediation can help children form less traditional and less stereotyped attitudes about sex roles.

Specifically, in their experiment, 5- to 11-year-old children watched an episode of *All in the Family* that featured characters engaged in nontraditional sex roles (e.g., the husband, Frank, cooked and the wife, Irene, fixed appliances). Some children heard an adult make comments during viewing that highlighted the violations of traditional sex roles and cast them in a positive light (e.g., "Look, Irene fixed Edith's mixer all by herself," "There's Frank cooking. He seems to really like cooking."). Children in the control group heard the adult make neutral comments that were not about the show. The authors found that although all children reported less stereotyped sex-role attitudes after viewing, compared to their pretest scores, children in the experimental group experienced the largest attitude shift and reported the least stereotyped postviewing attitudes.

In addition to altering children's attitudes, active mediation has been shown to affect children's perceptions. In particular, researchers have explored the role of active mediation in shaping children's perceptions of television's realism. For example, in a survey of mothers and their first-, third-, and fifth-grade children, Messaris and Kerr (1984) found a negative correlation between parents telling children that television is "make-believe" and children's beliefs that television is representative of the real world. A similar result was found by Austin (1993a), who found a positive correlation between active mediation and adolescents' skepticism about television news. In fact, active mediation emerged as a significant (and sometimes stronger) predictor of skepticism and other variables (e.g., adolescents' public affairs media use and involvement in public affairs) than more general family communication norms.

Not all forms of active mediation produce desirable perceptual outcomes, however. Austin and Chen (1999) found that positive active mediation was related to potentially dangerous attitudes and perceptions regarding alcohol and alcohol-related advertisements. In their study, college students recalled the positive mediation messages they received as teenagers (e.g., how often parents voiced approval of television advertising or characters, how often parents repeated something they heard on television). The authors found that recalled positive active mediation was related to perceptions the students currently held, such as less skepticism toward advertising, more perceived desirability of alcohol-related advertising (e.g., how much they believed the people in these ads are popular, smart, and attractive), and more positive expectancies for alcohol use (e.g., how much they believed alcohol connotes good times, friendship, and happiness). Some of these perceptions were also directly related to first experimenting with alcohol at a younger age and relatively high levels of current alcohol consumption. It is possible, then, that positive active mediation can lead children to more readily accept television's messages, including those that can have harmful effects.

Active mediation and children's emotional responses. A separate body of literature has explored techniques for reducing children's negative emotional responses to frightening television portrayals. Although this work is not typically labeled as mediation research, much of it is quite relevant to understanding parents' potential for modifying children's reactions to television.

In a series of experiments, it has been shown that the provision of certain previewing instructions or information can reduce the likelihood that children will become frightened by scary media content.[3] According to Cantor (1994), these "cognitive strategies" involve using verbal information to encourage children to process the frightening source from a perspective that renders it less threatening. There are several types of cognitive strategies that can be used. The first involves telling children that the frightening stimulus is not real (Cantor & Wilson, 1988). For example, Cantor and Wilson (1984) conducted an experiment in which some of the children were told, prior to viewing a scary movie scene, to remember that what they are watching is just a story and is not real. Other children in the experiment either received a different set of pre-viewing instructions or did not receive any pre-viewing information. The researchers found that the fright reactions of older children in the study (ages 9–11) who received the treatment experienced less fear than older children who did not receive the treatment. Younger children's (ages 3–5) fright reactions did not vary across conditions. Other work also highlights the effectiveness of this strategy for reducing older children's fright reactions (Wilson & Weiss, 1991) and the fright reactions of children at various developmental stages (Cantor, Sparks, & Hoffner, 1988).

A second type of cognitive strategy is appropriate for more realistic frightening media content and involves minimizing children's perceptions of the severity of the threat by providing supplemental information (Cantor & Wilson, 1988). For example, Wilson and Cantor (1987) found that second and third graders were less frightened by a scary movie scene that involved snakes after learning general information about snakes, including the fact that most of them are not poisonous. However, the pre-viewing information increased fear responses of kindergartners and first graders.

Perhaps the younger children did not understand the language contained in this mediation message—as a result, the effect of mediation for the younger group may have been solely to increase their attention to stimulus. In fact, misunderstanding the mediation has been cited as a potential reason why Cantor and Hoffner (1990) were unable to modify children's fear responses. Their mediation strategies used varying degrees of probability (e.g., "very likely," "probably"), which research indicates are difficult for children as old as third-graders to understand (Hoffner, Cantor, & Badzinski, 1990). This explanation might be relevant to understanding younger children's responses in Wilson and Cantor's (1987) study as well. Hence, mediation strategies will not produce uniform results and must be age appropriate.

A third type of cognitive strategy involves giving children information regarding the outcome of a frightening film prior to viewing the stimulus (Hoffner, 1997; Hoffner & Cantor, 1990). Specifically, presenting children with the knowledge that a movie scene they are about to see has a happy ending has been shown to reduce fright reactions (Hoffner, 1997). However, Hoffner found that individual differences in children's coping style sometimes modified her results, indicating that certain mediation techniques may be more or less suited to certain types of children.

Clearly, not all interventions of this nature are successful for all children. The studies described above highlight that individual differences among the children must be considered. Further, when the mediation is not appropriate for the target children, it may backfire by simply drawing children's attention to negative content.

Active mediation and children's real-world behaviors. Another class of research on active mediation has investigated its potential to influence children's real-world behavior. For example, Prasad et al. (1978) explored whether active mediation can affect children's interest in and requests for advertised products. In an experiment, the authors explored 8- to 10-year-old boys' reactions to two forms of active mediation: a power assertive technique, where mothers were trained to provide their child with information that forcefully negated the claims of a toy advertisement their child had just seen, and a reasoning technique, where mothers were trained to provide their children with negative information by engaging them in a discussion about the qualities and value of the product. In the control condition, mothers simply conversed with children about the program, but did not provide any information about the advertised toys. After receiving the mediation and then playing a game that was fixed so that the children would always win, children were allowed to choose a prize: the advertised toy or another toy that was not featured in the commercials they had viewed.

The authors found that boys who heard either form of mediation took longer to decide whether they wanted the targeted toy than control-group boys. In addition, whereas only 25% of the boys who received the reasoning mediation selected the advertised product, 75% of the boys who heard the power-assertive technique chose the targeted product. Half of the boys in the control condition selected the product. Thus, the more forceful technique of the two seemed to backfire and induce children to disobey their mothers' commands. However, Prasad et al. (1978) also found that when the advertised product was perceived as highly attractive, no form of mediation worked. That is, when the product was highly attractive, children in all three conditions selected it. This study demonstrates, then, that the effectiveness of these kinds of mediation techniques may be limited and that children's desires, if strong enough, will override maternal advice.

In another study of real-world behaviors, Coates and Hartup (1969) found that 4- and 5-year-olds best learned novel behaviors observed on television when an adult provided descriptive commentary of the behaviors immediately before viewing. That is, these children were best able to learn the behaviors when the adult explicitly verbalized what the television model would be doing in the program (by reference to a real-life model).

Another real-world behavior that has been explored in connection with active mediation is children's imitation of televised violence. In an early study, Hicks (1968) exposed a group of 5- to 9-year-olds to a film that featured aggression. One group of children heard an adult make negative statements about the aggressive acts (e.g., "That's awful," "That's wrong,") and another group heard positive statements (e.g., "He sure is a tough guy," "Boy, look at him go"). A third group of children heard no commentary from the adult. When the children were observed during a postviewing play session, Hicks found that children who heard the negative statements were less aggressive than children who heard the positive comments or no comments. Similarly, Grusec (1973) found that 10-year-olds were more likely to imitate a film character's aggressive and neutral behaviors when an experimental confederate made positive comments about the behaviors than when the confederate made negative comments. These studies suggest that negative active mediation decreases children's aggression whereas positive active mediation increases it.

It is important to note, however, that the effect observed in Hicks's study was only found when the adult who delivered the mediation was in the room during the postviewing play session. That is, when the children were allowed to play alone, there were no differences among the groups. Hicks's study suggests that, in an experimental context where children's postviewing behavior is observed, active mediation effects may really be effects of social desirability. In other words, if active mediation was truly effective in teaching children that violence on television is not acceptable, then the effect should have remained even when the adult was not present in the postviewing play room. As a result, this alternative explanation should be kept in mind when reviewing the results of active mediation experiments.

Horton and Santogrossi's (1978) experiment on the effects of active mediation on children's postviewing aggression also provokes this alternative explanation. In their study, second- through fifth-grade boys viewed an aggressive television clip. Some boys heard anti-aggressive comments that condemned the depicted violence, others heard nonaggressive comments that offered nonviolent alternatives to the aggressive acts, and others heard neutral comments that merely described the action. A fourth group of children viewed a nonviolent film without any mediation. After viewing, the children, who were tested individually, were asked if they could do the experimenter a favor and watch a group of preschoolers while he made an important phone call (the preschoolers were displayed via a television monitor, and their interaction was actually staged and recorded earlier). Each child was instructed to get the experimenter if the preschoolers managed to "get into trouble." Aggression was thus measured by the amount of time that children witnessed the actual aggression among the preschoolers before contacting the experimenter.

The authors found that children in both the anti-aggressive and the nonaggressive conditions were significantly faster in seeking the experimenter's help than children in the neutral commentary condition. However, since experimental-treatment children were informed of the experimenter's "opinions" of violence and then were asked to do the experimenter a favor, it is likely that their motivation to appear in a socially desirable manner was high. As a result, it is difficult to estimate how long-lasting these effects would be and whether they would generalize to other situations.

Corder-Bolz (1980) conducted an experiment that may have avoided some of the social desirability problems inherent in the previous experiments. Rather than set up a situation where it was clear to the children that their behavior was going to be judged, Corder-Bolz measured children's aggressive attitudes with a more private and anonymous paper-and-pencil questionnaire. In his study, groups of 5- to 10-year-old children watched an episode of *Batman* with a teacher. During viewing, one group heard the teacher make judgmental comments about aggression (e.g., "It is bad to fight. It is better to help.") and another group of children heard the teacher make neutral comments.

Corder-Bolz found that children in the experimental treatment condition experienced a significant pre- to posttest decrease in their approval of aggression, whereas children who heard neutral comments experienced an increase in approval scores across the two testing sessions. This kind of experiment, because it reduces the effects of social desirability, provides more convincing evidence that active mediation can reduce television-induced aggression.

Other experiments, also involving paper-and-pencil measures of aggression, complement Corder-Bolz's work. For example, Nathanson and Cantor (2000) found that second- through sixth-grade boys who were asked to think about the feelings of a victim of televised cartoon violence were less aggressive after viewing the cartoon than boys who had not been asked to consider the victim's perspective. In addition, both boys and girls who received this form of mediation had more critical attitudes toward the content than the children who received no mediation.

Although these experiments might allow children more anonymity in expressing aggressive attitudes than studies that observe children's behavior, it is unlikely that they have eliminated the influence of social desirability altogether. That is, children might still be able to anticipate what the researchers "want" and feel compelled to provide it. For example, in the case of Corder-Bolz's study, the mediation information offered to children and the postviewing survey questions were very similar in content. Hence, in reporting their own attitudes toward aggression, children may have felt compelled to repeat back the attitudes that the teacher expressed while delivering the mediation. And, the children in Nathanson and Cantor's mediation condition might have guessed that they were "supposed" to like the victim of violence more and adopt a critical attitude toward the violent cartoon. Perhaps because of the artificiality of the laboratory setting, it is very difficult to eliminate children's desire to second-guess the purpose of an experimental confederate's mediation messages.

Survey work on the relationship between parents' reports of mediation and children's reports of aggression avoids some of the problems detailed above. This kind of research has shown that active mediation may be a useful strategy for preventing children from learning aggression from television. For example, Nathanson (1999) found that second through sixth graders whose parents reported more negative active mediation of violent television were less aggressive both on a day-to-day basis and after watching a violent cartoon in a laboratory setting. It seems, then, that parental active mediation of this type of content makes children less vulnerable to learning violence from television, even when the children watch without their parents. Moreover, Nathanson (1999) found that negative active mediation of violent television was associated with less perceived importance of violent television on the part of children, which in turn was associated with less aggression. Hence, just as Reiser et al. (1984, 1988) suggested, negative active mediation may teach children that certain types of programs are not valuable or important—this orientation, then, may contribute to outcomes such as decreased aggression.

Of course, this explanation only applies to negative active mediation. Because there is limited evidence that heightened aggression is related to positive active mediation (Grusec, 1973; Hicks, 1969) and neutral active mediation (Corder-Bolz, 1980), we might suspect that these strategies communicate to children that programs are valuable, important, and worth attending to. For example, in a longitudinal design, Hucsmann, Eron, Klein, Brice, and Fischer (1983) found no significant differences between the change in aggression scores of first and third graders who heard relatively neutral information (e.g., information about special effects) while watching violent programs and those who discussed nonviolent programs. The authors suggested that the treatment children may have actually learned the aggressive acts they saw during the intervention and that "the context made these excerpts highly salient, and such a modeling effect could counteract any weak mitigating effect" (p. 903). When the authors tested the effects of an intervention that highlighted the undesirability of television violence and warned children not to imitate this content, they found that it reduced children's aggression and made them less vulnerable to learning violence from television.

It seems possible, then, that sheer comprehension and enhanced attention to television, in the absence of strong negative active mediation, may not be enough to counteract antisocial content that is portrayed in a glamorous fashion and may even produce the opposite effect. As Austin and Johnson (1997) state "children's logical, realism-based decision-making processes can be overwhelmed by a more affective, wishful-based process" (p. 326). Further, Austin and Chen (1999) suggest that communication campaigns designed to reduce undesirable behaviors (e.g., drinking, smoking) may want to address the desirability of media messages rather than simply focusing on sheer education. If children's attention to and interest in content intervenes in the relationship between mediation and outcomes, future research may want to explore whether certain forms of active mediation have the unintended effect of enhancing children's learning of a variety of things about television, including how to perform antisocial behaviors.

Summary. Overall, it seems that active mediation can have a generally positive effect on children's outcomes. It has been shown to improve children's comprehension of television and learning of educational content, foster healthier attitudes toward nontraditional sex roles and more critical perceptions of television, reduce their fear responses to frightening content, and decrease the likelihood they will engage in undesirable forms of real-world behavior. Neutral or positive active mediation of undesirable messages seems to produce undesirable outcomes.

Unfortunately, many of the studies included in this body of literature are limited by either (a) simply testing children's ability to recall information presented in the mediation condition or (b) inducing in children a strong motivation to appear socially desirable. Moreover, explanations for why active mediation is associated with outcomes are usually not provided. However, it seems plausible that active mediation, depending on its valence, socializes children into an orientation toward televised content that is either generally positive and accepting or negative and discounting. Positively or nonvalenced messages may communicate that parents approve of the content or deem it important, which then might lead children to readily accept its messages. Negatively valenced messages, however, may be interpreted as parental rejection of the material and encourage children to question the validity of what they see.

Restrictive Mediation

Research indicates that parents who engage in restrictive mediation tend to be educated mothers who are concerned about the negative effects of television (Brown et al., 1990; Bybee et al., 1982; Valkenburg et al., 1999; van der Voort et al., 1992).[4] In addition, younger children are typically the recipients of restrictive mediation. Restrictive mediation does not appear to vary by the child's gender, but, as stated earlier, is more likely with children who consume relatively little television overall (Abelman, 1999; Brown et al., 1990; Brown & Linne, 1976; Roberts, 1981).[5] On the one hand, this relationship might indicate that one effect of restrictive mediation is a reduction in children's access to television. On the other hand, it could signal that children who receive restrictive mediation are the ones who, as Abelman (1999) suggested, need it the least. Because the research in this area is correlational, it is difficult to select one interpretation over the other.

Although research exists on the precursors of restrictive mediation, fewer studies have explored the effects of restricting children's access to television. In some cases, evidence of the effectiveness of restrictive mediation is found in studies that have included measures of restrictive mediation but did not focus on this construct per se. For example, in a study on the relationship between children's television viewing and reading achievement, Roberts, Bachen, Horby, and Hernandez-Ramos (1984) found that sixth graders who reported having more television-related rules earned higher reading achievement scores than other youngsters. However, this relationship did not hold for second and third graders, and disappeared when other variables (including amount of television viewing) were controlled.

The research that has focused, at least in part, on restrictive mediation includes Desmond et al.'s (1985) survey, which found that kindergarten and first-grade children whose parents restricted television viewing were better able to understand an episode of a television program shown in the laboratory than other children. Furthermore, these children tended to understand the distinction between television and the real world better than other children. In subsequent analyses of the same data set, Desmond et al. (1987) found that this relationship was particularly strong among the girls in the sample.

In addition, restrictive mediation has been found to relate to various attitudes and perceptions that are often believed to be shaped by television. For example, in a study of adolescents, Rothschild and Morgan (1987) found that children whose parents controlled their television viewing tended to express less cultivation-like attitudes (e.g., endorsements of stereotypical sex roles) and cultivation-like perceptions (e.g., fear of the outside world).

Restrictive mediation has been associated with various sorts of real-world behaviors in children. In a qualitative study, Reid (1979) examined the relationship between parental rules about television viewing and children's requests for products advertised on television. Reid observed that children whose parents had firm rules about television viewing were less likely to ask for products advertised on television and, therefore, less likely to be involved in parent-child conflict.

Reid speculated that televised ads are not directly linked to parent-child conflict over product requests. Instead, he suggested that parent-child conflict occurs in an environment in which parents have failed to use rules and restrictions regarding television to establish the medium's place in their home. For example, parents who establish rules over television viewing teach their children that televised information is not especially valued or worthwhile. Therefore, when children see advertisements for products, they are less likely to ask for them. Or, if they do ask for them, they are less likely to engage in conflict when their requests are denied. As Reid states "television commercials do not dictate children's responses, but are acted toward in relation to those events, activities, and rules which surround viewing situations and are subsequently internalized and carried to other viewing situations in later life" (p. 25). The importance of rules, then, may be in the underlying message they communicate about the value and importance of television in the home.

Another real-world behavioral outcome that has been examined in conjunction with restrictive mediation is children's aggression. In a longitudinal study, Singer et al. (1984) explored the relationship between mothers' rules about television (along with many other predictors) and children's aggression, restlessness, ability to restrain themselves, school behavioral adjustment, and belief in a "mean and scary world." The measure of maternal rules about television was averaged with responses to other items to form an index reflecting the general "television environment." The authors found that children who lived in an environment with fewer rules about television, more television sets in the home, access to cable and premium channels, access to television during mealtimes, and heavy parental television viewing were more aggressive, more restless, less able to restrain themselves, less well-adjusted in school, and more likely to believe that the world is generally mean and scary than other children. The relationship between the television environment and aggression remained even when prior aggression levels were controlled.

Although these findings are interesting, it is difficult to understand the unique contribution of viewing rules to children's outcomes because the study included viewing rules in a more general television environment index. Nonetheless, it seems fair to conclude that children are less well-adjusted when they live in an environment that exerts little control over the child's television viewing.

Similarly, Nathanson (1999) found that children whose parents engaged in restrictive mediation of violent television were less aggressive—both in general and after watching a violent cartoon in a laboratory—than other youngsters. However, there was weak evidence that the relationship between restrictive mediation and children's aggression was curvilinear in that either very low or high amounts of this form of mediation was linked with more aggression. This finding introduced the possibility that restrictive mediation techniques may backfire.

However, McLeod et al.'s (1972a, 1972b) findings on the relationship between parental control over adolescents' television viewing and adolescents' aggressive behavior were inconsistent. In one analysis (1972a), the relationship was significant, but rather small. In another analysis (1972b), the relationship was nonsignificant. It seems, then, that if there is a relationship between the two variables, it is very weak.

The fact that restrictive mediation has a weak relationship with outcomes— combined with the possibility that viewing rules may backfire—casts doubts on its effectiveness. In addition, its practicality is suspect, as rules may be ignored when children view without parents.

On the other hand, with Reid's (1979) study in mind, it seems plausible to expect that the relationship between restrictive mediation and children's aggression is indirect. Moreover, the indirect relationship could signal that the effects of restrictive mediation are long-lasting in that they socialize children into an orientation toward television that makes them less vulnerable to negative effects. That is, perhaps children whose parents restrict television tend to perceive television as a less valuable and less important source of information. This perception, then, may help children discount the aggressive messages they receive from the medium.

Desmond, Singer, and Singer (1990) have offered a similar explanation for why restrictive mediation is related to various effects among children. Specifically, they suggested that the existence of viewing rules may communicate to children that the parents, and not the television, will raise the children. They seem to imply, then, that children's attitudes toward and beliefs about television may be important intervening variables. Although the authors did not provide any data to test this hypothesis, their speculation is helpful in moving us toward an understanding of why restrictive mediation has certain effects. Moreover, this speculation is somewhat consistent with that offered by Reiser et al. (1988) to explain why active mediation of educational television promotes learning.

In fact, Nathanson (1999) found evidence for an indirect effect of restrictive mediation on children's aggression via two intervening variables. Specifically, restrictive mediation of violent television was associated with less perceived importance of violent television and less attention to violent television on the part of children. Less perceived importance of and attention to this content, in turn, was linked with less aggression. Nathanson argued that restrictive mediation of violent television might socialize children into a generally negative orientation toward this content, which then makes children less vulnerable to learning from it. In fact, this study contains evidence that the effects of restrictive mediation are long-lasting and do extend to viewing contexts outside the home.

Summary. Research on restrictive mediation suggests that, compared to children whose parents do not enforce television viewing rules, children whose parents restrict television viewing tend to better understand television and are better able to resist negative television-related effects, such as perceiving the world as similar to the television world and aggressive behavior. However, the fact that the relationship between restrictive mediation and children's outcomes is typically weak raises the possibility that researchers have overlooked some important intervening variables, such as children's perceptions of the value and importance of television.

Coviewing

Before discussing the effects of coviewing, it is first helpful to understand who is likely to give and receive this form of mediation. Coviewing is most likely to occur among mothers (Bybee et al., 1982; McDonald, 1986; van der Voort et al., 1992), parents with lower incomes (Austin et al., 1998), and parents who have a generally positive orientation toward television (Austin & Pinkelton, 1997; Dorr et al., 1989; Nathanson, in press-b). Coviewing is equally likely to occur for boys and girls (Valkenburg et al., 1999; van der Voort et al., 1992). However, it is unclear how the frequency of coviewing varies with the age of the child. In a longitudinal study, St. Peters, Fitch, Huston, Wright, and Eakins (1991) found that parental coviewing of a variety of genres of television decreased as children aged. Moreover, they demonstrated that coviewing primarily occurred when children watched parents' favorite programs, and not because parents wanted to share in their children's viewing. That is, parents tended to "allow" their children to coview programs they enjoyed, such as sitcoms, crime shows, soap operas, variety shows, and news, and coviewed children's programs relatively infrequently. The authors concluded that children are socialized to share their parents' viewing interests and that parents rarely make an effort to share their children's interests.

However, there is also evidence that coviewing increases as children age. For example, Dorr et al. (1989) found that parents coviewed programs with their sixth graders more than with their second graders, and coviewed more with their tenth graders than their sixth graders. The authors concluded that coviewing may result from a similarity in program preferences. Bybee et al.'s (1982) study also demonstrated that unfocused guidance increased with the age of the child. Finally, although Sang, Schmitz, and Tasche (1992) found that within a 2-year period, parent-child coviewing decreased among adolescents, it should be noted that nearly 51% of 14-year-olds reported coviewing television with parents. Thus, even if coviewing does decrease as children age, substantial numbers of older children and teenagers watch television with their parents.

Interestingly, parental coviewing may be less common than other forms of coviewing. Lawrence and Wozniak (1989) found that the most common form of family coviewing among 6- to 17-year-olds was sibling coviewing. Rubin (1986) also found that sibling coviewing occurred more frequently among 5- to 12-year-olds than parental coviewing. In fact, Alexander et al. (1984) reported that "sibling coviewing is the predominant television viewing pattern of American children" (p. 345). Peer coviewing might be another form of coviewing that occurs with regularity (Nathanson, in press-a), although Kubey and Larson (1990) suggest that peer co-use of other media forms, such as video games, is more prevalent than peer coviewing of television. Little research exists on this topic (Alexander et al., 1984); the work that has been done has focused on its effects on children's attention to or involvement in television and has yielded mixed results (Anderson, Lorch, Smith, Bradford, & Levin, 1981; Sproull, 1973). Certainly, more research on sibling and peer coviewing—and how they compare to parental coviewing—is needed.

Very little work has been done on the relationship between parental coviewing and children's outcomes. However, Salomon (1977) studied the effects of maternal coviewing on children's learning of and reactions to *Sesame Street*. He encouraged some mothers of kindergartners to always coview the program with their kindergartners, and he told another group of mothers simply to watch the program as they pleased. No observations of the mothers were taken, as Salomon assumed that mothers in the treatment group complied with instructions.

Salomon found that coviewing significantly affected how much lower socioeconomic children learned from and enjoyed *Sesame Street*. To explain why coviewing was related to increased learning, Salomon suggested that, because coviewing was strongly related to children's affective responses to the program, it was possible that "the sheer presence of the mother . . . may have been a source of nonspecific general arousal, thus acting as a general energizer of all responses which were likely to be emitted in the learning situation" (p. 1150). Although it was impossible to assess what kinds of interactions coviewing mothers had with their children, Salomon's conclusion suggests that the mere presence of mothers may have communicated to children that the material viewed was important and worthy of their attention.

Wilson and Weiss (1993) explored the effects of *sibling* coviewing on preschoolers' reactions to a suspenseful movie that involved somewhat confusing dream sequences. They predicted that older siblings would help their younger, preschool siblings understand the dream sequences. They also predicted that preschoolers who coviewed the movie would find it more enjoyable than preschoolers who viewed alone. Although the authors assumed that the siblings would discuss the movie, they only manipulated coviewing; as a result, their results will be interpreted in light of what was manipulated.

Wilson and Weiss (1993) found mixed support for their predictions. Preschoolers were not better able to recognize the dream sequences when they coviewed with an older sibling than when they viewed alone. This is consistent with Haefner and Wartella's (1987) study, which did not find that coviewing with an older sibling increased first- and second-grade children's understanding of an adult-oriented program (it should be noted that the older siblings in Haefner and Wartella's study were encouraged to help the younger children understand the program).

However, consistent with Salomon's (1977) finding, Wilson and Weiss (1993) found that preschoolers who watched either the confusing movie version or a version that did not have the confusing dream sequence with an older sibling enjoyed it more than preschoolers who viewed it alone. Thus, it seems as though the effects of coviewing on children are primarily affective.

However, as Salomon (1977) suggested, the positive affective responses that children experience as the result of coviewing may produce arousal that can enhance their learning of television material. Survey research on the effects of coviewing extends this work, but also offers some rather surprising and counterintuitive findings. In their study of parents and their second-, sixth-, and tenth-grade children, Dorr et al. (1989) failed to find a significant relationship between coviewing and children's perceptions of television realism. However, they did find that children whose parents tended to engage in coviewing of family series were more likely to view family series for learning purposes but not for escape. This complements Salomon's (1977) suggestion that the mere presence of parents during viewing subtly communicates to children that programs are important and useful to them.

Given the possibility that coviewing sends a message to children about the value and importance of television, we might expect that children whose parents coview will learn more from television. Certainly, then, parent-child coviewing of educational or prosocial television should be endorsed. However, if we expect coviewing to contribute to learning from television, then we should also expect that children whose parents coview antisocial material (in the absence of negative active mediation) are at a greater risk for learning or accepting negative messages. In this case, coviewing should clearly have a negative influence on children.

In fact, some survey work indicates that coviewing has a detrimental effect on children's outcomes. For example, Rothschild and Morgan (1987) found that adolescents whose parents coviewed television with them were more likely to endorse stereotyped conceptions of sex roles and express greater fear of the outside world than adolescents whose parents did not coview with them. Further, in a study of first, third, and fifth graders, Messaris and Kerr (1984) found that children whose mothers coviewed programs were more likely to believe that television characters are representative of "real life" people. The authors, citing Salomon, later suggested that "the mere *fact* of maternal involvement in a child's TV viewing—regardless of what exactly a mother may say about a TV program—makes a child more attentive and receptive to information presented on the screen" (p. 665). Finally, research has shown that parental coviewing is positively related to children's day-to-day aggression (Nathanson, 1997) and the aggression they experience after watching a violent cartoon (Nathanson, 1999).

Consistent with previous reasoning, it is possible that parents who coview negative material with their children, but do not contradict or condemn the socially undesirable behaviors occurring on the screen, may subtly communicate that they approve of the content. That is, in the child's eyes, sheer coviewing may be interpreted as parental endorsement of content. In fact, Nathanson (in press-b) found support for this. Children who believe their parents approve of certain types of depictions may develop a generally positive or accepting orientation toward the material, which may make them more vulnerable to learning from it.

Summary. Research indicates that children whose parents coview television tend to enjoy programs more than other youngsters. It is possible that children interpret the mere presence of their coviewing parent as a sign that the parent likes and approves of the content viewed. This may then lead children to perceive the material as valuable and to become involved in the content, making it more likely that they will learn from what they see. As a result, in the case of educational programming, parental coviewing should produce welcomed effects. However, because we should expect the same interpretational processes to occur when parents coview negative material, coviewing may also amplify television's antisocial effects rather than curb them.

Summary of Research on the Effects of Active Mediation, Restrictive Mediation, and Coviewing

A review of the research indicates that mediation can affect children's processing of, interpretation of, and reactions to television. However, the effects of active mediation, restrictive mediation, and coviewing do not appear to be uniform.

In general, some forms of active mediation are linked with positive outcomes in children. Active mediation helps them understand televised plots and educational messages, appreciate the difference between television and reality, avoid intense fright responses to scary content, and resist advertising ploys and negative television messages, such as those pertaining to stereotypical sex roles and aggressive behavior. However, the interaction between the kind of active mediation and the type of content that is mediated must be considered, as both positive and neutral mediation of antisocial content can have harmful effects. Although less work has been conducted on restrictive mediation, it seems that imposing rules or limits on children's viewing improves their understanding of television when they do view, decreases their requests for products advertised on television, and helps them resist or discount negative televised messages relating to sex roles, crime, and aggression. Finally, there is evidence that coviewing is linked with enjoyment of and learning from television. However, it also seems that coviewing may amplify television's negative effects, such as increasing children's aggression, fear of the outside world, and endorsement of stereotypical sex roles.

Although explanations for mediation effects have not been explored very much, it is plausible that active mediation, restrictive mediation, and coviewing work by sending a message to children about the value and importance of television. Above and beyond the literal message that a parent delivers, children may view mediation as indicator of their parents' general attitudes toward the mediated content. If the children internalize what they perceive to be their parents' attitudes, then this perception of television may contribute to the effects associated with mediation. More specifically, if children interpret the presence of negative active mediation and restrictive mediation to mean that their parents disapprove of the mediated content—and they adopt a similarly critical orientation—they may be less likely to be affected by what they view. In addition, if children interpret the presence of positive active mediation and mere coviewing as indicative of parental endorsement of the content—and they adopt a similarly favorable orientation—they may be more likely to accept what they view. Future research should empirically test this and other explanations of mediation to help us gain a better understanding of how it affects children's reactions to television.

CONCLUSION

Mediation research is important and can teach us how to prepare children to handle their inevitable exposure to television. Through mediation, parents or other adults can shape the way that children watch television and help them experience its positive effects while avoiding some of its more negative outcomes. This is an area that deserves more attention, but has been at a disadvantage because of the lack of conceptual clarity regarding the term mediation. If the conceptualization of this construct continues to be ignored, the body of work on mediation will remain incoherent and disorganized. Researchers must come to a consensus regarding what mediation is and what it is not. Hopefully, by coming to an agreement regarding what mediation is and what behaviors its various forms encompass, researchers will be able to proceed from a shared understanding that will allow this body of work to move forward. This shared understanding can aid us in both interpreting the findings of previous work and guiding future research questions.

As a result, this paper offers the following recommendations for future work:

1. Mediation should only refer to interactions with children *that relate to television.*
2. Mediation should be regarded as a three-dimensional construct encompassing active mediation, restrictive mediation, and coviewing.
3. Mediation behaviors should be regarded as content-specific, both conceptually and methodologically.
4. The decision to use either parents or children (or both) as respondents in measuring mediation should be carefully considered and theoretically driven.
5. In statistical analyses on the effects of mediation, researchers must control for sources of spuriousness, including (and especially) the amount that children view television.
6. The nature of active mediation should be carefully considered. Positive active mediation should be distinguished from negative and neutral active mediation, both conceptually and methodologically.
7. Restrictive mediation should not be thought of in terms of its amount. Instead, the *presence, types,* and *severity* of rules should be assessed. In addition, the means by which viewing rules are arrived at (e.g., via parent-child discussion or simple parental enforcement) should be explored.

8.   Coviewing should be distinguished from active mediation and should simply refer to the presence of parents during children's television viewing. Measures of coviewing must assess mere coviewing. Or, analyses of coviewing (based on measures that do not ensure this distinction) should statistically control for the influence of active mediation.

9.   Since active mediation, restrictive mediation, and coviewing are conceptually distinct (and have been shown to have different outcomes), research should explore the effect of each form. Likewise, it should not necessarily be presumed that each form will function identically; hence, unique explanations for how each type of mediation works should be advanced.

10. Researchers should explore the direct effect of mediation on children's perceptions of the content that is being mediated. Children's interpretations of mediation messages (e.g., whether they are processed as parental endorsement or condemnation of content) may be important intervening variables in the relationship between mediation and children's outcomes. This kind of research could help the literature gain an understanding of why mediation operates as it does.

NOTES

1. For example, Nathanson (1999) computed residualized coviewing scores by removing the variance in coviewing contributed by active mediation to preserve the conceptual distinction between the two concepts.

2. However, it should be noted that parents are also prone to overreporting of communication variables, as Alexander, Wartella, and Brown (1981) found that mothers' estimates of their children's television viewing were higher than the children's estimates of their own viewing.

3. The research on the reduction of media-induced fear includes analyses of "noncognitive strategies" as well. However, noncognitive strategies do not require children to process verbally presented information and instead involve distracting or comforting the child via certain activities (Cantor, 1994). As a result, noncognitive strategies cannot be classified as active mediation strategies and will not be reviewed in this article.

4. However, Lin and Atkin (1989) found that restrictive mediation was more likely among less educated parents.

5. The research is not clear regarding the relationship between restrictive mediation and children's *violent* television viewing. Whereas Nathanson (1999) found a negative relationship between the two in her sample of second through sixth graders, McLeod et al. (1972b) found a positive relationship in their sample of adolescents. This discrepancy may be due to differences between the samples or measures (i.e., Nathanson measured restrictive mediation of violent television and McLeod et al. measured restrictive mediation of television in general).

REFERENCES

Abelman, R. (1985). Styles of parental disciplinary practices as a mediator of children's learning from prosocial television portrayals. *Child Study Journal, 15*, 131–145.

Abelman, R. (1990). From "The Huxtables" to "The Humbards": The portrayal of family on religious television. In J. Bryant (Ed.), *Television and the American family* (pp. 164–184). Hillsdale, NJ: Erlbaum.

Abelman, R. (1999). Preaching to the choir: Profiling TV advisory ratings users. *Journal of Broadcasting and Electronic Media, 43*, 529–550.

Abelman, R., & Courtright, J. (1983). Television literacy: Amplifying the cognitive level effects of television's prosocial fare through curriculum intervention. *Journal of Research and Development in Education, 17*, 46–57.

Alexander, A., Wartella, E., & Brown, D. (1981). Estimates of children's television viewing by mother and child. *Journal of Broadcasting, 25*, 243–252.

Alexander, A., Ryan, M. S., & Munoz, P. (1984). Creating a learning context: Investigations on the interaction of siblings during television viewing. *Critical Studies in Mass Communication, 1*, 345–364.

Atkin, D. J., Greenberg, B. S., & Baldwin, T. F. (1991). The home ecology of children's television viewing. *Journal of Communication, 41*(3), 40–52.

Anderson, D. R., Lorch, E. P., Smith, R., Bradford, R., & Levin, S. R. (1981). Effects of peer presence of preschool children's television-viewing behavior. *Developmental Psychology, 17*, 446–453.

Austin, E. W. (1992). Parent-child TV interaction: The importance of perspective. *Journal of Broadcasting and Electronic Media, 36*, 359–361.

Austin, E. W. (1993a). Exploring the effects of active parental mediation of television content. *Journal of Broadcasting and Electronic Media, 37*, 147–158.

Austin, E. W. (1993b). The importance of perspective in parent-child interpretations of family communication patterns. *Journalism Quarterly, 70*, 558–568.

Austin, E. W., & Chen, Y. J. (1999, May). *The relationship of parental reinforcement of media messages to college students' alcohol-related behaviors, age of experimentation and beliefs about alcohol.* Paper presented at the annual meeting of the Association for Education in Journalism and Mass Communication, New Orleans, LA.

Austin, E. W., Bolls, P., Fujioka, Y., & Engelbertson, J. (1999). How and why parents take on the tube. *Journal of Broadcasting and Electronic Media, 43*, 175–192.

Austin, E. W., & Johnson, K. K. (1997). Immediate and delayed effects of media literacy training on third graders' decision making for alcohol. *Health Communication, 9*, 323–349.

Austin, E. W., Knaus, C., & Meneguelli, A. (1998). Who talks how to their kids about TV: A clarification of demographic correlates of parental mediation patterns. *Communication Research Reports, 14*, 418–430.

Austin, E. W., & Pinkelton, B. E. (1997, May). *Parental mediation as information source use: Political socialization effects.* Paper presented at the annual conference of the International Communication Association, Montreal, Quebec, Canada.

Austin, E. W., Roberts, D. F., & Nass, C. I. (1990). Influences of family communication on children's television-interpretation processes. *Communication Research, 17*, 545–564.

Ball, S. J., & Bogatz, G. A. (1970). *The first year of Sesame Street: An evaluation.* Princeton, NJ: Educational Testing Center.

Brown, J. D., Childers, K. W., Bauman, K. E., & Koch, G. G. (1990). The influence of new media and family structure on young adolescents' television and radio use. *Communication Research, 17*, 65–82.

Brown J. R., & Linne, O. (1976). The family as a mediator of television's effects. In R. Brown (Ed.), *Children and television* (pp. 184–198). Beverly Hills, CA: Sage.

Bryce, J. W., & Leichter, H. J. (1983). The family and television: Forms of mediation. *Journal of Family Issues, 4*, 309–328.

Bybee, C., Robinson, D., & Turow, J. (1982). Determinants of parental guidance of children's television viewing for a special subgroup: Mass media scholars. *Journal of Broadcasting, 26*, 697–710.

Carlson, C. I. (1990). Assessing the family context. In C. R. Reynolds & R. W. Kamphaus (Eds.), *Handbook of psychological and educational assessment of children: Personality, behavior, and context* (pp. 546–575). New York: Guildford Press.

Cantor, J. (1994). Fright reactions to mass media. In J. Bryant & D. Zillmann (Eds.), *Media effects: Advances in theory and research* (pp. 213–245). Hillsdale, NJ: Erlbaum.

Cantor, J., & Hoffner, C. (1990). Children's fear reactions to a televised film as a function of perceived immediacy of depicted threat. *Journal of Broadcasting and Electronic Media, 34*, 421–442.

Cantor, J., Sparks, G. G., & Hoffner, C. (1988). Calming children's television fears: Mr. Rogers vs. The Incredible Hulk. *Journal of Broadcasting and Electronic Media, 32*, 271–288.

Cantor, J., & Wilson, B. J. (1984). Modifying fear responses to mass media in preschool and elementary school children. *Journal of Broadcasting, 28*, 431–443.

Cantor, J., & Wilson, B. J. (1988). Helping children cope with frightening media presentations. *Current Psychology: Research and Reviews, 7*, 58–75.

Chaffee, S. H., & McLeod, J. M. (1972). Adolescent television use in the family context. In G. A. Comstock & E. A. Rubinstein (Eds.), *Television and social behavior: Vol. 3. Television and adolescent aggressiveness* (pp. 149–172). Washington, DC: U.S. Government Printing Office.

Chaffee, S. H., McLeod, J. M., & Atkin, C. K. (1971). Parental influences on adolescent media use. *American Behavioral Scientist, 14*, 323–340.

Coates, B., & Hartup, W. W. (1969). Age and verbalization in observational learning. *Developmental Psychology, 5*, 556–562.

Collins, W. A., Sobol, B. L., & Westby, S. (1981). Effects of adult commentary on children's comprehension and inferences about a televised aggressive portrayal. *Child Development, 52*, 158–163.

Corder-Bolz, C. R. (1980). Mediation: The role of significant others. *Journal of Communication, 30*(3), 106–118.

Corder-Bolz, C. R., & O'Bryant, S. (1978). Teacher vs. program. *Journal of Communication, 28*(1), 97–103.

Desmond, R. J., Singer, J. L., Singer, D. G., Calam, R., & Colimore, K. (1985). Family mediation patterns and television viewing: Young children's use and grasp of the medium. *Human Communication Research, 11*, 461–480.

Desmond, R. J., Hirsch, B., Singer, D., & Singer, J. (1987). Gender differences, mediation, and disciplinary styles in children's responses to television. *Sex Roles, 16*, 375–389.

Desmond, R. J., Singer, J. L., & Singer, D. G. (1990). Family mediation: Parental communication patterns and the influence of television on children. In J. Bryant (Ed.), *Television and the American family* (pp. 293–309). Hillsdale, NJ: Erlbaum.

Dorr, A., Graves, S. B., & Phelps, E. (1980). Television literacy for young children. *Journal of Communication, 30*(3), 71–83.

Dorr, A., Kovaric, P., & Doubleday, C. (1989). Parent-child coviewing of television. *Journal of Broadcasting and Electronic Media, 33*, 35–51.

Eron, L. D., & Huesmann, L. R. (1984). The relation of prosocial behavior to the development of aggression and psychopathology. *Aggressive Behavior, 10*, 201–212.

Friedrich, L. K., & Stein, A. H. (1975). Prosocial television and young children: The effects of verbal labeling and role playing on learning and behavior. *Child Development, 46*, 27–38.

Fujioka, Y., & Austin, E. W. (1999, May). *The relationship of family communication patterns to parental mediation styles*. Paper presented at the annual conference of the International Communication Association, San Francisco.

Greenberg, B. S., Ericson, P. M., & Vlahos, M. (1972). Children's television behaviors as perceived by mother and child. In E. A. Rubinstein, G. A. Comstock, & J. P. Murray (Eds.), *Television and social behavior: Television in day-to-day life: Patterns of use.* (Vol. 4, pp. 395–409). Washington, DC: U.S. Government Printing Office.

Grotevant, H. D., & Carlson, C. I. (1987). Family interaction coding systems: A descriptive review. *Family Process, 26*, 49–74.

Grotevant, H. D., & Carlson, C. I. (1989). *Family assessment: A guide to methods and measures.* New York: Guildford Press.

Grusec, J. E. (1973). Effects of co-observer evaluations on imitation: A developmental study. *Developmental Psychology, 8*, 141.

Haefner, M. J., & Wartella, E. A. (1987). Effects of sibling coviewing on children's interpretation of television programs. *Journal of Broadcasting and Electronic Media, 31*, 153–168.

Hicks, D. J. (1968). Effects of co-observer's sanctions and adult presence on imitative aggression. *Child Development, 39*, 303–309.

Hobbs, R., & Frost, R. (1997, May). *The impact of media literacy education on adolescents' media analysis and news comprehension skills.* Paper presented at the annual conference of the International Communication Association, Montreal, Quebec, Canada.

Hoffman, L. W., & Lippitt, R. (1960). The measurement of family life variables. In P. H. Mussen (Ed.), *Handbook of research methods in child development* (pp. 945–1013). New York: Wiley.

Hoffner, C. (1997). Children's emotional reactions to a scary film: The role of prior outcome information and coping style. *Human Communication Research, 23,* 323–341.

Hoffner, C., & Cantor, J. (1990). Forewarning of a threat and prior knowledge of outcome: Effects on children's emotional responses to a film sequence. *Human Communication Research, 16,* 323–354.

Hoffner, C., Cantor, J., Badzinski, D. M. (1990). Children's understanding of adverbs denoting degree of likelihood. *Journal of Child Language, 17,* 217–231.

Horton, R. W., & Santogrossi, D. A. (1978). The effect of adult commentary on reducing the influence of televised violence. *Personality and Social Psychology Bulletin, 4,* 337–340.

Huesmann, L. R., Eron, L. D., Klein, R., Brice, P., & Fischer, P. (1983). Mitigating the imitation of aggressive behaviors by changing children's attitudes about media violence. *Journal of Personality and Social Psychology, 44,* 899–910.

Krcmar, M. (1996). Family communication patterns, discourse behavior, and children's television viewing. *Human Communication Research, 23,* 251–277.

Kubey, R., & Larson, R. (1990). The use and experience of the new video media among children and young adolescents. *Communication Research, 17,* 107–130.

Lawrence, F. C., & Wozniak, P. H. (1989). Children's television viewing with family members. *Psychological Reports, 65,* 395–400.

Lin, C. A., & Atkin, D. J. (1989). Parental mediation and rulemaking for adolescent use of television and VCRs. *Journal of Broadcasting and Electronic Media, 33,* 53–67.

Lull, J. (1980). Family communication patterns and the social uses of television. *Communication Research, 7,* 319–334.

Mattern, K. K., & Lindholm, B. W. (1983). Effect of maternal commentary in reducing aggressive impact of televised violence on preschool children. *Journal of Genetic Psychology, 146,* 133–134.

Matthews, D., & Desmond, R. (1997, May). *"To get you to buy:" Effects of a parent workshop on young children's understanding of television advertising.* Paper presented at the annual conference of the International Communication Association, Montreal, Quebec, Canada.

Meadowcroft, J. M. (1986). Family communication patterns and political development: The child's role. *Communication Research, 13,* 603–624.

Meadowcroft, J. M., & Fitzpatrick, M. A. (1988). Theories of family communication: Toward a merger of intersubjectivity and mutual influence processes. In R. P. Hawkins, J. M. Wiemann, & S. Pingree (Eds.), *Advancing communication science: Merging mass and interpersonal processes* (pp. 253–275). Newbury Park, CA: Sage.

Messaris, P. (1982). Parents, children, and television. In G. Gumpert & R. Cathcart (Eds.), *Inter/Media* (pp. 580–598). New York: Oxford University Press.

Messaris, P., & Kerr, D. (1984). TV-related mother-child interaction and children's perceptions of TV characters. *Journalism Quarterly, 61,* 662–666.

McDonald, D. G. (1986). Generational aspects of television coviewing. *Journal of Broadcasting and Electronic Media, 30,* 75–85.

McGhee, P. E., & Frueh, T. (1980). Television viewing and the learning of sex-role stereotypes. *Sex Roles, 6,* 179–188.

McLeod, J. M., Atkin, C. K., & Chaffee, S. H. (1972a). Adolescents, parents, and television use: Adolescent self-report measures from Maryland and Wisconsin samples. In G. A. Comstock & E. A. Rubinstein (Eds.), *Television and social behavior: Vol. 3. Television and adolescent aggressiveness* (pp. 173–238). Washington, DC: U.S. Government Printing Office.

McLeod, J. M., Atkin, C. K., & Chaffee, S. H. (1972b). Adolescents, parents, and television use: Self report and other-report measures from the Wisconsin sample. In G. A. Comstock & E. A. Rubinstein (Eds.), *Television and social behavior: Vol 3. Television and adolescent aggressiveness* (pp. 239–313). Washington, DC: U.S. Government Printing Office.

McLeod, J. M., & Chaffee, S. H. (1972). The construction of social reality. In J. T. Tedeschi (Ed.), *The social influence processes* (pp. 50–99). Chicago: Aldine-Atherton.

Morgan, M. (1982). Television and adolescents' sex role stereotypes: A longitudinal study. *Journal of Personality and Social Psychology, 43*, 947–955.

Nathanson, A. I. (1997, May). *The relationship between parental mediation and children's anti- and pro-social motivations*. Paper presented at the annual conference of the International Communication Association, Montreal, Quebec, Canada.

Nathanson, A. I. (1998, May). *The immediate and cumulative effects of television mediation on children's aggression*. Unpublished doctoral dissertation, University of Wisconsin-Madison.

Nathanson, A. I. (1999). Identifying and explaining the relationship between parental mediation and children's aggression. *Communication Research, 26*, 124–143.

Nathanson, A. I. (in press-a). Parents versus peers: Exploring the significance of peer mediation of antisocial television. *Communication Research*.

Nathanson, A. I. (in press-b). Parent and child perspectives on the presence and meaning of parental mediation. *Journal of Broadcasting and Electronic Media*.

Nathanson, A. I., & Cantor, J. (2000). Reducing the aggression-promoting effect of violent cartoons by increasing children's fictional involvement with the victim. *Journal of Broadcasting and Electronic Media, 44*, 125–142.

Paik, H, & Comstock, G. (1994). The effects of television violence on aggressive behavior: A meta-analysis. *Communication Research, 21*, 516–546.

Prasad, V. K., Rao, T. R., & Sheikh, A. A. (1978). Mother vs. commercial. *Journal of Communication, 28*(1), 91–96.

Rapaczynski, W., Singer, D. G., & Singer, J. L. (1982). Teaching television: A curriculum for young children. *Journal of Communication, 32*(2), 46–54.

Reid, L. N. (1979). Viewing rules as mediating factors of children's responses to commercials. *Journal of Broadcasting, 23*, 15–26.

Reid, L. N., & Frazer, C. F. (1980). Children's use of television commercials to initiate social interaction in family viewing situations. *Journal of Broadcasting, 24*, 149–158.

Reiser, R. A., Tessmer, M. A., & Phelps, P. C. (1984). Adult-child interaction in children's learning from *Sesame Street*. *Educational Communication and Technology Journal, 32*, 217–223.

Reiser, R. A., Williamson, N., & Suzuki, K. (1988). Using *Sesame Street* to facilitate children's recognition of letters and numbers. *Educational Communication and Technology Journal, 36*, 15–21.

Ridley-Johnson, R., Chance, J. E., & Cooper, H. (1984). Correlates of children's television viewing: expectancies, age, and sex. *Journal of Applied Developmental Psychology, 5*, 225–235.

Roberts, C. (1981). Children's and parent's television viewing and perceptions of violence. *Journalism Quarterly, 66*, 556–564, 578.

Roberts, D. F., Bachen, C. M., Horby, M. C., & Hernandez-Ramos, P. (1984). Reading and television: Predictors of reading achievement at different age levels. *Communication Research, 11*, 9–49.

Roberts, D. R., Christenson, P., Gibson, W. A., Mooser, L., & Goldberg, M. E. (1980). Developing discriminating consumers. *Journal of Communication, 30*(3), 94–105.

Rose, G. M., Bush, V. D., & Kahle, L. (1998). The influence of family communication patterns on parental reactions toward advertising: A cross-national examination. *Journal of Advertising, 27*, 71–85.

Rothschild, N., & Morgan, M. (1987). Cohesion and control: Adolescents' relationships with parents as mediators of television. *Journal of Early Adolescence, 7*, 299–314.

Rubin, A. M. (1986). Age and family control influences on children's television viewing. *Southern Speech Communication Journal, 52*, 35–51.

Rushton, J. P. (1982). Television and prosocial behavior. In D. Pearl, L. Bouthilet, & J. Lazar (Eds.), *Television and behavior: Ten years of scientific progress and implications for the eighties, Vol. 2: Technical reviews* (pp. 248–257). Washington, DC: U.S. Government Printing Office.

Salomon, G. (1977). Effects of encouraging Israeli mothers to co-observe *Sesame Street* with their five-year-olds. *Child Development, 48*, 1146–1151.

Sang, F., Schmitz, B., & Tasche, K. (1992). Individuation and television coviewing in the family: Developmental trends in the viewing behavior of adolescents. *Journal of Broadcasting and Electronic Media, 36,* 427–441.

Schramm, W. (1972). What the research says. In W. Schramm (Ed.), *Quality in instructional television* (pp. 44–67). Honolulu: University Press of Hawaii.

Schramm, W. (1977). *Big media, little media.* Beverly Hills, CA: Sage.

Singer, D. G., & Singer, J. L. (1998). Developing critical viewing skills and media literacy in children. *Annals of the American Academy of Political and Social Science, 557,* 164–179.

Singer, J. L., Singer, D. G., Desmond, R., Hirsch, B., & Nicol, A. (1988). Family mediation and children's cognition, aggression, and comprehension of television: A longitudinal study. *Journal of Applied Developmental Psychology, 9,* 329–347.

Singer, J. L., Singer, D. G., & Rapaczynski, W. S. (1984). Family patterns and television viewing as predictors of children's beliefs and aggression. *Journal of Communication, 34*(2), 73–89.

Singer, D. G., Zuckerman, D. M., & Singer, J. L. (1980). Helping elementary school children learn about TV. *Journal of Communication, 30*(3), 84–93.

Sproull, N. (1973). Visual attention, modeling behaviors, and other verbal and nonverbal meta-communication of prekindergarten children viewing *Sesame Street. American Educational Research Journal, 10,* 101–114.

St. Peters, M., Fitch, M., Huston, A. C., Wright, J. C., & Eakins, D. J. (1991). Television and families: What do young children watch with their parents? *Child Development, 62,* 1409–1423.

Stoneman, Z., & Brody, G. H. (1982). An in-home investigation of maternal teaching strategies during *Sesame Street* and a popular situation comedy. *Journal of Applied Developmental Psychology, 3,* 275–284.

Tangney, J. P. (1988). Aspects of the family and children's television viewing content preferences. *Child Development, 59,* 1070–1079.

Thompson, M., Pingree, S., Hawkins, R. P., & Draves, C. (1991). Long-term norms and cognitive structures as shapers of television viewer activity. *Journal of Broadcasting and Electronic Media, 35,* 319–334.

Tolan, P. H., Gorman-Smith, D., Huesmann, L. R., & Zelli, A. (1997). Assessment of family relationship characteristics: A measure to explain risk for antisocial behavior and depression among urban youth. *Psychological Assessment, 9,* 212–223.

Valkenburg, P. M., Krcmar, M., & de Roos, S. (1998). The impact of a cultural children's program and adult mediation on children's knowledge of and attitudes toward opera. *Journal of Broadcasting & Electronic Media, 42,* 315–326.

Valkenburg, P. M., Krcmar, M., Peeters, A. L., & Marseille, N. M. (1999). Developing a scale to assess three styles of television mediation: "Instructive mediation," "restrictive mediation," and "social coviewing." *Journal of Broadcasting & Electronic Media, 43,* 52–66.

van der Voort, T. H. A., Nikken, P., & van Lil, J. E. (1992). Determinants of parental guidance of children's television viewing: A Dutch replication study. *Journal of Broadcasting and Electronic Media, 36,* 61–74.

Watkins, B., Calvert, S., Huston-Stein, A., & Wright, J. C. (1980). Children's recall of television material: Effects of presentation mode and adult labeling. *Developmental Psychology, 16,* 672–674.

Weaver, B., & Barbour, N. (1992). Mediation of children's televiewing. *Families in Society: The Journal of Contemporary Human Services, 73,* 236–242.

Wilson, B. J., & Cantor, J. (1987). Reducing children's fear reactions to mass media: Effects of visual exposure and verbal explanation. In M. M. McLaughlin (Ed.), *Communication yearbook 10* (pp. 553–573). Newbury Park, CA: Sage.

Wilson, B. J., & Weiss, A. J. (1991). The effects of two reality explanations on children's reactions to a frightening movie scene. *Communication Monographs, 58,* 307–326.

Wilson, B. J., & Weiss, A. J. (1993). The effects of sibling coviewing on preschoolers' reactions to a suspenseful movie scene. *Communication Research, 20,* 214–248.

CHAPTER CONTENTS

5 Convergence: Informatization, World System, and Developing Countries

SHELTON A. GUNARATNE
Minnesota State University Moorhead

This essay reviews the arguments of the utopians and the dystopians on the ongoing Third Communication Revolution—the convergence of telecommunication, computers, and digitization—and makes the point that the state of *capitalism* stimulated by this revolution has left nations—small or big—with little option but to *informatize* so they could effectively compete in the world material economy. Because dependency theory offers no solution for these nations to escape from the quagmire of underdevelopment, a persuasive argument has surfaced to view the longitudinal "capitalist" dynamics of the world economy in nonideological terms. Global competition and interdependence reflect to some extent the end of the nation in the orthodox sense. One can reconfigure structural theory—the dependency-world system theory formulation—to reflect the emerging state of globalization. This essay uses an *informatization* model founded on the basic variables of the old paradigm of modernization—urbanization, literacy, education, and media participation—to explain 3 essential variables denoting informatization—economic status, telephone density, and Internet host penetration. It also points out that the Human Development Index (HDI) itself is based on related variables: literacy, education, health (life expectancy), and economic status (GNP).

IN 1997, *Time* magazine chose Andrew Steven Grove, chairman and CEO of Intel, as the Man of the Year (Isaacson, 1997) because he was "the person most responsible for the amazing growth in the power and innovative potential of microchips" (p. 48). The magazine claimed that the "Digital Revolution is now transforming the end of this century the way the Industrial Revolution transformed the end of the last one" (p. 48). The microchip has caused the dawn of the Tera Era, when digital bits-per-second are measured in trillions (tera), rather than in millions (mega) or billions (giga). The global communication grid is going through "an explosive expansion in capacity and speed"—a "bandwidth boom"—

AUTHOR'S NOTE: This essay is a revision of a paper presented at the 21st scientific conference of the International Association of Media and Communication Research in Glasgow, Scotland, July 1998.

Correspondence: Shelton A. Gunaratne, Mass Communications Department, Minnesota State University Moorhead, 1104 Seventh Ave. S., Moorhead, MN 56563; email: gunarat@mnstate.edu

(Erickson, 1998) resulting from projects such as FLAG, China-U.S. Cable Network, Sea-Me-We3, and Oxygen.[1] By the turn of the century, a surge of new communication technologies—digital subscriber lines, microwave (fixed wireless) links, broadband cellular (cellphone) networks, low-earth-orbit satellites, interactive cable, and multimedia satellites—added to the "bandwidth boom" (Whitmore & Erickson, 1999).

BACKGROUND: THE THIRD COMMUNICATION REVOLUTION

The Digital Revolution, also known as the Third Communication Revolution, is the result of the convergence of telecommunication, computers, and digitization. Digitization, which converts all information—text, sound, and pictures—into a binary code, has dismantled the barriers that once separated the three sectors of the information industry: telecommunications, computing, and audiovisual (or entertainment). A global information infrastructure (GII) encompassing high-performance *computers*, *multimedia*, and *interactive television* has thus emerged. The GII facilitates interactive television because of its abundant multimedia capacity to convey video in conjunction with data, image, text, and voice (International Telecommunication Union [ITU], 1995, p. 2).

The first two communication revolutions were the evolution of writing and the invention of printing. Stevenson (1994) wrote, "Written language ended the power monopoly of the elders who preserved and passed on the oral sagas and poems that contained the accumulated knowledge of preliterate tribes . . . [Printing] challenged the church's monopoly of information, its monopoly of truth, and changed the world for ever" (p. 262). The third revolution might shift the national and global power structure in ways yet to be seen. The Commission on Freedom of the Press (1947) titled the third chapter of its report "The Communication Revolution," which, it said, was "far from completed" (p. 31). That revolution, which brought in computers, satellites and fiber optics, multimedia, and so forth as the century progressed, has continued on to the new millennium. Glaeser (1997) observed, "The dramatic spread of new communication technologies in the past 15 years is unprecedented, and it implies that we are truly living through a worldwide information revolution" (p. 50). Sachs (1998) asserted that because the information technology revolution was "deeply changing the way that economies operate," the effective introduction and use of information technology (IT) would be a crucial factor in international competitiveness (p. 19).

The Third Communication Revolution is also what Toffler (1980) and Toffler and Toffler (1993) chose to call the Third Wave. They analyzed the historical progress of societies in terms of three waves: agricultural (first-wave), industrial (second-wave), and information-intensive (third-wave). Although Toffler and Toffler's First Wave encompassed the first communication revolution, their Second Wave followed the second communication revolution. Their three-wave analysis provides a magnificent framework to understand the tensions and crises of the contemporary global economy. These eruptions, they explained, sparked from the trisection—collision or overlapping—of the three waves, which clashed simultaneously even within contemporary societies, such as in India and China. Taylor (1997), who used the Toffler framework to expound on global communications and international affairs, saw the Internet, which symbolized the Third Communication Revolution, as the first truly Third-Wave "mass medium" (p. 15). Taylor asserted that the Internet allowed people to access information from the network of globally linked computers directly and individually without the mediation of gatekeepers as in the case of second-wave mass media. The Third Wave, Taylor (1997) said, was in the process of producing "information intensive third-wave powers whose economies depend[ed] not on the plough or the assembly-line but on 'brainpower'" (p. 14).

The GII has created new services and newer technologies. Intranets and extranets have appeared to help alleviate the clutter of the Internet and cater to the more specialized needs of industry, education, government, and other special interest organizations. A global debate is in full swing on the positive and the negative facets of the GII. The predominant view is that electronic information infrastructures are critical for expediting "economic, social and cultural benefits as well as for conferring competitive advantage" (ITU, 1995, p. 3). Therefore, countries as diverse as Canada and China have invested heavily on such infrastructures (ITU, 1995; Lee, 1997; Mueller & Tan, 1997).

ITU (1995) asserted the world was becoming dependent on electronic communication. The daily financial transactions conducted through one network of the GII was about $2.3 trillion, an "example of the increasing flow of electronic information" (p. 7). This dependence, which was "altering businesses, life styles and societies," had important implications considering that the service sector already accounted for more than half of national economic output in many countries. Even in the world's low-income countries (excluding China and India), the service sector (41% of the gross domestic product) surpassed agriculture (33%) and industry (25%) in 1995 (World Bank, 1997).

ITU (1995) further asserted that developing countries, already behind in various measures of information penetration (see Table 3 & 4, pp. 187–189), could not afford to wait and see whether the benefits of the communication revolution would outweigh the costs. Several aspects of the GII were "particularly appropriate for the needs of developing countries" (p. 13). First, an electronic infrastructure could help *deliver electronic health and learning services*. Second, such an infrastructure would promote *competitiveness* among these countries in an increasingly information-driven world. Third, an electronic infrastructure could *fundamentally alter the entire development paradigm* by enabling countries to skip whole stages of development. Fourth, those countries with better communication facilities would be in a better position to attract business *investment* in a more competitive world. Fifth, an electronic infrastructure could help *attract and retain skilled manpower* that countries would need for building national information industries. It could also minimize the brain drain. Last, developing countries could *leapfrog* developed countries because they—the developing countries—could install the latest facilities "often costing no more than traditional infrastructure" (p. 14).

Glaeser (1997) argued that information technology mattered in development. His research for the World Economic Forum has shown a significant relationship between a country's level of technology and the amount of inward foreign direct investment or trade. He asserted that a link existed between growth in production and improvements in technology, for example, increases in gross domestic product per capita and increases in the number of telephone lines. He found a significant correlation between the rate of growth of Internet hosts and subsequent national economic growth. Mustafa, Laidlaw, and Brand (1997) confirmed this view when they said, "Telecommunications infrastructure lies at the heart of the information economy. Countries lacking modern telecommunications infrastructure cannot compete effectively in the global economy" (p. 1). For countries in sub-Saharan Africa, they said, each new telephone line contributed about $4,500 to gross national product.

Kelly and Petrazzini (1997) have pointed out that the Internet has taken off "at a stunning pace throughout the world" even though its growth has been uneven (p. 5). More than 56.2 million Internet hosts supported an estimated 179 million users by July 1999. However, 64% of the Internet hosts (with 102 million users) were in Canada and the United States; 24.3% (with 42 million users) in Europe; and 6.3% in Japan, Australia, and New Zealand (19 million users) leaving only 5.4% (16 million users) for the developing countries (ITU, 1999b).[2] Because it would be unrealistic to expect widespread ownership of personal computers in low-income countries, Kelly and Petrazzini have argued that a more feasible approach would be "to disperse PCs with Internet access in public places" (p. 3).

Smaller countries with a literate and educated populace are well placed to take advantage of the communication revolution. Schumacher (1973) popularized the phrase "small is beautiful" in relation to the problem of production. He saw merit in the principle of right livelihood in Buddha's Noble Eightfold Path because it implied "such a thing as Buddhist economics" (p. 44). Gunaratne (1997) argued that Buddhist values did not stand in the way of countries like Sri Lanka taking advantage of the Third Communication Revolution to compete in the world material economy and enter the portals of the information society. Carrying Schumacher's metaphor further, one can argue that relatively small countries, whether Buddhist (e.g., Sri Lanka), Islamic (e.g., Malaysia), or Hindu (e.g., Mauritius), as well as "fertile spots" in big countries (e.g., Bangalore, India), have a good chance of becoming influential players in the world economy (Gunaratne, Safar Hasim, & Kasenally, 1997). The World Economic Forum's Competitiveness Index (Hu, Sachs, &Warner, 1997) placed "*the dynamic, small, open economies*" of Singapore and Hong Kong at the very top both in 1996 and 1997—ahead of all other industrialized countries because those two economies consistently excelled "in nearly every major area that matters for competitiveness" (p. 20). These two entrepot economies retained their top ranks in 1998 as well (World Economic Forum [WEF], 1998).

The much-disparaged old development paradigm—the "neo-liberal account," as McDowell (1997) calls it—associated with Lerner (1958), Rostow (1960), and Schramm (1964) served as a predictor of *modernization*. Rostow (1960) had argued that change in Europe had evolved slowly until a critical mass of people and resources had reached a takeoff point, at which time economic growth became self-sustaining. Lerner (1958) found in the Middle East some of the same patterns Rostow had described in Europe. Lerner, however, found that mass media use had an apparent influence in stimulating rapid change through the users' inculcation of empathy—the ability to imagine what might be. Lerner's semitheory postulated that urbanization and literacy, followed by media participation and political participation, produced the critical mass of "modernity" that propelled countries to the takeoff point of self-sustaining economic and social growth.[3] Lerner defined the goal of development as Western-style democracy. Schramm (1964) added to this paradigm by advocating the use of mass media as a key component of development programs because they functioned as the "great multiplier."[4]

This paper explores the hypothesis that the variables constituting the old paradigm, with refined operational definitions to fit the Information Age, can serve as predictors of informatization as well. Nora and Minc (1980) used the term *informatization* to describe the widespread use of computer networks in organizational operations, as well as the growing importance of information in societal development. To compete in the world system's material economy, countries require the educational and technological sophistication to exploit the global information infrastructure. An informatized society is a knowledge-based society that has ready access to communication media, telecommunication, and computer networks. Kuo (1993, p. 324; 1994, p. 143) looked at informatization in terms of three dimensions: *people, infrastructure*, and *economy*. He used two indicators to measure the people dimension: literacy rate and level of education. He measured the infrastructure dimension with indicators on the use of mass media, telecommunications, and computerization; and the economy dimension with indicators on information workers and the information economy. Kuo argued that the economy dimension represented the level of "informatization." To informatize, a nation still must have the prerequisites of the old paradigm—*literacy* and *media participation*—plus some more attributes: a better-educated people, a higher propensity to use telecommunications, and competence to apply computer technology. Kuo's model omitted the old paradigm's prerequisite of *urbanization*.

To explore our hypothesis, we revised Kuo's informatization model by restoring urbanization as an antecedent variable and placing literacy and educational level (tertiary enrollment ratio) as independent variables, with economic status (per capita GNP), telephone density, and Internet host density as dependent variables (see Figure 1, p. 182). The revised model retained the indicators of media participation—penetration of daily newspapers, TV, and radio—as the intervening variables that would generate empathy and political participation[5] and facilitate the interactive growth of the three dependant variables. It omitted Kuo's Telex indicator because electronic mail is in the process of displacing it. It replaced Kuo's computer density variable, as well as his computer application and IT expenditure variables, with a single *Internet host density* variable as the main indicator of informatization,[6] provided it is based on a strong national telecommunication infrastructure, that is, telephone density. The revised model excluded the share of the information sector in the economy and the proportion of information workers in the labor force—the two variables denoting Kuo's economy dimension—because data on these variables are not available for the majority of developing countries. It substituted economic status, that is, per capita income, as one of the three interactive dependent variables that stimulated and denoted the level of informatization.

This essay will, first, provide a general review of the recent literature on telecommunication and development paying attention to both the positive, *utopian*, and the negative, *dystopian*, views. Then, it will examine the impact of electronic infrastructures on the state of *capitalism* and point out the relevance of macroscopic theory to dissect global interconnections in terms of economic and trade relations. Finally, it will assess the state of global informatization using our revised informatization model, and demonstrate that even the Human Development Index, formulated by the U.N. Development Program, is highly related to elements associated with informatization.

PROS AND CONS: A LITERATURE REVIEW

One may analyze the literature reviewed in this section through the theoretical lens developed by Lee (1997) and McDowell (1997). Lee (1997) says the concept of development has at least three dimensions: *economic growth, equitable distribution*, and *satisfaction of basic needs*. The concept may also encompass political democracy, equitable distribution of world wealth, and environmental quality. He outlines three broad theoretical models—*individual deficiency* (e.g., Lerner, 1958; Schramm, 1964), *social-institutional deficiency* (e.g., Lipton, 1977), and *international deficiency* (e.g., Wallerstein, 1974; Galtung, 1980)—that explain the obstacles to development so conceived. The individual deficiency model assigns information and communication high priority and the other two a lower priority. However, telecommunications has an important role to play in development because it helps "to reduce the time and distance in information transmission, and improve efficiency in synthesizing and generating new information" (p. 8). Lee (1997) endorsed Parker's (1992) view that economic growth was the basic core of development and that the key to wealth creation was mobilizing the resources of the country focusing on three key factors: *investment in human capital, investment in basic infrastructure*, and *institutional reform*. Telecommunication infrastructure can help develop human information power and intelligence in the process of wealth creation thereby achieving the goals of development.

McDowell (1997), who used a historical and critical perspective in a case study of India, called the dominant theoretical models of communication and development "conventional or neo-liberal" approaches (p. 6). He identified three such models (see Figure 2, p. 183): *modernization* (equivalent to Lee's individual deficiency), *transnational communications* (based on the concepts of liberal economics such as market and trade theory in contrast to Lee's international deficiency), and *telecommunications for development*. (Lee's telecommunication model of development, based on Parker's approach, is an outgrowth of the three models to which Lee refers. Lee's model combines what McDowell identifies as transnational and telecommunication for development models.)

McDowell finds fault with the "neo-liberal account" as "both eclectic and inconsistent" because "it uses liberal economic theory to point to the necessity of policy liberalization, draws upon public choice political theory to explain why these required policy changes did not take place, and then turns to statist political and development theory to explain why these changes became possible in the early 1990s" (p. 7). He uses a theoretical framework that Cox (1987) developed (by applying Gramsci's concept of *hegemony*) to "link the investigation of social groups related to production, of historical forms of state, and of world order" (p. 7). Alongside this framework, he considers the relevance of dependency analysis of communications (what Lee calls international deficiency model), democratic communications, and gender and social-group analysis of communications processes and content. He challenges the main theoretic elements of the neo-liberal account and provides an alternative interpretation of India's transition from statism to greater liberalism in economic and communication policies.

McDowell (1997) says the modernization (and developmental communication) model, borrowed from neo-liberal political and economic analysis, defined development as economic growth with the North providing "the essential view of the future" (p. 24). The transnational communications (and liberalization) model defined development as the fastest economic growth produced by the most efficient use of economic and human resources through "capital mobility, transnational investment and production, and trade according to comparative advantage" (p. 31). This approach reflected economic theories of globalization, as well as technological determinist theories of technological convergence (e.g., telecommunications, computing, and mass media). The telecommunications for development model, which follows from the tradition of modernization, focused "less on attitude change and institutional shifts to promote development and more on the role of efficient physical infrastructure in allowing economic expansion and social integration" (p. 27). It "borrows most directly from engineering concepts and some inductive studies of telecommunication benefits rather than from the a priori assumptions of micro-economic theories" (p. 30). It makes little differentiation among transnational, national, and local economic uses of telecommunications.

McDowell's (1997) systematic analysis and critique of development models help us to differentiate between the utopians and the dystopians. The utopians are those who see merit in the "neo-liberal account." (Thus McDowell may also be skeptical of the perspectives of the new institutional economists[7] such as Spiller [Levy & Spiller, 1996] and Greenstein, 1993, on conditions promoting investment in information infrastructure and the relationship between information technology investments and development.) The dystopians are those who seek alternative explanations through "historical and critical analysis," including the political economy approach that focuses on Marxism and dependency. In this sense, Lee's (1997) telecommunications model represents the "neo-liberal account" because it presumes that economic growth is the basic core of development. It hypothesizes that *telecommunications infrastructure* (via the development of domestic brainpower) produces *capital for development*; and that the latter (via the primary, secondary, and tertiary sectors) leads to *wealth* as reflected in higher living standards, satisfaction of basic needs, greater national security, democracy, equality, fewer class and ethnic cleavages, and so forth. (p. 11).

Lee (1997) admits that empirical studies confirming the presumed beneficial effects of telecommunications "are few and the findings are far from conclusive" (p. 10). Ang (1993) has pointed out that modern telecommunications studies, which began to emerge from the 1970s, consistently showed an association between telecommunications and economic development (e.g., Berry, 1981; Hardy, 1980; Hudson, 1984; Moss, 1986; Parker, 1981; Pierce & Jequier, 1983; and Saunders, Warford, & Wellenius, 1983). Jipp (1963) had conducted the first study showing such a correlation, and Kellerman (1990) had found that trade, rather than tourism, explained telecommunications except in Britain and the United States. Stone's (1993) study of four countries found that telecommunications investments were more effective in upper middle-income countries than in lower middle-income countries. Ang (1993) reviewed the aforementioned literature in reporting his own study, which, contrary to expectation from previous studies, showed that the economic sectors caused international telephone traffic. His study, which used quarterly data on international telecommunication traffic as the independent variable, yielded mixed results.

Hukill (1993), developed "a proactive approach to the study of telecommunications rather than a reactive (impacts and effects) or passively derived (statistical representation) approach" (p. 333). He formulated a framework for the study of telecommunication policy from a problem-oriented, interdisciplinary perspective. However, his was not an empirical study that analyzed data. Samarajiva and Shields (1990), who arrived at the conclusion that an adequate theory of telecommunication and development required an adequate treatment of power implications of communication technologies, reviewed much of the literature that backed the Parsonian assumption of the desirability of the integration of the two variables.

On the basis of the ITU (1995) rationale outlined in the previous section, as well as the new thinking of Frank (1993), a founding father of dependency theory (or the international deficiency model), this essay takes the view that the state of capitalism engendered by the Third Communication Revolution has given nations—big and small—little option but to effectively compete in the world material economy. As Ihonvbere (1996) puts it, "Nations of the world really have no choice about joining or opting out of the new information age" (p. 351). Although this essay takes a predominantly utopian ("neo-liberal") view of the revolution, it also recognizes the need to take into account the negative consequences that the dystopians (historical and critical analysts) have described. For instance, planners and researchers should pay serious attention to Castells's (1996–1998) assertion that the rise of a global network society has greatly enhanced the prospects for grassroots social mobilization while it has also restructured and exacerbated poverty worldwide.

The Utopians

As Lee (1997) has already pointed out, researchers have not conclusively established the causal effect of telecommunications on economic growth. The correlation, however, is very clear. The utopians, starting with the Independent Commission for Worldwide Telecommunications Development (1984), better known as the Maitland Commission, have placed their faith on this correlation to express their views on the direct and indirect benefits of telecommunications. It established the objective that by the early part of the 21st century "virtually the whole of mankind should be brought within easy reach of a telephone." The commission said, "Our study of the role they can play has persuaded us that telecommunications can increase the efficiency of economic, commercial and administrative activities, improve the effectiveness of social and emergency services and distribute the social, cultural and economic benefits of the process of development more equitably throughout a community and a nation" (pp. 10–11). However, it warned:

> While the benefits of an efficient telecommunications system in individual cases can readily be quantified, the same is not true of the benefits conferred at the national level. *[Although] a strong correlation has been established between the number of telephones per capita and economic development measured by gross domestic product, it has not been clear whether investment in telecommunications contributes to economic growth or economic growth leads to investment in telecommunications* [italics added]. That there is a link between the two is, however, beyond question. (p. 9)

Following the Maitland Report, particularly the World Bank and the ITU have emphasized the need to improve telecommunications services for development. Thus Mustafa, Laidlaw, and Brand (1997) lament the relative neglect of telecommunications in sub-Saharan Africa in an age when the general trend for economic activity throughout the world has been to become more communications intensive. They have also pointed out the "specific ability of telecommunications to enable producers to overcome difficulties of distance from and access to regional and world markets," as well as the "sustained decline in costs of provision of services under the impact of technological change" (p. 1).

Mansell and Wehn (1998), in their "source book" synthesizing the deliberations of the working group of the U.N. Commission on Science and Technology for Development, offered the central conclusion that information and communication technologies (ICTs) could "make a major contribution to sustainable development" but that major risks might accompany such opportunities (p. 256). They concluded that the effective use of ICTs as tools of development required "investment in a combination of technological and social capabilities," and that countries could enter into new partnerships or coalitions "to address a variety of coordination, investment mobilization, and social problems" (p. 256).

Because the distinctive elements of the *transnational model* and the *telecommunication development model* are not always easy to flesh out in much of the utopian literature, it is not easy to clearly classify the utopian literature under the threefold McDowell (1997) rubrics. However, the institutional utopianism of the World Trade Organization (WTO), the World Bank, the Organization for Economic Cooperation and Development (OECD), and similar international organizations seems to fit the transnational model. The views of Al Gore (1996), who extols the benefits of telecommunications in promoting the Global Information Infrastructure, also fit this model. Gore has called for a global consensus to ensure five core principles to accommodate the best information network: *private investment, competition, flexible regulation, open access*, and *universal service*.[8] ITU (1998), however, points out that "reconciling the three contending criteria of contemporary universal service—availability, accessibility, and affordability—has proven a difficult task for most governments" (p. 65).

The views of Mahathir (1996) are more in consonance with the telecommunications for development model. He asserted that the "Internet-worked" electronic global village offered opportunities for national and local problem resolution, although equity and universal access continued to remain key issues in multiracial and multireligious societies. Mahathir argued that electronic governance might help realize the ideals of participatory democracy with greater transparency. The responsibility for censorship[9] might pass on from public agencies to societal organizations and institutions—the family, the school, the corporation, and the community. Read and Youtie's (1996) work also fits the telecommunication for development model. They concluded that "government policies that facilitate the growth of telecommunications businesses are certain economic winners" (p. 7). Their case studies showed that Singapore and Richardson, Texas, had become telecommunications winners, primarily because of their local quality-of-life conditions and their geographical positions. New Jersey and LaGrange, Georgia, which had adopted "build it and they will come" (p. 109) strategies, could be judged as winners or losers depending on whether their telecommunications-infrastructure investments would pay off in education, health care, and new jobs.

The views of Hudson (1997), Stevenson (1994), Solomon (1997), and Menzies (1996) appear to fit the transnational model. Hudson (1997) wrote that four major technological trends—capacity, digitization, ubiquity, and convergence—were driving the current telecommunications revolution, which paralleled the emergence of a global economy. She contended that investment in telecommunications could in itself contribute to economic, social, and political development. Reliable tele-communications networks could improve the productivity and efficiency of agriculture, industry, and social services. New approaches to financing telecommunications in the developing countries were also creating incentives for investment that should help to close the information gaps between the advanced and the developing regions. Stevenson (1994) surmised that the Third Communication Revolution was ending government monopolies on information, allowing insurgents to organize, destroying the legitimacy of repressive governments, and bringing down governments. Solomon (1997) argued that society would evolve along the complex international pathways of the global information superhighway just like the way that "American society evolved along the telegraph lines and railroads that opened up the West, and in the spaces created by the interstate highway network built after World War II" (p. 7). The new technologies would have profound implications in relation to decentralization and centralization; fragmentation, yet integration; transparency, mobilization, and rationalization; acceleration, and virtuality. Menzies (1996), just as much as Hudson, had no doubt that the emerging information highway was becoming the axis of the new economy. It was increasingly the place where work was dispatched to new global and local labor markets, where work was done and supervised, and where "value" was added.

The utopian views of Irving (1996), Knight (1996), Goldstein (1996), and Rudenstein (1996) are also weighted toward the transnational model though some elements of the telecommunications for development model are also present. Irving (1996) posited that developing countries could and must become a part of the information age because no country could be truly rich unless it had a robust tele-communications and information industry. Developing countries had the potential to leapfrog into sophisticated technologies such as wireless and satellites at a fraction of the cost of laying wire. Knight (1996), who endorsed Irving's utopianism, asserted that countries that failed to embrace the revolution were bound to become further marginalized and left out. The new technologies were lowering the cost of storing, processing, and transmitting information, knowledge, and even wisdom. Therefore, Knight contended that the less-developed countries must build new learning systems, and mobilize international resources to create massive programs, community information and learning centers. He said that Brazil, Russia, and South Africa were among the countries that had great potential in building their information infrastructures primarily because of military reasons. Goldstein (1996) said that different countries had used different ways to establish information networks. In Costa Rica, an early adopter of the Internet for government business, the law required all citizens to be computer literate. The commercial and the academic sectors were also highly involved in extending Costa Rica's information network. On the other hand, the Spanish Post, Telegraph, and Telecommunication administration (PTT), which had acquired the monopoly rights to a number of PTTs in

Latin America, was trying to crush the academic Internet services. China's Ministry of Post and Telecommunications was also trying to control the Internet to the detriment of the country's academic network. Rudenstein (1996) compared the advent of the World Wide Web to that of research libraries at the end of the 19th century. Through the Internet, people could roam through the electronic equivalent of book stacks, with assistance from the electronic equivalent of reference librarians. Moreover, the Internet could provide unusually rich course materials—densely woven, multilayered, and highly demanding new course materials.

Finally, the modernization model appears to fit the views of Fukuyama (1996) and Rheingold (1993). Fukuyama (1996) asserted that the new technologies had promoted the democratic revolution at the level of ideology and institutions and that, in the future, the real impact of these technologies would be at the levels of civil society and culture. Rheingold (1993) asserted that at the political level, computer-mediated communication (CMC), popularized by the communication revolution, had created the "capacity to challenge the existing political hierarchy's monopoly on powerful communications media, and perhaps thus revitalize citizen-based democracy" (p. 14). CMC had the potential to change people's lives at two other levels: At the individual level, young people could migrate to CMC spaces to try new ways of experiencing the world; and at the interpersonal level, CMC offered a new capability of "many to many" communication.

The Dystopians

McDowell (1997) and other adherents of the historical and critical school—including scholars who apply the political economy approach to communication analysis on the lines of Smythe (1957), H. Schiller (1969, 1996), and D. Schiller (1999)—exemplify the general dystopian view of informatization. H. Schiller (1996) asserted that two characteristics marked the 20th century American experience with new communication technologies: the overblown promise greeting its appearance and the rapid exploitation of the technology by commercial interests. The information superhighway would be the "latest blind alley" (p. 75). In his view, "A privately constructed and owned electronic information system . . . will embody the fundamental features of a private enterprise economy: inequality of income along with the production of goods and services for profit (pp. 96–97). D. Schiller (1999) has pursued on the same lines to argue that digital capitalism has further empowered transnational corporations while exacerbating existing social inequalities; offered supple tools to promote consumerism on a transnational scale; and placed education at the mercy of proprietary market logic.

Rideout and Mosco (1997), who follow the political economy approach, have pointed out the need to balance the tendency to assess communication policy on largely economic grounds by also paying attention to "the *political* dimension of communication policy" (p. 81), particularly in relation to democracy. They examined the four central tendencies in contemporary communication policy: *commercialization, deregulation, privatization*, and *internationalization*. They argued that each of these processes suggested the value of the class power perspective, and challenged the potential to create the conditions for democratic communication. They claimed that commercialization was reshaping public communication institutions to operate along private business lines, and that deregulation was diminishing or entirely scrapping public interest requirements to allow private industry to more explicitly pursue their market interests. They said that privatization was eliminating public communication organizations through sale to private interests whereas internationalization was encouraging the development of transnational media markets "by eliminating restrictions on corporate expansion and by establishing a global regulatory apparatus to manage the transition from national to global markets" (p. 100).

Mosco (1996) has pointed out that the changes that have occurred with the opening of telecommunication markets to more than one dominant service provider have caused political economists to react in three ways. First, they have examined this development in comparison to the cartel arrangements that characterized the early days of telecommunication. Second, they have "shifted attention from service providers to business and government users, arguing that their concentrated power means that whatever competition exits will be managed to benefit their needs for efficient and cost-effective services" (pp. 90–91). Third, they have "examined the changes in discourse that accompany structural changes, specifically by exploring the roots of a shift in the dominant rhetoric from that of 'public' service provided by regulated monopolies to 'cost-based' service offered by market competitors" (p. 91).

McChesney (1997) has argued that increasing private concentration and commercialization of the information superhighway would negate democracy; and that the new communication technologies would not solve social problems—such as poverty, environmental degradation, sexism, racism, and militarism—without conscious human intervention. In his view, the current "pro-market" policies would be "little short of disastrous for the quality of life for a majority of people" worldwide; "the tension between democracy and capitalism is becoming increasingly evident, and communication—so necessary to both—can hardly serve two masters at once" (p. 74). Taking the opposite view of Rudenstein (1996), McChesney has asserted that the rise of the Internet and the information highway would place the future of communication research at U.S. universities in jeopardy because of the "pressure on universities to elicit support from the corporate sector" and to link "education and research explicitly to the needs of business" (p. 74). McChesney (1999), McChesney, Wood, and Foster (1998), and Herman and McChesney (1997) have expanded on these ideas.

Vincent (1997b) has cast doubts on the technologically driven visions of a universally accessible GII that "government officials, industry, and the majority of communication scholars" are trying to sell to the world's people. The GII would "serve little more than narrowly defined instrumental interests rather than the much larger and more encompassing goals" (p. 401) of the New World Information and

Communication Order (NWICO). Vincent (1997a) has also argued that the guiding principle in striving for a NWICO should be the notion of achieving social equity through communication. He has called on the WTO, the ITU, the World Bank, and other bodies to conduct a "dialogue on communication access" to achieve "a truly equitable situation" (p. 205). Following the same line of argument, Roach (1997) has pointed out that "information society thinking has been a hallmark of the Western world since the 1970s and that this reality was not unconnected to its strategy *vis-à-vis* the NWICO" (p. 111).

Winseck (1997) has documented such negatives in relation to Canada, where the driving forces of technological and social change have been "privatization, the commoditization of information, increased industry concentration, commercialization of the policy sphere, and the centralization of political authority" (p. 108). Thus, Canada's experience failed to reflect the "idea that new communication technologies will radically alter social relations and democratize communication" (p. 129). Winseck and Cuthbert (1997), who analyzed the recent international communication policies of North American Free Trade Agreement and the General Agreement of Trade and Tariffs, concluded that these policies "*shield* the new technologies and information services from citizens' interventions." In doing so, "they institutionalize[d] the biases of limited democracy against extensive citizen participation in public affairs, social change and the communicative generation of norms to guide the new technologies" (p. 17).

Sussman (1997), who examined both the political issues and the global dimensions of the *information society*, has claimed that the people in Third World countries who made the commodities or provided the services for foreign consumption were "the least likely to get access to the products of their labor" (p. 253). The absorption of the Third World elites into the mainstream of transnational culture would marginalize the poor even further and leave them "few, often only the most extreme, alternatives, including war" (p. 260). Sussman and Lent (1998) have drawn attention to the new international division of labor (NIDL) caused by the restructuring of telecommunications and "information society," under which transnational corporations have been able to integrate and "third worldize" labor forces in the leading and emerging industrial countries (p. 11).

Hamelink (1994), who analyzed the four major trends in world communication—digitization, consolidation, deregulation, and globalization—has argued that the accumulation of these trends have disempowered the people in important ways. "They make people powerless vis-à-vis the control of their own lives. They create a culture of silence in which people become beings for others. Disempowerment matters [because] it represents a basic violation of human rights" (p. 148). The proliferation of digital technologies, for instance, disempowered people through new forms of dependence and vulnerability. The solution would be a people's self-empowerment on a global scale—a global public sphere "in which people can freely express themselves, share information, opinions, ideas, and cultural experiences, challenge the accountability of power holders, and take responsibility for the quality of our 'secondary environment'" (p. 149). In similar vein, Dunn (1995) lamented that debt, dependency, and underdevelopment fashioned the Caribbean telecommunications policy; that global restructuring had benefited the monopoly operators; and that additional competition and externally generated policy initiatives could place the Caribbean "in a wider net of dependency" without resort to national and regionally based strategies (p. 221)

Mody, Bauer, and Straubhaar (1995) have skeptically referred to telecommunication investments in the developing world as a "present-day gold rush" (p. xv). They have claimed that the technologically driven rhetoric has failed to address the economic, social, organizational, administrative, and political aspects of communication problems; that the "information highway and other such proposals driven by economics and technology are not socially and spatially neutral" (p. xvii), and, therefore, do not benefit the hundreds of millions with limited purchasing power. Referring to sub-Saharan Africa, Pratt (1996) advised policy makers to "debunk the notion that having every form of communication technology will result in the modernization of their countries" (p. 58). In his view, what the African countries require is "a pragmatic, issues-management approach, which emphasizes long-term planning and the practical utility of technologies in benefiting the public at large" (p. 58). Pratt's approach, however, fails to recognize the consequences of the failure of indigenous cultures to adapt to the changes wrought by the ongoing communication revolution: their inability to compete effectively in the world material economy.[10] Mustafa, Laidlaw, and Brand (1997) have pointed out the absence of a consensus among the interest groups in sub-Saharan African countries on the benefits they can secure from expanded and modernized telephone networks. These countries, they argued, should accelerate the pace of change by adopting innovative methods "of reform, of sector organization, and of investment finance" (p. 11). Ihonvbere (1996) lamented that Africa, which increasingly lacked the capacity to generate foreign exchange and attract the inflow of investments, stood "nowhere" in the new globalization of the financial marketplace.

Rota and Rodriguez (1996) claimed that modern information technologies had become another source of domination. They said "the incongruous ways" in which Latin American societies adopted modern technologies led to widening the gap that excluded "large majorities from participating in national decision-making process" (p. 250). Petrazzini (1995) used the political economy approach to analyze the telecommunication reform experiences of Argentina and Mexico while also briefly examining the reforms in eight other countries: Chile, Colombia, Jamaica, Malaysia, Thailand, South Africa, Venezuela, and Uruguay. He found that the whole productive system quickly felt the mistakes committed in the design of new telecom regimes, which clearly had multiplier effects. He found that the success or failure of telecom privatization depended on two variables: "(1) state autonomy from opposition of local interest groups, and (2) cohesiveness of policy makers, or, in its absence, the concentration of power in the head of the executive branch" (p. 192). He contended that "privatization and liberalization are intricately linked, yet different processes" (p. 194). The main beneficiaries of the reform process were the telecom service suppliers and the financial institutions that purchased the state-owned enterprises. He noted that "the opening of the economy to private ownership calls for a closing of the polity to widespread participation" (p. 197).

Interpretation and Summary

Research so far has not conclusively established telecommunications as the causal agent of economic development. However, little doubt exists on the high correlation between these two variables. The historical and critical school of thought, including the adherents of the Marxist and dependency typologies of political economy, has challenged the "neo-liberal" approaches to promote development through the models that McDowell (1997) identifies as *modernization and development communication, telecommunication for development*, and *liberalization and transnational communications*. Lee (1997) has conceptualized a "neo-liberal" telecommunications model encompassing the elements of the three models that McDowell has distinguished. Lee apparently sees his broad telecommunications model as an outgrowth of the modernization model, which he describes as the individual deficiency model, as well as what he calls the social-institutional deficiency and international deficiency (dependency) models. McDowell sees the dependency model as part of an alternative framework based on Gramsci's concept of hegemony and supplemented by the concepts of democratic communication, and social and gender participation.

This essay identifies the adherents of the "neo-liberal" theories as utopians and their critics as dystopians. It takes the pragmatic view that informatization is in the interest of all countries. However, it sees merit in the dystopian views to which policy makers must pay attention when they make decisions to expand their telecommunication and computerization infrastructure to compete in the world material economy.

The utopians believe that countries can best achieve open access and universal service within a framework of competition, flexibility, and private enterprise. They also believe that the global village offers vast opportunities for countries to solve national and local problems, and enable students to access knowledge through multilayered electronic libraries along the global information highway. Investment in telecommunications, moreover, would produce multiplier effects leading to economic, social, and political development. They assert that the new communication technologies will undercut monopolies on information, curtail censorship, and promote citizen-based democracy. They also point out that developing countries can leapfrog into the new sophisticated technologies.

The dystopians say that the economic arguments for the new technologies must be balanced against the political effects, as well as against the social, organizational, and administrative aspects. Countries must pay heed to their security and sovereignty whereas citizens ought to be concerned with privacy and surveillance. They point out the negative effects of commercialization, privatization, deregulation, and internationalization. They say that the tension between capitalism and democracy will further erode the latter and lead to commercialization of education as well. Such an environment would further downgrade the goals of NWICO. They point out case studies to document that the new technologies will not democratize communication. They assert that these technologies will disempower people through new forms of dependence. Moreover, a wrong decision on a telecommunication regime would have negative multiplier effects, and the main beneficiaries would be telecom service suppliers and investors. They also say that the large majority of the world's poor cannot bear the cost of accessing the new technologies.

Some internal contradictions, however, are apparent within the work of some of those who fall into one or other of the two groups. As Mansell puts it, "Many of the 'dystopians' are coming to regard ICTs in the form of decentralized cyberspace networks used by actors supporting democratic movements and some NGO activities as a 'good' thing despite the fact that in order to participate in these networks, an infrastructure of some kind is needed—and that generally means the imposition of technology and market arrangements that are normally associated by these writers with 'bad' outcomes."[11] Hamelink (1994), for instance, asserts that people's networks can emerge "to create a public sphere in 'cyber space'" (p. 144). Sussman (1997) concedes that ICTs have enabled people "to preserve some form of dyadic relations" (p. 265). Vincent (1997) recognizes that private agencies and NGOs can use the GII to promote "the interests and role of people in democratizing communication" (p. 403).

THE STATE OF CAPITALISM

Globalization: The End of Nation?

Contemporary economists and political scientists (e.g., Greider, 1997; Jameson & Miyoshi, 1998; Sassen, 1996) have taken a fresh look at Marx and Engels's *Communist Manifesto*, published in 1848. Lewis (1998) says that the manifesto has made a "vivid, even visionary presentation of capitalism as an untamable force that could sweep away the Middle Ages and anything else in its way"—a description of capitalism that "resembles the restless, anxious and competitive world of today's global economy." The manifesto had "recognized the unstoppable wealth-creating power of capitalism, predicted it would conquer the world, and warned that this inevitable globalization of national economies and cultures would have divisive and painful consequences" (p. B9). Scholars have drawn attention to some of the warnings in the manifesto such as the destruction of all old-established national industries and their replacement by "new industries whose introduction becomes a life or death question for all civilized nations . . . industries whose products are consumed not only at home but in every quarter of the globe" (p. B9). It elucidated that the constant revolutionizing of production, uninterrupted disturbance of social conditions, everlasting uncertainty, and agitation distinguished the bourgeois epoch from all earlier ones. The manifesto's warnings about capitalism's periodic crises foreshadowed the Great Depression of the 1930s and the more recent crises in Mexico and Asia.

Castells (1996–1998), who has attempted "a definitive account of the transition to an information society" (Calabrese, 1999, p. 172) through interdisciplinary discourse, argues that within a new global system of power characterized by many sources of authority, nation-states will lose their sovereignty and band together in multilateral networks. Sakamoto (1994) and other scholars have examined in some depth the internationalization of the state, the globalization of political economy, as well as transnational social movements, all of which are related to the state of capitalism shaped by the Third Wave and the GII. Falk (1994) asserts that the "primacy of the territorial state is being challenged as never before" (p. 498), even though by "aligning with market and other globalizing tendencies, the state may be reconceived, but not superseded, especially as long as market forces depend on militarism" (p. 498). Although the state may lose its territorial sovereignty in the Westphalian sense, Falk says it can try to retain its ascendancy by co-opting environmentalist tensions, including the concerns of the emerging forces of global civil society, and by strengthening the structures of global governance.

Transnational corporations clearly impinged on the Westphalian attributes of the nation state as a facet of the globalization of political economy in the closing decades of the 20th century. The global spread and the financial power of these corporations had rendered the lower-income states vulnerable. Schiller (1996) asserted that some "37,000 companies currently occupied the command posts of the world economic order" with the largest 100 of them, as of 1990, accounting for $3.2 trillion in global assets more than 37% of which was outside their home countries (p. 94). These megafirms had reduced the influence of the nation state.

Frank (1993), a founding father of dependency theory, now argues that "delinking" the developing countries from the "capitalist" world, as he had advocated in the 1960s, was no longer a realistic policy because the Third World could "not escape dependence" (p. 13). He states that "a materialist comparative examination of recent and past—including several millennia-old—material and ideal reality" (p. 25) shows no validity on the claims of various "isms" (e.g., capitalism and socialism). Calling the world system structure or the process of political-economic competition "capitalist" merely obfuscated the reality of that structure, which obliged all to compete effectively irrespective of public or private ownership of production. He concluded, "No economic, political, social, or cultural 'model' or 'ism' offers a guarantee for success. . . . No such model marks the end of history" (p. 25). The contemporary communication revolution has added to the momentum of global "capitalism." Robertson (1994) has argued that globalization involves both homogenizing and heterogenizing aspects—"the creation and the incorporation of locality, a process which itself largely shapes, in turn, the compression of the world as a whole" (p. 48). He called it "glocalization."

Center Views: "New Global Age"

The Organization for Economic Cooperation and Development (1997b)[12] says that a "New Global Age" has dawned, "where all countries can be active players, where people currently trapped in poverty can aspire to much better levels of material well-being" (p. 12). Rapid technological advances and an "unprecedented increase in worldwide trade of goods, services and financial assets" (p. 11) have been among the contributory factors. This "New Global Age" was predicated upon realizing at least four major challenges by 2020: *Strengthening the free and open multilateral system, pushing ahead with domestic policy reform, consolidating the integration of non-OECD countries into the global economy*, and *ensuring sustainable development.*

The World Trade Organization[13] has promulgated views similar to those of the OECD. Ruggiero (1997), the former director-general of WTO, asserted that technology had created the "global village" that McLuhan (1964) had predicted. In the global economy, knowledge had become a more important production factor than *labor, raw materials*, or *capital*. A new and more equitable relationship was emerging between the developed and the developing countries thereby paving the way for a single, borderless global economy. The World Bank (1997, 1999) too saw the positive aspect of the borderless global economy. However, the bank pointed out that despite globalization, the state would continue to play a vital role in defining "the policies and rules for those within [the state's] jurisdiction" (p. 12).

Ruggiero (1997) pointed out that the services sector had the greatest potential for global free trade because digital and communications technologies were creating the possibility of borderless electronic trade in key services sectors. Ruggiero saw four broad characteristics of the emerging borderless service economy: the increasing indifference to geography, distance, and time; the creation by the services industries—especially financial services, telecommunications, and transport—of a global infrastructure for the world economy; the emergence of a knowledge-based global services economy; and the equalization of relations between countries and regions by borderless technology. Ruggiero asserted that globalization had caused a significant shift in economic power to the South—a shift that was likely to continue at a growth rate of 5 to 6% a year up to the year 2020. The developing countries would almost double their share of world output, from about 16% in 1992 to about 30% in 2020.

WTO handles three areas of agreements: the General Agreement on Tariffs and Trade (GATT), which deals with trade in goods; the General Agreement on Trade in Services (GATS), which deals with trade in services; and the Agreement on Trade-Related Aspects of Intellectual Property (TRIPS), which deals with such issues as copyright, trademarks, patents, industrial designs and trade secrets. WTO conducted three major negotiations on the infrastructural services—telecommunications, financial, and transport—after the Uruguay Round.

Periphery View

World leaders have generally succumbed to the advent of globalization. For example, Kumaratunge (1997), the president of Sri Lanka, referred to the reality of the onset of globalization even though its effects were by no means entirely beneficial. She said,

> In theory, galloping globalization, and the rapid dissolution of national boundaries—economic, political and social—open up vast new possibilities, hitherto unimaginable, of improving the lot of humanity. The process of globalization should render possible the realization of equal opportunities for all peoples, and the guarantee of a level playing field for all nations, through the marvels of modern science and technology, especially information technology and the knowledge industry, so that the full benefit of the liberalization of economic systems could be obtained by all. The age-old practice of the stronger nations imposing their will on the weaker should come to an end. But in essence the impact of globalization on developing countries has been unfair. The distribution of the benefits of accelerated trade and capital flows have, so far, been highly uneven. It is true that some developing countries are among the beneficiaries of globalization, but their number is small. The income gap between the rich and poor is widening, when it should be narrowing. . . . Globalization also tends to aggravate inequalities within countries, both developed and developing, resulting in the exacerbation of internal tensions and problems such as crime, drug abuse, environmental damage and urban squalor. (Kumaratunge, 1997)

Global Theories

A "New Global Age" requires more refined global (or macrolevel) theories to dissect the reality of the world as an interconnected unit. Although microlevel and midrange theories have their uses, a clear need exists to use and refine macrolevel theories in the age of globalization. Galtung (1993) laments:

> Surprisingly little is known about the world, *geo, gaia*, as one economic system. Liberal economics is the economics of countries . . . or the economics of enterprises . . . and their relations. Marxist-Leninist economics is the economics of class relations, within and among societies, and is more global. Liberal economics focuses on growth, Marxist economics on distribution. Both are necessary, neither of them sufficient to answer the key question: how is the world doing, seen as one country, one enterprise, one class? (pp. 33–34)

Wallerstein (1974) conceptualized a world system that had the characteristics of an organism. Core states and peripheral areas constituted a world-economy. Semiperipheral areas, a necessary structural element in a world-economy, existed "between the core and the periphery on a series of dimensions, such as the complexity of economic activities, strength of the state machinery, cultural integrity, etc." (p. 349). A hierarchy of occupational tasks characterized a world-economy, where "tasks requiring higher levels of skill and greater capitalization" were reserved for higher-ranking areas (p. 350). Wallerstein (1974) applied the term *world-economy* to describe the widespread economic links that European colonialism had fostered in the late 15th and early 16th century. Frank and Gills (1993) have attempted to document the thesis that the contemporary world system, the motor force of which is the process of capital accumulation, has a history of at least 1,000 years. Both Wallerstein (1974) and Frank (1993) agree on the center-periphery "capitalist" structure of the world material economy. However, whereas Wallerstein traces this world system to the Middle Ages, Frank traces it to at least 1,000 years back. Galtung and Vincent (1992) applied the center-periphery structure embedded in the world-system theory to explain the phenomenon of world communication heavily colored by "occidental cosmology" (p. 13). Dependency theorists used the center-periphery structure to explain underdevelopment in the world system (Gunaratne & Conteh, 1988).

Because economic power reflects the ability of states to compete in the world material economy, a structural division of the world based on share of world trade— *center, semiperiphery,* and *periphery*—appears to be quite pertinent for analyzing how the world works (Gunaratne, 1999). Although Galtung (1980) theorized the existence of five types of imperialism (or dominance) in the center-periphery relationships—*economic, political, military, communication,* and *cultural*—one can argue that economic dominance can indeed be more basic than the others. Economic success enabled the Four Dragons to reach the level of *first-tier semiperiphery.*[14] Galtung (1980) explained that the world consisted of Center and Periphery nations; each nation, in turn, had its center and periphery. He described the phenomenon of the Center-Periphery inequality as a major form of *structural violence. Disharmony of interest* existed between the periphery in the Periphery and the periphery in the Center whereas *harmony of interest* prevailed between the *bridgeheads* at the center in the Periphery and the center in the Center. Galtung's structural formulation is a formidable construct upon which to build a global theory sans the bias of what Frank (1993) calls ideal-"isms" of the right or the left.

The basic premise of dependency/world-system theory has been the focus of the work of Barnett et al. (1996), who have examined the global telecommunication network structure, and the structure of physical communication—trade volume, mail, and so forth. Their examination of telecommunication indicators such as system density, connectedness, centrality, and integrativeness revealed a similar structure for the network at three points in time. The results supported the basic premise of the dependency/world-system theory "that position in the world communication system affected a country's economic and social development" (p. 40). Barnett et al. have found a similar structure in the international transportation network. Their extended research will examine international computer networks as well. Various other researchers (e.g., Brams, 1966; Breiger, 1982; Chase-Dunn, 1975; Smith & Nemeth, 1988; Snyder & Kick, 1979) have also analyzed aggregated cross-national data to test the dependency/world-system theory. A major problem for researchers using this theoretical perspective is the difficulty of gathering global data showing dependency.

The modest aim of this paper is to examine the process of informatization, the turn-of-the century equivalent of modernization, by extracting and extending the variables associated with the classical modernization theory—*urbanization, literacy* (expanded to include *tertiary-level education*), and *media participation* (Lerner 1958, p. 57) as predictors of *economic status, telephone density*, and *Internet host density*—three essential informatization variables associated with the telecommunication and transnational models of development.

AN OVERVIEW OF GLOBAL INFORMATIZATION

In the context of the compelling need to go global, it is pertinent to ascertain the degree of informatization the countries of the world have reached. Glaeser (1997) has already compiled a ranking of 45 countries by information technology using an index based on three fundamental variables: *the availability of direct-dial international service, the number of fax machines per capita*, and *the computing power in MIPS (millions of instructions per second) per capita*.[15] These three variables, he says, "explain almost all of the variations in overall quality of technology" (p. 53). When controlled for these three, Glaeser says, no other information technology item showed a significant correlation with the overall technology ranking. The three variables, which have a high degree of complementarity, appear in the same countries "because some countries have the human, physical and legal infrastructure for using new technologies and other countries do not" (p. 53). Thus, contrary to Pratt's (1996) issues-management approach of technology selection, Glaeser points out the need to introduce many technologies simultaneously.

Measuring Informatization

Researchers have adopted complex methods to measure what the ITU (1995) has officially termed informatization. Muchlup (1962), Porat (1976), OECD (1981), and Katz (1988) represent one tradition of measuring informatization. They have measured informatization by estimating the share of the information sector in the total labor force of the economy. Jussawalla, Lamberton, and Karunaratne (1988) have also provided some theoretical and methodological guidelines for the measurement of the information sector. These estimates, however, leave out other dimensions and indicators of the informatization process. Japanese scholars, particularly those in Tokyo's Research Institute of Telecommunications and Economics, represent the other major tradition of measuring informatization (Ito, 1980). They use complicated composite indexes based on information-related expenditure as a proportion of total household expenses. Other Japanese scholars have generated complicated formulas to measure the flow, supply, and consumption of information (Kuo, 1993).

The National Computerization Agency (NCA, 1997) of South Korea has devised an *informatization index* comprising three subindexes: information infrastructure, information use, and informatization support. The *information-infra-*

structure subindex includes data on the number of public telephone lines, lines for data communication, private communication-information devices, and TV sets. The *information-use* subindex includes data on the number of international calls made during the year and people's use of fax machines, mobile phones, pagers, the Internet, and databases. The *informatization-support* subindex uses data on telecom-related investment, the publication of academic information-related papers and the size of IT-related manpower and research personnel. NCA has set Korea's 1990 index at 100 and used it as a base for comparison. On this basis, the NCA claimed that Korea had a 90% growth in informatization in 1994–1995, just behind Germany's 99.4% growth.[16]

The Korean index seems appropriate for measuring informatization in advanced countries that have reliable databases. However, its usefulness is limited, just like the indexes developed by the Japanese scholars and the Muchlup School. Kuo (1993, 1994) has criticized such indexes because they take a unidimensional approach. He says that, because the movement toward an information society is multidimensional, a more appropriate model would be one comprising indicators that collectively measure the level and the process of informatization of a given society. He used two criteria to identify "good" indicators: availability of relevant data gathered over a period and the availability of such data from many societies for cross-national analysis. Kuo proposed a more modest three-dimensional informatization model comprising 12 indicators that, not surprisingly, overlap with the classical modernization variables. As Mowlana (1996) correctly points out, following the end of the Cold War the "'rise' of the dominant paradigm was indeed real, [and] its reported decline was only a myth" (p. 207).

Table 1 through Table 4 provide the data on *population* and nine variables associated with informatization for 108 economies with a population of a million or more. Table 1 (see pp. 184–185) provides the data for 29 (of the 51) *high-income economies* with a GNP per capita of $9,656 or more. These countries are predominantly in the advanced First World. Table 2 (see p. 186) provides the data for 23 (of the 37) *upper middle-income economies* with a per capita GNP of $3,126 to $9,655. Table 3 (see pp. 187–188) provides the data for 40 (of the 59) *lower middle-income economies* with a per capita GNP of $786 to $3,125. Finally, Table 4 (see p. 189) provides the data for 16 (of the 61) *low-income economies* with a per capita GNP of $785 or less. Although the World Bank has listed 61 economies in the lower-income category, Table 4 excluded three quarters of them because they each had less than one telephone per 100 people or less than one Internet host per 1,000 people.

Test of Informatization Model

The correlation matrix (see Table 5, p. 190), based on data for all 108 economies, show statistically significant ($p < 0.001$ at 95% confidence level) covariations of the nine variables in the revised informatization model (Figure 1) adapted from that of Kuo (1993, 1994).

Antecedent variable: Urbanization, which we introduced as the antecedent variable, has a definite but small correlation (0.38) with X_1, literacy, and a moderate correlation (0.54) with X_2, tertiary enrollment ratio—the two independent variables. Lerner (1958) had hypothesized that after reaching the "critical optimum" of 25%, urbanization ceased to play a determinant role in the modernization process (p. 63). In the contemporary world system, only Rwanda and Burundi have not reached the 10% level of urbanization needed for "take-off." Those still below the "critical optimum" are Nepal, Uganda, Malawi, Papua New Guinea, Eritrea, Niger, Bangladesh, Vietnam, Thailand, and Sri Lanka. Clearly, the high-income economies are very high on urbanization with Portugal, at 37%, occupying the lowest end. Urbanization is high in the upper middle-income economies as well—the lowest being 50% for South Africa. In the lower middle-income category, urbanization exceeds 50% in most countries, with Papua New Guinea (17) occupying the lowest end. In the low-income economies, urbanization is highest in Armenia (69) with the average at 28%. Because urbanization explains only about 14% of the variability of literacy, it appears that an informatization model need not include urbanization as a significant variable.

Independent variables: With a correlation of 0.60, X_1, literacy, explains about 36% of the variability of X_2, tertiary enrollment. Literacy is quite high in the high-income economies with the United Arab Emirates (UAE) at the lower end—75%. Tertiary enrollment (as a percentage of the 20 to 24 age group) is also high for the majority of these economies with the UAE, at 12%, occupying the lower end. In the upper middle-income economies, Saudi Arabia and Gabon, with 66% literacy, are at the low end. Tertiary enrollment, however, is relatively low, with Argentina and Estonia's 42% the highest. In the lower middle-income category, literacy exceeds 80% in most economies, with Morocco (46%) at the lowest end. Several economies have high tertiary enrollments with Belarus (44%) at the top. At the lowest end is Papua New Guinea (3%). In the low-income category, literacy is highest in Moldova (98.3) with the average at 54%. However, tertiary enrollment is dismal with an average of only 5%.

Intervening variables: X_2, tertiary enrollment, has a high correlation with Z_1, radio density (0.79), and Z_2, TV density (0.78), and a moderate correlation with Z_3, newspaper penetration (0.54)—the hypothesized intervening variables. Literacy alone has only a moderate correlation with radio density (0.45) and TV density (0.55), and a low correlation (0.37) with newspaper penetration. Within the cluster of intervening variables—constituting the mass media infrastructure—radio density explained 69% of the variability of television density, which, in turn, explained 53% of the variability of newspaper penetration.

Radio penetration (i.e., receivers per 100 people) is extremely high in the large majority of high-income economies, particularly in the United States (211), the United Kingdom (144), Australia (138), Finland (138), Denmark (115), Canada (108), and South Korea (104). In the upper middle-income economies, radio penetration ranges from 15.5 in Botswana to 89.2 in Lebanon; and in the lower middle-income economies from 7.3 in Guatemala to 87.2 in Ukraine. In the low-income economies, the average radio density is about 10—well above the minimum standard of 5 per 100 people that the U.N. Educational, Scientific and Cultural Organization (UNESCO) set in 1962.

Television penetration (i.e., receivers per 100 people) is significant as a measure of informatization because digitization has enabled the merger of television sets and computers. In 1997, the average TV penetration for the world was 27.7 per 100 people—64.7 for high-income economies, 28.3 for upper middle-income economies, 24.9 for lower middle-income economies, and 5.7 for low-income economies (World Bank, 1999). TV penetration is quite high in the large majority of high-income economies, particularly in the United States (80.6), Canada (70.9), Japan (70), and the United Kingdom (61.2). At the lowest end is UAE (29.4). In the upper middle-income economies, TV penetration ranges from the low-end of 2.7 in Botswana to 60.2 in Oman; and in the lower middle-income economies from the low-end of 2.4 in Papua New Guinea to the high-end of 59.2 in Latvia.

Newspaper penetration (i.e., circulation per 100 people) is relatively high in the majority of high-income economies, particularly in Hong Kong (73.9), Norway (58.8), Japan (57.8), Finland (45.5), and Sweden (44.6). At the lower end are Portugal (7.5), Spain (9.9), and Italy (10.4). In contrast to the commanding heights in radio and TV penetration, the United States (21.5) and Canada (15.7) occupy a lesser status on this indicator. In the upper middle-income economies, newspaper penetration ranges from 1.4 in Libya to 50.4 in Oman; and in the lower middle-income economies from 0.3 in Uzbekistan to 29.9 in Romania. In the selected low-income economies, Moldova has the highest penetration—6 copies. The minimum standard that UNESCO set in 1962 was 10 newspaper copies per 100 people. We used the mean of the penetration of newspapers, radio, and television as a *media participation index* for each economy. The correlation between X_2, tertiary enrollment, and Z, the media participation index, was a statistically significant 0.80 ($p = 0.00$)

Dependent variables: X_2, tertiary education, showed a substantial relationship with Y_1, economic status, that is, per capita GNP (0.66); and a high correlation with Y_2, telephone penetration (0.82), and Y_3, Internet host penetration (0.73)—the three dependent variables signifying informatization. Literacy alone, however, showed only a small relationship with economic status (0.35) and Internet density (0.33), and a moderate correlation with telephone density (0.53). The mass media—newspapers, radio, and TV—showed a high correlation with economic status (0.72) and telephone density (0.72 to 0.83), and a substantial relationship with Internet density (0.59 to 0.76).

A partial correlation analysis, however, showed that Z, media participation index, was indeed the intervening variable that accounted for the high correlation between tertiary enrollment and the three dependent variables. When controlled for Z, the predictive power of X_2 on Y_1, Y_2, and Y_3 was reduced to 0.3%, 11.36%, and 5.9% respectively. Thus the media participation component of the modernization paradigm remains extremely relevant to an informatization model because the media, *inter alia*, help engender empathy and propagate knowledge.

Within the cluster of dependent variables—constituting the economic dimension and the telecommunication and computer subdimensions of the infrastructure dimension—Y_1, economic status, explained 76% of the variability of Y_2, telephone penetration, which, in turn, explained 60% of the variability of Y_3, Internet host penetration.

Economic status (i.e., per capita GNP) reflects the economic dimension of informatization. It stimulates and is stimulated by the telecommunication and computer subdimensions of the infrastructure dimension.

Telephone penetration (i.e., main telephone lines per 100 people) is a vital indicator of informatization. The 1997 world average was 11.8 per 100 people. The average for high-income economies was 50.6; for upper middle-income economies, 15.0; for lower middle-income economies, 7.1; and for low-income economies, 1.6 (World Bank, 1999). Telephone penetration for high-income economies varies from 22.7 in Kuwait to 67.9 in Sweden; for upper middle-income economies, from 3.3 in Gabon to 33.5 in Croatia; for lower middle-income economies, from the low-end of 1.1 in Papua New Guinea to the high-end of 32.3 in Bulgaria; and for low-income economies from fewer than 1 for several economies to 15.4 in Armenia.

Internet host penetration (i.e., number of hosts per 1,000 people) has become the major indicator of informatization. Kuo (1993) wrote, "Computerization is an indicator that is commonly believed to be most closely associated with the level of informatization. Similar to telecommunications, computerization also has a mutually causal relationship with economic development and the level of per capita income" (p. 329). Informatization requires computerization coupled with global reach. Thus the more pertinent measure of informatization is the penetration of Internet host computers. The 1999 world average of Internet hosts was 7.4 per 1,000 people. The Internet host average for high-income economies was 45.2 per 1,000 people; for upper middle-income economies, 2.5; for lower middle-income economies, 0.7 and for low-income economies, 0.06. Internet-host penetration for high-income economies varies from 3.4 per 1,000 people in Kuwait to 111.4 in Finland; for upper middle-income economies, from 0 in Libya to 16.9 in Estonia; for lower middle-income economies, from 0 in a number of economies to 6.1 in Latvia; and for low-income economies, fewer than 1 across the board.

ITU (1995) estimated that in 1994 the size of the global information sector was $1,425 billion by defining that sector as *telecommunication services and equipment; computer software, services, and equipment; sound and television broadcasting and equipment*; and *audiovisual entertainment*. ITU data showed that telecommunication services and equipment (46%) dominated the world information industry in 1994, followed by computer hardware and software (33%), and audiovisual (21%). Furthermore, ITU said the global information sector was "growing faster than overall economic growth," and that this sector appeared to be "relatively immune to economic downswings" (p. 11).

Observations and Summary

Measurement of informatization for comparison of economies worldwide requires an international consensus on what constitutes the information sector. ITU (1995) has recognized four areas—telecommunications, computers, television, and audiovisual—as relevant to developing such a measurement index. The indexes developed by the Muchlup School and the Japanese scholars have limitations because of the dearth of relevant data for developing economies. Moreover, such indexes lack multidimensionality.

The revised informatization model, adapted from the multidimensional model proposed by Kuo (1993, 1994), provides a better understanding of the process of informatization that determine the place of each country's placement in the core-periphery structure of the world system. It borrows heavily from the modernization and developmental communication model and backs up the infrastructure and telecommunication for development model. In the rudimentary form used in this essay, it falls short of accommodating the concepts of the liberalization and transnational communication model. Because it demonstrates a process—urbanization, literacy, tertiary-level education, and mass media participation—it goes beyond merely quantifying informatization.

The variables in the people and infrastructure dimensions clearly show a vertical relationship among clusters of economies, as postulated by world system (structural) theorists. Economies in the Center are generally at the high end of informatization. Gunaratne (1999) identified the structural makeup of Asia based on world exports of merchandise and services (WTO, 1997). Data showed Japan as the clear center; Hong Kong, China, South Korea, Singapore, and Taiwan as the first-tier semiperiphery; Malaysia, Thailand, Indonesia, India, and the Philippines as the second-tier semiperiphery; and all other Asian economies as the periphery. One could similarly determine the structural makeup of the world to test the relationship between informatization and the competitive success in the world material economy.

DISCUSSION AND CONCLUSION

This essay posits that the state of capitalism revitalized by the Third Communication Revolution has left the nations—small or big—with little option but to informatize so they could effectively compete in the world material economy. Read and Youtie (1996) buttress Schumacher's (1973) belief in "small is beautiful" when they point out the informatization successes of small cities, not just of states or countries. Because knowledge has become a decisive factor of production (Ruggiero, 1997) in the progress toward a more global economy in the next century, smaller countries, as well as "fertile spots" in larger countries, with high achievements on the people dimension, have the potential to leapfrog into "cyberspatial heights" in the global information society.

This explains the success of the Four Dragons, and of Bangalore, the "fertile spot" in India, which will take many years to informatize as a nation.[17] Naisbitt (1996) writes: "Bangalore, with its seven software development parks and 5 million people, is one of the world's largest exporters of computer software" (p. 184). Glaeser (1997), who concurs with our "fertile spot" concept, says, "The example of India and Bangalore, which is a very well connected informational area, shows that, although a country may lack information technology on a broad scale, specific parts of that country may be well developed" (p. 54). He takes the view that a focus on entire countries tends to blur important regional differences. Similarly, Putrajaya will be the "fertile spot" in Malaysia, which has a vision of informatizing as a nation by 2020. Such "fertile spots" are likely to generate multiplier effects throughout a country. The World Bank (1995) asserts that for small countries like Mauritius, foreign investment can be an effective instrument of accelerated technology transfer because such investment can allow countries to leapfrog stages of economic development.

Frank (1993) has made a persuasive argument to view the reality of "capitalism," which he identifies as the world material economy, in nonideological terms because historically "capitalist" dynamics have been the operating force of the global economy. Global competition and interdependence reflect to some extent the end of the nation in the orthodox sense. Despite the immense disparities within the world economy, globalization offers disciplined countries in the peripheries the opportunity to foster development through global collective action (World Bank, 1997).

However, as the World Bank (1997) points out, "globalization" is not yet truly global. Half of the Third World people have been left out of "the rise in the volume of international trade and capital flows since the early 1980s" partly because of the hesitation "to open up to the world economy" (p. 12). Astounding disparities exist in the global economic system. The GNP per capita for the world's population of 5.82 billion in 1997 was $5,180. The GNP per capita for the 927 million people (16% of the world population) in the high-income countries was $25,890; for the 574 million people (9.9%) in the upper middle-income countries, $4,540; for the 2.28 billion people (39.2%) in the lower middle-income countries, $1,230; and for the 2.04 billion people (35%) in the low-income countries, $350 (World Bank, 1999). Thus one can reconfigure structural theory—the dependency-world system theory formulation—to reflect the emerging state of globalization. Such a global theory, which reflects the reality of the global material economy, would be devoid of "isms," and help further our understanding of the dynamics of the world material economy in order to change it.

The nine variables in the informatization model explored in this paper are clearly related to the old paradigm of modernization. Glaeser (1997) found a striking connection between the computing power of a country (MIPS per 1,000 people) and tertiary enrollment, which is highly correlated with telephones, Internet use, and fax machines as well. He constructed a supplementary index connecting his information technology index with the basic national characteristics that engendered a fertile environment for information technology. He detected three such characteristics: *enrollment in tertiary schools, quality of scientific research institutions,* and *sufficient power generation capacity.* Glaeser points out that "all the new technologies rely critically on the stable presence of electricity" (p. 57). He adds that countries also need "a legal environment that protects ideas" and helps technology flourish (p. 57). Glaeser's index, however, requires further replication to establish its reliability.

As Glaeser's (1997) analysis makes very clear, the two variables, telephone penetration and computer penetration, are essential to achieve a high degree of informatization. High achievement on the people dimension, particularly in tertiary education, must precede or go hand-in-hand with the infrastructure dimension. The available data indicate vast improvements in urbanization and literacy for the large majority of developing countries since Lerner (1958) studied modernization in the Middle East. However, the level of tertiary education in most developing countries shows a dismal picture in comparison to the Center countries. Informatization will be a slow process until countries achieve near-full literacy and emphasize higher education. Informatization also requires countries to improve their power generation capacity.

Levinson (1998), however, points out the possibility of a disconnect between traditional educational standards and the improved economic performance necessary for global competition. WEF (1998) data from transitional economies (i.e., the former Soviet bloc) show that educational improvement alone may be insufficient to overcome the disparities created by globalization. Although these transitional economies score well on their educational systems, particularly on the teaching of basic science and math, they are at the bottom of the competitiveness rankings. Porter (1998) says, "High rates of public investment in schooling will not ultimately pay off unless a nation's microeconomic circumstances create the demand for skill in companies and appropriate institutions and practices are present to translate general education into specialized business knowledge" (p. 48). The lesson for developing countries is that technological "leapfrogging" should go hand in hand with the training of a workforce that can compete both at the microeconomic and macroeconomic levels.

Developing countries have been instrumental in getting the U.N. Development Program to devise a Human Development Index (see Table 6, p. 191) to reflect progress on a multidimensional framework rather than on the sole economic criterion of per capita income. The HDI is a composite index of four variables: life expectancy at birth, adult literacy, gross school enrollment at all three levels, and real GDP per capita. Thus constructed, the HDI still produces very high scores for the Center countries in comparison to the Periphery countries. The 1997 HDI showed an average score of 0.706 for the world population. The industrial countries had an index of 0.919 compared to 0.637 for all developing countries. The index for sub-Saharan Africa was 0.463, and for the least developed countries, 0.430.

Therefore, even from the human development angle, developing countries have little option but to join the Information Superhighway to improve the well being of their inhabitants, because literacy, education, per capita income and life expectancy too are intimately related to economic development. Three of these variables belong to our informatization model as well.

With the qualifiers already mentioned, technological developments may enable the periphery countries to "leapfrog" in the global/glocal economy (Noam & Steinborn, 1997) despite the negative scenarios painted by the dystopians (e.g., Schiller, 1996; Negrine, 1997). Global cellular communication using intermediate-circular-orbit and low-earth-orbit satellites bodes well for rural communities in developing countries (Noam & Steinborn, 1997). Four mobile satellite network operators have developed such systems to offer a global system by 2000—Globalstar, Odyssey, Iridium, and Inmarsat ICO (*The APT Yearbook,* 1997). The current cost of such global cellular phones is beyond the reach of rural folks in the periphery countries. However, Grove's amazing microchip, combined with the amazing progress of technology, has the potential of turning the tables around.

FIGURES AND TABLES

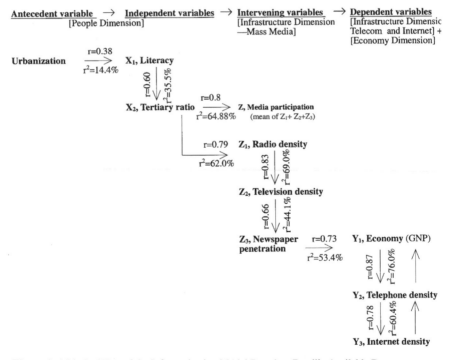

Figure 1. A Limited Test of the Informatization Model Based on Readily Available Data
NOTES: The statistics are derived from the data in Tables 1 through 4 ($N = 108$ economies).
   The **r** is the Pearson correlation coefficient of the two variables in the direction of the arrow.
   Statistical significance: $p < 0.000$ for each coefficient.
   The **r^2** shows the proportion of variance explained in each "successor" variable by its adjoining "predecessor" variable.

Modernization and developmental communications model (Origin: post-World War II)	Telecommunications for development model (Origin: early 1980s)	Liberalization and transnational communications model (Origin: 1980s)
Development Move to modernity through changes in: • Individual attitudes • Social institutions Emphasis on mass media for persuasion and attitude change	Development Social and economic growth with telecom as key to integration, infrastructure, efficiency of services Emphasis on interactive telecommunications for economic growth and social integration. (Follows from modernization tradition. Borrows most directly from engineering concepts and inductive studies.)	Development Fastest economic growth produced by most efficient use of economic and human resources. Emphasis on economic rather than sociological or engineering concepts. (Also follows modernization tradition. Borrows most directly from liberal economics, e.g., market and trade theory.)
Key concepts Urbanization Literacy Mass media Empathy Political participation Opinion leaders Modernity vs. tradition Innovations Two-step flow	Key concepts Telecom infrastructure (core) Investment capital Economic growth/wealth New technologies Technology transfer Market modernization Informatization Leapfrogging State intervention Integration with global economy	Key concepts Markets Competition Export infrastructure Liberalization/privatization Capital mobility Globalization Technological convergence Transnational investment Comparative advantage Media commercialization Information economy

Figure 2. McDowell's (1997) Classification of Communication Models

TABLE 1
Indicators for High-Income Countries—Population of More Than 1 Million
(Per Capita GNP of $9,656 or More)

Country	(1) GNP per capita (US $) 1997	(2) Population (000,000) 1997	(3) Urban population % 1997	(4) Adult literacy % 1997	(5) Tertiary enrollment ratio (gross) 1996	(6) Main telephone lines per 100 people 1997	(7) Internet hosts per 1,000 people 1999	(8) TV receivers per 100 people 1997	(9) Newspaper circulation per 100 people 1996	(10) Radio receivers per 100 people 1996
Switzerland	43,060	7	62	99	33	64.2	51.5	53.6	33.0	96.9
Japan	38,160	126	78	99	43	48.9	13.4	70.6	57.8	95.7
Norway	36,100	4	74	99	62	52.8	80.1	57.9	58.8	92.0
Denmark	34,890	5	85	99	48	63.3	75.2	56.9	30.9	114.6
Singapore	32,810	3	100	91.4	39	44.8	26.0	35.4	36.0	73.9
U.S.	29,080	268	77	99	81	64.3	94.2	84.7	21.5	211.5
Germany	28,280	82	87	99	45	55.0	23.2	57.0	31.1	94.6
Austria	27,920	8	64	99	48	48.4	25.6	49.6	29.6	74.0
Belgium	26,730	10	97	99	57	46.8	26.0	51.0	16.0	79.2
France	26,300	59	75	99	52	57.4	15.5	60.6	21.8	94.3
Netherlands	25,830	16	89	99	50	54.0	51.9	54.1	17.7	93.3
Sweden	25,200	9	83	99	49	67.9	72.1	53.1	44.6	90.7
Finland	24,790	5	64	99	71	55.7	111.4	53.4	45.5	138.5
Hong Kong	24,290	7	95	92.4	28	56.1	35.7	41.2	73.9	69.5
Australia	20,650	19	85	99	76	51.4	48.6	63.8	29.7	138.5
Italy	20,170	58	67	98.3	43	44.0	10.1	48.3	10.4	87.4
U.A.E.	19,743	3	85	74.8	12	35.1	7.8	29.4	15.6	35.4
U.K.	19,640	59	89	99	50	52.2	34.3	64.1	33.2	144.5

(continued)

TABLE 1 Continued

Country	(1) GNP per capita (US $) 1997	(2) Population (000,000) 1997	(3) Urban population % 1997	(4) Adult literacy % 1997	(5) Tertiary enrollment ratio (gross) 1996	(6) Main telephone lines per 100 people 1997	(7) Internet hosts per 1,000 people 1999	(8) TV receivers per 100 people 1997	(9) Newspaper circulation per 100 people 1996	(10) Radio receivers per 100 people 1996
Canada	19,020	30	77	99	90	60.2	85.4	70.8	15.7	107.8
Ireland	17,790	4	58	99	40	38.3	21.7	45.6	15.0	70.3
Kuwait	17,705	2	97	80.4	27	22.7	3.4	49.1	37.4	68.8
Israel	16,180	6	91	95.4	44	45.0	24.6	32.1	29.0	53.0
New Zealand	15,830	4	86	99	59	48.6	39.6	50.1	22.3	102.7
Spain	14,490	39	77	97.2	51	40.3	12.4	50.6	9.9	32.8
Taiwan*	12,240	22	58	86	46	46.6	14.3	32.7	33.0	40.1
Greece	11,640	11	60	96.6	43	50.9	5.8	46.6	15.3	47.7
Portugal	11,010	10	37	90.8	38	38.4	6.9	37.2	7.5	30.6
Korea South	10,550	46	83	97.2	60	44.4	6.0	34.2	39.3	103.7
Slovenia	9,840	2	52	99	36	36.4	12.7	35.3	20.6	41.6
World (210 economies)	5,180	5,820	46	78	19	18.9	7.4	27.7	...	29.5

SOURCES: (Table 1–Table 4): World Bank (1999) *World Development Indicators* (Ccls. 1, 2, 3, 5, 9, & 10); UNDP (1999) *Human Development Report* (Col. 4); ITU (1999) *Challenges to the Network*. (Cols. 6, 7, & 8); Highlighted data are from other sources. Aggregates refer to *all* countries in the relevant category. (*World Bank does not list Taiwan.)

TABLE 2
Indicators for Upper Middle-Income Countries—Population of More Than 1 Million (Per Capita GNP $3,126 to $9,655)

Country	(1) GNP per capita (US $) 1997	(2) Population (000,000) 1997	(3) Urban population % 1997	(4) Adult literacy % 1997	(5) Tertiary enrollment ratio (gross) 1996	(6) Main telephone lines per 100 people 1997	(7) Internet hosts per 1,000 people 1999	(8) TV receivers per 100 people 1997	(9) Newspaper circulation per 100 people 1996	(10) Radio receivers per 100 people 1996
Argentina	8,950	36	89	96.5	42	17.4	2.6	28.9	12.3	67.7
Saudi Arabia	7,150	20	84	73.4	16	11.7	0.6	26.0	5.7	31.9
Oman	6,693	2	79	67.1	6	8.3	1.2	60.2	50.4	58.2
Uruguay	6,130	3	91	97.5	29	23.1	4.7	30.4	29.3	61.0
Czech Republic	5,240	10	66	99	23	27.3	8.9	44.7	25.4	80.6
Chile	4,820	15	84	95.2	30	15.6	2.3	23.3	9.9	35.4
Brazil	4,790	164	80	84	12	9.6	1.8	31.6	4.0	43.5
Malaysia	4,530	22	55	85.7	11	19.5	3.0	16.6	15.8	43.2
Hungary	4,510	10	66	99	25	26.1	10.2	43.7	18.6	69.7
Trinidad-Tobago	4,250	1	73	97.8	8	19.0	3.4	33.2	12.0	51.7
Gabon	4,120	1	52	66.2	6	3.3	0.0	13.5	2.9	18.2
Croatia	4,060	5	57	97.7	28	33.5	1.8	26.7	10.8	33.3
Mauritius	3,870	1	41	83	7	19.5	0.5	22.8	7.5	36.8
Mexico	3,700	94	74	90.1	16	9.6	1.4	25.1	9.7	32.4
Slovakia	3,680	5	60	99	22	25.9	4.5	40.1	18.5	58.0
Poland	3,590	39	64	99	24	19.4	3.9	41.3	11.3	51.8
South Africa	3,210	41	50	84	19	10.7	3.8	12.5	3.2	31.6
Venezuela	3,480	23	86	92	25	12.1	1.1	17.2	20.6	47.1
Estonia	3,360	1	74	99	42	32.1	16.9	47.9	17.4	68.0
Lebanon	3,350	4	88	84.4	27	14.9	2.1	35.4	10.7	89.2
Botswana	3,310	2	65	74.4	6	4.8	0.4	2.7	2.7	15.5
Turkey	3,130	64	72	83.2	18	24.1	1.4	28.6	10.9	17.8
Libya	...	5	86	76.5	20	13.5	0.0	14.3	1.4	23.2
Upper middle-income economies (37)	4,540	574	74	88	19	14.43	2.5	28.3	9.2	36.1

TABLE 3

Indicators for Lower Middle-Income Countries—Population of More Than 1 Million (Per Capita GNP $786 to $3,125)

Country	(1) GNP per capita (US $) 1997	(2) Population (000,000) 1997	(3) Urban population % 1997	(4) Adult literacy % 1997	(5) Tertiary enrollment ratio (gross) 1996	(6) Main telephone lines per 100 people 1997	(7) Internet hosts per 1,000 people 1999	(8) TV receivers per 100 people 1997	(9) Newspaper circulation per 100 people 1996	(10) Radio receivers per 100 people 1996
Panama	3,080	3	56	91.1	32	12.2	2.9	23.2	6.2	29.9
Thailand	2,740	61	21	94.7	21	7.9	0.7	23.4	6.3	20.4
Russia	2,680	147	77	99	41	18.19	1.2	39.0	10.5	34.4
Costa Rica	2,680	3	50	95.1	33	16.9	2.9	40.3	9.4	27.1
Peru	2,610	24	72	88.7	31	6.7	0.2	14.3	8.4	27.1
Latvia	2,430	2	73	99	33	30.2	6.1	59.2	24.7	69.9
Lithuania	2,260	4	73	99	31	28.3	2.7	37.7	9.3	29.2
Colombia	2,180	40	74	90.9	19	13.0	0.7	21.7	4.6	56.5
Belarus	2,150	10	72	99	44	22.6	0.1	31.4	17.4	29.0
Namibia	2,110	2	38	79.8	9	6.2	1.6	3.2	1.9	14.3
Tunisia	2,110	9	63	67	14	7.0	0.0	18.2	3.1	21.8
El Salvador	1,810	6	46	77	17	5.6	0.1	25.0	4.8	46.1
Iran	1,780	61	60	73.3	17	10.7	0.0	14.8	2.8	23.7
Dominican Rep	1,750	8	63	82.6	23	8.8	1.0	8.4	5.2	17.7
Guatemala	1,580	11	40	66.6	8	4.1	0.2	12.6	3.3	7.3
Ecuador	1,570	12	60	90.7	26	7.5	0.4	29.4	7.0	34.2
Jamaica	1,550	3	55	85.5	8	14.0	0.1	32.3	6.2	48.2
Jordan	1,520	4	73	87.2	17	7.0	0.8	4.3	5.8	28.7
Yugoslavia	1,510	11	58	93.3	23	19.7	0.7	25.5	11.0	14.3
Algeria	1,500	29	57	60.3	13	4.7	0.0	6.8	3.8	23.9
Romania	1,410	23	57	97.8	23	14.0	1.2	22.6	29.9	31.7

(continued)

TABLE 3 Continued

Country	(1) GNP per capita (US $) 1997	(2) Population (000,000) 1997	(3) Urban population % 1997	(4) Adult literacy % 1997	(5) Tertiary enrollment ratio (gross) 1996	(6) Main telephone lines per 100 people 1997	(7) Internet hosts per 1,000 people 1999	(8) TV receivers per 100 people 1997	(9) Newspaper circulation per 100 people 1996	(10) Radio receivers per 100 people 1996
Kazakhstan	1,350	16	60	99	32	11.6	0.1	23.4	3.1	38.4
Cuba	1,291	11	77	95.9	12	3.3	0.0	24.1	11.8	35.1
Morocco	1,280	27	53	45.9	11	5.0	0.1	16.0	2.6	24.1
Egypt	1,200	60	45	52.7	23	5.6	0.1	12.7	4.0	31.6
Philippines	1,200	74	56	94.6	35	2.8	0.3	10.9	8.2	15.9
Bulgaria	1,170	8	69	98.2	41	32.3	1.4	36.6	25.7	53.1
Syria	1,120	15	53	71.6	15	8.8	0.0	9.2	2.0	27.4
Indonesia	1,110	200	37	85	11	2.5	0.2	13.4	1.4	15.5
Macedonia	1,100	2	61	94	18	17.4	0.5	25.2	1.9	18.4
Ukraine	1,040	51	71	99	42	18.6	0.4	49.3	5.4	87.2
Uzbekistan	1,020	24	42	99	36	6.7	0.0	27.3	0.3	45.2
Paraguay	1,000	5	54	92.4	11	3.6	0.2	10.1	4.3	18.2
Bolivia	970	8	62	83.6	24	6.9	0.1	11.5	5.5	67.2
Papua NG	930	5	17	73.7	3	1.1	0.0	2.4	1.5	9.1
Korea, North	900	23	62	99	...	4.9	0.0	11.5	19.9	14.7
Georgia	860	5	59	99	40	10.5	0.1	47.3	1.7	55.3
China	860	1,227	32	82.9	6	5.6	0.13	27.0	4.2	19.5
Sri Lanka	800	19	23	90.7	5	1.7	0.37	9.1	2.9	21.0
Iraq	...	22	75	58	11	3.3	0.0	8.3	1.9	22.8
Lower middle-income economies (59)	1,230	2,283	42	84	14	7.1	...	24.9	...	23.0

TABLE 4

Indicators for Selected Low-Income Countries—More Than 1 Million People
(Per Capita GNP of $785 or Less)

Country	(1) GNP per capita (US $) 1997	(2) Population (000,000) 1997	(3) Urban population % 1997	(4) Adult literacy % 1997	(5) Tertiary enrolment ratio (gross) 1996	(6) Main telephone lines per 100 people 1997	(7) Internet hosts per 1,000 people 1999	(8) TV receivers per 100 people 1997	(9) Newspaper circulation per 100 people 1996	(10) Radio receivers per 100 people 1996
Albania	760	3	38	85	11	2.3	0.03	16.1	3.5	23.5
Honduras	740	6	45	70.7	11	3.7	0.02	9.0	5.5	40.9
Zimbabwe	720	11	33	90.9	7	1.7	0.08	2.9	1.9	9.6
Turkmenistan	640	5	45	97.7	20	7.8	0.26	17.5	…	9.6
Armenia	560	4	69	98	12	15.4	0.12	21.8	2.3	0.5
Senegal	540	9	45	34.6	3	1.3	0.08	4.1	0.5	14.1
Azerbaijan	510	8	56	96.3	18	8.7	0.06	21.1	2.8	2.0
Pakistan	500	128	35	40.9	3	1.8	0.02	6.5	2.1	9.2
Kyrgyzstan	480	5	39	97	12	7.5	0.41	4.4	1.5	11.5
Moldova	460	4	53	98.3	26	14.5	0.12	30.2	6.0	72.0
Nicaragua	410	5	63	63.4	13	2.9	0.17	19.0	3.0	28.3
Mongolia	390	3	62	84	17	3.7	0.01	6.3	2.7	13.9
India	370	962	27	53.5	7	1.9	0.08	6.9	3.1	10.5
Gambia	340	1	30	33.1	2	2.1	0.00	0.4	0.2	16.4
Vietnam	310	77	20	91.9	5	2.1	0.00	18.0	0.4	10.6
Yemen	270	16	35	42.5	4	1.3	0.00	27.3	1.5	6.4
Low-income economies (61)	350	2,036	28	54	5	1.6	…	5.7	…	9.9

NOTE: Countries with a telephone density lower than 1 per 100 people (Col. 6) are excluded from the table.

TABLE 5

Correlation (Pearson) Matrix of Nine Variables
(for 108 Countries) Listed in Tables 1 Through 4

	Internet density	Telephone density	Per capita GNP	Newspaper penetration	Radio density	TV density	Tertiary ratio	Literacy
Telephone	0.779 0.000							
Per capita GNP	0.767 0.000	0.875 0.000						
Newspaper penetration	0.587 0.000	0.725 0.000	0.726 0.000					
Radio density	0.763 0.000	0.787 0.000	0.725 0.000	0.624 0.000				
TV density	0.659 0.000	0.832 0.000	0.724 0.000	0.657 0.000	0.830 0.000			
Tertiary ratio	0.732 0.000	0.819 0.000	0.663 0.000	0.544 0.000	0.787 0.000	0.782 0.000		
Literacy	0.326 0.001	0.528 0.000	0.349 0.000	0.386 0.000	0.448 0.000	0.548 0.000	0.596 0.000	
Urbanization	0.361 0.000	0.558 0.000	0.528 0.000	0.553 0.000	0.560 0.000	0.552 0.000	0.537 0.000	0.379 0.000

NOTE: Cell contents: Correlation (top)
                     p-value (bottom)

TABLE 6
Human Development Index—High Human Development
(Top 10 of 45 Countries)

HDI rank	Country	Life expectancy at birth (years)	Adult literacy rate (%)	Combined 1st, 2nd & 3rd level gross enrollment ratio (%)	Real GDP per capita (PPP$)*	Human Development Index (HDI) value	Real GDP per capita (PPP$)* rank minus HDI rank
		1998	1998	1998	1998	1998	
1	Canada	79.1	99.0	100	23,582	0.935	8
2	Norway	78.3	99.0	97	22,342	0.934	1
3	United States	76.8	99.0	94	29,605	0.929	-1
4	Australia	78.3	99.0	114	22,452	0.929	9
5	Iceland	79.1	99.0	89	25,110	0.927	1
6	Sweden	78.7	99.0	102	20,659	0.926	15
7	Belgium	77.3	99.0	106	23,223	0.925	4
8	Netherlands	78.0	99.0	99	22,176	0.925	6
9	Japan	80.0	99.0	85	23,257	0.925	1
10	United Kingdom	77.3	99.0	105	20,336	0.918	13

*PPP$ = purchasing power parity dollars
SOURCE: *Human Development Report 2000*. New York: UNDP & OUP, 2000.

NOTES

1. The Fiber-optic Link Around the Globe (FLAG), which cost $1.5 billion, is a 28,000-km cable from Japan to Britain. The 80-Gbps China-U.S. Cable Network is a $1.2 billion direct fiber-optic link between the two countries; and the 40-Gbps Sea-Me-We3 is a 30,000-km submarine cable connecting Southeast Asia, Middle East, and Western Europe. The CTR Group's Project Oxygen, an interconnecting self-healing loop network around the globe, is the most ambitious of these cable projects. Other examples: the 40-Gbps Southern Cross connecting Australia and New Zealand with the United States, and the 160-Gpbs Pacific 1 connecting Japan and the United States (APT, 1997, 1999; Erickson, 1998).

2. See also Internet Software Consortium <http://www.isc.org/ds/WWW200007/index.html>; and Nua Internet how many online <http://www.nua.ie/surveys/how_many_online/index.html>. Nua analysis estimated 407.1 million Internet users in November 2000.

3. Lerner (1958, p. 63) reported the following multiple correlation coefficients of the four indexes he used to measure modernization:

         Urbanization   .61
         Literacy   .91
         Media participation .84
         Political participation .82

Lerner hypothesized that the historical function of urbanization was to stimulate take off; thereafter, it yielded "priority to other factors of self-sustaining growth" (p. 65).

4. Stevenson (1994) provides a good summary of the old paradigm (pp. 233–234). Mowlana (1997) provides a critique (pp. 185–196).

5. The voter turnout (i.e., political participation) at the latest elections in several developed countries has been poor: United States, 36%; Singapore, 41%; Switzerland, 42%; and Poland, 48% (UNDP, 1999, p. 217), but the voter turnout in the majority of developed countries has been in the 81% (Sweden) to 95% (Australia) range.

6. However, smaller economies with a very high Internet host density (e.g., Niue, which has more hosts than inhabitants; Anguilla, which has used its favorable tax laws to develop Internet business; and Tonga) may not necessarily reflect true informatization.

7. The objective of *new institutional economics* is to broaden and modify the microeconomic foundations of economic theory by considering how political and economic institutions affect the performance of economics over time. Thus it takes into account more dimensions than just price and quantity. Levy and Spiller (1996) and their cowriters have used NIE's empirical and comparative approach to study the interrelationship among the telecommunication regulatory regime, utility performance and the background political institutions of five countries—Argentina, Chile, Jamaica, the Philippines, and the United Kingdom.

8. A meeting of the International Telecommunications Union in Buenos Aires adopted these principles in 1994. The G-7 Telecommunications Ministerial in Brussels affirmed them in 1996. The Asia-Pacific Economic Cooperation (APEC) and the Summit of the Americas have reaffirmed them.

9. Santoso (1997) wrote that the Internet has been beyond the reach of state censorship in Indonesia, where an estimated 100,000 people were online. Schmitt (1997) described how a Serbian prodemocrat, Drazen Pantic, used the global character of the Internet to break President Slobodan Milosevic's control of Serbia's domestic news media. However, Eckholm (1997) reported on elaborate new rules that China adopted at the end of 1997 to restrict Internet use with the number of Internet users reaching 620,000 even though "controlling Web sites is a Sisyphean task because so many new ones are constantly being created" (p. A3).

10. In 1996, Africa's share of the world merchandise exports was a mere 2.3%. In comparison, Western Europe's share was 44.6%; Asia's, 25.6%; North America's, 16.2%; Latin America's, 4.9%; Eastern Europe and former Soviet Union's, 3.3%; and Middle East's 3.2%. The share of the world exports of commercial services showed a similar trend: Western Europe's, 48%; Asia's, 22.7%; North America's, 17.9%; and Latin America's, 3.7 (WTO, 1997, Vol. 2).

11. Robin Mansell in a personal communication dated Aug. 17, 1998.

12. Frank (1993) refers to OECD as "a wider sort of consultatory circle" of industrialized countries "with some voice but no vote" with the "charmed circle of real decision makers" in geoeconomics limited to Germany, Japan, and the United States within the Group of Seven (p. 22). The OECD comprises 24 high-income countries (Australia, Austria, Belgium, Canada, Denmark, Finland, France, Germany, Greece, Iceland, Ireland, Italy, Japan, Luxembourg, Netherlands, New Zealand, Norway, Portugal, South Korea, Spain, Sweden, Switzerland, United Kingdom, and United States), and six upper middle-income countries (Czech Republic, Hungary, Mexico, Poland, Slovac Republic, and Turkey). The OECD says it brings together countries sharing the principles of the market economy, pluralist democracy, and respect for human rights.

13. Late 2000, WTO comprised 140 members. It also had 32 observer countries, and seven international organization observers to the General Council. All observer countries, including China and Russia, have applied to join the WTO except the Holy See (Vatican), Ethiopia, Cape Verde, Bhutan, and Yemen. The WTO began life on Jan. 1, 1995, but its trading system is half a century older. Since 1948, the General Agreement on Tariffs and Trade (GATT) had provided the rules for the system.

14. WTO (1997) reported that in 1996, Hong Kong, South Korea, Singapore, and Taiwan were the 9th, 12th, 13th, and 14th largest exporters in the world merchandise trade. In world trade in commercial services, Hong Kong ranked ninth; Singapore, 12th; South Korea, 14th; and Taiwan, 18th.

15. The scores in the Glaeser Index ranged from 2.604 at the bottom to a high of 6.689. The Scandinavian countries were at the top. The United States was at the very top, followed by Sweden, Denmark, Finland, Australia, Hong Kong, Canada, Netherlands, Japan, United Kingdom, New Zealand, Switzerland, Ireland, France, Singapore, Israel, Austria, Germany, Belgium, Taiwan, Spain, Italy, Chile, Turkey, Malaysia, Slovakia, Portugal, Greece, Thailand, South Africa, Hungary, Czech Republic, Mexico, Colombia, Argentina, Brazil, Indonesia, Philippines, Peru, Venezuela, Russia, Ukraine, India, Poland, and China.

16. NCA's (1997) informatization index compares nine economies—Britain, France, Germany, Hong Kong, Japan, Singapore, South Korea, Taiwan, and the United States. It also compares the average of these nine countries with the average of European countries and the average of advanced countries. This index is accessible on the Web at <http://www.nca.or.kr/NCA97e/pub/fall/cont_8a.htm>

17. Singhal & Rogers (1989) have done a lengthy analysis of the pros and cons of high-technology development in India. In addition to Bangalore, India has set up six other software technology parks (STPs) in Pune, Bhubaneswar, Thiruvananthapuram, Hyderabad, Noida (near Delhi), and Gandhinagar (near Ahmedabad). The state governments of Rajasthan and West Bengal have also set up STPs in Jaipur and Calcutta respectively.

REFERENCES

Ang, P. (1993). The causal relationship between international telecommunications and economic development: Cause for re-analysis. In A. Goonasekera & D. Holaday (Eds.), *Asian communication handbook* (pp. 341–358). Singapore: Amic.

The APT Yearbook. (1996–1999). Sutton, UK: ICOM Publications; & Bangkok, Thailand: Asia-Pacific Telecommunity.

Barnett, G. A. (1998). The social structure of international telecommunications. In H. Sawhney & G. A. Barnett (Eds.), *Progress in communication sciences Vol. XV: Advances in telecommunications* (pp. 151–186). Stamford, CT: Ablex.

Barnett, G. A., Jacobson, T., Choi, Y., & Sun-Miller, S. (1996). An examination of the international telecommunication network. *Journal of International Communication, 3*(2), 19–43.

Berry, J.- F. (1981). *Comments on the contribution of telecommunications to development: The case of France and Spain.* Marnes-la-Coquette, France: Association Francaise des Utilisateurs du Tele phone et des Telecommunications.

Brams, S. (1966). Transnational flows in the international system. *American Political Science Review,* *60,* 880–898.

Breiger, R. (1982). Structures of economic interdependence among nations. In P. Blau & R. Merton (Eds.), *Continuities in structural inquiry* (pp. 353–380). London: Sage.

Calabrese, A. (1999). The information age according to Manuel Castells. *Journal of Communication, 49*(3), 172–186.

Castells, M. (1996–1998). *The information age: Economy, society and culture* (Vols. 1–3). Malden, MA: Blackwell.

Chase-Dunn, C. (1975). The effects of international economic dependence on development and in equality: A cross-national study. *American Sociological Review, 40,* 720–738.

The Commission on Freedom of the Press (The Hutchins Commission). (1947). *A free and responsible press.* Chicago: University of Chicago Press.

Cox, R. W. (1987). *Production, power and world order: Social forces in the making of history.* New York: Columbia University Press.

Dunn, H. S. (1995). Caribbean telecommunications policy: Fashioned by debt, dependency and under-development. *Media, Culture & Society, 17,* 201–222.

Eckholm, E. (1997, December 31). China cracks down on dissent in cyberspace. *New York Times,* p. A3.

Erickson, J. (1998, April 17). The world on a wire. *Asiaweek, 24,* 46–56.

Falk, R. A. (1994). Democratizing, internationalizing, and globalizing. In Y. Sakamoto (Ed.), *Global transformation: Challenges to the state system* (pp. 475–502). Tokyo: United Nations University Press.

Frank, A. G. (1993). No end to history! History to no end? In K. Nordenstreng & H. I. Schiller (Eds.), *Beyond national sovereignty: International communication in the 1990s* (pp. 3–27). Norwood, NJ: Ablex.

Frank, A. G., & Gills, B. K. (Eds.). (1993). *The world system.* London: Routledge.

Fukuyama, F. (1989, Summer). The end of history? *National Interest,* pp.3–18.

Fukuyama, F. (1996, September). Implications of the revolution in communications. *Global Issues, 1*(12) [Online]. Available: http://www.usia.gov/journals/itgic/ 0996/ijge/jgcom5.htm

Galtung, J. (1980). A structural theory of imperialism. In I. Vogeler & A. R. de Souza (Eds.), *Dialectics of Third World development* (pp. 261–298). Montclair, NJ: Allanheld, Osmun.

Galtung, J. (1993). Geopolitical transformation and the 21st century world economy. In K. Nordenstreng & H. I. Schiller (Eds.), *Beyond national sovereignty: International communication in the 1990s* (pp. 28–58). Norwood, NJ: Ablex.

Galtung, J., & Vincent, R. C. (1992). *Global Glasnost: Toward a New World Information and Communication Order?* Cresskill, NJ: Hampton Press.

Glaeser, E. L. (1997). Information technology's role. In *The global competitiveness report 1997* (pp. 50–59). Geneva, Switzerland: World Economic Forum.

Goldstein, S. (1996, September). The Internet: Creating a democratic global village. *Global Issues, 1*(12) [Online]. Available: http:// www.usia.gov/ journals/itgic/ 0996/ijge/foc3.htm

Gore, A. (1996, September). Basic principles for building an information society. *Global Issues, 1*(12) [Online]. Available: http://www.usia.gov/journals/itgic/0996/ijge/oc1.htm

Greenstein, S. (1993, December 1). Markets, standards and the information infrastructure. *IEEE Micro, 13*(6), 36–51.

Greider, W. (1997). *One world, ready or not: The manic logic of global capitalism.* New York: Simon & Schuster.

Gunaratne, S. A. (1997). Sri Lanka and the third communication revolution. *Media Asia, 24,* 83–89.

Gunaratne, S. A. (1999). The media in Asia: An overview. *Gazette, 61,* 197–223.

Gunaratne, S. A., & Conteh, A. (1988). *Global communication and dependency: Links between the NIEO and NWICO demands and the withdrawals from UNESCO.* Moorhead, MN: Moorhead State University.

Gunaratne, S. A., Safar Hasim, M., & Kasenally, R. (1997). Small is beautiful: Informatization potential in three Indian Ocean rim countries. *Media Asia, 24,* 188–205.

Hamelink, C. J. (1994). *Trends in world communication: On disempowerment and self-empowerment.* Penang, Malaysia: Southbound Third World Network.

Hardy, A. (1980, December). The role of the telephone in economic development. *Telecommunications Policy, 4,* 278–286.

Herman, E. S., & McChesney, R. W. (1997). *The global media: The new missionaries of corporate capitalism.* London and Washington, DC: Cassell.

Hu, F., Sachs, J. D., & Warner, A. M. (1997). Executive summary. In *The global competitiveness report 1997* (pp. 20–27). Geneva, Switzerland: World Economic Forum.

Hu, F., & Zhang, T. (1997). Catching up and convergence. In *The global competitiveness report 1997* (pp. 74–78). Geneva, Switzerland: World Economic Forum.

Hudson, H. E. (1984). *When telephones reach the village: The role of telecommunications in rural development.* Norwood, NJ: Ablex.

Hudson, H. E. (1997). *Global connections: International telecommunications infrastructure and policy.* New York: Van Nostrand Reinhold.

Hukill, M. (1993). Getting beyond the statistics: Towards a problem orientation and interdisciplinary approach to telecommunication policy studies. In A. Goonasekera & D. Holaday (Eds.), *Asian communication handbook* (pp. 333–339). Singapore: Amic.

Ihonvbere, J. O. (1996). Africa and the new globalization: Challenges and options for the future. In H. F. Didsbury, Jr., *Future vision: Ideas, insights and strategies* (pp. 345–366). Bethesda, MD: World Future Society.

Independent Commission for Worldwide Telecommunications Development (Maitland Commission). (1984). *The missing link* (Report of commission chaired by Sir Donald Maitland). Geneva, Switzerland: International Telecommunications Union.

International Telecommunication Union (ITU). (1995). *World telecommunication development report.* Geneva, Switzerland: ITU.

International Telecommunication Union (ITU). (1997a). *World telecommunication development report.* Geneva, Switzerland: ITU.

International Telecommunication Union (ITU). (1997b). *Challenges to the network: Telecoms and the Internet.* Geneva, Switzerland: ITU.

International Telecommunication Union (ITU). (1998). *World telecommunication development report.* Geneva, Switzerland: ITU.

International Telecommunication Union (ITU). (1999a). *Yearbook of statistics: Telecommunication services 1988-1997.* Geneva, Switzerland: ITU

International Telecommunication Union (ITU). (1999b). *Challenges to the network: Internet for development.* Geneva, Switzerland: ITU.

Irving, I. (1996, September). New technology benefits all nations. *Global Issues, 1*(12) [Online]. Available: http://www.usia.gov/journals/itgic0996/ijge/foc2.htm

Isaacson, W. (1997, December 29). The Digital Age . . . driven by the passion of Intel's Andrew Grove. *Time, 150,* 48–51.

Ito, Y. (1980). The "Johoka Shakai" approach to the study of communication in Japan. *Keio Communication Review, 1,* 13–40.

Jameson, F., & Miyoshi, M. (Eds.). (1998). *The cultures of globalization.* Durham, NC: Duke University Press.

Jipp, A. (1963, July). Wealth of nations and telephone density. *Telecommunications Journal,* 199–201.

Jussawalla, M., Lamberton, D. M., & Karunaratne, N. D. (Eds.). (1988). *The cost of thinking: Information economies of ten Pacific countries.* Norwood, NJ: Ablex.

Katz, R. L. (1988). *The information society: An international perspective.* New York: Praeger.

Kellerman, A. (1990). International telecommunications around the world: A flow analysis. *Telecommunications Policy, 14*(6), 461–475.

Kelly, T., & Petrazzini, B. (1997, September). *What does the internet mean for development.* Paper presented at the Telecom Interactive Development Symposium, Geneva, Switzerland.

Knight, P. (1996, September). The electronic revolution and developing countries. *Global Issues, 1*(12) [Online]. Available: http://www.usia.gov/journals/itgic/0996/ijge/gjcom1.htm

Kumaratunge, C. B. (1997, December 27). South Asia: Into the next century (address to the Institute of Regional Studies, Islamabad). *The Island* [Online]. Available: http://www.upali.lk/island/sat/islfetrs.htm#features

Kuo, E. C. Y. (1993). Informatization among Asian NIEs: A comparative study. In A. Goonasekera & D. Holaday (Eds.), *Asian communication handbook* (pp. 319–332). Singapore: Amic.

Kuo, E. C. Y. (1994). Singapore. In G. Wang (Ed.), *Treading different paths: Informatization in Asian nations* (pp. 141–159). Norwood, NJ: Ablex.

Lee, P. S. N. (Ed.). (1997). *Telecommunications and development in China.* Cresskill, NJ: Hampton Press.

Lerner, D. (1958). *The passing of traditional society: Modernizing the Middle East.* Glencoe, IL: Free Press.

Levinson, M. (1998). Globalization: Who looks after the people? In *The global competitiveness report 1998* (pp. 64–68). Geneva, Switzerland: World Economic Forum.

Levy, B., & Spiller, P. T. (1996). *Regulations, institutions and commitment: Studies in telecommunications.* New York: Cambridge University Press.

Lewis, P. (1998, June 27). Marx's stock resurges on a 150-year trip. *New York Times*, pp. B9, B11.

Lipton, M. (1977). *Why poor people stay poor: Urban bias in world development.* London: Temple Smith.

Mahathir, M. (1996, December 19). *Speech by the prime minister* (address to Infotech Malaysia, Kuala Lumpur) [Online]. Available: http://www.jaring.my/nitc/events/infotech/main.html

Mansell, R., & Wehn, U. (Eds.). (1998). *Knowledge societies: Information technology for sustainable development.* New York: Oxford University Press (for the U.N. Commission Science and Technology Development).

Marx, K., & Engels, F. (1848/1998). *The communist manifesto* (with an introduction by Eric Hobsbawm). London: Verso.

McChesney, R. W. (1997). The communication revolution: The market and the prospect for democracy. In M. Bailey & D. Winseck (Eds.), *Democratizing communication? Comparative perspectives on information and power* (pp. 57–78). Cresskill, NJ: Hampton Press.

McChesney, R. W. (1999). *Rich media, poor democracy: Communication politics in dubious times.* Champaign: University of Illinois Press.

McChesney, R. W., Wood, E. W., & Foster, J. B. (Eds.). (1998). *Capitalism and the information age: The political economy of the global communication revolution.* New York: Monthly Review Press.

McDowell, S. D. (1997). *Globalization, liberalization and policy change: A political economy of India's communications sector.* New York: St. Martin's Press.

McLuhan, M. (1964). *Understanding media: The extension of man.* New York: McGraw-Hill.

Menzies, H. (1996). *Whose brave new world? The information highway and the new economy.* Toronto, Canada: Between the Lines.

Mody, B., Bauer, J. M., & Straubhaar, J. D. (Eds.). (1995). *Telecommunications politics: Ownership and control of the information highway in developing countries.* Mahwah, NJ: Erlbaum.

Mosco, V. (1996). *The political economy of communication.* London: Sage.

Moss, M. (1986). Telecommunications and the future of cities. *Land Development Studies, 3*, 33.

Mowlana, H. (1996). *Global communication in transition: The end of diversity?* Thousand Oaks, CA: Sage.

Mowlana, H. (1997). *Global information and world communication* (2nd ed.). London: Sage.

Muchlup, F. (1962). *The production and distribution of knowledge in the United States.* Princeton, NJ: Princeton University Press.

Mueller, M., & Tan, Z. (1997). *China in the Information Age: Telecommunications and the dilemmas of reform.* Westport, CT: Praeger.

Mustafa, M. A., Laidlaw, B., & Brand, M. (1997). *Telecommunication policies for Sub-Saharan Africa* (World Bank Discussion Paper No. 353). Washington, DC: The World Bank.

Naisbitt, J. (1996). *Megatrends Asia: Eight Asian megatrends that are reshaping our world.* New York: Simon & Schuster.

National Computerization Agency (NCA), Republic of Korea. (1997, Fall). *Informatization index of Korea* [Online]. Available: http://www.nca.or.kr/NCA97e/ pub/fall/cont_8.htm

Negrine, R. (1997). Communication technologies: An overview. In A. Mohammadi (Ed.), *International communication and globalization* (pp. 50–66). London: Sage.

Noam, E. I., & Steinborn, D. (1997). Introduction. In E. I. Noam (Ed.), *Telecommunications in Western Asia and the Middle East* (pp. ix–xix). New York: Oxford University Press.

Nora, S., & Minc, A. (1980). *The computerization of society: A report to the president of France.* Cambridge, MA: MIT Press.

Organization for Economic Cooperation & Development (OECD). (1981). *Information activities, electronics and telecommunication technologies*, Vols. 1 & 2. Paris: OECD.

Organization for Economic Cooperation & Development (OECD). (1997a). *Communications outlook 1997*, Vols. 1 & 2. Paris: OECD.

Organization for Economic Cooperation & Development (OECD). (1997b). *Towards a new global age: Challenges and opportunities—Policy report.* Paris: OECD.

Parker, E. B. (1981). *Economic and social benefits of the Rural Electrification Administration telephone loan program.* Stanford, CA: Equatorial Communications.

Parker, E. B. (1992). Developing third world telecommunications market. *The Information Society, 8,* 147–167.

Petrazzini, B. A. (1995). *The political economy of telecommunications reform in developing countries: Privatization and liberalization in comparative perspective.* Westport, CT: Praeger.

Pierce, W., & Jequier, N. (1983). *Telecommunications for development.* Geneva, Switzerland: International Telecommunications Union.

Porat, M. (1976). *The information economy.* Unpublished doctoral dissertation, Stanford University, Stanford, CA.

Porter, M. E. (1998). The microeconomic foundations of economic development. In *The global competitiveness report 1998* (pp. 38–49). Geneva, Switzerland: World Economic Forum.

Pratt, C. B. (1996). Africa south of the Sahara: New technologies, their implications, and special issues. In P. J. Jetter, K. R. Rampal, V. C. Cambridge, & C. B. Pratt, *International Afro mass media: A reference guide* (pp. 45–61). Westport, CT: Greenwood Press.

Read, W. H., & Youtie, J. L. (1996). *Telecommunications strategy for economic development.* Westport, CT: Praeger.

Rheingold, H. (1993). *The virtual community: Homesteading on the electronic frontier.* Reading, MA: Addison-Wesley.

Rideout, V., & Mosco, V. (1997). Communication policy in the United States. In M. Bailey & D. Winseck (Eds.), *Democratizing communication? Comparative perspectives on information and power* (pp. 81–104). Cresskill, NJ: Hampton Press.

Roach, C. (1997). The Western world and the NWICO: The challenge for the next millennium. In P. Golding & P. Harris (Eds.), *Beyond cultural imperialism: Globalization, communication & the new international order* (pp. 94–116). London: Sage.

Robertson, R. (1994), Globalization or glocaliztion? *Journal of International Communication, 1*(1), 33–52.

Rogers, E. M., with Svenning, L. (1969). *Modernization among peasants: The impact of communication.* New York: Holt, Rinehart & Winston.

Rostow, W. W. (1960). *The stages of economic growth.* Cambridge, UK: Cambridge University Press.

Rota, J., & Rodriguez, C. (1996). Information technology, culture, and national development. In D. L. Paletz (Ed.), *Political communication research: approaches. studies, and assessments*, Vol. 2. (pp. 237–252). Norwood, NJ: Ablex.

Rudenstein, N. (1996, September). The Internet is changing higher education. *Global Issues, 1*(12) [Online]. Available: http://www.usia.gov/journals/itgic/0996/ijge/gjcom2.htm

Ruggiero, R. (1997, October 23). *Services in a borderless economy.* Address to the second DEBIS (Daimler-Benz Interservices AG) Services Conference "Services for the Working World in the 21st Century" in Berlin, Germany.

Sachs, J. D. (1998). Ten trends in global competitiveness in 1998. In *The global competitiveness report 1998* (pp. 14–21). Geneva, Switzerland: World Economic Forum.

Sakamoto, Y. (Ed.). (1994). *Global transformation: Challenges to the state system.* Tokyo: United Nations University Press.

Samarajiva, R., & Shields, P. (1990). Integration, telecommunication, and development: Power in the paradigms. *Journal of Communication, 40*(3), 84–105.

Santoso. (1997). Into cyberspace. *Index on Censorship, 26*(2), 58.

Sassen, S. (1996). *Losing control?: Sovereignty in an age of globalization.* New York: Columbia University Press.

Saunders, R. J., Warford, J. J., & Wellenius, B. (1983). *Telecommunications and economic development.* Baltimore, MD: Johns Hopkins University Press (for the World Bank).

Schiller, D. (1999). *Digital capitalism: Networking the global market system.* Cambridge, MA: MIT Press.

Schiller, H. I. (1969). *Mass communication and American empire.* Boston: Beacon Press.

Schiller, H. I. (1996). *Information inequality: The deepening social crisis in America.* New York: Routledge.

Schmitt, B. (1997, March 31). An Internet answer to repression. *Washington Post,* p. A21.

Schramm, W. (1964). *Mass media and national development.* Stanford, CA: Stanford University Press.

Schumacher, E. F. (1973). *Small is beautiful: A study of economics as if people mattered.* London: Blond & Briggs.

Singhal, A., & Rogers, E. M. (1989). *India's information revolution.* New Delhi, India: Sage.

Smith, D., & Nemeth, R. (1988). An empirical analysis of commodity exchange in the international economy: 1965–80. *International Studies Quarterly, 32,* 227–240.

Smythe, D. W. (1957). *The structure and policy of electronic communication.* Urbana: University of Illinois Press.

Solomon, R. H. (1997, April 1). *The global information revolution and international conflict management.* Address to the Virtual Diplomacy Conference of the U.S. Institute of Peace, Washington, DC.

Snyder, D., & Kick, E. (1979). Structural position in the world system and economic growth, 1955–1970: A multiple network analysis of transnational interactions. *American Journal of Sociology, 84,* 1096–1126.

Stevenson, R. L. (1994). *Global communication in the twenty-first century.* New York: Longman.

Stone, P. B. (1993). Public-private alliances for telecommunications development: Intracorporate Baby Bells in the developing countries. *Telecommunications Policy, 17*(4), 459–469.

Sussman, G. (1997). *Communication, technology, and politics in the Information Age.* Thousand Oaks, CA: Sage.

Sussman, G., & Lent, J. A. (Eds.).(1998). *Global productions: Labor in the making of the "information society."* Cresskill, NJ: Hampton Press.

Taylor, P. M. (1997). *Global communications, international affairs and the media since 1945.* London & New York: Routledge.

Toffler, A. (1980). *The third wave.* New York: Morrow.

Toffler, A., & Toffler, H. (1993). *War and anti-war: Survival at the dawn of the 21st century.* Boston: Little, Brown.

United Nations Development Program. (1999, 2000). *Human development report.* New York: Oxford University Press.

Vincent, R. C. (1997a). The future of the debate: Setting an agenda for a New World Information and Communication Order, 10 proposals. In P. Golding & P. Harris (Eds.), *Beyond cultural imperialism: Globalization, communication & the new international order* (pp. 175–207). London: Sage.

Vincent, R. C. (1997b). The New World Information and Communication Order (NWICO) in the context of the information superhighway. In M. Bailey & D. Winseck (Eds.), *Democratizing communication? Comparative perspectives on information and power* (pp. 377–406). Cresskill, NJ: Hampton Press.

Wallerstein, I. (1974). *The modern world-system: Capitalist agriculture and the origins of the European world economy in the 16th century.* New York: Academic Press.

Wang, G. (Ed.). (1994). *Treading different paths: Informatization in Asian nations.* Norwood, NJ: Ablex.

Whitmore, S., & Erickson, J. (1999, September 3). Meeting the need for speed. *Asiaweek, 25,* 32–37

Winseck, D. (1997). Democratic potentials versus instrumental goals in Canadian telecommunications. In M. Bailey & D. Winseck (Eds.), *Democratizing communication? Comparative perspectives on information and power* (pp. 105–134). Cresskill, NJ: Hampton Press.

Winseck, D., & Cuthbert, M. (1997). From communication to democratic norms: Reflections on the normative dimensions of international communication policy. *Gazette, 59,* 1–20.

World Bank. (1995). *Mauritius: Sustaining the competitive edge* [Online]. Available: http://worldbank.org/aftdr/findings/english/find37.htm

World Bank. (1997). *World development report: The state in a changing world.* New York: Oxford University Press.

World Bank. (1999). *World development report: Knowledge for development.* New York: Oxford University Press.

World Economic Forum (WEF). (1997, 1998). *The global competitiveness report.* Geneva, Switzerland: WEF.

World Trade Organization (WTO). (1997). *Annual report 1997,* Vols. 1 & 2. Geneva, Switzerland: WTO.

CHAPTER CONTENTS

6 Communication Ethics: Centrality, Trends, and Controversies

RICHARD L. JOHANNESEN
Northern Illinois University

The centrality of ethics, both theoretically and professionally, to the field of communication is demonstrated. Then 7 trends in communication ethics scholarship are illustrated: (a) the proliferation of books on media and journalism ethics; (b) stress both on individual ethics and on social or institutional ethics; (c) recognition of the interrelationship of freedom and responsibility; (d) scholarship on ethics in organizational communication contexts; (e) diverse feminist contributions to communication ethics; (f) scholarship from a feminist viewpoint on an "ethic of care"; and (g) applications of the ancient Greek tradition of virtue ethics to contemporary communication contexts. Finally, 6 controversies or challenges in the development of communication ethics are probed. (a) Can we develop a viable concept of the "self" as an ethical agent in communication? (b) Can we develop a postmodern ethic or ethics of communication? (c) Can we legitimately search for some minimum transcultural ethical standards for communication? (d) Can we recognize the roles that diversity and marginalization play in developing communication ethics? (e) Can we develop a viable communication ethic for the internet and cyberspace? (f) Can some conception of "shame" be legitimate for communication ethics?

AT the dawn of the 21st century, it is well to take stock of key assumptions, trends, issues, controversies, and challenges within the sub-areas of communication study. First, I will demonstrate the centrality of ethics to the human communication process and to the communication profession. Then I will illustrate seven current trends in communication ethics scholarship. Finally, I will investigate six controversies or challenges in the development of communication ethics for a postmodern age.

Correspondence: Richard L. Johannesen, Department of Communication, Watson Hall, Northern Illinois University, DeKalb, IL 60115; email: rjohannesen@niu.edu

Communication Yearbook 25, pp. 201–235

CENTRALITY

Theoretical

Matters of ethics, of degrees of rightness and wrongness, virtue and vice, and moral obligation, I believe are inherent in the human communication process. Traditional ethicists argue that ethical issues may arise in human behavior whenever the behavior involves conscious choice of means and ends, whenever the behavior could have significant impact on other persons, and whenever that behavior is subject to judgment of standards of right and wrong (Wellman, 1988, pp. xiii–xviii, 267; Williams, 1993, pp. 55, 66). If there is little possible significant physical or symbolic impact of our behavior on other humans, matters of ethics have been deemed minimally relevant. If we have little or no opportunity for conscious free choice in our behavior, if we are forced or coerced, matters of ethics are seen as minimally relevant for our behavior.

It seems to me that the human communication process is a paradigm of human behavior that inherently involves matters of ethics, no matter how we resolve them or even whether we face them. Generally in human communication we make conscious choices about our means and ends. And generally we communicate to have some impact on other persons. In each case some of our choices and impacts are subject to judgments of degrees of moral right and wrong. Here, as throughout my essay, I use the concepts ethics and morals more or less interchangeably.

Ethical concerns have been central to communication theory and practice at least since Plato condemned rhetoric as sophistry and characterized it as no more intellectually respectable than mere cookery. In contrast, Aristotle in his *Rhetoric* (1356a) described rhetoric as an "offshoot" of ethics. Today, diverse scholars in philosophy, rhetoric, sociology, and communication contend that, indeed, ethics is a central dimension of the human communication process. Kenneth Burke and Richard M. Weaver, politically liberal and conservative rhetoricians respectively, both argue that all human use of language necessarily involves matters of ethical responsibility (Burke, 1961, pp. 41, 187; Weaver, 1953, pp. 6, 24). Wallace Matson describes the fundamentally human capacity to create and use symbols as leading inevitably to the ethical norms of truth telling and promise keeping (Matson, 1994, pp. 163–165).

Philosopher Martin Buber sees the self or person as constituted through continuous human interaction in the realm of the "between"—symbolic interaction that to varying degrees is dialogical or monological. This communication is to varying degrees more or less ethical and our ethical responsibilities derive from the I-Thou relationship (Buber, 1965; Johannesen, 1996a, pp. 63–85; Johannesen, 2000). For philosopher Emmanuel Levinas (1969, 1985, 1987), the bedrock of ethics is the direct or indirect encounter I have with the Other. My ethical obligation is to hear and respond to the call addressed to me by the Other, especially the Other as stranger or one in need (Ediger, 1994; Smith, 1997; Wyschogrod, 2000). Following Levinas, Zygmunt Bauman argues in his *Postmodern Ethics* that my obligation to respond to the Other does not depend on whether or how the other responds to me. My ethical obligation rests on "that unfounded, non-rational, un-arguable, no-excuses given and non-calculable urge to stretch towards the other, to caress, to live for, happen what may" (1993, pp. 85–86, 247; see also Bauman, 1997, pp. 46–70).

German critical theorist Jurgen Habermas has developed a comprehensive theory of communicative competence or communicative action. Because he views humans as unique in the social and communicative construction of their "selves," Habermas emphasizes the fundamental ethical principles of justice and solidarity in his book, *Moral Consciousness and Communicative Action* (1990, pp. 56–67, 200; see also Benhabib & Dallmayr, 1990; Thomassen, 1992). Justice requires equal rights and equal respect for individuals whereas solidarity demands "empathy and concern for the well-being of one's neighbor." Feminist critical theorist Seyla Benhabib (1992) argues that "the exercise of moral judgment is pervasive and unavoidable" because we are "immersed in a network of human relationships." In fact, the "domain of the moral is so deeply enmeshed" with these relationships that "to withdraw from moral judgment is tantamount to ceasing to interact, to talk and act in the human community" (pp. 125–126).

The philosophic tradition of American pragmatism undergirds rhetorician James Mackin's book, *Community Over Chaos: An Ecological Perspective on Communication Ethics* (1997). Mackin sees social systems as communicative ecosystems subject both to health and pollution. His premise is that

> the community must protect its communicative ecosystem in order to support all of its members. What everybody is doing may be polluting that communicative system, just as what everybody does often pollutes our biological ecosystems. In both cases the pollution is unethical. Audiences and speakers are moral agents, responsible for the results of their communicative actions on the larger ecosystem. (pp. 1–2)

Mackin considers the individual as "a system made up of subordinate systems, existing alongside parallel systems, within superordinate systems." For him, individualism and communitarianism are "just different levels of analysis of the ecosystem." The basic principle of Mackin's communication ethics "is that the individual should support the communicative ecosystem that supports the individual. Supporting the ecosystem, however, does not mean blind loyalty to the way things are but includes building, maintaining, and remodeling the system" (pp. 31–34, 58).

Professional

At the outset, a brief comment on the history of academic study of communication ethics is appropriate. One of the earliest articles in a national scholarly communication journal was that by William Schrier (1930) on the ethics of persuasion. In the mid-1950s, Karl Wallace (1955) published his widely quoted, adapted, and reprinted classic, "An Ethical Basis of Communication." Johannesen's (1967) anthology reprinted some of the key articles and book chapters on ethics in persuasion, public address, advertising, and public relations published during the 1950s and early 1960s. A landmark book was Thomas Nilsen (1966), *The Ethics of Speech Communication*, in which he developed his "significant choice" standard for public discourse rooted in the values fundamental to representative democracy. Nilsen also suggested how this view might apply to interpersonal communication.

Four surveys of the early literature prove invaluable. Jensen (1959, 1985) twice examined the available literature on teaching ethics in speech communication. Clifford Christians (1977) assessed "Fifty Years of Scholarship in Media Ethics." And Ronald Arnett (1987) evaluated "The Status of Communication Ethics Scholarship in Speech Communication Journals from 1915 to 1985." Arnett grouped his analyses into five categories: democratic ethics; universal/humanitarian ethics; codes, procedures, and standards; contextual ethics; and narrative ethics.

The activities of our national professional associations and the scholarship of their members now clearly recognize the centrality of ethics to human communication theory and practice. Three current general textbooks sketch the broad parameters of the subject matter and dimensions of communication ethics. *Communication Ethics: Methods of Analysis*, by James Jaksa and Michael Pritchard (1994), focuses on veracity and truth telling as a recurrent theme, suggests approaches to justification of ethical decisions, presents numerous brief case studies for discussion, and develops three case studies in depth. My own *Ethics in Human Communication* (1996a), explores seven fundamental ethical perspectives that undergird most contemporary communication ethics, probes ethics in the contexts of interpersonal, small group, organizational, and intercultural/multicultural communication, examines over a dozen basic issues, discusses formal codes of ethics, describes feminist contributions to communication ethics, and reprints four lengthy case studies. *Ethical Issues in the Communication Process*, by J. Vernon Jensen (1997), examines a wide range of issues in communication ethics as they manifest themselves in the various dimensions of the communication process: communicator; message; medium; receivers, and situation. A special contribution, based on his earlier journal article, is Jensen's analysis of the ethics of whistleblowing.

At least seven scholarly anthologies of original essays now probe various aspects of communication ethics, and I will mention some of them more specifically as I proceed (Casmir, 1997; Christians & Traber, 1997; T. W. Cooper et al., 1989; Denton, 1991, 2000; Greenberg, 1991; Jaksa & Pritchard, 1996; Makau & Arnett, 1997). Three literature review essays in the *Communication Yearbook* sponsored by the International Communication Association include significant discussion of ethical issues in varied communication contexts (Allen, Gotcher, & Seibert, 1993; Cameron, Sallot, & Curtin, 1997; Rimal, Fogg, & Flora, 1995). Two extensive bibliographies of sources on communication ethics are in print (Johannesen, 1996a, pp. 337–365; Jensen 1997, pp. 203–228) and a lengthy essay on ethics appears in the *Encyclopedia of Rhetoric and Composition* (Johannesen, 1996b).

Since 1972 the National Communication Association has had a Credo for Free and Responsible Communication in a Democratic Society. Also NCA now has policy statements on electronic communication networks, political communication, diversity, and campus speech codes that in part address matters of ethics (*Spectra*, July 1997, pp. 4–5). Recently NCA has formulated a professional code of responsibility for its members and a more general credo on communication ethics. At least four presidential addresses by NCA leaders have focused specifically on communication ethics: Robert Jeffrey in 1973, Frank Dance in 1982, Kenneth Andersen in 1983, and James Chesebro in 1996. In 1995 the Association for Communication Administration agreed on a definition of the field of communication that in part says that the "field promotes the effective and ethical practice of human communication" (Jensen, 1997, p. 4).

Since its formation in 1985, the Communication Ethics Commission of NCA has promoted both teaching and scholarship on communication ethics. Since 1990 the Commission has cosponsored a biannual National Communication Ethics Conference. At each NCA convention since 1985, the Commission has sponsored 6–10 programs of competitively selected papers or competitively selected programs. As the concern for discussion of ethical issues has widened and deepened in the association, other divisions and commissions increasingly have programs that examine communication ethics.

Are matters of ethics central to the theory and practice of human communication? Should communication ethics be a fundamental topic of our scholarship, our teaching, and our professional association concerns? Clearly, I believe, we must answer yes to both questions.

SELECTED TRENDS

Media Ethics

I turn my attention now to illustrating seven trends in communication ethics scholarship. Certainly one trend is the proliferation of texts and scholarly books on media and journalism ethics. Clifford Christians's review (1995) noted that the "34 books in media ethics published during the decade so far [1990–1995] already exceed the total number published in the 1980s"; academia, he observed, "is being flooded" (p. 545). Some of these books focus on case studies for analysis, although most of these also briefly discuss ethical theory. Here I think of such books as *Media Ethics: Cases and Moral Reasoning*, by Christians, Fackler, and Rotzoll (1998); *Media Ethics: Issues and Cases*, by Philip Patterson and Lee Wilkins (1998); *Ethics in Media Communications*, by Louis Day (1997); *Doing Ethics in Journalism: A Handbook With Case Studies*, by Black, Steele, and Barney (1995); and *Electronic Media Ethics*, by Val Limburg (1994).

Whereas they do discuss ethical theory somewhat and do discuss cases briefly, another group of books focus on an array of specific ethical issues facing the media and journalism. Of special note here is *Controversies in Media Ethics*, by Gordon and Kittross (1999). For each issue they carefully craft a pro and con argument and present a concluding critical commentary by John Merrill. Also included in this issues-oriented group would be, for example, Conrad Fink, *Media Ethics* (1995); Eugene Goodwin and Ron Smith, *Groping for Ethics in Journalism* (1994); Michael Bugeja, *Living Ethics: Developing Values in Mass Communication* (1996); Carl Hausman, *Crisis of Conscience: Perspectives on Journalism Ethics* (1992); Matthew Kieran, *Media Ethics: A Philosophical Approach* (1997); and Philip Seib and Kathy Fitzpatrick, *Public Relations Ethics* (1995; see also Hulteng, 1985; Meyer, 1987; Pippert, 1989; Rivers & Mathews, 1988; Seib, 1994).

Significant contributions in building ethical theory for print and broadcast journalism are made by a small cluster of books. In *Good News: Social Ethics and the Press*, Christians, Ferre, and Fackler (1993) propose fundamental reforms in press theory and institutional practice. They develop a communitarian ethic "that features the dialogic self, community commitment, civic transformation, and mutuality in organizational culture" (p. 13). John Merrill's recent *Journalism Ethics* (1997) surveys a wide range of philosophical tributaries that he believes must contribute and in the end briefly sketches a stance he calls "ethical mutualism"—an interactive balance between individualism and communitarianism, egoism and altruism, religion and science, rationalism and emotivism, legalism and consequentialism, absolutism and relativism (p. 214). In an earlier book, *The Dialectic in Journalism* (1989), Merrill presents at length what he terms a "deontelic ethics" for journalism that combines features both of deontological ethics and teleological ethics. Edmund Lambeth, in his *Committed Journalism* (1992), argues for and applies five principles to guide journalistic ethics: truth telling, humaneness, justice/fairness, freedom, and stewardship. Jeremy Iggers's book, *Good News, Bad News: Journalism Ethics and the Public Interest* (1998), examines key journalistic concepts such as impartiality, objectivity, neutrality, and social responsibility and develops a pragmatist ethical theory for civic journalism. Finally, as part of the proliferation of publication on media ethics, note that the *Journal of Mass Media Ethics* now is a well-established scholarly outlet for both theoretical and applied research.

Individual and Social Ethics

Continued urging to have communication ethics scholarship and teaching stress both individual ethics and social or institutional ethics represents a second trend. Elsewhere I put the point this way: "What are the ethical virtues of character and central ethical standards that should guide individual choices? What are the ethical standards and responsibilities that should guide the communication of organizations and institutions—public and private, corporate, governmental, or professional? For an ethically suspect communication practice, where should individual and collective responsibility be placed? The study of communication ethics should suggest standards both for individual daily and context-bound communication choices and also for institutional systemic policies and practices" (Johannesen,

1996a, pp. 16–17). Christians, Ferre, and Fackler lament that most past ethical advice for journalists was "tailored to individual professionals. Media ethics stressed the duties of reporters and editors, downplaying the responsibility they share with the newspapers, broadcast stations, chains, corporations, and conglomerates that employ them" (1993, pp. ix, 18–48). The appropriate dual concern both for individual and social communication ethics crystallizes in the words of Christians, Fackler, and Rotzoll: "For all the emphasis in this book on social ethics, individual practitioners ought not become lost. The individual is the authentic moral agent." Whereas "corporate obligation is a meaningful notion," the

> point is that responsibility, to be meaningfully assigned and focused, must be distributed among the individuals constituting the corporation. Individuals are not wholly discrete, unrelated, atomistic entities; they always stand in a social context with which they are morally involved. But individuals they nevertheless remain. And it is with each person that ethics is fundamentally concerned. (1998, p. 22; see also Merrill, 1989, p. 3)

Lambeth (1992, pp. 57–71) employs an entire chapter to examine the "ways in which news organizations affect the nature, range, and impact of the ethical decisions journalists make" and some "ways journalists can and do respond to organizational influences on their professional lives." The Jaksa and Pritchard text (1994) probes both the individual and social ethics dimensions while recognizing their connections.

Freedom and Responsibility

Continued recognition of the interrelationship, often tension, between freedom and responsibility represents a third trend. The intertwined concerns are for the boundaries of constitutionally and legally protected freedom of expression and for the ethically responsible exercise of those freedoms (Johannesen, 1996, pp. 6–9, 110–111, 136–137, 197–198; see also Klumpp, 1997). Christians, Ferre, and Fackler (1993, p. 22) believe that the philosophy of the Enlightenment bequeathed "to us the universal problem of integrating human freedom with moral order." That "freedom from legal constraints is a special privilege that demands increased awareness of moral obligation" is an assumption of Klaidman and Beauchamp (1987, p. 12). In his *The Dialectic in Journalism*, Merrill depicts the freedom-responsibility relationship as a creative tension:

> Freedom and responsibility are, in a real sense, contraries of great importance in journalism; they are the tension agents that bring conflict to the dialectic. Freedom clashes with ethics to gain more flexibility and individualism. Ethics conflicts with freedom to supplant personal licentiousness with social concern. Neither ever completely wins the battle, and neither falls completely vanquished. Instead, a reconciliation, a hybridization, a mediation—a *dialectical synthesis*—results. (1989, pp. 10–11; see also 37–39, 197–202, 214)

Sociologist Edward Sampson, in developing his non-Buberian conception of dialogic human interaction and a related dialogic ethic, describes the roles of both freedom and responsibility more in positive than negative terms:

> We currently consider both freedom and responsibility negatively. We are free in so far as another's will does not impose itself on us. We are acting responsibly in so far as we do not harm others, intrude upon their "space" or infringe on their own freedom. Dialogism insists on recasting both of these in positive terms. We are free not because we are detached from others, but literally because we and they are interconnected. We are responsible, not in order to avoid harming others or intruding on their turf, but because we and they are mutually involved in one another's completion as human beings and in sustaining the very social world that makes our life and its values even possible to consider. (1993, pp. 171–172)

Although Vernon Jensen notes that people "constantly struggle with the tension between rights and responsibilities" and generally "seek to balance the tensions in meaningful and fair ways," he strongly believes that they are not separate entities nor are they simply two sides of the same coin. In fact Jensen suggests that their "intimate enmeshing" is captured best in a newly coined word—"rightsabilities." This word, he contends, does capture the "total integration of rights and responsibilities, like the intertwining strands of a rope or the encircling figures on a totem pole or a Hindu temple." The two words rights and responsibilities embody "the yin and yang in Eastern cultures, the supposed opposites that are really complementary, each contributing to the other's fulfillment" (1997, pp. 9–10).

Organizational Communication Ethics

I now turn to a *fourth trend*, namely the accumulating scholarship in our field concerning ethics in organizational communication contexts (Jaksa & Pritchard, 1997, p. 17; Johannesen, 1996, pp. 173–196). At the First National Communication Ethics Conference in 1990, W. Charles Redding (1990, pp. 121–147), the acknowledged founder in our field of research on organizational communication, severely and at length chastised our scholars of organizational communication for their "culpable neglect" for virtually ignoring research on ethics, both descriptive and normative inquiry. Also he urged that for the immediate future those scholars should have as their "highest research priority" the "relationships among communication, ethical choices, and behavioral consequences" (p. 134). Jaksa and Pritchard characterize Redding's address as a "landmark" that "stimulated significant research in organizational communication ethics" (1996, p. xiii). Certainly at subsequent national communication ethics conferences and at NCA and ICA conventions, an increasing number of papers examined matters of ethics in varied organizational communication contexts. In a paper completed in 1994 just prior to his death, Redding (1996, pp. 18–24), continued his criticism of neglect of ethics by organizational communication scholars in our field. But Redding answered his own previous call for research by explaining an exploratory typology of "unethical communication phenomena (messages or message-related events) as they are frequently observed in organizational life." He suggests the following categories as guides for both descriptive and normative research: coercive, destructive, deceptive, intrusive, secretive, and manipulative-exploitative (for an application, see Mattson & Buzzanell, 1999).

This trend of research on organizational communication ethics can be illustrated by mentioning a few of the key contributions from journal articles and conference papers both from the 1980s and 1990s. Ronald Arnett (1988) builds on the work of Ian Mitroff to propose a "choice-making ethic" for organizational communication. Eric Eisenberg (1984) contends that intentional (strategic) ambiguity often is a necessary and ethical technique in organizational communication. Both Ron Pearson (1989a, 1989b) and Carl Botan (1993) proposed a dialogical ethic for public relations practice. In a series of papers and journal articles, George Cheney and Phil Tompkins draw upon rhetorician Kenneth Burke and philosopher Henry Johnstone, Jr., to advocate four ethical duties applicable in organizational communication contexts: guardedness, accessibility, nonviolence, and empathy (summarized in Johannesen, 1996a, pp. 181–183). Based on their earlier organizational integrity audits, Julie Belle White and her colleagues develop a Model of Organizational Integrity that could guide individual and institutional practice. They present six ethical habits (along with specific commitments and practices to implement them): (a) solving ethical problems directly and reflectively, (b) interacting responsibly, (c) modeling integrity, (d) sharing organizational purposes and directions, (e) valuing stakeholder perspectives, and (f) practicing personal integrity (summarized in Johannesen, 1996a, pp. 180–181). Christopher Schroll (1995) offers an evaluative framework for critiquing communication ethics and technology.

Two anthologies of original essays and a scholarly book further illustrate this trend. Charles Conrad's anthology, *The Ethical Nexus* (1993), examines "the complex interrelationships between values, ethics, and organizational decision making, the matrix of concepts that comprise the 'ethical nexus'" (p. 2). Two chapters provide conceptual grounding, three explore communication and the origins of value-based decisions, three examine communication and the management of value incongruities, and two probe future application in policy decision making of a framework of organizational meaning systems and of value-oriented arguments. With roots in two conference programs they organized on communication in high-risk (hazardous) technologies, James Jaksa and Michael Pritchard edited *Responsible Communication: Ethical Issues in Business, Industry, and the Professions* (1996). The 20 essays in the volume cluster around four themes: (a) issues in organizations, (b) communicating risk, (c) sharing and controlling information, and (d) educational challenges. And we have a full-length book treatment by Matthew Seeger titled simply *Ethics and Organizational Communication* (1997). Seeger's wide range of significant topics includes the centrality of ethics to organizational communication, organizational theory and enacting ethics, individual and corporate responsibility and accountability, privacy and employee rights, free speech and employee voice, whistle-blowing, organizational legitimacy, stakeholder perspectives, advertising, organizational change, leadership, and integrating ethics into the organization's agenda.

Feminist Communication Ethics

Increasing feminist contributions that enrich communication ethics constitute a fifth trend (Johannesen, 1996a, pp. 221–222, 230–239; see also Brennan, 1999). With a grounding in feminist "muted group theory" and inspiration from a poem by Emily Dickinson, Gillian Michell (1984) contends that the practice of women "telling it slant" (rather than outright lying or telling the truth straight up) is ethically justifiable in our male-dominated culture. Sally Miller Gearhart (1979) attacks the tradition of rhetoric-as-persuasion because it represents a masculine "conquest/conversion mentality" and constitutes violence (but see Condit, 1997). Rather she proposes a particular view of "communication" as a more desirable and ethical alternative. Her "womanization of rhetoric" fosters a collective rather than competitive mode, equalizes power, enhances voluntary self-persuasion, and risks openness to change rather than adamancy in one's position. Although they accept much of Gearhart's critique of the rhetoric of conquest, conversion, and control, Sonja Foss and Cindy Griffin (1995; see also Foss, Griffin, & Foss, 1997) believe that rhetoric-as-persuasion should be one among several rhetorics available to us. In their move "beyond persuasion," they develop an "invitational rhetoric" rooted in feminist assumptions. "Invitational rhetoric," say Foss and Griffin, invites the "audience to enter the rhetor's world and see it as the rhetor does" (p. 5). The invitational rhetor aims to establish a "nonhierarchical, nonjudgmental, nonadversarial framework" for the interaction with the audience, a "relationship of equality, respect, and appreciation" (pp. 5–6). Invitational rhetors make no assumptions that their "experiences or perspectives are superior to those of audience members and refuse to impose their perspectives on them." Whereas change is not the intent of invitational rhetoric, change may occur in the "audience or rhetor or both as a result of new understandings and insights gained in the exchange of ideas" (pp. 5–6). Foss and Griffin remark that invitational rhetoric may require a "new scheme of ethics" to fit its goals and purposes (p. 16). Bonnie Dow (1995) has taken issue with some of the assumptions and arguments not only of Gearhart but also of Foss and Griffin.

From her stance as a feminist teacher and scholar, Lana Rakow (summarized in Johannesen, 1996a, pp. 234–235) employs the norms of "trust, mutuality, justice, and reciprocity" as touchstones for ethical communication relationships. She suggests three ground rules for an ethic that would promote healthy, egalitarian, and respectful communication in varying contexts between individuals, cultures, organizations, and countries: (a) *Inclusiveness* means openness to multiple perspectives on truth, an encouragement of them, and a willingness to listen. Persons are not dehumanized because of their gender, race, ethnicity, sexual orientation, country, or culture. (b) *Participation* means ensuring that all persons must have the "means and ability to participate, to be heard, to speak, to have voice, to have their opinions count in public decision making." All persons "have a right to participate in naming the world, to be a part of the discussion in naming and speaking our truths." (c) *Reciprocity* assumes that participants be considered equal partners in communication. There should be a "reciprocity of speaking and listening, of knowing and being known as you wish to be known." Lea Stewart (1997) surveys a broad range of issues in feminist ethics, including the intersections of race/ethnicity, gender/sex, and economic/social class. She offers potential ethical guidelines for communication: foster dialogue (in the Buberian sense), embrace multiple discourses, empower all people, and abandon the notion of "women's" issues.

In her article, "Feminist Theorizing and Communication Ethics," Linda Steiner (1989) explores applications to mass communication. A feminist ethic for mass communication questions "who the communicators are, who is allowed to communicate and who is excluded, in part because this controls what is communicated, how, and to whom" (p. 168). Media institutions would be challenged to broaden their definition of news to include "communications by, for, and about peoples who are ignored, suppressed, or oppressed" (p. 168). Views of those who are outside of or who resist conventional authority structures should be sought actively. The feminist ethic advocated by Steiner would challenge the objectification both of mass media sources and of audiences. Respect for dignity and integrity and the promotion of a collaborative and egalitarian process are goals of the ethic. Journalists, for example, could allow sources to raise issues as they see them, to ask questions, or to redirect questions. Or journalists might "share information and/or interpretations with sources before publication" and thus secure the sources' sense of accuracy and completeness of a story (p. 169). In a more recent essay, Steiner (1997) infuses feminist ethical perspectives into her enlargement and extension of the Potter Box framework for ethical analysis: (a) definition of the situation; (b) values and ideals; (c) ethical principles; (d) loyalties; (e) options; and (f) harms (for an application, see Mattson & Buzzanell, 1999). She provides a penetrating illustration of how she would employ her schema to decide, as a booking agent for a cable TV variety entertainment show, whether to book a "gangsta" rap group whose lyrics and visuals are sexist and demeaning.

Sandra Davidson Scott (1995) proposes a feminist theory of ethics for journalists that goes "beyond reason." She contends that a larger and more significant role in journalists' ethics must be made for emotion and empathy. Scott offers four guidelines as aids to making journalistic decisions, for example whether to take or publish a photo: (a) "Listen to one's emotions. Maybe the situation will require that one listen more than once" (p. 31). (b) "Quit rationalizing. . . . If one's gut says 'don't,' then one should avoid looking to one's head to concoct some fancy reason to go ahead" (p. 31). (c) Use one's moral imagination through empathizing with (seeing from the viewpoint of) victims, their families, and the reading/viewing audience. (d) "Last, trust emotions. One should not be duped into believing that one has to go through fancy mental machinations to come up with the right ethical decision" (p. 32). Finally, Tanni Haas and Stan Deetz (2000; see also Deetz, Cohen, & Edley, 1997) draw upon feminist theorists, especially the work of feminist critical theorist Seyla Benhabib (1992), to suggest ethical procedures for corporations that require them to seriously identify and allow representation of multiple stakeholder interests. In their application of Benhabib, they argue that corporations must simultaneously assume the standpoints both of the "generalized other" and of the "concrete other" through an continuing "moral conversation" with multiple stake-holders about their values and political interests.

An Ethic of Care

Surely a sixth and related trend is the continually expanding scholarly literature that explores from feminist viewpoints an "ethic of care" as a complement to or alternative to a more traditional "ethic of justice" (Johannesen, 1996a, pp. 222–230). *In a Different Voice: Psychological Theory and Women's Development* was published in 1982 by Carol Gilligan, a developmental psychologist, and generated considerable scholarly response that supported or criticized, modified or extended her view. Gilligan contends that most earlier studies of human moral development generalized the experiences and views of men as adequate to describe human moral development generally and that, thus, women's moral development usually is judged as deficient. In contrast, based on her own research, Gilligan argues that in con-temporary American culture there are two different but valuable and potentially complementary moral "voices" of adulthood. These male and female voices, al-though typically manifested in men and women respectively, are modes of thought and themes that could be found in either men or women (pp. 2, 14, 18, 155–156, 173–174; but for a contradictory reading of Gilligan on this point, see Wood, 1994, pp. 62–85; also Wood, 1992).

The traditional *ethic of justice*, according to Gilligan, characterizes the male moral voice. It is rooted in the primacy of individual autonomy and independence. The ethic of justice judges competing rights and embodies a logic of equality and fairness. Reciprocal noninterference with rights describes an individual's obliga-tion. Abstract, universalizable, impartial principles and rules concerning rights and justice are applied to a specific case. An *ethic of care*, says Gilligan, characterizes the female moral voice. It is rooted in the primacy of actual relationships and the interdependence of self and others. Compassion, empathy, and nurturance help resolve conflicting ethical responsibilities to all concerned, including the self. The ethic of care considers the needs both of self and others, not just the survival of one's self and not just the avoidance of hurting others. Focus is on the concrete circumstances of particular relational situations to guide moral deliberation rather than solely on abstract rules and principles. In Gilligan's view, then, these are the contrasting characteristics of an ethic of justice and an ethic of care (pp. 19, 63, 69, 73–74, 100–101, 127, 143, 156–165, 174).

In the intervening years, a number of issues relevant to Gilligan's assumptions, research methods, and implications have been debated by feminist and nonfeminist scholars from diverse disciplines. Treatments that support, attack, modify, or sug-gest new avenues are represented by books (Bowden, 1997; Clement, 1996; Hekman, 1995; Koehn, 1998; Tong, 1993), by anthologies on the topic (Brabeck, 1989; Held, 1995; Larrabee, 1993), and by special issues of journals (On *In a*

Different Voice, 1986). In addition, four books by feminist scholars each present their own more or less complete versions of an ethic of care (Manning, 1992; Noddings, 1984; Tronto, 1993; Wood, 1994). Virginia Held (1993) sees an ethic of care as central to the project of developing an adequate feminist ethics. Whereas she acknowledges the diversity and ferment within contemporary feminist ethics, Held believes that "the ethic of care" is the "phrase which is gathering most support as a way of designating an alternative feminist outlook. While no label seems adequate yet, 'care' seems to come closest, and to contrast well with traditional approaches based on rationality, rules, and the conception of morality in terms of . . . justice, liberty, or equality" (p. 169).

What are some of the issues that have been and continue to be debated concerning versions of an ethic of care? Here are clusters of some of the major questions: (a) What grounding or basic assumptions are offered to undergird a care ethic? How is an ethic of care rooted in "natural" capacities common to all humans? To what degree is an ethic of care rooted in biology, maternal experience, cultural construction, or all of these? (b) Must an ethic of justice be essentialized only to men and a care ethic only to women? To what degree can or should the ethics of justice and care be available to both women and men? (c) How do such factors as race/ethnicity, economic/social class, and sexual orientation affect the development and functioning of an ethic of care? Is an ethic of care mostly reflective of the experiences of White, middle-class women? (d) What are some of the central dimensions or characteristics of an ethic of care that might help clarify or implement it? (e) What view of the "self" as moral agent is embedded in the care ethic? (f) What roles should ethical rules or principles play, if any, in an ethic of care? (g) Are an ethic of care and an ethic of justice best seen as complementary, antagonistic, interdependent, or mutually exclusive? If both are valuable and applicable, does one uniformly take precedence over the other, or might it depend on the situation? Is care best seen as supplementary to justice or justice as supplementary to care? (h) Do an ethic of justice and an ethic of care, if both are broadly conceived, adequately cover the entire domain of moral decision making? How adequately can Kantian universalism, Rawlsian impartial justice, Ross's prima facie duties, versions of utilitarianism, and the tradition of virtue ethics be subsumed under one or the other labels? Are there multiple moral "voices" rather than just two? (i) How might the norms of a care ethic actually function to perpetuate the cultural subordination of women as the "natural" caregiver (rather than men also), as confined to the private sphere of home, family, and close relationships (rather than also as viable in the public sphere of politics, policy, and work), and as engaged in expected duty more than respected work? Is the focus of a care ethic on the maintenance of relationships as primary over all other concerns and at all costs to the caregiver? Or is the focus on maintaining relationships wherein the needs/interests of both caregiver and cared-for have serious recognition and protection? (j) How might an ethic of care apply to voluntary and involuntary relationships and to equal and unequal power relationships? (k) To what degree can an ethic of care apply both to the private and public spheres of life? How might an ethic of care effectively be embedded in the policies and practices of institutions?

Joan Tronto (1993) and Julia Wood (1994) demonstrate how their versions of a care ethic might apply in the public sphere. Clement (1996), Minow (1990), and Robinson (1997, 1999) also suggest applications in the realms of pacificism, eldercare, law, and international relations. The research program of Patricia Sullivan and Steven Goldzwig explores applications to decision making in the public spheres of Supreme Court decisions (1994, 1996) and of political communication (1994; Sullivan, 1993; Sullivan & Turner, 1996). Their conception of a relational ethic, or care ethic, incorporates dimensions from Gilligan (1982), Noddings (1984), Tronto (1993), and Minow (1990).

Virtue or Character Ethics

The seventh and final trend I have selected for illustration is the steadily growing interest in how the ancient Greek philosophical tradition of virtue ethics, or character ethics, might be applied or modified for contemporary communication contexts (Johannesen, 1996a, pp. 11–13, 177–178). An emphasis on duties, obligations, rules, principles, calculation of consequences, and the resolution of complex ethical dilemmas has dominated the contemporary philosophy of ethics. Ethicists of virtue or character generally see that perspective as a complement to the current dominant ethical theories. Ethicists describe virtues variously as deep-rooted dispositions, habits, skills, or traits of character that incline persons to perceive, feel, and act in ethically right and sensitive ways. In times of crisis or uncertainty, our decision concerning ethical communication may stem less from deliberation than from our formed character. Furthermore, our ethical character influences the terms with which we describe a situation and whether we believe the situation contains ethical issues.

In Judeo-Christian or Western cultures, good moral character usually is associated with the habitual embodiment of such virtues as courage, temperance, prudence (or practical wisdom), justice, fairness, generosity, patience, truthfulness, and trustworthiness. Contemporary feminist scholars would interject additional vital virtues: caring for self and others, compassion, nurturance of relationships, facilitation of growth and change, and attentive and realistic love. Martin Buber's dimensions of true dialogue could be viewed as virtues of ethical character: authenticity, inclusion, confirmation, and presentness (Johannesen, 1996a, pp. 66–67). Other cultures may praise additional or different virtues that they believe constitute ethical character. Instilled in us as habitual dispositions to see and act, virtues guide the ethics of our communication when careful or clear deliberation is not possible. Some of the key books by philosophers that trace the ancient Greek virtue ethics tradition and which explore that tradition's applicability for contemporary life are: Crisp and Slote (1997); Hudson (1986); Krushwitz and Roberts (1987); Kupperman (1991); Sherman (1989); Slote (1992); and Taylor (1991).

I want to describe briefly some attempts to apply this virtue ethics tradition in communication-related fields. I have explored, for example, the implications of virtue ethics for the role played by "character" in contemporary American political rhetoric (Johannesen, 1991). In what way and to what degree should ethical character be an legitimate political issue? James Herrick (1992, 1995, pp. 45–55) examined the nature of rhetoric as a human practice and extracted "rhetorical virtues" that would allow rhetoric to flourish as an ethical practice: rhetorical acumen, honesty, cooperation, respect for persons, and respect for rhetorical contexts. These rhetorical virtues, each with their several subvirtues, Herrick contends are "enacted habits of character" that aid persons in perceiving the "ethical nuances" of a rhetorical situation and in conducting rhetoric in ways that facilitate that person being true to self, audience, and topic. In their book, *The Virtuous Journalist* (1987), Stephen Klaidman and Tom Beauchamp examine the practice of journalism to determine some key moral virtues, fixed dispositions to do what is morally right, that enable journalism to flourish: reaching for the truth, avoiding bias, avoiding harm to others, serving the public, maintaining trust, escaping manipulation, inviting criticism, and being accountable.

Oliver Williams and Patrick Murphy (1990, 1992) investigate virtue ethics as a moral theory for marketing, specifically, and business, generally. They believe that ethical virtues can be shaped by our individual choices and encouraged by the institutions and organizations within which we work. Virtue theory would prompt the developer of a proposed marketing decision or policy to ask two questions: What sort of person am I shaping? What sort of organization am I shaping? They argue: "Underpinned by a theory of virtue, an ethical corporate culture, through an ingrained set of habits and perspectives, trains all those in its purview to see things in a certain way and hence is likely to predispose them toward ethical behavior" (1992, p. 18). Several psychologists (Jordan & Meara, 1990; Pettifor, 1996) suggest applications of virtue ethics to the training and practice of professional psychologists. In part they endorse the moral virtues elaborated for all professionals by William May (1984): honesty, respect, benevolence, promise keeping, prudence, perseverance, courage, integrity, concern for the public good, compassion, justice, and humility (see also LeBacqz, 1985, pp. 77–91). Finally, David H. Smith (1993) argues that virtue ethics, as part of an educational orientation for physicians that emphasizes paradigm-case ethics and narrative ethics, provides a better approach than a principles-based ethics.

CONTROVERSIES AND CHALLENGES

I now explore some controversies and challenges that face the development of communication ethics. Most of these controversies and challenges stem from one significant question: Can communication ethics survive the devastating critique posed by postmodernism (Audi, 1995, pp. 634–635; Caputo, 1993; Cornell, 1985;

Bauman, 1993; Best & Kellner, 1991; Lyotard, 1984; Richardson et al., 1998, pp. 498–503; Taylor & Winquist, 2001, pp. 252–253)? More concretely, what would be the result for communication ethics: If there is no individual moral agent, no autonomous, unencumbered, individual "self" deciding ethical questions objectively about abstract others apart from the social, economic, and institutional contexts in which that self is imbedded and constructed (see Christman, 1995)? If there are no personal "speakers" in communication with attendant ethical responsibilities for choice but only interchangeable "role" players whose communication is dictated by the discourse "rules" of a hegemonic culture? If there are no grand master narratives or absolute universal values that warrant general allegiance across groups and cultures? If probing the nature of "human nature" is but a delusion or an exercise in political power? If the alternative to absolutism and universalism is nothing but fragmentation and alienation? If there can no longer be ethics as we have known it?

Self as an Ethical Agent

First controversy/challenge: Can we develop a viable concept of self as an ethical agent in communication? Must we go all the way with some postmodernists to a self so decentered as to be completely fragmented, alienated, impotent, and determined—indeed to the death of the self? Must we simply agree with Best and Kellner's (1991) estimate?: "However, all postmodern theory lacks an adequate theory of agency, of an active creative self, mediated by social institutions, discourses, and other people" (p. 283). Some feminist scholars and some communitarian scholars envision a situated or contextualized self imbedded in a web of relationships and responsibilities, making decisions about and responding to concrete, particular persons (Benhabib, 1992, pp. 148–177, 215–216; Manning, 1992, pp. 2–5, 28; Sandel, 1984, pp. 5–6; see also Meyers, 1997; Schrag, 1997). Bauman (1993, pp. 44–47), however, worries about possible abuses stemming from a communitarian notion of a situated self.

From the vantage point of rhetoric and English composition studies, Michael Hassert (1995) urges us toward a "perspective that will enable us to see some sort of ethical responsibility for the writer while still allowing the reader to participate in the meaning-making process. And this perspective has to place the author and reader in a relationship that is not agonistic" (p. 180). Hassert turns to the works of Kenneth Burke for a "conception of writer as agent, as acting upon language, while still understanding the writer as being acted upon by language." He also speculates that the ethic he proposes "might even be easier in some ways to incorporate within speech communication than within written composition" (p. 180). Martha Cooper (1994) is concerned with the construction through discourse of an ethical agent who both is responsible and "response-able." For her, responsibility is something created by the agent continually, not something possessed. "To be able to respond requires a reaching out, a recognition of the other, followed by careful listening that allows the other to be heard, and followed yet again by empathy that validates what is heard. Responsibility is based on connection and valorizes the importance of relationships" (pp. 305–306).

Julia Wood (1994, pp. 108–110) describes an "interdependent sense of self" as undergirding an ethic of care. She builds upon Keller's (1985) concept of "dynamic autonomy" as "an awareness of both one's own desires, plans, motives, and viewpoints and those of others, as being comfortable thinking and acting independently and thinking and acting cooperatively or in relationship with others" (Wood, 1994, pp. 108–110). Clifford Christians (1995, pp. 550, 552) urges a "revitalized notion of human agency as we face the demise of the ethical and the transition to a new era beyond duty," and he contends that the "idea of institutions as moral agents is still seriously underdeveloped." In arguing for their communitarian social ethic for journalism, Christians, Ferre, and Fackler (1993, pp. 13, 61–75) assume a "dialogic self"—a "self-in-relation" as opposed to an autonomous self. They agree with Martin Buber's view that our sense of self or personhood develops only in and through I-Thou and I-It relationships (for a non-Buberian view of the dialogic self see Sampson, 1993, pp. 165–175). In explaining "Communication and the Ground of Dialogue," Kenneth Cissna and Rob Anderson (1994) build a conception of the socially constructed interdependent "self" rooted in the works of Buber, Bakhtin, Gadamer, and various conversation analysts. They articulate an important reminder: "Just as we reject an entirely monadic and individual conception of the self, we cannot accept an entirely social model in its place. Human beings, even human infants, are not some variety of sponge, soaking up whatever self-definitions might spill our way. And, although the self is a social construction, one in which other people—and hence our society, our culture—are completely involved, we also know that the self is unique, individual" (p. 16; see also Richardson et al., 1998, pp. 504–513).

Postmodern Communication Ethics

Second controversy/challenge: Can we develop a postmodern communication ethic that responds to the postmodern critique without capitulating to its excesses (Gergen, 1994)? Although there may be other communication scholars presently addressing this challenge, I will focus on the research programs of two. In a chapter in his book, *Audience and Rhetoric* (1992, pp. 119–126), James Porter briefly introduces several postmodern viewpoints that he believes hold useful implications for rhetorical ethics. Based on the works of Lyotard and Foucault, in a later essay Porter (1993) develops a locally and communally based postmodern ethics for rhetoric and English composition that centers on how the values of the individual, community, discipline/field, and tradition/culture intersect in the composing process. In *Rhetorical Ethics and Internetworked Writing*, Porter (1998; see also Porter, 1997) develops a postmodern "critical rhetorical ethics" that he sees as especially appropriate for discourse on electronic networks. He adapts parts of traditional sources such as Aristotle and Kenneth Burke but also draws heavily on postmodernist, critical theorist, and feminist sources such as Foucault, Lyotard, Benhabib, and Irigaray. His view condemns static, decontextualized, universal ethical rules and principles but focuses on how rules are created and changed and how competing principles may be decided among in concrete contexts. His approach offers not certain and specific answers to issues of rhetorical ethics but heuristic questions and guiding principles for exploring what ethical judgments might be probable and appropriate in a given case. Porter's critical rhetorical ethics examines how one (and one's discourse) is situated in a web of economic, class, and gender relationships and constraints and it prioritizes concern for the marginalized and oppressed. His view critiques both liberal individualism and communitarianism and moves toward solidarity in the sense of harmony not homogeneity (pp. 68–69, 134–135, 143–146, 149–151, 162–166). As ethical principles to guide both rhetor stance toward audience and rhetorical procedures, Porter (pp. 151–162) offers the following: (a) respect the audience and audience differences, (b) care for the audience and for concrete Others, (c) do not harm or oppress the audience, (d) consult dialogically with diverse sources, (e) focus on contexualized elements and the situated moment, and (f) recognize the complexity and ambiguity of ethical judgment.

Martha Cooper's book chapter in 1991 represented her first overt explanation of the possibility of a postmodern communication ethic. That chapter, "Ethical Dimensions of Political Advocacy from a Postmodern Perspective," built upon the works of Habermas, Foucault, and Nancy Fraser to present an ethic that focuses on the need to re-create the citizen, on procedures that can open up citizen access to means of communication, and on consequences of political discourse that preserve citizens as agents who genuinely can participate in government. Her 1994 conference presentation, "Postmodernism, Feminism, and the Ethical Subject," ventured a depiction of a viable moral agent in communication who is both responsible and response-able. Her brief 1996 conference position paper sketches three dimensions of the possible postmodern ethic she envisions. In a book chapter, "Decentering Judgment: Towards a Postmodern Communication Ethic," Cooper (1998) presents a kind of culmination of her project. Cooper grounds her ethic in the primacy of discourse in human existence and in the inherent human moral impulse variously called obligation or conscience. We have a sense of obligation or call to conscience when we hear and must respond to the call of a marginalized or needy Other. In her view, there are three alternative responses that are available, as appropriate, in a well-rounded postmodern communication ethic: (a) a *discourse ethic* (adapted from Habermas) that involves the practice of questioning through argument, deliberation, and judgment; (b) an *ethic of care* (rooted in feminist theorizing) that involves the practice of responding through narrative, empathy, and identification; and (c) an *ethic of resistance* (adapted from Foucault and Fraser) that involves the practice of the Other affirming herself or himself through ritual celebration, detachment/connection, and tolerance/empowerment. Cooper carefully explains each of these key concepts, examines ways that each of the three alternatives may be carried to unethical extremes, and notes ways in which each may offset or compensate for potential defects of the other alternatives. Finally, at length Cooper presents an illuminating example of what she sees as an instance of sexual harassment and describes how each of the three alternatives might be employed by her in response to the call of the Other.

Transcultural Ethical Standards

Third controversy/challenge: Can we legitimately search for some minimum transcultural ethical standards for communication? If these transcultural ethical values are to be considered universal, in what sense should we mean universal? In his book, *Through the Moral Maze: Searching for Absolute Values in a Pluralistic World*, Robert Kane (1994) offers several relevant insights. Universal or absolute does not have to mean that we are absolutely certain about the values or that we have a right to impose them on others through fanaticism or authoritarianism. Universal simply means that we believe these values are valid for all persons, times, or points of view. "The real issue," says Kane, "is whether we can have good reasons for believing in (at least some) universal values and truths despite not being certain" (pp. 9, 15–16). Kane also argues that we need not be adamant about the "requirement that the ethically relevant human traits we are seeking be completely universal human traits and provably so, rather than merely *common* human traits." It is enough, he says, "to know that human beings commonly need certain things. For we can reason that *since we are human, there is high probability that we need these things as well for a fulfilling human life*" (p. 51). Joanna Hodge (1992) suspects "that an ethics for a postmodern community will have to retain some of the characteristics of a transcendental subjectivity and transcendent value, alongside the incompatible emphases on location more characteristic of the postmodern." The task facing postmodern ethics, she believes, is "to explain how such a conjunction of incompatible elements can be thought about at all" (p. 135).

Two recent books represent attempts by scholars outside of the communication discipline to uncover universal transcultural values to guide our moral choices (see also Dalai Lama, 1999). *Shared Values for a Troubled World: Conversations with Men and Women of Conscience* reflects Rushworth Kidder's (1994) interviews with 24 "ethical thought leaders" from diverse positions in diverse world cultures. Kidder discerns a transcultural ethical code rooted in the widely shared values of love, truthfulness, fairness, freedom, unity, tolerance, responsibility, and respect for life (see also Loges & Kidder, 1997). Sissela Bok's book, *Common Values* (1995), presents her argument for a "minimalist" starting point for the search, one that "seeks out the values that are in fact broadly shared, without requiring either absolute guarantees for them or unanimity regarding them" (pp. 74, 78). Such minimalist values can serve as a basis for communication and cooperation across cultures and for discussion of how they might be applied or might be extended in scope. Such common values "provide criteria and a broadly comprehensible language for critique of existing practices" both within a particular society or culture and also across societal boundaries (pp. 1, 18–19, 75). Bok identifies a small cluster of minimalist moral values that are held in common by most human beings and that have had to be worked out by all human societies: positive duties of mutual support, care, loyalty, and reciprocity; negative duties to refrain from the hurtful actions of deceit, betrayal, and violence; and the standards for "rudimentary fairness and procedural justice" when conflicts arise (pp. 13–19, 26, 57, 70, 778–779). Bok's effort embodies her own admonition to take seriously the doubts raised against simplistic views of human nature and universal values "without relying so uncritically on those doubts as to reject all study of what human beings have in common" (p. 49).

Now I turn to three books and an article by communication scholars that engage in the search for transcultural ethical standards for communication. The first three works I will mention briefly and the fourth will be described more fully. An anthology of original essays, *Ethics in Intercultural and International Communication*, was edited by Fred Casmir (1997). Several of the essays in the book probe the degree to which transcultural ethical norms for communication are feasible and, equally important, how they might be applied and adapted in differing cultural contexts (pp. 23, 145–148, 153–182). Thomas Cooper (1998, pp. 92–94, 164, 187) suggests that the sacredness of all life—respect for all human and nonhuman life—is a virtually universal ethical standard guiding the communication of indigenous or native cultures of the world. Vernon Jensen (1992) examines the ancient Eastern and Western religions of Hinduism, Buddhism, Taoism, Confucianism, Judaism, Christianity, and Islam. Despite significant differences in core values, views of the deity, and sacred truths, he finds that these seven world religions hold in common six ethical standards for communication: (a) Tell the truth and avoid lies; (b) do not slander anyone; (c) do not blaspheme, dishonor, or profane the sacred persons, symbols, or rituals central to the religion; (d) avoid communication that demeans other persons or life in general; (e) aim habitually to embody ethical virtues in your character as preparation for ethical communication and aim to be trustworthy—to earn trust; and (f) go beyond communicating to inform, persuade, or please to aim at "edifying" others, that is, showing them how close to excellence humans can become. Jensen argues that we need not be "believers" in these religions in order to benefit from the power of these standards.

Clifford Christians and Michael Traber (1997) edited an anthology of original essays titled *Communication Ethics and Universal Values*. In their own introductory and concluding essays (viii–xv, 3–23, 327–343), Christians and Traber search for universal values rooted not solely in anthropological sameness, although some relevant commonalities exist, but rooted primarily in philosophical assumptions about human nature. The ethical values they identify are not foundational a priori certainties; they are commitments open to reexamination (p. 17). "The universality of these values," they believe, "is beyond culture. It is rooted ontologically in the nature of human beings. It is by virtue of what it means to be human that these values are universal" (p. 341). In addition, no matter the cultural differences concerning individualism or community, there "is a growing consensus that certain universal standards for the social accordance of human dignity must be upheld, regardless of cultural differences" (p. 337). As the protonorm underlying most cultures and at the heart of what it means to be human is the sacredness of life, the "irrevocable status" of respecting human life (pp. x–xii, 6–7, 13, 17). Christians and Traber identify the universal ethical principles that follow from the protonorm as guides for our uniquely human capacity to use language: truth telling, human dignity, no harm to the innocent, unconditional acceptance of the Other as a person, and solidarity with the weak and vulnerable (pp. x–xv, 13–15, 330, 334–336, 339–340).

Before leaving discussion of the challenge or controversy of the search for transcultural ethical values, I would also urge that we examine contributions that might be made by natural scientists and social scientists. James Q. Wilson (1993) explores insights from the biological and social sciences to contend that humans have a natural "moral sense" formed from the interactions of their innate human nature with their family experiences and culture. In all people to some but differing degrees, the moral sense shapes how we believe we and others ought to behave. As nonexhaustive examples of the moral sense, Wilson mentions sympathy, fairness, self-control, duty, and integrity. Mark Johnson (1993) examines the implications of cognitive science for ethics and develops the central thesis that "human beings are fundamentally *imaginative* moral animals." He argues that the "quality of our moral understanding and deliberation depends crucially on the cultivation of our moral imagination" (p. 1). What is needed, he contends, "is a new, empirically responsible moral philosophy" that is "grounded on what the cognitive sciences teach us about concepts, understanding, and reasoning." This "new account of moral understanding" shows us the "imaginative nature of morality" and makes us "aware of the variety of possible framings for any given situation and the variety of metaphorical concepts that define our most important moral concepts" (pp. 11–12). Finally, the field of evolutionary ethics is one in which pro and con positions have emerged as to whether, or to what degree, scientific evidence demonstrates that our moral capacity is rooted in biological, genetic, and developmental evolution (Bradie, 1994; Nitecki & Nitecki, 1993; Thompson, 1995; Wilson, 1998, pp. 238–256; Wright, 1994).

Role of Diversity

Fourth controversy/challenge: Can we recognize the roles that diversity and marginalization play in developing communication ethics? At this point in human history, this is a major challenge as we attempt to move beyond ethics equated with an elite White male Western cultural view (Kidder, 1994, pp. 15–16; Christians & Traber, 1997, p. 5). Clifford Christians (Christians & Traber, 1997, p. 18) argues for a "worldview pluralism" in which ethical beliefs are held in good faith and debated openly and in which "a commitment to universals does not eliminate all differences" of view. "The only question," he says, "is whether our worldviews and community formations contribute in the long run to truth telling, human dignity, and nonmaleficence." Sissela Bok agrees: "Cultural diversity can and should be honored, but only within the context of respect for common values. Any claim to diversity that violates minimalist values . . . can be critiqued on cross cultural grounds invoking basic respect due all human beings" (1995, p. 24).

In his book, *Ethnic Ethics*, Anthony Cortese (1990) argues at length that "morality must be bound to a particular cultural or sociocultural context" (p. 41). His position is "that people are more important than principles, that relationships are more crucial than conceptions of justice, and that subcultural moral systems are more relevant than universal standards of ethics" (p. 91). "The key to morality is in social relations," Cortese contends, "not in abstract rational principles" (p. 2). "Ethnic background, gender, role demands, and socioeconomic status" are key factors in his view (p. 2). On the matter of how diversity should be taken into account in doing ethics, the views of Cortese and those of Christians and Bok just discussed clearly differ. Can they be accommodated? At least we should recognize that all three reject the rationalist position of a priori foundationalist absolutely certain universal values.

I now turn to some recent scholarly efforts that examine ways in which diversity and marginalization play roles in developing communication ethics. *Communication Ethics in an Age of Diversity* is an anthology of original essays recently edited by Josina Makau and Ronald Arnett (1997). The book's goal is to "help frame the communicative ethics needed to guide interactions and actions in the emerging age of diversity" and the essays explore issues of race, ethnicity, gender, and sexual orientation (p. viii). The editors note that many of the essays share elements of the postmodernist critique, including giving serious attention to the role of emotions. At the same time, most of the authors "reject the postmodern tendency to abandon the quest to find meaningful ways to deliberate across differences about ethical issues" (pp. x–xi). Several of the essays problematize the idea of "tolerance" either by exploring potential negative functions or by urging a move beyond mere tolerance to a celebration or appreciation of the positive values of diversity (pp. 48–67, 137–138). Several others examine both positive and negative dimensions of the idea of "community" as an alternative to hyper-individualism (pp. 27–47, 197–200). My own essay investigates how freedom, responsibility, and diversity intertwine in such controversial communication contexts as obscene rap and rock lyrics, as pornography, and as campus "hate" speech (pp. 157–186).

In an article in *College Composition and Communication*, Gregory Clark (1994) criticizes the discourse about "community" for privileging agreement while often overlooking, minimizing, or excluding difference. He sketches an ethics for a rhetoric that has as its end an "accommodation of the contradictory demands of difference and collectivity" (p. 64). This is a discourse that "directs people to identify and explore their conflicts," thereby binding them together "in a collectivity of equals" (pp. 62, 64). Willie Hopkins, in his book *Ethical Values and Diversity in Organizations* (1997), presents a theoretical model to support his speculation that "the ethics paradigms subscribed to by U.S. organizations are susceptible to being influenced by the ethical values brought to the workplace by individuals from diverse racial, ethnic, cultural, and otherwise diverse backgrounds" (pp. 55–71).

By reconsidering the ethics of plagiarism (Johannesen, 1995), I attempt to illustrate how an ethical standard assumed to be universal by persons of one cultural heritage may not be an ethical issue at all for persons of other cultural heritages. Our conception of plagiarism as unethical deception and theft of words or ideas is deeply imbedded in the Euro-American traditions of print orientation, individual originality, capitalistic commodification of ideas, and private ownership. In contrast, people in many primarily oral cultures view words and ideas as communal intellectual resources to be shared and adapted; for them, borrowing without acknowledgment would not be an ethical issue.

Clifford Christians (Christians & Traber, 1997) believes that "reverence for life" as an ethical protonorm undergirding a communication ethic can only be embodied in the "creaturely and corporeal" lived experience of "geography, ethnicity, and ideology" (p. 12). In his view, the ethical touchstone of a culture's or subculture's authenticity is its willingness to move toward common citizenship for the excluded, the alienated, and the "voiceless along the fringes" (Christians, 1997, p. 201). A current trend among historians is away from history as a "view from above"—the notable words and deeds of the elite and powerful—toward writing "history from below"—the views and activities of ordinary people and of marginalized people (Burke, 1995, pp. 1–23). Is there an analogous tendency, even embryonic, among scholars of communication ethics? Two brief conference position papers by Anne Pym (Makus, 1994) and by Dolores Tanno (1994) seem to reflect such an impulse. In harmony with the spirit of Caputo's *Against Ethics* (1993), Pym writes about "ethics in the flesh": "I find ethics floating rather too high, while I find myself faced with events happening from below" (Makus, 1994, p. 313). Tanno finds a kindred view in Bauman's (1993, pp. 6–7) postmodern critique of traditional ethics viewed from the top. For Tanno (1994), the view from below is quite different. Whereas marginalized groups have "been viewed as the manifestation of postmodernism," in fact "they have been the foreshadowers of it" (p. 313). Tanno vividly describes how the characteristics of postmodernism that challenge traditional ethics

> have been reality for the oppressed throughout history. . . . All oppressed groups have intimately known fragmentation and anomie. All oppressed groups continually experience what it means to have nothing to hold on to. All oppressed groups have historically recognized the irrationality of a "rational" stance that has been curiously selective in determining how far its "humanizing force" should extend, which groups it would embrace, and which behaviors it would endorse. (p. 318)

Ethics for Cyberspace

Fifth controversy/challenge: Can we develop a viable communication ethic for the internet and cyberspace? Can we develop a communication ethic for this mind-boggling medium that so clearly embodies the tensions between freedom and responsibility and that offers the potential not only for connection and community but also for fragmentation and alienation? Perhaps we might gain some general orientation from two anthologies by scholars outside the communication field: *Social and Ethical Effects of the Computer Revolution* (Kizza, 1996) and *Computers, Ethics, and Society* (Ermann, Williams, & Shauf, 1997). Other orienting starting points for discussion might be the "Ten Commandments of Computer Ethics" promulgated by the Computer Ethics Institute (Kizza, 1996, p. 313) or the NCA's "Credo for Free and Responsible Use of Electronic Communication Networks" (*Spectra*, April 1997, p. 20).

I will describe briefly some efforts by communication scholars to examine ethical issues for computer communication and cyberspace. James and Paula Gilchrist (1996) explore the ethical implications of the proliferating corporate and government practice of computer monitoring of employees. They conclude: "The ethical issue, then, must precede the technological one. Instead of asking about the possible uses of technology, individuals in organizations must first ask what view will be used to judge human beings and their work, what work of organizations is most worth doing, and what kind of relationships are expected to be maintained among people" (p. 128). Michael Pritchard (1996) probes ethics for computer professionals and suggests applications of the virtue ethics tradition—ethical virtues that function even when no one is watching. In suggesting ethical guidelines for communication in the cyberspace realm of the Internet, World Wide Web, listservs, news groups, and chat rooms, John Courtright and Elizabeth Perse (1998) view ethics simply as "doing the right thing, even when no one is looking" and as "behaving properly, even when their is not a chance of being caught" (pp. 16, 33, 64, 82).

James Porter (1998) at length applies his postmodern critical rhetorical ethics to the realm of internetworked writing—to "the Internet, the World Wide Web, electronic mail, and the networked classroom" (p. xi). He argues that the "expectations and ethics from the print world and from the face-to-face conversational world" do not fit very well in the realm of internetworked writing (p. xii). Also we must go beyond purely legal issues and standards in this realm and develop an appropriate ethics for electronic writing (see pp. 1–22, 101–131). Although they do not label the issues they examine as ethical ones, David and Ann Gunkel (D. J. Gunkel & A. H. Gunkel, 1997; see also D. J. Gunkel, 1998, 2001) critique matters of power disparity, voicelessness, and marginalization in "The New World of Cyberspace." They bring to our awareness for evaluation the corrosive implications imbedded in the "new world" metaphor for the internet and cyberspace with its assumptions of ethnocentrism, commercialism, and utopianism inherited from European and American colonialism. At one point they argue: "Far from resolving the crises of the multicultural society, cyberspace could perpetuate and reinforce current systems of domination" (p. 131). Their critical analysis of the "new world" metaphor is rooted in their assumption about the power of naming and labeling: "The future of cyberspace, therefore, will be determined not only through the invention of new hardware and software but also through the names we employ to describe it. What cyberspace becomes will, to a great extent, depend upon what we call it" (p. 133).

Jana Kramer and Cheris Kramerae (1997) use feminist perspectives to critique "Gendered Ethics on the Internet." They, too, scrutinize dominant metaphorical images that are guiding our thinking about the use of the Internet: anarchy, frontier, democracy, and community. In their judgment, all four of the metaphorical models do little to foster desirable change but do much to "validate the dominant social structures." For each of the four dominant metaphorical images, they describe the "logic" of the metaphor (often an unnoticed logic), they identify the ethical standards imbedded in each, and they show how those standards disadvantage or harm women and other marginalized groups. In contrast, they describe an alternative feminist ethic for the Internet—an ethic that takes the loving, caring, parent-child relationship as its analogical starting point. Here, too, they describe the logic underlying this metaphor, its intrinsic ethical standards, and its positive effects on the lives of women and others who are marginalized.

Role of Shame

Sixth and final controversy/challenge: Can some conception of "shame" be legitimate for communication ethics? Certainly this is not a topic that has been much on the mind of those writing about communication ethics (a major exception is Planalp, Hafen, & Adkins, 2000). For instance, as an index item "shame" does not appear in the three general communication ethics textbooks or in the numerous media and journalism ethics books. With one significant exception (Barrett, 1998), textbooks on interpersonal communication seem not to treat shame as relevant.

Yet articles spanning 3 decades in such disparate sources as the *New York Times* (Hoffer, 1974), *Harper's* (Kaus, 1982), *The Nation* (Lasch, 1992), and *Newsweek* (Alter & Wingert, 1995) urge the rehabilitation of shame as a legitimate ethical force in American society. Other examples of this impulse appear in the news from time to time (Lipson, 1997). Republican House Majority Leader Dick Armey condemned President Bill Clinton as a "shameless person" concerning Clinton's personal sexual behavior (Barbs fly, 1998). And a syndicated political columnist condemned President Clinton for "routine and unending deceptions" on matters not only of personal behavior but also of public policy: "What inhibits most people from routine lies is a sense of shame. Clinton seems to lack this" (Samuelson, 1998, p. 17).

In his 1995 presidential campaign speech attacking sex and violence in the entertainment media, Bob Dole warned: "But those who cultivate moral confusion for profit should understand this: we will name their names and shame them as they deserve to be shamed" (Dole, 1997, p. 246). Media scholar Marvin Olasky (1985/1986) has urged a similar public shaming of ethical lapses to make more effective the Code of Professional Standards of the Public Relations Society of America. If the PRSA Board of Directors expels a member, Olasky believes it should publicly explain "the reasons for the expulsion, with names named. PRSA would thus bring shame into play." In addition, says Olasky, since "neither buyers or sellers of public relations services seem ready to publicize shameful activities," there is need for persons, groups, and the media to monitor the ethicality of public relations practice and through exposure "help to restore a sense of shame" (pp. 45–46). At a more private and personal level, consider legal scholar Stephen Carter in his book, *Integrity*, as he reflects on a childhood classroom chastisement he received for cheating: "I do remember that I was made to feel terribly ashamed; and it is good that I was made to feel that way, for I had something to be ashamed of. The moral opprobrium that accompanied that shame was sufficiently intense that it has stayed with me ever since, which is exactly how shame is supposed to work. As I grew older, whenever I was tempted to cheat . . . I would remember . . . the humiliation of sitting before my classmates, revealed as a cheater" (Carter, 1996, pp. 3–4).

In probing the usefulness of a conception of shame for communication ethics, I am not thinking of the current dominant views in psychiatry and psychology that tend to view shame negatively as a corrosive self-destroying pathology or as a threat to a person's fragile self-esteem (Broucek, 1991; Lansky & Morrison, 1997; Lasch, 1992; Karen, 1992). Rather I am thinking more about what some have called normal or situational shame (Karen, 1992, pp. 42, 58, 62). I am thinking about the view of philosopher Gabriele Taylor (1985, pp. 53–84) who sees shame as an emotion with positive roles in moral self-assessment and self-protection (see also Boolin, 1983; Liszka, 1999, pp. 12–39; Thrane, 1979). And philosopher Bernard Williams (1993) believes that shame should play an essential moral role for us: "By giving through the emotions a sense of who one is and of what one hopes to be, it mediates between act, character, and consequence, and also between ethical demands and the rest of life" (p. 102). Our search should be for a "reasonable mean, one that avoids suggesting that we need never feel shame or that we need always feel it" (Schneiderman, 1995, p. 55). The thrust of this sixth and final controversy or challenge can be captured in a question: Is there literally nothing anymore that persons could speak, write, or depict for which they justifiably should feel a sense of shame?

CONCLUSION

I believe that the trends, controversies, and challenges in communication ethics that I have examined point to a significant research agenda for the immediate decades. First, we should continue exploration of both individual and social ethics. That is, we should continue emphasis on issues and standards to guide individual ethical choices. But also we vigorously must probe standards, procedures, and unspoken guidelines that do or should influence the systemic ethical norms of organizations and institutions. Second, and clearly related to the first item, we must determine what role the individual or self as an ethical agent can play in communication ethics. Even if the notion of an independent, autonomous, unencumbered self no longer is appropriate, what vision of a situated, imbedded, socially constructed self is most viable? Third, how should an "ethic of care" best be conceptualized and applied both for the private and public spheres? What are the similarities and differences, the strengths and weaknesses, of the versions of a care ethic by Noddings, Manning, Tronto, and Wood? In what ways can an ethic of care influence communication institutions and practices in the public sphere? Fourth, we must continue the search for a small or minimal core of transcultural ethical norms to guide intercultural and multicultural communication while acknowledging that at another level ethical standards for communication legitimately may vary between and within cultures. We need, I believe, some transcultural norms to avoid complete relativism. But also, I believe, we must understand and respect, much more than we have, the necessary and legitimate role of cultural, ethnic, gender, and other types of diversity in communication ethics. Fifth, and finally, we should explore in all seriousness the potential role of "shame" in a system of communication ethics. Why has it fallen into disfavor among academics in psychiatry, psychology, communication, and, to some degree, philosophy? Yet why does it seem to persist as a meaningful ethical concept in the public mind, one that periodically resurfaces as an important cultural component of ethics and character? While admitting the undesirability of using shame as a punishment in a classroom setting, can we approve the public shaming of public officials and public figures for their ethical lapses? What role can shame (in the sense of feeling ashamed for violating or not living up to our own personal ethical standards) play as an internal ethical guidance mechanism, perhaps even as a component of what we term conscience?

What might the future hold for the theory and practice of communication ethics as the 21st century dawns? This reminder of the centrality of ethics to communication and this survey of some significant trends and controversies of the 1980s and 1990s may provide some clues. Perhaps several observations from two scholars who have thought deeply about ethics for a postmodern age will underscore the opportunities and uncertainty ahead. In developing a dialogic ethic for the postmodern age that is rooted in the works of Bernstein, Apel, and Gadamer, Drucilla Cornell (1985) concluded: "The most we can expect from a ethical ideal is an orientation for our practice. It cannot protect us from the uncertainty of history or shield us from the risk of commitment" (p. 380). Zygmunt Bauman (1993) warns at the outset of his book, *Postmodern Ethics*: "The kind of understanding of the moral self's condition which the postmodern vantage point allows is unlikely to make moral life *easier*. The most it can dream of is making it a bit more *moral*" (p. 15). But in the end he concluded optimistically that "the moral conscience—that ultimate prompt of moral impulse and root of moral responsibility—has only been anesthetized, not amputated. It is still there, dormant perhaps, often stunned . . . but capable of being awoken" (p. 249).

NOTE

Portions of an earlier version of this essay were given as a Sharing the Wealth presentation at the National Communication Association conference, Chicago, November 20, 1997.

REFERENCES

Allen, M. W., Gotcher, J. M., & Seibert, J. H. (1993). A decade of organizational communication research: Journal articles 1980–1991. In S. A. Deetz (Ed.), *Communication yearbook 16* (pp. 252–330). Newbury Park, CA: Sage.

Alter, J., & Wingert, P. (1995, February 6). The return of shame. *Newsweek*, pp. 21–25.

Arnett, R. (1987). The status of communication ethics scholarship in speech communication journals from 1915 to 1985. *Central States Speech Journal, 38*, 46–61.

Arnett, R. C. (1988). A choice-making ethic for organizational communication: The work of Ian Mitroff. *Journal of Business Ethics, 7*, 151–161.

Audi, R. (Ed.). (1995). The Cambridge dictionary of philosophy. Cambridge, UK: Cambridge University Press.

Barbs fly over whether Clinton should quit. (1998, April 8). *Chicago Tribune*, Sec. 1, p. 3.

Barrett, H. (1998). *Maintaining the self in communication*. Incline Village, NV: Alpha & Omega Book Publishers.

Bauman, Z. (1993). *Postmodern ethics*. Oxford, UK: Blackwell.

Bauman, Z. (1997). *Postmodernism and its discontents*. New York, NY: New York University Press.

Benhabib, S. (1992). *Situating the self: Gender, community, and postmodernism in contemporary ethics*. New York: Routledge.

Benhabib, S., & Dallmayr. (Eds.). (1990). *The communicative ethics controversy*. Cambridge, MA: MIT Press.

Best, S., & Kellner, D. (1991). *Postmodern theory: Critical interrogations*. New York: Guilford.

Black, J., Steele, B., & Barney, R. (1995). *Doing ethics in journalism: A handbook with case studies* (2nd ed.). Boston: Allyn & Bacon.

Bok, S. (1995). *Common values*. Comumbia: University of Missouri Press.

Boolin, L. (1983). Guilt, shame, and morality. *Journal of Value Inquiry, 17*, 295–304.

Botan, C. (1993). A human nature approach to image and ethics in international public relations. *Journal of Public Relations Research, 5*, 71–81.

Bowden, P. (1997). *Caring: Gender-sensitive ethics*. London: Routledge.

Brabeck, M. M. (Ed.). (1989). *Who cares? Theory, research, and educational implications of the ethic of care*. New York: Praeger.

Bradie, M. (1994). *The secret chain: Evolution and ethics*. Albany: State University of New York Press.

Brennan, S. (1999). Recent work in feminist ethics. *Ethics, 109*, 858–893.

Broucek, F. J. (1991). *Shame and the self*. New York: Guilford.

Buber, M. (1965). *Between man and man* (R. G. Smith, Trans.). New York: Macmillan.

Bugeja, M. J. (1996). *Living ethics: Developing values in mass communication*. Boston: Allyn & Bacon.

Burke, K. (1961). *The rhetoric of religion*. Boston: Beacon Press.

Burke, P. (Ed.). (1992). *New perspectives on historical writing*. University Park: Pennsylvania State University Press.

Cameron, G. T., Sallot, L. M., & Curtin, P. A. (1997). Public relations and the production of news: A review and theoretical framework. In B. R. Burleson (Ed.), *Communication yearbook 20* (pp. 111–155). Thousand Oaks, CA: Sage.

Caputo, J. D. (1993). *Against ethics: Contributions to a poetics of obligation with constant reference to deconstruction*. Bloomington: Indiana University Press.

Carter, S. L. (1996). *Integrity*. New York: Basic Books.

Casmir, F. L. (Ed.). (1997). *Ethics in intercultural and international communication*. Mahwah, NJ: Erlbaum.

Christians, C. (1977). Fifty years of scholarship in media ethics. *Journal of Communication, 27*(4), 19–29.

Christians, C. G. (1995). Review essay: Current trends in media ethics. *European Journal of Communication, 10*, 545–558.

Christians, C. G. (1997). Social ethics and media practice. In J. M. Makau & R. C. Arnett (Eds.), *Communication in an Age of Diversity* (pp. 187–205). Urbana: University of Illinois Press.

Christians, C. G., Fackler, P. M., & Rotzoll, K. B. (1998). *Media ethics: Cases and moral reasoning* (5th ed.). New York: Longman.

Christians, C. G., Ferre, J. P., & Fackler, P. M. (1993). *Good news: Social ethics and the press*. New York: Oxford University Press.

Christians, C. G., & Traber, M. (Eds.). (1997). *Communication ethics and universal values*. Thousand Oaks, CA: Sage.

Christman, J. (1995). Feminism and autonomy. In D. E. Bushnell (Ed.), *"Nagging" Questions: Feminist ethics in everyday life* (pp. 17–30). Lanham, MD: Rowman & Littlefield.

Cissna, K. N., & Anderson, R. (1994). Communication and the ground of dialogue. In R. Anderson, K. N. Cissna, & R. C. Arnett (Eds.), *The reach of dialogue: Confirmation, voice, and community* (pp. 9–30). Cresskill, NJ: Hampton.

Clark, G. (1994). Rescuing the discourse of community. *College Composition and Communication, 45*, 61–74.

Clement, G. (1996). *Care, autonomy, and justice: Feminism and the ethic of care*. Boulder, CO: Westview.

Condit, C. M. (1997). In praise of eloquent diversity: Gender and rhetoric in public persuasion. *Women's Studies in Communication, 20*, 91–116.

Conrad, C. (Ed.). (1993). *The ethical nexus*. Norwood, NJ: Ablex.

Cooper, M. (1991). Ethical dimensions of political advocacy from a postmodern perspective. In R. E. Denton, Jr. (Ed.), *Ethical dimensions of political communication* (pp. 23–47). New York: Praeger.

Cooper, M. (1994). Postmodernism, feminism, and the ethical subject. In J. J. Jaksa (Ed.), *Proceedings of the third national communication ethics conference* (pp. 305–308). Annandale, VA: Speech Communication Association.

Cooper, M. (1996, May). *Postmodern communication ethics*. Paper presented at the Fourth National Communication Ethics Conference, Kalamazoo, MI.

Cooper, M. (1998). Decentering judgment: Towards a postmodern communication ethic. In J. M. Sloop & J. P. McDaniel (Eds.), *Treading judgment* (pp. 63–83). Boulder, CO: Westview.

Cooper, T. W. (1998). *A time before deception: Truth in communication, culture, and ethics*. Santa Fe, NM: Clear Light Press.

Cooper, T. W., et al. (Eds.). (1989). *Communication ethics and global change*. New York: Longman.

Cornell, D. (1985). Toward a modern/postmodern reconstruction of ethics. *University of Pennsylvania Law Review, 133*, 291–380.

Cortese, A. (1990). *Ethnic ethics: Restructuring of moral theory*. Albany: State University of New York Press.

Courtright, J. A., & Perse, E. M. (1998). *Communicating online: A guide to the internet*. Mountain View, CA: Mayfield.

Crisp, R., & Slote, M. (Eds.). (1997). *Virtue ethics*. New York: Oxford University Press.

Dalai Lama. (1999). *Ethics for the new millennium*. New York: Riverhead.

Day, L. A. (1997). *Ethics in media communications: Cases and controversies* (2nd ed.). Belmont, CA: Wadsworth.

Deetz, S., Cohen, D., & Edley, P. P. (1997). Toward a dialogic ethic in the context of international business organization. In F. L. Casmir (Ed.), *Ethics in intercultural and international communication* (pp. 183–226). Mahwah, NJ: Erlbaum.

Denton, R. E., Jr. (Ed.). (1991). *Ethical dimensions of political communication*. New York: Praeger.

Denton, R. E., Jr. (Ed.). (2000). *Political communication ethics: An oxymoron?* Westport, CT: Praeger.

Dole, B. (1997). *Sex and violence in the entertainment media.* In R. L. Johannesen, R. R. Allen, W. A. Linkugel, & F. J. Bryan (Eds.), *Contemporary American Speeches* (8th ed., pp. 242–247). Dubuque, IA: Kendall-Hunt.

Dow, B. J. (1995). Feminism, difference(s), and rhetorical studies. *Communication Studies, 46,* 106–117.

Ediger, J. (1994). An ethics of address-ability in Emmanuel Levinas. In J. J. Jaksa (Ed.), *Proceedings of the third national communication ethics conference* (pp. 200–216). Annandale, VA: Speech Communication Association.

Eisenberg, E. M. (1984). Ambiguity as a strategy in organizational communication. *Communication Monographs, 51,* 227–242.

Ermann, D. M., Williams, M. B., & Shauf, M .S. (Eds.). (1997). *Computers, ethics, and society* (2nd ed.). New York: Oxford University Press.

Foss, S. K., & Griffin, C. L. (1995). Beyond persuasion: A proposal for an invitational rhetoric. *Communication monographs, 62,* 2–18.

Foss, S. K., Griffin, C. L., & Foss, K. A. (1997). Transforming rhetoric through feminist reconstruction: A response to the gender diversity perspective. *Women's Studies in Communication, 20,* 117–135.

Fink, C. C. (1995). *Media ethics.* Boston: Allyn & Bacon.

Gearhart, S. M. (1979). The womanization of rhetoric. *Women's Studies International Quarterly, 2,* 195–201.

Gergen, K. J. (1994). The limits of pure critique. In H. W. Simons & M. Billig (Eds.), *After postmodernism: Reconstructing ideology critique* (pp. 58–78). Thousand Oaks, CA: Sage.

Gilchrist, J. A., & Gilchrist, P. S. (1996). Communication ethics and computer technology: The case of computer monitoring. In J. A. Jaksa & M. S. Pritchard (Eds.), *Responsible communication* (pp. 107–131). Cresskill, NJ: Hampton.

Gilligan, C. (1982). *In a different voice: Psychological theory and women's development.* Cambridge, MA: Harvard University Press.

Gilligan, C., Ward, J. V., & Taylor, J. M. (1988). *Mapping the moral domain.* Cambridge, MA: Harvard University Graduate School of Education.

Goodwin, H. E., & Smith, R. F. (1994). *Groping for ethics in journalism* (3rd ed.). Ames: Iowa State University Press.

Gordon, A. D., & Kittross, J. M. (1996). *Controversies in media ethics.* Overview and commentary by J. C. Merrill. New York: Longman.

Greenberg, K. J. (Ed.). (1991). *Conversations on communication ethics.* Norwood, NJ: Ablex.

Gunkel, D. J. (1998). Virtually transcendent: Cyberculture and the body. *Journal of Mass Media Ethics, 13,* 111–123.

Gunkel, D. J. (2001). *Hacking cyberspace.* Boulder, CO: Westview.

Gunkel, D. J., & Gunkel, A. H. (1997). Virtual geographics: The new worlds of cyberspace. *Critical Studies in Mass Communication, 14,* 123–137.

Haas, T., & Deetz, S. (2000). Between the generalized and the concrete other: Approaching organizational communication ethics from feminist perspectives. In P. Buzzanell (Ed.), *Rethinking organizational and managerial communication from feminist perspectives* (pp. 24–46). Thousand Oaks, CA: Sage.

Habermas, J. (1990). *Moral consciousness and communicative action.* (C. Lenhart & S. W. Nicholson, Trans.). Cambridge, MA: MIT Press.

Hassert, M. (1995). Constructing an ethical writer for the postmodern scene. *Rhetoric Society Quarterly, 25,* 179–196.

Hausman, C. (1992). *Crisis of conscience: Perspectives on ethics in journalism.* New York: HarperCollins.

Hekman, S. (1995). *Moral voices, moral selves: Carol Gilligan and feminist moral theory.* University Park: Pennsylvania State University Press.

Held, V. (1993). *Feminist morality: Transforming culture, society, and politics.* Chicago: University of Chicago Press.

Held, V. (Ed.). (1995). *Justice and care: Essential readings in feminist ethics*. Boulder, CO: Westview.

Herrick, J. A. (1992). Rhetoric, ethics, and virtue. *Communication Studies, 43,* 133–149.

Herrick, J. A. (1995). *Argumentation: Understanding and shaping arguments*. Scottsdale, AZ: Gorsuch.

Hodge, J. (1992). Genealogy for a postmodern ethics: Reflections on Heel and Heidegger. In P. Berry & A. Wernick (Eds.), *Shadow of spirit: Postmodernism and religion* (pp. 135–148). New York: Routledge.

Hoffer, E. (1974, October 18). Long live shame! *New York Times*, p. 41.

Hopkins, W. E. (1997). *Ethical dimensions of diversity*. Thousand Oaks, CA: Sage.

Hudson, S. (1986). *Human character and morality*. Boston: Routledge.

Hulteng, J. L. (1985). *The messenger's motives: Ethical problems of the media* (2nd ed.). Englewood Cliffs, NJ: Prentice-Hall.

Iggers, J. (1998). *Good news, bad news: Journalism ethics and the public interest*. Boulder, CO: Westview.

Jaksa, J. J., & Pritchard, M. S. (1994). *Communication ethics: Methods of analysis* (2nd ed.). Belmont, CA: Wadsworth.

Jaksa, J. J., & Pritchard, M. S. (Eds.). (1996). *Responsible communication: Ethical issues in business, industry, and the professions*. Cresskill, NJ: Hampton.

Jensen, V. R. (1959). An analysis of recent literature on teaching ethics in public address. *Speech Teacher, 8,* 219–228.

Jensen, V. R. (1985). Teaching ethics in speech communication. *Communication Education, 4,* 324–330.

Jensen, V. R. (1992). Ancient Eastern and Western religions as guides for contemporary communication ethics. In J. Jaksa (Ed.), *Proceedings of the second national communication ethics conference* (pp. 58–67). Annandale, VA: Speech Communication Association.

Jensen, J. V. (1997). *Ethical issues in the communication process*. Mahwah, NJ: Erlbaum.

Johannesen, R. L. (Ed.). (1967). *Ethics and persuasion: Selected readings*. New York: Random House.

Johannesen, R. L. (1991). Virtue ethics, character, and political communication. In R. R. Denton, Jr. (Ed.), *Ethical dimensions of political communication* (pp. 69–90). New York: Praeger.

Johannesen, R. L. (1995). The ethics of plagiarism reconsidered: The oratory of Martin Luther King, Jr. *Southern Communication Journal, 60,* 185–194.

Johannesen, R. L. (1996a). *Ethics in human communication* (4th ed.). Prospect Heights, IL: Waveland.

Johannesen, R. L. (1996b). Ethics. In T. Enos (Ed.), *Encyclopedia of rhetoric and composition* (pp. 235–240). New York: Garland.

Johannesen, R. L. (1997). Diversity, freedom, and responsibility in tension. In J. M. Makau & R. C. Arnett (Eds.), *Communication ethics in an age of diversity* (pp. 157–186). Urbana: University of Illinois Press.

Johannesen, R. L. (2000). Nel Nodding's uses of Martin Buber's philosophy of dialogue. *Southern Communication Journal, 65,* 151–160.

Johnson, M. (1993). *Moral imagination: Implications of cognitive science for ethics*. Chicago: University of Chicago Press.

Jordan, A. E., & Meara, N. M. (1990). Ethics and the professional practice of psychologists: The role of virtue and principles. *Professional Psychology: Research and Practice, 21,* 107–114.

Kane, R. (1994). *Through the moral maze: Searching for absolute values in a pluralistic world*. New York: Paragon.

Karen, R. (1992, February). Shame. *Atlantic Monthly*, 40–70.

Kaus, R. (1982, August). There's no shame anymore. *Harper's*, 8–15.

Keller, E. F. (1985). *Reflections on gender and science*. New Haven, CT: Yale University Press.

Kidder, R. M. (1994). *Shared values for a troubled world: Conversations with men and women of conscience*. San Francisco: Jossey-Bass.

Kieran, M. (1997). *Media ethics: A philosophical approach*. Westport, CT: Praeger.

Kizza, J. M. (Ed.). (1996). *Social and ethical effects of the computer revolution*. Jefferson, NC: McFarland.

Klaidman, S., & Beauchamp, T. L. (1987). *The virtuous journalist*. New York: Oxford University Press.
Klumpp, J. F. (1997) Freedom and responsibility in constructing public life: Toward a revised ethic of discourse. *Argumentation, 11*, 113–130.
Koehn, D. (1999). *Rethinking feminist ethics: Care, trust, and empathy*. London: Routledge.
Kramer, J., & Kramerae, C. (1997). Gendered ethics on the internet. In J. M. Makau & R. C. Arnett (Eds.), *Communication ethics in an age of diversity* (pp. 226–243). Urbana: University of Illinois Press.
Krushwitz, R. B., & Roberts, R. C. (Eds.). (1987). *The virtues: Contemporary essays on moral character*. Belmont, CA: Wadsworth.
Kupperman, J. (1991). *Character*. New York: Oxford University Press.
Lambeth, E. B. (1992). *Committed journalism: An ethic for the profession* (2nd ed.). Bloomington, IN: Indiana University Press.
Lansky, M., & Morrison, A. P. (Eds.). (1997). *The widening scope of shame*. Hillsdale, NJ: Analytic Press.
Larrabee, M. J. (Ed.). (1993). *An ethic of care: Feminist and interdisciplinary perspectives*. New York: Routledge.
Lasch, C. (1992, August 10). For shame. *The New Republic*, 29–34.
LeBacqz, K. (1985). *Professional ethics*. Nashville, TN: Abingdon Press.
Levinas, E. (1969). *Totality and infinity* (A. Lingis, Trans.). Pittsburgh, PA: Duquesne University Press.
Levinas, E. (1985). *Ethics and infinity* (R. Cohen, Trans.). Pittsburgh, PA: Duquesne University Press.
Levinas, E. (1987). *Time and the other* (R. Cohen, Trans.). Pittsburgh, PA: Duquesne University Press.
Limburg, V. E. (1994). *Electronic media ethics*. Boston: Focal Press.
Lipson, C. (1997, June 12). Rodman's shameful spews. *Chicago Tribune*, sec. 1, p. 27.
Liszka, J. J. (1999). *Moral competence: An integrated approach to the study of ethics*. Upper Saddle River, NJ: Prentice-Hall.
Loges, W. E., & Kidder, R. M. (1997). *Global values, moral boundaries: A pilot summary*. Camden, ME: Institute for Global Ethics.
Lyotard, J.- F. (1984). *The postmodern condition: A report on knowledge* (G. Bennington & B. Massumi, Trans.). Minneapolis: University of Minnesota Press.
Mackin, J. A., Jr. (1997). *Community over chaos: An ecological perspective on communication ethics*. Tuscaloosa: University of Alabama Press.
Makau, J. M., & Arnett, R. C. (Eds.). (1997). *Communication ethics in an age of diversity*. Urbana: University of Illinois Press.
Makus, A. P. (1994). Ethics in the flesh. In J. A. Jaksa (Ed.), *Proceedings of the third national communication ethics conference* (pp. 313–316). Annandale, VA: Speech Communication Association.
Manning, R. C. (1992). *Speaking from the heart: A feminist perspective on ethics*. Lanham, MD: Rowman & Littlefield.
Matson, W. I. (1994). The expiration of morality. In E. F. Paul, F. D. Miller, & J. Paul (Eds.), *Cultural Pluralism and Moral Knowledge* (pp. 159–178). Cambridge, UK: Cambridge University Press.
Mattson, M., & Buzzanell, P. M. (1999). Traditional and feminist organizational communication ethical analyses of messages and issues surrounding an actual job loss case. *Journal of Applied Communication Research, 27*, 49–72.
May, W. F. (1984). The virtues in a professional setting. *Soundings: An Interdisciplinary Journal, LXVII*, 245–266.
Merrill, J. C. (1989). *The dialectic in journalism: Toward a responsible use of press freedom*. Baton Rouge: Louisiana State University Press.
Merrill, J. C. (1997). *Journalism ethics: Philosophical foundations for the news media*. New York: St. Martin's Press.
Meyer, P. (1987). *Ethical journalism*. New York: Longman.
Meyers, D. T. (Ed.). (1997). *Feminists rethink the self*. Boulder, CO: Westview.
Michell, G. (1984). Women and lying: A pragmatic and semantic analysis of "telling it slant." *Women's Studies International Forum, 7*, 375–383.

Minow, M. (1990). *Making all the difference: Inclusion, exclusion, and American law.* Ithaca, NY: Cornell University Press.

Nilsen, T. R. (1966). *The ethics of speech communication.* Indianapolis, IN: Bobbs-Merrill.

Nitecki, M. H., & Nitecki, D. V. (Eds.). (1993). *Evolutionary ethics.* Albany: State University of New York Press.

Noddings, N. (1984). *Caring: A feminine approach to ethics and moral education.* Berkeley: University of California Press.

Olasky, M. N. (1985/1986). Ministers or panderers: Issues raised by the Public Relations Society Code of Standards. *Journal of Mass Media Ethics, 1,* 43–49.

On *In a different voice*: An interdisciplinary forum. (1986). *Signs: A Journal of Women in Culture and Society, 11,* 304–333.

Patterson, P., & Wilkins, L. (1998). *Media ethics: Issues and cases* (3rd ed.). Dubuque, IA: Wm. C. Brown.

Pearson, R. (1989a). Business ethics as communication ethics: Public relations practice and the idea of dialogue. In C. H. Botan & V. Hazelton, Jr. (Eds.), *Public Relations Theory* (pp. 111–131). Hillsdale, NJ: Erlbaum.

Pearson, R. (1989b). Beyond ethical relativism in public relations: Coorientation, rules, and the idea of communication symmetry. In J. E. Grunig & L .A. Grunig (Eds.), *Public Relations Research Annual,* Vol. 1 (pp. 67–86). Hillsdale, NJ: Erlbaum.

Pettifor, J. L. (1996). Ethics: Virtue and politics in the science and practice of psychology. *Canadian Psychology, 37,* 1–12.

Pippert, W. G. (1989). *An ethics of news.* Washington, DC: Georgetown University Press.

Planalp, S., Hafen, S., & Adkins, A. D. (2000). Messages of shame and guilt. In M. Roloff (Ed.), *Communication yearbook 23* (pp. 1–65). Thousand Oaks, CA: Sage.

Porter, J. E. (1992). *Audience and rhetoric.* Englewood Cliffs, NJ: Prentice-Hall.

Porter, J. E. (1993). Developing a postmodern ethics of rhetoric and composition. In T. Enos & S. Brown (Eds.), *Defining the new rhetorics* (pp. 207–226). Newbury Park, CA: Sage.

Porter, J. E. (1997). Legal realities and ethical hyperrealities: A critical approach to cyberwriting. In S. S. Selber (Ed.), *Computers and technical communication: Pedagogical and programmatic perspectives* (pp. 45–73). Norwood, NJ: Ablex.

Porter, J. E. (1998). *Rhetorical ethics and internetworked writing.* Greenwich, CT: Ablex.

Pritchard, M. S. (1996). Computer ethics: The responsible professional. In J. A. Jaksa & M. S. Pritchard (Eds.), *Responsible communication* (pp. 135–150). Cresskill, NJ: Hampton.

Redding, W. C. (1990). Ethics and the study of organizational communication: A case of culpable neglect. In J. A. Jaksa (Ed.), *Proceedings of the first national communication ethics conference* (pp. 121–147). Annandale, VA: Speech Communication Association.

Redding, W. C. (1996). Ethics and the study of organizational communication: When will we wake up? In J. A. Jaksa & M. S. Pritchard (Eds.), *Responsible communication* (pp. 17–40). Cresskill, NJ: Hampton.

Richardson, F. C., Rogers, A., & McCarroll, J. (1998). Toward a dialogical self. *American Behavioral Scientist, 41,* 496–515.

Rimal, R. N., Fogg, B. J., & Flora, J. A. (1995). Moving toward a framework for the study of risk communication: Theoretical and ethical considerations. In B. R. Burleson (Ed.), *Communication yearbook 18* (pp. 320–342). Thousand Oaks, CA: Sage.

Rivers, W. C., & Mathews, C. (1988). *Ethics for the media.* Englewood Cliffs, NJ: Prentice-Hall.

Robinson, F. (1997). Globalizing care: Ethics, feminist theory, and international relations. *Alternatives, 22,* 113–133.

Robinson, F. (1999). *Globalizing care: Ethics, feminist theory, and international relations.* Boulder, CO: Westview.

Samuelson, R. (1998, January 30). Clinton's problems with the other "L word." *Chicago Tribune,* Sec. 1, p. 17.

Sampson, E. E. (1993). *Celebrating the other: A dialogic account of human nature.* Boulder, CO: Westview.

Sandel, M. (1984). *Liberalism and its critics.* New York: New York University Press.

Schneiderman, S. (1995). *Saving face: America and the politics of shame.* New York: Knopf.

Schrag, C. O. (1997). *The self after postmodernity.* New Haven, CT: Yale University Press.

Schrier, W. (1930). The ethics of persuasion. *Quarterly Journal of Speech, 16,* 476–486.

Schroll, C. J. (1995). Technology and communication ethics: An evaluative framework. *Technical Communication Quarterly, 4,* 147–164.

Scott, S. D. (1993). Beyond reason: A feminist theory of ethics for journalists. *Feminist Issues, 13,* 23–40.

Seeger, M. W. (1997). *Ethics and organizational communication.* Cresskill, NJ: Hampton.

Seib, P. (1994). *Campaigns of conscience: The ethics of political journalism.* Westport, CT: Praeger.

Seib, P., & Fitzpatrick, K. (1995). *Public relations ethics.* Fort Worth, TX: Harcourt Brace.

Sherman, N. (1989). *The fabric of character: Aristotle's theory of virtue.* New York: Oxford University Press.

Slote, M. (1992). *From morality to virtue.* New York: Oxford University Press.

Smith, A. R. (1997). The limits of communication: Lyotard and Levinas on otherness. In M. Huspek & G. P. Radford (Eds.), *Transgressing discourses: Communication and the voice of the other* (pp. 329–351). Albany: State University of New York Press.

Smith, D. H. (1993). Stories, values, and health care decisions. In C. Conrad (Ed.), *The ethical nexus* (pp. 123–148). Norwood, NJ: Ablex.

Spectra. (1997 July). Annandale, VA: National Communication Association.

Steiner, L. (1989). Feminist theorizing and communication ethics. *Communication, 12,* 157–173.

Steiner, L. (1997). A feminist schema for analysis of ethical dilemmas. In F. L. Casmir (Ed.), *Ethics in intercultural and international communication* (pp. 59–88). Mahwah, NJ: Erlbaum.

Stewart, L. P. (1997). Facilitating connections: Issues of gender, culture, and diversity. In J. M. Makau & R. C. Arnett (Eds.), *Communication ethics in an age of diversity* (pp. 110–125). Urbana: University of Illinois Press.

Sullivan, P. A. (1993). Women's discourse and political communication: A case study of Congressperson Patricia Schroeder. *Western Journal of Communication, 57,* 530–545.

Sullivan, P. A., & Goldzwig, S. R. (1994). Constructing a postmodern ethic: The feminist quest for a new politics. In L. H. Turner & H. M. Sterk (Eds.), *Differences that make a difference: Examining the assumptions of gender research.* Westport, CT: Bergin & Garvey.

Sullivan, P. A., & Goldzwig, S. A. (1995). A relational approach to moral decision-making: The majority opinion in *Planned Parenthood v. Casey. Quarterly Journal of Speech, 81,* 167–190.

Sullivan, P. A., & Goldzwig, S. R. (1996). Abortion and undue burdens: Justice Sandra Day O'Connor and judicial decision-making. *Women and Politics, 16,* 27–54.

Sullivan, P. A., & Turner, L. H. (1996). *From the margins to the center: Contemporary women and political communication.* Westport, CT: Praeger.

Tanno, D. V. (1994). The meaning of morality: Views of ethics from above and below. In J. A. Jaksa (Ed.), *Proceedings of the third national communication ethics conference* (pp. 317–319). Annandale, VA: Speech Communication Association.

Taylor, G. (1985). *Pride, shame, and guilt: Emotions of self-assessment.* Oxford, UK: Clarendon Press.

Taylor, R. (1991). *Virtue ethics: An introduction.* Interlaken, NY: Linden.

Taylor, V. E., & Winquist, C. E. (Eds.). (2001). *Encyclopedia of postmodernism.* London: Routledge.

Thomassen, N. (1992). *Communicative ethics in theory and practice.* New York: St. Martin's Press.

Thompson, P. (Ed.). (1995). *Issues in evolutionary ethics.* Albany: State University of New York Press.

Thrane, G. (1979). Shame and the construction of the self. *Annual of Psychoanalysis, 7,* 321–341.

Tong, R. (1993). *Feminine and feminist ethics.* Belmont, CA: Wadsworth.

Tronto, J. C. (1993). *Moral boundaries: A political argument for an ethic of care.* New York: Routledge.

Wallace, K. R. (1955). An ethical basis of communication. *Speech Teacher, 4,* 1–9.

Weaver, R. M. (1953). *The ethics of rhetoric.* Chicago: Regnery.

Wellman, C. (1988). *Morals and ethics* (2nd ed.). Englewood Cliffs, NJ: Prentice-Hall.

Williams, B. (1993). *Shame and necessity*. Berkeley: University of California Press.

Williams, O. F., & Murphy, P. E. (1990). The ethics of virtue: A moral theory for marketing. *Journal of Macromarketing, 10*, 19–29.

Williams, O. F., & Murphy, P. E. (1992). The ethics of virtue: A moral theory for business. In O. F. Williams & J. W. Houck (Eds.), *A virtuous life in business* (pp. 9–27). Lanham, MD: Rowman & Littlefield.

Wilson, E. O. (1998). *Consilience: The unity of knowledge*. New York: Knopf.

Wilson, J. Q. (1993). *The moral sense*. New York: Free Press.

Wood, J. T. (1992). Gender and moral voice: Moving from women's nature to standpoint epistemology. *Women's Studies in Communication, 15*, 1–24.

Wood, J. T. (1994). *Who cares? Women, care, and culture*. Carbondale: Southern Illinois University Press.

Wright, R. (1994). *The moral animal: The new science of evolutionary psychology*. New York: Pantheon.

Wyschogrod, E. (2000). *Emmanuel Levinas: The problem of ethical metaphysics*. New York: Fordham University Press.

CHAPTER CONTENTS

7 Investigating the Role of Communication in Culturally Diverse Work Groups: A Review and Synthesis

JOHN G. OETZEL
TRUDY E. BURTIS
MARTHA I. CHEW SANCHEZ
FRANK G. PÉREZ
University of New Mexico

The purpose of the current study is to provide a narrative literature review to synthesize the research investigating the role of communication in culturally diverse work groups. A review of the extant literature revealed 3 predominant roles of communication: (a) communication as affected by cultural and contextual factors, (b) communication as affecting group outcomes, and (c) communication as a constitutive element for group culture. The research for each role is reviewed and summarized in order to identify what we do and do not know about communication in culturally diverse work groups. We conclude the essay by identifying five unanswered questions to guide future research.

I NCREASED cultural and ethnic diversity in the workplace is altering the composition and environment of organizations in the United States and around the world. If current trends continue, the majority of the net new entrants into organizations in the U.S. by the year 2020 will be of Latin, Asian, or African decent (listed in descending order; Judy & D'Amico, 1997). These demographic changes have led organizational scholars to focus upon the effects of cultural diversity on

AUTHORS' NOTE: An earlier version of this essay was presented at the annual convention of the National Communication Association, Seattle, WA, November 2000. The second through fourth authors are listed alphabetically.

Correspondence: John G. Oetzel, Department of Communication and Journalism, University of New Mexico, Albuquerque, NM 87131; email: joetzel@unm.edu

Communication Yearbook 25, pp. 237–269

workgroup behavior. Cultural diversity "means the representation, in one social system, of people with distinctly different group affiliations of cultural significance" (Cox, 1994, p. 6). National culture, ethnicity, language, gender, job position, age, or disability can index cultural diversity. For the purposes of the current review, cultural diversity is limited to considerations of national or ethnic culture in work groups. The rationale for this decision is threefold. First, other researchers have investigated and reviewed factors such as functional, gender, age, or tenure diversity (e.g., Cox & Finley, 1995; Milliken & Martins, 1996; Williams & O'Reilly, 1998). Second, there is a great deal of research examining national and ethnic diversity and a thorough review of other types of diversity is beyond the scope of a single essay. Third, the focus on work groups, groups that perform primarily problem-solving and decision-making tasks, is due to the fact that the majority of research in this line investigates work groups, as opposed to social groups.

A number of initial studies of culturally diverse groups examined how group composition (i.e., homogeneous or heterogeneous) affected group outcomes. Both benefits and costs have been attributed to cultural diversity. Researchers have found that cultural heterogeneity in group composition is associated with lower group cohesion and higher turnover of members (Jackson et al., 1991; O'Reilly, Caldwell, & Barnett, 1989; Wiersema & Bird, 1993), low group performance on a problem-solving task during initial meetings (Watson, Kumar & Michaelsen, 1993), and low member satisfaction and identification with the group (Milliken & Martins, 1996). On the other hand, other scholars have found that diversity has benefits for the group including increased feasibility and effectiveness of idea generation (McLeod, Lobel, & Cox, 1996), greater personal satisfaction, and higher perceived group creativity and effectiveness (Rodríguez, 1998).

Despite the importance of these findings, a significant limitation of the previous research has been the omission of communication processes (Pelled, Eisenhardt, & Xin, 1999). In the current essay, we define communication processes as messages that are exchanged among members of a work group (i.e., interactions among group members). We include studies that focus on messages in actual groups (laboratory or field), as well as studies that focus on messages in hypothetical work groups (e.g., "What would you do in this situation?"). Communication processes are the medium through which cultural diversity affects group outcomes (Hackman & Morris, 1975; Lawrence, 1997; Oetzel, 1995). In recent years, a number of studies have addressed this limitation and have examined group communication from a variety of perspectives. Unfortunately, these studies are scattered across disciplines and topics and thus determining the role of communication in the culturally diverse group is difficult.

The purpose of the current essay is to organize the extant literature through a narrative literature review in order to identify the role of communication for culturally diverse work groups. We argue that there are three roles that communication has served in previous studies: (a) communication as affected by cultural and contextual factors, (b) communication as affecting group outcomes, and (c) communication as a constitutive element for group culture.

The first role is communication as affected by cultural and contextual factors. Studies that view communication from this perspective examine communication as the outcome of other factors. The main goal of this type of research is to identify which cultural and contextual factors influence group interaction. These studies focus especially on understanding potential difficulties and misunderstandings that can arise when group members from culturally different backgrounds interact. The second role is communication as affecting group outcomes. From this perspective, communication is the determining factor of the quality of group products and relationships. In some studies, communication is viewed as a mediator of cultural diversity and group outcomes. These studies focus on understanding what types of communication variables allow groups to leverage cultural diversity. That is, how can groups communicate in order to establish strong interpersonal relationships and allow for the benefits and avoid the costs of diversity? The third role is communication as a constitutive element for group culture. From this perspective, communication is the creator of group culture. Thus culture is the outcome of group interaction. Scholars examining the constitutive element of communication seek to understand how communication alters previously held assumptions and biases of other cultural members in order to become a unified, integrated group. In this essay, we review the literature on culturally diverse work groups from the three predominant roles of communication. At the end of each role, we provide a summary and critique of each area of research. Finally, we conclude with a set of unanswered questions for future research.

COMMUNICATION AS AFFECTED BY CULTURAL AND CONTEXTUAL FACTORS

Identifying how and why cultural diversity impacts group communication has been important to scholars for several reasons. First, communication has a direct impact on group outcomes. Second, scholars have argued that an understanding of how cultural diversity influences communication will enable group members and facilitators to avoid (or at least reduce or resolve) problems and misunderstandings that often result when groups are composed of culturally diverse members. Previous studies have investigated the effects of culture and cultural diversity from one of three perspectives. The first perspective is to examine the influence of group composition on communication. The second focus posits that cultural values affect group communication. The third argument is that contextual features impact group communication. We describe and review each of these in turn.

Group Composition and Communication

Group composition is the pattern of its members' characteristics and varies in degree from homogeneous to heterogeneous (McGrath, Berdahl, & Arrow, 1995). For the current review, the national or ethnic cultural background of the individual members is the important group composition characteristic. A consistent finding about group composition is that culturally heterogeneous groups have less effective interaction processes (or more process difficulty) than culturally homogeneous groups (Watson et al., 1993). Process difficulty is communication process that potentially interferes with the productivity of a group and includes high levels of conflict and tension, power struggles, lack of cooperation, lack of respect for group members, and inequality in turn taking (Watson & Michaelsen, 1988). Previous research has examined process difficulty in regards to leadership, participation, cooperation, and problem solving.

Zamarripa and Krueger (1983) investigated the effects of cultural diversity on leadership. The authors compared three homogeneous and three heterogeneous groups in terms of leadership rules and message types during group interactions regarding a hypothetical diplomatic situation in the U.S. The heterogeneous groups were composed of three or four U.S. Americans and three or four French or Arab students, whereas the homogeneous groups were composed of seven U.S. Americans.[1] Zamarripa and Krueger found that homogeneous groups presented an internally consistent set of leadership rules compared to the heterogeneous groups' internally varied rules. Further, heterogeneous groups used more evaluative responses and fewer reciprocal behaviors during interaction.

Several empirical studies have found that cultural diversity relates negatively to participation in the group's task. Kirchmeyer and Cohen (1992) studied 45 student groups in Canada working on a task that involved making a decision about hypothetical layoffs for an engineering firm. Most of the groups had four members composed of two men and two women, with one ethnic minority. Kirchmeyer and Cohen found that ethnic minorities contributed considerably less to decisions than did nonminorities, based on the assessments of the other group members. Oetzel (1998a) studied homogeneous and heterogeneous groups working on a hypothetical decision-making task about a student allegedly caught cheating on a test. There were two sets of homogeneous groups (Japanese and European American), while the heterogeneous groups were composed of two Japanese and two European Americans. All of the groups interacted in the U.S. and in English. Oetzel found that the heterogeneous groups utilized fewer consensus decisions and had more inequality in the distribution of turns than homogeneous groups. These findings were discovered even when controlling for language competency. Finally, Cady and Valentine (1999) explored the effects of race and gender diversity on perceptions of teaming consideration and quality and quantity of ideas. Perception of teaming consideration is the members' felt level of consideration from others (e.g., ideas are considered). The authors examined 50 teams of a high-tech, Fortune 500 company (it is not specified where the company is located). The diversity of the teams was measured by an entropy-based formula to find a range of homogeneity and heterogeneity. They found that diversity due to race and sex had a negative relationship with perceptions of teaming consideration and race also had a negative effect on the number of ideas produced.

Other empirical studies have identified power struggles and conflicts as the result of culturally diverse composition. One study examined the effects of diverse composition on problem solving during risky situations. Watson and Kumar (1992) examined how decision making differed between culturally heterogeneous and homogeneous student groups engaged in risk-taking assignments. The homogeneous groups consisted of White Americans, whereas the heterogeneous groups had at least three of the following four backgrounds: Black Americans, Hispanic Americans, White Americans, and foreign nationals. Groups were asked to make decisions related to everyday life situations, including questions about investing, careers, and sports strategies. The authors found that diverse groups had more difficulty handling problem solving in high-risk situations than did homogeneous groups. Their study allowed them to propose that the more diverse a group, the more conservative it will behave in terms of risk-taking.

Fiedler (1966) compared 48 homogeneous and 48 heterogeneous groups composed of French-speaking and Dutch-speaking sailors and chief petty officers in Belgium. The groups performed three tasks that varied in structure and verbal interaction under conditions of strong leadership (groups led by petty officers) and weak leadership (groups led by recruits). Neither group composition nor leadership status was found to significantly alter group success. However, heterogeneous groups initially faced a greater degree of communication difficulty than homogeneous groups.

Watson et al. (1993) compared the processes of ethnically homogeneous and heterogeneous student groups working on four business case studies over the course of a semester. The homogeneous groups were composed of European Americans, whereas the heterogeneous groups were predominantly composed of an African American, European American, Latin American, and a foreign national from an Asian, African, Middle Eastern, or Latin American country. Group process was measured with 23 items from Watson and Michaelsen's (1988) Group Style Description, which allowed group members to self-report the effectiveness of the process in their group. Homogeneous groups were found to have more effective processes than heterogeneous groups during initial meetings. The effective processes included few power struggles, cooperative interaction, and equal participation. Over a period of 12 weeks, the heterogeneous groups made adjustments and had processes at the level of effectiveness experienced by homogeneous groups.

The finding that heterogeneous groups have process difficulty initially, but not over a period of time is a popular conclusion of diversity scholars. However, a recent study produced conflicting findings. Millhous (1999) studied the interaction between 17 Americans and 18 Russians in ongoing, business-related collaborations (some short-term and some long-term) in Russia. Millhous interviewed each individual and asked what strengths and weaknesses occurred in the groups. She found that long-term groups reported more communication difficulties than did short-term groups.

Two explanations appear possible for these seemingly contradictory results. First, the nature of the work could affect the existence of difficulties. Pelled et al. (1999) found that the longer diverse groups were together and the more routine their task, the less likely there was to be process difficulty in culturally diverse groups. The students in Watson et al.'s (1993) study were engaged in the same type of tasks over the course of a semester and thus the work had likely become routine. In contrast, the business collaborations of the Russian and American groups were not likely to be routine. The longevity of the Russian/American groups was not reported and thus we cannot speculate as to this factor. Second, the motivation of the group members can affect the degree of process difficulty. If individual members want to work in a culturally diverse group, they are likely to work with the other members and try to make adjustments to overcome difficulties. In contrast, a lack of motivation to work with culturally diverse others likely results in rigid behavior and further problems. However, these speculations were not directly addressed in either study.

In sum, culturally diverse groups tend to have more communication difficulties than culturally homogeneous groups. The communication difficulties include inequality in participation, conflict and power struggles, and difficulties in problem solving during risky situations. Many researchers speculate that process difficulties abate over time, but there is some inconsistency with this conclusion. The reason for this inconsistency is that although researchers know that diversity affects group communication, it is not known exactly why this occurs (Sessa & Jackson, 1995). Clearly there are other factors that affect the relationship between group composition and group interaction. In the next two sections, we review research that offers explanations for why cultural diversity impacts group communication.

Cultural Differences and Group Communication

Cultural differences provide one of the two predominant approaches that explain why cultural diversity influences communicative behavior. Cultural differences are general patterns of cultural values, attitudes, and communicative behavior associated with specific sets of individuals (Chemers & Murphy, 1995). The following section is devoted to a review and synthesis of studies that have taken a cultural difference approach to the study of communication in work groups. First, studies comparing work groups across two different cultures (i.e., cross-cultural) are summarized. Second, and more importantly given the focus of this essay, studies that have used cultural differences to explain culturally diverse work groups (i.e., intercultural) are discussed.

Cross-cultural studies of work groups. The purpose of cross-cultural studies is to provide an understanding of how members of different cultures communicate. There are a number of dimensions on which cultures can vary. Most cross-cultural studies of work groups focus on the individualism and collectivism (I/C) of members because I/C is the primary dimension upon which cultures vary (Hui & Triandis, 1986). In individualistic cultures, people tend to focus on personal goals that overlap slightly with group goals, whereas people in collectivistic cultures consider it socially desirable to put group goals ahead of individual goals (Triandis, 1995). Previous studies have examined the influence of I/C on reward allocation, social loafing, cooperation, consensus decision making, and event management. We also discuss one study that considers dimensions of cultural variability other than I/C.

A few studies investigate the influence of I/C on reward allocation and social loafing. Bond, Leung, and Wan (1982) studied how U.S. Americans and Hong Kong Chinese allocated rewards in hypothetical student work group situations. The U.S. Americans represented the individualistic culture and the Hong Kong Chinese the collectivistic culture. U.S. Americans tended to use an equity principle (rewards allocated given the amount or quality of work performed by a member), whereas Hong Kong Chinese used an egalitarian principle (equal rewards among all group members). Earley (1989, 1993) studied the effects of I/C in the work styles of U.S. and Chinese managers in groups. He has found that group interaction led to social loafing (i.e., not doing a fair share of the work) by U.S. participants, but to social striving (i.e., doing more work than one would do individually) by Chinese participants.

Several studies have examined the effects of I/C on cooperative and consensus communicative behavior in work groups. Harris and Nibler (1998) studied consensus processes and outcomes of Hong Kong Chinese and U.S. American undergraduate students in previously established ingroups. The authors found that in terms of ability to reach a consensus decision, Hong Kong Chinese individuals performed more effectively in ingroups than outgroups, whereas U.S. American individuals performed more effectively in outgroups than ingroups. In addition, the Hong Kong Chinese participants emphasized the importance of presenting an appropriate image in the presence of others. However, they also reported feeling dominated, rebellious, and pressured during their group interactions.

Oetzel (1998b) compared 234 European Americans and 115 Latino/as to examine the impact of self-construal and ethnicity on self-reported conflict style in a hypothetical group situation. Self-construal is one's perception of self as either independent or interdependent; the independent construal of self involves the view that an individual is a separate entity with a unique repertoire of feelings and thoughts, whereas the interdependent construal of self involves an emphasis on a person feeling connected to those around her or him (Markus & Kitayama, 1991). Gudykunst et al. (1996) argued that independent self-construals predominate in individualistic cultures, whereas interdependent self-construals predominate in collectivistic cultures. Self-construals are more direct measures of an individual's value orientation than static ethnicity or nationality (Gudykunst et al., 1996; Kim et al., 1996; Singelis & Brown, 1995). The participants, a combination of students and members of the workforce, received one of six scenarios involving the hypothetical discussions of a group of managers. Oetzel (1998b) discovered that self-construal is a better predictor of conflict styles than ethnic background. Specifically, he found that independent self-construal is associated positively with dominating conflict styles, whereas interdependent self-construal is associated positively with avoiding, obliging, compromising, and integrating conflict styles.

Finally, two studies examined the effects of cultural differences on event management. An event is "a partially abstracted bit of social reality that serves as a unit of information processing, interpretation, or meaning constructed by a social actor in interaction with other social actors" (Peterson, 1993, as cited in Maznevski & Peterson, 1997, p. 64). Event management is the process of attaching meaning and making sense of events (Smith & Peterson, 1988). Smith, Peterson, and Misumi (1994) studied event management in work teams in four electronics assembly plants in Great Britain (20 teams), Japan (29 teams), and the U.S. (12 teams), in order to determine the role of I/C on the management of routine and nonroutine events. Japan is a collectivistic culture and Great Britain and the U.S. are individualistic. The authors discovered that team members in Britain and the U.S. give more emphasis to their own experience and training than to asking supervisors for advice than those from Japan, whereas Japanese employees are more likely to seek the advice of co-workers than those from the U.S. or Britain. The authors also concluded that whereas differences may exist in the event management processes and performance criteria of collectivistic and individualistic cultures, the type of event also plays a role in the management processes used by the teams.

Maznevski and Peterson (1997) also theorized about the role of culture on a team's event management. They speculate that five specific differences in cultural orientation (Kluckhohn & Strodtbeck, 1961) influence the way a team reacts to an event: relationship to nature (mastery, subjugation, or harmony), perceptions of time (past, present, or future), the nature of humans (good or evil), relationships between humans (individualistic, collectivistic, or hierarchical), and mode of activity (doing-achieving, being-feeling, or thinking-reflecting). Although Maznevski and Peterson did not study specific national or ethnic cultures, they constructed a taxonomy to illustrate how cultural orientations influence the management of events. For example, those with a cultural orientation of respect for the past and traditional practices will be better able to identify similarities between past and present situations and to learn from the past than people from cultures with a future orientation. People with a future orientation are likely to incorporate the long-term implications of events into current planning and action.

Although these studies do not provide direct evidence of the importance of a cultural difference perspective in the study of culturally diverse work groups, they do have important implications for such a perspective. For example, individualists are likely to take a competitive stance, utilize majority decision-making procedures, and loaf during group situations, whereas collectivists are likely to cooperate, utilize consensual decision making, and strive during group situations. These communication patterns help to illustrate why process difficulty occurs in culturally diverse groups composed of members from individualistic and collectivistic cultures.

Intercultural studies of work groups. Although cross-cultural differences certainly have important implications for scholars and group members alike, the question remains whether cultural differences are useful in explaining the interaction patterns (especially problems and misunderstandings) of culturally diverse work groups. Problems, misunderstandings, and conflicts likely occur in groups that demonstrate cultural diversity because individuals tend to view norms and practices of interaction from their own cultural perspective (Nadler, Keeshan-Nadler, & Broome, 1985). For example, during interactions in heterogeneous groups, members from one culture use communication styles that may not correspond to the styles of members of a different culture. In essence, differences in the cultural backgrounds of the members of heterogeneous groups lead to different, and potentially difficult, communication processes more than in homogeneous groups. We now review intercultural studies that examine cooperation, conflict, participation, and respect to help illustrate how cultural differences can lead to communication problems.

I/C is also the most popular approach to study ethnically diverse groups. Cox, Lobel, and McLeod (1991) studied the effects of I/C on the cooperative and competitive choices made by individuals during a prisoner's dilemma game. They assigned 136 U.S. undergraduate and graduate students to one of 16 all-Anglo or 17 culturally diverse groups (with one member each from Asian American, Hispanic American, Black American, and Anglo American ethnic groups). The groups also received cooperative feedback (i.e., others had made a cooperative choice) or no feedback during the experiment. They found that all of the groups in the study produced more competitive than cooperative responses, but that groups composed of members from a collectivistic tradition (Asian American, Hispanic American, and Black American) displayed more cooperative choices overall than groups composed of members with an individualistic cultural tradition. This study not only showed the importance of I/C on group behavior, but also illustrated the importance of a group norm being established in culturally diverse groups that is reflective of the summative cultural values of the individual members (as opposed to being dominated by one cultural group).

A second study utilizing I/C also examined conflict and cooperation. Thomas (1999) studied the influence of collectivism on evaluations of conflict and cooperation in culturally diverse groups. Seventy-seven undergraduates representing 14 nationalities at a New Zealand university were randomly assigned to 24 three- or four-person groups and required to perform five business case studies. The participants registered their opinions about a variety of processes including conflict, cooperation and citizenship (i.e., helping others), and satisfaction with the group and the process. Thomas found that an individual's degree of collectivism was positively related to cooperation and citizenship, but not related to substantive and emotional conflict.

In a third set of studies, Oetzel (1998a, 1998c) utilized I/C, measured at the individual level, to investigate turn taking and conflict behavior. He compared the communication patterns of homogeneous European American groups (an individualistic culture) composed of four members, homogeneous Japanese groups (a collectivistic culture) composed of three or four members, and heterogeneous groups composed of two Japanese and two European Americans working on a decision-making task (in English and in the U.S.). In addition to using national culture, he measured participants' self-construals. Oetzel found that: (a) homogeneous Japanese groups had fewer conflicts and used more cooperative conflict tactics and fewer competitive conflict tactics than homogeneous European American groups; (b) groups composed of members with high independent self-construals were more likely to use competitive tactics and less likely to use cooperative tactics than groups composed of members with low independent self-construals; and (c) because of their cultural background and self-construals, European Americans took more turns, initiated more conflicts, and used more competitive conflict tactics than did Japanese in both homogenous and heterogeneous groups.

Furthering this line of research, Oetzel (2001) explored the relationship between member self-construal and communication processes (equal participation, cooperation, and respect) in groups of varying levels of diversity (in terms of age, gender, and ethnicity). The 36 total groups were composed of three to six undergraduate students in the U.S. engaged in three group tasks relevant to a course in which the students were enrolled. Oetzel found that self-construals explain the communication processes used by the group better than the composition of the group. Specifically, equal participation, cooperation, and respect were positively associated with the average interdependent self-construal of the individual members.

In a final study emphasizing I/C, Kim and Paulk (1994) sought to understand the cultural differences that occur in daily interactions between Japanese and U.S. Americans in a Japanese multinational organization. Eighteen individuals (12 U.S. Americans and 6 Japanese), primarily at the managerial level, who had frequent contact with the other culture were interviewed in their native languages. The authors found three areas of difficulty for the interviewees: language/communication behavior, work style, and management style. The differences were consistent with differences in I/C. For example, Japanese reported that U.S. Americans focus on speaking, emphasize the individual's career, and are unwilling to compromise personal interests, whereas U.S. Americans reported that Japanese lack verbal clarity, demonstrate absolute adherence to the "company way," and utilize a lengthy decision-making process.

We could locate only two studies in this area that examined cultural factors other than I/C. Bochner and Hesketh (1994) studied the power distance and I/C in an Australian bank where 28 different nationalities were represented. Power distance refers to the extent that subordinates in an institution accept as appropriate an unequal distribution of power, with high-power distance cultures emphasizing status and power more so than low-power distance cultures (Hofstede, 1991). Based on 263 respondents, the authors discovered that individuals from high-power distance cultures (who also tended to be collectivistic) were more likely to (a) have formal superior-subordinate relationships; (b) prefer close supervision; (c) be more task-oriented; and (d) believe people need to be made to work hard, as opposed to individuals from low-power distance cultures (who tended to be individualistic). The study also concluded that workers from collectivistic cultures display more attachment to the company and fellow workers and place greater importance on group goals and recognition than on individual goals and rewards.

Thomas, Ravlin, and Wallace (1996) examined the influence of cultural differences on communication processes in student work groups. The authors examined 13 groups over 5 weeks. There were five homogeneous Japanese groups and eight heterogeneous groups composed of Japanese and other nationalities (16 total). All group interactions took place in Japan and in English. The authors examined the relative cultural distance of group members using Hofstede's (1991) dimensions and scores for national cultures (i.e., I/C, power distance, uncertainty avoidance, and masculinity) and psychological distance using a variety of individual-level measurements including locus of control, tolerance for ambiguity, and importance of national identity. Communication process was self-rated by the group members and included measures of constructive conflict, frequency of conflict, cohesion, and shared leadership. The authors found that: (a) the greater the cultural distance, the lower the rating of group process; and (b) the greater the psychological distance, the lower the rating of group cohesion. Further, Japanese participants, especially in diverse groups, rated the group process lower than other nationalities. The authors utilized follow-up comments from the participants to conclude that the type of task group and its interaction violated Japanese norms.

In sum, collectivism is associated with interdependence, high-power distance, avoiding and cooperating during conflict, respect of others, and equal participation, whereas individualism is associated with independence, low-power distance, competition during conflict and the taking of individual turns. These findings are consistent with the cross-cultural research. Additionally, I/C was found to be a good explanatory factor for differences in culturally diverse groups. Finally, there are two limitations with previous research into cultural values. First, I/C dominates the research efforts of both cross-cultural and intercultural explorations of work groups, and other variability dimensions are given limited, if any, attention. Second, this line of research investigates cultural differences of groups in a container (Putnam & Stohl, 1990). That is, contextual features that influence interaction are not considered. We move to this point in the next section.

Contextual Factors and Group Communication

Putnam and Stohl (1990) argued that groups are not isolated entities devoid of context. Groups operate in a specific context and are interdependent with this context. In this section, we examine five contextual factors and how they frame communication in culturally diverse work groups: (a) organizational structure, (b) integration of the workforce, (c) ingroup identification, (d) type of task, and (e) external stakeholders. Organizational structure, integration of the workforce, and ingroup identification result in vertical differences that influence individual group members. Vertical differences are status differences that exist in a group because of various factors, including ethnicity, nationality, sex, tenure, knowledge, and position in the organizational hierarchy, which serve as cues that are used to assign people to positions in a hierarchy within a group or organization (Sessa & Jackson, 1995). Vertical differences offer an alternative approach to cultural differences for explaining why cultural diversity affects group communication. Type of task and external stakeholders do not necessarily result in status distinctions, but can directly influence members' communicative behaviors.

Organizational structure. Sessa and Jackson (1995) discussed how democratic and hierarchical structures affect culturally diverse work group communication. They argued that only a democratic/horizontal structure provides the optimal condition for group members of diverse backgrounds and characteristics to have the potential to create a wide variety of ideas, alternatives, and solutions. Hierarchical structures tend to institutionalize competition, personal dominance, and status. When the structure is hierarchical, work groups focus on status of members and groups. Ideas generated and discussed by low status members and in low status groups tend to be censored and not considered. Under hierarchical structures, decision-making processes seldom fit the idealized, rational model of decision making. The main characteristics of horizontal structures (openness, respect, mutual concern, and trust) are replaced with asymmetry, status, and egocentrism in hierarchical structures.

Sessa and Jackson (1995) used status characteristics theory to explain how status created via hierarchy affect group members' communication. Status characteristics theory (Berger, Cohen, & Zelditch, 1973; Berger, Wagner, & Zelditch, 1985) "specifies the process through which evaluations of, and beliefs about, the characteristics of team members become the basis of observable inequalities in face-to-face social interactions" (Sessa & Jackson, 1995, p. 144). Status characteristics are hierarchical factors that influence evaluations of self and others, and include both task-specific and diffuse characteristics. Task-specific characteristics are related to the level of expertise relevant to the task at hand. Diffuse characteristics focus on broad master statuses that have little relationship with the actual competence or job performance of the individuals (e.g., physical attractiveness, sex, age, nationality, and ethnic or cultural group membership).

Using the principles of status characteristics theory, Sessa and Jackson (1995) reviewed a variety of studies and concluded that higher status members (in terms of both diffuse and task-specific characteristics) tend to participate more in group discussions, are more assertive, challenge contradictory ideas and have more influence on group outcomes than lower status members. Further, available resources provided by the diversity of members in organizations may not be fully identified and used by the teams. Thus important decisions may be shaped by irrelevant and unintentional dynamics among team members (e.g., diffuse status characteristics).

Integration of the workforce. Another approach to studying the effects of contextual factors is to consider the degree to which the workforce is culturally integrated. An interesting approach to examining workforce integration is Kanter's (1977) tokenism hypothesis, which states that the relative proportion of social types (salient external statuses, such as ethnicity and sex) in an organization results in organizations that are uniform (100% of the same social type), skewed (minority members are 1–15%), tilted (minority members are 16–34%), or balanced (minority members are 35–65%). In skewed organizations, minority members tend to be viewed as "tokens," and a variety of adverse effects occur for such members, including interactional isolation, fewer opportunities for power, and being forced into playing stereotypical roles. The tokenism hypothesis predicts that as minority and majority social types within a group reach numerical parity, interactional isolation between the members of the two groups diminish (Kanter, 1977).

Larkey (1996b) used the ideas of the tokenism hypothesis to explain how diversity in organizations can affect work group interaction. She explains that group members can engage in two types of information processing: category-based and difference-based processing. Category-based processing focuses on stereotyping or ingroup/outgroup differentiation, whereas difference-based processing focuses on interpreting differences on an individual basis, even if one considers cultural information as part of understanding. On the basis of these two types of information processing, Larkey offered three general arguments: (a) Members of work groups in monolithic organizations (organizations with token representation of minority group members) are likely to use category-based processing and, as a result, are likely to negatively evaluate and exclude ethnic minorities; (b) members of work groups in plural organizations (organizations with uneven representation of ethnic minorities) use both category- and difference-based processing and, as a result, will have divergent cultural patterns in the group, ideation that conforms to the dominant management standards, and frequent misunderstanding; and (c) members of work groups in multicultural organizations (organizations that have ethnic majority and minority members integrated at all levels of the organization) will use difference-based processing and, as a result, will demonstrate positive evaluation of differences, inclusion of all members, adjustment to other members, understanding of one another, and varied ideation. In essence, Larkey argued that cultural balance in work groups results in positive interactions among members, whereas imbalance results in negative interactions.

Bochner and Hesketh's (1994) study of the Australian bank had some consistent findings with Larkey's theory. The bank had 28 different nationalities represented. These employees represented an ingroup (Anglo-Celtic Australian) and an outgroup (all others). They found that outgroup members more than ingroup members reported a greater incidence of discrimination, regarded cultural diversity in the workplace more favorably, and engaged in more behaviors that the host culture would regard as counternormative. These findings are consistent with Larkey's theory in that the members of the outgroup are a numerical minority and not integrated into the organizational culture. Thus they received negative evaluations based on category-based processing.

An alternative approach to examining workforce integration is to utilize social identity theory. Social identity consists of views of self shared by other members of an ingroup (Turner, 1987). Social identity theory focuses on how the social categorization of people into groupings affects interactions between people of different social identities (e.g., national or ethnic culture; Tajfel, 1978). According to social identity theory, awareness of membership in a social group is the most important factor influencing intergroup behaviors. Awareness of group membership results in a process of comparing oneself (and one's group) to others for the purpose of establishing a positive social identity. The desire to achieve a positive social identity results in a positive bias favoring the ingroup (Tajfel & Turner, 1986). Individuals tend to engage in social competition to preserve a positive social identity when interacting with members of outgroups (Turner, 1975). A number of factors influence whether people representing different social categories will compete rather than cooperate when working with one another in groups. These conditions include unequal status, competition for resources, and imbalance between ingroup and outgroups members.

Espinoza and Garza (1985) and Garza and Santos (1991) conducted studies to test the effects of social identity on cooperation and competition in diverse work groups. In the first study, Espinoza and Garza randomly assigned Anglo Americans and Hispanics to one of two conditions (three-to-one or one-to-three ratio of ingroup to outgroup composition) and required them to make a choice in a prisoner's dilemma-type game. They also received feedback controlled by the experimenter to make participants believe they were in a cooperative or competitive group during the experiment. In the second study, Garza and Santos used similar research procedures and participants as in the previous study, but employed ratios varying from one-to-five to six-to-zero. In both studies, they found that Hispanics competed with others when they were in the minority group and cooperated when they were equal in number with the Anglo members, in a majority, or in an exclusive group. In contrast, Anglos were minimally affected by changes in the ingroup/outgroup balance.

The researchers explained the findings in terms of social identity theory. Specifically, they argued that ethnic majority groups (e.g., Anglo Americans in the U.S.) already have a number of socially valued dimensions along which they can positively differentiate themselves from others (e.g., education and occupation). As a result, they do not have to consider the ethnic minority group members as a relevant group for social comparison and do not feel the need to compete with them. The Anglo American groups do not have to explicitly rely on their ethnic background, not necessarily because race or ethnic group composition was not important to them, but because the structure, rules, and ideology of the work are set up according to the Anglo American ideology. In contrast, the researchers argued that ethnic minority members (e.g., Hispanic Americans) lack a preexisting positive social identity, and therefore perceive the majority group as a relevant social comparison. Consequently, ethnic minority group members feel the need to compete when they are in a numerical minority in a group to achieve a positive social identity. In further support of the usefulness of social identity theory, Espinoza and Garza (1985) noted that most research shows that Hispanic cultural values indicate that Hispanics would cooperate with others.

Ingroup identification. Ingroup identification is the strength with which an individual emphasizes his or her group identity (Gagnon & Bourhis, 1996). A number of studies have utilized social identity theory and the minimal group technique to illustrate the impact of ingroup identification on intergroup behavior. As we noted above, social identity theory explains that individuals with a strong ingroup identification discriminate in favor of the ingroup as a result of striving for positive social identity. The minimal group technique is utilized frequently to test the social identity theory and involves members of two arbitrary social groups (i.e., created by the researchers) allocating resources to anonymous members of the ingroup and outgroup. There is no previous history of relations between the social groups, there is no social interaction within or between group members, and there are no instrumental links between individuals' responses and their self-interest (Gagnon & Bourhis, 1996; Perreault & Bourhis, 1999). That is, individuals are place in a hypothetical work group composed of ingroup and outgroup members and assigned an ingroup identity. Then, the individuals allocate rewards to each of the hypothetical group members. Although there is no social interaction, the choices made by individuals help to illustrate how individuals communicate in diverse work groups because decisions about reward allocation likely reflect communication behavior and the social categories represent relevant social groups, such as gender and ethnicity (Gagnon & Bourhis, 1996).

Two recent studies illustrate the importance of ingroup identification for group processes. Gagnon and Bourhis (1996) examined the impact of ingroup identity on the distribution of extra points in a hypothetical work group. Using the minimal group technique, 94 students were randomly assigned in a two (autonomous/interdependent from other members) by two (high/low ingroup identification) factorial design. The authors found that the greater an individual's ingroup identification, the more likely she or he was to discriminate in favor of the ingroup.

Perreault and Bourhis (1999) not only examined the effects of ingroup identification on reward allocation, but also considered the antecedents of ingroup identification. In Phase I of the study, the authors administered measures of ethnocentrism, authoritarianism, and personal need for structure to 121 students. In Phase II, the authors randomly assigned half of the students to a group identity and allowed the other half to choose their own group identity in the minimal group design. The participants allocated a monetary reward to their hypothetical work group members. The authors found that level of ethnocentrism and the ability to choose a group were positively related to ingroup identification, which consequently led to discrimination in favor of the ingroup.

Type of task. Many studies have noted the importance of group tasks on individual communication in small groups (Hackman, 1990; McGrath, 1984). Group task refers to the work that the group is assigned (McGrath, 1984). The group's task structures the activity of the group and thus guides the interactions of the group members. There are many tasks that a group could be involved with. We consider two factors here: (a) cooperative/competitive tasks and (b) routineness of task.

One way to categorize group tasks is along the dimension of cooperation and competition (McGrath, 1984). Cooperative tasks (e.g., brainstorming) require the group members to work together in order to complete the work successfully. In contrast, competitive tasks (e.g., mixed-motive tasks) require the group members to resolve conflict of interest and can influence group members to form coalitions. A number of research investigations illustrate the impact of cooperative and competitive tasks on attitudes and behavior. Breer and Locke (1965) found that people engaged in disjunctive tasks (tasks that can be solved by one person) reported higher levels of individualism and lower levels of collectivism than people engaged in conjunctive tasks (tasks that require others' contributions). Espinoza and Garza (1985) examined group members' choices during a prisoner's dilemma type game under conditions of cooperative or competitive feedback. The feedback informed the participants whether the other members were cooperating or competing in the game. Participants who received cooperative feedback made choices that benefited the group more than participants who received competitive feedback. Similarly, Cox et al. (1991) found that participants in a prisoner's dilemma type game who received cooperative feedback about group members were more likely than participants who received no feedback about group members to make cooperative choices.

Another study examined not only cooperative/competitive tasks, but also considered ingroups and outgroups. Oetzel (1999) examined the influence of these situational features on self-construal and conflict style for 504 participants in the U.S. Students and members of the workforce received a questionnaire about a hypothetical group in one of four settings: (a) cooperative/ingroup; (b) cooperative/outgroup; (c) competitive/ingroup; and (d) competitive/outgroup. The major findings of his study were: (a) competitive group tasks lead to more dominating, avoiding, and third-party help and a greater emphasis of the independent self-construal than do cooperative group tasks; (b) ingroup situations lead to less avoiding and emotional expression, and lesser emphasis of the independent self-construal than do outgroup situations; and (c) cooperative/ingroup situations lead to more integrating and more compromising than either cooperative/outgroup our competitive/ingroup situations, and a greater emphasis of the interdependent self-construal than cooperative/outgroup situations.

The second factor regarding the type of task is routineness (whether the task is repetitive and mundane). Pelled et al. (1999) investigated whether task routineness moderated the relationship between diverse composition and task and emotional conflict. Emotional conflict refers to disagreements among people due to categorization of others, whereas task conflict refers to disagreements over the work and the way to complete the work (Pelled et al., 1999). The authors utilized a questionnaire to study 45 diverse teams at three electronics firms in the U.S. The diversity of the teams was measured with an entropy-based formula. They found that cultural diversity was positively associated with emotional conflict and functional diversity (e.g., job differences) was positively associated with task conflict. However, task routineness moderated the positive relationship between emotional conflict and diversity. Specifically, the positive relationship was eliminated when the routineness of task was considered.

External stakeholders. A final contextual factor is the influence of external stakeholders on culturally diverse groups. External stakeholders are individuals who are not directly involved in the group's interaction, but impact, or are impacted by, the group's outcomes. Only one study could be located that examines this factor. Millhous's (1999) study of the interaction between 17 Americans and 18 Russians engaged in collaborations investigated the impact of external stakeholders on group interaction. Millhous found that external stakeholders were strong influences on the groups. Specifically, Americans were concerned with specific stakeholders, such as bosses or investors, whereas Russians focused on general stakeholders, such as the economic environment or the social system. A few Americans in short-term collaborations also saw the Russian mafia as having an important role.

In sum, the previous section has revealed that the environmental context has an impact on communication in culturally diverse work groups. In the cases of organizational structure, integration, and ingroup identification, contextual features serve as vertical differences that result in status differences and competition among group members. These processes are detrimental to effective communication in culturally diverse work groups. In the cases of type of work and external stakeholders, contextual features serve to influence directly the type of communicative behavior of group members. Overall, these studies emphasize the importance of considering a variety of factors when attempting to understand the communication processes of culturally diverse groups. A limitation of this research is that cultural differences are not considered in these studies. Tannen (1994) argued that a cultural difference perspective is critical for identifying and explaining misunderstandings, conflicts, and other troubling aspects of interactions between women and men. Tannen's arguments center on the complementary, rather than dichotomous, nature of cultural and vertical differences and also apply to culturally diverse work groups. First, cultural differences show how status and power are created (at least in part) in interaction. Group member roles are created through interaction, not given. Through joint production by the parties involved, group members create position in a hierarchy. Hence, power and dominance are created and recreated through social interaction. Second, a focus on cultural differences does not preclude attention to vertical differences. Cultural differences work to the disadvantage of members of groups who do not have power, and to the advantage of members who have power. Essentially, researchers need to consider cultural, vertical, and contextual factors when investigating cultural diversity in work groups (Ragins, 1995).

COMMUNICATION AFFECTING GROUP OUTCOMES

The second role of communication in culturally diverse work groups is the influence on group outcomes. Group scholars have long been concerned with understanding how communication relates to the outcomes of a group in terms of what makes an effective group. What does it mean to be an effective group? There are two important, interrelated, dimensions to task-oriented groups: a task dimension and a social or relational dimension (Bales, 1950). The task dimension refers to the productivity of the group (e.g., the quality of the decision), whereas the relational dimension refers to the cohesiveness of the group members (e.g., the quality of the relationships). Thus a group can be evaluated in terms of both task and relational effectiveness.

Individual definitions of effectiveness are influenced by cultural differences. Hofstede (1991) explained that I/C influences the views of group effectiveness, arguing that people from individualistic cultures tend to be task-oriented, whereas people from collectivistic cultures tend to be relational-oriented. This difference influences group behavior as individualists are likely to want to "get down to business," whereas collectivists want to establish strong interpersonal relationships before worrying about tasks or business. Oetzel and Bolton-Oetzel (1997) empirically tested whether certain individuals prefer a particular dimension of group effectiveness to others. The authors asked 535 culturally diverse individuals from the U.S. to describe their self-construals and their ratings of what is important for a group to be effective. Oetzel and Bolton-Oetzel found that independent and interdependent self-construals were positively associated with both task and relational effectiveness. However, task effectiveness was better explained by independent, rather than interdependent, self-construals, whereas relational effectiveness was better explained by interdependent, rather than independent, self-construals. In this section, we review the literature relating communication to both task and relational outcomes.

Task Effectiveness

There are a number of studies that examine the impact of communication on task outcomes. We begin with three theoretical models examining this relationship and then proceed to empirical studies. Shaw and Barrett-Power (1998) developed a model to show the way in which diversity affects group development and performance. The authors argue that individuals' diversity management skills are moderating factors between differences in cultural background and the development and performance of a culturally diverse work group. Diversity management skills include willingness to communicate, relational development, self-monitoring, evaluation flexibility, and communication skill.

In a similar manner, Maznevski (1994) developed a model to explain performance in decision-making groups that are characterized by high diversity in composition. Consistent with prior research, she explained that diversity in decision-making groups provides several advantages (e.g., creativity) and disadvantages (e.g., process difficulty). Maznevski argued that the key for diverse groups to be task effective is integration. Integration is "the combining of elements into a unified result" (Maznevksi, 1994, p. 537). Integration leads to effective decisions when group members share social reality, display the ability to decenter, have confidence and motivation to communicate, have the ability to negotiate and endorse norms of communication, and have the ability to attribute difficulties appropriately. Maznevski and Peterson (1997) also supported these communicative behaviors. They argue that diverse groups need to decenter and recenter to be effective. Decentering is taking the perspective of others and recentering calls for building a common view of the situation and the common set of norms. These processes help diverse groups develop synergistic approaches to their work.

Whereas the previous studies are theoretical, there are several empirical investigations into what communication behaviors are associated with task effectiveness. Hofner Saphiere (1996) studied 56 business people representing 12 global business teams to identify patterns of behavior correlated with team productivity. She found productive teams, more than unproductive teams: (a) communicated in informal and social ways, (b) communicated frequently, (c) used task and affect behaviors, (d) desired to work together again, (e) acted as cultural interpreters, and (f) frequently disagreed with one another.

Watson, Johnson, Kumar, and Critelli (1998) reanalyzed the data from Watson et al. (1993) to understand the effect of group process on problem-solving tasks. Factor analysis of the Group Style Instrument (Watson & Michaelsen, 1988) utilized in the study revealed two dimensions of behaviors: team orientation and individual orientation. Team orientation consists of communicative behaviors such as coordination, consensus decision making, and support. Individual orientation consists of avoiding conflict, power struggles, and dominating discussion. The authors found that individual orientation was associated negatively with performance, whereas team orientation was associated positively with performance. Performance consisted of receiving a good grade on a case study for a class project.

Pelled et al.'s (1999) study of 45 diverse teams in three electronic firms also investigated the effects of task and emotional conflict on performance (in addition to diverse composition and task routineness). Team supervisors rated performance based on the efficiency of the teams and the number of innovations introduced by the teams. They found that cultural diversity was associated positively with emotional conflict and functional diversity (e.g., job differences) was associated positively with task conflict. Further, emotional conflict was associated negatively with performance and task conflict was associated positively with performance.

Finally, Chatman, Polzer, Barsade, and Neale (1998) studied the effects of demographic composition and cultural emphasis on work processes and outcomes. They utilized an organizational simulation for 258 M.B.A. students in the U.S. to study the frequency of communication, conflict among members, idea quality, and productivity. They found that groups that emphasized collectivism engaged in communication more frequently and had fewer incidents of conflict than groups that emphasized individualism. Further, increased diversity was related to decreased interaction, but also to increased productivity. The authors speculated that this negative relationship between interaction and productivity may be due to two factors: (a) individuals can complete the tasks better than groups; or (b) the frequency of interaction may be due to social and not task issues. However, the content of the interactions was not measured so the latter speculation could not be confirmed.

In sum, previous theoretical and empirical work illustrates that effective communication processes are associated positively with task effectiveness. Effective communication processes consist of integrating multiple viewpoints, frequent communication, willingness to communicate, support, and task conflict.

Relational and Task Effectiveness

We could locate no studies that focus on relational effectiveness alone. However, there are two studies that examine both relational and task outcomes in culturally diverse groups. Tjosvold, Sasaki, and Moy (1998) examined several components of interactions between 29 Japanese workers in two Hong Kong organizations: cooperative goals, open discussion of differing positions, work relationships, productivity, and commitment to their organizations. The participants in the study were interviewed about critical incidents that influenced their willingness to stay with and work hard for their current company. The participants were asked to describe the setting, what occurred, and the consequences of one critical incident that influenced them positively and one that had a negative influence. Utilizing a structural equation model, the authors determined that cooperative goals lead to open discussion, open discussion results in productive work and strong interpersonal relationships, and productive work results in commitment from the workers.

Oetzel's (2001) study of 36 culturally diverse and culturally homogeneous student groups in the U.S. examined the effects of three communication variables (equal participation, cooperation, and respectful communication) and the outcome variables of performance, satisfaction, and withholding effort (in addition to examining the effects of self-construals on the communication processes discussed earlier). Oetzel found that the more groups had equal participation, cooperation, and respectful communication the more satisfied were the group members and the less likely they were to withhold effort. Withholding effort harms the performance of the group in an indirect manner because the available resources of a group are not being used to their full potential. However, the communication processes did not directly relate to performance measures (i.e., a grade on the assignment). Thus the communication processes are associated positively with relational effectiveness, but only indirectly associated with task effectiveness.

In sum, the majority of studies examine the impact of communication on task outcomes such as productivity and performance. The amount of focus on task effectiveness reflects the Western bias of concern for the bottom line. However, Oetzel (1995) argued that a culturally appropriate model of group effectiveness must consider both task and relational effectiveness, at least for groups composed of both individualistic and collectivistic individuals. Thus more research on how communication processes relate to relational effectiveness in culturally diverse work groups is needed.

COMMUNICATION PROCESS CREATING GROUP CULTURE

The third role of communication in culturally diverse groups is constitutive. That is, the interaction of group members creates a group culture and alters the ways in which group members think and communicate. The constitutive role of communication has been demonstrated in research on group culture (Adelman & Frey, 1994; Bormann, 1997). Group (and organizational) culture is emergent and can only be understood by considering "the way individuals make sense of their world through their communicative behaviors" (Putnam, 1983, p. 31). Group scholars have investigated the creation of group culture via understanding the sharing of fantasies (Bormann, 1997) and the investigation of symbols and rituals (Adelman & Frey, 1994). For example, Adelman and Frey (1994) examined the rituals of the Bonaventure House—a home for people livings with AIDS. Rituals are the repeating of activities and can occur on a daily basis or for special occasions. For example, when a person dies, residents at the Bonaventure House attach a message to a balloon and let the balloon go as they say good-bye. Rituals contribute to a group's sense of solidarity, cohesiveness, and community. However, there is limited research examining how communication creates group culture in culturally diverse work groups. In this section, we examine the theoretical models and empirical research focusing specifically on communication creating group culture in culturally diverse work groups.

One of the popular approaches to understanding how members of distinct cultures come together to create a common culture is the contact hypothesis. The contact hypothesis (Allport, 1954) argues that participants from two different cultures who are of equal status and working toward a superordinate goal (one that requires efforts and commitment from both cultures) will be able to reduce intercultural conflict and prejudice. Gaertner, Dovidio, and Bachman (1996) extended the contact hypothesis by arguing that intercultural conflict and prejudice can be reduced by factors that transform members' cognitive representations of the group as being composed of one, inclusive group identity instead of multiple group identities. Common ingroup identity is achieved under conditions of equal status between members, cooperative interdependence, the opportunity for self-revealing interactions, and egalitarian norms. Gaertner et al. (1996) described a study of three-person laboratory groups to test the common ingroup identity hypothesis. The authors found that cooperative interaction leads to the perception of a common group identity, which subsequently reduces bias toward outgroup members.

A recent study by Hubbard (1999) also helps to illustrate factors of the contact hypothesis. Hubbard investigated a grassroots organization composed of Jewish Americans, Palestinian Americans, and other U.S. Americans concerned about working for peace in the Middle East over the course of five years. The group came together on an equal status level to dialogue and resolve conflicts. The focus of the group was internally oriented, as opposed to an externally oriented, social mobilizing group. Overall, the group utilized consensus building and cooperative dialogue to create a successful group. Success was defined as the ability of the group to maintain its membership (for the most part) and reach mutually agreeable decisions. However, the success was largely due to the influence of two Palestinian Americans who were well-respected group members. These two members were able to balance power differences that resulted from cultural differences between the Jewish and Palestinian American members. The cultural differences led to particular communication styles that created a power imbalance among members. The quality of interaction was able to overcome the imbalance in some ways and create a group that bridged the Arab and Jewish communities. However, the bridge was tenuous because the Palestinian Americans were more responsible for adjusting than were the Jewish Americans. Hubbard emphasized the consideration of cultural differences when examining equal status contact and its impact on reducing intercultural bias.

Other empirical investigations that we have previously reviewed also provide some support for the constitutive role of communication. Hofner Saphiere's (1996) investigation of global business teams revealed that productive teams unanimously desired to work together again. Although not directly addressed, we can assume that the desire to work together is the result of the quality of interactions. Similarly, Tjosvold et al. (1998) found that cooperative goals led to open discussion, which led to productive work and subsequently to greater commitment in employees of a Japanese multinational firm operating in Hong Kong. Thus open discussion indirectly affected the degree of commitment in these employees. These two studies reveal that quality interaction increases the motivation for group members to continue to work together. This finding, however, does not directly illustrate how communication creates group culture.

Finally, three studies help to illustrate that "culture is an ongoing process whereby norms and expectations evolve among the participants in face-to-face interaction" (Millhous, 1999, p. 299). Zamarripa and Krueger's (1983) study of leadership in homogeneous and heterogeneous groups revealed indications that rule negotiation takes place to form implicit contracts that regulate leadership behavior. Watson et al.'s (1993) study of ongoing heterogeneous groups illustrated that culturally diverse groups learn their own norms, which replace original cultural programming. During the first task, the groups in the study had process difficulty, but this difficulty had relatively disappeared (compared to homogeneous groups) by the fourth and final task. Millhous's (1999) research on collaborative groups composed of Russians and U.S. Americans demonstrated that differences in culture did not predict conflict or failures. Most of the groups were engaged in productive ventures and were evaluated positively by the members. Thus the quality of the group interactions influenced the feelings of the groups.

In sum, it appears that communication can create culture in culturally diverse work groups. The strongest evidence in previous research is that cooperative interactions lead to the reduction of intercultural conflicts and prejudice. This finding is important because one of the key questions facing culturally diverse groups is

"What can be done to create an inclusive, supportive group?" However, the fact that communication influences affective feelings is not direct evidence that communication creates group culture. It is not clear exactly what (and how) communication processes lead to the creation of an inclusive culture as there is limited search investigating the use of symbols, rituals, or fantasies in culturally diverse groups. Further, there is no research investigating whether a group culture is truly inclusive or whether one group is expected to assimilate to the norms of the other.

UNANSWERED QUESTIONS: WHERE DO WE GO FROM HERE?

The literature review revealed three main approaches to understanding the role of communication in culturally diverse groups: (a) communication as affected by cultural and contextual factors, (b) communication as affecting group outcomes, and (c) communication as a constitutive element for group culture. Each of these roles was reviewed and limitations were discussed. In this section, we conclude by noting what we feel are the most important questions for understanding the role of communication in culturally diverse groups. Additionally, we provide a review of theories and empirical work that may be useful for answering these questions.

What Are the Important Communicative Processes in Culturally Diverse Groups?

Previous research on culturally diverse work groups has examined a variety of communication variables including conflict, leadership style, decision making, turn taking, and perspective taking. However, few studies have attempted to identify which communication variables are important to consider for culturally diverse groups. As we noted earlier, Oetzel (1995) argued that to be culturally inclusive any evaluation of a work group composed of members from both individualistic and collectivistic cultures should include both task and relational outcomes. As a result, Oetzel argued further that the communication processes studied in culturally diverse groups should relate positively with both task and relational outcomes. In a survey of the extant literature, he identified three communication processes that meet this criterion: (a) equal distribution of turns, (b) consensus decision-making style, and (c) cooperative conflict style. However, follow-up research indicates that there may be different sets of behaviors that relate to task and relational effectiveness (Oetzel, 2001). Specifically, it appears that relationally effective groups participate equally and resolve conflicts in a cooperative manner, whereas task effective groups are vigilant during discussions (Hofner Saphiere, 1996).

Another alternative is to examine dimensions of communication that are associated with and prevalent in culturally diverse work groups. Larkey (1996a) identified five dimensions of workgroup interaction in culturally diverse groups through a review of the extant literature: (a) inclusion—the degree to which certain people are marginalized in a group; (b) ideation—the amount of varied ideas or creativity in a group; (c) understanding—the matching of expectations and meanings of other group members; (d) treatment—positive or negative evaluations of behavior; and (e) adjustment—the degree to which individuals converge their communication patterns to those of other group members. Through subsequent interviews with 35 members of two organizations, Larkey created the Workforce Diversity Questionnaire in order to measure these five dimensions. She was able to confirm the measurement scales of four of the five dimensions (not adjustment) by having 280 organizational members and 182 students complete versions of the questionnaire. The questionnaire may be utilized to assess the quality of interactions in culturally diverse groups and help to predict successful task and relational outcomes.

Are All Culturally Diverse Groups Alike?

One assumption that has guided the majority of research in this area is that all culturally diverse groups are alike. That is, so long as conditions are the same, communication in the culturally diverse group will function in a consistent matter. Thus groups composed of Japanese and European Americans will have similar process difficulties as groups composed of Mexicans and Chinese. However, this is not intuitive. Every culture has unique aspects that work well with some cultures and not so well with others. Further, this assumption does not take into consideration the degree to which two cultures have a history of unsuccessfully resolved conflicts (e.g., Palestine and Israel). For example, I/C may explain the difficulties that occur in one group, whereas unresolved conflicts may explain the difficulties in another group.

Further, one methodological limitation of the research on culturally diverse groups encourages the viewpoint that all diverse (and homogeneous) groups are alike. The majority of research comparing homogeneous and heterogeneous groups utilizes only European American homogeneous groups (exceptions are Oetzel, 1998a, 1998c; Thomas, 1999; Thomas et al., 1996). The comparison group is any set of heterogeneous individuals. This choice is often one of convenience, but it serves to normalize European American communication patterns and treat heterogeneous groups as the same (Cox, 1990). The consequence is that we gloss over potentially meaningful differences and conclude that cultural diversity (regardless of the origin) is associated with process difficulty. The solution is to conduct research on a variety of homogeneous and culturally diverse groups in order to identify similarities and differences in group communication.

How Do Cultural and Contextual Factors Relate to Each Other in Their Influence on Communication in Culturally Diverse Work Groups?

It is important to try to understand how cultural and contextual factors relate because both are relevant to culturally diverse groups. Unfortunately, there is a lack of research that considers both factors in the same study. Further, when both are included, the relationship between the factors is usually not considered (e.g., Millhous, 1999; Oetzel, 1999). An exception is Hubbard's (1999) study of a group composed of Jewish and Palestinian Americans. Hubbard's findings revealed that cultural differences in communicative styles create unequal status among the members. Thus the cultural features frame the vertical factors in this situation. In another exception, Pelled et al. (1999) examined multiple factors such as type of task and cultural factors and found that type of task moderated the influence of culture on work group communication.

We want to note two sets of seemingly inconsistent studies to help illustrate how multiple factors can help to explain inconsistencies. Earlier, we discussed the effects of diverse composition on group communication. Watson et al. (1993) found that over time culturally diverse groups adjust norms and alleviate process difficulties, whereas Millhous (1999) found that long-term groups reported more process difficulties than short-term groups. We noted earlier that understanding the individuals' motivations and the routineness of the task could explain these apparent inconsistencies.

A second example is the research of Espinoza and Garza (1985), Garza and Santos (1991), and Oetzel (1998a, 1998c). Oetzel found that Japanese and European Americans in heterogeneous groups communicated in a manner consistent with individual and group self-construals (i.e., cultural differences). In contrast, Garza and his colleagues found that Hispanic Americans have different behaviors in various group compositions because of competition resulting from social comparison and social identity (i.e., contextual differences). The difference in these studies is that the participants in Oetzel's studies were in a balanced group (equal numbers of both cultural groups) and the participants in studies by Garza and his colleagues were in imbalanced groups.

Both of these examples help to illustrate the importance of situational features for understanding communication in culturally diverse groups. Maznevski and Peterson (1997) argue that certain situations influence whether or not these value orientations affect behavior. Strong situations are those in which social cues to behavior are clear, whereas in weak situations there are ambiguous cues guiding behavior. Culturally diverse groups will likely experience process difficulty in weak situations because of differences in value orientations, but not in strong situations because behavior is not the result of cultural values. However, it is not clear exactly what are strong and weak situations.

Two recent theoretical pieces offer some starting points for investigating these relationships and understanding situational impacts. Kim (1994) proposed a model of contextual and behavioral factors relevant to interethnic communication. Drawing from a pragmatic and systems theoretical point of view, Kim argued that associative (inclusion and connection with others) and disassociative (autonomy and separation from others) communication behaviors are embedded within three contextual features: communicator, situation, and environment. That is, these contextual features directly influence and frame association and dissociation in interethnic communication. The communicator includes an individual's cognitive structure (e.g., cognitive complexity), identity (e.g., ingroup loyalty), and bias (e.g., prejudice). The situation focuses on the immediate social milieu, such as heterogeneity of participants' ethnic background, salience of ethnicity, and interaction structure. Finally, environment is the larger social milieu consisting of institutional equity/inequity, ethnic group strength, and degree of interethnic contact. Although Kim does not provide specific propositions for culturally diverse work groups, her organizing model provides a framework for drawing hypotheses about the relationship between contextual and cultural factors for communication behavior.

Oetzel (in press) posited that cultural, vertical, and contextual factors work in concert together to influence group communication. The starting point of the model is context. Four contextual elements are considered: (a) a history of unsuccessfully resolved conflict among cultural/ethnic groups (e.g., the conflict between Israelis and Palestinians), (b) group composition (ingroup/outgroup balance), (c) cooperative versus competitive tasks, and (d) status differences among members (e.g., boss and employee). Oetzel argued that the contextual factors influence the degree to which cultural or vertical differences are more important for explaining communication in culturally diverse work groups. Under certain conditions (history of unsuccessfully resolved conflict, imbalance between ingroup and outgroup members, competitive tasks, and inequality of status among group members), vertical differences have a greater impact on group communication than cultural differences. Under the opposite conditions, cultural differences have a greater influence on group communication than vertical differences. The model does not provide an explication of strong versus weak situations, but does provide testable hypotheses for understanding the relationships among contextual and cultural factors.

How Does Communication Function to Create Inclusive and Divisive Groups?

This question focuses on the need to further investigate the constitutive role of communication for group cultures. We know very little about the creation of norms in culturally diverse groups. Earlier, we noted that culturally diverse groups appear to develop their own norms over time (Millhous, 1999; Watson et al., 1993). However, we do not know what these norms are or how they are negotiated. Do norms develop in such a way as to privilege the mainstream cultural group or are norms created equally by members of all cultural groups? The answer to this question can be illuminating for understanding how culturally diverse groups utilize the diversity in their groups. It is easy to imagine groups that utilize communication in such a way to create an open and supportive atmosphere, whereas other groups create a suspicious and closed atmosphere. However, we do not know much about how this process occurs.

Two theories have the potential to inform these questions. Brewer (1991, 1996) proposed the theory of optimal distinctiveness for explaining successful intergroup interactions (i.e., interactions with people from different cultural groups). The theory is a critique of the notion of cooperative interdependence (i.e., superordinate goals) reducing intergroup conflict and prejudice. Specifically, she explained that the failure of many cooperative ventures provides evidence for the inability of the contact hypothesis and cooperative interdependence to explain intergroup interaction. Brewer (1996) argued that "social identity is derived from two opposing motivational systems that govern the relations between self-concept and membership in social groups" (p. 296): inclusion with others and differentiation from others. The motives are in opposition because as one is satisfied, the other is more likely to be activated. However, equilibrium is possible and the result is the search for optimal distinctiveness. Brewer noted that optimal distinctiveness is maximized when social category boundaries are clearly defined enough to insure inclusion and exclusion. She suggested that a solution in the search for optimal distinctiveness is to have a salient superordinate goal that allows individuals to be members of subgroups (e.g., we have a group goal, but we are still unique individuals). Thus communication that emphasizes both common goals and uniqueness of the individual members will likely result in an inclusive group culture.

The communication accommodation theory (Gallois, Giles, Jones, Cargile, & Ota, 1995) also provides a potential explanation for understanding how groups include and divide individuals. The purpose of the theory is to understand how and why individuals in intercultural encounters utilize communication patterns that converge with and diverge from others. The theory includes several stages moving from context to behavior to evaluation. The starting point for communication accommodation theory is sociohistorical context (e.g., societal norms, cultural variability such as I/C, historical and economic relations). The next step is accommodative orientation, which includes an individual's tendency to perceive encounters as intergroup, interpersonal, or both, as well as his or her initial orientation to converge. The immediate situation (e.g., level of formality or stress) is the next factor for determining behavior followed by individual goals and addressee focus. As a result of these various factors, individuals utilize a variety of sociolinguistic strategies and verbal/nonverbal behaviors to converge or diverge with the other party. The final steps are labeling and attributing behavior, followed by an evaluation of the encounter. Gallois et al. posited 17 propositions about the relationships among these variables. Although a detailed description of this theory is beyond the scope of the current essay, communication accommodation theory helps to explain why individuals converge or diverge (i.e., the result of sociohistorical context, immediate situation, and individual orientations) and why convergence and divergence results in positive or negative evaluations. An important point of the theory is that convergence of communication behavior is not always a positive factor for intercultural encounters and that divergence can be beneficial under certain conditions.

What Methods Should Be Utilized to Further This Line of Research?

Before addressing this question, it is helpful to summarize and describe the methods of the studies we have reviewed. One predominant approach is a laboratory design involving a homogeneous control group (as noted above, the control is usually European Americans) and a heterogeneous group. The groups are composed of students and interact for a predetermined amount of time. At the conclusion of the interaction, self-report ratings of the communication processes and outcomes (if relevant) are administered (an exception is Oetzel 1998a, 1998c with videotaped interactions). The two sets of groups are compared to determine whether differences exist. The second predominant design is to utilize existing culturally diverse groups of both students and members of the workforce. These groups interact in their natural settings and self-report measures of process and outcomes are administered and related to the relative diversity (usually measured by an entropy-based formula) of the group. There are two other types of designs: (a) in-depth interviews or observations of naturally occurring diverse groups (Hofner Saphiere, 1996; Hubbard, 1999; Kim & Paulk, 1994; Millhous, 1999); and (b) laboratory experiments of individuals in hypothetical groups (Gagnon & Bourhis, 1996; Oetzel, 1999; Perreault & Bourhis, 1999).

The focus on the majority of these studies has been attempting to relate cultural diversity, cultural values, or contextual cues to communication process and communication process to group outcomes. The strength of these studies is internal validity; valid conclusions have been reached, and replicated, about the relationship between cultural diversity and group communication and outcomes. Although these studies have revealed valuable insights about culturally diverse work groups, there are also limitations that have resulted in several unanswered questions about this line of research. We briefly discuss two limitations.

The majority of the studies utilized student groups (approximately 70%) and did not focus on contextual features. For example, a study of student groups working on a task for a class typically does not consider the larger social milieu (e.g., power dynamics of individuals within the society). Thus external validity of the research is questionable. Is what we find in student laboratories relevant to the larger society? It is important to extend research from the laboratory and determine if the conclusions are applicable elsewhere. Similarly, the external validity of studies conducted primarily in the U.S. and in English also is limited. The solution is to include a variety of participants from various cultural groups and social classes in their context.

The majority of the studies reviewed also utilized quantitative designs (approximately 85%). We see two limitations of quantitative design for this line of research. First, the communication processes, group outcomes, and contextual features are specified by the researcher (frequently without the guidance of a theory) and may not be applicable to the participants. Second, quantitative designs limit the ability of researchers to examine the process of group development, which inhibits the understanding of the constitutive role of communication in culturally diverse groups. Interviews with individuals can help to identify the factors that are important to individuals in a culturally diverse group. Ethnographic observations and interviews are useful for understanding how communication creates inclusive and exclusive group environments.

Overall, our recommendation for future research on communication in culturally diverse groups is for balance. First, a balance in the type of participants (e.g., all ethnic groups within the U.S., multiple national cultures, multiple languages, and multiple socioeconomic classes) is necessary to fully understand the role of communication in culturally diverse work groups. Many groups remain invisible in this literature (e.g., Native Americans, Africans, and the poor). Second, a balance of quantitative and qualitative studies and laboratory and field studies is important because the strengths of each type of study help to overcome the weaknesses of the other.

In conclusion, we have identified three roles of communication in the extant literature: (a) communication as affected by cultural and contextual factors, (b) communication as affecting group outcomes, and (c) communication as a constitutive element for group culture. This review provides a synthesis to what has been done and reveals some unanswered questions for future research. In particular, future research is needed to investigate the relationship between group communication and outcomes, as well as the constitutive role of communication. This future research will help us to come to a better understanding of how cultural diversity and communication relate in work groups.

NOTE

1. Throughout this essay, we utilize the labels for national and ethnic groups given by the authors of the studies.

REFERENCES

Allport, G. W. (1954). *The nature of prejudice.* Cambridge, MA: Addison-Wesley.

Adelman, M. B., & Frey, L. R. (1994). The pilgrim must embark: Creating and sustaining community in a residential facility for people with AIDS. In L. R. Frey (Ed.), *Groups in context: Studies of natural groups* (pp. 3–22). Hillsdale, NJ: Erlbaum.

Bales, R. F. (1950). *Interaction process analysis: A method for the study of small groups.* Reading, MA: Addison-Wesley.

Berger, J., Cohen, B. P., & Zelditch, M. (1973). Status characteristics and social interaction. In R. Ofshe (Ed.), *Interpersonal behavior in small groups* (pp. 194–216). Englewood Cliffs, NJ: Prentice-Hall.

Berger, J., Wagner, D. G., & Zelditch, M. (1985). Introduction: Expectation states theory: Review and assessment. In J. Berger & M. Zelditch (Eds.), *Status, rewards, and influence* (pp. 1–72). San Francisco: Jossey-Bass.

Bochner, S., & Hesketh, B. (1994). Power distance, individualism/collectivism, and job-related attitudes in a culturally diverse work group. *Journal of Cross-Cultural Psychology, 25,* 233–257.

Bond, M. H., Leung, K., & Wan, K. C. (1982). How does cultural collectivism operate? The impact of task and maintenance contributions on reward distribution. *Journal of Cross-Cultural Psychology, 13,* 186–200.

Bormann, E. G. (1997). Symbolic convergence theory and communication in group decision making. In R. Y. Hirokawa & M. S. Poole (Eds.), *Communication in group decision making* (2nd ed., pp. 81–113). Thousand Oaks, CA: Sage.

Breer, P. E., & Locke, E. A. (1965). *Task experience as a source of attitudes.* Homewood, IL: Dorsey Press.

Brewer, M. B. (1991). The social self: On being the same and different at the same time. *Personality and Social Psychology Bulletin, 17,* 475–482.

Brewer, M. B. (1996). When contact is not enough: Social identity and intergroup cooperation. *International Journal of Intercultural Relations, 20,* 291–303.

Cady, S. H., & Valentine, J. (1999). Team innovation and perceptions of consideration: What difference does it make? *Small Group Research, 30,* 730–750.

Chatman, J. A., Polzer, J. T., Barsade, S. G., & Neale, M. A. (1998). Being different yet feeling similar: The influence of demographic composition and organizational culture on work processes and outcomes. *Administrative Science Quarterly, 43,* 749–780.

Chemers, M. M., & Murphy, S. E. (1995). Leadership and diversity in groups and organizations. In M. M. Chemers, S. Oskamp, & M. A. Costanzo (Eds.), *Diversity in organizations: New perspectives for a changing workplace* (pp. 157–188). Thousand Oaks, CA: Sage.

Cox, T. H. (1990). Problems with research by organizational scholars on issues of race and ethnicity. *Journal of Applied Behavioral Science, 26,* 5–23.

Cox, T. H. (1994). *Cultural diversity in organizations: Theory, research, and practice.* San Francisco: Berret-Koehler.

Cox, T. H., & Finley, J. A. (1995). An analysis of work specialization and organization level as dimensions of workforce diversity. In M. M. Chemers, S. Oskamp, & M. A. Costanzo (Eds.), *Diversity in organizations: New perspectives for a changing workplace* (pp. 62–89). Thousand Oaks, CA: Sage.

Cox, T. H., Lobel, S. A., & McLeod, P. L. (1991). Effects of ethnic group cultural differences on cooperative and competitive behavior on a group task. *Academy of Management Journal, 34,* 827–847.

Earley, P. C. (1989). Social loafing and collectivism. *Administrative Science Quarterly, 34,* 565–581.

Earley, P. C. (1993). East meets West meets Mideast: Further explorations of collectivistic and individualistic work groups. *Academy of Management Journal, 36,* 319–348.

Espinoza, J. A., & Garza, R. T. (1985). Social group salience and intergroup cooperation. *Journal of Experimental Social Psychology, 21,* 380–392.

Fiedler, F. E. (1966). The effect of leadership and cultural heterogeneity on group performance: A test of the contingency model. *Journal of Experimental Social Psychology, 2,* 237–264.

Gaertner, S. L., Dovidio, J. F., & Bachman, B. A. (1996). Revisiting the contact hypothesis: The induction of a common ingroup identity. *International Journal of Intercultural Relations, 20,* 271–290.

Gagnon, A., & Bourhis, R. (1996). Discrimination in the minimal group paradigm: Social identity or self interest? *Personality and Social Psychology Bulletin, 22,* 1289–1301.

Gallois, C., Giles, H., Jones, E., Cargile, A. C., & Ota, H. (1995). Accommodating intercultural encounters: Elaborations and extensions. In R. L. Wiseman (Ed.), *Intercultural communication theories* (pp. 115–147). Thousand Oaks, CA: Sage.

Garza, R. T., & Santos, S. J. (1991). Ingroup/outgroup balance and interdependent interethnic behavior. *Journal of Experimental Social Psychology, 27,* 124–137.

Gudykunst, W. B., Matsumoto, Y., Ting-Toomey, S., Nishida, T., Kim, K. S., & Heyman, S. (1996). The influence of cultural individualism-collectivism, self construals, and individual values on communication styles across cultures. *Human Communication Research, 22,* 510–543.

Hackman, J. R. (1990). *Groups that work and those that don't.* San Francisco: Jossey-Bass.

Hackman, J. R., & Morris, C. G. (1975). Group tasks, group interaction process, and group performance effectiveness: A review and proposed integration. In L. Berkowitz (Ed.), *Advances in experimental social psychology* (Vol. 8, pp. 45–99). New York: Academic Press.

Harris, K. L., & Nibler, R. (1998). Decision making by Chinese and U.S. students. *Journal of Social Psychology, 138,* 102–114.

Hofner Saphiere, D. M. (1996). Productive behaviors of global business teams. *International Journal of Intercultural Relations, 20,* 227–259.

Hofstede, G. (1991). *Cultures and organizations: Software of the mind.* Maidenhead, UK: McGraw-Hill.

Hubbard, A. S. (1999). Cultural and status differences in intergroup conflict resolution: A longitudinal study of a Middle East dialogue group in the United States. *Human Relations, 52,* 303–325.

Hui, C., & Triandis, H. C. (1986). Individualism-collectivism: A study of cross-cultural researchers. *Journal of Cross-Cultural Psychology, 17*, 225–248.

Jackson, S. E., Brett, J. F., Sessa, V. I., Cooper, D. M., Julin, J. A., & Peyronnin, K. (1991). Some differences make a difference: Individual dissimilarity and group heterogeneity as correlates of recruitment, promotions, and turnover. *Journal of Applied Psychology, 76*, 675–689.

Judy, R. W., & D'Amico, C. (1997). *Workforce 2020: Work and workers for the 21st century*. Indianapolis, IN: Hudson Institute.

Kanter, R. M. (1977). *Men and women of the corporation*. New York: Basic Books.

Kim, M. S., Hunter, J. E., Miyahara, A., Horvath, A., Bresnahan, M., & Yoon, H. (1996). Individual-vs. cultural-level dimensions of individualism and collectivism: Effects on preferred conversational styles. *Communication Monographs, 63*, 28–49.

Kim, Y. Y. (1994). Interethnic communication: The context and the behavior. In S. Deetz (Ed.), *Communication yearbook 17* (pp. 511–538). Thousand Oaks, CA: Sage.

Kim, Y. Y., & Paulk, S. (1994). Intercultural challenges and personal adjustments: A qualitative analysis of the experiences of American and Japanese co-workers. In R. L. Wiseman & R. Shuter (Eds.), *Communicating in multinational organizations* (pp. 117–140). Thousand Oaks, CA: Sage.

Kirchmeyer, C., & Cohen, A. (1992). Multicultural groups: Their performance and reactions with constructive conflict. *Group & Organization Management, 17*, 153–170.

Kluckhohn, F. R., & Strodtbeck, F. L. (1961). *Variations in value orientations*. Evanston, IL: Row, Peterson.

Larkey, L. K. (1996a). The development and validation of the workforce diversity questionnaire: An instrument to assess interactions in diverse workgroups. *Management Communication Quarterly, 9*, 296–337.

Larkey, L. K. (1996b). Toward a theory of communicative interactions in culturally diverse groups. *Academy of Management Review, 21*, 463–491.

Lawrence, B. S. (1997). The black box of organizational demography. *Organization Science, 8*, 1–22.

Markus, H. R., & Kitayama, S. (1991). Culture and self: Implications for cognition, emotion, and motivation. *Psychological Review, 98*, 224–253.

Maznevski, M. L. (1994). Understanding our differences: Performance in decision-making groups with diverse members. *Human Relations, 47*, 531–552.

Maznevski, M., & Peterson, M. F. (1997). Societal values, social interpretation, and multinational teams. In C. S. Granrose & S. Oskamp (Eds.), *Cross-cultural work groups* (pp. 61–89). Thousand Oaks, CA: Sage.

McGrath, J. E. (1984). *Groups: Interaction and performance*. Englewood Cliffs, NJ: Prentice-Hall.

McGrath, J. E., Berdahl, J. L., & Arrow, H. (1995). Traits, expectations, culture, and clout: The dynamics of diversity in work groups. In S. E. Jackson & M. N. Ruderman (Eds.), *Diversity in work teams: Research paradigms for a changing workplace* (pp. 17–45). Washington, DC: American Psychological Association.

McLeod, P. L., Lobel, S. A., & Cox, T. H. (1996). Ethnic diversity and creativity in small groups. *Small Group Research, 27*, 248–264.

Millhous, L. (1999). The experience of culture in multicultural groups: Case studies of Russian-American collaboration in business. *Small Group Research, 30*, 280–308.

Milliken, F. J., & Martins, L. L. (1996). Searching for common threads: Understanding the multiple effects of diversity in organizational groups. *Academy of Management Review, 21*, 402–433.

Nadler, L. B., Keeshan-Nadler, M., & Broome, B. J. (1985). Culture and the management of conflict situations. In W. Gudykunst, L. Stewart, & S. Ting-Toomey (Eds.), *Communication, culture, and organizational processes* (pp. 87–113). Newbury Park, CA: Sage.

Oetzel, J. G. (1995). Intercultural small groups: An effective decision-making theory. In R. L. Wiseman (Ed.), *Intercultural communication theories* (pp. 247–270). Thousand Oaks, CA: Sage.

Oetzel, J. G. (1998a). Culturally homogeneous and heterogeneous groups: Explaining communication processes through individualism-collectivism and self-construal. *International Journal of Intercultural Relations, 22*, 135–161.

Oetzel, J. G. (1998b). The effects of self-construals and ethnicity on self-reported conflict styles. *Communication Reports, 11,* 133–144.

Oetzel, J. G. (1998c). Explaining individual communication processes in homogeneous and heterogeneous groups through individualism-collectivism and self-construal. *Human Communication Research, 25,* 202–224.

Oetzel, J. G. (1999). The influence of situational features on perceived conflict styles and self-construals in small groups. *International Journal of Intercultural Relations, 23,* 679–695.

Oetzel, J. G. (2001). Self-construals, communication processes, and group outcomes in homogeneous and heterogeneous groups. *Small Group Research, 32,* 19–54.

Oetzel, J. G. (in press). The effects of culture and cultural diversity on communication in work groups: Synthesizing vertical and cultural differences with a face-negotiation perspective. In L. Frey (Ed.), *New directions in group communication.* Thousand Oaks, CA: Sage.

Oetzel, J. G., & Bolton-Oetzel, K. D. (1997). Exploring the relationship between self-construal and dimensions of group effectiveness. *Management Communication Quarterly, 10,* 289–315.

O'Reilly, C. A., Caldwell, D. F., & Barnett, W. P. (1989). Work group demography, social integration, and turnover. *Administrative Science Quarterly, 34,* 21–37.

Pelled, L. H., Eisenhardt, K. M., & Xin, K. R. (1999). Exploring the black box: An analysis of work group diversity, conflict, and performance. *Administrative Science Quarterly, 44,* 1–28.

Perreault, S., & Bourhis, R. (1999). Ethnocentrism, social identification, and discrimination. *Personality and Social Psychology Bulletin, 25,* 92–103.

Putnam, L. L. (1983). The interpretive perspective: An alternative to functionalism. In L. L. Putnam & M. E. Pacanowsky (Eds.), *Communication and organizations: An interpretive approach* (pp. 31–54). Newbury Park, CA: Sage.

Putnam, L. L., & Stohl, C. (1990). Bona fide groups: A reconceptualization of groups in context. *Communication Studies, 41,* 248–265.

Ragins, B. R. (1995). Diversity, power, and mentorship in organizations: A cultural, structural, and behavioral perspective. In M. M. Chemers, S. Oskamp, & M. A. Costanzo (Eds.), *Diversity in organizations: New perspectives for a changing workplace* (pp. 91–132). Thousand Oaks, CA: Sage.

Rodríguez, R. (1998). Challenging demographic reductionism: A pilot study investigating diversity in group composition. *Small Group Research, 29,* 744–759.

Sessa, V. I., & Jackson, S. E. (1995). Diversity in decision-making teams: All differences are not created equal. In M. M. Chemers, S. Oskamp, & M. A. Costanzo (Eds.), *Diversity in organizations: New perspectives for a changing workplace* (pp. 133–156). Thousand Oaks, CA: Sage.

Shaw, J. B., & Barrett-Power, E. (1998). The effects of diversity on small work group processes and performance. *Human Relations, 51,* 1307–1325.

Singelis, T. M., & Brown, W. J. (1995). Culture, self, and collectivist communication: Linking culture to individual behavior. *Human Communication Research, 21,* 354–389.

Smith, P. B., & Peterson, M. F. (1988). *Leadership, organizations, and culture: An event management model.* London: Sage.

Smith, P. B., Peterson, M. F., & Misumi, J. (1994). Event management and work team effectiveness in Japan, Britain, and USA. *Journal of Occupational and Organizational Psychology, 67,* 33–43.

Tajfel, H. (1978). The achievement of group differentiation. In H. Tajfel (Ed.), *Differentiation between social groups: Studies in the social psychology of intergroup relations* (pp. 77–98). New York: Academic Press.

Tajfel, H., & Turner, J. C. (1986). The social identity theory of intergroup behavior. In S. Worchel & W. G. Austin (Eds.), *Psychology of intergroup relations* (2nd ed., pp. 7–24). Chicago: Nelson-Hall.

Tannen, D. (1994). *Gender and discourse.* New York: Oxford University Press.

Thomas, D. C. (1999). Cultural diversity and work group effectiveness: An experimental study. *Journal of Cross-Cultural Psychology, 30,* 242–263.

Thomas, D. C., Ravlin, E. C., & Wallace, A. W. (1996). Effect of cultural diversity in work groups. In P. A. Bamberger, M. Erez, & S. B. Bacharach (Eds.), *Research in the sociology of organizations: Cross-cultural analysis of organizations* (pp. 1–33). Greenwich, CT: JAI Press.

Tjosvold, D., Sasaki, S., & Moy, J. W. (1998). Developing commitment in Japanese organizations in Hong Kong: Interdependence, interaction, relationship, and productivity. *Small Group Research, 29,* 560–582.

Triandis, H. C. (1995). *Individualism and collectivism.* Boulder, CO: Westview.

Turner, J. C. (1975). Social comparison and social identity: Some prospects for intergroup behaviour. *European Journal of Social Psychology, 5,* 5–34.

Turner, J. C. (1987). *Rediscovering the social group: A self-categorization theory.* Oxford, UK: Blackwell.

Watson, W. E., Johnson, L., Kumar, K., & Critelli, J. (1998). Process gain and process loss: Comparing interpersonal processes and performance of culturally diverse and non-diverse teams across time. *International Journal of Intercultural Relations, 22,* 409–430.

Watson, W. E., & Kumar, K. (1992). Differences in decision making regarding risk taking: A comparison of culturally diverse and culturally homogeneous task groups. *International Journal of Intercultural Relations, 16,* 53–65.

Watson, W. E., Kumar, K., & Michaelsen, L. K. (1993). Cultural diversity's impact on interaction process and performance: Comparing homogeneous and diverse task groups. *Academy of Management Journal, 36,* 590–602.

Watson, W. E., & Michaelson, L. K. (1988). Group interaction behaviors that affect group performance on an intellective task. *Group & Organizational Studies, 13,* 495–516.

Wiersema, M. F., & Bird, A. (1993). Organizational demography in Japanese firms: Group heterogeneity, individual dissimilarity, and top management team turnover. *Academy of Management Journal, 36,* 996–1025.

Williams, K. Y., & O'Reilly, C. A. (1998). Demography and diversity in organizations: A review of 40 years of research. In B. M. Staw & L. L. Cummings (Eds.), *Research in organizational behavior* (Vol. 20, pp. 77–140). Greenwich, CT: JAI Press.

Zamarripa, P. O., & Krueger, D. L. (1983). Implicit contracts regulating small group leadership: The influence of culture. *Small Group Behavior, 14,* 187–210.

CHAPTER CONTENTS

8 Three Decades of Developing, Grounding, and Using Symbolic Convergence Theory (SCT)

ERNEST G. BORMANN
University of Minnesota

JOHN F. CRAGAN
Illinois State University

DONALD C. SHIELDS
University of Missouri-St. Louis

For 30 years, good fortune has enabled us to contribute to the development of symbolic convergence theory (SCT). SCT is a general theory of communication that helps explain broad aspects of interpersonal, small group, public, organizational, mass, and intercultural communication. SCT explains the communicative force of fantasy-sharing on human action as stemming from its ability to forge a symbolic consciousness that is constitutive of reality. In this chapter, we first depict SCT's heuristic value. Next, we highlight its historical development and grounding research. Then, we set out its anatomical elements providing a clear view of the relationship among its 18 technical concepts. Specifically, we highlight its basic, message, dynamic, communicator, medium, and evaluative concepts. Then, we depict its utility by describing its use in solving real-world problems ranging from physician recruitment to relationship building to creating a new corporate identity and culture. Thereupon, we synthesize the answers to its major criticisms. Finally, we discuss potential avenues for future research and development. We highlight the need for researchers to develop a propensity to fantasize scale and work toward the unification of the force of fantasy and the other communicative forces.

A ESOP related the following fable:

A traveling scorpion came to a stream. She asked a frog, "Will you take me across?" The frog expressed concern, "But you will sting me!" The scorpion replied, "No! To do so would mean your death. I would then drown and that's not in my self-interest."

Correspondence: Donald C. Shields, 504 NE Jasper Circle, Lee's Summit, MO 64064; email: sdschie@worldnet.att.net

Communication Yearbook 25, pp. 271–313

Upon reflection, the frog agreed to serve as transport. All went well until they reached the middle of the stream. Suddenly, the scorpion stung the frog. The dying frog asked the drowning scorpion, "Why did you do that knowing we both will die?" The scorpion replied: "It's onto-logical, baby—it's my nature—that's what I do."

The moral of our rendition of the fable is twofold. First, it highlights that hu-mans ask why actions occur? Second, it highlights that humans respond to such *why questions* with explanatory accounts. In the venue of the sciences, social sci-ences, and humanities, we call such explanatory accounts *theory*. Cragan and Shields (1995a) indicated that humans possess a natural theory-making ability. Humans respond readily to the impetus of the why question, and in so doing, theorize, that is, provide a *why explanation* of *phenomena* (p. 18). Communication scholars do that, too, as they develop theories to provide communication-based explanations of communication phenomena. One such contemporary communication theory is the symbolic convergence theory of communication (SCT). For 30 years, good fortune has enabled us to contribute to SCT's development. One aspect of this chapter's importance flows from the opportunity to preserve in one spot a review of the nearly 160 published works that represent SCT's research program.

The fable also reminds us that the beginning point of theory building is often an ontological assumption regarding the nature of human kind. Our insight concern-ing the ontological assumption that human beings are natural dramatizers (fantasizers) helped spawn the SCT research program in 1970. That program en-abled us to test, verify, and modify the theory through observational communica-tion studies and experiments using a technique called *grounded theory* (B. A. Fisher & Hawes, 1971; B. Glaser, & Strauss, 1967). SCT is the product of a long-term, programmatic, research effort. Here, we seek to describe SCT's heuristic value, highlight its historical development and grounding research, set out its anatomical elements, depict its use in solving real-world problems, synthesize our answers to its major criticisms, and discuss avenues for future research.

SCT'S HEURISTIC VALUE

One of the unique characteristics of SCT is that it is a *general theory* built on the model of the natural sciences. By examining phenomena, researchers develop general theories. In turn, the theories are tested, verified, and modified by studies and experiments with phenomena. Newton's theory of gravity is an example of a general theory. Newton's theory is also general due to its applicability across time and cultures. His theory explained the operation of gravity in England in the 17th century as well as England in the 12th century. It also explained the operation of gravity in England as well as China. One drama, often shared, depicts Newton under an apple tree. He is trying to explain the path of the planets at the same time he is studying the acceleration of freely falling bodies on the surface of the earth. An apple fell and Newton suddenly had a flash of insight. Maybe the fall of the earth toward the sun and the apple falling from the tree toward the earth were one and the same phenomenon (Greene, 1999). Newton does not yet have a general theory—he has a hunch or hypothesis. Newton soon started the studies and experiments necessary to check out his hunch. His studies and experiments enabled him to ground his theory. Part of Newton's grounding process even included the development of a new kind of mathematics—calculus—to enable the testing of many more predictive hypotheses (Greene, 1999).

SCT, like Newton's gravitational theory, works across time and culture. Indeed, SCT exhibits a rich heritage of accounting for those dramatizing, communicative processes that create and sustain a community, group, or organization's consciousness (Bormann, 1985a). SCT accounts for the use of imaginative language. It also accounts for the development of shared fantasies that coalesce into a rhetorical vision (the shared symbolic ground exhibited by a vision's participants). As well, it accounts for the creation, rise, and sustainment of a group or community's consciousness (Bormann, Cragan, & Shields, 1994).

Another characteristic of SCT is that it places the audience in the center of its communication paradigm. Although SCT posits that the loci of meaning, emotion, value, and motive for action are in the message, it also posits that the message is co-created with the audience. By placing the locus of meaning in a jointly created message, we provided a sharp contrast to the dominant communication theories of that day (the early 1970s). For example, it contrasted with Aristotle's (trans. 1960) view that meaning existed in the rhetor or speaker who picks the words to create a message. As well, it contrasted with McLuhan's (1964) view that the medium conveying the message provides meaning. Finally, it contrasted with Watzlawick, Beavin, and Jackson's (1967) view that meanings reside in people, the receivers of messages. Today, after those working with SCT have demonstrated extensively its usefulness, the wisdom of such a change hardly seems groundbreaking. Nonetheless, it seemed so initially. Indeed, at the time, it represented a significant, paradigmatic shift (see Kuhn, 1970). Concomitantly, SCT eventually incorporated all elements of the communication situation within its purview including message, competing communication message dynamics, communicators, medium, and evaluative components (Bormann, Knutson, & Musolf, 1997).

Bormann et al. (1994) indicated that SCT is also a general communication theory that "accounts for broad classes of events" (p. 266). It explains the use of imaginative language, including its discursive form. As Bormann et al. put it, "the force of fantasy accounts not only for the irrational and non-rational aspects of persuasion but . . . it creates the ground for the rational elements as well" (p. 265). Additionally, SCT is a general communication theory. Its explanation holds within and across the traditional communication contexts, such as interpersonal, small group, organizational, public, mass, and intercultural communication (Bormann et al., 1994; Cragan & Shields, 1995a, 1998). Specifically, SCT explains the effect of the communicative force of fantasy (fantasy-sharing and fantasy-chaining) on human action (Bormann, 1985b; Cragan & Shields, 1998). Humans share such symbolic facts as fantasies, cues, and types. Then, others use the proffered symbolic facts. They reiterate, reconfigure, and embellish them. Ultimately the shared symbolic facts coalesce into a composite drama. The composite drama, called a rhetorical vision, represents the consciousness of its adherents regarding a particular topic (Bormann, 1972). A major tenet of the theory is that a rhetorical community—by way of the process of fantasy-sharing—creates a symbolic reality that both denotes and becomes its consciousness (Bormann et al., 1994). The resultant symbolic structure (consciousness) is constitutive of the collectivity's view of reality.

SCT, like Newton's theory of gravity, also explains seemingly divergent phenomena with the same principle. On the one hand, it explains the constitutive consciousness of collectivities. On the other hand, it explains the historical phenomena that provide the knowledge necessary for the participation in and the critique of communication styles and episodes (Shields, 2000). SCT does so by positing the same communicative force—fantasy—as undergirding both phenomena (Bormann, 1980). The researchers working with SCT named the second phenomenon *special theories* (Bormann, 1980). In part, it is SCT's ability to explain special theories that enables us to say that the theory explains discursive as well as imaginative language (Shields, 2000). For example, Bormann et al. (1994) noted that "the prior sharing of requisite fantasies provides the necessary and sufficient cause for the creation of a special theory with an ideal model [rationality] that provides the rules, warrants, and grounds for argument" (p. 268).

SCT provides the account of how consciousness is created, raised, and sustained and how it effects human action (Bormann et al., 1997). It does so by recognizing the existence of the communicative force of fantasy—a force that continuously effects symbolic consciousness in individuals, groups, and large publics due to our intrinsic nature as fantasizers (Bormann, 1985b). In other words, SCT posits the communicative force of fantasy (fantasizing and fantasy-chaining)—interlinked with the ontological need to provide explanation—as the causative component that ignites the creation, raising, and sustenance of symbolic consciousness.

HISTORICAL DEVELOPMENT AND GROUNDING RESEARCH

SCT is a theory built from both rhetorical and social scientific studies of communication. As a general theory of communication, SCT explains how humans come to share a common symbolic consciousness (reality) such as that of the cold war or the American Dream (Bormann, 1972). It allows us to look at human talk and explain how collectivities of people build a shared consciousness that provides emotion, meaning, motive, and value for human action (Bormann, 1972, 1982a, 1982b, 1982c). Finally, SCT provides a viable interpretive framework for distinguishing facts from nonfacts as scholars conduct research (Cragan & Shields, 1992b, 1995a, 1995b, 1998).

The formal research program began in 1970 at the University of Minnesota. The program drew upon earlier work done by Bales and his colleagues and students at Harvard and Bormann and his colleagues and students at Minnesota. To examine the distinctive nature of the SCT, we begin by explaining the grounded-theory methodology used in its discovery and development. The developers of SCT merged two lines of research. The first line was that of Bales and his associates at Harvard who were studying the dynamics of groups by means of content analysis of group communication. He and his associates had developed a coding system they called *interaction process analysis* (Bales, 1950). They used the system for observing and coding task-group communication. Another line was that of the Minnesota studies conducted by Bormann and his associates. They were studying ongoing groups by a number of techniques including content analysis, participant journals and interviews, and voice and video recordings. Through this line of research, Geier (1963) discovered an emergent process for natural leadership. B. A. Fisher (1968, 1970a, 1970b, 1971) found similar emergent processes for decision-making. As well, Bormann (1969) again found a general emergent process for all group roles that supported Geier's findings about leadership.

Another area that was under investigation was very different from those using social scientific research methods. This was an effort to use rhetorical criticism methods to examine the communication dynamics in task groups. The investigators examined the nature and results of the use of persuasion techniques, ethos-building efforts, logical argument, and so forth. In the tradition of rhetorical criticism, they also experimented with making evaluative judgments about the rhetoric in group communication.

At this point in the work at Minnesota, the Bales group published their latest findings in the book, *Personality and Interpersonal Behavior* (Bales, 1970). The fact that the Harvard group had changed one of the categories on their content analysis scale struck Bormann as important. The category had previously been called *shows tension release* and had been described by a series of words about laughing, smiling, giggling, and so forth. The Harvard group now called the category *dramatizing* and defined it by listing things like double entendre, stories, jokes, narratives, analogies, metaphors, and so forth. Bormann promptly announced at a noon research meeting at Minnesota that Bales had discovered rhetorical criticism.

What the Bales team had actually discovered was that, from time-to-time, as a group member used imaginative language it triggered within the group an explosion of further imaginative language, laughter, excitement, sometimes sadness and other strong emotions. During these episodes the entire climate of the meeting changed. The discussion group that was often subdued or quiet and sometimes tense would suddenly change to excited involvement. Bales and his team characterized such moments as dramatizing fantasy themes. They saw such shared fantasies as helping the group members create group *cohesiveness*.

What struck the Minnesota group was that here was a melding of two modes of scholarship, social science and rhetorical criticism. Scholars in communication had used both methods of research but seldom were they used in conjunction. The Minnesota researchers viewed fantasy themes as the key element in integrating social science with humanism and began to use the concept in studies in rhetorical criticism. They grew excited by the potential of fantasy theme analysis to provide a distinctive, rewarding, and intellectually fruitful way to conduct rhetorical studies. They began to conduct and publish fantasy theme analysis studies. The method did several things. First, it emphasized the function of imaginative language in building collective consciousness and group cohesion. Second, it brought the audience back into the paradigm that had once been speaker, speech, audience, and occasion. Over time, the audience had essentially disappeared and the emphasis shifted to the text. Here was a new paradigm that once again placed the audience in the center of communication studies. Third, fantasy theme analysis was a social approach that studied communication in the context of collectives. Fourth, the fantasy emphasis enabled a more complex analysis of fictitious and nonfictitious imaginative language.

Meanwhile, the Minnesota research group continued its study of groups and organizations using the methods of observation, interview, and content analysis. An early project was to replicate the Bales group's description of the process of sharing fantasies. Next, the research group examined the influence of the sharing process on cohesion and *group consciousness*. Such studies led to positive results. One of the earmarks of grounded theory is that replications of the same experiments should yield the same results (B. Glaser & Strauss, 1967). The Minnesota researchers began to see the shape of a scientific theory that could explain communication. They called the emerging theory the *symbolic convergence theory*. The team used the word *symbolic* because the theory dealt with language and fantasy and lots of symbolic (as opposed to material and social) facts. They used the word *convergence* because the theory's basic theorem described the dynamic communicative process of sharing group fantasies as the cause of the union of the participants' symbolic world.

For several years, the Minnesota group met monthly at the Bormann home. Participants in those Wednesday night sessions became known euphemistically as Turtle Racers. During the early years, the Turtle Racer team included: Charles Bantz, Ernest Bormann, Nancy Bormann, John Breitlow, James Chesebro, Catherine Collins, John Cragan, Charles Fahey, Marlene Fine, William Henderson, Wayne Hensley, Richard Ilka, Charles Kauffman, Virginia Kidd, James Klumpp, Charles Larson, Patti McCullough, Dan Miller, Jerie Pratt, Laurinda Porter, Linda Putnam, David Rarick, Jerry Sanders, William Semlak, Barbara Sharf, Donald Shields, Michael Stano, Julie Belle White, and Gordon Zimmerman.

In addition to laying the foundation for SCT, the early Turtle Racers made another noteworthy contribution. They represented the team, as opposed to the sole-scholar, approach to communication theory building (G. R. Miller, 1979). The sciences had long known the importance of the laboratory team in regard to contributing to a meaningful product. The Turtle Racers were in the vanguard of disciplinary scholars demonstrating the efficacy of the programmatic, team approach to the development of communication theory.

A central feature of SCT's development concerned the discovery, observation, and grounding of its key concepts. In turn, additional research led to clarification of those concepts. At other times, new research pointed to the need for additional concepts and suggested future lines of research (Bormann, 1982b). Bormann (1980, 1982a, 1982b, 1982c, 1985a) often emphasized that, with the SCT research program, contributors espoused the same scholarly viewpoint—that is, used the same assumptions and technical concepts—from study to study. In actuality, in the early 1970s, things did not go quite that smoothly. The Turtle Racers displayed fits and starts, but culminated those with dozens of novel applications. They discovered and uncovered what many considered an exponential growth in assumptions and technical concepts. As well, they tried out various names for what proved out to be similar things. However, all worked out in the end.

The development of SCT began with the study of small group communication. Researchers studied the creation and effect of symbolic consciousness and symbolic reality on *group identity* (Chesebro, Cragan, & McCullough, 1973). Cragan and Shields (1995a, 1998) indicated that SCT differentiated *symbolic reality* (symbolic facts like ideographs, ideologies, orientations, visions, and worldviews) from *social reality* (social facts like hierarchies, positions, and roles) and *material reality* (material facts like objects and things). Work with SCT soon spread to the other traditional communication contexts. In each context, SCT provided a general theoretical explanation of the effect of *fantasizing* on consciousness-creating, -raising, and -sustaining communication.

As the investigations continued, it became apparent that the complexity of the process of convergence encompassed more than the sole concept of *fantasy theme*. The first additional concept resulted from the findings that groups often shared fantasies that resulted in a larger coherent structure, that is a complex of fantasy themes. People created and used these complexes of fantasy themes in the same way that they created and used individual, shared fantasies. The Minnesota researchers labeled the new phenomenon *rhetorical vision*. The team chose the name *rhetorical* because rhetorical imaginative language triggering shared fantasies produced the larger symbolic structures. The team chose the name *vision* because the rhetorical structures were of the scope of other visions such as the views of large landscapes.

The continuing investigations required unique methods to study the dynamic process of fantasy-sharing. By now, the Minnesota researchers had discovered that the process of sharing fantasies was not confined to small task-groups. They found the process operating in the media, in other audience and speaker situations, in reading texts, and in historical documents. Indeed, they found the process in every communication situation they observed. Observation techniques and interviews of subjects worked well enough in controlled studies in which the communication could be monitored. However, historical studies and studies in field contexts, where such methods and controls were difficult or impossible, required other techniques.

The first breakthrough came with the discovery of a middle-sized structure; that is, a generalizable type of shared fantasy in the middle range between a fantasy theme and a rhetorical vision. The new phenomenon appeared as a generalized statement incorporating the central kernel of a number of similar fantasies. For example, the researchers found that a group might share a fantasy theme about the Puritan treatment of women accused of being witches who were then burned at the stake. The story portrayed the Puritan leaders as the evil ones and the women as victims. Subsequently, the group shared another fantasy theme about a committee of the congress that was investigating communists in the state department. The story portrayed the leaders of the committee as the villains and the people accused of being communists or fellow travelers as being the victims. One of the group's members says, "It's like the Salem witch-hunts." This statement triggered an exciting sharing of this new drama with Senator McCarthy dressed up as a Puritan minister. Then, the group suddenly refers to the hearings as witch-hunts. Subsequently, another group more than 20 years later shared a fantasy about a new set of congressional hearings in the here-and-now. That new group saw the hearings as led by a right-wing group of Christian conservatives seeking to impeach a President. They labeled the situation as, "another witch-hunt." The Minnesota researchers would say that the initial and new groups have now created and shared a *fantasy type* that they understand and that places a number of prior, shared fantasy themes with similar scenarios into a genre. This witch-hunting fantasy type is now available to explain new events as witch-hunts. The appearance of fantasy types in the consciousness of a rhetorical community is evidence that the members have shared fantasies of a certain sort in the past. When found in the historical records of texts and films, fantasy types provide information for the rhetorical critic without the need for developing and implementing an experiment to ground the existence of fantasy-sharing among the members of a collectivity.

A second phenomenon also provides evidence of a community having shared a fantasy. Illustrated by the inside joke, the investigators called the new phenomenon a *symbolic cue*. A symbolic cue is a cryptic feature of the verbal and nonverbal communication that triggers for the listener who participated in the original fantasy-chaining a similar response. If the cue is for a joke, the response is laughter or smiling. If the cue were making a *V* with one's fingers, it would trigger memories of victory fantasies. If someone does not participate in the shared fantasies that created the cue, the response would be confusion. Like fantasy types, inside cues evidence fantasies shared in the past.

The SCT research program relied upon both rhetorical and social scientific studies of people communicating to discover and isolate the concepts necessary to explain the creating, raising, sustaining, and eventual dimming and death of symbolic consciousness (Bormann, Cragan, & Shields, 1996). Bormann (1982b) explained that a researcher could discover a technical concept through the systematic observation of communication phenomena. Bormann et al. (1996) reported that researchers "on the basis of what they discovered . . . developed concepts and generalizations" that led to the development of a general theory of communication (p. 2). Cragan and Shields (1998) indicated that "a theory is mere armchair speculation until researchers ground its concepts to observable phenomena" (p. 25).

With SCT, the early observation of communication phenomena occurred through the use of a special *qualitative method* called *fantasy theme analysis* (Bormann, 1972). Then, in 1972, Professor David Rarick introduced Stephenson's (1953) Q-sorts and Van Tubergen's (n.d.) Q-Type Quantitative Factor Analysis (QUANAL) program to us as a means for grounding the evolving SCT concepts. By adopting, adapting, and integrating Stephenson's methods, the social science component of SCT's research program flowered. Stephenson created Q-methodology to develop a science of subjectivity from the viewpoint of the subject's own interpretation of events. Stephenson claimed that the penetrating analyses of famous novelists had been rejected because they dealt with particular events. He argued that those using Q-sorts preferred the penetrations of humanists and only needed to bring them to heel for scientific purposes like the good hunters they had been. For the SCT researchers, the qualitative method became that of content analysis and the merged quantitative method relied upon Q-type, multivariate, factor analysis using the QUANAL computer program to sort-out the various rhetorical communities within a sample audience. The integration of rhetorical criticism and social scientific methods occurred when the QUANAL program revealed the shared fantasies of the communities studied. In other words, the investigators used fantasy theme analysis to make a rhetorical criticism of the consciousness of the audience(s) under study. They then used the QUANAL analysis to provide concurrent and construct validity for the findings (D. C. Shields, 1981f).

In this manner, the researchers intertwined rhetorical criticism and social scientific methods into a symbiotic relationship undergirding the development of SCT. By combining the methods, the research team achieved a mechanism to bridge the gap between qualitative ideographic and quantitative nomothetic research. The mechanism was Rarick's suggestion to use a Q-sort to operationalize SCT's emerging rhetorical vision concept. Bormann (1980), Cragan and Shields (1981d), and Shields and Cragan (1975, 1981a, 1981b, 1981c) provided early discussions of the philosophical issues related to bridging the gap. In any case, the genie could not be put back in the bottle.

Poole, Seibold, and McPhee (1985) called the link between a theory and its attendant methods, the theory-method complex. Poole (1990) defined the complex as "an interdependent whole in which methods shape theory and vice versa" (p. 238). The links between SCT's theory, the message, and its qualitative and quantitative methods evolved and became grounded in a way similar to how the gravitational theory evolved and became grounded. SCT owed its grounding to the application of Q-type factor analysis and a survey method (Q-sorts) that got at the cognitive subjectivity of individuals (Van Tubergen & Olins, 1979, 1982). Use of the new quantitative method empowered the SCT researchers and allowed them to capture empirically and thus ground the symbolic reality of collectivities of people.

Early studies (e.g., Bormann, 1972; Hensley, 1975; Ilka, 1977) found the Turtle Racers using fantasy theme analysis to find rhetorical visions in the historic record. Others (e.g., Bantz, 1972, 1975, 1979; Chesebro et al., 1973) sought to use FTA to find chaining fantasies in the live communication of face-to-face groups and TV newscasts. As well, Bormann, Koester, and Bennett (1978), Cragan and Shields (1977, 1978b, 1981b, 1981c, 1981d, 1992b), Endres (1989, 1994, 1997), McFarland (1985), Rarick, Duncan, Lee, and Porter (1977), and D. C. Shields (1974, 1981f) contributed a series of studies demonstrating the viability of using Q-sorts to quantify the acceptance of fantasy themes. These studies enabled the researchers to segment rhetorical communities by vision participation and ground SCT's technical concepts including the righteous, social, and pragmatic deep structure of rhetorical visions. Then, by using vision-participation as a breaker-variable for discriminant analysis procedures, Cragan and Shields (1981b, 1981c, 1981d, 1992b), Cragan, Shields, and N. E. Nichols (1981a, 1981b), and Endres (1997) were able to predict the demo-, psycho-, and socio-graphic characteristics of the adherents to specific, rhetorical visions.

Breakthroughs in research design continued. Cragan, Semlak, and Cuffe (1984), K. A. Foss and Littlejohn (1986), and Rosenfeld and Schrag (1985) added questionnaires and ANOVA designs to ground rhetorical visions to the avowed consciousness of the audience. Bormann, Kroll, Watters, and McFarland (1984) used marker themes reflective of participation in a Q-sort, derived vision to conduct large-sample, telephone surveys and type respondents' vision participation by their answers. Cragan and Shields (1995a) and Vasquez (1994) reported studies that moved SCT-based, Q-sort, market-segmentation designs into the world of standard Likert-type scales. Here, pencil and paper responses to 15–20 fantasy themes proved sufficient to sort out segments, based on rhetorical vision participation, for selling and advertising purposes.

ANATOMY OF SCT

The social sciences and the communication discipline readily accept the use of several metatheoretical concepts (for example, power and scope, heuristic and isomorphic, elegance and parsimony, and validity and utility) to evaluate the quality of theories (Cragan & Shields, 1998). There is less agreement about the metatheoretical concepts that would allow us to compare the anatomy (muscles, bones, arteries) of one theory with the anatomy of another. Recently, Cragan and Shields (1995a, 1998, 1999), following D. C. Shields and Preston (1985), offered a metatheory for anatomizing a communication theory's concepts. Their metatheory enables us to highlight the anatomical elements (basic, message, dynamic, communicator, medium, and evaluative elements) that help us distinguish SCT's various concepts. We rely upon this communication metatheory as our next way of organizing the research studies that grounded SCT's 18 technical concepts (see Table 1). For those unfamiliar with SCT's anatomy, we do provide brief examples

TABLE 1
Selected Studies Grounding SCT's Technical Concepts

• *Fantasy theme*
Bantz (1972, 1975, 1979); Bormann (1973); Bormann et al. (1996, 1978).
• *Fantasy type*
Ball (1990, 1992); Bormann (1977, 1982a); Bormann et al. (1996); Ford (1989); Mayerle (1987); Sharf (1987).
• *Saga*
Bormann (1982c, 1983b); Csapó-Sweet & Shields (2000).
• *Symbolic cue*
Bormann (1982c, 1983b, 1985b); Bormann et al. (1994, 1996); Koester (1982).
• *Rhetorical vision*
Bastien & Hostager (1995); Bormann (1972); Bormann et al. (1994, 1996); Callahan (1992); Chesebro (1980); Cragan & Shields (1977); Daniel (1995); Duffy & Gotcher (1996); Endres (1989, 1994, 1997); Kidd (1975); Hensley (1975); Huxman (1996); Ilka (1977); Matthews (1995); Rosenfeld & Schrag (1985); Roth (1993); Schrag et al. (1981).
• *Dramatis personae*
Bormann (1973); Bormann et al. (1994, 1996); Callahan 1992); Cragan & Cutbirth (1984); Cragan & Shields (1978b, 1981c); Rarick et al. (1977); D. C. Shields (1974, 1981f); K. J. Shields & D. C. Shields (1974).
• *Plot lines*
Barton & O'Leary (1974); Bormann (1972, 1977, 1985b); Bormann et al. (1994, 1996); Cragan et al. (1981a; 1981b); Duffy & Gotcher (1996); Putnam et al. (1991).
• *Scene*
Bormann (1989b); Bormann et al. (1994, 1996); Campbell (1982); Corcoran (1983); Cragan (1975); S. K. Foss (1979); Haskins (1981); Ritter (1977).
• *Sanctioning agent*
Bormann (1972); Bormann et al. (1994, 1996); D. C. Shields (1981a; 1981e).
• *Righteous, social, and pragmatic deep structure*
Bormann et al. (1994, 1996, 1997); Cragan (1981); Cragan & Shields (1977, 1978a, 1978b, 1981b, 1981c, 1981d, 1992b, 1995a); Cragan et al. (1981a, 1981b); Duffy (1997); Endres (1989, 1994, 1997); Shields & Cragan (1981d); Vasquez (1994).
• *Communicator style*
Bormann et al. (1978), Cragan et al. (1985), Doyle (1985), Duffy & Gotcher (1996), Garner et al. (1998), Hubbard (1985), Kidd (1975), Shields (2000).
• *Propensity to fantasize*
Bormann & Itaba (1992); Bormann et al. (1997).
• *Group-chaining*
Barton & O'Leary (1974); Bormann (1986, 1990); Bormann et al. (1995); Chesebro et al. (1973); Cragan & Shields (1995b); Cragan et al. (1996); Kroll (1983); Porter (1976); D. C. Shields (1981b, 1981c, 1981d, 1981f).
• *Public-chaining*
Bormann (1983c); Bormann, Koester et al. (1978); Bormann et al. (1984, 1985); Corcoran (1983); Cragan et al. (1984); Cragan & Shields (1977, 1978b, 1981d); Duffy (1997); Endres (1994), K. A. Foss & Littlejohn (1986), Rarick et al. (1977).
• *Artistry*
Bormann et al. (1995, 1996, 1997); Bormann & Itaba (1992), Cragan (1975); Cragan & Cutbirth (1984); Cragan & Shields (1992a, 1994); Duffy (1997).
• *Shared consciousness*
Bormann et al. (1994, 1996); Cragan (1975); Darsey (1995); Kroll (1983); McIllwraith & Schallow (1983); Monaghan et al. (1974).
• *Reality-links*
Bormann et al. (1996); Cragan & Shields (1977); Darsey (1995).

from other general communication theories to aid in understanding the following discussion. In each of the following subsections, the examples that we draw from the other general communication theories exist at the same metatheoretical level of analysis as the concepts that we introduce from SCT. We trust that these brief examples will allow a ready comparison of SCT's concepts to those in other mainstay communication theories.

Basic Concepts

Cragan and Shields (1998) indicated that the metatheoretical term *basic concept* points to the thing one must be able to find and identify to use a given theory. Scholars often refer to it as the basic unit of analysis (Bormann, 1980). For example, with information systems theory (IST), the basic concept is *information*. With uncertainty reduction theory (URT), the basic concept is *social information*. With rational argumentation theory (RAT), the basic concept is *argument*. With narrative paradigm theory (NPT), the basic concept is *narration* (story). With SCT, the basic concept is *fantasy theme* and its associated basic concepts include *symbolic cue, fantasy type*, and *saga*.

A fantasy theme is a dramatizing message that depicts characters engaged in action in a setting that accounts for and explains human experience (Bormann, 1972). Bormann et al. (1996) indicated that the development of a new consciousness is guided by the principle of explanatory power. They indicated that "when events become confusing and disturbing, people are likely to share fantasies that provide them with a plausible and satisfying account that makes sense out of experiences" (p. 3). A fantasy theme is not something imaginary, but rather it is a "creative or imaginative interpretation of events which fulfills a psychological or rhetorical need" (Bormann, 1983a, p. 434), thus giving meaning to human action (Duffy, 1997). It may be a word, phrase, sentence, or paragraph in length (D. C. Shields, 1981a). Bormann (1973) reported an early study grounding the concept of fantasy to observable communication. He did so through his study of the Eagleton Affair that concerned the resignation of Thomas Eagleton as a vice-presidential nominee on the Democratic Party's ticket (due to the public disclosure of Eagleton's having partaken of electric shock therapy to combat depression).

A number of studies represent the critical mass of works analyzing the fantasy themes present in various types of rhetorical discourse. For example, Bantz (1972, 1975, 1979) reported on the fantasies contained in the evening news. Bormann and Itaba (1992) and Bormann et al. (1997) studied why people share fantasies. Bormann, Koester, et al. (1978) looked at the complexity of shared fantasy patterns of voters and their relation to the cartoon mediated dramatizations of the presidential campaign. Cragan (1975) analyzed the strategic failure of fantasies within the contemporary Native American movement. Doyle (1985) examined the symbolic consciousness portrayed by Barbara Cartland's romance novels. Duffy (1997) reported on the strategic use of fantasies and visions to legalize gambling. Duffy and Gotcher (1996) analyzed the central fantasies concerning how to get the guy. Garner, Sterk, and Adams (1998) reported on the fantasy themes depicting sexual etiquette. Mayerle (1987) studied the failed fantasies of the TV program *a. k. a. Pablo*. Putnam, Van-Hoeven, and Bullis (1991) looked at the strategic fantasies in teacher bargaining. As well, D. C. Shields (1981e) reported on the modal societal fantasies used by Malcolm X to gain converts to his new Black Nationalist organization. Through such studies, the researchers observed the chaining of fantasy themes. They did so by noting the use of reiteration, reconfiguration, embellishment, fantasy types and inside cues in print discourse coupled with excitement and laughter in live groups and audiences. In each case, they used fantasy theme analysis to flesh-out the symbolic reality and consciousness of a particular rhetorical community.

Illustratively, Cragan and Shields (1995a) reported on the observation of several dentists discussing the decline of their practices due to a saturation of dentists. Suddenly, one dentist said, "The days of drill, fill, and bill are over . . . I should have gone to medical school and specialized in plastic surgery. Then, I could cut, suck, and tuck for $3,000 a whack" (pp. 35–36). Cragan and Shields reported that the statement chained-out, as indicated by the embellishment and laughter of the other dentists in the group. They then showed how the fantasy theme "pointed to specific aspects of a larger symbolic reality shared by members of the dentistry profession" (p. 36). Such rhetorical and social scientific studies enabled the grounding of the fantasy theme concept to observable communication.

A symbolic cue is a shorthand indicant or code that stands for a fantasy theme such as a sign or symbol or an inside joke (Bormann, 1982c; Cragan & Shields, 1995a). For example, in regard to the Eagleton Affair, in the State of Missouri, where Eagleton then served as Senator, the words, *Electric Tom*, became a symbolic cue (inside joke) among Missourians that triggered a sharing of the whole Eagleton Affair drama. Emerging visions, following the principle of imitation, are often cued by words like *new* (New Deal, New Populism, New Isolationism, New Feminism). Also, they are often cued by the prefix *neo-* (neoclassicism, neocolonialism, neoimpressionism) or *post-* (postmillennialism, postmodernism). The adjective *new* and the prefixes *neo-* and *post-* illustrate the ways creators of a new vision use historical personae and dramas as the basis for the creation of a new consciousness (Bormann et al., 1996). The symbolic cue phenomenon appears to be cross-cultural. For example, Bormann et al. (1996) and D. C. Shields (1990) indicated that the rhetorical team developing messages for the USSR's mid-1980s leader, Gorbachev, promulgated a new, humanist vision using such inside cues as *perestroika* (economic restructuring) and *glasnost* (openness). A number of other reports represent the critical mass of studies grounding the symbolic cue concept to observable communication. For example, Bormann (1983b) reported on the symbolic cue phenomenon in building organizational culture. Bormann (1985b) reported on such symbolic cues associated with the American Dream. Bormann, Koester, et al. (1978) described the symbolic cues present in political cartoons. Bormann, Bormann, and Harty (1995) looked at the symbolic cue phenomenon in reducing teenage tobacco use. As well, Koester (1982) studied the symbolic cues present in organizations viewing managers as Machiavellian princesses.

A fantasy type is a stock scenario used to explain new events in a well-known, dramatic form such as Watergate, Irangate, and Whitewatergate. Each of these -*gate* forms depicts governmental corruption and cover-up using the *gate* symbolic cue as a fantasy type (Cragan & Shields, 1998). Bormann et al. (1996) indicated that "fantasy type is the workhorse of rhetorical visions; it is also the driving force behind the principle of imitation," that is, the tendency, with boredom or confusion, for "people to share fantasies that give some old familiar drama a new production" (p. 3). Bormann (1977) initially grounded the concept with his study of the rhetorical use of calamity and reported the use of *fetching good out of evil* as a fantasy type to explain away the horrendous outcomes of adversity. A number of other studies contributed to the critical mass of research grounding the fantasy type concept to observable communication. For example, Ball (1990, 1992) looked at the various sports-based fantasy types undergirding Vietnam War decision making. Bormann (1982a) examined the restoration fantasy type and its effect on the hostage release and the Reagan inaugural. Also, Bormann (1985b) examined the communicative force of fantasy types in his study of American public address since the Puritans. Bormann et al. (1996) and Cragan (1981) reported on the use of WWII fantasy types as master analogies creating and sustaining the cold war. Ford (1989) analyzed the fantasy type *fetching good out of evil* in her study of *The Big Book* of Alcoholics Anonymous. Goodnight and Poulakos (1981) examined the use of the *conspiracy* fantasy type in American public address. Porter (1976) looked at *the best defense is a good offense* as a fantasy type in her study of the Nixon White House transcripts.

A *saga* is a detailed account of the achievements in the life of a person, group, community, organization, or nation (Bormann, 1982c, 1983b). It appears to be a concept unique to the study of rhetorical communities that exist over time as an actual physical entity, such as an organization. A saga typically represents the symbolic consciousness of an organization as culture and in so doing may tie together organizational members who participate in diverse rhetorical visions (Bormann, 1983b). Cragan and Shields (1992b) grounded the concept in observable communication with their study of the privatization of a Fortune 500 company. They identified four latent, long-standing sagas whose impact had been lost with a corporate buyout and privatization. Most recently, Csapó-Sweet and Shields (2000) grounded the creation of a saga in observable communication with their case study of the event of Serbia's Radio B-92 going into cyberspace. Together, these studies indicated that a saga often dramatizes the founding of the organization and its founder (Bormann, 1983b). For example, Csapó-Sweet and Shields indicated that B92's founding saga stressed its roots as an *alternative* station. The alternative fantasy type had allowed B92 to expand over 10 years to stress first alternative music, then alternative news, and finally economically viable life-style promotions such as alternative arts theatrical shows, concerts, and books. They also reported on the genesis of a new Radio B92 saga. The new saga, spawned by the station's shutdown by Serbia's President, Slobodan Milosevic, in early December 1996, usurped the alternative founding saga and indeed replaced it. The new saga exhibited fantasy themes relating to B92's new cyberspace role as an independent media providing free speech and promoting democracy. The Csapó-Sweet and Shields study also provided insights into how consciousness-creating, dramatizing messages may promote cultural change.

Message Structure Concepts

At the metatheoretical level of analysis, message structure concepts dress-up and flesh-out the form of the communication viewed through the lens of a particular theory (Cragan & Shields, 1998). For example, with IST, the major message structure concept is called a *message* as represented by a *code-set*. With RAT, the major message structure concept is called a *case*. With URT, the major message structure concept is called a *memory organization packet*.

SCT's major message structure concept is *rhetorical vision*, that is, "a composite drama that catches up large groups of people in a symbolic reality" (Bormann, 1972, p. 398). Communicators weave fantasy themes into the substructural elements of a rhetorical vision as character, action, setting, and legitimizing themes (Bormann, 1972; D. C. Shields, 1981a). Thus, a rhetorical vision's substructural elements include *dramatis personae* or characters, *plot lines* or action, elements of the *scene* or setting, and *sanctioning agent* or legitimizer for the rhetorical vision (Bormann, 1972; D. C. Shields, 1981a). Again, it is participation in a rhetorical vision that creates for its adherents a symbolic consciousness that spurs people to human action (Bormann, 1972; Cragan & Shields, 1995a, 1998). A number of SCT studies grounded the concept of rhetorical vision to observable communication. Table 2 offers a glimpse of the breadth of work with the rhetorical vision concept. The table indicates that researchers studied competing, emerging, contemporary, and extant rhetorical visions in such diverse contexts as interpersonal, mass, public, organizational, and small group communication.

From the beginning, the research program sought to capture both old and contemporary rhetorical visions. For example, studies by Bormann (1972), Cragan (1981), Haskins (1981), Huxman (1996), and Ilka (1977) captured extant rhetorical visions from the historic record. In addition, studies by Bastien and Hostager (1992), Callahan (1992), Campbell (1982), Daniel (1995), Duffy and Gotcher (1996), Endres (1989, 1994), K. A. Foss and Littlejohn (1981), Kidd (1975), Matthews (1995), and Roth (1993) captured contemporary rhetorical visions in various stages of maturity. Such studies grounded the concepts of dramatis personae, plot line(s), scenic attributes, and sanctioning agent(s). As well, the studies enabled the discovery of the presence of fantasy themes, fantasy types, and symbolic cues in differing rhetorical domains.

Some rhetorical visions fall on a flexible-to-inflexible continuum in relation to their ability to change (Bormann, 1978). Others fall on a pure-to-mixed continuum in relation to their underlying pragmatic, righteous, or social deep structure (Cragan

TABLE 2

Selected Studies of Rhetorical Visions by Author(s) and Subject(s)

• *Competing vision studies:*

Bormann et al. (1996)	Cold war, neo-isolationism, power politics
Cragan (1981); Cragan & Shields (1977)	Cold war, one world, power politics
Cragan & Shields (1981b)	Commercial, family, quality hog operation
Cragan & Shields (1978b, 1981c)	Fire education, inspection, suppression
Cragan & Shields (1992b)	Pragmatic, righteous, social at Beta
Cragan et al. (1981a)	Mr. Doane, family, and corporate Doane
Endres (1989, 1994)	Unmarried mothers; father-daughter relations
McFarland (1985)	Pragmatic, righteous, social law professors

• *Emerging vision studies:*

Brown (1976)	Prime-time TVs
Huxman (1996); Kroll (1983)	Women's rights
Schrag et al. (1981)	TV's new humane collectivity

• *Individual's vision studies:*

Aden (1981)	Ronald Reagan
Callahan (1992)	Jesse Jackson
Darsey (1995)	Joseph McCarthy
Huxman (1996)	M. Fuller, A. Grimke, and M. Wollstonecraft
King (1974)	Booker T. Washington
Roth (1993)	Louis Sullivan
D. C. Shields (1981e)	Malcolm X

• *Interpersonal vision studies:*

Duffy & Gotcher (1996)	How to get the guy
Garner et al. (1998)	Teenage sexual etiquette
Hubbard (1985); Kidd (1975)	Relationship styles

• *Media vision studies:*

Bantz (1975, 1979)	Television news
Bormann, Koester et al. (1978)	Carter vision, Ford vision
Daniel (1995)	Intifada
K. A. Foss and Littlejohn (1986)	*The Day After*
Grainey, Pollack, & Kushmierek (1984)	Three Chicago newspapers
Haskins (1981)	Southern Black press
Kapoor et al. (1992)	TV newsrooms
Schrag et al. (1981)	New humane collectivity
Turner (1977)	Cartoons

• *Organizational vision studies:*

Cragan & Shields (1992b)	Beta company's pragmatic, righteous, social
Cragan et al. (1981b)	Doane Agricultural Service farm managers
Endres (1994)	Knights of Columbus
Lee & Hoon (1993)	Men and women managers in Singapore
McFarland (1985)	Law professors
D. C. Shields (1974, 1981f)	Firefighters' private and public personae

---

(continued)

TABLE 2 Continued

• *Movement vision studies:*

Bormann (1972, 1985)	Puritans
Endres (1994)	Knights of Columbus
S. K. Foss (1979); Kroll (1983)	Women's movement
Heisey & Trebing (1983)	Shah's White, Ayatollah's Islamic revolutions
Hensley (1975)	The Disciples of Christ
Ilka (1977)	American communism
Kroll (1983)	Women's movement
Solomon (1980)	Stop ERA

• *Political vision studies:*

Ball (1990, 1992)	Vietnam decision making
Bormann et al. (1996)	Cold war
Bormann, Koester et al. (1978)	Voters' visions of Carter and Ford
Campbell (1982)	The New South
Chesebro (1980)	Social science visions of homosexuality
Cragan (1981)	Origins of the cold war
Cragan & Shields (1977)	Cold war, neo-isolationism, power politics
Kapoor et al. (1992)	Political visions in TV newsrooms
Rarick et al. (1977)	Voters visions of Carter, Ford
Stano (1972)	Political visions of radio commentators

& Shields, 1992b). Then, too, others fall on a paranoid-to-healthy continuum in relation to the amount of conspiracy underlying them (Bormann et al., 1996). Finally, some rhetorical visions fall on a secretive-to-proselytizing continuum in relation to the participants' views toward new members (Bormann et al., 1996). A vision's place on a continuum affects the rhetorical strategies used to sustain it. For example, Bormann et al. (1996) indicated that rhetoricians involved in consciousness-sustaining communication in inflexible rhetorical visions often seek one of three overriding goals. The first is *restoration*, the effort to reclaim lost rhetorical ground and return to the essential position of the founders of the rhetorical vision. The second is *conservation*, the effort to keep whatever remains of the vision and integrate changing positions into it without diluting it so much that the participants lose important values, emotions, and motives. The third goal is *preservation*, the effort to keep the rhetorical vision pure and unchanging.

Bormann et al. (1996) provided a definitive study of the life cycle of the cold war rhetorical vision as they compared it to other research on the rhetorical vision concept. Studying the cold war rhetoric as a paradigm case of SCT's message-structure concept, rhetorical vision, the authors found that the cold war rhetorical vision traveled through five stages: consciousness-creating, consciousness-raising, consciousness-sustaining, consciousness-decline, and consciousness-terminus. They reported that up to 12 rhetorical principles drive the stages of a rhetorical vision. Seven principles (novelty, explanatory power, imitation, critical mass, dedication, rededication, and reiteration) apply to the consciousness-creating, -raising, and -sustaining communication undergirding all rhetorical visions. Five principles (shielding, explanatory deficiency, exploding free speech, resurfacing of competitive rhetorical visions, and implosion) apply to the decline and terminus stages of those visions whose life cycle resembles the cold war.

Dynamic Structure Concepts

At the metatheoretical level of analysis, the dynamic structure concepts of any communication theory refer to the deep structure tension or war underlying a message's cast, form, or mold (Cragan & Shields, 1998). For example, with IST the war is over whether or not the system's dynamic is *linear, interactional,* or *transactional.* With RAT, the war is over whether or not the dynamic is *dialectical, logical,* or *rhetorical.* With URT, the dynamic concerns whether or not the social information seeking and giving is *benign* or *strategic.* With NPT, the dynamic concerns whether or not the deep structure of a story represents an *idealistic-moralistic* or *materialistic* aspect of the American Dream.

With SCT the war occurs between *righteous, social,* and *pragmatic* fantasy themes and ultimately competing rhetorical visions (Cragan & Shields, 1981c, 1992b, 1995a). Rhetorical visions steeped in a righteous master-analogue rely upon fantasy themes that stress correctness, the right way, morality, and so forth. Those visions steeped in a social master-analogue stress such elements as humaneness, social concern, family, brotherhood and sisterhood, and so forth. Those visions steeped in a pragmatic master-analogue stress such elements as the bottom line, what will work, what is expedient, and so forth. Studies by Bormann and Itaba (1992), Bormann et al. (1997), Cragan et al. (1984), Cragan and Shields (1977, 1978b, 1981b, 1981c, 1992b), and Endres (1989, 1994, 1997) confirmed the competing deep structure of rhetorical visions. Studies by Bormann et al. (1997), Cragan and Shields (1992b), and Endres (1994, 1997) confirmed that the deep structures of some rhetorical visions represent mixed combinations of the master-analogues.

Communicator Structure Concepts

At the metatheoretical level of analysis, communicator concepts focus on the names given to communicators from the lens of a particular theory. As well, this metatheoretical level of analysis allows a researcher to determine the important attributes of communicators as posited by a given communication theory (Cragan & Shields, 1998). For example, with IST the communicators are called *senders, receivers,* and *observers.* With RAT, the communicators are called *arguers, audience,* and *critics.* With URT, depending upon the ascribed dynamic, the communicators are called *co-interactants,* or *strategic communicators* and *targets.* With NPT, the communicators are called *storytellers* and *audience.* With SCT the major communicator concepts are *fantasizers* and *rhetorical community* along with their attributes such as *propensity to fantasize* and *dramatistic communication style.*

TABLE 3
Rhetorical Communities Studied Using SCT—by Author(s)

• *Alcoholics Anonymous*
  Ford (1989)
• *Baseball fans*
  Matthews (1995)
• *Cold warriors*
  Bormann et al. (1996); Cragan (1971, 1981); Cragan & Shields (1977)
• *Farmers/feed dealers*
  Cragan & Shields (1981b, 1992b); D. C. Shields (1981c, 1981d)
• *Fire educators/firefighters*
  Cragan & Shields (1978b, 1981c); D. C. Shields (1974, 1977, 1979, 1981f)
• *Interpersonal communicators*
  Bormann et al. (1995); Doyle (1985); Duffy & Gotcher (1996); Endres (1989, 1997); Garner et al. (1998); Kidd (1975)
• *Japanese citizens*
  Bormann & Itaba (1992)
• *Journalists, newspapers*
  Bantz (1972, 1975, 1979); Bormann (1982a); Daniel (1995); Kapoor et al. (1992); Haskins (1981); Kauffman (1972); Nimmo & Combs (1982, 1983); Turner (1977)
• *Lawyers, law professors*
  Cragan & Shields (1995b); McFarland (1985)
• *Media users, TV programs*
  Brown (1976); K. A. Foss & Littlejohn (1986); Lindloff (1982); Mayerle (1987); McIlwraith & Schallow (1983); Rosenfeld & Schrag (1985); Schrag et al. (1981)
• *Movements, radical revolutionaries*
  Chesebro et al. (1973); Cragan (1975); Endres (1994); Hensley (1975); Ilka (1977)
• *Organizations, personnel*
  Bormann (1983b); Bormann, Pratt et al. (1978); Chesebro (1980); Cragan & Shields (1992b); Cragan et al. (1981a, 1981b, 1984); Faules (1982); Koester (1982); Lee & Hoon (1993); Putnam et al. (1991); Vasquez (1994)
• *Physicians, psychiatrists*
  Barton & O'Leary (1974); Sharf (1987)
• *Politicians, presidents, campaign planners*
  Aden (1986); Ball (1992); Bormann (1982c); Cragan & Shields (1977); Porter (1976); Putnam (1972); D. C. Shields & Preston (1985)
• *Public communicators*
  Bormann (1977), Bormann et al. (1996); Callahan (1992); Goodnight & Poulakos (1981); Heisey & Trebing (1983); Huxman (1986); Kiewe & Houck (1989); Roth (1993); D. C. Shields (1977, 1981f); D. C. Shields & Preston (1985); Vasquez (1994)
• *Voters*
  Bormann, Koester et al. (1978); Bormann et al. (1984); Cragan & Shields (1977, 1978a); Rarick et al. (1977)

Across the years, all SCT studies examined fantasizers. As well, a number of studies concerned diverse rhetorical communities ranging from baseball fans to voters (see Table 3).

Studies concerning dramatistic communication styles included those by Bormann, Pratt, and Putnam (1978); Cragan, Cuffe, Pairitz, and Jackson (1985); Doyle (1985); Duffy and Gotcher (1996); Garner et al. (1998); Hubbard (1985);

Kidd (1975); and Lee and Hoon (1993). Studies on the propensity to fantasize included those by Bormann and Itaba (1992) and Bormann et al. (1997). In general, these studies found that participation in differing visions often prompted and identified communicator attributes representing different styles of communication. For example, Lee and Hoon (1993) found the media in Singapore portrayed both men and women managers as people-centered, but differed in portraying their other communicator attributes. For example, the media portrayed men managers as innovative and outgoing with interests in sports and women managers as sociable and helpful with interests in family life, community, and social work. The results of these studies indicated that the rhetoric of a specific rhetorical community often reflects a particular communication style as part of their vision (Bormann, 1980).

Medium Structure Concepts

This metatheory concept allows us to conceive of medium as a propagating substance, such as in the statement: corn grows best in sandy loam soil (Cragan & Shields, 1998). For example, IST grows best in *open* and *mixed* communication systems and not well in *closed* communication systems. RAT grows differently in *field invariant* and *field dependent* media. URT operates differently in *high-context, collectivist cultures* than it does in *low-context, individualist cultures*. Likewise, NPT grows best in an *open, democratic society* and does not do well in a *closed, totalitarian state*.

Fantasies (and thus SCT) grow best in a medium that fosters group sharing or public sharing as opposed to just personal fantasizing. As Bormann (1972) noted, fantasies that begin in small groups often are worked into public speeches, become picked up by the mass media, and "spread out across larger publics" (p. 399). With both group and public sharing the tendency for fantasies to be embellished, reconfigured, reworked, and evolved increases. The result is that members of groups and public rhetorical-communities come to have a stake in the symbolic construction. The resultant symbolic construction has then entered their consciousness through the causative entity of the communicative force of fantasy (fantasy-sharing and fantasy-chaining).

Barton and O'Leary (1974); Bormann (1986, 1990); Bormann et al. (1995); Chesebro et al. (1973); Cragan and Shields (1995b); Cragan, Shields, and Wright (1996); Cragan and Wright (1999); Kroll (1983); Lesch (1994); Porter (1976); Putnam (1972); and Shields (1981b, 1981c, 1981d, 1981f) reported studies of fantasy-chaining occurring in the fertile medium of small group communication. These studies concerned group communication in both simulated laboratory and natural settings and provided the grounding evidence of the fantasizing, fantasy-sharing and fantasy-chaining processes.

Bormann (1983c); Bormann, Koester et al. (1978); Bormann et al. (1984); Bormann, Olson, Percy, and Tremaine (1985); Brown (1976); Bush (1981); Corcoran (1983); Cragan et al. (1984); Cragan and Shields (1977, 1978b, 1981a, 1981c, 1981d, 1992a); Daniel (1995); Duffy (1997); and Rarick et al. (1977) reported studies of fantasy-chaining within and to large publics. These studies concerned fantasizing communication within large rhetorical communities. They provided the grounding evidence that *public chaining* does occur in the public communication context. They demonstrated that the symbolic structures conveyed in the public fantasizing become part of the symbolic consciousness of the adherents within various rhetorical communities. The studies of group communication and public communication confirmed the similarity of the chaining processes in both media. Analogous to the physical force of gravity effecting planets and apples, the communicative force of fantasy effects large, public audiences and small, face-to-face groups.

Evaluative Concepts

At the metatheoretical level of analysis, all communication theories posit one or more technical concepts that allow for the evaluation of communication that falls within the purview of a particular theory (Cragan & Shields, 1998). For example, with IST, the primary evaluative concepts are *fidelity, capacity*, and *uncertainty reduction*. With RAT, the primary evaluative concepts are *prima facie* (believability), *validity*, and *ethical*. With URT, the primary evaluative concepts are *goal attainment* and *uncertainty reduction*. With NPT, the primary evaluative concepts are *narrative probability* (hangs together) and *narrative fidelity* (rings true).

With SCT, three primary technical concepts enable the evaluation of the quality and effects (outcomes) of fantasy-sharing among the members of rhetorical collectivities: *fantasy theme artistry, shared group consciousness*, and *rhetorical vision reality-links*. Fantasy theme artistry is an evaluative concept that concerns the rhetorical creativity, novelty, and competitive advantage of fantasy themes, symbolic cues, fantasy types, rhetorical visions, and sagas (Cragan & Shields, 1995a; 1998). Studies by Bormann et al. (1995) on stopping teenage tobacco use, Bormann and Itaba (1992) and Bormann et al. (1997) on why people share fantasies, and Cragan and Cutbirth (1984) on political ad hominem are typical of the studies that focus on issues related to fantasy theme artistry. For example, Duffy (1997) reported an SCT-based case study of the professional public relations campaign that contributed to the legalization of riverboat gambling in Iowa. Duffy noted that the deep structure of the public relations firm's emphasis on scenic attributes—in a social, Mark Twain-like drama of riverboats plying Iowa's waterways—helped to disperse the countering righteous drama of the evils of gambling. In the vision of the public relations professionals, the riverboat scene would be historically accurate with gambling merely ancillary to the scene of sternwheelers, lazy-hazy rivers, and family river excursions. The public relations professionals backed the Mark Twain-like, social drama with pragmatic fantasy themes about economically revitalizing Iowa's river towns.

Duffy focused on SCT's evaluative concept of *fantasy theme artistry* as she traced the chaining of themes from press releases to news media reports. She emphasized the success of the artistic, fantasy themes of the social and pragmatic visions over the inartistic, righteous, thematic portrayals offered by gambling's opponents. Her implicit advice: increase rhetorical success by using artistic fantasy themes.

Cragan and Shields (1992a) reported on the New World Order rhetorical vision. They noted that the Bush administration's attempts to promulgate the New World Order vision suffered too much from the proponents' tendencies to rely upon the straightforward symbolic cue—New World Order—and not enough on detailing the completeness of the rhetorical vision. As a result (although the symbolic cue chained-out through the media), the meat or heart of the rhetorical vision did not. The symbolic cue alone lacked *rhetorical sufficiency* (Bormann et al., 1996).

Cragan and Shields (1994) offered an example to illustrate the skill of rhetorical sufficiency as it pertains to fantasy theme artistry. They noted that the Manifest Destiny rhetorical vision depicted Americans as spreading democratic institutions over the entire American continent. They traced its first usage to an 1845 statement by Horace Greeley, editor of the New York *Tribune*. Greeley wrote exuberantly of "America's manifest destiny to over spread and possess the whole of the continent which Providence has given us for the development of the great experiment of liberty and the federated self-government entrusted to us" (cited in Blum et al., 1963, p. 261). They then offered several famous depictions of the vision that remain extant. These included: Senator Albert Beveridge's (1989) address in 1898, *The March of the Flag*, and the Reverend Josiah Strong's (1963/1885) statements about the country's Anglo-Saxon mission and manifest destiny. They also referenced the editorial that contained perhaps the most remembered symbolic cue, Greeley's: "Go West young man" (cited in Blum et al., 1963, p. 261). Cragan and Shields (1994) noted that such artistically complete renditions of manifest destiny overshadow many rhetorically deficient expressions of the vision. They offered the example of the New Jersey politician who shouted from the stump: "Make way, I say, for the young Buffalo. He has not yet got land enough" (cited in Blum et al., 1963, p. 261).

A *closeness of fit* standard for fantasy theme artistry also exists (Cragan & Shields, 1994, 1995a). The fit standard implies that a fantasy theme should fit its rhetorical community and be consistent with other fantasy themes of the rhetorical vision. In other words, "one doesn't often hear a fundamentalist, Baptist preacher shouting, 'There is no hell!'" (Cragan & Shields, 1994, p. 7). Similarly, public discussion of President Clinton's Whitewater investments soon broke down the Republican-offered link between the new fantasy of Whitewatergate and the initial fantasy type of Watergate. The analogy of the *-gate* fantasy type was not a good fit. For example, the Whitewater River appeared to be more aptly named "Clearwater"—one could see clear to the bottom and there was nothing there: no act of obstructing justice, no smoking gun, no evidence of cover-up, and no break-in. The Republicans' attempts to plant the fantasy type of Whitewatergate to describe President Clinton's Whitewater investments failed to chain into the public's consciousness as symbolic reality because the planted fantasy type failed the closeness of fit standard of fantasy theme artistry (Cragan & Shields, 1994, 1995a).

Shared group consciousness is an evaluative concept that reminds one using SCT to check for the occurrence of symbolic convergence. Bormann et al. (1996) reported that the principles of *novelty, critical mass,* and *channel access* help symbolic convergence to catch-up larger numbers of people and build a collection of fantasy themes, fantasy types, and symbolic cues into a widely accepted rhetorical vision. Studies by Cragan (1975) on the contemporary Native-American movement, Kroll (1983) on mainstreaming the women's movement, and Mayerle (1987) on producing a television situation-comedy give insights into other failed attempts to ignite group and public-sharing. Darsey (1995), in his study of the rhetoric of Joe McCarthy, provided an insightful analysis of how fantasy themes not grounded in reality-links offer a rhetoric that is *fantastic* and *imaginary* that proves infertile for the constitutive chaining of a rhetorical vision in the public arena. Overall, these studies traced the failure to achieve a common consciousness to: inartistic renditions of fantasy themes, the absence of reality-links, a lack of novelty, the denial of channel access, and the emergence of competing, symbolic consciousnesses that provided a better accounting of the phenomena being explained. On the other hand, studies by Duffy (1977) on the selling of riverboat gambling in Iowa; Monaghan, Plummer, Rarick, and Williams (1974) on predicting television viewer preferences; and McIllwraith and Schallow (1983) on adult fantasy life and patterns of media use celebrated shared fantasies, as do the majority of SCT studies.

Rhetorical vision reality-links tie rhetorical visions and fantasies to the objective reality of the public record and material facts (Bormann, 1982a; Cragan & Shields, 1995a, 1998). Several studies directly concerned the concept of reality-links and their importance to sustaining a vision. For example, Bormann et al. (1996) reported that the lack of reality links in the dimming days of the cold war lead to the vision's disintegration. D. C. Shields (1981e) noted that Malcolm X's use of modal, societal fantasies that were as American as apple-pie explained the hollowness of his Black Nationalism movement. Vasquez (1994) reported on the reality-links needed to attract students to a private school. Darsey (1995) explained that when fantasy is so devoid of links to reality as to be imaginary and thus a special genre of fiction, then no constitutive creation of consciousness can be expected to take place. Using Senator Joseph McCarthy's anti-Communist rhetoric as an exemplar of the *fantastic* genre, Darsey penetratingly characterized McCarthy's rhetoric as not a vision that would provide structure but "fragmented and disjointed . . . really just the hyperbolic, irrational discourse of the fantastic parading as politics" (p. 79). SCT's evaluative concept of rhetorical vision reality-links serves to remind those who would use SCT to delineate the fantastic from fantasizing and symbolic fiction from symbolic reality.

We have now concluded our highlighting of the technical concepts of SCT. In a nutshell, the anatomizing structure of the metatheory offered by Cragan and Shields (1998) allowed us to see that the communicative force of fantasy flows from communicators (fantasizers and rhetorical communities) communicating (fantasy-chaining and fantasy-sharing) by presenting messages (fantasy themes, fantasy types, rhetorical visions, sagas, and symbolic cues) propagated through a medium (group-sharing or public-sharing) affected by a communication dynamic (pragmatic, righteous, or social deep structures of fantasies and rhetorical visions) and evaluated for fantasy theme artistry, rhetorical vision reality-links, and shared group consciousness.

APPLYING SCT TO COMMUNICATION PROBLEMS

What makes SCT rewarding and intellectually fruitful is that, across the traditional contexts of communication study, the researchers using SCT have been able to do several novel things. For example, they provided SCT-based answers to marketing and advertising problems (Cragan & Shields, 1981a, 1992b, 1995a, 1995b). They used SCT to guide political and public relations campaigns (Cragan & Shields, 1978a, 1981d; Duffy, 1997; D. C. Shields, 1977, 1979; K. J. Shields & D. C. Shields, 1974; Vasquez, 1994). They used SCT to provide cultural analyses of the mass media (Bantz, 1975; Csapó-Sweet & Shields, 2000). They showed SCT's use in synthesizing large segments of American public address (Ilka, 1977; Bormann, 1985b; Bormann et al., 1996). In addition, the research program also included studies to determine the viability of SCT in each of the traditional communication contexts. Many of these studies sought to use the theory to solve real-world communication problems. We weave these two threads throughout the following discussion as another way of organizing the large body of research that is the tapestry of SCT.

Interpersonal Communication Studies

In the context of interpersonal communication, scholars such as Doyle (1985), Endres (1989, 1994), S. R. Glaser and Frank (1982), Hubbard (1985), and Kidd (1975) used SCT to gain insights into problematic communication. For example, several scholars captured the dramatis personae of women in mediated portrayals of interpersonal relationships with men. Kidd (1975) analyzed the portrayals in popular magazines in the 1950s and 1960s. She found a constraining vision and an emerging rhetorical vision reflecting a negotiated, process-of-becoming relationship. Kidd highlighted the changing portrayal of the ideal relationship. Hubbard (1985) examined relationship portrayals in popular romance novels. She reported four distinct visions ranging from Cinderella as Virgin Earth Mother and the Prince as Benign Dictator (1950s) to Cinderella as Liberated Heroine and the Prince as Equal Partner (1980s). Hubbard's work reaffirmed the changing nature of the ideal relationship and pointed to the importance of our symbolic constructions in achieving relationship satisfaction. Such theory-based research warrants the conclusion that the visions we hold have an impact on how we define ideal relationships and how we act in relationships (Cragan & Shields, 1999).

Small Group Communication Studies

In the context of group communication, studies by Barton and O'Leary (1974), Bormann (1986, 1990), Bormann et al. (1995), Chesebro et al. (1973), Cragan and Shields (1995b), Kroll (1983), Lesch (1994), D. L. Miller (1971), Porter (1976), Putnam (1972), and D. C. Shields (1981b, 1981f) examine the impact of fantasizing on the building of identity and culture in groups. For example, Chesebro et al. (1973) identified the use of fantasy themes in the four stages of consciousness-raising (credentialing, polarization, new identity, and relating to other groups). Subsequent research confirmed that new groups spend a lot of time in Stages 1 and 2 (Cragan et al., 1996), whereas established groups spend most of their time in Stages 3 and 4 (Lesch, 1994). Porter (1976) studied the discourse of the Nixon White House transcripts on Watergate. She also used SCT to identify chaining, group fantasies. She found fantasies concerning the group's attempts to control the mass media and a recurring fantasy type: "The best defense is a good offense" (p. 277). As well, Bormann (1990), Cragan and Wright (1991, 1999), and Cragan et al. (1996) provided extensive discussions of the functioning of SCT in small group communication. They indicated its role in consciousness-raising, group culture building, and group motivation.

Public Communication Studies

Aden, (1986), Bormann (1983c), Bormann et al. (1996), Campbell (1982), Cragan (1971, 1981), Cragan and Cutbirth (1984), Cragan and Shields (1977, 1978a), Duffy (1997), Endres (1994), S. K. Foss (1979), Goodnight and Poulakas (1981), Hensley (1975), Huxmann (1996), Kiewe and Houck (1989), Matthews (1995), Ritter (1977), D. C. Shields (1974), D. C. Shields and Preston (1985), K. J. Shields and D. C. Shields (1974), and Solomon (1978) reported SCT-based studies regarding persuasion in the public arena. For example, Barton and O'Leary (1974) used SCT to help alleviate the crisis of physician-less communities. They needed to recruit physicians for six rural, Minnesota towns. They reported that the fantasy themes espoused in small group discussions involving rural Minnesotans—such as "a quiet, independent life"—produced negatively chaining fantasies among young medical doctors (Barton & O'Leary, 1974, p.148). Based upon their discussions with physicians, they then fashioned new fantasy themes. For example, they dramatized one plot line as adjoining rural communities "cooperating" to provide "support services" for rural physicians (p. 150). They dramatized another plot line as "supporting special-needs patients" through such services as emergency transport to large city hospitals for patient advanced care (p. 151). They showed that fantasy themes could be discovered, refashioned, and used in a public relations campaign to recruit physicians.

Interestingly, the rhetorical vision concept proved useful to a number of otherwise non-SCT researchers conducting work on public communication. For such scholars, the rhetorical vision concept exuded a special heuristic benefit. For example, several scholars first captured and synthesized a particular collectivity's rhetorical vision and then offered analysis and insight through the lens of some other communication theory. Reid (1983) depicted the Puritan rhetorical vision and then analyzed it from a non-SCT frame. Lucaites and Condit (1990) described the black martyr rhetorical vision and Short (1994) depicted the rhetorical vision of progress. Upon describing the respective rhetorical visions, these researchers turned to McGee's (1980) concept of ideograph to provide critical insight into public communication. Similarly, Heisey and Trebing (1983) first used SCT to capture the Shah's White Revolution and the Ayatollah's Islamic Revolution rhetorical visions and then turned to Burkean-based ratio-analysis to analyze the differences in strategies employed by the adherents of the respective visions.

Organizational Communication Studies

In the organizational communication context, Bormann (1982c, 1983b, 1989); Bormann, Pratt et al. (1978); Callahan (1992); Chesebro (1980); Cragan et al. (1981a, 1981b, 1984, 1985); Cragan and Shields (1978b, 1981b, 1981c, 1992b, 1995b); Csapó-Sweet and Shields (2000); Eyo (1992); Faules (1982); Ford (1989); Koester (1982); McFarland (1985); and Putnam et al. (1991) examined organizational visions, sagas, and cultures. For example, Cragan and Shields (1992b) reported on the re-creation of a corporate symbolic reality for a national company whose members and customers had experienced privatization. They captured the discrete rhetorical visions held by the corporation's customers. They then developed repositioning statements for the company, segmented its marketplace into five distinct buying types (segments), and developed hot buttons (salient fantasy themes) keyed to each market segment for nationally distributed media advertisements and sales stories. Their study grounded the use of SCT to create new symbolic realities for companies, to segment markets, and to target sales campaigns. As well, by using vision participation as the breaker variable for use with discriminant analysis, they were able to determine the demo-psycho-socio-product-graphics of vision participants so that members of the sales force could predict the vision participation of their customers from observable characteristics.

Mass Communication Studies

In the mass communication context, scholars such as Bantz (1972, 1975, 1979); Bormann (1973, 1982a); Bormann, Koester et al. (1978); Brown (1976); Cragan and Shields (1977); Daniel (1995); Doyle (1985); Duffy (1997); Duffy and Gotcher (1996); K. A. Foss and Littlejohn (1986); Garner et al. (1998); Haskins (1981); Heisey and Trebing (1983); Kapoor, Cragan, and Groves (1992); Kauffman (1972); Kidd (1975); Lee and Hoon (1993); Lindlof (1982); Mayerle (1987); McIllwraith and Schallow (1983); Monaghan et al. (1974); Nimmo and Combs (1982, 1983); Nimmo and Savage (1976); Rarick et al. (1977); Rosenfeld and Schrag (1985); Schrag, Hudson, and Bernado (1981); and Sharf (1987a, 1987b) used SCT to capture media-situated rhetorical visions.

For example, Lee and Hoon (1993) designed a concurrent validity study. They used profile, word, and fantasy theme analysis to examine the media-based rhetorical vision of men and women managers in Singapore. They sought to use SCT to explain the low participation of women in upper-level management positions. Lee and Hoon validated that "the mass media depicted different rhetorical visions for the women and men managers" and that "each portrayed a distinctive view of social [symbolic] reality" (p. 540). They then noted that the articles intended "to provide 'role models' for the young professionals, especially for the young aspiring women executives" but that readers "caught-up in the [media's] depiction of reality may develop a set of expectations which can serve as a filter to influence their interpretation of daily experiences . . . [that] can possibly limit the career expectations of women" (p. 540). This study also showed how SCT may be used to frame symbolic facts and provides a feminist critique of organizations.

Intercultural Communication Studies

In the intercultural context, scholars such as Bormann and Itaba (1992), Bormann et al. (1997), Callahan (1992), Chesebro (1980), Cragan (1975), and Lee and Hoon (1993) used SCT to facilitate our understanding of communication among culturally diverse communities. For example, Bormann and Itaba (1992) and Bormann et al. (1997) demonstrated the transcultural nature of the predisposition to share fantasies. Bormann et al. (1992, 1997) grounded that people in Japan and the U.S. display a predisposition to share fantasies. These scholars reported finding a predominantly righteous, moral, sentimental vision or event; a social, humane, communal vision or event; and a pragmatic, expedient, material vision or event in both cultures. They translated their research by suggesting that the use of righteous, social, or pragmatic role-taking fantasies by intercultural interactants will increase the likelihood of both communicative interaction and intercultural problem solving.

These applications of SCT to the traditional contexts of interpersonal, small group, public, organizational, mass, and intercultural communication provide ample evidence of SCT's status as a general communication theory. As well, these and other studies demonstrate its viability in solving real-world communication problems.

RESPONDING TO CRITICAL COMMENTARY

Theoretical advancement in communication depends upon good criticism. We review the critical commentary to provide our final way of organizing the contributed research on SCT. Scholars such as Balthrop (1979), Cathcart (1986), Combs (1980), Eadie (1982), Measell (1982), and Mickey (1982) offered valuable, constructive, critical input that furthered the development of SCT as a general communication theory. Others such as Zarefsky (1977) advised those who would use SCT in their academic pursuits. For example, Zarefsky disclosed that he had encouraged S. K. Foss's (1979) social movement study to help explain "why one set

of fantasy themes rather than another chains out successfully" to "permit predic-
tion of the rhetorical behavior of a movement" (p. 372). Similarly, Swanson (1977)
wondered if fantasy theme analysis was not "the study of the creation of social
reality [symbolic reality] or the constitutive phenomenology of the natural attitude?" (p. 214). Others offered explanations of SCT in their books (e.g., Bormann,
1980, 1990; Bormann, Howell, R. G. Nichols, & Shapiro, 1982; Brock, Scott, &
Chesebro, 1990; Cragan & Shields, 1981a, 1995a, 1998; Cragan & Wright, 1991,
1999; Daniels, Spiker, & Papa, 1997; S. K. Foss, 1989; S. K. Foss, K. A. Foss, &
Trapp, 1985; Frey, 1995; Golden, Berquist, & Coleman, 1983; Griffin, 1996; Hart,
1990; Infante, Rancer, & Womack, 1996; Larson, 1998; Littlejohn, 1999; Nimmo
& Combs, 1983; Rybacki & Rybacki, 1991; and C. A. Smith, 1990). Such critical
insights and syntheses contributed to SCT's move from a method of rhetorical
analysis to its advancement as a general communication theory with wide respect
and use in the discipline.

Of course, some criticized SCT. Leff and Mohrmann shared a series of criticisms from a 1977 convention paper, first as a topic of a National Communication
Association seminar program (Leff & Mohrmann, 1978), and then as a Central
States Communication Association spotlight program (Leff & Mohrmann, 1982).
Soon, a small group of preeminent rhetoricians became caught-up in the symbolic
reality of the critical stance. They were motivated by the critical constitutive message to begin critiquing SCT in the pages of our discipline's most prestigious journals. For example, Black (1980), Brummett (1984), Farrell (1980, 1982), Goodall
(1983), Gronbeck (1980), Hart (1986), Ivie (1987), Leff (1980), Mohrmann (1980,
1982a, 1982b), Osborn (1986), and R. R. Smith and Windes (1993, 1995) presented criticisms running the gamut from rhetorical asides in non-SCT-based articles to critical reviews of scholarly SCT books, to article-length attacks.

Across the years, Bormann (1982b, 1995), Bormann et al. (1994), Cragan and
Shields (1995a, 1998), Grainey (1983), and Sharf (1987b) offered refutations of
the critics. Then, too, Bormann (1980, 1982a, 1982c, 1983a, 1983b, 1983c, 1985a,
1986, 1989, 1990), Bormann et al. (1996), Cragan and Shields (1981a, 1995a,
1998), and D. C. Shields (1991) provided updates of new developments. As well,
Bormann et al. (1994) answered SCT's criticisms in full detail and explained the
presuppositions of the theory. We incorporate a synthesis of our responses as the
heart of this section of the chapter.

Not a General Theory

Critics such as Mohrmann (1982a, 1982b) contended that SCT is not a general
theory by arguing that fantasy-chaining is true of small groups but is not demon-
strable in the case of mass publics. As we saw in the earlier discussion of the
medium structure concepts of SCT, studies conducted across 25 years—such as
those reported by Bormann (1973), Bormann and Itaba (1992), Bormann et al.
(1997), Bormann, Koester et al. (1978), Cragan and Shields (1977, 1978a, 1992b),
Duffy (1997), Endres (1989, 1994, 1997), K. A. Foss and Littlejohn (1986), Nimmo

and Combs (1982), Rarick et al. (1977), and D. C. Shields (1981f)—empirically grounded and reaffirmed the sharing of group fantasies by large mediated publics. As the previous discussion indicated, a similarity exists regarding the group- and public-chaining processes in both group and mass mediated contexts. As well, the various applications and studies across contexts demonstrated that SCT's scope is general. In other words, studies reflected the vitality of SCT's use to explain the communicative force of fantasy in the interpersonal, small group, organizational, public, mass, and intercultural communication contexts. Again, it is SCT's ability to explain both group- and public-chaining by way of the same communicative force—the force of fantasy—that lies at the heart of SCT's development as a significant, discipline-indigenous, general communication theory.

Freudian-Based

Mohrmann (1982a, 1982b) made much of the fact that Robert Bales, a Harvard psychologist, used a Freudian definition of fantasy in his studies of fantasy-chaining in small groups (Bales, 1970). Mohrmann concluded that SCT must be Freudian and not an indigenous communication theory. Although Bales may be indebted to Freud, SCT is not. The clearest way to see that SCT's theoretical concept of a rhetorical fantasy is not Freudian is to examine the SCT studies to see if there is a Freudian interpretation in the grounding research. As Hyde (1980) pointed out, a truly Freudian analysis must contain such psychoanalytic concepts as Oedipus complex, castration, phallus, primal regression, and transference. A reading of the technical definitions of SCT's concepts, and their use in basic and applied research studies, indicates no such use of Freudian concepts or interpretations.

Researcher Dependent

Mohrmann (1982a, 1982b) argued that the insights found in the SCT studies did not flow from the use of the theory; rather they flowed from just bright people doing good work. Although Mohrmann's approbation appeared sincerely offered, the fact that bright people do good work is not in itself cause to dismiss the contributions of a theoretical frame. We believe that if our basic unit of analysis had not been a rhetorical fantasy theme, then we would have had no reason to look for fantasies. As well, we would have had no way of knowing how to identify them. Indeed, Bormann (1972) provided several examples of well known rhetorical illusions that had always appeared puzzling in the absence of the new dramatistic frame. We would add that although a rose is a rose, it still must be classified as something with like qualities (genus, specie, smell, shape, texture) to identify, count, and analyze it. In other words, all systematic research needs theoretical concepts with technical definitions. To sort out raw phenomena, one must have an implicit or explicit theory, even if it is only categorical, to distinguish raw communication phenomena. The SCT researchers systematically developed and grounded an explicit theory. They have used it scores of times to capture dramatistic communication and study its effect on human action.

Mere Category System

Black (1980), Farrell (1982), and Hart (1986) called SCT a mere taxonomy with a cookie-cutter mentality producing the same predictable analysis from study to study. SCT's researchers accept this characterization as high praise. Accurate *taxonomies* in the sciences, social sciences, and humanities—such as the periodic table of elements in chemistry, the classifications of scalar structure in organizations, the parts of speech in the English language—are important. The goal of the SCT research program has been to identify and name the recurring regularities observed in communication. That programmatic effort now allows us to see dramatizing messages, rhetorical fantasy themes, fantasy types, symbolic cues, rhetorical visions, sagas, the righteous, social, and pragmatic deep structures of visions, fantasizers, rhetorical communities, the propensity to fantasize, group-sharing, public-sharing, shared group consciousness, rhetorical vision reality-links, and fantasy theme artistry. Of course, these technical concepts now comprise the theory. In addition, the qualitative method of fantasy theme analysis allows us to capture them in actual communication. The question of whether or not the SCT taxonomy is complete is one we will consider in the final section of this chapter.

We accept the description of fantasy-theme analysis as *cookie-cutter*. For us, systematic investigation—the ability to generalize across cases and the replication of findings in research—requires a consistent template. With the application of a consistent template, theories can be grounded across contexts and become general in scope. Again, SCT's grounding, research studies crossed the interpersonal, small group, public, organizational, mass, and intercultural communication contexts. The taxonomy and the template have stood the test of time.

Across 3 decades, SCT has proven itself to be a useful theory. It has allowed us to explain the impact of the communicative force of fantasy on creating a consciousness that entails meaning, emotion, motive, and value for action for the participants in a chaining fantasy or a rhetorical vision. SCT's development is the product of 30 years of doing rhetorical and social scientific research and scholarship. The result is that we now have a grounded, viable, discipline-indigenous communication theory. SCT's importance rests in the knowledge that it posits fantasy-sharing and fantasy-chaining as the causal engine that, when coupled with the ontological propensity to fantasize, provides explanatory power and predictive capacity for human action.

CONCLUSION

Having delineated the origin and roots of SCT, described its heuristic value, traced its development as a tested and verified general theory of communication, set forth its anatomy of technical concepts, highlighted its use to solve real-world communication problems, and reiterated the answers to its most prevalent criticisms, it now appears useful to look ahead. What follows are our brief suggestions for future research for those interested in sustaining SCT's research program in the 21st century.

TABLE 4
Tentative Taxonomy of SCT

• *Classes of rhetorical fantasy themes*
  fantasy theme
  fantasy type
  saga
  symbolic cue
	• *Life-cycle of rhetorical visions*
	  consciousness-creating
	  consciousness-raising
	  consciousness-sustaining
	  consciousness-terminus

• *Elements of rhetorical fantasy themes*
  stylistic qualities
  substantive qualities
  structural qualities
	• *Qualities of rhetorical fantasy themes*
	  pragmatic
	  righteous
	  social

• *Forms of rhetorical fantasy themes*
  constructive
  destructive
  discursive
  factious
  fantastic
  nonfiction
	• *Rhetorical vision continua*
	  flexible to inflexible
	  intense to passive
	  paranoid to healthy
	  pure to mixed
	  secretive to proselytizing

• *Kinds of rhetorical fantasy themes*
  consciousness-creating
  consciousness-raising
  consciousness-sustaining
	• *Strategies for sustaining rhetorical visions*
	  conservation
	  preservation
	  restoration

• *Kinds of sagas*
  founders
  genesis
  latent/inactive	

Directions for Future Research

After 3 decades of research on SCT, we now know a number of things. For example, we now know that there are different kinds of rhetorical fantasies, rhetorical visions, sagas, and fantasy types. We suggest that the time is right to begin the development of a taxonomy of SCT. Taxonomies enable scholars to arrange a number of artifacts into an ordered pattern. Botanists have organized various kinds of trees into taxonomies. Geologists have created taxonomies of rocks. The scholars who search for genres in rhetorical practice are essentially seeking taxonomies. Although our discipline exhibits no general theories based solely on taxonomies in the study of communication, we believe a taxonomy of the anatomy of SCT might prove useful in providing some order and symmetry to the understanding of SCT. In line with this suggestion, we present an initial taxonomy of SCT as Table 4. Of course, we present it not as the finished product, but as a beginning upon which to build.

Additionally, we believe that SCT's research program could benefit immediately from the development of a propensity to fantasize scale. Just as we know from the communication apprehension research program that some people are more able and willing to communicate and some are less able and willing to do so, it would appear that a person's affinity for and ability to use imaginative language varies across populations and perhaps across settings. We believe a fruitful extension of the SCT research program might flow from the development of new ways of measuring the propensity to fantasize. One way would be a propensity to fantasize scale. Such a scale would provide those within the research program the ability to identify high fantasizers from low fantasizers.

We envision the *propensity-to-fantasize* aspect of the research program potentially becoming tied to the discovery of a gene that is the basis for the risk-taking communicative behavior that is rhetorical fantasizing. If that is the case, we can also see a future in linking the propensity to fantasize to a research program such as Beatty, McCroskey, and Heisel (1998) proposed for the communibiology paradigm. In the context of small group communication, scholars have long observed the group-role of the tension-releaser and the importance of that role in breaking primary and secondary tension in small work groups (Bormann, 1969; Cragan & Wright, 1999). It may be that individuals who have a high propensity to fantasize, that is, have the rhetorical skill to fashion fantasy themes that will chain-out in the group play the tension-releasing role. One aspect of the tension-releaser's ability seems innate and another aspect seems teachable. The goal would be to design, develop, and conduct controlled studies that assess the abilities of trained and untrained fantasizers to create group identity and raise the consciousness of work groups.

In the medium of public-chaining, one of the central characteristics of speech writers appears to be their skill at using imaginative language to create rhetorical fantasy themes that chain across the republic. The memorable fantasy themes of former Presidents—Reagan with his *shining city upon a hill*, Bush with his *thousand points of light*, and Truman with his *containment of the cancer of communism*—provide lasting examples of such successful chaining fantasies. A propensity to fantasize scale, coupled with the proper design of studies, would enable the testing of the hypothesis that successful speech writers and public relations directors possess a higher propensity to fantasize (the ability to create and use rhetorical fantasies) than do their less successful counterparts.

It is clear that the SCT predicts that, just as the force of fantasy effects small groups of communicators and mass publics, the force of fantasy should effect individuals by way of their personal fantasizing. Although the literature contains more than a half dozen published studies of the rhetorical visions of individuals (see Table 2), at the moment, a propensity-to-fantasize instrument that would allow us to measure the impact of personal fantasy on human action does not exist. What is it that initiates the beneficial visions of a Martin Luther King or Ghandi on the one hand and the vicious, personal visions of a Hitler, Jim Jones, Joseph McCarthy, or Ted Kaczynski on the other? Darsey (1995) has indicated it is reliance on the fantastic. The development of a propensity to fantasize scale would appear to enable us to begin testing the impact of personal fantasies on individuals.

Unifying the Communicative Forces

Cragan and Shields (1998, 1999) identified the general communication theories that respectively explain the impact of six different communicative forces on human action. The communicative forces are information sharing, social information sharing, argument making, narration (storytelling), fantasy-sharing (-chaining), and diffusing innovation-talk. These forces are akin to the four forces of nature: strong nuclear, electromagnetic, weak nuclear, and gravity. Epistemologically, it may be possible to group communicative forces just as the once separate electric and magnetic forces were grouped in physics. For example, information, social information, and innovation diffusion-talk may just be refinements belonging to the same set. As well, W. R. Fisher (1987) has argued that narration subsumes argument. Similarly, one may use SCT to view argument as a style-specific, special theory. Thus, there is some evidence that reductions are possible. At this time, we cannot say if these or further reductions are possible, but they may be. However, whether or not there are further reductions of the communicative forces for human action, the experiences of our colleagues in physics point to the need to develop a theory that would unify and explain the workings of the separate forces (Greene, 1999).

At the very least, the different communicative forces need to be accounted for within a single unifying explanation. Such an endeavor will require the commitment of the discipline, and the foregoing of the often prevalent, deep-seated allegiances to the respective research programs undergirding the half dozen general communication theories that individually explain a separate communicative force. At first, even with a sizable disciplinary commitment, the research needed to explain the diverse communicative forces will seem like we are returning to the late 1960s and starting over with our programmatic research. We say this because we believe that reaching the goal of a unified explanation of the communicative forces will require a more complex research design that would allow us to operationalize simultaneously material, social, and symbolic facts (Cragan & Shields, 1995a).

The force particles of communication represent different kinds of facts (Cragan & Shields, 1998). Information and argument primarily represent material facts. Social or disclosive information and innovation diffusion-talk primarily represent social facts. Narrative and rhetorical fantasies primarily represent symbolic facts. At the very least, our observations must begin to take into account the separate communicative forces in our theorizing and theory-grounding research programs. Then, we need to develop instruments and use operational definitions that will enable us to code simultaneously for information, social information, diffusing innovation-talk, argument, narrative, and fantasy. Such new instruments will allow us to move beyond the advancement of competitive general theories toward the development of a unified theory of communication (see Cragan et al., 1996). Just as, in the absence of a theory, a researcher does not know the communicative phenomena that represent a basic concept neither will she know how the communicative forces simultaneously impact human action in the absence of a unified coding instrument. In other words, all talk is just babble in the absence of an inter-pretive theory. All data is uninterpretable without some kind of theory. A full, uni-fied explanation of the communicative forces is only possible in the presence of an adequate coding instrument that stands at the heart of any future unified theory's theory-method complex.

It may also be that the discipline is going to need an epistemological break-through in method and measurement within the theory-method complex required of the quest for a unified theory of communication. Newton needed to work out the calculus of differential equations before he could prove out his theory of grav-ity. The SCT team needed to work out the applications of Q-sorts and Q-type factor analysis to large populations (Cragan & Shields, 1981d). The discipline may need one or more clever scholars (or scholar-teams) to invent some new meth-ods and measurements to provide a unified explanation of the communicative forces. In other words, total unification may only come with the advent of a new theory-method complex that is unknown at this time. We know that a given communica-tion theory may blend material and social facts (for example, uncertainty reduc-tion theory and diffusion of innovation theory) or material and symbolic facts (for example, narrative paradigm theory and symbolic convergence theory). Such blend-ing would seem to indicate that we are not that far from sensing the need for a new theory-method complex that allows the simultaneous capturing of material, social, and symbolic communicative facts.

We believe that concern about the communicative forces, and how one might provide a unified explanation of them, will provide the big research questions of the twenty-first century. Already, some general theories appear to account for more than one communicative force in their explanations. Given a widespread disciplin-ary effort, by 2025 we predict that hindsight will validate our foresight about the quest for a unified theory. There may yet be a universal theory of communication. Our work with SCT and the communicative force of fantasy across the past 3 decades has led us to this conclusion.

REFERENCES

Aden, R. C. (1986). Fantasy themes and rhetorical visions in the 1984 presidential campaign: Explain-ing the Reagan mandate. *Speaker and Gavel, 23*(3), 87–94.

Bales, R. F. (1950). *Interaction process analysis: A method for the study of small groups.* Reading, MA: Addison-Wesley.

Bales, R. F. (1970). *Personality and interpersonal behavior.* New York: Holt, Rinehart, & Winston.

Ball, M. A. (1990). A case study for the Kennedy administration's decision-making concerning the Diem coup of November, 1963. *Western Journal of Speech Communication, 54,* 557–574.

Ball, M. A. (1992). *Vietnam on the Potomac.* New York: Praeger.

Balthrop, B. (1979). [Review of the book *Rhetorical fantasy in the Webster-Calhoun debate on the revenue collection bill of 1833*]. *Southern Speech Communication Journal, 45,* 101–104.

Bantz, C. R. (1972). The rhetorical vision of the *ABC Evening News:* June 12 to July 10. *Moments in Contemporary Rhetoric and Communication, 2*(2), 34–37.

Bantz, C. R. (1975). Television news: Reality and research. *Western Speech Journal, 39,* 123–130.

Bantz, C. R. (1979). The critic and the computer: A multiple technique analysis of the *ABC Evening News. Communication Monographs, 46*, 27–39.

Barton, S. N., & O'Leary, J. B. (1974). The rhetoric of rural physicians procurement campaigns: An application of Tavistock. *Quarterly Journal of Speech, 60*, 144–154.

Bastien, D. T., & Hostager, T. J. (1992). Cooperation as communicative accomplishment: A symbolic interaction analysis of an improvised jazz concert. *Communication Studies, 43*, 92–104.

Beatty, M. J., McCroskey, J. C., & Heisel, A. D. (1998). Communication apprehension as temperamental expression: A communibiological paradigm. *Communication Monographs, 65*, 197–219.

Beveridge, A. (1989). The march of the flag. In J. Andrews & D. Zarefsky (Eds.), *American voices: Significant speeches in American history, 1640–1945* (pp. 374–378). New York: Longman. [Originally delivered in 1898.]

Black, E. (1980). A note on theory and practice in rhetorical criticism. *Western Journal of Speech Communication, 44*, 331–336.

Blum, J. M., Catton, B., Morgan, E. S., Schlesinger, A. M., Jr., Stampp, K. M., & Woodward, C. V. (1963). *The national experience: A history of the United States.* New York: Harcourt, Brace, & World.

Bormann, E. G. (1969). *Discussion and group methods.* New York: Harper & Row.

Bormann, E. G. (1972). Fantasy and rhetorical vision: The rhetorical criticism of social reality. *Quarterly Journal of Speech, 58*, 396–407.

Bormann, E. G. (1973). The Eagleton affair: A fantasy theme analysis. *Quarterly Journal of Speech, 59*, 143–159.

Bormann, E. G. (1977). Fetching good out of evil: A rhetorical use of calamity. *Quarterly Journal of Speech, 63*, 130–139.

Bormann, E. G. (1978, April). *The tentative and certain in rhetoric: The role of corroboration in the relative rigidity or flexibility of rhetorical visions.* Paper presented at the meeting of the Central States Speech Association, Chicago, IL.

Bormann, E. G. (1980). *Communication theory.* New York: Holt, Rinehart, & Winston.

Bormann, E. G. (1982a). A fantasy theme analysis of the television coverage of the hostage release and the Reagan inaugural. *Quarterly Journal of Speech, 68*, 133–144.

Bormann, E. G. (1982b). Fantasy and rhetorical vision: Ten years later. *Quarterly Journal of Speech, 68*, 133–144.

Bormann, E. G. (1982c). The symbolic convergence theory of communication: Applications and implications for teachers and consultants. *Journal of Applied Communication Research, 10*, 50–61.

Bormann, E. G. (1983a). Rhetoric as a way of knowing: Ernest Bormann and fantasy theme analysis. In J. L. Golden, G. F. Berquist, & W. E. Coleman (Eds.), *The rhetoric of western thought* (pp. 431–449). Dubuque, IA: Kendall Hunt.

Bormann, E. G. (1983b). Symbolic convergence: Organizational communication and culture. In L. L. Putnam & M. E. Pacanowsky (Eds.), *Communication and organizations: An interpretive approach* (pp. 99–122). Beverly Hills, CA: Sage.

Bormann, E. G. (1983c). The symbolic convergence theory of communication and the creation, raising, and sustaining of public consciousness. In J. I. Cisco (Ed.), *The Jensen lectures: Contemporary communication studies* (pp. 71–90). Tampa: Department of Communication, University of South Florida.

Bormann, E. G. (1985a). Symbolic convergence theory: A communication formulation. *Journal of Communication, 35*, 128–138.

Bormann, E. G. (1985b). *The force of fantasy: Restoring the American dream.* Carbondale: Southern Illinois University.

Bormann, E. G. (1986). Symbolic convergence theory and communication in group decision-making. In R. Y. Hirokawa & M. S. Poole (Eds.), *Communication and group decision-making* (pp. 219–236). Beverly Hills, CA: Sage.

Bormann, E. G. (1989). The "empowering organization" as a heuristic concept in organizational communication. In J. A. Anderson (Ed.), *Communication yearbook 11* (pp. 391–404). Beverly Hills, CA: Sage.

Bormann, E. G. (1990). *Small group communication: Theory and practice* (3rd ed.). New York: HarperCollins.

Bormann, E. G. (1995). Some random thoughts on the unity or diversity of the rhetoric of abolition. *Southern Communication Journal, 60*, 266–274.

Bormann, E. G., Bormann, E., & Harty, K. C. (1995). Using symbolic convergence theory and focus group interviews to develop communication designed to stop teenage smoking. In L. R. Frey (Ed.), *Innovations in group facilitation: Applications in natural settings* (pp. 200–232). Cresskill, NJ: Hampton.

Bormann, E. G., Cragan, J. F., & Shields, D. C. (1994). In defense of symbolic convergence theory: A look at the theory and its criticisms after two decades. *Communication Theory, 4*, 259–294.

Bormann, E. G., Cragan, J. F., & Shields, D. C. (1996). An expansion of the rhetorical vision concept of symbolic convergence theory: The cold war paradigm case. *Communication Monographs, 63*, 1–28.

Bormann, E. G , Howell, W. S., Nichols, R. G., & Shapiro, G. L. (1982). *Interpersonal communication in modern organizations* (2nd ed.). Englewood Cliffs, NJ: Prentice-Hall.

Bormann, E. G., & Itaba, Y. (1992). Why do people share fantasies? An empirical investigation of the symbolic convergence theory in a sample of Japanese subjects. *Human Communication Studies, 20*, 1–25.

Bormann, E. G., Koester, J., & Bennett, J. (1978). Political cartoons and salient rhetorical fantasies: An empirical analysis of the '76 presidential campaign. *Communication Monographs, 45*, 312–329.

Bormann, E. G., Knutson, R. L., & Musolf, K. (1997). Why do people share fantasies? An empirical investigation of a basic tenet of the symbolic convergence communication theory. *Communication Studies, 48*, 254–276.

Bormann, E. G., Kroll, B. S., Watters, K., & McFarland, D. (1984). Rhetorical visions of committed voters in the 1980 presidential campaign: Fantasy theme analysis of a large sample survey. *Critical Studies in Mass Communication, 1*, 287–310.

Bormann, E. G., Pratt, J., & Putnam, L. (1978). Power, authority and sex: Male response to female leadership. *Communication Monographs, 45*, 119–155.

Bormann, E. G., Olson, G., Percy, V., & Tremaine, R. (1985). A fantasy theme analysis of the Growe Boschwitz senatorial campaign in the Minnesota state election of 1984. *Speech Association of Minnesota Journal, 12*, 39–60.

Brock, B. L., Scott, R. L., & Chesebro, J. W., (Eds.). (1990). *Methods of rhetorical criticism* (3rd. ed.). Detroit, MI: Wayne State University.

Brown, W. R. (1976). The prime-time television environment and emerging rhetorical visions. *Quarterly Journal of Speech, 62*, 389–399.

Brummett, B. A. (1984). Rhetorical theory as heuristic and moral: A pedagogical justification. *Communication Education, 33*, 97–107.

Bush, R. R. (1981). Applied q-methodology: An industry perspective. In J. F. Cragan & D. C. Shields (Eds.), *Applied communication research: A dramatistic approach* (pp. 367–371). Prospect Heights, IL: Waveland.

Callahan, L. F. (1992). Corporations, the news media and other villains within Jesse Jackson's rhetorical vision. *Western Journal of Black Studies, 16*, 190–198.

Campbell, J. L. (1982). In search of The New South. *Southern Speech Communication Journal, 47*, 361–388.

Cathcart, R. S. (1986). [Review of the book *The force of fantasy: Restoring the American dream*]. *Quarterly Journal of Speech, 72*, 108–110.

Chesebro, J. W. (1980). Paradoxical views of 'homosexuality' in the rhetoric of social scientists: A fantasy theme analysis. *Quarterly Journal of Speech, 66*, 127–139.

Chesebro, J. W., Cragan, J. F., & McCullough, P. W. (1973). The small group technique of the radical revolutionary: A synthetic study of consciousness raising. *Communication Monographs, 40*, 136–146.

Combs, J. (1980). [Review of the book *Applied communication research: A dramatistic approach*]. *Political Communication Review, 5*, 34–38.

Corcoran, F. (1983). The bear in the back yard: Myth, ideology, and victimage ritual in Soviet funerals. *Communication Monographs, 50*, 305–320.

Cragan, J. F. (1971). Johnson, Goldwater, and the cold war phantasy. *Moments in Contemporary Rhetoric and Communication, 1*(1), 9–16.

Cragan, J. F. (1975). Rhetorical strategy: A dramatistic interpretation and application. *Central States Speech Journal, 26*, 4–11.

Cragan, J. F. (1981). The origin and nature of the cold war rhetorical vision, 1946–1972: A partial history. In J. F. Cragan & D. C. Shields (Eds.), *Applied communication research: A dramatistic approach* (pp. 47–66). Prospect Heights, IL: Waveland.

Cragan, J. F., Cuffe, M., Pairitz, L., & Jackson, L. H. (1985). What management style suits you? *Fire Chief Magazine, 26*, 24–30.

Cragan, J. F., & Cuthirth, C. W. (1984). A revisionist perspective on political ad hominem argument. *Central States Speech Journal, 26*, 4–11.

Cragan, J. F., Semlak, W. D., & Cuffe, M. (1984). Measuring chairperson/faculty satisfaction in various academic sub-cultures. *Proceedings of academic chairpersons: Administrative responsibilities* (Vol. 13: pp. 106–117). Manhattan: Kansas State University.

Cragan, J. F., & Shields, D. C. (1977). Foreign policy communication dramas: How mediated rhetoric played in Peoria in Campaign '76. *Quarterly Journal of Speech, 63*, 274–289.

Cragan, J. F., & Shields, D. C. (1978a). Communication in American politics: Symbols without substance. *USA Today, 108*, 60–62.

Cragan, J. F., & Shields, D. C. (with Pairitz, L. A., & Jackson, L. H.). (1978b, October). The identifying characteristics of public fire safety educators. *Fire Chief Magazine, 41*(10), 44–50.

Cragan, J. F., & Shields, D. C. (Eds.). (1981a). *Applied communication research: A dramatistic approach*. Prospect Heights, IL: Waveland.

Cragan, J. F., & Shields, D. C. (1981b). Communication-based market segmentation study: Illustrative excerpts. In J. F. Cragan & D. C. Shields (Eds.), *Applied communication research: A dramatistic approach* (pp. 357–365). Prospect Heights, IL: Waveland.

Cragan, J. F., & Shields, D. C. (with Pairitz, L. A., & Jackson, L. H.). (1981c). The identifying characteristics of public fire safety educators: An empirical analysis. In J. F. Cragan & D. C. Shields (Eds.), *Applied communication research: A dramatistic approach* (pp. 219–234). Prospect Heights, IL: Waveland.

Cragan, J. F., & Shields, D. C. (1981d). Uses of Bormann's rhetorical theory in applied communication research. In J. F. Cragan & D. C. Shields (Eds.), *Applied communication research: A dramatistic approach* (pp. 31–42). Prospect Heights, IL: Waveland.

Cragan, J. F., & Shields, D. C. (1992a, April). *Images of the New World Order: Emergent rhetorical vision or act of political expediency?* Paper presented at the meeting of the Central States Communication Association, Cleveland, OH.

Cragan, J. F., & Shields, D. C. (1992b). The use of symbolic convergence theory in corporate strategic planning: A case study. *Journal of Applied Communication Research, 20*, 199–218.

Cragan, J. F., & Shields, D. C. (1994, May 20). *Advancing symbolic convergence theory: A paper in honor of Ernest G. Bormann*. Paper presented at the University of Minnesota, Minneapolis.

Cragan, J. F., & Shields, D. C. (1995a). *Symbolic theories in applied communication research: Bormann, Burke, and Fisher*. Cresskill, NJ: Hampton.

Cragan, J. F., & Shields, D. C. (1995b). Using SCT-based focus group interviews to do applied communication research. In L. Frey (Ed.), *Innovations in group facilitation: Applications in natural settings* (pp. 233–256). Cresskill, NJ: Hampton.

Cragan, J. F., & Shields, D. C. (1998). *Understanding communication theory: The communicative forces for human action*. Needham Heights, MA: Allyn & Bacon.

Cragan, J. F., & Shields, D. C. (1999). Translating scholarship into practice: Communication studies reflecting the value of theory-based research to everyday life. *Journal of Applied Communication Research, 27*, 92–106.

Cragan, J. F., Shields, D. C., & Nichols, N. E. (1981a). Marketing farm management services: An internal study. In J. F. Cragan & D. C. Shields (Eds.), *Applied communication research: A dramatistic approach* (pp. 271–307). Prospect Heights, IL: Waveland.

Cragan, J. F., Shields, D. C., & Nichols, N. E. (1981b). Doane farm management study: Structured matrix and dramatistic q-deck. In J. F. Cragan & D. C. Shields (Eds.), *Applied communication research: A dramatistic approach* (pp. 387–394). Prospect Heights, IL: Waveland.

Cragan, J. F., Shields, D. C., & Wright, D. W. (1996). A unified theory of small group communication. In J. F. Cragan & D. W. Wright (Eds.), *Theory and research in small group communication* (pp. 69–92). Edina, MN: Burgess.

Cragan, J. F., & Wright, D. W. (1991). *Communication in small group discussions: An integrated approach*. St. Paul, MN: West.

Cragan, J. F., & Wright, D. W. (1999). *Communication in small groups: Theory, process, skills*. Belmont, CA: Wadsworth.

Csapó-Sweet, R., & Shields, D. C. (2000). Explicating the saga component of symbolic convergence theory: The case of Serbia's Radio B92 in cyberspace. *Critical Studies in Media Communication, 17,* 316–333.

Daniel, A.- M. A. (1995). U.S. media coverage of the Intifada and American public opinion. In Y. R. Kamalipour (Ed.), *The U.S. media and the Middle East: Image and perception* (pp. 62–72). Westport, CT: Greenwood.

Daniels, T. D., Spiker, B. K., & Papa, M. J. (1997). *Perspectives on organizational communication* (4th ed.). Boston, MA: McGraw Hill.

Darsey, J. (1995). Joe McCarthy's fantastic moment. *Communication Monographs, 62,* 65–86.

Doyle, M. V. (1985). The rhetoric of romance: A fantasy theme analysis of Barbara Cartland novels. *Southern Speech Communication Journal, 51,* 24–48.

Duffy, M. (1997). High stakes: A fantasy theme analysis of the selling of riverboat gambling in Iowa. *Southern Communication Journal, 62,* 117–132.

Duffy, M., & Gotcher, M. (1996). Crucial advice on how to get the guy: The rhetorical vision of power and seduction in the teen magazine *YM. Journal of Communication Inquiry, 20*(1), 32–48.

Eadie, W. F. (1982). [Review of the book *Applied communication research: A dramatistic approach*.] *Journal of Applied Communication Research, 10,* 75–78.

Endres, T. G. (1989). Rhetorical visions of unmarried mothers. *Communication Quarterly, 37,* 134–150.

Endres, T. G. (1994). Co-existing master analogues in symbolic convergence theory: The Knights of Columbus quincentennial campaign. *Communication Studies, 45,* 294–308.

Endres, T. G. (1997). Father-daughter dramas: A Q-investigation of rhetorical visions. *Journal of Applied Communication Research, 25,* 317–340.

Eyo, B. A. (1992). Innovation and organizational communication in corporate America: The rhetorical visions of managers, facilitators, and employees on quality circles. *Bulletin of the Association for Business Communication, 55*(1), 52–63.

Farrell, T. B. (1980). Critical models in the analysis of discourse. *Western Journal of Speech Communication, 44,* 300–314.

Farrell, T. B. (1982). [Review of the book *Applied communication research: A dramatistic approach*]. *Quarterly Journal of Speech, 68,* 96–97.

Faules, D. (1982). The use of multi-methods in the organizational setting. *Western Journal of Communication, 46,* 150–161.

Fisher, B. A. (1968). *Decision emergence: A process model of verbal task behavior for decision-making groups*. Unpublished doctoral dissertation, University of Minnesota, Minneapolis.

Fisher, B. A. (1970a). Decision emergence: Phases in group decision-making. *Communication Monographs, 37,* 53–66.

Fisher, B. A. (1970b). The process of decision modification in small group discussions. *Journal of Communication, 20,* 136–149.

Fisher, B. A. (1971). Communication research and the task-oriented group. *Journal of Communication, 21,* 136–149.

Fisher, B. A., & Hawes, L. (1971). An interact system model: Generating a grounded theory of small groups. *Quarterly Journal of Speech, 57*, 444–453.

Fisher, W. R. (1987). *Human communication as narration: Toward a philosophy of reason, value, and action.* Columbia: University of South Carolina.

Ford, L. A. (1989). Fetching good out of evil in AA: A Bormannean fantasy theme analysis of *The Big Book* of Alcoholics Anonymous, *Communication Quarterly, 37*, 1–15.

Foss, K. A., & Littlejohn, S. W. (1986). "The day after": Rhetorical vision in an ironic frame. *Critical Studies in Mass Communication, 3*, 317–336.

Foss, S. K. (1979). Equal rights amendment controversy: Two worlds in conflict. *Quarterly Journal of Speech, 65*, 275–288.

Foss, S. K. (Ed.). (1989). *Rhetorical criticism: Exploration and practice.* Prospect Heights, IL: Waveland.

Foss, S. K., Foss, K. A., & Trapp, R. (1985). *Contemporary perspectives on rhetoric.* Prospect Heights, IL: Waveland.

Frey, L. (Ed.) (1995). *Innovations in group facilitation: Applications in natural settings.* Cresskill, NJ: Hampton.

Garner, A., Sterk, H. M., & Adams, S. (1998). Narrative analysis of sexual etiquette in teenage magazines. *Journal of Communication, 48*(4), 59–78.

Geier, J. (1963). *A descriptive analysis of an interaction pattern resulting in leadership emergence in leaderless group discussion.* Unpublished doctoral dissertation, University of Minnesota, Minneapolis.

Glaser, B., & Strauss, A. (1967). *The discovery of grounded theory.* Chicago: Aldine.

Glaser, S. R., & Frank, D. A. (1982). Rhetorical criticism of interpersonal discourse: An exploratory study. *Communication Quarterly, 30*, 353–358.

Golden, J. L., Berquist, G. F., & Coleman, W. E. (Eds.) (1983). *The rhetoric of Western thought.* Dubuque, IA: Kendall Hunt.

Goodall, H. L., Jr. (1983). The nature of analogic discourse. *Quarterly Journal of Speech, 69*, 171–179.

Goodnight, G. T., & Poulakos, J. (1981). Conspiracy rhetoric: From pragmatism to fantasy in public discourse. *Western Journal of Speech Communication, 45*, 299–316.

Grainey, T. F. (1983). A reply to G. P. Mohrmann. *Quarterly Journal of Speech, 69*, 190–191.

Grainey, T. F., Pollack, D. R., & Kushmierek, L. A. (1984). How three Chicago newspapers covered the Washington-Epton campaign. *Journalism Quarterly, 61*, 352–355.

Greene, B. (1999). *The elegant universe: Superstrings, hidden dimensions, and the quest for the ultimate theory.* New York: Norton.

Griffin, E. A. (1996). *A first look at communication theory* (3rd ed.). New York: McGraw Hill.

Gronbeck, B. E. (1980). Dramaturgical theory and criticism: The state of the art (or science?). *Western Journal of Speech Communication, 44*, 315–330.

Hart, R. P. (1986). Contemporary scholarship in public address: A research editorial. *Western Journal of Speech Communication, 50*, 75–95.

Hart, R. P. (Ed.). (1990). *Modern rhetorical criticism.* Glenville, IL: Scott Foresman.

Haskins, W. A. (1981). Rhetorical vision of equality: An analysis of the southern Black press during reconstruction. *Communication Quarterly, 29*, 116–122.

Heisey, D. R., & Trebing, J. D. (1983). A comparison of the rhetorical visions and strategies of the Shah's white revolution and the Ayatollah's Islamic revolution. *Communication Monographs, 50*, 158–174.

Hensley, C. W. (1975). Rhetorical vision and the persuasion of a historical movement: The disciples of Christ in nineteenth century American culture. *Quarterly Journal of Speech, 61*, 250–264.

Hubbard, R. C. (1985). Relationship styles in popular romance novels, 1950–1983. *Communication Quarterly, 33*, 113–125.

Huxman, S. S. (1996). Mary Wollstonecraft, Margaret Fuller, and Angelina Grimke: Symbolic convergence and a nascent rhetorical vision. *Communication Quarterly, 44*, 16–28.

Hyde, M. J. (1980). Jacques Lacan's psychoanalytic theory of speech and language [Review of the book *Ecrits, a selection and the four fundamental concepts of psycho-analysis*]. *Quarterly Journal of Speech, 66*, 96–108.

Ilka, R. J. (1977). Rhetorical dramatization in the development of American communism. *Quarterly Journal of Speech, 63*, 413–427.

Infante, D. A., Rancer, A. S., & Womack, D. F. (1996). *Building communication theory* (3rd ed.). Prospect Heights, IL: Waveland.

Ivie, R. L. (1987). The complete criticism of political rhetoric. *Quarterly Journal of Speech, 73*, 98–107.

Kapoor, S., Cragan, J., & Groves, J. (1992). Political diversity is alive in TV and newspaper rooms. *Communication Research Reports, 9*, 89–97.

Kauffman, C. (1972). Rhetorical visions of two professional journalists. *Moments in Contemporary Rhetoric and Communication, 2*(2), 28–34.

Kidd, V. V. (1975). Happily ever after and other relationship styles: Advice on interpersonal relations in popular magazines. *Quarterly Journal of Speech, 61*, 31–39.

Kiewe, A., & Houck, D. W. (1989). The rhetoric of Reagonomics: A redemptive vision. *Communication Studies, 40*, 97–108.

King, A. A. (1974). Booker T. Washington and the myth of heroic materialism. *Quarterly Journal of Speech, 60*, 323–327.

Koester, J. (1982). The Machiavellian princess: Rhetorical dramas for women managers. *Communication Quarterly, 30*, 165–172.

Kroll, B. S. (1983). From small group to public view: Mainstreaming the women's movement. *Communication Quarterly, 31*, 139–147.

Kuhn, T. S. (1970). *The structure of scientific revolutions* (2nd ed.). Chicago: University of Chicago.

Larson, C. U. (1998). *Persuasion: Reception and responsibility* (8th ed.). Belmont, CA: Wadsworth.

Lee, S. K. J., & Hoon, T. H. (1993). Rhetorical vision of men and women managers in Singapore. *Human Relations, 46*, 527–542.

Leff, M. C. (1980). Interpretation and the act of rhetorical criticism. *Western Journal of Speech Communication, 44*, 337–349.

Leff, M. C., & Mohrmann, G. P. (1977, November). *Old paths and new: A fable for critics.* Paper presented at the annual meeting of the Speech Communication Association, Washington, DC.

Leff, M. C. & Mohrmann, G. P. (1978, November). *Fantasy theme analysis.* Seminar conducted at the annual meeting of the Speech Communication Association, San Francisco, CA.

Leff, M. C. & Mohrmann, G. P. (1982, April). *Fantasy theme analysis.* Spotlight program presented at the annual meeting of the Central States Communication Association, Milwaukee, WI.

Lesch, C. L. (1994). Observing theory in practice: Sustaining consciousness in a coven. In L. R. Frey (Ed.), *Group communication in context: Studies of natural groups* (pp. 57–82). Hillsdale, NJ: Erlbaum.

Lindlof, T. R. (1982). A fantasy construct of television viewing. *Communication Research, 9*, 67–112.

Littlejohn, S. W. (1999). *Theories of human communication* (6th ed.). Belmont, CA: Wadsworth.

Lucaites, J. L., & Condit, C. M. (1990). Reconstructing <equality>: Culturetypal and countercultural rhetorics in the martyred Black vision. *Communication Monographs, 57*, 5–24.

Matthews, G. (1995). Epideictic rhetoric and baseball: Nurturing community through controversy. *Southern Communication Journal, 60*, 1995.

Mayerle, J. (1987). A dream deferred: The failed fantasy of Norman Lear's *a. k. a. Pablo. Central States Speech Journal, 38*, 223–239.

McFarland, D. D. (1985). Self-images of law professors: Rethinking the schism in legal education. *Journal of Legal Education, 35*, 232–260.

McIllwraith, R. D., & Schallow, J. R. (1983). Adult fantasy life and patterns of media use. *Journal of Communication, 33*, 78–91.

McLuhan, M. (1964). *Understanding media.* New York: McGraw Hill.

Measell, J. S. (1982). [Review of the book *Applied communication research: A dramatistic approach*]. *Communication Education, 31*, 101–102.

Mickey, T. J. (1982). [Review of the book *Applied communication research: A dramatistic approach*]. *Journal of Communication, 32*(1), 226.

Miller, D. L. (1971). Fantasy themes and roles in the small group. *Moments in Contemporary Rhetoric and Communication, 1*(1), 4–8.

Miller, G. R. (1979). The research team concept: An approach to graduate training. *Communication Education, 28*, 322–327.

Monaghan, R. R., Plummer, J. T., Rarick, D. L., & Williams, D. A. (1974). Predicting viewer preference for new TV program concepts. *Journal of Broadcasting, 18*, 131–142.

Mohrmann, G. P. (1980). Elegy in a critical graveyard. *Western Journal of Speech Communication, 44*, 265–274.

Mohrmann, G. P. (1982a). An essay on fantasy theme criticism. *Quarterly Journal of Speech, 68*, 109–132.

Mohrmann, G. P. (1982b). Fantasy theme criticism: A peroration. *Quarterly Journal of Speech, 68*, 306–313.

Nimmo, D., & Combs, J. E. (1982). Fantasies and melodrama in television network news: The case of Three Mile Island. *Western Journal of Speech Communication, 46*, 45–55.

Nimmo, D., & Combs, J. E. (1983). *Mediated political realities.* New York: Longman.

Nimmo, D., & Savage, R. L. (1976). *Candidates and their images: Concepts, methods, and findings.* Pacific Palisades, CA: Goodyear.

Osborn, M. (1986). [Review of the book *The force of fantasy: restoring the American dream*]. *Communication Education, 35*, 204–205.

Poole, M. S. (1990). Do we have any theories of group communication? *Communication Studies, 41*, 237–247.

Poole, M. S., Seibold, D. R., & McPhee, R. D. (1985). Group decision-making as a structurational process. *Quarterly Journal of Speech, 71*, 74–102.

Porter, L. W. (1976). The White House transcripts: Group fantasy events concerning the mass media. *Central States Communication Journal, 27*, 272–279.

Putnam, L. L. (1972). The rhetorical vision and fantasy themes of McGovern campaign planners. *Moments in Contemporary Rhetoric and Communication, 2*(2), 13–20.

Putnam, L. L., Van-Hoeven, S. A., & Bullis, C. A. (1991). The role of rituals and fantasy themes in teachers' bargaining. *Western Journal of Speech Communication, 55*, 85–103.

Rarick, D. L., Duncan, M. B., Lee, D. G., & Porter, L. W. (1977). The Carter *persona*: An empirical analysis of the rhetorical visions of Campaign '76. *Quarterly Journal of Speech, 63*, 258–273.

Reid, L. F. (1983). Apocalypticism and typology: Rhetorical dimensions of a symbolic reality. *Quarterly Journal of Speech, 69*, 229–249.

Ritter, K. (1977). Confrontation as moral drama: The Boston Massacre in rhetorical perspective. *Southern Speech Communication Journal, 42*, 114–136.

Rosenfeld, L. B., & Schrag, R. L. (1985). Empirical validation for the critical construct "humane collectivity." *Central States Speech Journal, 36*, 193–200.

Roth, N. J. (1993). Dismantling the mosaic of misery: Louis Sullivan's paradoxical rhetorical vision. *Howard Journal of Communication, 4*, 234–248.

Rybacki, K., & Rybacki, D. (1991). *Communication criticism: Approaches and genres.* Belmont, CA: Wadsworth.

Schrag, R. L., Hudson, R. A., & Bernado, L. M. (1981). Television's new humane collectivity. *Western Journal of Speech Communication, 45*, 1–12.

Sharf, B. F. (1987a). Sending in the clowns: The image of psychiatry during the Hinckley trial. *Journal of Communication, 36*, 80–93.

Sharf, B. F. (1987b). A response to Vatz and Weinberg. *Journal of Communication, 37*, 169–171.

Shields, D. C. (1974). Firefighters' self-image, projected-image, and public-image. *Fire Command, 41*, 26–28.

Shields, D. C. (1977). *Beyond the bumper sticker: Communication strategies for fire service public relations* (Tech. Rep. No. EP–12, 7/77). St. Louis, MO: University of Missouri, Continuing Education/Extension.

Shields, D. C. (1979). Public fire education planning. In J. W. Laughlin (Ed.), *Public fire education* (pp. 9–34). Stillwater: Oklahoma State University.

Shields, D. C. (1981a). A dramatistic approach to applied communication research: Theory, methods, and applications. In J. F. Cragan & D. C. Shields (Eds.), *Applied communication research: A dramatistic approach* (pp. 5–13). Prospect Heights, IL: Waveland.

Shields, D. C. (1981b). Dramatistic communication-based focus group interviews. In J. F. Cragan & D. C. Shields (Eds.), *Applied communication research: A dramatistic approach* (pp. 313–319). Prospect Heights, IL: Waveland.

Shields, D. C. (1981c). Feed dealer focus group interview on Shell's gestation litter conditioner. In J. F. Cragan & D. C. Shields (Eds.), *Applied communication research: A dramatistic approach* (pp. 335–349). Prospect Heights, IL: Waveland.

Shields, D. C. (1981d). Hog producer focus group interview on Shell's gestation litter conditioner. In J. F. Cragan & D. C. Shields (Eds.), *Applied communication research: A dramatistic approach* (pp. 321–334). Prospect Heights, IL: Waveland.

Shields, D. C. (1981e). Malcolm X's black unity addresses: Espousing middle-class fantasy themes as American as apple-pie. In J. F. Cragan & D. C. Shields (Eds.), *Applied communication research: A dramatistic approach* (pp. 79–91). Prospect Heights, IL: Waveland.

Shields, D. C. (1981f). The St. Paul fire fighters' *dramatis personae*: Concurrent and construct validation for rhetorical vision. In J. F. Cragan & D. C. Shields (Eds.), *Applied communication research: A dramatistic approach* (pp. 235–270). Prospect Heights, IL: Waveland.

Shields, D. C. (1990, June). *Perestroika, glasnost and communication equality in the Soviet Union: Reporting Eastern European democratization in the United States.* Paper presented at the annual conference of the International Communication Association, Dublin, Ireland.

Shields, D. C. (1991). Drug education and the communication curricula. In S. H. Decker, R. B. Rosenfeld, & R. Wright (Eds.), *Drug and alcohol education across the curriculum* (pp. 30–60). Saratoga Springs, CA: R & E.

Shields, D. C. (2000). Symbolic convergence and special communication theories: Sensing and examining dis/enchantment with the theoretical robustness of critical autoethnography. *Communication Monographs, 67,* 392–421.

Shields, D. C., & Cragan, J. F. (1975). Miller's humanistic/scientific dichotomy of speech communication inquiry: A help or a hindrance? *Western Speech Journal, 40,* 278–283.

Shields, D. C., & Cragan, J. F. (1981a). A communication-based political campaign: A theoretical and methodological perspective. In J. F. Cragan & D. C. Shields (Eds.), *Applied communication research: A dramatistic approach* (pp. 177–196). Prospect Heights, IL: Waveland.

Shields, D. C., & Cragan, J. F. (1981b). Media critique of the dramatistic based, computer generated, political speech. In J. F. Cragan & D. C. Shields (Eds.), *Applied communication research: A dramatistic approach* (pp. 197–213). Prospect Heights, IL: Waveland.

Shields, D. C., & Cragan, J. F. (1981c). New technologies for market research: A methodology for ad test segmentation and market segmentation studies. In J. F. Cragan & D. C. Shields (Eds.), *Applied communication research: A dramatistic approach* (pp. 351–356). Prospect Heights, IL: Waveland.

Shields, D. C., & Preston, C. T., Jr. (1985). Fantasy theme analysis in competitive rhetorical criticism. *National Forensic Journal, 3,* 102–115.

Shields, K. J., & Shields, D. C. (1974). Politics 1974: The year of the woman. *Kansas City Woman, 1*(1), 12–13.

Short, B. (1994). "Reconstructed, but unregenerate": *I'll take my stand's* rhetorical vision of progress. *Southern Communication Journal, 59,* 112–124.

Smith, C. A. (1990). *Political communication.* San Diego, CA: Harcourt Brace Jovanovich.

Smith, R. R., & Windes, R. R. (1993). Symbolic convergence and abolitionism: A terministic reinterpretation. *Southern Communication Journal, 59,* 45–59.

Smith, R. R., & Windes, R. R. (1995). The interpretation of abolitionist rhetoric: Historiography, rhetorical method, and history. *Southern Communication Journal, 60,* 303–311.

Solomon, M. (1978). The rhetoric of STOP ERA: Fatalistic reaffirmation. *Southern Speech Communication Journal, 44*, 42–59.

Stano, M. (1972). The 1972 presidential contenders: Visions, dramas, and fantasy themes of radio commentators. *Moments in Contemporary Rhetoric and Communication, 2*(2), 21–27.

Stephenson, W. (1953). *The study of behavior: Q-technique and its methodology.* Chicago: University of Chicago.

Strong, J. (1963). *Our country* (J. Herbst, Ed.). Cambridge, MA: Belknap Press of Harvard University Press. (Original work published 1885)

Swanson, D. L. (1977). A reflective view of the epistemology of critical inquiry. *Communication Monographs, 44*, 201–219.

Turner, K. J. (1977). Comic strips: A rhetorical perspective. *Central States Speech Journal, 28*, 24–35.

Van Tubergen, G. N. (n.d.). *Q-analysis (QUANAL).* Unpublished manuscript, University of Iowa, School of Journalism, Mass Communication Research Bureau, Iowa City.

Van Tubergen, G. N., & Olins, R. A. (1979). Mail vs. personal interview administration for q-sorts: A comparative study. *Operant Subjectivity, 3*, 51–59.

Van Tubergen, G. N., & Olins, R. A. (1982). Reflections on a test for construct validity in some q-typologies. *Operant Subjectivity, 6*, 36–50.

Vasquez, G. (1994). A *Homo narrans* paradigm for public relations: Combining Bormann's symbolic convergence theory and Grunig's situational theory of publics. *Journal of Public Relations, 5*, 201–216.

Watzlawick, P., Beavin, J. H., & Jackson, D. D. (1967). *Pragmatics of human communication: A study of interaction patterns, pathologies, and paradoxes.* New York: Norton.

Zaretsky, D. D. (1977). President Johnson's war on poverty: The rhetoric of three "establishment" movements. *Communication Monographs, 44*, 352–373.

CHAPTER CONTENTS

9 Mental Imagery and Intrapersonal Communication: A Review of Research on Imagined Interactions (IIs) and Current Developments

JAMES M. HONEYCUTT
Louisiana State University

SHERRY G. FORD
University of Alabama-Birmingham

Imagined interactions (IIs) are a type of social cognition and mental imagery grounded in symbolic interactionism in which individuals imagine conversations with significant others for a variety of purposes. The II construct has provided a beneficial mechanism for operationalizing the study of intrapersonal communication. IIs are a type of daydreaming that have definitive characteristics and serves a number of functions including rehearsal, self-understanding, relational maintenance, managing conflict, catharsis, and compensation. For example, the conflict management function explains how conflict is difficult to manage in everyday life such that it is hard to "forgive and forget." Over a decade of research is reviewed in terms of requisite characteristics and functions. Current and future research endeavors are discussed.

A recent college graduate prepares herself for her first job interview. She buys the right suit, reads the right books, conducts the right company research, and prepares herself for the questions that the potential employer may propose. In preparing herself for those questions, she develops a mental picture of the situation, including likely dialogue. She imagines the questions the interviewer may propose while also developing possible answers she may offer. This mental representation of likely interpersonal interaction is the concept that has become known as the imagined interaction, or II.

Correspondence: James M. Honeycutt, Department of Communication Studies, Louisiana State University, Baton Rouge, LA 70803; email: sphone@lsu.edu

Communication Yearbook 25, pp. 315–345

The II described in the previous paragraph would potentially serve to prepare the first-time interviewee for a variety of possible questions, which in turn may help her feel more confident in her preparedness for the interview. She may also achieve a clearer understanding of how she is likely to answer the questions, thus providing her with a better understanding of herself. The types of benefits and characteristics associated with imagined interactions have been identified in past research centering on the construct; this review offers a thorough discussion of that research, which has spanned more than a decade. More specifically, this review examines how IIs developed out of symbolic interactionism and script theory followed by a brief discussion of measurement issues related to IIs. We discuss different types of imagery used in IIs as well as the characteristics and functions associated with IIs. Finally, current and future research developments are discussed.

THEORETICAL FOUNDATION OF IMAGINED INTERACTIONS

Honeycutt, Zagacki, and Edwards (1989) define IIs as a process of social cognition through which individuals imagine themselves in anticipated or recalled interaction with others. They proposed that IIs are actually an extended form of intrapersonal communication, which allows one to talk to oneself and imagine talking to others as well. In the early proposal, IIs were suggested as a means to operationalize the study of intrapersonal communication as it works to shape communication interpersonally.

Imagined interactions were initially discussed by Rosenblatt and Meyer (1986) as a tool used in clinical settings for allowing patients to visualize interaction with others who were not emotionally or physically available to them. IIs were seen as possessing many of the same characteristics as real conversations in that they may be fragmentary, extended, rambling, repetitive, or coherent. They proposed imagined interactions as a means of problem solving by allowing an individual to think through a problem.

IIs are a type of mindful activity as opposed to being mindless (Honeycutt, 1991). Langer, Blank, and Chanowitz (1978) demonstrated how individuals process information mindlessly, not carefully attending to information in their immediate environment. There is an absence of flexible cognitive processing. Mindlessness occurs when the individual relies on old, established ways of thinking and uses script such as saying "Hi" as a greeting ritual. Scripts are overlearned rituals specifying a sequence of behaviors to finish a goal. For example, a person turns left out of his or her division thinking they are going to work, but forget that on this morning they initially must go someplace else and are habituated to turning left. Honeycutt and Cantrill (2001) discuss how scripts are a type of automatic pilot that provide guidelines on how to act when one encounters new situations. Scripts are activated mindlessly.

Mindlessness is a type of perception that is rigid to the extent that individuals rely on previous distinctions (Langer, Chanowitz, & Blank, 1985). On the other hand, mindfulness implies creative thought and attention to information. Mindfulness enables one to make distinctions and create categories. Individuals are likely to be mindful or engaging in thought when encountering novel situations for which no script can be utilized (Langer, 1978). IIs play a role here by envisioning contingency plans for actions in which the confidence that a given plan will be initiated is low.

Honeycutt and his colleagues (1989) discuss how IIs have their theoretical foundation in the work of symbolic interactionists and phenomenologists, including Mead (1934), Dewey (1922), and Schutz (1962). Mead discussed the internalized conversation of gestures in which individual actors are able consciously to monitor social action by reviewing alternative endings of any given act in which they are involved. Individuals use internal dialogues to test out within their minds the various possible scenarios of an event in advance of the act. Mead (1934) indicates that individuals choose a scenario that is most desirable to perform explicitly and think about carrying it into action.

Mead (1934) illustrates, "One separates the significance of what he is saying to the other from the actual speech and gets it ready before saying it. He thinks it out, and perhaps writes it in the form of a book" (p. 118). This sort of precommunicative mental activity, explain Manis and Meltzer (1978), "is a peculiar type of activity that goes on in the experience of the person. The activity is that of the person responding to himself, of indicating things to himself" (p. 21). Mead adds that such activity is essential to the constitution of the self: "That the person should be responding to himself is necessary to the self, and it is this sort of social conduct which provides behavior within which that self appears" (p. 118). What is important about this type of mental activity is that (a) one may consciously take the role of others, imagining how they might respond to one's messages within particular situations, and thus (b) one can test and imagine the consequences of alternative messages prior to communication.

Schutz (1962) describes Dewey's (1922) notion of deliberation as planning activity which precedes action; actors plan by imagining a future instance where an action will have already been accomplished "and reconstruct[ing] the future steps which will have brought forth this future act" (p. 69). For Schutz (1962), deliberation is a rehearsal in imagination of various lines of action. Hence, in their intrapersonal experience, individuals imagine desirable and undesirable future states of events and imagine ways in which to obtain or avoid these states. IIs provide a means by which to plan conversations using visual and verbal imagery.

While discussing cognitive editing, Meyer (1997) describes the process of message formulation, which occurs as an individual activates a message goal, such as a asking for a favor, and recalls appropriate situational schema. The individual may find it necessary to rehearse a message mentally in order to assess its potential impact on relational outcomes prior to actually transmitting the message. This mental rehearsal enables one to detect potential problems prior to message production, an important tool for competent communicators and key to the functioning of imagined interactions.

Honeycutt et al. (1989) discuss how imagined interactions are communication examples of what Abelson (1976) called collections of "vignettes," or representations of events of short duration similar to a panel in a cartoon strip where a visual image is accompanied by a verbal caption. A coherent collection of vignettes forms a script, just as the panels of a cartoon strip form a story. Like the cartoon reader, an individual having an imagined interaction has the luxury of moving back and forth over the panel, even "rewriting" the story if desired. The analogy to cartoon strips is important to understanding imagined interactions. For like these strips, imagined interactions may be visual and verbal. Moreover, communicators may possess, like cartoon characters, much power over the imagined conversation (e.g., topic changes, anticipating the other's response, time-travel, pause, and so on) not afforded real-life communicators (Honeycutt et al., 1989).

Imagined interactions provide information for individuals to use during real encounters. Greene (1984) refers to "procedural records" in terms of the information-production function of cognition. He indicates that cognitive research assumes that cognitive systems have developed to facilitate action and that the functions of cognitive systems are best understood in terms of their implications for behavior. As a type of cognitive information bank, a procedural record specifies communicative actions associated with particular interaction goals. Honeycutt and his associates (1989) proposed that as individuals engage in imagined interactions, procedural records—which inform behavior related to specific situational exigencies—are activated and reconstituted.

Mulling, rumination, planning, and intrusive thoughts are broader than IIs because the thoughts may be nonverbal and do not necessarily involve imagined dialogue. IIs are different from internal monologues and private speech. Internal monologues are self-talk in which an individual talks to him- or herself in both speaking and listening roles. It is speech directed toward the self from the self. Private speech is speech in which an individual speaks aloud to him- or herself. Roloff and Ifert (1998) discuss how private speech may occur in isolation as well as in the presence of others. When enacted in the presence of others, private speech may not elicit a response from an interaction partner because the partner perceives the speech is not directed toward him- or herself.

Honeycutt and his colleagues (1989) clearly articulate the difference between an II and a fantasy. They clarify the difference by stating that IIs simulate communication encounters that a person expects to actually experience or has experienced during his or her interpersonal life. They do note, however, that for various reasons, these "real life" interactions may never occur or may take place in ways quite different from the imagined situation. However, fantasies involve highly improbable or even impossible communicative encounters. For example, imagining oneself chatting with an idolized movie star or professional athlete would be quite unlikely to actually occur, thus would qualify as pure fantasy. These imagined encounters would not, or at least rarely would, serve as the basis for actual communicative exchanges. The researchers suggest that they "are not dismissing the psychological importance of fantasies" but note their irrelevance to the study of imagined interactions as currently defined. Reports support the notion that IIs do not occur with strangers or celebrities but with real-life significant others. Honeycutt et al. (1989) found that college students had most of their IIs with romantic partners (33%), followed by friends (16%), family members (12%), authority figures (9.4%), coworkers (8%), ex-relational partners (6%), and prospective partners (4%).

Measuring Imagined Interactions

From the conception of imagined interactions and their application to communicative encounters, researchers were faced with the same difficulty as other cognitive researchers in that measuring imagined interactions depends largely on inferences based on external behavior (Honeycutt et al., 1989). Measuring mental states is a lofty and difficult task. The study of imagined interactions presents researchers with several important problems. A problem is that, like cognitive researchers in general, investigators of imagined interactions must largely infer the existence of internal cognitive states from external behavior (Ericsson & Simon, 1980). Whereas physiological measures allow researchers to document the occurrence of mental states, they inform us very little about these states beyond the physiological level. Hence, self-reports must be used to measure IIs through survey administration, journal accounts, or interviews (see Honeycutt et al., 1989, for a discussion of these areas).

Using self-reports about cognition requires introspection despite questions over the unreliability of introspective self-reports. Yet, Caughey (1984) mentions an impressive list of social science research that has depended heavily on self-report data, especially in anthropology (Wallace, 1972; Turner & Turner, 1978). Ericsson and Simon (1980) addressed the issue of using self-reports as data and offer guidelines when retrospective verbalization is made. For example, providing contextual information and prompts to participants aids recall from long-term memory. Honeycutt et al. (1992–1993) used a survey instrument called the Survey of Imagined Interactions (SII) to measure imagined interaction characteristics and functions. The SII prompts individuals to think about the concept of imagined interactions following Newell and Simon's (1972) suggestions that questions directed to individuals about the task itself often provide strong indications of the adequacy of verbalized information, especially where there is a large number of alternative responses. The SII contains items on the ease of reporting imagined interactions as well as requesting if they experienced or re-experienced the II as they write samples of them on the survey.

The SII describes IIs as "those mental interactions we have with others who are not physically present" and follows with a description of sample characteristics such as "being ambiguous or detailed and how they may address a number of topics or examine one topic exclusively. The interactions may be one-sided where the person imagining the discussion does most of the talking, or they may be more interactive where both persons take an active part in the conversation" (Honeycutt, 1991). Part 1 of the initial survey consisted of statements about IIs which required responses on a 7-point Likert scale. These items were designed as a means of measuring the frequency and occurrence of imagined interactions, as well as their emotional intensity, content, and degree of specificity (Honeycutt et al., 1989). Part 2 consisted primarily of open-ended response items that asked for a list of topics they recalled in their most recent II, with whom they have most of their IIs, and specific details of the last II they had. They also reported how long ago it took place, with whom, and the location or scene of the imagined encounter. In addition, they were asked to write sample lines of dialogue said by each speaker in their II such as they might find in a play script. Confirmatory factor analysis supported the dimensions of imagined interactions that were originally identified in earlier studies (Honeycutt, Zagacki, & Edwards, 1992–1993). This analysis resulted in a shortened version of the SII that has adequately reflected the II dimensions. The statements were initially derived from Rosenblatt and Meyer's (1986) discussion of IIs with therapists and clients. We also discussed the concept with colleagues, graduate, and undergraduate students enrolled in interpersonal communication courses.

IMAGINED INTERACTIONS AND IMAGERY

Individuals describing their IIs have reported differences in their use of imagery (Honeycutt, 1989). They can make use of verbal or visual imagery exclusively, or there may be a mixing of imagery forms. The specificity index is a gestalt measure of the degree of verbal or visual imagery in the II. Verbal imagery involves imagining the lines of dialogue and is concerned with the content of messages. Visual imagery involves "seeing" the scene of the interaction. For example, many IIs occur in an office or a room in a home (Honeycutt et al., 1989). According to data reported by Zagacki et al. (1992) on the three modes of imagery, few individuals'reported IIs that were primarily of the visual mode. Those reporting a mixed mode also indicated more pleasantness than did those reporting primarily verbal modes (Zagacki et al., 1992). Less pleasantness has been associated with more conflict-related IIs. Hence, IIs associated with conflict tend to involve more verbal imagery. This helps individuals in planning their messages as they use the rehearsal function of IIs, which is discussed in more detail later. According to Zagacki et al.

(1992), individuals experiencing relational conflict rely primarily on the single mode (verbal only) form of imagery. This finding suggests that individuals process conflict versus nonconflict information through different modes of representation. "This leads us to suspect either that the verbal mode entails certain unaccounted for advantages to interpreting conflict information, or that individuals reveal a general mental 'laziness' when it comes to examining conflict information through multi-mode (both verbal and visual) means" (Zagacki et al., 1992, p. 66).

Associated with this idea of imagery mode is the various perspectives which can be taken in the view of the person using mental imagery (Honeycutt, 1989). Some IIs may be viewed from a direct perspective, whereas others may be viewed from an omniscient perspective. The direct perspective allows an individual to see only other interactors, much like actual interaction. An omniscient perspective gives the imaginer the view to see him- or herself along with the other interactors. Indeed, individuals have an imagery consideration dealing with II operation. One can use immediate or reflective modes of operation (Honeycutt, 1989). The immediate mode is the experience of actually having an II; the reflective mode involves the experience of moving out of the immediate mode of the II in order to deliberate over the happenings in the imagined interaction. One can switch between the modes quite readily.

Each of the characteristics and functions of IIs is discussed in full in sections to follow; however, a brief description is included here which lists the II factors as they were measured according to a confirmatory factor analysis (Honeycutt et al, 1992–1993). *Frequency*, also referred to as *activity*, is measured by an index representing how often individuals report having IIs (e.g., "I have imagined interactions all the time"). *Proactivity* is an index measuring how often IIs occur before anticipated encounters (e.g., "Before important meetings, I frequently imagined them"). The index measuring *retroactivity* (e.g., "After I meet someone important, I imagine my conversations with them") assesses the occurrence of IIs after an encounter. The *variety* factor measures topic and partner diversity (e.g., "Most of my imagined interactions are with different people"). *Discrepancy* is an index measuring the incongruity between IIs and actual interaction. (e.g., "More often than not, what the other actually says in a real conversation is different from what I imagined s/he would say"). The index *self-dominance* measures the extent to which an individual reports him- or herself talking in IIs as opposed to the II partner (e.g., "When I have imagined interactions, the other person talks a lot"). The *valence* factor measures the degree of conflict or pleasantness of IIs (e.g., "My imagined interactions are usually quite pleasant"). Finally, *specificity* measures the degree of detail in the II in terms of verbal and visual imagery as opposed to being vague or abstract (e.g., When I have imagined interactions, they tend to be detailed and well-developed"). Table 1 is a summary of II characteristics and their relationship with selected communication variables.

TABLE 1
Summary of II Characteristics and Their Relationship
to Selected Communication Variables

Communication variable	Frequency	Proactivity	Retroactivity	Variety	Discrepancy	Self-dominance	Positive valence	Specificity
Communication competence					−			
Detecting meanings			+					+
Conversational memory			+				−	+
Conversational alternatives				+				+
Perceiving affinity		+						
Interpretation	+							
Conversational dominance			+					
Eavesdropping enjoyment					+			
Loneliness		+		−	+			−
Locus of control			−	+				
Overall conversational sensitivity			+	+				+

NOTE: − (Refers to a negative relationship between the II characteristic and the communication variable).
       + (Refers to a positive association between the II characteristic and the communication variable).

IMAGINED INTERACTIONS AND THEIR CHARACTERISTICS

With a description of the construct's development and its components estab-lished, it is appropriate to take a more detailed look at the various dimensions and functions of IIs. The characteristics of IIs, along with the empirical support for each, will be articulated first. This discussion will be followed by a delineation of each of the functions and the research supporting their existence. The first of the II characteristics to be described will be that of frequency.

Frequency

Frequency is a characteristic of IIs, referring to the frequency and regularity at which IIs occur for an individual. Research assessing the association between the occurrence of IIs and an individual's level of loneliness has revealed a negative relationship between the two variables (Honeycutt, Edwards, & Zagacki, 1989–

1990). In other words, those who are chronically lonely experience fewer imagined interactions. Findings also suggest that those who report higher levels of II activity also report more self-dominance.

Increased use of IIs, or higher frequency, has been found to be associated with decrease in discrepancy for individuals competing in debate tournaments (Gotcher & Honeycutt, 1989). Couples experiencing geographical separation from one another have reported that they experience an increase in the number of IIs when they are separated (Allen, 1994). Honeycutt and Wiemann (1999) found that marital status is related to the use of IIs in that engaged couples report having more imagined interactions compared to married couples. Their IIs were more pleasant and compensated for the lack of real interaction to the extent that the engaged partners were not living together. As revealed in Table 1, frequency is positively associated with conversational interpretation. This is the ability to detect irony or sarcasm in what others say and to paraphrase what others have said (Daly, Vangelisti, & Daughton, 1987).

Proactivity

It is important to note that IIs can have characteristics of being proactive or retroactive. Proactivity refers to those IIs which are engaged in prior to actual interaction, and research has shown that such IIs tend to occur prior to actual interactions rather than after (Zagacki et al., 1992). Research has suggested, for instance, that individuals who measure high in Machiavellianism experience more proactive IIs. Proactivity emerges as an important characteristic in the context competitive debate, showing correlation with imagined success during competition rounds but not with actual success (Gotcher & Honeycutt, 1989). The use of IIs appears to aid competitors in psychologically preparing for actual competition and may serve to create success through self-fulfilling prophecy (Honeycutt & Gotcher, 1991).

Table 1 reveals that proactivity is positively associated with perceiving affinity. Daly and his associates (1987) define this as a communication skill in sensing liking, attraction, or affiliation between communicators. Proactivity is positively correlated with loneliness. Hence, lonely individuals may sometimes anticipate encounters that actually do not occur. This also could reflect compensating for the lack of actual encounters.

Retroactivity

Retroactivity involves reviewing the interaction once it has taken place. For example, a worker may desire a raise, so she decides to approach her boss concerning the matter. Using an II proactively, she may visualize herself going into her boss's office and may even devise a plan for what she will say. Once the real-life interaction has taken place, she may reflect on the interaction, analyzing it to determine what worked and what did not. This is an example of a retroactive II.

While discussing the planning process, Berger (1993) recognized the likelihood that individuals recall previous interaction with others in order to determine if past interactions have or will have bearing on a present goal, calling indirect attention to the importance of retroactive IIs.

Research reveals that conflict is associated with low communication satisfaction with IIs (Zagacki et al.,1992). At first glance this finding may appear inconsequential. However, Zagacki and his colleagues (1992) indicated that the finding "indicates that at least some individuals do not use imagined interactions to think through their conflict toward more satisfactory conclusions by composing alternate message scenarios for future use, but instead review and rehearse the negative dimensions as a total experience" (p. 65).

Retroactive IIs that review and rehearse negative messages reflect rumination. Self-focused rumination is where individuals repetitively dwell on themselves in terms of the cause and outcome of their negative feelings (Lyumbomirsky, Tucker, Caldwell, & Berg, 1999). Rumination results in heightened feelings of depression, hopelessness, and sadness. The more that ruminators dwell on their problems, the less motivation they have to solve problems. Ruminators believe that they lack the strength or resources to effectively solve their problems. Lyumbomirsky et al. (1999) discussed how ruminators may acknowledge that there are ways of solving their problems but lack the energy to do.

Along with the negative thoughts of rumination, Zagacki et al. (1992) found that IIs associated with positive emotions occur less frequently and with lower levels of retroactivity than those with mixed emotions. However, their findings suggested that when pleasant encounters occur, they are taken for granted and not often recalled. Kellermann (1984) makes a similar point by noting, "Even when the actual probabilities for pleasant and unpleasant events are identical, pleasant events have been judged to more likely than unpleasant events" (p. 39).

Zagacki and his associates (1992) suggested a second possibility for why positive emotions occurred less in their II reports. They suggested that individuals avoid reviewing what they perceive to have been pleasant communicative episodes through the use of IIs for fear of finding potentially discrepant information that could possibly lead to an unpleasant state. Apparently, it may be functional for some individuals to think negatively and be surprised at pleasant discrepancies rather than uplifting one's hopes only to be disappointed later by negative information.

Retroactivity is correlated with proactivity ($r = .34$, Honeycutt et al., 1989–1990). Honeycutt (1995) notes how many IIs are linked together to form themes of relationships. Even though a retroactive II is experienced, it may be immediately linked with a proactive II (e.g., "Last time, I bit my lip. Next time, I see him/her, I am going to say exactly how I feel."). Given that IIs tend to occur with significant others, it may be that many of them are linked and occur between encounters reviewing and previewing conversations.

Honeycutt (1999) examined the themes of marriages based on Gottman's (1994) oral history interview. Couples are asked to recall periods of happy times and hard times in the marriage as well as to how different their marriage currently is compared to when they first got married. They are asked about their beliefs about what makes a marriage work. Honeycutt (1999) used Fitzpatrick's (1988) classification of marital types to examine individual differences in themes of relationships and their association with retroactive IIs.

Traditionals are interdependent with a high degree of sharing and have little personal space. They maintain physical and psychological closeness. They share conventional ideological beliefs with an emphasis on stability over spontaneity. Traditionals often talk through conflict but avoid issues that are unimportant, yet report an expressive communication style. Independents display medium interdependence, enjoy novelty, change, and uncertainty. They confront and will argue about matters no matter how trivial they may seem. Independents use aversive remarks (e.g., criticizing partner, denying responsibility, use of hostile jokes or sarcasm). Independents are psychologically close, but maintain separate physical spaces with more room to move around (Fitzpatrick, 1988). They also report an expressive communication style similar to the Traditionals.

Separates emphasize autonomy and are nonexpressive. They do not share a sense of togetherness. They are physically and psychologically differentiated. Separates endorse some traditional beliefs. They are conventional in marital issues but at the same time support the values of individual freedom upheld by Independents (Fitzpatrick, 1988). Separates may hold one value in a public setting while believing another value privately. They are not very interdependent and report little expressiveness in their communication. They are emotionally withdrawn and have different physical spaces. According to Fitzpatrick (1988), Separates seek emotional support outside the relationship and experience little direct conflict in their marriage. A fourth type of marriage that Fitzpatrick (1988) discusses is the mixed types in which each partner endorses different philosophies about marriage.

Honeycutt (1999) found that both husbands' and wives' marital happiness was predicted by pleasant IIs. However, an intriguing profile of the Separates emerged. Their oral histories revealed fewer themes of "we-ness" in which "we" or "our" signifies bonding. Other spouses use "I," "you," or "my" as a means of communicating differences from the partner (Knapp & Vangelisti, 1996). Separates' IIs were less pleasant than Traditionals and Independents.

Gottman (1994) speculates that Separates live with the pain of unsolved, solvable problems. He discusses how negative emotions are frightening for Separates and that Separates lack the communication skills to work out unavoidable conflict. If this is the case, then conflict may be kept alive in the minds of Separates through retroactive and proactive IIs as partners may imagine what might be said in future arguments (Honeycutt, 1995).

As revealed in Table 1, retroactivity is associated with a number of communication variables. It is positively correlated with detecting meanings, which is the tendency to sense the purposes and the hidden meanings in what individuals are saying in conversations (Honeycutt et al., 1992). It is associated with memory about conversations as individuals report a high level of recall for prior conversations. It is related to conversational dominance, a skill about determining who has power and control within conversations (Daly et al., 1987).

Variety

Variety refers to the diversity of topics and partners within IIs. Variety has been shown to be moderately correlated with II proactivity and retroactivity (Honeycutt et al., 1989–1990). IIs that involve various individual and different topics are related to the imaginer's internal locus of control as well, and this finding lends credence to the idea that the chronically lonely lack variety in their IIs. Research suggests that IIs involve a wide variety of topics including conflict, dating, activities, school, family/home, and include various partners such as family members, dating partners, friends, and roommates (Edwards et al., 1988).

As revealed in Table 1, variety is positively associated with conversational alternatives. This refers to a flexibility in talking and being skilled at wording the same thought in a number of ways. Variety is negatively associated with loneliness but positively associated with an internal locus of control and overall conversational sensitivity.

Discrepancy

Sometimes actual conversations proceed very smoothly in accordance with what what was previously imagined. Yet, they also may be very discrepant from what was envisioned (Honeycutt, 1991; Honeycutt et al., 1992). IIs can be similar to or different from relevant interaction. Discrepancy is the II characteristic that provides for the incongruity between IIs and the actual interaction they address. Research suggests that individuals who are chronically lonely have highly discrepant IIs, which researchers suggest serves to perpetuate their lonely state (Edwards et al., 1988). Lonely people have limited prior interactions upon which to base their IIs, so imagined interactions they experience prior to new interaction are likely to be high in discrepancy. Discrepancy also is reported to be negatively correlated with communication competence (Honeycutt et al., 1992).

Research has also looked at the role of IIs used by individuals preparing for forensics competition, which includes competitive debate. Gotcher and Honeycutt's (1989) findings indicate that higher frequency of IIs decreases discrepancy, alluding to the increased ability to construct an imagined situation that closely mirrors reality through the use of IIs (Honeycutt & Gotcher, 1991). This finding, the researchers note, seems to relate to the self-fulfilling prophecy.

IIs are also recognized as significant to the planning process (Allen & Honeycutt, 1997). In their study, Allen and Honeycutt (1997) conducted an experiment developed to investigate the effects of independent variables, including planning task and discrepant IIs, on a dependent variable of anxiety as operationalized through the use of object adaptors. The participants completed the SII and then participated in the experimental part of the study, which was videotaped. In this portion of the study, participants were asked to devise a plan for convincing a friend with a drinking problem to seek help. One group of the participants was placed in a distractor-task condition for the purpose of minimizing message planning time. The other group was given time solely to rehearse its plan for convincing a friend to seek help. Both groups then engaged in the role-playing activity with a "friend." These role-playing tasks were videotaped and assessed for frequency of object adaptor use by participants. Findings emerged that suggest those experiencing high levels of discrepancy between their plan and the actual encounter more frequently used object adapters than did those reporting low discrepancy.

Other research has examined the association between discrepancy and attachment styles. Low discrepancy is associated with a secure attachment style. According to attachment theory, individuals develop internal schemata of self and others that persist throughout life (Bowlby, 1982). Those with secure attachments believe that others will be loving and responsive. Love is experienced as happy, friendly, and trusting. Secure attachment types emphasize the importance of openness and closeness, while seeking to retain individual identity (Feeney & Noller, 1991).

Conversely, the anxious/ambivalent attachment type is characterized by obsession, jealousy, having emotional extremes, having an intense sexual attraction for another, and desiring a strong bond (Ainsworth, Blehar, Waters, & Wall, 1978).

The anxious/ambivalent attachment type is preoccupied with having close relationships and has a dominating style of resolving conflict as opposed to compromising (Ainsworth, 1989). Those with anxious attachments have high discrepancy in their IIs with their relational partners. It is possible that anxiety evolves after a series of discrepant encounters (Honeycutt, 1998–1999). Anxious/ambivalents also report more loneliness than the other attachment types (Hazan & Shaver, 1987). As noted above, Edwards et al. (1988) found that loneliness is associated with IIs that are discrepant. Those who report an anxious attachment style experience higher levels of discrepancy in their IIs.

The relationship between the mode of imagery and its affects on discrepancy has been explored. Zagacki et al. (1992) note that verbally based IIs are usually less similar to the actual communication they represent. Additionally, IIs involving conflict are likely more verbal. Thus, taking a syllogistic approach to the findings reported by Zagacki et al. (1992), if conflictual IIs are more verbal, and verbally based IIs are usually discrepant, then conflictual IIs are more discrepant, thus distort reality.

Table 1 shows that discrepancy is negatively associated with communication competence and positively associated with loneliness. In addition, it is correlated with eavesdropping enjoyment, which is the extent to which individuals enjoy listening to conversations.

Self-Dominance

Imagined interactions also include the characteristic of self-dominance. This addresses who is more prominent in the II, self or other. Early research suggested that self-dominance in the II was associated with having less pleasant IIs (Honeycutt et al., (1989–1990). Research also suggests that a person engaging in IIs concerned with matters of conflict will likely find the self being more dominant than the II partner. Typically, we see ourselves doing more of the talking while the other interactor says less and is in more of a listening role (Edwards et al., 1988). Analysis of II protocols reveals more words and lines of dialogue by the self contrasted with the other says. In addition, the self tends to start the conversation in the II (Zagacki et al., 1992). Again, the rehearsal function of IIs is an important consideration here. Recall that verbal imagery is associated with having conflictual IIs (Zagacki et al., 1992). The rehearsal function of IIs reflects self-dominance as attention is concentrated on one's messages.

Valence

A second II characteristic is the degree of emotional affect produced while having an II and is referred to as valence in terms of pleasantness. Honeycutt, Edwards, and Zagacki (1989–1990) report that females indicate having more pleasant IIs. Those experiencing less pleasantness in their IIs report higher levels of self-dominance. Additionally, research suggests that more pleasant IIs elicit positive affect, whereas those that are less pleasant often involve conflict eliciting negative affect. And though it may be contrary to what is assumed, II pleasantness negatively predicts memory (Honeycutt et al., 1992–1993). That is, the more pleasant the II, the less memory an individual has of it. Thus, it follows that individuals have a better memory for IIs that involve less pleasantness. "This finding suggests that recalling past conflictual or unpleasant interactions is a means by which memory about conversations operates so that when a person is remembering an interaction, he or she may be going back and replaying a previous encounter that was unpleasant" (Honeycutt et al., 1992, p. 154). Perhaps this explains why negative information, or IIs, may be recalled more readily and have higher informational value than positive information, or IIs.

Imagined interactions share a relation to the personality characteristic of Machiavellianism (Allen, 1990). Machiavellianism is a reflection of the degree to which an individual believes that other individuals are manipulatable in interpersonal situations, the degree to which an individual is willing to manipulate others in interpersonal situations, and an individuals' skill or ability is manipulated. The research suggests that those measuring high in Machiavellianism are more likely to report IIs that are less pleasant than those low in Machiavellianism.

Also associated with II pleasantness is mode of imagery (Zagacki et al., 1992). Less pleasant IIs concern conflict and are usually more verbal, as opposed to visual, in nature. As revealed in Table 1, positive valence impedes one's ability to remember conversations. Thus, individuals may be more likely to recall arguments rather than positive encounters. There is research on initial impressions and the negativity effect in which negative impressions are remembered more than positive ones. For example, negative adjectives are recalled more in impression formation than positive adjectives (Feldman, 1966). Kellermann (1984) reviews research indicating the pervasiveness of the negativity effect in employment interviews, evaluations of the police, government agencies, and political candidates. Negative information is more important than positive information in rendering impressions.

When we have retroactive IIs, we often reconstruct negative messages and themes of conversations in light of preinteraction expectations about speakers. We often recall prior actual conversations through retroactive IIs. For example, the perceived status of a speaker affects conversational recall. Individuals recall remarks by high status speakers as being more assertive as opposed to recalling remarks from equal status speakers (Holtgraves, Srull, & Socall, 1989).

In terms of conversational memory, recall is poor even after only 5 minutes with individuals recalling no more than 10% of their conversations in terms of what was said (Stafford, Burggraf, & Sharkey, 1987; Stafford & Daly, 1984). Furthermore, only 4% is remembered within a week after the conversation occurred (Stafford, Waldron, & Infield, 1989). Themes of conversations are more accurately recalled as opposed to literal lines of dialogue (Stafford & Daly, 1984; Stafford et al., 1987, 1989). Negative remarks are more likely to be remembered including sarcasm, wittiness, and criticism (Kellermann, 1995; Kemper & Thissen, 1981).

Specificity

A final II characteristic is specificity, which refers to the level of detail and distinction of images contained within IIs. Honeycutt (1998–1999) found that those individuals reporting a secure attachment style experience high levels of detailed visual and verbal imagery, suggesting high levels of specificity. This level of specificity aids in greater recall of the IIs. Honeycutt, Zagacki, and Edwards (1992) conducted a study for the purpose of assessing the use of IIs and the correlation with communication competence as well as conversational sensitivity. Their results suggest that the level of detail in IIs, or specificity, positively predicts several dimensions of conversational sensitivity including the ability to detect meanings in another's messages, conversational memory, and conversational alternatives (see Table 1).

Summary

There are eight characteristics of IIs. Frequency simply represents individual differences in how individuals experience them. Proactivity and retroactivity are concerned with the timing of the II in relation to actual conversations. Proactive IIs occur before an anticipated encounter whereas retroactive IIs occur after the encounter. Proactive and retroactive IIs can occur simultaneously as individuals replay prior conversations in their minds while preparing for ensuing interactions.

Discrepant IIs occur when what was imagined is different from what happens in actual conversations. IIs are used for message planning. Hence, most of the imagined talk comes from the self with less emphasis being placed on what the interaction partner says. This reflects the self-dominance characteristic. The variety characteristic of IIs reflects individual differences in the number of topics that are discussed in the IIs and whom they are with. IIs tend to occur with significant others such as relational partners, family, and friends. They do not occur with people we rarely see. Finally, IIs vary in their specificity or how vague the imagined lines of dialogue are as well as the setting where the imaginary encounter occurs.

IMAGINED INTERACTIONS AND THEIR FUNCTIONS

Although several II characteristics are identified, there are also several functions that research suggests are connected with their use. More specifically, imagined interactions function in the following ways: (a) they keep a relationship alive, (b) they maintain conflict as well as resolving it, (c) they are used to rehearse messages for future interaction, (d) they aid people in self-understanding through clarifying thoughts and feelings, (e) they provide emotional catharsis by relieving tension, and (f) they compensate for lack of real interaction (Honeycutt, 1991, 1995). The following sections review research resulting in the designation of these II functions, beginning with the relationship maintenance function.

Relational Maintenance

In terms of keeping relationships alive, earlier studies of imagined interactions sought to uncover their role in impacting interpersonal communication. Honeycutt, Zagacki, and Edwards (1989) suggested that often the most important determinants of relational development occur outside of immediate conversation in the cognitive realm that includes imagined interactions. Individuals report having IIs that involve relational partners such as romantic partners, friends, family members, individuals in authority, people from work, ex-relational partners, and prospective partners (Honeycutt et al., 1989). As the data suggest, IIs are predominated by thoughts of significant others rather than with strangers or acquaintances.

Duck (1980) has suggested that explorations of relational communication should involve interpersonal research that looks at interpersonal relationships as they evolve outside of direct relational encounters in terms of processes such as replaying relational events during time spent alone, planning future encounters, and remembering the pleasures of encounters. The study of imagined interactions has provided for a means of investigating such phenomena (Honeycutt, 1989). "IIs can psychologically maintain relationships by concentrating thought on relational scenes and partners" (Honeycutt, 1995, p. 143).

Research demonstrates that geographically separated couples use IIs as a means of maintaining their relationships (Allen, 1994). Suggesting that IIs establish relational significance and serve specific purposes for anticipated relational encounters, Allen designed a study to explore II usage in relieving tension caused by separation. Sampling 40 couples, half of whom were in geographically separated relationships, Allen used a revised version of the SII to make her assessments. Indications are that couples who are geographically separated experience increases in the number of IIs during times of separation and view their use as a coping strategy. This would seem to suggest that IIs are tools allowing individuals to continue their relationships when circumstances prevent actual interaction. The study's findings also suggest that relational couples geographically separated experience increased understanding as a result of their II usage, as well as greater use of IIs for rehearsal. Together these findings imply that IIs can and do serve a significant role in perpetuating relationships. Whereas imagined interactions may create a relationship, they also shape it as it goes through certain stages of development. Individuals have expectations about what is likely to happen in different types of relationships based on memory and experience.

Honeycutt and Cantrill (2001) discuss how relationship memory structures are hierarchically ordered on the basis of recall of particular scenes (e.g., meeting an individual for the first time at a specific place) and scripts for behavior embedded within various scenes. People's complex personal memories (scripts) create the bias people read into one another's signals. When partners interact, they often think about what they are going to say in the form of IIs, mentally processing what has been said, sorting through their experiences to compare and contrast new information with their experience (Honeycutt & Cantrill, 2001). As relationships develop, people create not only their views of themselves, but their views of their partner and the ways in which they think about themselves in relation to the other person. As new observations of relationships are made, they are assimilated into the expectations and revisited in the form of IIs. These IIs may serve to keep an existing relationship intact, or maybe to rehearse for the initiation of a new one. In these terms, IIs enable the process of thinking about a relationship, even through its various developmental phases.

The memory structure approach assumes that individuals have particular expectations some of which are more mindful than others in terms of what should happen in the progression of a relationship that can be used as an anchor prototype for categorizing the type of relationship observed between others as well as one's own relationships (Honeycutt & Cantrill, 2001). Relationship expectations may be reinforced as observed behavior is assimilated into existing categories (e.g., self-disclosure). Occasionally, accommodation takes place in which the expectancies are modified to account for new observed behavior. For example, a "faithful partner" loses trustworthiness after being discovered for infidelity. Regardless if assimilation or accommodation takes place, the person may play over in their mind images of conversations with their relational partner. These IIs may relive previ- ous encounters and link these to anticipated conversations. The IIs may serve a function of keeping relationships intact, rehearsing for the ending of relationships as well as the initiation of relationships, such as planning to ask someone for a date (Berger & Bell, 1988). The function of imagined interaction in keeping conflict alive as well as resolving it in personal relationships is discussed in the next section.

Conflict Management

Keeping the relationship alive has a downside in that conflict within a relation- ship can also be kept alive. In his discussion of the "retroactivity" and "proactivity" characteristics of IIs, Honeycutt (1991) notes that IIs may occur before or after actual encounters, with these characteristics not necessarily being mutually exclu- sive. Thus, he indicates that some IIs may have simultaneous features, meaning they occur after an encounter and prior to the next. This idea suggests that IIs can link one interpersonal episode, including conflict, to the next. Research in various areas has served to support this idea of IIs linking interactional episodes.

IIs can also be used to manage conflict. Empathy, apology, and rumination are associated with forgiving (McCullough et al., 1998). Yet, as noted earlier, follow- ing a stressful event many individuals ruminate about the event, which increases psychological distress. Humor is an effective way to diffuse some conflict. Honeycutt and Brown (1998) examined the retroactive and proactive roles of IIs in marriage in terms of rehearsing jokes. While having a proactive II, a spouse may rehearse a joke before telling it to their partner. The couple then interacts, at which time the joke is shared. The joke-teller may experience retroactive IIs for the purpose of reviewing the positive or negative responses of their partner. "This retroactive II may lead the person to further rehearse the joke hoping to improve delivery, decide to never try the joke again, or think of another person that may appreciate the joke" (Honeycutt & Brown, 1998, p. 4). Thus, the spouse can re- hearse or replay a past joke-telling interaction mentally for the purpose of becom- ing better prepared for the next interaction that may involve the telling of the joke.

In his article addressing the oral history interview as a means of studying mari- tal couples and their use of imagined interactions, Honeycutt (1995b) recounts discussion of questions concerning IIs and conflict that took place during the inter- view. Memories of conflict, reexperienced as retroactive IIs, are acknowledged by couples as keeping conflict alive. However, some couples reported that the IIs serve as a mechanism for dealing with suppressed conflict that is not being dis- cussed openly. Honeycutt (1995b, 1999) reports that using the oral history inter- view in the study of marital couples reveals that spouses often tell of imagining conversations with their partner concerning a number of topics when not in the other's presence. The oral history interview is a semistructured narrative that al- lows married couples to reconstruct events from the relationship's past. The inter- view includes discussion of how the couple met, what attracted them to one an- other, philosophy of marriage, problems in the marriage, and the like. Spouses' imagined conversations include the issue of conflict, where one may replay an encounter involving conflict and regret not having said various things currently in one's mind. This replaying involves the use of retroactive IIs, or reviewing past interaction, as well as proactive IIs, used to rehearse for the next encounter with the spouse, such that the conflict picks up where it was left. Honeycutt (1995b) indicates that when discussing this notion during the oral history interview, "couples eagerly relate to the concept and provide examples of imagining conflict in their minds with their partner over some issue" (p. 66).

As previously mentioned, the "retroactivity" and "proactivity" features of imagined interaction can work simultaneously to link one interaction to the next with a specific interactional other (Honeycutt, 1991). Thus, if person X and person Y experience conflictual interaction which is characterized by conflict, person X may reflect on the conflict making use of imagined interaction's dimension of retroactivity. Person X may re-experience the negative affect associated with the original conflict and use this reflection as a means of envisioning exactly what will be said to person Y during the next interaction between the two individuals. It is possible that the retroactive II that occurs as a product of the initial conflict acts as a preinteraction stimulus for the next encounter with that partner (Honeycutt, 1995).

Klos and Singer (1981) induced IIs in adolescents as a means of eliciting emotions about parental conflict. They examined the effects of resolved versus unresolved situations with parents, mutual nonconflictual parental interaction versus mutual conflictual interaction, and simulated coercive parental interaction versus simulated collaborative parental interaction. Proposing that exposure through simulated interaction to these conditions would later affect recurrence of simulation-relevant thoughts, the researchers had individuals participate in one of six conditions: (a) collaborative decision-making with parent, resolved; (b) collaborative decision-making with parent, unresolved; (c) collaborative confrontation with parent, resolved; (d) collaborative confrontation with parent, unresolved; (e) coercive confrontation with parent, resolved; (f) coercive confrontation with parent, unresolved. The participants engaged in simulated interactions with a parent while they were read a predeveloped parental script for the appropriate situation. The participants were asked to think about the last visit with the same-sex parent that was three days or longer in duration.

The operationalization for each of the conditions was as follows: *coercive confrontation* involved a parent's trying to win an argument without listening to the subject's viewpoint, whereas *collaborative confrontation* involved a parent's expressing her or his viewpoint while trying to understand the subject's viewpoint. *Collaborative decision-making* involved a parent and subject working together to find a solution to a shared interpersonal problem external to the relationship. *Resolution/nonresolution* focused on whether or not subjects were able to reach a solution at the end of three imagined interactions.

After the IIs, subjects were taken to a separate room and given a 20-minute period in which thought samples were elicited by sounding a buzzer at 20 random intervals. At each interval, subjects were to report their thoughts, feelings, and mental images. Thoughts were coded as "simulation-related" if they were directly relevant to the simulation conditions. Affect was measured before and after the simulations using 5-point Likert that reflected interest, anger, distress, joy, disgust, and contempt. Stress with parents was also measured by items which assessed the level of interpersonal conflict and need satisfaction including acceptance, recognition, and support.

Anger was higher in the coercive, as opposed to collaborative, conditions. Once exposed to a simulated parental conflict, students with a history of stress with parents reported as much as 50% of their later thoughts concerning the simulations. Klos and Singer (1981) concluded that a reawakening of unpleasant past experiences is enough to sustain arousal and recurrent thought even if the conflict is resolved. Their research appears to lend credence to Honeycutt's (1995) idea that conflict is kept alive and managed through proactive and retroactive IIs. The thoughts of adolescents who have a history of parental stress could be so unpleasant as a result of environmental cues, such as television plots and films, that recurrent thoughts of conflict are provoked. Whether an episode is resolved or unresolved depends on the particular scripts that are evoked by the situation and their reconstitution in the given scenario. That is to say, resolution is contingent upon the retroactive IIs that are recalled and the ways in which they are transformed through the use of proactive IIs. Long-standing child-parent conflict may be kept alive and maintained as a result. As Honeycutt (1995) noted, "Given that IIs tend to occur with significant others, it may be that many of them are linked and occur between encounters reviewing and previewing conversations" (p. 142).

Although such linking occurs in both positive (e.g., relationship maintenance for geographically separated couples) and negative (e.g., conflict maintenance) situations, research may suggest that the more common occurrence is that involving conflict. Zagacki et al. (1992) discovered that the most common case of reported IIs involve conflict. In an attempt to assess the role of emotion and mental imagery on the use of IIs, respondents were asked to complete the Survey of Imagined Interactions. Participants were to describe the topics they discussed in their imagined interactions. The following topics were coded: conflicts/problems, dating, school/class, work/job, activities, family, money, friends, ex-partners, small-talk, and miscellaneous. The topic most reported involved conflict, with those of dating, family, and friends following. With such a high occurrence of IIs involving conflict, it seems that much cognitive effort and time is invested in dealing with such topics. For example, Caprara (1986) and Collins and Bell (1997) report that aggression follows insult and threats to self-esteem. Ruminating over these intrusive thoughts maintains distress concerning the insult. Furthermore, some individuals have a desire to seek revenge against offenders even though base rates of seeking revenge are low. Approximately 8% of the U.S. population indicate that they seek revenge against an offender (Gorsuch & Hao, 1993). Yet, this figure may be too low because half of all interpersonal delinquency (e.g., fighting at school or work) is motivated by revenge and anger (Pfefferbaum & Wood, 1994).

A study conducted by Johnson and Roloff (1998) assessed factors contributing to the problem of serial arguing in relationships and its effects on relationship quality. Looking at the factors influencing perceptions of resolvability of a given conflict, researchers found that perceived resolvability is negatively associated with the following items: (a) arguments arising from violated expectations, (b) counter-complaining and partner initiated demand-withdrawal, (c) predictability of argumentative episodes, (d) overall discord, (e) withdrawal after a conflict episode, and (f) mulling over the argument. The relevant factor from this study in relation to conflict-linkage is the last item—mulling. Mulling, which includes mentally reliving the argument over and over, seems to be related to the use of retroactive IIs, allowing an individual to revisit an episode once it has taken place. The revisiting of conflict may be accompanied by the reformulation of points and counterpoints for future interaction (Honeycutt, 1991, 1995). Thus, IIs can help link unresolved, or serial, conflict episodes together.

Whether an individual's emotional state is causally linked to her or his II experiences or whether a person's imagined interactions affect her or his emotional state is a question that may necessitate further investigation. However, research does suggest that the nature of IIs is a function of the communicator's situational experiences (Zagacki et al., 1992). If a person is currently not experiencing stressful activities or relationships, imagined interactions are likely to involve mixed imagery, which have been shown to be more pleasant. A person experiencing stress may engage in IIs that are less pleasant, thus more likely to involve certain levels of conflict. This suggests that stress may induce conflict-laden IIs.

Current II research is examining how everyday conflict is kept alive and managed in our minds through reliving old arguments as we are exposed to environmental cues such as music that may remind us of unresolved conflict (Honeycutt & Eidenmuller, 2000). In addition, listening to certain songs may remind someone of an old flame. When this occurs, people may have a retroactive II in which they replay old conversations in their mind that mentally takes them back to a certain time or place. Smeijsters (1995) reports that 41% of individuals indicated that music reminds them of things from the past and that they used music to vent frustration.

Rehearsal

A large body of research has grown out of the study of strategic communication, especially in terms of the planning process (for a thorough discussion, see Berger, 1997). This line of research acknowledges the vital role communication plays in converting plans to action. Berger (1997) notes that when individuals engage in the planning process by themselves, they likely engage in internal dialogue as a means of testing out several alternatives before enactment. In essence, the individual can rehearse the plan(s) mentally prior to activation (Berger, 1995).

Research has directly linked imagined interactions and the planning process, providing empirical evidence for the rehearsal function of IIs. Proactive IIs are a means by which to plan anticipated encounters. Wilensky (1983) discusses how "planning includes assessing a situation, deciding what goals to pursue, creating plans to secure these goals, and executing plans" (p. 5). Plans are broaders than IIs since rehearsal is just one function. Plans may be nonverbal in the pursuit of actions or goals (e.g., realizing it's your anniversary coming up and buying a gift that does not involve any communication). When used for rehearsal, IIs allow for a decrease in the number of silent pauses and shorter speech onset latencies during actual encounters (Allen & Edwards, 1991a), and allow for an increase in message strategy variety (Allen & Edwards, 1991b). Individuals also report a decrease in the use of object adaptors when allowed to rehearse a message prior to real-life interaction as opposed to being distracted from rehearsal (Allen & Honeycutt, 1997).

Two studies suggest that IIs can be used strategically for rehearsing anticipated encounters and for relieving stress in such settings as forensics competition (Gotcher & Honeycutt, 1989; Honeycutt & Gotcher, 1991). Participants involved in forensics competition must be aware of the communication environment and in control of the messages they convey. The nature of such competition is that those most adept at such message conveyance receive the highest rewards (Honeycutt & Gotcher, 1991). Competitors who were surveyed reported using IIs for rehearsal to prepare arguments and counter-arguments in debates (Gotcher & Honeycutt, 1989). This suggests that IIs can be used to practice various messages when several possibilities exist for playing out of the interaction (Honeycutt & Gotcher, 1991).

Studying the use of IIs by student protesters who were present at the Tian-an-men Square demonstrations in Beijing, China, Petress (1990) found that student-protesters reported using IIs for various purposes including (a) rehearsing and preparing messages in the case they were taken in for interrogation by the authorities, (b) the rehearsal of conversations with family members and friends enabling the student to remain calm during the riots, and (c) reflecting on actual experiences and interactions endured after the riots were stopped.

Petress (1995) also explored the use of IIs by Chinese foreign exchange students preparing to study abroad in the United States. Oral interview results indicate that students used IIs for rehearsal purposes. They reported using IIs for the purpose of rehearsing meetings and interviews with local officials and foreign advisers who would portentially provide help during the process of securing admission to a U.S. university. Geographically separated couples (GSCs) also make particular use of IIs for the purpose of rehearsing future interactions (Allen, 1994). In comparison to couples who are not geographically separated, GSCs report greater use of imagined interactions for the purpose of preparing for the next interaction with their partners. Such a result seems to suggest that GSCs emphasize an efficiency meta-goal that is in operation during times of separation.

Finally, rehearsal has been analyzed in relation to attachment styles. Regression analysis revealed that a secure attachment is predicted by rehearsal as compared to other attachment types (Honeycutt, 1998–1999). Perhaps strategic planning for various encounters may enhance security in romantic relationships. This use of IIs seems also to be linked to cognitive editing, which allows adjustments to messages after their potential effects on a given relationship have been assessed (Meyer, 1997). The implication here is that individuals rehearse messages, presumably through the use of IIs, and make changes as necessary for achieving desired outcomes.

Developing Self-Understanding

Rosenblatt and Meyer's (1986) original conception of imagined interaction for use in therapy recognized that imagining interaction that involves explaining ideas or relating information to another person aids in the clarification of the self. Imagined interactions may help to uncover opposing or differing aspects of the self. Zagacki and his associates (1992) indicated that those IIs involving conflict increase understanding of the self. Self-understanding involves more verbal imagery with the self playing a greater role in the II, or being more dominant.

Imagined interactions' role in bettering self-understanding was also revealed in research assessing the use of IIs by couples who were experiencing geographical separation. Geographically separated couples (GSCs) suggest they do experience IIs as a means for increasing self-understanding more than do couples who are not geographically separated (Allen, 1994). The results suggest that GSCs have a greater need to develop better understanding prior to interaction because of the limit on interaction time due to their geographic circumstances. The use of IIs helps to create a better understanding of the partner as well as the self. Allen (1994) suggests that GSCs may also use IIs to discuss certain issues with the relational partner so as not to be forced to deal with a given issue that may be deemed unimportant during precious and limited interaction time.

Catharsis

Imagined interactions have been recognized for their ability to relieve tension and reduce uncertainty about another's actions (Honeycutt, 1989). Rosenblatt and Meyer (1986) proposed IIs as a means of emotional catharsis in counseling sessions having found that IIs served as an outlet for their patients to release unresolved tension. Patients had noted feeling less relational tension after having experienced IIs.

Allen and Berkos (1998) note that individuals use IIs as a means of "getting things off their chest" when they know that certain behaviors or the expression of certain emotions is inappropriate in actual interactions. The use of IIs is also associated with a reduction in anxiety level (Allen & Honeycutt, 1997). When planning for an interaction, making use of IIs results in a lower occurrence of object adaptors. This seems to suggest that when one uses IIs, one experiences anxiety relief, perhaps experiencing a release of certain emotions in the form of catharsis. Honeycutt (1991) provides numerous accounts of individuals reporting how their IIs made them feel better and release anxiety.

Compensation

Another function of IIs is that they can serve to compensate for the lack of interaction. From their initial development, IIs have been purported to serve in the place of real interaction when it is not possible to actually communicate with a given individual (Rosenblatt & Meyer, 1986). In their discussion of IIs used for therapeutic purposes, Rosenblatt and Meyer (1986) indicate that an individual may choose to use IIs in place of actually confronting a loved one in fear that the loved one would be hurt by the message.

Honeycutt (1989b) discusses the use of IIs as a means of compensation by the elderly who may not see their loved ones as often as they would like. For example, residents in retirement centers imagine talking with children as well imagine talking with friends who live at the center. Research focusing on geographically separated individuals and their increased use of IIs during separation for the purposes of coping provides additional support for the notion that IIs are used in the place of real interaction (Allen, 1994).

Summary

To summarize, there are six functions of IIs. IIs serve to maintain relationships as intrusive thinking occurs in which the partner is thought about outside of his or her physical presence. IIs are used to manage conflict. Individuals relive old arguments while imagining statements for ensuing encounters. Hence, the argument may pick up where it left off from a prior interaction. A major function of IIs is rehearsing and planning messages. Individuals report how they prepare for important encounters and even think of various messages depending on the response of the interaction partner. IIs allow people to clarify their own thoughts and promote understanding of their own views. The catharsis function allows people to release feelings and vent feelings of frustration or joy. Finally, IIs may be used to compensate for the lack of actual conversations. These functions are not independent of each other. Some of them may occur simultaneously. For example, compensating for the lack of real interaction in a long-distance relationship may be used to keep the relationship alive as well as rehearsing what will be said at the next telephone conversation.

CURRENT AND FUTURE RESEARCH DEVELOPMENT

Using research supporting the idea that IIs link interaction, such as with studies of joke-telling and interview preparation, Honeycutt (1991) began discussing the idea of taking that concept a step further. In that study, he describes an argument with one's relational partner in which "X may recreate in his/her mind what was said while being in the immediate mode" (Honeycutt, 1991, p. 124). This recreation provokes negative affect. The switch from an immediate II mode to a reflective II mode may be accompanied by X's feeling of distress or anger while reflecting on the past encounter and envisioning what will be said during the next encounter with Y. The result is the experience of a retroactive II that is immediately linked with a proactive II. It is this line of thinking that has lead to the articulation of a theory seeking to articulate this phenomenon, II conflict-linkage theory.

Honeycutt and Cantrill (2001) discuss II conflict-linkage theory. It has taken the form of an axiomatic theory containing three axioms and nine theorems explaining why conflict endures, how it is maintained, why it may be constructive or destructive and how it can erupt at any time during interpersonal communication. The theorems reveal that intrapersonal communication, through the form of IIs, allows conflict to be kept alive in everyday life. This is done through linking imagined interaction that involves a given conflict episode while anticipating future encounters. Current testing of this theory will provide additional direct empirical support for its axioms and theorems. This testing includes an examination of how everyday conflict is kept alive in the minds of individuals as they relive old arguments through memories that are triggered by certain environmental cues.

We are also examining conflict management in terms of inducing IIs. Relational partners fill out a modified version of the SII asking about IIs with their partner. They examine a list of issues in relationships (e.g., shared goals, issues of equality, treatment of family or friends, social life). They are asked to examine the list and imagine talking with their partner about the issue. They write down some sample lines of dialogue. Following this, they are taped for 5 minutes discussing one of the issues. Part of this research deals with agenda-setting in terms of how they decide whose topic to discuss. After the interaction period, they are asked questions dealing with the discrepancy between their induced II and what actually happened.

Although conflict-linkage and management is an area currently being explored, there are other studies underway. One area is adjustment to spousal bereavement. Couched within Mead's (1934) theory of symbolic interaction is the notion of identity, which McCall and Simmons (1978) and Stryker (1980) have purported to be a compilation of individual role-identities. The spousal role-identity, which is disrupted by the death of one's husband or wife, must be reconciled in order for the widow or widower to adjust to life without the spouse (Farnsworth, Pett, & Lund, 1989). Parkes (1996) likens the bereavement process to a psychosocial transition, or PST, requiring reformulation of identity.

The symbolic interactionist perspective on the formulation of identity suggests that it is a social construction, meaning that a person becomes who he or she is through social interaction (Mead, 1934). The notions of the looking-glass self and the generalized other are means through which one comes to know how he or she is viewed socially. Imagined interactions, described in an earlier section of this review in light of Mead's (1934) internalized conversation of gestures, allow one to test how he or she will interact with others. It may be that IIs aid in the bereavement process by enabling the widow or widower to envision socially interacting as a widow or a widower prior to real-life interaction, thus allowing for identity adjustment. Imagined interactions may also function in cathartic ways as well, allowing for the release of anxiety as plans are developed and enacted for dealing with the new "widow" or "widower" role, as well as providing an increased understanding of the self in the new role. Research is currently underway assessing the potential significance of imagined interactions in aiding the process of psychosocial adjustment to bereavement.

We are examining cross-cultural differences in IIs among Americans, Thai, and Japanese and cultural patterns of horizontal and vertical individualism and collectivism. Individualism has been of great interest to cross-cultural researchers because the construct links individualistic Western countries to collectivistic Asian cultures, which are the largest populations in the world. This research is one attempt to respond to Singelis and Brown (1995) who argue that the popular use of individualism-collectivism "requires an explanation of the mechanisms and intermediate steps through which the various pressures inherent in this broad-based construct shape individual behavior" (p. 355). One mechanism shaping individualism-collectivism is self-talk in the form of IIs.

Singelis and his colleagues (1995) define horizontal collectivism as a cultural pattern in which the individual views the self as part of an in-group to the extent that the self is merged with other members of the in-group, all of whom are very similar to each other. Horizontal collectivists merge with in-groups (family, co-workers, country) but do not feel subordinate to the in-groups (Triandis, Chen, and Chan, 1998). An extreme example was theoretical communism.

Vertical collectivism is a cultural pattern in which members of the in-group have status differences. Whereas the self is interdependent with other in-group members, inequality is accepted and people are not viewed as being the same. Rural villages in India are examples of this cultural pattern.

Horizontal individualism is a cultural pattern in which the self is important and independent, but is more or less equal in status with others. There is a desire for high equality and freedom. They do their own thing but do not necessarily compare themselves with others (Triandis et al., 1998). Sweden, Australia, and the British Labor party are examples of this cultural pattern. There is the desire to bring those down who have high status.

Vertical individualism is a cultural pattern in which the self is also important, yet individuals see each other as different. Competition characterizes social relations. There are differences in authority based on status, low equality, high freedom, and a market democracy (Singelis et al., 1995). The United States and France are examples of this cultural pattern as are middle and upper classes in many Western democracies and in the United States.

We are examining which characteristics of IIs predict the four types of cultural patterns and differences between the countries. For example, since self-dominance concentrates attention on one's own imagined talk, this characteristic of IIs could be associated with horizontal and vertical individualism. Through message planning and thinking about one's own statements, attention is focused on the self.

SUMMARY

As has been demonstrated by the work of this review of literature surrounding the construct of imagined interactions as it relates to intrapersonal communication and social cognition, IIs have a number of characteristics and serve a variety of functions. Imagined interactions involve various levels of discrepancy, activity, specificity, retroactivity, proactivity, self-dominance, variety, and pleasantness. The use of IIs along these dimensions may prove to aid in maintaining relationships, providing catharsis, creating a better sense of self-understanding, allowing for rehearsal of anticipated encounters, but also allowing for the review of past interactions. They may provide some level of compensation for the lack of real interaction or may substitute for interaction. IIs function to maintain conflict as well as resolve it. II conflict-linkage theory explains how conflict is ruminated and thought about long after episodes of arguing have occurred.

The past decade of imagined interaction has served to illuminate what an II is, its role as an intrapersonal process, and how it shapes actual interaction. Continued research on IIs and their various applications furthers our understanding in terms of why conflict persists, whether individuals can be taught to utilize IIs in a more constructive manner for the purpose of creating better and stronger relationships, and how IIs are used to adjust to certain life events such as the birth of a child or the loss of a spouse. Interpersonal communication processes can only be informed by a better understanding of intrapersonal processes that affect interpersonal experiences. Continued study of the II construct allows communication scholars to better understand the communication process from beginning to end.

REFERENCES

Abelson, R. P. (1976). Script processing in attitude formation and decision-making. In J. S. Carroll & J. W. Payne (Eds.), *Cognition and social behavior* (pp. 33–45). Hillsdale, NJ: Erlbaum.

Ainsworth, M. D. S. (1989). Attachments beyond intimacy. *American Psychologist, 44,* 709–716.

Ainsworth, M. D. S., Blehar, M. C., Waters, E., & Wall, S. (1978). *Patterns of attachment: A psychological study of the strange situation.* Hillsdale, NJ: Erlbaum.

Allen, T. H. (1990). The effects of Machiavellianism on imagined interaction. *Communication Research Reports, 7,* 116–120.

Allen, T. H. (1994, November). *Absence makes the mind work harder: Imagined interactions and coping with geographical separation.* Paper presented at the annual convention of the Speech Communication Association, New Orleans, LA.

Allen, T. H., & Berkos, K. M. (1998, November). *A functional approach to imagined interaction: Examining conflict-linkage and aggression.* Paper presented at the annual convention of the National Communication Association, New York.

Allen, T. H., & Edwards, R. (1991a, November). *The effects of imagined interaction and planning on message strategy use.* Paper presented at the annual convention of the Speech Communication Association, Atlanta, GA.

Allen, T. H., & Edwards, R. (1991b, November). *The effects of imagined interaction and planning on speech fluency*. Paper presented at the annual convention of the Speech Communication Association, Atlanta, GA.

Allen, T. H., & Honeycutt, J. M. (1997). Planning, imagined interaction, and the nonverbal display of anxiety. *Communication Research, 24*, 64–82.

Berger, C. R. (1993). Goals, plans and mutual understanding in relationships. In S. Duck (Ed.), *Individuals in relationships* (pp. 30–59). Newbury Park, CA: Sage.

Berger, C. R. (1995). A plan-based approach to strategic communication. In D. E. Hewes (Ed.), *The cognitive bases of interpersonal communication* (pp. 141–179). Hillsdale, NJ: Erlbaum.

Berger, C. R. (1997). *Planning strategic interaction: Attaining goals through communcative action*. Mahwah, NJ: Erlbaum.

Berger, C. R., & Bell, R. A. (1988). Plans and the initiation of social relationships. *Human Communication Research, 15*, 217–235.

Bowlby, J. (1982). *Attachment and loss: Vol. 1. Attachment* (2nd ed.). New York: Basic Books.

Caprara, G. V. (1986). Indicators of aggression: The dissipation-rumination scale. *Personality and Individual Differences, 7*, 763–769.

Caughey, J. L. (1984). *Imaginary social worlds*. Lincoln: University of Nebraska Press.

Collins, K., & Bell, R. (1997). Personality and aggression: The dissipation-ruminative scale. *Personality and Individual Differences, 22*, 751–755.

Daly, J. A., Vangelisti, A., & Daughton, S. M. (1987). The nature and correlates of conversational sensitivity. *Human Communication Research, 14*, 167–202.

Dewey, J. (1922) *Human nature and conduct: An introduction to social psychology*. New York: Henry Holt.

Duck, S. (1980). Personal relationships research in the 1980s: Towards an understanding of complex human sociality. *Western Journal of Speech Communication, 44*, 114–119.

Edwards, R., Honeycutt, J. M., & Zagacki, K. S. (1988). Imagined interaction as an element of social cognition. *Western Journal of Speech Communication, 52*, 23–45.

Ericsson, K. A., & Simon, H. A. (1980). Verbal reports as data. *Psychological Review, 87*, 215–251.

Farnsworth, J., Pett, M. A., & Lund, D. A. (1989). Predictors of loss management and well-being in later life widowhood and divorce. *Journal of Family Issues, 10*, 102–121.

Feeney, J. A., & Noller, P. (1991). Attachment style and verbal descriptions of romantic partners. *Journal of Social and Personal Relationships, 8*, 187–215.

Feldman, S. (1966). Motivational aspects of attitudinal elements and their place in cognitive interaction. In S. Feldman (Ed.), *Cognitive consistency: Motivational antecedents and behavioral consequents* (pp. 75–108). New York: Academic Press.

Fitzpatrick, M. A. (1988). *Between husbands and wives: Communication in marriage*. Newbury Park, CA: Sage.

Gorsuch, R. L., & Hao, J. Y. (1993). Forgiveness: An exploratory factor analysis and its relationship to religious variables. *Review of Religious Research, 34*, 333–347.

Gotcher, J. M., & Honeycutt, J. M. (1989). An analysis of imagined interactions of forensic participants. *National Forensic Journal, 7*, 1–20.

Gottman, J. M. (1994). *What predicts divorce?* Hillsdale, NJ: Erlbaum.

Greene, J. O. (1984). A cognitive approach to human communication: An action-assembly theory. *Communication Monographs, 51*, 289–306.

Hazan, C., & Shaver, P. (1987). Romantic love conceptualized as an attachment process. *Journal of Personality and Social Psychology, 52*, 511–524.

Holtgraves, T., Srull, T. K., & Socall, D. (1989). Conversation memory: The effects of speaker status on memory for the assertiveness of conversation remarks. *Journal of Personality and Social Psychology, 56*, 149–160.

Honeycutt, J. M. (1989). A functional analysis of imagined interaction activity in everyday life. In J. E. Shorr, P. Robin, J. A. Connella, & M. Wolpin (Eds.), *Imagery: Current perspectives* (pp. 13–25). New York: Plenum.

Honeycutt, J. M. (1989b). A pilot analysis of imagined interaction accounts in the elderly. In R. Marks & J. Padgett (Eds.), *Louisiana: Health and the elderly* (pp. 183–201). New Orleans, LA: Pan American Life Center.

Honeycutt, J. M. (1991). Imagined interactions, imagery and mindfulness/mindlessness. In R. Kunzendorf (Ed.), *Mental imagery* (pp. 121–128). New York: Plenum Press

Honeycutt, J. M. (1995). Imagined interactions, recurrent conflict and thought about personal relationships: A memory structure approach. In J. E. Aitken & L. J. Shedletsky (Eds.), *Intrapersonal communication processes* (pp. 138–150). Plymouth, MI: Speech Communication Association and Midnight Oil Multimedia.

Honeycutt, J. M. (1995b). The oral history interview and reports of imagined interactions. *Journal of Family Psychotherapy, 6,* 63–69.

Honeycutt, J. M. (1998-99). Differences in imagined interactions as a consequence of marital ideology and attachment. *Imagination, Cognition, and Personality, 18,* 269–283.

Honeycutt, J. M. (1999). Typological differences in predicting marital happiness from oral history behaviors and imagined interactions. *Communication Monographs, 66,* 276–291.

Honeycutt, J. M., & Brown, R. (1998). Did you hear the one about? Typological and spousal differences in the planning of jokes and sense of humor in marriage. *Communication Quarterly, 46,* 1–11.

Honeycutt, J. M., & Cantrill, J. C. (2001). *Cognition, communication, and romantic relationships.* Mahwah, NJ: Erlbaum.

Honeycutt, J. M., Edwards, R., & Zagacki, K. S. (1989–1990). Using imagined interaction features to predict measures of self-awareness: Loneliness, locus of control, self-dominance, and emotional intensity. *Imagination, Cognition, and Personality, 9,* 17–31.

Honeycutt, J. M., & Eidenmuller, M. E. (2000). An exploration of the effects of music and mood on intimate couples' verbal and nonverbal conflict-resolution behaviors. In V. Manusov & J. H. Harvey (Eds.), *Attribution, communication behavior, and close relationships* (pp. 37–60). London: Cambridge University Press.

Honeycutt, J. M., & Gotcher, J. M. (1991). Influence of imagined interactions on communicative outcomes: The case of forensic competition. In R. Kunzendorf (Ed.), *Mental Imagery* (pp. 139–143). New York: Plenum Press

Honeycutt, J. M., & Wiemann J. M. (1999). An analysis of functions of talk and reports of imagined interactions (IIs) during engagement and marriage. *Human Communication Research, 25,* 399–420.

Honeycutt, J. M., Zagacki, K. S., & Edwards, R (1992-1993). Imagined interaction, conversational sensitivity, and communication competence. *Imagination, Cognition, and Personality, 12,* 139–157.

Honeycutt, J. M., Zagacki, K. S., & Edwards, R. (1989) Intrapersonal communication, social cognition, and imagined interactions. In C. V. Roberts & K. W. Watson (Eds.), *Intrapersonal Communication Processes* (pp. 166-184). Scottsdale, AZ: Gorsuch Scarisbrick and Spectra.

Johnson, K. L., & Roloff, M. E. (1998). Serial arguing and relational quality: Determinants and consequences of perceived resolvability. *Communication Research, 25,* 327–343.

Kellermann, K. (1984). The negativity effect and its implications for initial interaction. *Communication Monographs, 51,* 37–55.

Kellermann, K. (1995). The Conversation MOP: A model of patterned and pliable behavior. In D. E. Hewes (Ed.), *The cognitive bases of interpersonal communication* (pp. 181–221). Hillsdale, NJ: Erlbaum.

Kemper, S., & Thissen, D. (1981). Memory for the dimension of requests. *Journal of Verbal Learning and Verbal Behavior, 20,* 552–563.

Klos, D. S., & Singer, J. L. (1981). Determinants of the adolescent's ongoing thought following simulated parental confrontations. *Journal of Personality and Social Psychology, 41,* 975–987.

Knapp, M. L., & Vangelisti, A. L. (1996). *Interpersonal communication and human relationships* (3rd ed.). Boston: Allyn & Bacon.

Langer, E. (1978). Rethinking the role of thought in social interaction. In J. Harvey, W. Ickes, & R. Kidd (Eds.), *New directions in attribution research* (pp. 35–58). Hillsdale, NJ: Erlbaum.

Langer, E. J., Blank, A., & Chanowitz, B. (1978). The mindlessness of ostensibly thoughtful action: The role of placebic information in interpersonal interaction. *Journal of Personality and Social Psychology, 36,* 635–642.

Langer, E. J., Chanowitz, B., & Blank, A. (1985). Mindlessness-mindfulness in perspective: A reply to Valerie Folkes. *Journal of Personality and Social Psychology, 48,* 605–607.

Lyumbomirsky, S., Tucker, K. L., Caldwell, N. D., & Berg, K. (1999). Why ruminators are poor problemsolvers: Clues from the phenomenology of dysphoric rumination. *Journal of Personality and Social Psychology, 77,* 1041–1060.

Manis, J. G., & Meltzer, B. N. (1978). *Symbolic interaction: A reader in social psychology.* Boston: Allyn & Bacon.

McCall, G., & Simmons, J. (1978). *Identities and interactions.* New York: Free Press.

Mead, G. H. (1934). *Mind, self and society.* Chicago: University of Chicago Press.

Meyer, J. R. (1997). Cognitive influences on the ability to address interaction goals. In J. O. Greene (Ed.), *Message production: Advances in communication theory* (pp. 71–90). Mahwah, NJ: Erlbaum.

McCullough, M. E., Rachal, K. C., Sandage, S. J., Worthington, E. L., Jr., Brown, S. W., & Hight, T. L. (1998). Interpersonal forgiving in close relationships: II. Theoretical elaboration and measurement, *75,* 1586–1603.

Newell, A., & Simon, H. A. *Human problem solving.* Englewood Cliffs, NJ: Prentice-Hall.

Parkes, C. M. (1996). *Bereavement: Studies in adult life* (3rd ed.). London, Routledge.

Petress, K. C. (1995). Coping with a new educational environment: Chinese students' imagined interactions before commencing studies in the US. *Journal of Instructional Psychology, 22,* 50–63.

Petress, K. C. (1990, June). *The role imagined interactions played in the Tian-an-men Square student demonstrations: An analysis of participants' self-reporting.* Paper presented at a conference of the American Association for the Study of Mental Imagery, University of Massachusetts, Lowell.

Pfefferbaum, B., & Wood, P. B. (1994). Self-report study of impulsive and delinquent behavior in college students. *Journal of Adolescent Health, 15,* 295–302.

Roloff, M. E., & Ifert, D. E. (1998). Exploring the role of private thought, Imagined interaction and serial interaction in mutual influence. In M. T. Palmer & G. A. Barnett (Eds.), *Volume 14: Progress in communication sciences* (pp. 113–133).

Rosenblatt, P. C., & Meyer, C. (1986). Imagined interactions in the family. *Family Relations, 35,* 319–324.

Schutz, A. (1962). Choosing among projects of action. In M. Natanson (Ed.), *Collected Papers, Vol. I: The Problem of Social Reality* (pp. 67–96). The Hague, Netherlands: Martinus Nijhoff.

Singelis, T. M., & Brown, W. J. (1995). Culture, self, and collectivist communication: Linking culture to individual behavior. *Human Communication Research, 21,* 354–389.

Singelis, T. M., Triandis, H. C., Bhawuk, D. P. S., & Gelfand, M. J. (1998). Horizontal and vertical dimensions of individualism and collectivism: A theoretical and measurement refinement. *Cross Cultural Research, 29,* 240–275.

Smeijsters, H. (1995). The functions of music in music therapy. In T. Wigram, B. Saperston, & R. West (Eds.), *The art and science of music therapy: A handbook* (pp. 385–394). Chur, Switzerland: Harwood.

Stafford, L., & Daly, J. A. (1984). The effects of recall mode and memory expectancies on remembrances of natural conversation. *Human Communication Research, 10,* 379–402.

Stafford, L., Burggraf, C. S., & Sharkey, W. F. (1987). Conversational memory: The effects of time, recall mode, and memory expectations on rememberances of natural conversations. *Human Communication Research, 14,* 203–229.

Stafford, L., Waldron, V. R., & Infield, L. L. (1989). Actor-observer differences in conversational memory. *Human Communication Research, 15,* 590–611.

Stryker, S. (1980). *Symbolic interactionism: A social structural version.* Palo Alto, CA: Benjamin Cummings.

Triandis, H. C., Chen, X. P., & Chan, D. K. S. (1998). Scenarios for the measurement of collectivism and individualism. *Journal of Cross-Cultural Psychology, 29,* 275–289.

Turner, V., & Turner, E. (1978). *Image and pilgrimage in Christian culture: Anthropological perspectives.* New York: Columbia University Press.

Wallace, A. F. C. (1972). Driving to work. In J. P. Spradley (Ed.), *Culture and cognition* (pp. 311–313). San Francisco: Chandler.

Wilensky, R. (1983). *Planning and understanding.* Reading, MA: Addison-Wesley.

Zagacki, K. S., Edwards, R., & Honeycutt, J. M. (1992). The role of mental imagery and emotion in imagined interaction. *Communication Quarterly, 40,* 56–68.

CHAPTER CONTENTS

10 Attitudes Toward Language: A Review of Speaker-Evaluation Research and a General Process Model

AARON CASTELAN CARGILE
California State University-Long Beach

JAMES J. BRADAC
University of California-Santa Barbara

Language attitudes are typically inferred from hearers' evaluative reactions to speech variations. Although they are central to human communication, their social scientific study has been reported mainly in journals outside of the communication discipline. This chapter first reviews the multidisciplinary work in the area that has looked to evaluations of speakers as a means of assessing language attitudes. Although this research has resulted in pragmatically interesting generalizations, more recent research and theorizing suggests that such generalizations may be limited due to assumptions and methodologies that neglect the complex process through which language attitudes reveal themselves. An emergent understanding of the speaker-evaluation process is discussed herein and represented by a recently developed model. Our assessment of the area concludes with suggested directions for future research.

T HE complexity of human communication has made researchers receptive to a multitude of voices, each encouraging the use of a different method or definition in its study. As a result, most communication scholars recognize that their endeavor is truly multidisciplinary and that they must often look outside the field in their attempts to understand phenomena that are central, and a fortiori those that are ancillary, to their study. Such is the case with language attitudes.

Attitudes toward varieties of speech (i.e., dialects, accents, and styles) affect evaluations of many interpersonal, mass, organizational, and intercultural events. As humans develop both direct and indirect experience communicating with one

Correspondence: Aaron Castelan Cargile, Department of Communication Studies, California State University, 1250 Bellflower Blvd., Long Beach, CA 90840-2407; email: acargile@sculb.edu

Communication Yearbook 25, pp. 347–382

another, they rely on this experience to navigate through future interactions. In our view, attitudes are a heuristic summary of experience; thus language attitudes are invoked every time interlocutors encounter a variety of speech that they have heard (or heard of) before. Despite the centrality of this process to nearly all communication, its investigation has occurred largely outside the pages of communication journals and outside the awareness of many communication scholars. Instead, the social scientific study of language attitudes has been left mainly to researchers trained in linguistics, psychology, or sociology; although recently researchers in communication have increasingly examined attitudinal consequences of "molecular" language variables (more about this below). It seems accurate to say that researchers in communication and those in other fields have often studied particular aspects of the language-attitudes process with low mutual knowledge. Given this state of affairs, this essay aims to review and critique speaker-evaluation research published both inside and outside the field of communication in order to explicate a construct foundational to human communication—language attitudes. Our review is necessarily selective, given over 40 years worth of international research on the topic, and in this respect it resembles earlier reviews (e.g., Bradac, 1990; Cargile, Giles, Ryan, & Bradac, 1994; Giles & Powesland, 1975; Giles & Ryan, 1982). Particularly, we focus on research conducted both on and in varieties of English, a limitation that reflects length constraints primarily; however, research on non-English languages is by no means ignored altogether, as evidenced in the following section. Additionally, we offer a model of the speaker-evaluation process that indicates the complex relationship between language attitudes and evaluations of speakers.

LANGUAGE-ATTITUDES RESEARCH AND FINDINGS: THE SPEAKER-EVALUATION TRADITION

From the time of Aristotle, at least, rhetorical scholars have assumed and proposed that lexical and vocal variations can affect the impressions that audiences form of communicators. However, it was not until the mid-20th century that the effects of language variations were studied empirically and systematically. Although an enormous variety of language variables could have been studied (e.g., speech rate, lexical diversity, or vocal quality), the early researchers' attention was directed mostly to differences among languages and dialects. In some sense, comparing levels or types of the macrovariable "language" (German, Italian, Spanish, etc.) is the most basic starting point imaginable for the study of language attitudes; it seems retrospectively logical. But it is probably the case that more than logic guided the decision to examine consequences of language differences—namely, an interest in linguistic manifestations of "national character" and cultural superiority or inferiority.

Since the 1960s, language-attitudes research has proliferated, relying mainly on three investigative techniques. First, content analyses have been conducted on the public treatment accorded to language varieties. Techniques here include observational, participant-observation, and ethnographic studies (e.g., Stevens, 1983); analyses of government and educational language policies (e.g., Bourhis, 1982); as well as analyses of literature, government and business documents, newspapers, and broadcasting media (e.g., Rickford & Traugott, 1985). Second, people have been asked directly about their attitudes toward language varieties through the use of questionnaires and interviews (e.g., Galindo, 1995; Labov, 1966). Third, language attitudes have been studied indirectly by asking listeners to evaluate one or more tape-recorded speakers (e.g., Buck, 1968; Cargile & Giles, 1997; Ryan & Carranza, 1975). Speaker evaluations are of interest because they are believed to reflect a listener's underlying attitude toward the language variety being examined. We focus herein on language-attitudes research from the speaker-evaluation tradition because this method has dominated social scientific approaches to the study of language attitudes.

A study by Buck (1968) is a good example of early speaker-evaluation research on language attitudes. This researcher was interested in the effects of "substandard" dialects on hearers' impressions of speakers. She observed that "substandardness" is associated with "people in lower socio-economic and educational levels" (p. 181) and that the users of "substandard" language "face negative evaluative reactions in spite of social, economic, and educational mobility" (p. 181). Four dialects were specified (standard White, standard or Northern U.S. "Negro," "New Yorkese," and "substandard" or Southern U.S. "Negro") and each was employed by one of four speakers who tape recorded a short prose passage (from *Alice in Wonderland*). Thus, each dialect was represented by a single speaker. Respondents, who were female students at a college in New York, heard one of the four versions and rated the speaker on scales reflecting the competence and trustworthiness dimensions of communicator credibility. Analyses indicated that both the White and "Negro" standard dialects produced higher competence ratings than did the two "substandard" dialects. Also, on the trustworthiness dimension the speakers using the two standard dialects received higher ratings than did the speaker using the White "substandard" dialect.

The study just described was conducted by a communication researcher and reported in a communication journal. More typical in terms of disciplinary identity are two early studies by psychologist Wallace Lambert and associates. In the first study, Lambert, Hodgson, Gardner, and Fillenbaum (1960) examined the effect of a prose passage recorded by four bilingual speakers in both French and English on respondents' assessments of a variety of speaker traits (e.g., leadership and intelligence). Respondents, who were themselves bilingual, heard all eight recordings and generally evaluated the English versions more favorably. In the second study, Lambert, Anisfeld, and Yeni-Komshian (1965) had bilingual and bidialectal speakers record a passage in Arabic and two dialects of Hebrew. Respondents were Jewish and Arab adolescents who evaluated each speaker after hearing each recording. In this case, the Jewish respondents made more favorable judgments of the Hebrew versions, whereas the Arab respondents were more favorable toward the versions presented in Arabic, an example of ingroup favoritism (Tajfel, 1981).

The Buck (1968) and Lambert et al. (1960, 1965) studies show some significant similarities that may reflect to some extent Buck's awareness of Lambert's research program, which is revealed by citations in Buck's article. The Buck and Lambert et al. studies are experiments in which languages or dialects constitute independent variables, and evaluative reactions to speakers, as measured by forced-choice instruments, constitute dependent variables. The independent variables are instantiated in prose passages, which are constant across conditions, so message content is not manipulated; this means that relationships between message content and dialect (or language) in the production of evaluative reactions are not examined. Situational context of message production is not specified to respondents, and therefore relationships between perceived communication situation and dialect (or language) in the production of evaluative reactions are also not examined. The use of experimental designs in which language or dialect are manipulated in a contextual and message-substantive vacuum in order to assess effects of the manipulation on respondents' evaluative reactions is highly typical of the early research on language attitudes.

In addition to being prototypical in terms of their methodology, the studies by Buck (1968) and Lambert (1960, 1965) also illustrate, in part, an important trend in speaker-evaluation findings: standard speakers are often evaluated more favorably than nonstandard speakers. According to Fishman (1971), nearly all languages, dialects, and accents can be classified by the degree to which they are considered "standard" or "nonstandard" within a particular community. A "standard" variety is that most often associated with status, the media, institutional control, and power, whereas a "nonstandard" variety is one that is often associated with lower levels of socioeconomic success. Despite lay ideas to the contrary, what makes a particular language variety "standard" has little to do with its intrinsic value or aesthetic appeal (see Trudgill & Giles, 1978). Instead, standard varieties of language are considered such because of historical influence; regardless of how they sound, the social group that dominates a particular milieu gets to set the standard (see Edwards, 1982).

As described by Ryan, Hewstone, and Giles (1984), speakers who use a standard language or accent tend to be rated highly on traits related to competence, intelligence, and social status, whereas nonstandard speakers are evaluated unfavorably along these same dimensions, even by listeners who themselves use the same nonstandard variety of speech. However, when these speakers are evaluated along traits related to kindness, solidarity, and overall attractiveness, speakers with a nonstandard accent often compare much more favorably, sometimes even being rated as more attractive, especially by nonstandard speaking listeners. It should be noted that this generalization applies only to settings in which a dominant language variety can be identified (e.g., mainstream U.S. English in an American court of law), and not to settings in which (language) domination is contested (e.g., Arabic and Hebrew in Israeli-occupied territories).

As the presented examples suggest, the above-described pattern holds for language evaluations throughout the world. For example, in France, Paltridge and Giles (1984) found that Parisian-accented speakers were rated more competent than speakers employing regional accents and languages (see also Vassberg, 1993). In the Netherlands, school children rated speakers of their own minority language, Frisian, as less intelligent and diligent but equally pleasant compared to Dutch speakers (Ytsma, 1990). In Spain, Castilian Spanish speakers were rated unfavorably on both status- and attractiveness-related traits by Catalonian listeners, and conversely, Catalonian Spanish speakers were rated poorly on the same traits by Castilian speakers (Wollard, 1984). In Costa Rica, nonstandard Spanish speakers were accorded less status and were less well liked than standard speakers (Berk-Seligson, 1984). In India, children favored standard Kannada- to Tamil-accented speakers on 14 different trait ratings (Sridhara, 1984). Finally, in China, speakers of standard Putonghua (Mandarin) were thought to be more successful but less empathetic than speakers of Cantonese-accented Putonghua (Kalmar, Zhong, & Xiao, 1989).

In addition to numerous speaker-evaluation studies conducted throughout the non-English-speaking world, the greatest number have been undertaken in English-speaking settings. Results from these studies also confirm the general speaker-evaluation pattern just discussed. Many studies have found nonstandard English speakers to rate unfavorably on status-related traits, but favorably on those associated with attractiveness. This is true for Greek-, Italian-, and Vietnamese-accented English in Australia (Nesdale & Rooney, 1990; Riches & Foddy, 1989); Lancashire-accented English and Welsh in England (Giles, Coupland, Henwood, Harriman, & Coupland, 1992; Giles, Wilson, & Conway, 1981); and Spanish-accented, Appalachian-accented, and African-American vernacular English in America (Bradac & Wisegarver, 1984; Buck, 1968; Galindo, 1995; Garner, 1986; Giles, Williams, Mackie, & Rosselli, 1995; Johnson & Buttny, 1982; Luhman, 1990; Speicher & McMahan, 1992).

Less frequently, nonstandard English speakers have been rated unfavorably on both status- and attractiveness-related traits (e.g., Arthur, Farrar, & Bradford, 1974; Bishop, 1979; Larimer, Beatty, & Broadus, 1988; Ryan, Carranza, & Moffie, 1977; Ryan & Carranza, 1975; White et al., 1998). And less frequently still, speakers of a select few varieties of nonstandard English in America (i.e., British and "Asian" varieties) have not been downgraded on status-related traits (Cargile & Giles, 1998; Gill, 1994; Podberesky, Deluty, & Feldstein, 1990; Rubin, DeHart, & Heintzman, 1991; Stewart, Ryan, & Giles, 1985). Although these last results appear contradictory, in our opinion they merely suggest an amendment to the pattern described above. Specifically, nonstandard speakers rate favorably on status-related traits when their representative social groups are perceived to be competitive with, and not entirely subordinate to, the dominant social group.

RECENT RESEARCH TRENDS

Discovering and understanding patterns of evaluation for standard and non-standard speakers alike is a project that has received the lion's share of attention within the study of language attitudes. Even so, since about 1975 there has been an increase of speaker-evaluation studies concerned with variables other than dialects, accents, or whole languages. This represents a shift from a "macro-orientation" to a "micro-" or "molecular orientation" (cf. Milroy & Preston, 1999) as researchers have become interested in specific subsets of features residing within languages and dialects (e.g., the devices used to convey an impression of politeness). In addition, this "macro" to "micro" shift has also been accompanied by a shift in interest away from the attitudinal effects of phonological features (as in the case of accent and, to a large extent, dialect) toward the effects of syntactic and semantic features (e.g., lexical and grammatical features associated with impressions of communicator power). Several examples of these more recently studied language variables are presented below.

New Variables

Among the new variables attracting attention, researchers have examined evaluative consequences of "hate speech"—direct insults, obscenities, and threats to members of negatively evaluated social groups. For example, Leets and Giles (1997) had respondents read a scenario in which a person either addressed hate speech to a member of a devalued group or used hate speech when discussing the group with an outsider; the speaker in the former situation was evaluated especially negatively, presumably as a result of high perceived intentionality. Also, respondents who were themselves members of the derogated group (an ethnic minority) reacted especially negatively when the hate speech was cast in indirect language, whereas respondents who were not members of the group were more negative when direct language was used.

The example of hate speech calls attention to the fact that groups may differ in social power. It has been argued that relatively powerless persons use language forms that are not used by their relatively powerful counterparts (O'Barr, 1982), and it has been shown that use of tag questions, hesitations, and hedges produce *perceptions* of low communicator power (Bradac & Mulac, 1984). The latter two forms have been shown to produce negative evaluations of communicators who use them (Hosman, 1989). One study has shown that evaluations of powerful and powerless language are mediated by a personality variable, locus of control; respondents with an external locus of control reacted relatively favorably to a powerful message (i.e., a message that did not contain powerless forms; Hosman, 1997).

Turning to variables with psychological, rather than social antecedents, strength of emotion and degree of attitudinal commitment can affect a speaker's language; specifically, strong emotion and deep commitment are associated with the use of lexical items that are perceived to be intense: "I despise hypocrites" vs. "I dislike hypocrites" (Bowers, 1963; Rogan & Hammer, 1995). High- and low-intensity language can affect evaluations of speakers; for example, Aune and Kikuchi (1993) found that both actual and perceived similarities between level of language intensity in a message and message recipients' own language-intensity styles are associated with positive impressions of source credibility. Speaker commitment is also linked to another language variable, verbal immediacy, which is the extent to which a speaker approaches or avoids a topic through lexical and syntactic variations (Wiener & Mehrabian, 1967): "We certainly will enjoy the party" vs. "I think you must enjoy the beef wellington at that party with me" (Bradac, Bowers, & Courtright, 1979, p. 262). Conville (1975) found that evaluations of speaker competence and trustworthiness were lowered when low-immediacy language was used.

Speaker anxiety is another psychological state that has also been related to language use (Siegman & Pope, 1972). Two language variables are of interest here: lexical diversity (or manifest vocabulary range) and speech rate. The simple hypothesis is that as speaker anxiety increases, speech rate will increase also but lexical diversity will decrease. However, an "inverted U" hypothesis may be more accurate: Both extremely high and extremely low anxiety will produce a slow speech rate and low lexical diversity, but moderate anxiety will produce a relatively high speech rate and high diversity. Most importantly in this context, both language variables affect evaluations of speakers. A number of studies have shown that a low level of lexical diversity (e.g., 7 words repeated per 25; Bradac, Desmond, & Murdock, 1977) leads to relatively negative evaluations of speaker competence and status (Bradac et al., 1979; Bradac, Mulac, & House, 1988). Similarly, many studies have shown that a slow speech rate (e.g., 140 syllables per minute) leads to negative competence and status evaluations and that increases in rate produce linear increases in the positivity of evaluations (e.g., Brown, 1980; Street, Brady, & Putman, 1983), although in this case there is evidence of factors that qualify the effect, e.g., the typical speech rate of the person evaluating the speaker (Street & Brady, 1982).

New Research Problems

In addition to including new language variables within its expanded scope, current language-attitudes research includes new nonlinguistic variables. Some of these new inclusions suggest research problems that differ considerably from those examined in the early research.

Early studies of language attitudes largely ignored the fact that language performance is always contextualized; usually respondents were told nothing about the (ostensible) circumstances surrounding the message that was the object of evaluation. Speakers (and writers) know that different situations demand different forms of discourse and different linguistic styles, and message recipients know this also. This knowledge constitutes a part of one's communicative competence, arguably universally in every culture, although the details of this knowledge vary cross-culturally (Gudykunst & Ting-Toomey, 1988). Thus, within cultures there are widely recognized relationships between situations and messages that should affect both message production and the evaluation of messages. For example, message recipients might expect speakers in formal situations to use lexically diverse language that avoids grammatical errors and colloquialisms (Joos, 1967), and if this expectation is violated these recipients might evaluate offending speakers negatively on the dimension of status.

Indeed, the effect of perceived situational formality when conjoined with language style has been investigated in contemporary research. Bradac, Konsky, and Davies (1976) predicted an interaction between lexical diversity and perceived formality, but instead obtained an additive effect such that a low-diversity message in a formal situation was evaluated especially negatively and a high-diversity message in an informal situation was evaluated especially positively, with the low-diversity informal and high-diversity formal combinations falling between these extremes. Similarly, Street and Brady (1982) predicted an interaction between speech rate and perceived formality, but obtained an additive effect indicating that respondents evaluated a speaker's competence and social attractiveness least favorably when a slow rate was used in a formal context and most favorably when a rapid rate was used in an informal context. Taken together, the studies indicate that individuals distinguish communication situations along the dimension of formality and that they tend to be more critical of speakers performing in formal contexts. However, Creber and Giles (1983) predicted and *obtained* an interaction between accent and formality such that an RP British accent was evaluated especially *favorably* on the dimension of status compared to a Welsh accent in a *formal* situation, which suggests that different varieties of language may relate to perceived formality in different ways or alternatively that there are differences between American and British respondents in their evaluations of contextualized language.

Apart from the issue of context, an important new line of research on the subjective mapping of language attitudes has been initiated by a group in Wales. This work follows the lead of Preston (1989) who demonstrated that objective geographical maps of English dialects in the U.S. established by linguists may not correspond to maps created on the basis of naive (nonlinguist) perceptions of U.S. dialects and their boundaries. Using Preston's logic and applying it to the domain of language evaluation, Williams, Garrett, and Coupland (1996) had 129 teachers dispersed throughout Wales identify dialect boundaries for English (as opposed to Welsh) on a map of Wales and then provided labels for the dialect regions identified. Additionally, they gave open-ended comments about each of the dialects labeled, from which the researchers extracted information about their evaluative reactions to the dialects. For example, a "Cardiff" dialect emerged and a relatively large number of affectively negative comments were made about this; on the other hand, more positive comments were made about a "Valleys" dialect. As in Preston's research (1989), the maps produced by the teachers were more complex than were corresponding objective geolinguistic maps (see also Garrett, Coupland, & Williams, 1995).

Perhaps the most important (and most radical) feature of the Wales research is its reliance upon the perceptions of nonexperts in creating the linguistic objects of evaluation, in this case dialects of English. Previous research on evaluative reactions to dialects and accents, both early and recent, relied upon standard, technical operationalizations, and no doubt future studies will continue to do so. However, given the demonstrated slippage between technical conceptions and naive perceptions, and given the fact that it is naive perceptions that directly energize stereotypical beliefs about ingroups and outgroups, future research on the evaluative consequences of standard versus nonstandard varieties, for example, should examine implications of operationalizing the variable of interest on the basis of naive views in addition to using standard operationalizations. There is information to be gained by juxtaposing expert and lay perspectives (Cole & Bradac, 1996). The same point can be made about studying evaluative consequences of the "new" language variables described previously. Here, too, research has generally relied upon technical conceptions. Research on powerful and powerless speech styles, for example, reflects a narrow range of linguistic devices originally hypothesized to correlate with social power by O'Barr and associates (1982). These devices have been validated against the perceptions of naive respondents (e.g., Bradac & Mulac, 1984), but it may be the case that many other linguistic devices reside in lay theories of interpersonal and public control and that these other, presently unknown devices have significant evaluative effects.

THE TRADITION REASSESSED

Although the speaker-evaluation tradition has provided researchers and laypersons alike with an important understanding of language attitudes, it is a tradition in need of reassessment. This need has been created by both research within the tradition (described above), and theoretical advances occurring outside the tradition (described below).

As speaker-evaluation studies underwent a "macro" to "micro" shift in independent variables investigated, a key insight was made possible, one that went beyond understanding the effects of a host of disparate variables. Namely, Giles and Coupland (1991) realized that because syntactic structures and semantic features were found regularly to have evaluative consequences, no message text could ever really be neutral, as most of the early speaker-evaluation studies had assumed. More problematic still, new research problems have pointed to a host of other variables beyond the message text (e.g., situational formality) that affect speaker evaluations. Together, these findings have challenged current conceptualizations of the relationship between language attitudes and speaker evaluations.

Speaker evaluations as a method for measuring language attitudes have been so widely used that the two constructs are treated synonymously. Manifest evaluations are assumed to reflect only latent language attitudes and this assumption is represented schematically in Figure 1. As the figure outlines, exposure to a par-

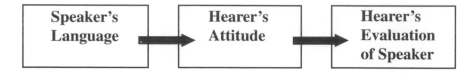

Figure 1. An Implicit Model of Speech Evaluation in Traditional Research

ticular language behavior is believed to evoke a corresponding language attitude possessed by the speaker. This attitude, in turn, presumably generates an observable evaluation of the speaker that is used as a measure of the hearer's language attitude. The strengths of this implicit model are its simplicity and common sense appeal. However, this model cannot accommodate the findings just discussed. For example, if a highly involved English-speaking hearer evaluates a known celebrity Spanish speaker reading her personal diary in a formal situation as intelligent, which language attitude, if any, is being measured?

As Giles and Coupland (1991) describe it, speaker evaluations are influenced by a whole host of discursive concerns such as a hearer's goals, identities, and interpretation of the situation at hand. Consequently, it is naive to suggest that a given evaluation reflects only a given language attitude. For example, even though a single language behavior might be controlled in a speaker-evaluation experiment, provided the nature of speech as a "multidimensional configuration of phonological forms, prosodic, paralinguistic, and rhetorical selections, questions arise as to *what it may be* in the stimulus materials that possibly generates social evaluations" (Giles & Coupland, 1991, p. 29). A researcher may infer that an evaluation reflects an attitude toward a tested accent, but it might instead reflect a reaction to a combination of the speaker's accent, voice, and message.

Although Giles and Coupland's critique and the findings from recent speaker-evaluation studies serve as an important starting point for constructing a model of the speaker-evaluation process, it will be useful first to consider a transitional question.

Wither Sociality?

A sociological dimension has always been apparent in language-attitudes research. The early studies, including those by Buck (1968) and Lambert et al. (1960, 1965) discussed above, typically focused on evaluations of speakers representing different social groups, groups that often were (and for the most part still are) ethnolinguistically distinct. This focus persists in much of the recent research on language attitudes (e.g., Cargile, 1997; Cargile & Giles, 1998; Galindo, 1995; Nesdale & Rooney, 1990; Rubin et al., 1991), although as suggested above, some of the "new" language variables that have been investigated reflect psychological states that may arise in a wide range of speakers, regardless of group membership. At the same time, the process of evaluating speakers representing these social groups has always been essentially psychological. Indeed, the construct "attitude" that has been assumed to undergird evaluations is generally viewed as a psycho logical predisposition to respond to classes of objects (Sarnoff, 1970).

However, much of the research cited or described above exhibits a limited, even impoverished, conception of the process of speaker evaluation, often over-looking the fact that language is rarely an isolated evaluative cue and erroneously conceptualizing the link between evaluation and attitude as a direct one, when instead it is mediated by a variety of influential cognitive variables. In our presentation of the model that follows, we attempt to capture some of the complexity inherent in the process of evaluating speakers. Social group membership and language are but two of the variables affecting speaker evaluations, and language attitudes typically play no more than an indirect role in the production of hearers' reactions.

A GENERAL PROCESS MODEL OF SPEAKER EVALUATIONS[1]

A large number of language-attitudes studies, both early and recent, have invoked an implicit model that is essentially behavioristic: A stimulus (some linguistic feature) elicits a response (an evaluative reaction). Presumably, the elicited response reflects a given message recipient's history of learning with regard to the variety of language constituting the stimulus. The model just described may be characterized more precisely as "neo-behavioristic," since an attitude is assumed to mediate the stimulus-response (language-evaluation) relationship (S-R or S-A-R, sometimes also rendered S-O-R, where "O" stands for "organismic" variable). In this S-R or S-A-R model, no attention is paid to particular cognitive and affective processes that may influence the responses of message recipients to language variation. In a sense, linguistic stimuli may interact with these mediating processes, and these processes may interact with specific language attitudes, to shape evaluative (and other) responses. In the model described below (Figure 2), we focus on attitudinal and non-attitudinal variables that mediate the language-response relationship (cf. Cargile, Giles, Ryan, & Bradac, 1994). The model should be treated broadly; it maps potential relationships among interdependent variables and processes, and should not be treated as a strict causal chain. Also, it should be noted that any stylistic behavior, verbal or nonverbal, toward which hearers can form attitudes resides within the model's domain. Thus, for example, a stylized walk indicating ethnic-group membership can serve as a basis for evaluation. In this respect, language and other behaviors would be viewed similarly, whereas from other standpoints linguistic and nonverbal expression are distinct; for example, nonverbal acts are continuous, whereas utterances are segmented.

The Speaker

We begin consideration of the model with a speaker (or writer) and his or her language behavior. This language behavior can be of any variety already discussed

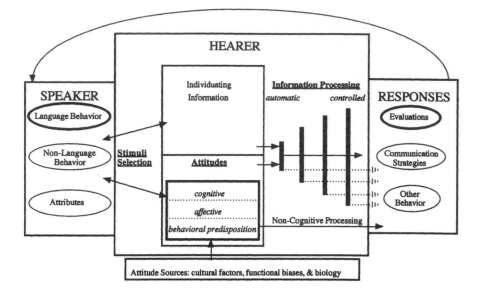

Figure 2. A General Process Model of Speaker Evaluations

(e.g., accent, politeness, or speech rate) and is the main focus of our model (indicated by the bold outline in Figure 2). Even so, we recognize that language is
embedded in a host of simultaneously interactive nonlanguage behaviors, along
with social and physical attributes (e.g., the speaker's ethnicity, sex, posture, and
age), that potentially affect a hearer's response.

Nonlanguage behaviors are all nonverbal behaviors produced by the speaker to
which hearers are exposed during a communication event (or to which they have
been exposed prior to the event, e.g., gestures, posture, movement, and so forth)
and these can reinforce or contradict language-based attributions available to hearers. In addition, physical features of a speaker may provide cues that function in
much the same way (Williams, 1976). That said, it is not necessarily the case that
nonlanguage behaviors change attributions made strictly on the basis of language.
It has been found that the evaluative potency of accent effects (i.e., Asian vs. British Received Pronunciation) was not diminished when the addition of visual cues
(via videotaped presentation) was contrasted with audiotape-only conditions
(Elwell, Brown, & Tutter, 1984). Indeed, contextual issues notwithstanding, we
maintain that language behaviors are among the most salient and often used cues
in social interaction. Several studies comparing the relative effects of language
and nonlanguage behaviors, such as dress and physical attractiveness, have all
found language behaviors to have a greater impact on listener attributions (Parsons & Liden, 1984; Seligman, Tucker, & Lambert, 1972; Sondermeyer, 1995).
Based on this, we can state that the privileged position of language as the focus of

study within the language-attitudes domain is well deserved. Even so, nonverbal behaviors have demonstrated a larger effect than verbal behaviors in other areas of inquiry (e.g., compliance gaining, see Segrin, 1993), thus we should be careful not to ignore completely the potential impact of nonlanguage behaviors on the language-attitudes process.

Alongside both language and nonlanguage behaviors, hearers typically also have access to information regarding the speaker's social attributes. Such attributes are considered separately here because, unlike nonlanguage behaviors, they have a well-established impact on a hearer's judgments and behaviors. Consider, for example, the social attribute of sex. Sex role stereotype research demonstrates that perceivers typically make different attributions about men and women. Women are often rated more highly on traits related to aesthetic quality (e.g., nice, sweet, beautiful), whereas men are often rated more highly on traits related to dynamism (e.g., active, strong, loud; Ashmore & Tumia, 1980; Ruble, 1983). In an experiment comparing the effects of sex role stereotypes to those of gender-linked language, Mulac, Incontro, and James (1985) found that the two phenomena operate independently. That is to say, effects resulting from both the speaker's sex and language behavior could be either added together (e.g., a speaker identified as "a man" using "male" linguistic forms was seen as very dynamic), or subtracted (e.g., a speaker identified as "a man" using "female" linguistic forms was seen as moderately dynamic, equal in dynamism to a speaker identified as "a woman" using "male" linguistic forms). From this it can be seen that hearer responses to language depend not only on the language stimulus itself, but also on perceived social attributes of the speaker. In addition to sex, other social attributes demonstrated to affect language-based judgments include the speaker's inferred age (Giles et al., 1992), nationality (Niedzielski, 1999), status (Gill & Badzinski, 1992; Stewart et al., 1985), and ethnicity (Rubin & Smith, 1988).

The Hearer

As suggested previously, cognitive and affective mediators of hearers' responses to language have been largely ignored in language-attitudes research. To a large extent, the hearer has been viewed as a passive, unanalyzed "given" and attention has been devoted to various aspects and types of language that can affect this inert entity. This is especially true of the "molecular" language-variable research described above. However, this is something of an overstatement, because language-attitudes research with an intergroup focus has examined hearer characteristics such as ethnicity and, more basically, because "attitudes" differentiate hearers and can serve as a basis for activity. But previous research has largely ignored the possibility that nonattitudinal cognitive and affective variables may be especially potent energizers of responses to language. These other variables are likely to interact with attitudes as hearers form responses to speakers. In the following discussion we consider several variables that mediate hearers' responses to a speaker's language.

Attitudes. An attitude is generally and traditionally viewed as "a disposition to react favorably or unfavorably to a class of objects" (Sarnoff, 1970, p. 279). Specifically, it includes cognitive, affective, and behavioral features of response (see Eagly & Chaiken, 1993; Edwards, 1982). First, attitudes are cognitive because they entail beliefs about the world, such as "French is a useful language to know" or "English people are refined." These beliefs are commonly described as stereotypes and are the most typically studied attitudinal component. Second, attitudes are affective because they involve feelings toward an attitude object, such as a passion for Irish poetry, or an awful taste in the mouths of Georgians when speaking Russian. Third, attitudes are behavioral because they encourage certain actions, such as enrolling in a Japanese language course, or hiring a standard-accented speaker for a job.

In addition to this traditional view, a nontraditional approach to attitudes advocated by Potter and Wetherell (1987) also deserves consideration here. According to these authors, the concept of an attitude has been made problematic by a number of concerns, two of which we highlight here. First, because meaning is not fixed, it is difficult to ensure that the same attitude "object" is evoked in research participants', researchers', or even readers' thoughts. For example, a study by Marsh (cited in Potter & Wetherell, 1987) asked people to express their attitude toward "coloured immigrants," but given a variety of connotative and denotative meanings for the term, who is to say that everyone involved in the study evaluated exactly the same "object"? Second, an additional difficulty encountered by use of the attitude construct is a lack of consistency; given the same attitude-object but different purposes or contexts, a very different evaluation may be expressed. In response to these concerns, Potter and Wetherell have abandoned the search for attitudes in underlying, internal states, and have instead chosen to view attitudes as public discourse that is evaluative in nature.

Although we agree with Potter and Wetherell that the attitude construct has, at times, been needlessly reified, and that more discursive treatment is often needed, we have chosen (obviously) not to give up on attitudes. It is our view that evaluations do correspond to internal states, and this view is grounded most persuasively in our own phenomenology; we have known a regularity of thought, feeling, and action when faced with particular "objects." Of course, that phenomenology may have been constructed itself through cultural discourse; regardless though, the attitude construct remains viable within certain cultural bounds.

Despite our continued faith in the attitude construct, Potter and Wetherell's concerns persist. Fortunately though, our model addresses some of them, in part. Realizing that traditional speaker-evaluation studies rarely question what the "object" under study is, our model forces consideration of the issue by incorporating nonlanguage behaviors and attributes as speaker characteristics to which the hearer is possibly responding. Similarly, as discussed below, our model accounts for variations in response to the same attitude-object by considering the impact that a hearer's goals or level of information processing will have on his or her responses. As these examples suggest, our design provides traditional treatment of the attitude construct while anticipating some problems normally associated with such treatment.

Having considered briefly the nature of attitudes, an equally relevant topic should now be addressed: The source of attitudes. It is important to ask the question, "Where do attitudes come from?" because a good answer increases knowledge of their functions and reasons for being. In response to this question, three important sources can be identified: perceived cultural factors, functional biases, and biology.

Perceived cultural factors include political, historical, social, economic, and linguistic realities that exert a large influence over the process of (language) attitude formation. Many of our attitudes toward varieties of language emerge from society and culture. If we observe that speakers with a particular accent (e.g., Appalacian-accented English) are rarely in positions of political or economic influence, and that hearers usually denigrate these speakers for not sounding "educated" or "cultured," we begin to learn a language attitude. Ryan, Giles, and Sebastian (1982) developed a scheme to describe in greater detail how cultural factors provide a basis for language attitudes. They suggest that a given variety of language can be characterized by two interrelated dimensions: standardization and vitality. Although these dimensions are conceivably "objective," language attitudes will only be affected by the speaker's and hearer's "subjective" or perceived assessment of such factors.

Standardization is a relatively static dimension and it describes the extent to which norms for correct usage have been codified, adopted, and promoted for a particular language variety (Fishman, 1971). This might be accomplished through the compilation of dictionaries and grammars, whereas the acceptance of a variety may be advanced by social elites and the government. Thus, for example, the English spoken among White, middle-class Americans would often be designated "standard," whereas Spanish-accented or West-Indian-accented English would often be designated "nonstandard" in most areas in the United States and the United Kingdom, respectively.

Vitality is a more dynamic dimension compared to standardization and it reflects the range and importance of functions served by a given language variety, along with social pressures toward shifts in language use. Giles, Bourhis, and Taylor (1977) have provided a taxonomy of relevant nonpsychological factors that constitute ethnolinguistic vitality: status (the economic, social, political, and historical power wielded by its speakers); demographic strength (the number and distribution of its speakers); and institutional support (the contribution made to the maintenance of the variety by national, governmental, and community bodies).

Using the two dimensions of standardization and vitality, we can see more clearly how perceived cultural factors may affect the development of language attitudes. Specifically, if a hearer perceives a social group to exhibit high vitality and believes that their language is standardized, favorable language attitudes, at least along status-related traits, will likely be attendant. Despite this effect, however, the perceived cultural factors represented by standardization and vitality do not guarantee the formation of any particular language attitude. This is because they must share their capacity to shape attitudes with other factors, including any functional biases brought about by the hearer's needs.

Attitudes are not created in a social vacuum. As just discussed, they develop in response to perceived cultural "facts." In addition, they can also develop as means of protecting and improving one's image. As Tajfel (1981) described, individuals may rely on their beliefs about others to preserve and defend their value systems whereas social groups can use these beliefs to preserve, create, or enhance positively valued differentiations between ingroups and outgroups. In this way, the formation of a particular attitude might enhance a hearer's image of him- or herself through denigration of an outgroup (e.g., an Anglo-American might think that Mexican Americans sound "illiterate" because this evaluation increases feelings of self-worth). Thus, individuals are motivated to develop attitudes that provide them both with better self- and social group-esteem. Of course, attitudes serve many functions other than an ego-protective one (see Eagly & Chaiken, 1993; Katz, 1960), but this sufficiently illustrates the point that the process of attitude formation can be biased in order to establish or improve an attitude's functionality.

A third source from which language attitudes may spring is biology. Although language itself is a learned behavior, the ability to learn language is an evolved trait (Pinker, 2000). Because human language proved to benefit the survival of our species, we will consider the possibility that at least one "hard-wired" evaluative response may have also been evolutionarily advantageous.

Among the language behaviors to which a biologically based response may have been shaped, perhaps the strongest case can be made for psychoacoustically described "low-pitched" or "deep" voices. In his model of the evolution of animal signals, Tanaka (1996) argues that when a signal comes to represent reliably a quality of the signaler, receivers evolve adaptive responses that allow them to exploit the information carried in the signal. For example, reliable signalers of dominance may achieve higher fitness because they can expend less energy in establishing their dominance, compared to fighting. Simultaneously, receivers who evolve means of recognizing these signals also achieve higher fitness because they less often provoke more dominant conspecifics. Tanaka's (1996) theory applies to the perception of "deep" (and conversely "high-pitched") voices because this vocal quality reliably signals body size.

A psychoacoustically described "low-pitched" or "deep" timbre is created by both closely spaced formants and low fundamental frequency (F_0; see Titze, 1994). Formant dispersion is inversely related to vocal tract length, and vocal tract length is positively correlated with body size in mammals (Fitch, 1999). In addition, larger animals possess a greater ability to produce sounds of low F_0 than smaller animals (Glenn, Glenn, & Forman, 1989; Morton, 1977; Sales & Pye, 1974). It follows then that larger mammals regularly produce deeper-sounding vocalizations and that humans have likely evolved responses that exploit information about the signaler's size from this reliable signal. What responses likely evolved? Clearly a response of perceived weakness regarding (and subsequent attack on) a large individual would not have led to higher fitness on the part of receivers. Instead, male receivers who responded with deference to deeper-sounding males, and females who responded with attraction, would have been more successful in the "environment of evolutionary adaptedness" (EEA)—the environment present 1.5 million years ago when our genus, *Homo*, first evolved from the Australopithecines, and to which our biology is suited (Barkow, Cosmides, & Tooby, 1992).

Considering the above, it stands to reason that humans today would evaluate speakers with deep-sounding voices as more dominant. Indeed, this is what a study by Buller and Burgoon (1986) found. Relatedly, several other studies have found low F_0 to be associated with perceptions of dominance (Ohala, 1982) and potency (e.g., stronger and more confident; Apple, Streeter, & Krauss, 1979; Tusing & Dillard, 1996). More impressive still are results showing that this type of response is not subject to cultural variation. Montepare and Zebrowitz-McArthur (1987) found that both American and Korean respondents rated speakers with childlike voices as weaker and less competent than their mature-sounding counterparts. Thus, there is limited evidence to suggest that attitudes toward vocal timbre may be biologically based.

Having discussed the nature of attitudes and several likely sources for these evaluative, affective, and behavioral predispositions toward language, we will now consider how attitudes are used in interaction by hearers.

Stimuli selection. In most natural settings, a particular language behavior (say, accent or intensity) will co-occur with many other language behaviors and with nonlanguage behaviors, as well as with indicators of a speaker's social class, gender, and ethnicity. As discussed earlier, any one or several of these speaker features may be stimuli to which a hearer will respond. However, as a result of attentional limitations, hearers must focus on a relatively small subset of stimuli (among all available stimuli).

The concept of attentional limitation was first articulated scientifically by Broadbent (1958), who argued that the brain has a finite capacity for information processing, and thus attention evolved as a mechanism to protect the brain from informational overload. In this view, attention selects some information for processing and shuts out any nonselected information from further analysis. Although the idea of "limited-capacity processing" remained popular for many years, it has been supplanted by conceptualizations of attention that are consistent with an evolving body of neuropsychological evidence. One such conceptualization has been popularized by Allport (1989). In his view, the primary purpose of attention is not to protect the brain from overload; the brain is perfectly capable of handling a nearly limitless number of stimuli in parallel, at a subconscious level. Instead, an attentional system is designed to ensure the coherence of behavior. As Posner (1982) argues, mental operations related to attention require time to perform. If humans are to behave in response to their environments, and this behavior necessitates certain mental operations, appropriate attentional engagement needs to be maintained or protected for some period. Without the attentional selection of stimuli, humans would not be able to concentrate sufficiently to formulate behavioral (or other) responses.

If hearers must select the stimuli that serve as a basis for their responses to speakers, how do they do it? According to Allport (1989), stimuli selection can be accomplished by employing a "top-down" mode of attention selection that is internally generated and controlled. In this case, hearers attend to stimuli perceived to be relevant as a result of accessible attitudes, expectancies, and goals.

Research by Fazio and others has shown that attitudes can strongly influence both perceptions of and response to social situations (Fazio, Sanbonsatsu, Powell, & Kardes, 1986; Fazio, Roskos-Ewoldsen, & Powell, 1994; Houston & Fazio, 1989). Correspondingly, Fazio's (1986) attitude-behavior model suggests that when an attitude is activated, attention becomes oriented to attitudinally relevant stimuli. Consider, for example, a highly prejudiced social perceiver who dislikes ethnic minorities. One of the first characteristics she would attend to in social interaction would be another's ethnic background. However, a second social perceiver may ignore this very same information if he is instead aware of his love for "foreign" sounding speech. In this second case, the perceiver would focus first (and perhaps exclusively) on the speaker's accent. As these examples illustrate, attitudes that are accessible to a hearer at any given moment may help focus the hearer's attention on particular stimuli. In our model, this is represented by one end of a double-headed arrow that runs from the hearer's attitudes toward the speaker (see Figure 2). Accessibility of these attitudes is affected in turn by cognitive elaboration, recency of activation, frequency of activation, and expectations (see Roskos-Ewoldsen, 1997).

As just indicated, expectations are one of several factors that influence the accessibility of an attitude. When a perceiver anticipates that a particular attitude (e.g., an attitude toward fast rates of speech) will be useful for responding in a social situation (e.g., interacting with a used-car salesperson), that attitude is "readied" through increased saliency (Roskos-Ewoldsen, 1997). Expectations can thus indirectly affect a hearer's attention by engendering the accessibility of an attitude which, in turn, forces consideration of particular stimuli. Expectations, or expectancies in the terms of expectancy violations theory (Burgoon, 1978), can also directly influence a hearer's attention by outlining which stimuli are most likely to be useful for responding in social situations. For example, if the situation is a college classroom, a student's expectancies usually orient her attention toward the professor's speech instead of toward the conversation of her neighbors or toward the wildlife outside the window. Similarly, if a woman is on a date, her male partner's expectancies may orient his attention toward her behaviors of nonverbal affiliation (e.g., prolonged touch or eye gaze) instead of her verbal assessment of the evening's success. As these examples imply, expectancies can be based on general cultural conventions (Burgoon, 1995). Additionally, they may also stem from person-specific knowledge. Thus, another man with knowledge that his date tends to be both physically flirtatious and bluntly honest may develop expectancies that lead him, unlike his counterpart above, to attend to the woman's verbal assessments of their time together. This feature of stimuli selection is represented in our model by a second double-headed arrow that runs from individuating information (possessed by the hearer) toward the speaker (see Figure 2).

In addition to attitudes and expectancies, goals are a third factor that help orient a hearer in this "top-down" mode of attention selection. Indeed, Allport (1987) argues that attention develops in response to the necessity of goal-directed action. Such actions require individuals to identify relevant stimuli for successful execution; for example, in order to catch a mouse, a cat must distinguish the mouse from all irrelevant stimuli and maintain a mouse-relevant focus. Thus, attention allows for the execution of goals. Unsurprisingly then, goals affect attention. For example, for some parole board members the goal of imprisonment is the protection of society from criminals; for others, it is rehabilitation. Different goals then can sometimes lead to differences in attributions for a given crime (Carroll & Weiner, 1982), attributions that may well be realized through language attitudes. One official with the protection goal may attend to a criminal's nonstandard accent and believe that he or she is a member of a particular social group stereotypically associated with the traits of cruelty and remorselessness. Another official with the rehabilitation goal may hear, at the same time, a criminal's slow rate of speech and redundant vocabulary, allowing attributions to be made about the criminal's impoverished educational upbringing. In this manner, the two officials' divergent goals can lead to contrasting yet suitable perceptions of the criminal based on the different language behaviors to which they attended.

Thus far in our discussion of stimuli selection we have treated attention exclusively as a "top-down" process (i.e., as internally directed). However, Allport (1989) points out that whereas any attentional system must be able to maintain and protect attentional engagement, it must also be able to interrupt such engagement when the environment offers threats or opportunities. This suggests that attention is also a "bottom-up" process that is sensitive to environmental contingencies. While a student concentrates on a professor's lecture, she must also be able to break focus to attend to the fire alarm, should it sound.

Based on the above, we can conclude that attention is simultaneously beholden to both internal and external inputs (Allport, 1989). Consequently, people will not orient to simply any external stimulus. According to Posner (1982), attentional processing biases people toward fresh or novel sources of stimulation. If a stimulus is familiar (e.g., a conversation among students in class), it will not engender a "bottom-up" orienting response. Reeves, Thorson, and Schleuder (1986) explain this in terms of short-term memory. Information in short-term store provides a template that perceivers use to judge the "match" or "mismatch" of any stimuli. If a stimulus does not match the information in short-term store, attention is directed toward the stimulus, regardless of the outcome of co-occurring internally directed attention processes. For our purposes, this short-term store can be viewed as the functional equivalent of an expectancy. Correspondingly, an expectancy violation will elicit attention and arousal, which in turn results in elaborated processing of the considered stimulus (Burgoon & Hale, 1988).

This process of "bottom-up" stimuli selection is represented in our model by opposite ends of the two double-headed arrows described previously (see Figure 2). Thus, unexpected language behaviors can compel a hearer's attention and in turn foster the acquisition of individuating information. These behaviors can also activate specific language attitudes. Similarly, these arrows also represent the second phase in any "top-down" attentional processes. Thus, attitudes, individuating information, expectancies, and goals can initially direct attention to particular language behaviors or speaker attributes that will provide a basis for speaker evaluation. After these behaviors or attributes are observed, they may once again foster the acquisition of individuating information and activate specific language attitudes. After the relevant attitudes and individual facts have been made salient through this complex interaction of attentional factors and processes, the next task that the hearer faces is processing these two types (and multiple pieces) of information.

Information Processing. There are two types of information that strongly influence the formation of person impressions: individuating information and stereotypes (Brewer, 1988; Fiske & Neuberg, 1990). Although this distinction may be ambiguous on occasion, the idea is that some of our information about a given individual is person-specific (i.e., based on idiosyncratic behaviors and unique characteristics), whereas other information reflects general and preexisting associations between nonverbal or linguistic stimuli (e.g., style of dress or accent) and traits (e.g., socio-intellectual status or attractiveness). Stereotypes, of course, describe the latter and are treated in our model as the cognitive component of attitudes (see Figure 2). After attending to certain traits and behaviors of a speaker, several (language) attitudes, along with other individuating information, may be activated. Consequently, a hearer must somehow synthesize both types of information as he or she works toward developing a response. Although no one can say definitively how this process occurs, Kunda and Thagard's (1996) parallel-constraint-satisfaction model (PCSM) offers some important insights.

To review briefly, this model indicates that stereotypes (i.e, cognitive attitudinal features), traits, and behaviors are represented as interconnected nodes in an network. Nodal activation occurs when either a stereotype or individuating information is made salient and spreads constrained both by the positive or negative associations between nodes and by the relative strength of these associations. For example, hearers may attend to a speaker's low level of lexical diversity and stereotypically associate it with the trait of "ignorance." Simultaneously, they may also observe that the speaker received good grades in college. These three nodes (i.e., "lexically simple," "ignorance," and "good grades") would be initially and automatically activated.

Unlike other, similar models (Brewer, 1988; Fiske & Neuberg, 1990), the PCSM gives priority to neither stereotypes nor individuating information, instead giving them equal weight in the process of impression formation. Inferred traits, activated by course of a stereotypical association, have the same impact on a hearer's impression as speaker-specific information, as the hearer interprets all of the activated nodes in the network. Of course, the network could consist of only attitudinally derived nodes, or of only person-specific information. In this way, the model incorporates the entire attitude/nonattitude continuum discussed by Fazio and his colleagues (e.g., Fazio, Sanbonsatsu, Powell, & Kardes, 1986; Roskos-Ewoldsen, 1997). Responses to attitude-objects can be generated in three ways: without use of a priori evaluations, through strict reliance on a highly accessible attitudes, or based on some combination of both attitude and nonattitude information.

When a hearer's nodal network is initially activated by some configuration of attitudinally derived or person-specific information, the information contained within the network may be quickly and automatically integrated for impression formation purposes. On the other hand, the network may also spread, sometimes widely, by repeatedly updating the activation of interrelated nodes. Such spread occurs over time and can require numerous iterations until a point is reached at which the network "settles." Although the PCSM attends primarily to the automatic integration of information, we contend that this model, when interpreted broadly, can also accommodate more elaborate and controlled information integration processes.

The recognition that hearers can process information about the speaker in either "automatic" or "controlled" fashions is important in order to account for recent empirical findings. Devine suggests that automatic processes "involve the unintentional or spontaneous activation of some well-learned set of associations," whereas controlled processes "are intentional and require the active attention of the individual" (1989, p. 6). Many recent experimental investigations provide evidence that when forming impressions of social actors persons may make two different kinds of evaluations, reflecting either automatic processes or controlled processes (e.g., Blair & Banaji, 1996; Dovidio, Kawakami, Johnson, Johnson, & Howard, 1997; Fazio, Jackson, Dunton, & Williams, 1995). This suggests that information that is automatically activated in an initial iteration of the nodal network may or may not affect a hearer's evaluation of a speaker. As Dovidio et al. (1997) describe it,

> the presentation of an attitude object may automatically activate an associated evaluation from memory which *may* influence subsequent judgments. However, as Gilbert and Hixon (1991) argue, automatic activation "does not mandate such use, nor does it determine the precise nature of its use. It is possible for [automatically] activated information to exert no effect on subsequent judgments or to have a variety of different effects" [due the impact of controlled processes]. (p. 511)

For our purposes, automatic processing of information occurs when few iterations occur in a hearer's activated nodal network that lead to a rapid response (e.g., an immediate evaluation of speaker status). On the other hand, controlled processing entails numerous iterations or elaborations of the network resulting in a relatively slow or delayed hearer response; in fact, in some cases elaboration may be so extensive that initially activated information will have little effect on this response. In even more controlled circumstances, the network may be said to migrate as the information elements present in the first iteration (and activated in response to observed stimuli) may be completely absent from the finally settled network. This would be true in the case of socially desirable responses, for example. A hearer may attend to the accent of the speaker, which in turn evokes an attitude represented in the initial nodal network as the activation of several negative traits. However, as attention is brought to bear, the hearer may realize the undesirability of responding based on the currently activated network. Consequently, the network may migrate as other, more positive behaviors and traits are activated, while the nodes that were initially active are deactivated.

The variability in processing described above should be regarded as a continuum such that sometimes hearer responses are based on the relatively automatic integration of information; other times these responses are based on a nodal network whose spread has been greatly controlled; and other times still these responses are based on a network whose nodes have been activated in both automatic and controlled manners. The possibility that hearers may process information about the speaker in a number of ways is depicted in our model as a series of increasingly long vertical bars, where each bar represents an iteration of the activated nodal network and the network's tendency toward complexity over time is shown by the increasing length of the bars (see Figure 2). At each point of iteration, a hearer's response may emerge from the activated network, or further elaboration may occur. Consequently, our model has been drawn both with dashed lines that connect each bar to the hearer's responses and with a solid line that joins all bars and ends in an arrow representing the possibility of even further elaboration.

Having now distinguished between the automatic processing and controlled elaboration of the hearer's nodal network, the important question becomes: What factors affect the probability of increasing iterations of the network? No doubt there are many such factors, all of them probably not yet identified. Even so, we can be reasonably sure that at least three broad categories of factors affect both the nature and extent of controlled processing that occurs. Two are borrowed from the elaboration likelihood model (Petty & Cacioppo, 1986a): motivation and ability; and the third we propose is mood.

First, a hearer must be sufficiently motivated to go beyond the initial state of the nodal network activated by accessed (language) attitudes and speaker-specific information. We assume that most hearers are cognitively lazy to such a degree that they will usually avoid the continued processing of information if that information has already been automatically and sufficiently integrated. Motivation is treated here as a broad construct because many specific factors fit within its umbrella. Petty and Cacioppo (1986a) suggest that it consists of at least three things: need for cognition, involvement, and diversity of argument.

The need for cognition is quite simply a variable of individual difference that recognizes outliers in the overall pattern of cognitive laziness. Most people will usually avoid elaborated processing if given the opportunity, so that established judgments of individual speakers ("Sally is fluent") and stereotypical judgments ("Women talk a lot") will tend to prevail. However, some people are especially analytic and enjoy extra cognitive work. Consequently, these individuals are said to possess a motivation to engage in controlled information processing.

Involvement is a second factor believed to engender controlled information processing: The more perceivers are involved with the sources, topics, or outcomes of information processing, the more likely they will be to control that processing actively. No other factor for motivation has been the topic of more debate and research than involvement (see Johnson & Eagly, 1989; Johnson & Eagly, 1990; Petty & Cacioppo, 1990). Although different definitions of the concept exist, and the research has been interpreted in multiple ways, there is no doubt that at least some types of involvement affect information processing. For example, in their review of the literature, Thomsen, Borgida, and Lavine (1995) describe multiple effects for outcome-relevant involvement. This type of involvement is typically created by leading perceivers to believe that they will later be interacting with a target person in some capacity. As a consequence, outcome-dependent participants have been found to take longer in making judgments (Monson, Keel, Stephens, & Genung, 1982), to better remember information (Berscheid, Graziano, Monson, & Dermer, 1976), and to use more complex reasoning strategies when thinking about the target person (Harkness, DeBono, & Borgida, 1985), than noninvolved participants. Thus, a person attending a lecture who anticipates interacting with the lecturer the next day may analyze carefully and mindfully both substantive and stylistic cues that pertain to the lecturer's competence and status.

Alongside involvement and need for cognition, Petty and Cacioppo (1986a) also discuss diversity of argument as a third factor that increases motivation. They chose the expression "diversity of argument" because they were focused on message characteristics while trying to explain the process of persuasion. Because our explanatory task is slightly different, we prefer to use a conceptually similar yet more inclusive expression: *nature of the information.* By this we mean that the make up of the activated nodal network itself can help determine whether or not elaborated processing occurs. As Kunda and Thagard (1996) suggest, "perceivers may initiate causal reasoning when they have trouble understanding the information they have observed (Kintsch, 1988), or when they find it particularly surprising (Kunda, Miller, & Claire, 1990; Wong & Weiner, 1981)" (p. 288).

In the spirit of Petty and Cacioppo's elaborated likelihood model, but in the terms of Kunda and Thagard's parallel-constraint-satisfaction model, we expect that hearers will consciously elaborate initially complex networks until information can be integrated and sense can be provided. Conversely, we expect that initially simple networks, generated by strong attitudes or by unambiguous individuating information, will settle automatically and lead directly to a hearer's response. In this manner, our model accounts for the "biased" or "selective" processing said to occur with the activation of robust attitudes (see Fazio et al., 1986). Additionally, our model accounts for behavior described by expectancy violations theory (Burgoon, 1978): Information contained in a nodal network that hearers find particularly surprising (i.e., in violation of their expectancies) will increase their motivation for controlled processing.

In addition to the three factors for motivation just discussed, we would also add the motivational factor of goals. As researchers have long recognized, goal setting is often the preeminent form of motivation (Lewin, Dembo, Festinger, & Sears, 1944). Goals can stem from the situation, the social perceiver, or a situation x perceiver interaction (Showers & Cantor, 1985). For example, hearers often adopt different goals for social interaction when they are at a family dinner (e.g., to establish connection), compared to being at a cocktail party (e.g., to appear friendly) or a political debate (e.g., to convince others of certain "truths"). Conversely, social actors may pay little attention to situational norms and instead import goals into situations based on their identity or task needs. For example, children are often guided by the abstract goal of self-socialization across many situations, which encourages social comparison in order to determine areas of competence (Ruble, 1983). By including goals in our model, we suggest that if a hearer seeks a particular outcome, he or she will likely engage in controlled (rather than automatic) processing as a means of achieving that outcome.

Whatever the source or factor involved in motivation, motivation is a necessary, but never a sufficient condition for elaborated processing; social perceivers must also have the ability to exert processing control (Petty & Cacioppo, 1986b). Ability, in turn, is a product of available time and cognitive capacity (Devine, 1989). As already mentioned, involved social perceivers, presumably engaged in more controlled information processing, have been found to take longer in making judgments (Monson et al., 1982). Similarly, Shiffrin and Schneider (1977) have demonstrated that controlled processing is demanding of attentional capacity and strongly dependent on cognitive load. Consequently, hearers must be motivated and have both the available time and cognitive capacity in order to elaborate the nodal network that is activated initially in response to the individuating information and attitudes evoked after selective observation of a speaker.

As just discussed, both motivation and ability are necessary conditions, and together they form a sufficient condition, for controlled processing to occur. That said, there is still one more factor relevant to information-processing that remains to be considered: mood. We expect that mood influences both the extent and direction of information processing.

Although the literature on mood effects is oftentimes inconsistent (Isen, 1984), the impact of mood on message elaboration has been found to be reliable (Schwarz, Bless, & Bohner, 1991). Specifically, people in bad moods have been found to elaborate spontaneously the content of persuasive messages, whereas people in good moods have not (e.g., Bless, Bohner, Schwarz, & Strack, 1990). This finding reviewed alongside a host of similar others led Schwarz et al. to conclude that negative moods serve to indicate a problem, and that people typically respond to this indication with a thorough assessment of the current situation in hopes that this will provide some basis for change. Positive feelings, on the other hand, indicate that all is well, and thus people prefer simple heuristics over more effortful information processing strategies, all else being equal (Schwarz et al., 1991). In view of this, we expect positive moods to bias hearers toward automatic processing, and negative moods toward controlled processing. Thus, a hearer who is feeling good is relatively likely to use linguistic cues (e.g., a speaker's accent) to make automatic judgments of speaker status, intelligence, attractiveness, and so forth.

In addition to the extent of information processing, moods also influence the direction of such processing. Research has found that informants in good moods express greater liking for others and form more positive impressions of them (Forgas & Bower, 1987; Forgas & Moylan, 1989). It has been suggested that this occurs because positive feelings serve as retrieval cues for positive material in memory (see Blaney, 1986). In addition, positive moods have also been observed to encourage positive behavioral responses to targets (Isen, Shalker, Clark, & Karp, 1978). Accordingly, a good mood in hearers is likely to bias their judgments of speakers in a positive direction. Linguistic cues that under other circumstances would be used as a basis for negative evaluations may be discounted or ignored. The effects of mood on the elaboration and direction of processing may be accounted for by a process whereby positive moods help determine which nodes in a perceiver's network get integrated, or help bias the spread of that network as additional nodes are activated.

People in negative moods, on the other hand, have been found to respond less consistently. In some cases, negative moods foster negative evaluations and behaviors. For example, participants feel more vulnerable (Davitz, 1969), rate themselves more negatively (Isen & Shalker, 1982), are less attracted to others (Gouaux, 1971), and have less favorable impressions of them (Forgas & Bower, 1987), when negative mood states are induced. At other times, however, negative moods produce positive and prosocial behaviors. Negative feeling states have been associated with increased self-reward (Cialdini, Darby, & Vincent, 1973) and a proclivity to help others (Isen, Horn, & Rosenhan, 1973). In these cases, negative moods encourage mood repair—people engage in positive, prosocial activities because they want to enhance their mood.

Taken together, these data are somewhat equivocal. We may generally expect positive moods to encourage benevolent responses to a speaker. Negative moods, however, may encourage mood congruent (i.e., negative) or mood incongruent evaluations, depending perhaps on the strength of the mood involved (cf. Blaney, 1986). Although not entirely reliable, emotions nonetheless likely bias the manner in which information about the speaker is processed.

Despite the emphasis we have placed on cognitive processes and the cognitive features of an attitude (i.e., stereotypes), it must be remembered that attitudes also include both an affective and a behavioral component. For example, it may be the case that a hearer's attitude toward nonstandard accented speech includes not only negative stereotypes (e.g., "this speaker sounds unintelligent"), but negative affect as well (e.g., "this speaker makes me feel uncomfortable" or "this speaker makes me angry"). On most occasions we imagine that this affect will be incorporated into the nodal network and influence the extent and direction of its spread. On rare occasions, however, the affective component of an activated attitude may be so strong as to render the results of any information processing moot. In the above example, if the hearer felt extremely uncomfortable in the presence of a nonstandard speaker, she may end up refusing the speaker's request based directly on this discomfort alone and without consultation of her activated nodal network. Although this sort of response can fit within an information processing framework (i.e., "mood as peripheral cue"; see Schwarz, Bless, & Bohner, 1991), we do not wish to overemphasize cognitions. Consequently, we allow for the possibility of noncognitive (i.e., emotion- or behavior-based) processing in our model (see Figure 2). The nodal network will be bypassed when responses to a speaker are influenced directly by the affective or behavioral predisposition component of an attitude.

Responses

As has been suggested throughout this paper, language attitudes are often closely related to evaluations of the speaker performing a given language behavior. In fact, most experimental studies infer language attitudes based on speaker evaluations, perhaps hazardously, as our model suggests—the connection between attitudes and evaluations is indirect, mediated by a number of variables. As our model indicates, speaker evaluations are one important consequence of perception that can reflect language attitudes, although these evaluations may reflect instead the interaction of attitudes with various cognitive and affective processes. Language-attitude outcomes, indirect though they may be, are not confined to speaker evaluations, however. They can also include various communication strategies (e.g., your language is unfamiliar to me which leads to judgments of dissimilarity and, consequently, particular strategies for uncertainty reduction) or other behaviors (e.g., disengagement). Moreover, language attitudes can lead to these behavioral outcomes indirectly by encouraging evaluations that, in turn, shape the hearer's strategies and behaviors. Because speaker evaluation is the primary outcome (or at least has been treated as such in research), we begin with this variable.

Speaker evaluations can consist of rating the speaker on any number of traits. Some researchers (Lambert et al., 1960; Williams, 1976) have emphasized the ecological validity of first impressions by conducting pilot studies for each specific respondent population to determine the dimensions used spontaneously to describe people. Within this framework, Lambert (1967) identified three frequently emerging dimensions (person integrity, personal competence, and social attractiveness), whereas Williams (1976) obtained two quite different factors in his work comparing speakers of standard and nonstandard English (confidence-eagerness and standardness). Others have sought to develop a general speech style assessment instrument by using post hoc and confirmatory factor analysis to validate generally useful dimensions (Mulac, Hanley, & Prigge, 1974; Zahn & Hopper, 1985). Finally, others have identified evaluative dimensions from a theoretical perspective and then used confirmatory factor analysis to establish the appropriateness of specific rating scales as reflections of the a priori dimensions (Brown, Strong, Rencher, & Smith, 1974; Ryan & Carranza, 1975).

As Giles and Ryan (1982) have argued, the evaluative dimensions of social status and ingroup solidarity have a universal importance for the understanding of attitudes toward contrasting language varieties. These theoretically based evaluative dimensions allow researchers to test contrasting predictions concerning the effects of various independent variables upon attitudes across a wide variety of settings. Within the framework, for example, one can make good sense of empirical findings of American listeners' preference for British English on status but for their own English on the solidarity dimension (Stewart et al., 1985). Similarly, Swiss listeners' preference for Swiss German on solidarity-related evaluations and for High German on those related to status (Hogg, Joyce, & Abrams, 1984) underlines the need for this type of distinction at a theoretical level. Even so, regardless of how researchers identify or measure speaker evaluations, they are a real and important outcome of language attitudes in social encounters.

In addition to speaker evaluations, language attitudes may also influence the listener's subsequent communication and communication strategies. Two studies offer the opportunity to examine specifically how this operates. Bourhis and Giles (1977) found that when Welsh respondents were threatened by a person speaking RP English, a situation of ingroup/outgroup confrontation, their Welsh accents broadened and in some cases Welsh words and phrases were included in their responses to the RP speaker. We would argue that such divergent speech choice conveyed, at least in part, their attitude toward the outgroup speaker as one of dissociation and displeasure. Also, divergence may have reflected automatic, as opposed to controlled, processing or it may have emerged directly from the affective component of an attitude toward standard English speakers. Language attitudes may also affect a wide variety of other listener behaviors, including co-operation. Kristiansen and Giles (1992) showed that cinema audiences in Denmark were more likely to assist the theater in completing an audience survey on site when the request was voiced in standard Danish rather than other less prestigious varieties (although this pattern was a variable function of the audience type). Research by Henry and Ginzberg (1985) illustrates a real-life paradigm in which individuals with different ethnic/racial accents made telephone inquires about jobs advertised in the newspaper. Certain kinds of speakers were told that a job was already filled whereas others, in contrast, received invitations to appear for a personal interview for this very same job. In other words, some people do sometimes indeed allow their actions to be shaped by their attitudes toward speakers of particular language varieties.

CONCLUSION

Whenever communicators produce messages, they make lexical, syntactic, and phonological decisions, and as the research reviewed in this chapter demonstrates, these decisions affect, among other things, the evaluative reactions of message recipients. In many (probably most) cases, these decisions are unconscious, but sometimes they are components of intricate plans (Berger, 1997), as in the case of political advertisements (Bradac, 1997). An important implication of recent research is that the message-evaluation connection is mediated by variables that are inevitably a part of the communication process, such as situational context and hearer (or reader) personality.

Our model calls special attention to variables residing in hearers, perhaps most notably variables that affect stimuli selection and information processing. Not only will differences in linguistic preferences produce different speaker evaluations among hearers, but so too will differences in attention, hearer goals, expectations, and depth of processing. Previous studies of language attitudes have not considered how hearers with dissimilar goals might respond to messages rendered in a powerful or powerless style, for example. It seems likely that hearers oriented to the goal of achieving dominance over a speaker will respond less favorably to the speaker's use of a powerful style than will hearers pursuing the goal of achieving personal abasement. To give another example, previous studies have not examined the effect of automatic versus controlled processing on responses to gender-linked language. Inducing a state of cognitive control might reduce the stereotypically high dynamism ratings given to male speakers and elevate the corresponding ratings of females. More generally, in future research it will be useful to examine the ways in which variations in hearers' moods, attentional foci, goals, expectations, and motivation to process messages may qualify the influence of language attitudes. One could, for example, directly assess attitudes toward particular standard and nonstandard dialects independently of speaker evaluations; induce in respondents differing attentional sets, levels of processing motivation, and so forth; expose respondents to messages exhibiting the dialects; and then measure evaluative reactions, comparing them with the independently assessed attitudes. It could be especially informative to conduct this type of experiment using previously examined language variations with known evaluative effects in order to compare obtained effects with the established ones. Might the advantage of standard dialects for evaluations of status/competence be reduced or even eliminated in a condition in which hearers are induced to focus on strength of the speaker's arguments and the standard speaker's arguments are, in fact, weak compared to those of the nonstandard speaker?

By including hearer variables in language-attitudes research, error variance may well be reduced, but much more importantly such inclusion seems likely to assist in the construction of *theories* of the language-attitudes process that depart increasingly from the simple stimulus-response model guiding much of the previous research.

NOTE

1. An earlier version of this model will appear in Bradac, J. J., Cargile, A. C., & Hallett, J. S. Language attitudes: Retrospect, conspect, and prospect. In H. Giles & W. P. Robinson (Eds.), *Handbook of language and social psychology* (2nd ed.). Chichester, UK: Wiley.

REFERENCES

Allport, A. (1987). Selection-for-action: Some behavioral and neurophysiological considerations of attention and action. In H. Heurer & A. F. Sanders (Eds.), *Perspectives on perception and action* (pp. 78–95). Hillsdale, NJ: Erlbaum.

Allport, A. (1989). Visual attention. In M. I. Posner (Ed.), *Foundations of cognitive science* (pp. 631–671). Cambridge, MA: MIT Press.

Apple, W., Streeter, L. A., & Krauss, R. M. (1979). Effects of pitch and speech rate on personal attributes. *Journal of Personality and Social Psychology, 37,* 715–727.

Arroyo, J. (1996). Psychotherapist bias with Hispanics: An analog study. *Hispanic Journal of Behavioral Sciences, 18,* 21–28.

Arthur, B., Farrar, D., & Bradford, G. (1974). Evaluation reactions of college students to dialect differences in the English of Mexican-Americans. *Language and Speech, 17,* 255–270.

Ashmore, R. D., & Tumia, M. L. (1980). Sex stereotypes and implicit personality theory: I. A personality description approach to the assessment of sex stereotypes. *Sex Roles, 6,* 501–518.

Aune, R. K., & Kikuchi, T. (1993). Effects of language intensity similarity on perceptions of credibility, relational attributions, and persuasion. *Journal of Language and Social Psychology, 12,* 224–238.

Barkow, J. H., Cosmides, L., & Tooby, J. (1992). *The adapted mind: Evolutionary psychology and the generation of culture.* Oxford, UK: Oxford University Press.

Berger, C. R. (1997). *Planning strategic interaction.* Mahwah, NJ: Erlbaum.

Berk-Seligson, S. (1984). Subjective reactions to phonological variation in Costa Rican Spanish. *Journal of Psycholinguistic Research, 13,* 415–442.

Berscheid, E., Graziano, W., Monson, T., & Dermer, M. (1976). Outcome dependency: Attention, attribution, and attraction. *Journal of Personality and Social Psychology, 34,* 978–989.

Bishop, G. D. (1979). Perceived similarity in interracial attitudes and behaviors: The effects of belief and dialect style. *Journal of Applied Social Psychology, 9,* 446–465.

Blair, I., & Banaji, M. R. (1996). Automatic and controlled processes in gender stereotyping. *Journal of Personality and Social Psychology, 70,* 1142–1163.

Blaney, P. H. (1986). Affect and memory: A review. *Psychological Bulletin, 99,* 229–246.

Bless, H., Bohner, G., Schwarz, N., & Strack, F. (1990). Mood and persuasion: A cognitive response analysis. *Personality and Social Psychology Bulletin, 16,* 331–345.

Bourhis, R. Y. (1982). Language policies and language attitudes: Le monde de la Francophonie. In E. Ryan & H. Giles (Eds.), *Attitudes towards language variation: Social and applied contexts* (pp. 34–62). London: Edward Arnold.

Bourhis, R. Y., & Giles, H. (1977). The language of integroup distinctiveness. In H. Giles (Ed.), *Language, ethnicity and intergroup relations* (pp. 119–133). London: Academic Press.

Bowers, J. W. (1963). Language intensity, social introversion, and attitude change. *Speech Monographs, 30,* 345–352.

Bradac, J. J. (1990). Language attitudes and impression formation. In H. Giles & W. P. Robinson (Eds.), *Handbook of language and social psychology* (pp. 387–412). Chichester, UK: Wiley.

Bradac, J. J. (1997). Aitchison's words in the mind: An introduction to the mental lexicon. *Journal of Language and Social Psychology, 16,* 79–84.

Bradac, J. J., Bowers, J. W., & Courtright, J.A. (1979). Three language variables in communication research: Intensity, immediacy, and diversity. *Human Communication Research, 5,* 257–269.

Bradac, J. J., Cargile, A. C., & Hallett, J. S. (in press). Language attitudes: Retrospect, conspect, and prospect. In H. Giles & W. P. Robinson (Eds.), *Handbook of language and social psychology* (2nd ed.). Chichester, UK: Wiley.

Bradac, J. J., Desmond, R. J., & Murdock, J. I. (1977). Diversity and density: Lexically determined evaluative and informational consequences of linguistic complexity. *Communication Monographs, 44*, 273–283.

Bradac, J. J., Konsky, C. W., & Davies, R. A. (1976). Two studies of the effects of lexical diversity upon judgments of communicator attributes and message effectiveness. *Communication Monographs, 43*, 70–79.

Bradac, J. J., & Mulac, A. (1984). A molecular view of powerful and powerless speech styles: Attributional consequences of specific language features and communicator intentions. *Communication Monographs, 51*, 307–319.

Bradac, J. J., Mulac, A., & House, A. (1988). Lexical diversity and magnitude of convergent versus divergent style shifting: Perceptual and evaluative consequences. *Language & Communication, 8*, 213–228.

Bradac, J. J., & Wisegarver, R. (1984). Ascribed status, lexical diversity, and accent: Determinants of perceived status, solidarity, and control of speech style. *Journal of Language and Social Psychology, 3*, 239–55.

Brewer, M. B. (1988). A dual process model of impression formation. In T. K. Srull & R. S. Wyer (Eds.), *Advances in social cognition* (pp. 1–36). Hillsdale, NJ: Erlbaum.

Broadbent, D. E. (1958). *Perception and communication*. New York: Pergamon Press.

Brown, B., Strong, W., Rencher, A., & Smith, B. (1974). Fifty-four voices from two: The effects of simultaneous manipulation of rate, mean fundamental frequency, and variance of fundamental frequency on ratings of personality from speech. *Journal of the Acoustical Society of America, 55*, 313–318.

Brown, B. L. (1980). Effects of speech rate on personality attributions and competency evaluations. In H. Giles, W. P. Robinson, & P. Smith (Eds.), *Language: Social psychological perspectives* (pp. 294–300). Oxford, UK: Pergamon.

Buck, J. F. (1968). The effects of Negro and White dialectal variations upon attitudes of college students. *Speech Monographs, 2*, 181–186.

Buller, D. B., & Burgoon, J. K. (1986). The effects of vocalics and nonverbal sensitivity on compliance: A replication and extension. *Human Communication Research, 13*, 126–144.

Burgoon, J. K. (1978). A communication model of personal space violations: Explication and initial test. *Human Communication Research, 4*, 129–142.

Burgoon, J. K. (1995). Cross-cultural and intercultural applications of Expectancy Violations Theory. In R. Wiseman (Ed.), *Intercultural Communication Theory* (pp. 194–214). Thousand Oaks, CA: Sage.

Burgoon, J. K., & Hale, J. L. (1988). Nonverbal expectancy violations: Model elaboration and application to immediacy behaviors. *Communication Monographs, 55*, 58–79.

Cargile, A. C. (1997). Attitudes toward Chinese-accented speech: An investigation in two contexts. *Journal of Language and Social Psychology, 16*, 434–443.

Cargile, A. C., & Giles, H. (1997). Understanding language attitudes: Exploring listener affect and identity. *Language & Communication, 17*, 195–217.

Cargile, A. C., & Giles, H. (1998). Language attitudes toward varieties of English: An American Japanese context. *Journal of Applied Communication Research, 26*, 338–356.

Cargile, A. C., Giles, H., Ryan, E. B., & Bradac, J. J. (1994). Language attitudes as a social process: A conceptual model and new directions. *Language and Communication, 14*, 211–236.

Carroll, J., & Weiner, R. (1982). Cognitive social psychology in court and beyond. In A. Hastorf & A. Isen (Eds.), *Cognitive social psychology* (pp. 213–253). New York: Elsevier.

Cialdini, R., Darby, B., & Vincent, J. (1973). Transgression and altruism: A case for hedonism. *Journal of Experimental Social Psychology, 9*, 502–516.

Cole, T., & Bradac, J. J. (1996). A lay theory of relational satisfaction with best friends. *Journal of Personal and Social Relationships, 13*, 57–84.

Conville, R. (1975). Linguistic nonimmediacy and self-presentation. *Journal of Psychology, 90,* 219–227.

Creber, C., & Giles, H. (1983). Social context and language attitudes: The role of formality-informality of the situation. *Language Sciences, 5,* 155–162.

Davitz, J. (1969). *The language of emotions.* New York: Academic Press.

Devine, P. G. (1989). Stereotypes and prejudice: Their automatic and controlled components. *Journal of Personality and Social Psychology, 56,* 5–18.

Dovidio, J. F., Kawakami, K., Johnson, C., Johnson, B., & Howard, A. (1997). On the nature of prejudice: Automatic and controlled processes. *Journal of Experimental Social Psychology, 33,* 510–540.

Eagly, A. H., & Chaiken, S. (1993). *The psychology of attitudes.* Fort Worth, TX: Harcourt Brace Jovanovich.

Edwards, J. (1982). Language attitudes and their implications among English speakers. In E. Ryan & H. Giles (Eds.), *Attitude towards language variation: Social and applied contexts* (pp. 20–33). London: Edward Arnold.

Edwards, J. (1999). Refining our understanding of language attitudes. *Journal of Language and Social Psychology, 18,* 101–110.

Elwell, C., Brown, R., & Tutter, D. (1984). Effects of accent and visual information on impression formation. *Journal of Language and Social Psychology, 3,* 297–299.

Fazio, R. H. (1986). How do attitudes guide behavior? In R. M. Sorrentino & E. T. Higgins (Eds.), *The handbook of motivation and cognition: Foundations of social behavior* (pp. 204–243). New York: Guilford Press.

Fazio, R. H., Jackson, J. R., Dunton, B. C., & Williams, C. J. (1995). Variability in automatic activation as an unobtrusive measure of racial attitudes: A bona fide pipeline? *Journal of Personality and Social Psychology, 69,* 1013–1027.

Fazio, R. H., Roskos-Ewoldsen, D. R., & Powell, M. C. (1994). Attitudes, perception, and attention. In P. M. Niedenthal & S. Kitayama (Eds.), *The heart's eye: Emotional influences in perception and attention* (pp. 197–216). Orlando, FL: Academic Press.

Fazio, R. H., Sanbonsatsu, D. M., Powell, M. C., & Kardes, F. R. (1986). On the automatic activation of attitudes. *Journal of Personality and Social Psychology, 50,* 229–238.

Fishman, J. A. (1971). *Sociolinguistics: A brief introduction.* Boston: Rowley.

Fiske, S. T., & Neuberg, S. L. (1990). A continuum of impression formation, from category-based to individuating processes: Influences of information and motivation on attention and interpretation. In M. Zanna (Ed.), *Advances in experimental social psychology* (pp. 1–74). San Diego, CA: Academic Press.

Fitch, W. T. (1999). Acoustic exaggeration of size in birds via tracheal elongation: Comparative and theoretical analyses. *Journal of Zoology, 248,* 31–48.

Forgas, J. P., & Bower, G. H. (1987). Mood effects on person perception judgments. *Journal of Personality and Social Psychology, 53,* 53–60.

Forgas, J. P., & Moylan, S. (1989). After the movies: Transient mood and social judgments. *Personality and Social Psychology Bulletin, 13,* 467–77.

Galindo, D. L. (1995). Language attitudes toward Spanish and English varieties: A Chicano perspective. *Hispanic Journal of Behavioral Sciences, 17,* 77–99.

Garner, T., & Rubin, D. L. (1986). Middle class Blacks' perceptions of dialect and style shifting: The case of southern attorneys. *Journal of Language and Social Psychology, 5,* 33–48.

Garrett, P., Coupland, N., & Williams, A. (1995). "City harsh" and "the Welsh version of RP": Some ways in which teachers view varieties of Welsh English. *Language Awareness, 4,* 99–107.

Gilbert, D. T., & Hixon, J. G. (1991). The trouble of thinking: Activation and application of stereotypic beliefs. *Journal of Personality and Social Psychology, 60,* 509–517.

Giles, H., Bourhis, R., & Taylor, D. M. (1977). Towards a theory of language in ethnic group relations. In H. Giles (Ed.), *Language, ethnicity, and intergroup relations* (pp. 307–348). London: Academic Press.

Giles, H., & Coupland, N. (1991). Language Attitudes: Discursive, contextual, and gerontological considerations. In A. Reynolds (Ed.), *Bilingualism, multiculturalism, and second language learning* (pp. 21–42). Hillsdale, NJ: Erlbaum.

Giles, H., Coupland, N., Henwood, K., Harriman, J., & Coupland, J. (1992). Language attitudes and cognitive mediation. *Human Communication Research, 18,* 500–527.

Giles, H., & Powesland, P. F. (1975). *Speech style and social evaluation.* London: Academic Press.

Giles, H., & Ryan, E. B. (1982). Prolegomena for developing a social psychological theory of language attitudes. In E. Ryan & H. Giles (Eds.), *Attitudes toward language variation* (pp. 208–223). London: Edward Arnold.

Giles, H., & Smith, P. (1979). Accommodation theory: Optimal levels of convergence. In H. Giles & R. N. S. Clair (Eds.), *Language and social psychology* (pp. 45–65). Baltimore, MD: University Park Press.

Giles, H., Williams, A., Mackie, D. M., & Rosselli, F. (1995). Reactions to Anglo- and Hispanic American accented speakers: Affect, identity, persuasion, and the English-only controversy. *Language and Communication, 14,* 102–123.

Giles, H., Wilson, P., & Conway, A. (1981). Accent and lexical diversity as determinants of impression formation and perceived employment suitability. *Language Sciences, 3,* 91–103.

Gill, M. (1994). Accent and stereotypes: Their effect on perceptions of teachers and lecture comprehension. *Journal of Applied Communication Research, 22,* 348–361.

Gill, M., & Badzinski, D. (1992). The impact of accent and status on information perception and recall formation. *Communication Reports, 5,* 99–105.

Glenn, E. C., Glenn, P. J., & Forman, S. H. (1989). *Your voice and articulation* (2nd ed.). Englewood Cliffs, NJ: Prentice Hall.

Gouaux, C. (1971). Induced affective states and interpersonal attraction. *Journal of Personality and Social Psychology, 20,* 37–43.

Gudykunst, W. B., & Ting-Toomey, S. (1988). *Culture and interpersonal communication.* Newbury Park, CA: Sage.

Hamilton, M. A. (1997). The phase interfaced omnistructure underlying the processing of persuasive messages. In G. A. Barnett & F. J. Boster (Eds.), *Advances in communication science* (pp. 1–42). Greenwich, CT: Ablex.

Hamilton, M. A. (1998). Message variables that mediate and moderate the effect of equivocal language on source credibility. *Journal of Language and Social Psychology, 17,* 109–143.

Harkness, A. R., DeBono, K. G., & Borgida, E. (1985). Personal involvement and strategies for making contingency judgments: A stake in the dating game makes a difference. *Journal of Personality and Social Psychology, 49,* 22–32.

Henry, F., & Ginzberg, E. (1985). *Who gets the work: A test of racial discrimination in employment.* Toronto, Canada: Urban Alliance on Race Relations and Social Planning Council of Metropolitan Toronto.

Hogg, M. A., Joyce, N., & Abrams, D. (1984). Diglossia in Switzerland? A social identity analysis of speaker evaluations. *Journal of Language and Social Psychology, 3,* 185–196.

Hosman, L. A. (1989). The evaluative consequences of hedges, hesitations, and intensifiers: Powerful and powerless speech styles. *Human Communication Research, 15,* 383–406.

Hosman, L. A. (1997). The relationship between locus of control and the evaluative consequences of powerful and powerless speech styles. *Journal of Language and Social Psychology, 16,* 70–78.

Houston, D. A., & Fazio, R. H. (1989). Biased processing as a function of attitude accessibility: Making objective judgments subjectively. *Social Cognition, 7,* 51–66.

Isen, A. (1984). Towards understanding the role of affect in cognition. In R. Wyer & T. Srull (Eds.), *Handbook of social cognition* (pp. 179–236). Hillsdale, NJ: Erlbaum.

Isen, A., Horn, N., & Rosenhan, D. L. (1973). Effects of success and failure on children's generosity. *Journal of Personality and Social Psychology, 27,* 239–247.

Isen, A., & Shalker, T. (1982). The influence of mood state on evaluation of positive, neutral, and negative stimuli: When you accentuate the positive, do you eliminate the negative? *Social Psychology Quarterly, 45,* 58–63.

Isen, A., Shalker, T., Clark, M., & Karp, L. (1978). Affect, accessibility of material in memory and behavior: A cognitive loop? *Journal of Personality and Social Psychology, 36,* 1–12.

Johnson, B. T., & Eagly, A. H. (1989). Effects of involvement on persuasion: A meta-analysis. *Psychological Bulletin, 106,* 290–314.

Johnson, B. T., & Eagly, A. H. (1990). Involvement and persuasion: Types, traditions, and the evidence. *Psychological Bulletin, 107,* 375–384.

Johnson, F. L., & Buttny, R. (1982). White listeners' responses to "sounding Black" and "sounding White": The effects of message content on judgments about language. *Communication Monographs, 49,* 33–49.

Joos, M. (1967). *The five clocks.* New York: Harcourt, Brace, & World.

Kalmar, I., Zhong, Y., & Xiao, H. (1989). Language attitudes in Guangzhou, China. *Language in Society, 16,* 499–508.

Katz, D. (1960). The functional approach to the study of attitudes. *Public Opinion Quarterly, 24,* 163–204.

Kintsch, W. (1988). The role of knowledge in discourse comprehension: A construction-integration model. *Psychological Review, 95,* 163–182.

Kristiansen, T., & Giles, H. (1992). Compliance-gaining as a function of accent: Public requests in varieties of Danish. *International Journal of Applied Linguistics, 2,* 17–35.

Kunda, Z., Miller, D. T., & Claire, T. (1990). Combining social concepts: The role of causal reasoning. *Cognitive Science, 14,* 551-577.

Kunda, Z., & Thagard, P. (1996). Forming impressions from stereotypes, traits, and behaviors: A parallel-constraint-satisfaction theory. *Psychological Review, 103,* 284–308.

Labov, W. (1966). *The social significance of English in New York City.* Washington, DC: Center for Applied Linguistics.

Lambert, W. (1967). A social psychology of bilingualism. *Journal of Social Issues, 23,* 91–109.

Lambert, W., Anisfeld, M., & Yeni-Kosmshian, G. (1965). Evaluational reactions of Jewish and Arab adolescents to dialect and language variations. *Journal of Personality and Social Psychology, 2,* 84–90.

Lambert, W., Hodgson, R., Gardner, R., & Fillenbaum, S. (1960). Evaluational reactions to spoken languages. *Journal of Abnormal and Social Psychology, 60,* 44–51.

Larimer, G. S., Beatty, E. D., & Broadus, A. C. (1988). Indirect assessment of interracial prejudices. *Journal of Black Psychology, 14,* 47–56.

Leets, L., & Giles, H. (1997). Words as weapons: When do they wound? Investigations of harmful speech. *Human Communication Research, 24,* 260–301.

Lewin, K., Dembo, T., Festinger, L., & Sears, P. A. (1944). Level of aspiration. In J. M. Hunt (Ed.), *Personality and the behavior disorders* (pp. 333–378). New York: Ronald Press.

Luhman, R. (1990). Appalachian English stereotypes: Language attitudes in Kentucky. *Language in Society, 19,* 331–348.

Milroy, L., & Preston, D. R. (1999). Attitudes, perception, and linguistic features [Special issue]. *Journal of Language and Social Psychology, 18.*

Monson, T. C., Keel, R., Stephens, D., & Genung, V. (1982). Trait attributions: Relative validity, covariation with behavior, and prospect of future interaction. *Journal of Personality and Social Psychology, 42,* 1014–1024.

Montepare, J. M., & Zebrowitz-McArthur, L. (1987). Perceptions of adults with childlike voices in two cultures. *Journal of Experimental Social Psychology, 23,* 331–349.

Morton, E. S. (1977). On the occurrence and significance of motivation-structural rules in some bird and mammal sounds. *American Naturalist, 111,* 855–869.

Mulac, A., Hanley, T. D., & Prigge, D. Y. (1974). Effects of phonological speech foreignness upon three dimensions of attitude of selected American listeners. *The Quarterly Journal of Speech, 60,* 411–420.

Mulac, A., Incontro, C. R., & James, M. R. (1985). Comparison of the gender-linked language effect and sex role stereotypes. *Journal of Personality and Social Psychology, 49,* 1099–1110.

Nesdale, A. R., & Rooney, R. (1990). Effect of children's ethnic accents on adult's evaluations and stereotyping. *Australian Journal of Psychology, 42,* 309–19.

Niedzielski, N. (1999). The effect of social information on the perception of sociolinguistic variables. *Journal of Language and Social Psychology, 18,* 62–85.

O'Barr, W. M. (1982). *Linguistic evidence: Language, power, and strategy in the courtroom.* New York: Academic Press.

Ohala, J. J. (1982). The voice of dominance. *Journal of the Acoustical Society of America, 72,* S66.

Paltridge, J., & Giles, H. (1984). Attitudes towards speakers of regional accents of French: Effects of regionality, age and sex of listeners. *Linguistiche Berichte, 90,* 71–85.

Parsons, C. K., & Liden, R. C. (1984). Interviewer perceptions of applicant qualifications: A multivariate field study of demographic characteristics and nonverbal cues. *Journal of Applied Psychology, 69,* 557–568.

Petty, R. E., & Cacioppo, J. T. (1986a). *Communication and persuasion: Central and peripheral routes to attitude change.* New York: Springer-Verlag.

Petty, R. E., & Cacioppo, J. T. (1986b). The elaboration likelihood model of persuasion. In L. Berkowitz (Ed.), *Advances in experimental social psychology* (Vol. 19, pp. 123–205). San Diego, CA: Academic Press.

Petty, R. E., & Cacioppo, J. T. (1990). Involvement and persuasion: Tradition versus integration. *Psychological Bulletin, 107,* 367–374.

Pinker, S. (2000). *The language instinct* (2nd ed.). New York: HarperCollins.

Podberesky, R., Deluty, R. H., & Feldstein, S. (1990). Evaluations of Spanish-and Oriental-accented English speakers. *Social Behavior and Personality, 18,* 53–63.

Posner, M. I. (1982). Cumulative development of attentional theory. *American Psychologist, 37,* 168–179.

Potter, J., & Wetherell, M. (1987). *Discourse and social psychology.* London: Sage.

Preston, D. (1989). *Perceptual dialectology: Nonlinguists' views of area linguistics.* Dordrecht, The Netherlands: Foris.

Ray, G. B. (1986). Vocally cued personality prototypes: An implicit personality theory approach. *Communication Monographs, 53,* 266–276.

Reeves, B., Thorson, E., & Schleuder, J. (1986). Attention to television: Psychological theories and chronometric measures. In J. Bryant & D. Zillman (Eds.), *Perspectives on media effects* (pp. 251–279). Hillsdale, NJ: Erlbaum.

Riches, P., & Foddy, M. (1989). Ethnic accent as a status cue. *Social Psychology Quarterly, 52,* 197–206.

Rickford, J., & Traugott, E. (1985). Symbol of powerlessness and degeneracy, or symbol of solidarity and truth? Paradoxical attitudes towards pidgins and creoles. In S. Greenbaum (Ed.), *The English language today* (pp. 252–261). Oxford, UK: Pergamon.

Robinson, J. A. (1996). The relationship between personal characteristics and attitudes toward black and white speakers of informal nonstandard English. *Western Journal of Black Studies, 20,* 211–220.

Rogan, R. G., & Hammer, M. R. (1995). Assessing message affect in crisis negotiations: An exploratory study. *Human Communication Research, 21,* 553–574.

Roskos-Ewoldsen, D. R. (1997). Attitude accessibility and persuasion: Review and a transactive model. In B. Burleson (Ed.), *Communication yearbook 20* (pp. 185–225). Thousand Oaks, CA: Sage.

Rubin, D., DeHart, J., & Heintzman, M. (1991). Effects of accented speech and culture-typical compliance-gaining on subordinates' impressions of managers. *International Journal of Intercultural Relations, 15,* 267–283.

Rubin, D. L., & Smith, K. A. (1988). Effects of accent, ethnicity, and lecture topic on undergraduates' perceptions of nonnative English-speaking teaching assistants. *International Journal of Intercultural Relations, 14,* 337–353.

Ruble, D. N. (1983). The development of social-comparison processes and their role in achievement related self-socialization. In E. T. Higgins, D. N. Ruble, & W. W. Hartup (Eds.), *Social cognition and social development* (pp. 134–157). New York: Cambridge University Press.

Ryan, E. B., Carranza, M., & Moffie, R. W. (1977). Reactions toward varying degrees of accentedness in the speech of Spanish-English bilinguals. *Language and Speech, 20,* 267–73.

Ryan, E. B., & Carranza, M. A. (1975). Evaluative reactions of adolescents toward speakers of standard English and Mexican-American accented English. *Journal of Personality and Social Psychology, 31,* 855–863.

Ryan, E. B., Giles, H., & Hewstone, M. (1988). The measurement of language attitudes. In U. Ammon, N. Dittmar, & K. J. Mattheier (Eds.), *Sociolinguistics: An international handbook of the science of language* (Vol. 2, pp. 1068–1081). Berlin, Germany: de Gruyter.

Ryan, E. B., Giles, H., & Sebastian, R. J. (1982). An integrative perspective for the study of attitudes toward language variation. In E. B. Ryan & H. Giles (Eds.), *Attitudes towards language variation: Social and applied contexts.* London: Edward Arnold.

Ryan, E. B., Hewstone, M., & Giles, H. (1984). Language and intergroup attitudes. In J. Eiser (Ed.), *Attitudinal judgment* (pp. 135–160). New York: Springer.

Sales, G. D., & Pye, J. D. (1974). *Ultrasonic communication by animals.* New York: Wiley.

Sarnoff, I. (1970). Social attitudes and the resolution of motivational conflict. In M. Jahoda & N. Warren (Eds.), *Attitudes* (pp. 279–284). Harmondsworth, UK: Penguin.

Schwarz, N., Bless, H., & Bohner, G. (1991). Mood and persuasion: Affective states influence the processing of persuasive communications. In M. P. Zanna (Ed.), *Advances in experimental social psychology* (Vol. 24, pp. 161–201). San Diego, CA: Academic Press.

Segrin, C. (1993). The effects of nonverbal behavior on outcomes of compliance gaining attempts. *Communication Studies, 44,* 169–187.

Seligman, C., Tucker, G. R., & Lambert, W. E. (1972). The effects of speech style and other attributes on teachers' attitudes toward pupils. *Language in Society, 1,* 131–142.

Shiffrin, R. M., & Schneider, W. (1977). Controlled and automatic human information processing: II. Perceptual learning, automatic attending, and a general theory. *Psychological Review, 84,* 127–190.

Showers, C., & Cantor, N. (1985). Social cognition: A look at motivated strategies. *Annual Review of Psychology, 36,* 275–305.

Siegman, A. W., & Pope, B. (1972). *Studies in dyadic communication.* New York: Pergamon Press.

Small, M. F. (1998). *Our babies, ourselves: How biology and culture shape the way we parent.* New York: Anchor Books.

Sondermeyer, C. (1995). *The interactive effects of clothing and powerful/powerless speech styles.* Unpublished doctoral dissertation, University of Southern Mississippi, Hattiesburg.

Speicher, B., & McMahan, S. (1992). Some African-American perspectives on Black English vernacular. *Language in Society, 21,* 383–407.

Sridhara, A. (1984). A study of language stereotype in children. *Journal of Psychological Researches, 28,* 45–51.

Stevens, P. (1983). Ambivalence, modernisation and language attitudes: French and Arabic in Tunisia. *Journal of Multilingual and Multicultural Development, 4,* 101–114.

Stewart, M. A., Ryan, E. B., & Giles, H. (1985). Accent and social class effects on status and solidarity evaluations. *Personality and Social Psychology Bulletin, 11,* 98–105.

Street, R. L., & Brady, R. M. (1982). Speech rate acceptance ranges as a function of evaluative domain, listener speech rate, and communication context. *Communication Monographs, 49,* 290–308.

Street, R. L., Brady, R. M., & Putman, W. B. (1983). The influence of speech rate stereotypes and rate similarity on listeners' evaluations of speakers. *Journal of Language and Social Psychology, 2,* 37–56.

Tanaka, Y. (1996). Social selection and the evolution of animal signals. *Evolution, 50,* 512–523.

Tajfel, H. (1981). Social stereotypes and social groups. In J. Turner & H. Giles (Eds.), *Intergroup Behavior* (pp. 144–165). Oxford, UK: Blackwell.

Thomsen, C. J., Borgida, E., & Lavine, H. (1995). The causes and consequences of personal involvement. In R. E. Petty & J. A. Krosnick (Eds.), *Attitude strength: Antecedents and consequences* (Vol. 4, pp. 191–214). Mahwah, NJ: Erlbaum.

Titze, I. R. (1994). *Principles of voice production*. Englewood Cliffs, NJ: Prentice Hall.

Trudgill, P., & Giles, H. (1978). Sociolinguistics and linguistic value judgments: Correctness, adequacy and aesthetics. In F. Coppiertiers & D. Goyvaerts (Eds.), *The functions of language and literature studies* (pp. 167–190). Ghent, Belgium: Storia Scientia.

Tusing, K. J., & Dillard, J. P. (1996, November). *The sounds of dominance: Vocal precursors of dominance during interpersonal influence*. Paper presented at the annual convention of the Speech Communication Association, San Diego, CA.

Vassberg, L. (1993). *Alsatian acts of identity*. Clevedon: Multilingual Matters.

White, M. J., Vandiver, B. J., Becker, M. L., Overstreet, B. G., Teple, L. E., Hagan, K. L., & Mandelbaum, E. P. (1998). African American evaluations of Black English and standard American English. *Journal of Black Psychology, 24*, 60–75.

Wiener, M., & Mehrabian, A. (1967). *Language within language: Non-immediacy, a channel in verbal communication*. New York: Appleton-Century-Crofts.

Williams, A., Garrett, P., & Coupland, N. (1996). Perceptual dialectology, folklinguistics, and regional stereotypes: Teachers' perceptions of variation in Welsh English. *Multilingua, 15*, 171–199.

Williams, F. (1976). *The explanation of the linguistic attitudes of teachers*. Newbury Park, CA: Rowley.

Wollard, K. (1984). A formal measure of language attitudes in Barcelona: A note from a work in progress. *International Journal of the Sociology of Language, 47*, 63–71.

Wong, P., & Weiner, B. (1981). When people ask "why" questions, and the heuristics of attributional search. *Journal of Personality and Social Psychology, 40*, 650–663.

Ytsma, J. (1990, June). *School children's language attitudes in Friesland*. Paper presented at the annual conference of the International Communication Association, Dublin, Ireland.

Zahn, C. J., & Hopper, R. (1985). Measuring language attitudes: The speech evaluation instrument. *Journal of Language and Social Psychology, 4*, 113–123.

AUTHOR INDEX

SUBJECT INDEX

ABOUT THE EDITOR

WILLIAM B. GUDYKUNST is a professor of speech communication and a faculty member in Asian American Studies at California State University, Fullerton. He is the author of *Bridging Differences* and *Asian American Ethnicity and Communication*, and coauthor of *Culture and Interpersonal Communication, Communicating With Strangers*, and *Bridging Japanese/North American Differences*, among others. He has edited or coedited numerous books including *Communication in Japan and the United States, Handbook of International and Intercultural Communication, Theories of Intercultural Communication*, and *Communication in Personal Relationships Across Cultures*, among others. *Communicating With Strangers* and *Culture and Interpersonal Communication* received the Outstanding Book Award from the International and Intercultural Division of the Speech Communication Association (now the National Communication Association [NCA]). He is a past editor of the *International and Intercultural Communication Annual* and a Fellow of the International Communication Association.

ABOUT THE CONTRIBUTORS

ERNEST G. BORMANN is emeritus professor of speech communication at the University of Minnesota. He is the author or coauthor of a number of books that include *Communication Theory*, *Small Group Communication* (3rd ed.), *The Force of Fantasy*, and *Effective Small Group Communication* (5th ed.). He received the B. Aubrey Fisher Mentorship Award from the International Communication Association (1988) and the Outstanding Teacher Award of the College of Liberal Arts at the University of Minnesota. He also has received the National Communication Association's Charles H. Woolbert Award for research projects withstanding the test of time (1983), the Distinguished Service Award (1990), and the Distinguished Scholar Award (1992).

JAMES J. BRADAC is a professor of communication at the University of California, Santa Barbara. He is interested in the social psychology of language and interpersonal communication and has published research reflecting these interests in journals in communication, psychology, and linguistics. He is coauthor of *Language and Social Knowledge* (with Charles Berger) and *Power in Language* (with Sik Hung Ng), past editor of *Human Communication Research*, and a Fellow of the International Communication Association.

TRUDY E. BURTIS is a doctoral student in the Department of Communication and Journalism at the University of New Mexico. Her primary research area is intercultural communication with an interest in the rhetorical analysis of (inter)cultural phenomena, especially followership and prejudice within diverse communities.

AARON CASTELAN CARGILE is an assistant professor in the Department of Communication Studies at California State University, Long Beach. His research interests include the social psychology of language and intercultural communication processes. His work has appeared in journals and edited volumes including the *Journal of Language and Social Psychology*, *The Handbook of Language and Social Psychology*, *Intercultural Communication Theory*, and *Communication Yearbook 19*.

JOHN F. CRAGEN is a professor of communication at Illinois State University. He is the author or coauthor of a number of books including *Applied Communication Research*, *Communication in Small Groups* (5th ed.), *Nationalized Medical Care*, *Understanding Communication Theory*, and *Symbolic Theories in Applied Communication Research*, which received the Applied Communication Book Award (1995) from the Speech Communication Association (now NCA).

SHARON DUNWOODY is Evjue-Bascom Professor and Director of the School of Journalism and Mass Communication at the University of Wisconsin, Madison. Her research interests focus on the public communication of scientific and technical information, from the behaviors of sources and journalists through the coping strategies of information consumers.

WILLIAM P. EVELAND, JR., is an assistant professor in the School of Journalism and Communication at Ohio State University. His research focuses on the roles of motivation and information processing in the influence of traditional media and the World Wide Web on users' knowledge, perceptions, and opinions.

LISA FALVEY is a doctoral student in the Department of Language, Literature, and Communication at Rensselaer Polytechnic Institute. Her teaching and research interests focus on computer-mediated communication, organizational communication, and feminism.

SHERRY G. FORD is a doctoral candidate at Louisiana State University and an instructor of communication studies at the University of Alabama at Birmingham. Her research interests are conflict management, self-identity and communication, relational maintenance, and communication strategies in dealing with bereavement.

SHELTON A. GUNARATNE is a professor of mass communication at Minnesota State University Moorhead. He has edited *The Handbook of the Media in Asia* (Sage, 2000) and a special issue of *Gazette* (Vol. 61, 1999) on Asia. He published "Old Wine in a New Bottle" in *Communication Yearbook 21*.

TERESA M. HARRISON is associate dean for graduate program and research initiatives in the School of Humanities and Social Sciences and associate professor in the Department of Language, Literature, and Communication at Rensselaer Polytechnic Institute. She is the managing editor of the *Electronic Journal of Communication/La revue Electronique de Communication* (http://www.cios.org/www/ejcmain.htm) and cofounder of the Communication Institute for Online Scholarship (http://www.cios.org), a Web-based center providing bibliographic tools for communication scholars.

JAMES M. HONEYCUTT is a professor of communication studies at Louisiana State University. He serves on a number of editorial boards and has published numerous articles in national and interdisciplinary journals. He is coauthor of *Cognition, Communication, and Romantic Relationships*. His research interests include developmental communication, music therapy, mental imagery, and nonverbal behavior.

RICHARD L. JOHANNESEN is a professor of communication at Northern Illinois University. His research interests focus on communication ethics, contemporary public address, and contemporary rhetorical theory. He is author of *Ethics in Human Communication* and *Ethics and Persuasion*, and the coeditor of *Contemporary American Speeches* and *Language Is Sermonic*. He is past chair of the Commission on Communication Ethics of the National Communication Association and was a consultant to the NCA for development of its professional code of ethics.

PHILIP M. NAPOLI is an assistant professor in the Communication and Media Management Program at the Graduate School of Administration at Fordham University. His research interests focus on media industries, media policy, and the policymaking process. His book, *Foundations of Communications Policy*, is forthcoming from Hampton Press.

AMY I. NATHANSON is an assistant professor in the School of Journalism and Communication at Ohio State University. Her research focuses on children and television, with particular attention to the role of parents in shaping television-related effects among children.

JOHN G. OETZEL is an assistant professor in the Department of Communication and Journalism at the University of New Mexico. His research interests include understanding the influence of cultural diversity in work groups and organizational communication, particularly conflict communication. His publications have appeared in journals such as *Human Communication Research*, *International Journal of Intercultural Relations*, and *Management Communication Quarterly*. He is coauthor of *Managing Intercultural Conflicts Effectively* (with Stella Ting-Toomey, Sage, forthcoming).

FRANK G. PÉREZ is a doctoral student in the Department of Communication and Journalism at the University of New Mexico. His research interests include intercultural communication and media theory. His earlier publications examine the representations of Chicanos in film and Spanish-language media advertising.

MARTHA I. CHEW SANCHEZ is a doctoral student in the Department of Communication and Journalism at the University of New Mexico. Her main areas of interest are intercultural communication and community development.

DONALD C. SHIELDS is a professor of communication at the University of Missouri-St. Louis. He is the author or coauthor of a number of books including *Applied Communication Research*, *Financing Education*, *Saga of Darkness—Vision of Light*, *Understanding Communication Theory*, and *Symbolic Theories in Applied Communication Research*, which received the Applied Communication Book Award (1995) from the Speech Communication Association (now NCA).